MW00998756

This edition is published to mark the bicentennial of the War of 1812 and the bicentennial of the 1813 attack on York.

"With a technique reminiscent of that in Walter Lord's finest work – in which extraordinary events come to vivid life through the recollections of ordinary people – Malcomson's account … is a mixture of poignancy, heroism, and violence. His analysis of its aftermath moves beyond the recital of the military and political consequences to address the human toll exacted by the grim events of that April." David S. Heidler, *The Historian*

"Here, at last, is a comprehensive, meticulously researched history of the battle of York… This brilliant book tells the whole story from both Canadian (i.e., British) and American points of view. It is basic reading, essential for understanding early Toronto as well as the war, and destined to become the definitive study of the subject." Chris Raible, *Ontario History*

"The story of the American capture and occupation of York in April 1813 is not an edifying one. Quite apart from marking a defeat for British and Canadian arms, it was a stew of inappropriate strategic plans, weak leadership, disloyalty, faction, and bad luck. This is the story told in brimming detail in Robert Malcomson's worthwhile new book …" Douglas Dodds, *Fife & Drum*

"Malcomson maintains an even, unbiased look at the British, Canadian and American participants and events and shies away from nothing … an excellent, well-researched and lucid look at a subject often mentioned in connection with the war, but never truly examined before … this is one for your bookcase." *The War of 1812 Magazine*

"Malcomson's coverage of the battle is masterful and comprehensive. His lively narrative is detailed and demonstrates a sound understanding of the dynamics of combat. He attacks the myths that grew up around the battle…" Richard V. Barbuto, *Journal of America's Military Past*

"… a model of how to present military history. There are good maps and many illustrations, a glossary of terms, a list of dramatis personae, and a series of appendices that offer up a host of useful information, including the terms of capitulation at York, lists of prisoners, orders of battle, and details on Fort York's layout." J. L. Granatstein, *Legion Magazine*

Capital in
FLAMES

THE
AMERICAN ATTACK
ON YORK, 1813

ROBERT

MALCOMSON

ROBIN BRASS STUDIO

To the memory of
Kurt Vonnegut
1922–2007

"It begins like this:
  Listen:
  Billy Pilgrim has come unstuck in time."

First published 2008 by Robin Brass Studio Inc., Montreal, and Naval Institute Press, Annapolis. Published in paperback 2013 by Robin Brass Studio Inc.
www.robinbrassstudio.com

ISBN-13: 978-1-896941-70-7
ISBN-10: 1-896941-70-2

Printed and bound in Canada by Marquis Imprimeur, Cap-Saint-Ignace, Quebec

Library and Archives Canada Cataloguing in Publication

Malcomson, Robert, 1949–
    Capital in flames : the American attack on York, 1813 / Robert Malcomson.

Reprint. Originally published: Montreal : Robin Brass Studio, 2008.
Includes bibliographical references and index.
ISBN 978-1-896941-70-7

    1. York, Battle of, Toronto, Ont., 1813. 2. Canada – History – War of 1812. I. Title.

FC446.T6M35 2013   971.03'4   C2012-908474-3

Contents

Introduction

I first saw Fort York in the spring of 1960 when my Grade Five friends and I made our end-of-the-year trip to Toronto with Mr. Pearce, our teacher and the principal of J. C. Bald Public School in Welland, Ontario. I admired Mr. Pearce, and the example he set fuelled a desire I had already stated to someday be a teacher. I wrote my first book as an assignment for him. It was about a young ice hockey goalie who played in the Stanley Cup Finals against Johnny Bower, the great Toronto Maple Leaf netminder of those days, another hero of mine.

Memories of that visit to Fort York remain; I was intrigued by the guns, and how they were used in that long-ago war. I was only eleven years old, so I had no idea that another great battle had been fought in the months before our visit. Construction of the Gardiner Expressway along Toronto's waterfront was underway and the original plans called for the elevated highway to cut across the property of the fort. An indefatigable line of twentieth-century defenders stood to oppose the route and its powerful advocates. They won; the course of the highway was changed and the plan to take the fort apart, brick by brick and log by log, and move it to a more convenient location on the artificially created lakeshore failed.

One result of the preservation of the fort was that it was still alive and open when I arrived as a boy from Welland to gather some images I would never lose. And here I am, nearly fifty years later, telling the story of the fort's most traumatic day back in 1813.

The point I am making is this: in their determination to prevent the evisceration of Fort York, its modern-day protectors unknowingly nurtured my early interest in things historical. Just as Mr. Pearce encouraged me to put my dreams on paper, they helped me along the path that has led to this book. So, many thanks to them and to my old teacher. In part, *Capital in Flames* is my way of passing their gifts forward.

"The true cause of our defeat must be attributed to the loss of the command of the lakes," declared six leading citizens of the town of York, chaired by the Reverend John Strachan, ten days after the Americans had arrived. Infuriated by what had happened on Tuesday, 27 April 1813, the group railed against "the pernicious consequences" of the government's defensive policy and the conduct of Major General Sir Roger Sheaffe, whose tactics they considered "ill calculated to meet and defeat the enemy." The headmen were trying to make sense of the insult suffered by the capital of Upper Canada and the people who lived there. They certainly hit the bull's-eye with their allegations, but there were plenty of other arrows that might have been fired and the target could easily have been bristling with explanations.

In writing this book, my role was basically the same as theirs: to explain what happened and why. Naturally, since the result of the day was not a personal affront to me as it was to Strachan and his peers, I viewed things from a more neutral position. And it was from that place that I read all the popular and lesser known accounts of the action and began to make the same list of questions that has guided me through previous books and papers: What happened? Who was there? What did they do? How and why did they do such things? What was the result? How does the event fit into the larger context of the war between Britain and the United States? And, particular to this topic, what was the story of a frontier town that went from standing on the fringe of hostilities to landing on the sharp point of the spring's military campaign?

The basic story that writers have told before about the landing, the battle and the outcome is here, but some old notions have been pushed aside by fresh insights, all based on fully referenced sources. York became a target for attack because of misguided strategic decisions at the highest levels in Canada. The Americans clung to their original campaign goals, but they were still unattainable at the beginning of 1813 and so they changed direction and sought a much-needed land victory at a vulnerable spot. Commanders in the field formed operational decisions which made them culpable for the results and, therefore, easy scapegoats, if such were necessary. Whatever amount of planning went into an operation, it was subject to unpredictable circumstances that could alter everything in a flash or with the mind-numbing slowness of a stalled weather system. Zebulon Pike was prophetic in the way he predicted the flow of events and his own fate. Sir Roger Sheaffe lived down to his reputation.

Their followers were a mixed bag of brave hearts and conflicted malcontents. The town was left in a state of shock akin to scenes of urban warfare in any century.

In the historiography of the War of 1812, it has been argued that the battle at York was a direct factor in the British defeat at Put-in-Bay the following September, but here, for the first time, are the facts about the guns and supplies and a critique of the myth-makers. The same sort of revision is given to the traditional view of the performance of the Upper Canada militia before, during and after the battle, showing that they really were not as unwilling to serve as some might allege. In a similar vein, the oft-repeated connection between the burnings at York in 1813 and the similar event at Washington in 1814 is challenged.

And a point of pride for Americans that no one has ever trumpeted loudly enough is that the amphibious attack on York was the first time in history that the U.S. Army executed a combined operation with the U.S. Navy. Compared to the army's logistical disaster of the river-crossing attack on Queenston the previous October, the landing at York was executed with remarkable speed and precision and laid the groundwork for a similarly successful assault on Fort George four weeks later. It was a momentous day in American military and naval history that was clouded by a cataclysmic event that no one anticipated.

It was a particular pleasure to discover some new characters and allow them to contribute to the narrative. Captain John Scott, of Pike's Fifteenth Infantry, finds his public voice for the first time in regards to army life, "Granny Dearborn" and the chaos of the landing that morning. Sergeant James Commins, 8th Foot, repeats the rumours about French reinforcements among the invaders. The papers of Amasa Trowbridge at the Library of Congress in Washington, D.C. tell how the surgeon from Connecticut volunteered to join the expedition and left an account that sheds new light on old questions. John York's Ojibwa memoir recorded in 1916 offers a rare native remembrance of events. Sixty-year-old Tito LeLièvre receives credit as the man who laid the crucial powder train and set the first blazes. Baptist Irvine, the firebrand from the Baltimore Volunteers, gets the point about the danger of friendly fire, and then helps mix the stew of post-battle controversy. And then there are the thousands of soldiers and seamen, militia and volunteers whose names fill the appendices, answering the question of who was there and giving the genealogists a new playing field.

Capital in Flames is more than just a book about a battle. York, as capital of Upper Canada, was at the centre of the tale, and so the book begins and ends with the town, since understanding what happened to it requires a knowledge of what it had been. As an effect of the engagement on 27 April, York became the scene of one of the first blatant examples of civil unrest in Canada during the war. The community leaders who had guided its early years and stood to defend it in battle were then required to deal with the societal aftershocks that kept reverberating through the spring and summer. They were disgusted by the men who avoided muster on the day of battle and then gave themselves up to get easy paroles, and by the citizens who rejoiced at the Americans' success and helped them reap their plunder. The culprits are named in these pages, their actions exposed and counted and then compared with events elsewhere.

It is unfortunate that there are not more records about the refugees of the battle. The stories of the women and children of the town remain thin and there is scant reference to the slaves and free blacks who lived there and the native families camped in the woods. The closest we can get to the view of the common folk is from the vantage points of Ely Playter, Isaac Wilson and John Lyon. Their parts in the tale represent the roles played by hundreds of virtually anonymous individuals.

I do not hesitate to admit that I have not solved every puzzle about the battle and its related strands. Someday someone will point out my errors and misconceptions and paint a more elaborate and truer picture. I am at ease with such a notion and have endeavoured to lay out my evidence in such a way as to help future researchers. I have wasted too much of my own time trying to figure out vague endnotes and hunting through documents for single supporting sentences to foist that annoyance on anyone who studies this work. I wondered during the process if I was overdoing it with too much detail in the notes, but then I saw what John Sugden did with his magnificently researched biography *Nelson, A Dream of Glory* and my decision was made.

Several technical points want explanation. As is becoming common practice among War of 1812 writers, I have used numerals to identify numbered British/Canadian units (e.g., 8th Regiment of Foot) and words for American units (Fifteenth Regiment of Infantry) to help the reader differentiate them. Although I write this is in a country that officially uses metric units of measure, I have employed the English standards. This was done for consistency's sake, since participants' references to yards and miles are quoted and repeated in the notes. I have offered metric conversions for most weights and measures in the notes. I did not convert monetary values into Canadian dollars, since the variety of currencies in use at the time made conversion unwieldy and potentially misleading. Lastly, American time frames were employed because they align closely with actual sunrise and sunset times for April 1813.

In the larger view of the world, the attack on York did not amount to much; it was not exactly the Battle of Waterloo. But although the town was often called "little" and would later be known as "muddy" York, it was still the capital city of the province and the taking of a capital city is no small potatoes. Had fate twisted the chronology in a different direction, it might have been the beginning of the end for Upper Canada. And, as with any traumatic or disastrous event, what happened at York meant everything to the people involved. To the men who planned the assault and those who prepared the defences, it was an obsession. To the soldiers who clashed in the woods and on the field and to the women, children and old people who fled the fighting, the experience was harrowing. For the survivors, 27 April was an indelible memory in their lives.

At the very least, a true accounting of the events surrounding the Battle of York will bring to the mind and conversations of the readers, the names of the mighty and the meek. If this narrative causes their lives to be reconsidered and their challenges to be better understood, their memory has been honourably served.

My publisher and editor, Robin Brass, and I discussed this book for several years before I set to work on it seriously. With his usual professional approach, he has nursed it through the various stages and produced this edition of which I am very proud. I am most appreciative of his talents and his devotion to the project.

I happily recognize again the generosity of Gary Gibson, the resident scholar of Sackets Harbor, New York, who for years has provided a flow of primary documents from sources only he has had the creativity and commitment to explore. He read an early draft and called me on the carpet for not presenting a balanced view; talk about a stinging criticism! I rewrote and he was satisfied and the book is better for his advice.

I thank Guy St. Denis for poring over the manuscript in such detail. He is researching Isaac Brock and he helped me to rethink one of the last lines that the general wrote, as well as a few dozen other interpretations. Likewise Stephen Otto greatly enhanced my understanding of York, providing references and advice. I think he may be disappointed that the chapters about the town are not longer, but at least he should be pleased to know that his influence on the final product is evident. Carl Benn must have flinched when he read an early draft, but in his steady and amiable manner he helped me straighten out the story and reconsider the tone with which I was treating some of the players. Readers will find many reference to his authoritative publications in the notes. Major John Grodzinski brought his military know-how and enthusiasm to his assessment of the text, especially with a last-minute chapter vet. And, the leading American historian of the War of 1812, Donald R. Hickey, took time from

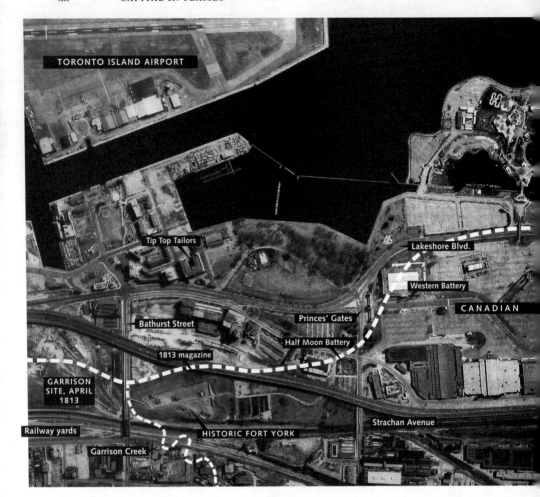

Bird's-eye view of the battlefield, as of 1992. As the city of Toronto grew during the nineteenth and twentieth centuries, soil, rocks and construction debris from the many building sites were dumped along the lakeshore. Wharves, roads, railway lines, depots and factories sprang up along the lake, which also became the location of the annual fair and eventually the recreational facilities at Ontario Place. As these overlapping aerial photos indicate, virtually nothing remains of the contours of the original land along the water, of the forest that covered the shore west of the Western Battery and of the numerous ravines where creeks spilled into the lake. (City of Toronto Archives, Sheet 92, 49G and 48G)

Lake Ontario

ONTARIO PLACE

Fort Rouillé

AMERICAN LANDING PLACE

NATIONAL EXHIBITION GROUNDS

Approx. 1813 shoreline

Gardiner Expressway

Dunn Avenue

Dufferin Street

Jameson Avenue

his teaching and publication activities to read an early draft and straighten out some details of American history. I am deeply grateful for his encouragement and support.

My son-in-law, Geoffrey MacGillivray, read the manuscript, although he professed no knowledge of military and naval history. If you find the *dramatis personae* of service, then it is thanks to Geoff, because it came about as a result of his admission that he had trouble keeping the characters and command structure straight. As well, he was fascinated by Pike, and when I restructured the middle of the book, I rescued the general from the centre of a chapter and brought him right up to the first line. He certainly deserves the attention.

The James A. Gibson Library at Brock University in St. Catharines is where I do the bulk of my research. I spend my days in the stacks, at the media machines and the computer databases and in the rich repository of the Special Collections and Archives, where David Sharron (who recently took over Lynn Prunskus's post as head of the collections), Edie Williams and Jen Goul enthusiastically assist my searches. If there is something the Gibson Library does not have, I turn to Jan Milligan, Susan Moskal and Annie Relic of the Interlibrary Loan office, who treat my requests for obscure titles with absolute attention.

A portion of the research was supported by a grant through the Hackman Research Residency Program of the Archives Partnership Trust at the Albany State Archives. I was grateful for this grant and for the help of Gracia Yaeger, Dr. James Folts and the staff at the archives and the state library during my visits. I thank the following individuals for their guidance while accessing material held by their institutions: Chad Leinaweaver, New Jersey Historical Society; Jeff Flannery, Library of Congress, Washington, D.C.; Jim Cheevers, U.S. Naval Academy Museum; Diane Cooter, Special Collection Research Center, Syracuse University Library; Lisa Buchanan, City of Toronto Collections and Conservation Centre; Nancy Mallett, Archives and Museum Committee, St. James' Cathedral, Toronto; Kevin Hebib and David Spittal, City of Toronto Museums and Heritage Services; Dave O'Hara and the staff of Historic Fort York; Kim Nusco, Massachusetts Historical Collection; Eric Voboril, The Flag House and Star-Spangled Banner Museum, Baltimore; Michael Taylor, Lilly Library, Indiana University at Bloomington; and Jim Bradley, MPP, and assistants at his St. Catharines riding office. To the staffs who administer the following institutions and the governments which fund them, I extend my sincere appreciation for the resources in their collections: the Library and Archives of Canada, Ottawa; the Archives of Ontario, Toronto; the United States National Archives, Washington, D.C.; the National Archives of the United Kingdom at Kew, London; the Niagara-on-the-Lake Public Library; Chicago History Museum; the Historical Society of Pennsylvania in Philadelphia; and the City of Toronto Archives.

Bob Gregory of Kanata opened the door to John Lyon; Stephen Sheaffe, of Queensland, Australia, shared his research into Sir Roger's family; Gene Towner encouraged my use of the letters by his ancestor Thomas Warner; John Fredriksen, renowned independent scholar and editor of a portion of the Scott papers, advised on the location of the originals; Chris Raible shared my search for Strachan's letter of protest to Jefferson and offered ideas on early York; James Elliott sent relevant documents; Jon Moore, Parks Canada, provided background about the *Scourge* and Charity Shoal; Brian Murphy of Chester, New Jersey, provided access to the letter by Lieutenant George Runk; Dr. J. Jakibchuk explained the symptoms and modern treatment for Lieutenant de Koven's case of *tic douloureux*; and Robert Ducat-Brown, Michael Caulfield, Larry Karp,

Robin Biggins and Frank Metzger provided information about musical snuff boxes. Vic Suthren and Peter Rindlisbacher invited me to participate in the 2005 "School of the Sailor" exercise at Fort George in Niagara-on-the-Lake, in which I experienced first-hand the difficulties of handling small boats during an amphibious landing, even without the hail of ball and whining shot.

My daughters, their husbands and the two little girls who call me "Bookie" encourage me with their kind words and loving appreciation. Janet somehow still enjoys hearing where I need to go next to do research and then plots out what other adventures we can have along the way. She is so patient and, usually, she is amused to see me drift off in my thoughts. "Are you counting dead soldiers again?" she'll ask.

One late night this past spring, after slogging away in this room for hours, I heard on the radio that Kurt Vonnegut had died in New York City at the age of eighty-four years. I immediately sent a comment off to a column in the *Globe and Mail* in which I mentioned that I had rarely felt more comfortable in the world than when I was immersed in something written by KV. I often repeat his line that reading allows us to meditate with great minds. Meditating with Kurt prompted me to begin writing seriously more than any other single experience I have had. It is my ultimate act of gratitude to Kurt Vonnegut to dedicate this book to his memory.

ROBERT MALCOMSON
St. Catharines, Ontario
18 August 2007

Overleaf **A view of Toronto, facing east, 1965.** This photograph provides a view of how the waterfront of Toronto changed between the early 1800s and mid-1900s. The rail yards (greatly reduced by the turn of the twenty-first century) dominated the transportation corridor, flanked by the recently built Gardiner Expressway. At the top left is Toronto City Hall at Nathan Phillips Square, nearly brand new in 1965, while Maple Leaf Stadium, the 20,000-seat baseball field, next to the Tip Top Tailors factory on the bottom right, would face the wrecking ball three years later. (AO, C30, Box B, 184, 1615, ES22, 58)

The following abbreviations are used in picture credits:
AO – Archives of Ontario
LAC – Library and Archives Canada
TRL – Toronto Reference Library
USNA – U.S. Naval Academy

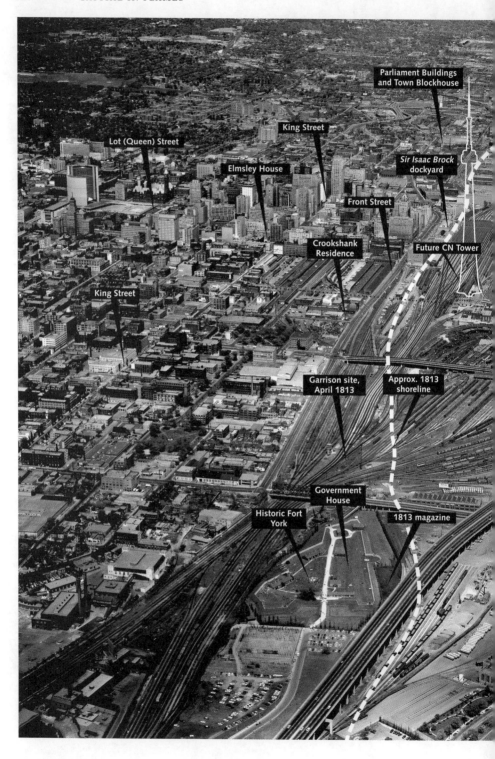

Lake Ontario

Toronto
Harbour

Gardiner Expressway

Canada Malting

Lakeshore Blvd.

Tip Top Tailors

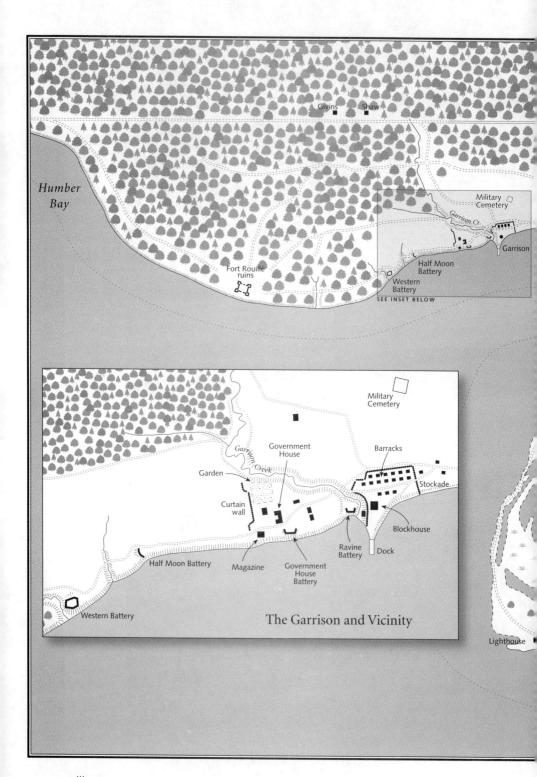

Givins Shaw

Humber Bay

Military Cemetery

Garrison Cr.

Garrison

Fort Rouillé ruins

Half Moon Battery

Western Battery

SEE INSET BELOW

Military Cemetery

Garrison Creek

Government House

Barracks

Garden

Stockade

Curtain wall

Blockhouse

Half Moon Battery

Magazine

Government House Battery

Ravine Battery

Dock

Western Battery

The Garrison and Vicinity

Lighthouse

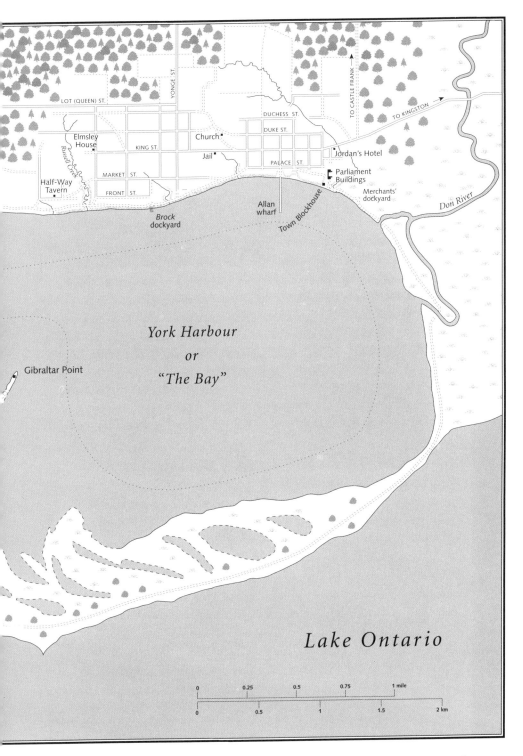

LOT (QUEEN) ST.

YONGE ST.

DUCHESS ST.

TO CASTLE FRANK →

TO KINGSTON

Elmsley
House

KING ST.

Church

DUKE ST.

Jail

PALACE ST.

Jordan's Hotel

Parliament
Buildings

Russell Creek

MARKET ST.

Merchants'
dockyard

Half-Way
Tavern

FRONT ST.

Allan
wharf

Brock
dockyard

Town Blockhouse

Don River

Gibraltar Point

York Harbour

or

"The Bay"

Lake Ontario

| 0 | | 0.25 | | 0.5 | | 0.75 | | 1 mile |
| 0 | 0.5 | | 1 | | 1.5 | | 2 km | |

DRAMATIS PERSONAE

Home Government, Britain

Duke of York: Commander-in-Chief, British army

Lord Liverpool: Prime Minister

Lord Bathurst: Secretary of State for War and the Colonies

British North America, Canadian Command at Quebec

Prevost, Lieutenant General Sir George: Captain General of H.M. Forces and Governor-in-Chief of British North America

Baynes, Colonel Edward: Adjutant General

Freer, Lieutenant Noah: Military Secretary

Gray, Captain Andrew: Acting Deputy Quarter Master General, Upper Canada

Myers, Colonel Christopher: Deputy Quarter Master General, Upper Canada

Clerk, Major Alexander: Assistant Deputy QMG, York

LeLièvre, Captain Tito: Assistant Deputy QMG, York

Bruyeres, Lieutenant Colonel Ralph: Commanding Royal Engineer

Upper Canada

Sheaffe, Major General Sir Roger Hale: Commander-in-Chief of H.M. Forces and Acting-President of Upper Canada

Loring, Captain Robert: Aide-de-Camp

Coffin, Lieutenant Colonel Nathaniel: Aide-de-Camp

British Army, Upper Canada

Vincent, Brigadier General John: Commander, Niagara

Heathcote, Lieutenant Colonel Rowland: Commander, York Garrison

Earl, Master and Commander Hugh: Provincial Marine Squadron Commander, Lake Ontario

Gauvreau, Lieutenant François: Provincial Marine

Plucknett, Thomas: Superintendent and Store Keeper, York

Ingouville, Lieutenant Philip: Acting Engineer, U.C.

Hughes, Lieutenant Colonel Philip: Commanding Royal Engineer, U.C.

Powell, Grant: Surgeon, Provincial Marine and York Garrison

Strachan, The Reverend John: Garrison Chaplain; Parish Pastor, York

Indian Department

Givins, Major James: Assistant Superintendent

Executive Council

Scott, Thomas: Chief Justice

Powell, William: Puisne Justice

McGill, John: Inspector of Public Accounts; Magistrate, York

Militia, Upper Canada

Shaw, Major General Æneas: Adjutant General

Chewett, Lieutenant Colonel William: Commanding Officer 3rd York, Magistrate

Allan, Major William: 3rd York; Magistrate

Town of York

Baldwin, Dr. William: Magistrate; lawyer

Cameron, Duncan: Magistrate; merchant

McLean, Donald: Magistrate; Clerk of the Assembly

Ridout, Thomas: Magistrate; Surveyor General

Wood, Alexander: Magistrate; merchant

Beikie, John: Sheriff

United States Federal Government

Madison, James: President

Monroe, James: Secretary of State

Gallatin, Albert: Secretary of the Treasury

Eustis, William: Secretary of War, 1812

Armstrong, John: Secretary of War, 1813

Hamilton, Paul: Secretary of the Navy, 1812

Jones, William: Secretary of the Navy, 1813

U.S. Army Northern Department/Ninth District

Dearborn, Major General Henry: Senior Officer Commanding

Conner, Lieutenant Colonel Samuel: Aide-de-Camp

FIRST BRIGADE

Pike, Brigadier General Zebulon: Commander

Pearce, Colonel Cromwell: Second in Command of Brigade, Commander Sixteenth Infantry

Fraser, Lieutenant Donald: Aide-de-Camp

Jones, Captain Charles: Aide-de-Camp

Nicholson, Captain Benjamin: Aide-de-Camp

Hunter, Captain Charles: Brigade Major

Swan, Major William: Senior Officer, Fifteenth Infantry

Forsyth, Major Benjamin: Commander, Rifle Regiment

Ripley, Lieutenant Colonel Eleazar: Commander, Twenty-first Infantry

McClure, Colonel Francis: Commander, Federal Volunteer Regiment

Macomb, Colonel Alexander: Sackets Harbor Garrison Commander, winter 1812/13

Scott, Captain John: Company Commander, Fifteenth Infantry

Beaumont, William: Surgeon's Mate, Sixth Infantry

Trowbridge, Amasa: Surgeon; expedition-volunteer

SECOND BRIGADE

Chandler, Brigadier General John: Commander

Mitchell, Lieutenant Colonel George: Commander, Third Artillery; expedition-volunteer

U.S. Navy, Great Lakes

Chauncey, Commodore Isaac: Senior Officer, Commanding the Lakes

Woolsey, Lieutenant Melancthon: Commander, *Oneida*

Elliott, Lieutenant Jesse: Commander, *Conquest, Madison*

Myers, Ned: Seaman, *Oneida, Scourge*

"Part of York the Capital of Upper Canada on the Bay of Toronto in Lake Ontario."
Elizabeth Frances Hale's 1804 version of the village of York omits its pattern of streets
and the numerous creeks flowing into the bay, but it presents a fair impression of the
clapboard houses with their outbuildings and fences. The mixed forest crowds the town
to the north while lofty elms and oaks left standing during the clearing of the town
site provide shade. Of particular interest is the Town Blockhouse at the foot of the bay,
with a large Union Flag at its peak. Nearby are the low brick structures of the Provincial
Parliament's Upper and Lower Houses. (LAC, 34334)

PART ONE

The Town and the War

The town, according to plan, is projected to extend to a mile and a half in length, from the bottom of the harbour, along its banks. Many houses are already completed, some of which display a considerable degree of taste.

GEORGE HERIOT, 1803

The Commander of the Forces submitted to the consideration of His Majesty's Government the propriety of strengthening the Post of York by a regular fortification, as the seat of Government of Upper Canada.

NOAH FREER, APRIL 1812

CHAPTER 1

"Reared as if by enchantment"[1]

YORK, UPPER CANADA, 1812

As the capital of Upper Canada, the town of York was to become a formidable military post. At least, this was the dream of Colonel John Graves Simcoe.

Simcoe made his name as an officer in the British army while leading his Queen's Rangers against the American rebels during the War of Independence. One outcome of the war was that thousands of colonists remained loyal to the Crown and wanted nothing to do with the new republic forming under the name of the United States. Many of these Loyalists sought refuge in the Maritime provinces of Canada or abroad, while the British government encouraged others to settle in the British territory north of Lakes Erie and Ontario and along the St. Lawrence River. To administer this vast region more efficiently and secure it from invasion, the government split it into the colonies of Lower and Upper Canada (approximately modern Quebec and Ontario) in 1791. Because of his reputation and familiarity with America, Simcoe was selected as the first lieutenant-governor of the upper province and was soon off to Canada to turn the wilderness into a model British community.

Simcoe's devotion to his task in Upper Canada was relentless. Although plagued by ill health, he personally examined the province's shores and settlements, its rivers and forests, from Kingston to the Detroit River and north to Georgian Bay. He dealt tirelessly with all the complexities of forming a new government and social structure and developed ambitious plans for the colony.

One of Lieutenant-Governor Simcoe's early worries was that the colony's original capital at the town of Niagara, situated across the mouth of the Niagara River from New York State, was easy prey for an American attack, fears of which rose and fell during his administration. Simcoe's preferred location was a site in the interior of the province on the Thames River that would someday become London, Ontario, but it would be years before a sufficient number of settlers could move into that area. As an alternative, he looked due north across Lake Ontario from Niagara to an expansive bay on a stretch of shoreline that was known in those days as Toronto.

The name derived from the Mohawk *Tkaronto*, meaning " where there are trees standing in the water."[2] This was actually an allusion to the stakes that natives drove into river and lake bottoms to form fish weirs along the shores of *Lac de Taronto* (later Lake Simcoe). As time passed, the term *Taronto* came to refer to the whole region extending 60 miles south to the shores of Lake Ontario, and when French explorers and fur traders began to map the area they used the name in various forms to label the region. One of the main routes from Lake Ontario northward, today's Humber River, was known as the *Rivière Taronto,* and when the French built a post near its mouth in the 1720s, it was called Fort Toronto. The buildings and stockade were abandoned after ten years of use, but a second fort, built in the 1750s and named Fort Rouillé, was also referred to as Fort Toronto.

A succession of native peoples had inhabited the region over the centuries. When British surveyors began their work along the Lake Ontario shoreline near the ruins of Fort Rouillé in the 1780s, it was the Mississauga, close relatives of the Ojibwa nation and frequently identified by that name, who lived in the area.[3] They were a migratory people, gathering in the late winter to form camps and collect maple sap before moving down to Lake Ontario in the spring. Here they planted corn on the river flats, built weirs to catch salmon, trout and eels through the summer, harvested rice and corn in the fall and, breaking up into family groups, headed for the winter hunting grounds inland. The Mississauga/Ojibwa chiefs met with British agents to discuss the use of the forests and lake shores that were their homes and, believing that the newcomers would share the land and leave it as unaltered as possible, they agreed to "sell" it. The 90-mile stretch west from the head of the Bay of Quinte to Etobicoke Creek (just west of Toronto) went for about £1,700 worth of clothing, muskets, iron tools and other goods in 1787 and 1788.

A Royal Engineer named Gother Mann drew plans for a town at Toronto in 1788, locating it east of old Fort Rouillé on the large bay that was formed by a long and low-lying sandy peninsula. Simcoe thought the bay a good location for the new capital and ordered the forest cleared for the town near the Don River at the eastern end of the bay. He was particularly impressed by the expansive basin, which he described as "the best Harbour on the Lakes, [which could] readily be made very strong at the slightest expence, and in the progress of the

John Graves Simcoe (1752-1806). Lieutenant-Governor Simcoe's term in Upper Canada lasted from 1792 until 1796. During this time his plans for the province drew criticism from some quarters. Kingston merchant Richard Cartwright wrote: "Our good Governor is a little wild in his projects, and seems to imagine that he can in two or three years put the country into a situation that it is impossible it can arrive at in a century."[1] (TRL, T34632)

Country, impregnable."[4] Creating a military stronghold in a central location, away from the American shores, was foremost in Simcoe's mind. He foresaw a naval arsenal and dockyard erected near the town while a military post with a heavily armed battery would be built to guard the entrance to the bay. The place would become the headquarters of the Provincial Marine, the small squadron of warships that gave Britain command of the lakes. In time of war Simcoe could direct the defence of the province's lakefront from this stronghold at the same time as he kept the relatively short overland route to Georgian Bay open for the fur trade companies. Although Simcoe's ideas seemed unrealistically ambitious, his superiors in England heartily approved his plans for the new town.

In the summer of 1793, Simcoe sent a detachment of the Queen's Rangers to clear the forest at Toronto for the garrison, settlement and roads. He was in the process of anglicizing place names across the province, and for the town he found inspiration in the news of the Duke of York's recent victory against the French in Holland. On 27 August 1793 Simcoe formally named the capital-to-be York.[5]

In the spring of 1812 as war clouds gathered along the frontier, York had grown into a settlement that spread for a mile and a half along the north shore of the bay.[6] People sometimes called it Little York as if to avoid confusion with New

York City, but it was a dubious comparison since there were only 700 inhabitants. The "old town" was located about 1000 yards west of the Don River with seven streets running north and south and four streets east and west, creating square blocks composed of one-acre lots that were nearly all taken up with homes and businesses. Beyond them to the north, where the land gradually rose above Lot Street, lay the "park lots" of 100 acres each, most of which had yet to be cleared of forest. In 1797, an opening to the west of the town was marked out for civic use, making space for a market, a court house, a church, jail, school and hospital. West of this corridor was situated the "new town" where the houses were still widely scattered in 1812. Only King Street, one avenue up from the bay in the old town, ran the entire length of the settlement, with bridges over the half dozen or so ravines where streams flowed down to the lake; one of the largest was Russell Creek, forming a natural boundary at the western end of King. The citizens had also raised funds to bridge the two channels of the mouth of the Don River and gain easy access to the peninsula, a perfect location for livestock to graze and the people to take their leisure. Although years later a critic would declare that York was still "a paltry little dirty hole … her streets as yet blocked up with stumps and mud," one visitor announced in 1807 that he had experienced "sentiments of wonder, on beholding a town which may be termed handsome, reared as if by enchantment, in the midst of a wilderness."[7]

The town was still very much surrounded by the wilderness. During Simcoe's time the nearest grants of land had been given to government officials, military veterans and leading merchants, in part to encourage their move to the town from Niagara and elsewhere.[8] By holding on to the properties until their value had risen, the owners prevented others from settling near York, which was a source of bitter grievance among some settlers. About 700 people lived in the outlying hamlets of York Township while more than 5,000 others had formed settlements and cleared remote farms in the fifteen other townships of the Home District, which stretched from Whitby in the east to West Flamboro overlooking Burlington Bay. Roads fanned out from York: Asa Danforth's byway heading east to the District of Newcastle and on toward Kingston; Dundas Street going west to the District of Niagara at Burlington Bay.[9] Yonge Street climbed inland toward Lake Simcoe, although its beginning was still situated north of the town at a junction that later became known as Yorkville.

The forest around the town was relatively untouched by settlement except for the patches of homesteads and hamlets and the strings of roads and lanes that had been cut out of it.[10] The forest was a general mixture of broadleaf and needle although there were places, such as the sandy hills east of the Humber River, where lofty pine, hemlock and cedar dominated. Oak and elm, beech and ash preferred the more fertile soil on the northern edge of town. There were stands of black walnut, curly maple and cherry of such high quality that they were harvested for export to the furniture makers at Quebec and beyond. The inhabitants made no mention of bears or cougars or lynx in the woods, but deer still roamed in large numbers and it was not unheard of for a pack of wolves to attack livestock grazing on the edge of town, prompting the release of hounds at the head of a search and kill expedition. Sportsmen found delight in such pursuits or in blasting away at the vast flocks of water fowl on the bay and in the marsh to the east. Passenger pigeons passed in such numbers during the spring and fall that they darkened the sky, and fish – Atlantic salmon, trout, pike, perch – were so plentiful that there was no stretch in the tale when a man said he took 300 in one night with a spear. In the warm months, mosquitoes that bred in the marsh joined the pestilent clouds of flies and gnats that not even smokey fires could disperse, while grubs and worms infested the abundant gardens of the settlers. Songbirds found plenty of food there to nurture their young and, soaring aloft above the forest and shore, ospreys, red-tails, peregrines and eagles surveyed a complete menu of fin, feather and fur.

York was in every way a pioneer community. The muddy streets were virtually impassable in the wet months, and dusty and rutted during the hot and humid summers, their only saving grace being that they froze in the winter and, with a frosting of snow, made travel by sleigh a pleasure by comparison. There were a few rough-hewn, round-log houses to be seen, but many more had been built of squared timbers and then clapboarded with pine with brick chimneys at either end and roofs covered with wooden shingles.[11] About half the houses were frame structures and many of these had a course of brick acting as insulation behind the pine weatherboard. The home and store of merchant Quetton St. George was a rarity in that it had a brick exterior and a tin roof. Many of the properties were fenced to a lawful height of five and a half feet to enclose the gardens, fruit trees, sheds, stables and sundry other outbuildings typical of frontier life. There were, in addition to the residences, eight or more shops, several storehouses, nine taverns (and up to sixty stills), most of which were located in the six hotels, a small private lending library and a single newspaper, a government organ, the *York Gazette*. Only a few public buildings had been erected, including a stockaded jail and the Home District Grammar School. Both of these were on King Street in the space between the old and new towns. Nearby was the plain, frame building put up in 1807 and known as the "Episcopal church," the only place of worship in the Anglican parish. On the lot next to his home and store at the foot of Frederick Street, merchant William Allan had erected a pier extending 200 yards into the bay, where the water was deep enough to allow

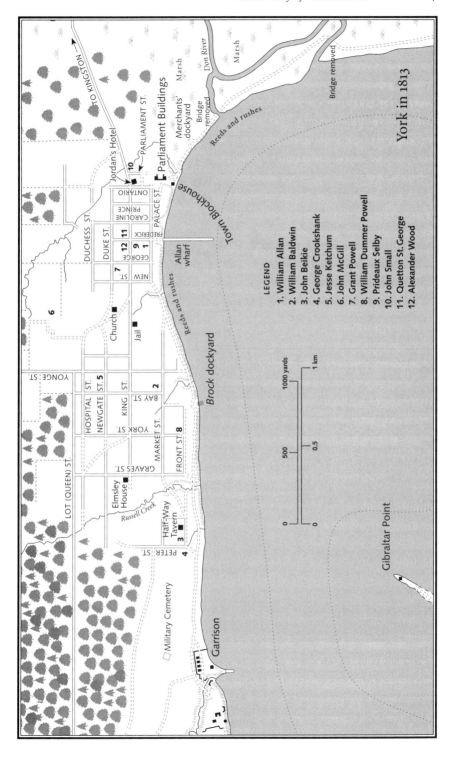

York in 1813

LEGEND
1. William Allan
2. William Baldwin
3. John Beikie
4. George Crookshank
5. Jesse Ketchum
6. John McGill
7. Grant Powell
8. William Dummer Powell
9. Prideaux Selby
10. John Small
11. Quetton St. George
12. Alexander Wood

View from York Barracks, 1796. Among the watercolours painted by Elizabeth Simcoe, wife of the lieutenant-governor, is a view from the original army post on the west side of Garrison Creek, showing the tree-lined shore of the bay stretching eastward toward the town. Before the turn of the century the army extended the wharf shown here and relocated the garrison to the east side of the creek, on the point of land above the wharf. (AO, F 47-11-1-0- 236)

York garrison and Government House. Lieutenant Sempronius Stretton, 49th Foot, drew this pen and ink sketch of the garrison and "The Generals," or Government House as it became known. The latter stood on the west bank of Garrison Creek, across from the blockhouse and barracks within the stockade on the east bank. The sketches, which Stretton drew one above the other in May 1803, are here placed side by side to provide a panoramic view. (LAC, C14822)

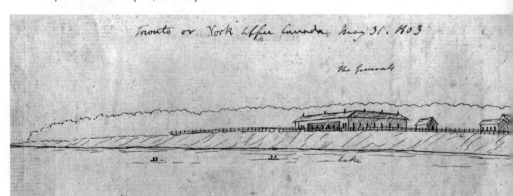

a vessel to tie up without fear of grounding. William Cooper's dock was a little farther west.

Despite the evidence that York was flourishing, Lieutenant-Governor Simcoe would have been disappointed that his scheme for a well-defended naval base had not come to fruition. Maintaining an empire upon which the sun never set and waging nearly continuous warfare in Europe and abroad were costly matters and the British home government could support only the bare essentials of administration and defence in Upper Canada. As a result, the only dockyard on the bay was a small private facility just north of the mouth of the Don River. And, at this place, as elsewhere on the bay, the water was too shallow for the easy launch of even the smallest schooner so that, compared to Kingston, where there were busier dockyards, very few vessels had been built at York. Before 1812, the government had constructed only one public schooner, the "yacht" *Toronto*, launched in 1798 primarily to serve the communications needs of provincial officials.[12]

The military presence was so weak as to prompt an officer in the Royal Engineers to report early in 1812 that York was "entirely open to attack, and no Works of any description have hitherto been constructed for its protection."[13] The fortification that Simcoe wanted constructed at Gibraltar Point, the western tip of the peninsula, consisted of two blockhouses filled with stores sent to Canada during the early 1790s but never fully distributed. There was a guardhouse beside it but it was weakly manned and there were no heavy guns mounted in the run-down old redoubt near by. The only other building of note nearby was the stone lighthouse standing over 60 feet tall on the southwest shore of the peninsula.

Opposite Gibraltar Point and on the eastern bank of Garrison Creek lay the main military post, known simply as "the garrison" or "the fort" rather than "Fort York." It consisted of a single two-storey blockhouse, designed to accommodate seventy men, at the brink of the 15-foot embankment overlooking the lake. A road had been cut down to the shore where a wharf ran out into the

water. A stockade protected the west side of the wharf and continued to the land and up the bank to surround the blockhouse and twenty or so cottage-like huts. Most of these were barracks, each large enough to house sixteen soldiers or a pair of officers, while the other buildings served as the hospital, bake house, canteen and guard house. Nearby was a wooden magazine in bad repair, a carriage shed and two storehouses. There were no batteries at the garrison, the only serviceable artillery being a pair of 6-pdr. field guns. A number of old guns and carronades, brought to York by Simcoe but never mounted, lay collecting dust in storage. About half a mile east of the fort was the home of George Crookshank, the acting commissary general, and on the shore near it there appears to have been a large storehouse for military supplies.[14]

The only other sign of military presence at York was another blockhouse erected two miles to the east of the garrison on the lake shore, just beyond the limit of the old town and close to the Don River. Like the others it was two-storeys, constructed of square timbers, covered with weatherboard and probably painted white. It was designed to house seventy men and to also serve as a storehouse. From the time of its construction in 1798, the Eastern or Town Blockhouse, as it was known, had been an unpopular station since the troops tended to get sick soon after being sent there; its proximity to the marsh at the mouth of the Don was said to be the cause. The blockhouse had likely never been filled to capacity, as the evidence suggests that the military contingent at York rarely exceeded the standard company strength of 100 officers and men.[15]

Simcoe's dream of a permanent capital rising at London having failed, York remained the centre of the colony, though without much in the way of governmental trappings. There had been an ambitious plan in the 1790s to construct an official residence with two large wings for the lieutenant-governor, but this was another scheme that had not been realized.[16] Construction began on the wings in 1797 at a site adjacent to the Town Blockhouse and resulted in two one-and-a-half-storey brick buildings each measuring 24 by 40 feet. They were built end to end on a roughly north-south line, separated by a 75-foot gap. A covered walkway joined them on the side facing the town and behind each wing was a smaller wooden structure used for offices. This pair of nearly identical brick structures became the first purpose-built Parliament Buildings of Upper Canada; the Legislative Council met in the southern building and the House of Assembly in the northern one. Until other public buildings were built, court sessions, town meetings and church services were also held in one or another of the wings, while most officials set aside rooms in their own homes for their civil work. To meet the rise in administrative business, private dwellings were rented for office space, the most prominent of these being Elmsley House, the home

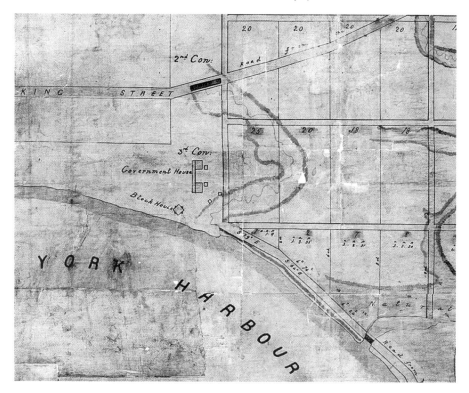

East end of York, 1810. A survey of the town identified the location and structure of the Parliament Buildings and the adjacent structures. The Town Blockhouse was nearer the lake. (LAC, H2/440/Toronto/1810, NMC 22818)

of the late Chief Justice John Elmsley. It occupied a large lot at the other end of town near the corner of King and Graves streets, close to Russell Creek. A room at Elmsley House held the town's public library, founded in 1810.

When money became available for the governor's "mansion" in 1800, the idea of filling in the space between the upper and lower houses was dropped and the new structure was erected at the other end of town on the west side of Garrison Creek across the ravine from the military buildings. Peter Hunter was the first lieutenant-governor and commander of the armed forces in the province to take up residence there. The new Government House was a one-storey frame building with a low peaked roof, plain in style, though much more comfortable in its accommodations than the timber structures of the garrison.[17] It faced eastward toward the garrison and the town, standing 90 feet wide across the front with two wings extending out the back to the west. Along the bank of the lake was a rail fence and near the house were sheds and other outbuildings and a large garden overlooking the Garrison Creek ravine.

As capital of the province and the largest town in the district, York was home to many of the leading officials in Upper Canada. By 1812 six different men had performed the duties of lieutenant-governor, each with his own predilections and goals, advised and assisted by the appointed members of the Executive and Legislative Councils.[18] These long-serving councillors and other senior officials, akin to modern cabinet ministers, judges and career bureaucrats, formed the core of administrative consistency and exercised great power and influence over the affairs of the province, much more than did the Legislative Assembly of twenty-four elected representatives of the province's ridings. One of the best known figures in Canadian history, Major General Isaac Brock, temporarily assumed the duties of lieutenant-governor in the autumn of 1811 and, as war clouds darkened and his military responsibilities became more demanding, he relied heavily upon these senior advisors.

The leading officials living at York during Brock's term included sixty-five-year-old Chief Justice Thomas Scott, who served on both councils and also as speaker of the Legislative Council, his multiple posts being typical of the leading men in the province.[19] William Dummer Powell was fifty-seven years old and, as Puisne Justice, he was next in line of authority to Scott. John McGill had been an officer in the Queen's Rangers and from 1801 was the inspector general of public accounts, in charge of the colony's finances. Another aging veteran of the British army who had been in Canada since before Simcoe's time was Prideaux Selby, who did double duty as the auditor- and receiver-general. Lastly came Æneas Shaw, a former Queen's Ranger, first appointed to the Executive Council in 1794. He had retired from public service in 1807 but four years later accepted promotion to major general in the British army and appointment as the adjutant general of the provincial militia.

Of this group William Powell was the only one who had not served in the military, though his Loyalist blood ran as red as that of the others.[20] He was born in 1755 in Boston to a family of some wealth and received his education abroad before returning home, where he met Anne Murray, who was working as a milliner with her sister and an aunt, their family having fallen on hard times. Anne's father disapproved of Powell, which eventually prompted the lovebirds to elope and move to England in 1775, where they started their family. William soon learned, however, that the Americans rebels had confiscated his father's property and, with it, his financial support, and so he undertook a career in law and went alone to Montreal in 1779 to open an office. There he prospered well enough to have his family join him and live in a home on Mount Royal until he won an appointment as a senior judge in 1789 and moved his family to the wilderness frontier at Detroit. He later played a key role in help-

The Powell residence. The ample, two-storey, wood-frame home overlooking the bay from Front Street in the "new town" was a suitable residence for Puisne Justice William Dummer Powell and his wife, Anne, and befitted their place of prominence in York society. (TRL, T11439)

ing Simcoe set up the administration of the new province of Upper Canada and in 1794 rose to the post of puisne justice. His heart was set on stepping up to become the chief justice, but despite his years of hard service, others were always picked to fill the vacancy when it came up, a fact that annoyed both Anne and him to no end. Like most of the other leading government officials, the Powells moved to the new capital at York, and they took up quarters in a handsome, two-storey frame house on the southeast corner of Front and York streets overlooking the bay.

The next tier of civil authorities included the magistrates or justices of the peace, as they were alternately called, and all the other local officers, from town clerk to jailer. The magistrates exercised wide powers under a system originated in twelfth-century England; in the Upper Canada application, the lieutenant-governor selected men who his councillors believed could handle the responsibility of this key post.[21] By tradition, they had to be familiar with the locale, possess a reasonably high level of material worth and demonstrate the strength of character and wisdom necessary to deal with all the many local issues competently and judiciously. They served for indefinite terms and were responsible for setting the budget for the district and identifying the priorities for improvement of the community. They also made sure that the men elected or appointed at the annual town meetings to be the sheriff, assessor, tax collector, path masters, pound keepers and so on did their jobs. The magistrates met publicly four times a year to hold the Court of General Quarter Sessions of the Peace, during which they dealt with administrative matters and also provided the initial level of the judicial process, hearing complaints, rendering verdicts, assessing fines when necessary and assembling juries for more contentious issues. Between sessions, they dealt, individually and in groups, with all the town and district matters informally, which, even in a thinly settled area like the Home District, incurred a significant expense in time and energy. In return, the magistrates received a salary and a portion of some of the many administrative fees. But, perhaps most importantly, their position gave them a place of high status in their community and great influence over the management of local affairs.[22]

There were as many as twelve men serving as magistrates for the Home District in 1811, the most active of whom was the Scottish merchant William Allan, who had been a magistrate since 1800.[23] Duncan Cameron had some commercial ties also, whereas Thomas Ridout was the surveyor general of Upper Canada, and Donald McLean held the prestigious and demanding post of clerk of the Legislative Assembly. Each of these individuals epitomized the industrious ambition, and good connections, necessary to achieve prominence in their town, district and province.[24] Allan, for example, emigrated from Scotland in 1787 as a seventeen-year-old clerk with a fur trading company in Montreal. The next year he moved to the company's post on the Niagara River and in 1795 relocated to York, by which time he had become an agent for another Montreal enterprise. He built the first commercial wharf at York in 1801 and worked in a number of different partnerships to become one of the leading merchants at the capital, dealing in commercial sales and contracts with the Indian Department and the army. Besides his responsibilities as a magistrate, over the years he also served as the treasurer for the Home District, the collector of customs, the district inspector of flour, potash and pearl ash (he owned a potashery), the postmaster for York and a returning officer. He was the treasurer for the Anglican parish, the people's warden for the church, a militia officer from 1795 and became the major of the 3rd Regiment of York Militia in 1812. He also had good social connections through his wife, Leah, who was the daughter of a surgeon in the Queen's Rangers and the niece of Colonel Samuel Smith, another magistrate, who became the province's administrator in 1817.

These two echelons of authority and their families formed the influential upper crust of York and the surrounding area. The majority of the inhabitants lived their lives and had little opportunity to gain anything more than passing notice. They formed the labour force, owned their shops and taverns, plied their trades, harvested their crops, cut their timber and left scant records of their daily lives. Nearly half the population, for example, was made up of boys and girls under the age of sixteen, but mention of them was limited to isolated comments such as when the young Robert Baldwin, who would grow up to play a vital role in the shaping of Canadian government, was considered to be "very noisy and unruly" due to having been spoiled by his grandfather.[25] A portion of the inhabitants were people of colour, labouring as free men or serving still as the property of their Loyalist owners, but there are only rare references to their presence.[26] And none of the Mississauga/Ojibwa seem to have taken up residence in the town, preferring only to visit there or to stop at the farm of James Givins, a Queen's Rangers veteran and the assistant superintendent of "Indian Affairs" for the Home District.[27]

A brief introduction to three men who figure in this story sheds some light on the lives of the common folk. The first, Ely Playter, was thirty-seven years old in

Playter's bridge, 1796. George Playter, Sr. settled his family on land beside the Don River and built one of its first rustic crossings in the vicinity of present-day Danforth Avenue, as recorded in this watercolour by Elizabeth Simcoe. (AO, F 47-11-1-0-233)

1812.[28] His father, George, was a native of Suffolk, England, who had married into the Quaker faith and moved to New Jersey, where he opened a shop as a cabinet maker. George's allegiance to the Crown cost him all his property during the American War of Independence and, after a period in Pennsylvania, he moved his wife and four sons to York in 1795, where they soon acquired land in the township about a mile and a half up the Don River. The Playters were part of the wave of "Late Loyalists," enticed to leave the United States when Lieutenant-Governor Simcoe eased land acquisition requirements in an attempt to bolster Upper Canada's population. George Playter's sons were ambitious and they soon all owned property by the Don and near Yonge Street and took turns helping their father with his farm. Ely became a successful farmer but also owned a tavern with his brother James for a number of years and engaged in the timber business with his brother George, Jr. Between 1801 and 1809 he was the town clerk and through the years he was an active member of the militia. In 1806 Ely married Sophia Beman, the daughter of Elisha Beman, another Late Loyalist, who owned a tavern and a farm. By 1812 they were raising three boys and two girls.

Similar in origins to Ely Playter but fated ultimately to walk a different path was John Lyon. He was born in 1767 on Long Island, New York, and emigrated to Upper Canada with his newly wed bride Elizabeth in 1794 in the Late Loyalist stream.[29] The vague records of Lyon's early years in the province show him to have been typical of the hard-working pioneers. He and his young family lived in town until 1796 and then moved to a lot on the east side of Yonge Street in Markham, where he kept a farm and ran a modest distillery. A local folk story has it that Mrs. Lyon matched her husband for strength and endurance by being able to carry a 180-pound bag of wheat on her back to have it ground at a mill a mile away from their farm. Her husband saved her from having to do that too frequently, however, by buying a second lot near their home, where by 1802 he had built a sawmill and a grist mill on a branch of the Don River. Lyon also kept a residence in York, where he answered to the yearly militia roll call, performed his civic duties by serving on several juries, completed brief terms as a path master and fence viewer in 1799 and as a constable in 1806, and probably sold his whiskey. By 1812, he was forty-five years old, had a household of teenaged children and was a well-established businessman; among the many visitors to his mills was Ely Playter.

It was almost by chance that the third fellow settled at York. His name was Isaac Wilson and in the spring of 1811 he and his father set out from the county of Cumberland in the northwest corner of England to sail to America. They landed at New York and ventured across the state, their purpose being to find a place where Isaac could seek his fortune. He was about to put down stakes near Oswego when someone convinced the pair to take a schooner across Lake Ontario to York. Here they visited a kinsman named John Wilson, who was an avowed Loyalist and, though well into his seventies, still busily operating the King's Mills on the Humber River. Wilson offered Isaac instant employment and an income of $120 a year, which, combined with the nest egg his father had given him, was all the young man needed to make his way. His father returned to England and Isaac was soon writing home that "the longer I remain in this country the better I like it."[30] He got along well with old Mr. Wilson and worked hard to earn his keep. The winter of 1811-12 was a trial but he kept at his labours even as frigid temperatures caused balls of ice "about the size of peas" to form on his eyelashes. He met other family acquaintances and was soon lending his money at good rates, reporting home in detail about the price of goods, the wealth of crops and the profits that could be made. Isaac was especially pleased to be free of the oppressive system of taxation that had burdened his father in England and, with his mind fixed only on hard work and self improvement, he urged his brother to join him in what he considered to be "this land of liberty."

On Sundays many of the inhabitants of York sought inspiration at the church, whereas others waited for a Methodist circuit rider to pass through or joined the quiet reflection of the Religious Society of Friends, the Quakers. The people also thronged together to attend theatrical performances, such as the "celebrated tragedy … [of] 'Douglas, or, *The Noble Shepherd!*'" put on by "the company of *Comedians from Montreal*" in September 1810.[31] On another occasion they assembled to witness *"Philosophical, Mathematical and Curious Experiments"* conducted by "Messrs. Potter and Thompson from London," and they lined up one day to pay a penny fee for the privilege of looking at an orangutan brought to town by a traveller.[32] Forms of recreation were simple but no less enjoyable. There was fishing and hunting, building and sewing bees, a billiard table in one of the taverns, horse racing on the peninsula to Gibraltar Point and back, and fox hunts in winter across the ice of the bay. The lieutenant-governor's celebration of the Queen's birthday each January drew more than 100 people who dined and danced from dusk until past dawn. Less formal were the shivarees that were held after weddings, where a crowd of masqueraded partiers, well-lubricated with whiskey, would gather in the street outside the house where the newlyweds had retired and bang pots and pans, sing, chant and do anything else that would inhibit any romancing in the matrimonial bed. If not suitably treated by the home owner, the revellers often returned the next night and the night after that until their good times drew complaints and turned into a brawl, with broken heads and blackened eyes, and the magistrates and constables in the thick of it trying to sort things out.

John Strachan (1778-1867). Apart from his drive for personal advancement, Strachan was also devoted to the loyal cause, as he expressed it to Governor-in-Chief Sir George Prevost in October 1812: "I am ready to exert myself in any way consistent with my Clerical character to contribute towards the defence and security of the Provinces."[2] (TRL, T13801)

The shepherd who came to tend to the souls at every level of York society in June 1812 was thirty-four-year-old John Strachan.[33] Like many other immigrants, he was a Scotsman with no end to his ambition. He took up teaching part time in his teens as he continued to attend university classes, and when it looked as if he would never be able either to complete the work for a full degree or to make a comfortable living as a parish school teacher, he accepted the invitation to teach the children of well-to-do families at Kingston, Upper Canada. He arrived there in 1799 and worked industriously to prove his abilities and earn the respect and patronage of his employers and their friends. Deciding that teaching would not lead to the level of prominence he wanted, Strachan fulfilled his mother's dreams for him by turning to the church and being ordained first a deacon in 1803 and then a priest in the Church of England in 1804.

Strachan's first parish was at Cornwall, on the St. Lawrence River, where he found the locals to have little interest at first in his Anglican sermons. In 1807 he married Ann McGill, the widow of one of the sons of the wealthy McGill family of Montreal, who brought a yearly pension to the marriage as well as a strong connection to a family of high status. Through his commitment to the church and the community, Strachan earned respect and an ever-widening circle of influence, which he enhanced by inaugurating a new school at Cornwall. Here he came to know and form lasting relationships with the sons of some of the province's leading citizens, making it a priority to prepare them for careers that would allow them to further their families' success. John Beverley Robinson was one of these, the son of the province's surveyor general, who, after his father's death, went to live with Strachan's family, forming a friendship that would span a lifetime. In 1811 Strachan received an honorary degree as Doctor of Divinity from the University of Aberdeen and was thereafter formally referred to as the Reverend Dr. John Strachan.

The next critical step in Strachan's career came in 1812 when he accepted appointment to the parish at York. He was hesitant to relocate, but when Isaac Brock offered to enhance Strachan's income by making him chaplain of the garrison and the Legislative Council, the pastor agreed. Although it took him some time to adjust to his new position, the Reverend Dr. Strachan and life in the capital proved to be a perfect fit. He was surrounded by the elite of the province and within walking distance of many of his former students, young men who were now studying law or commencing careers in commerce. He quickly established himself as a community leader, baptising and burying, tending to the ill, participating in local matters, offering his help, expressing his loyalty to the Crown, but never shying away from criticizing anyone he suspected of not having the best interests of York and Upper Canada in mind. And when he was not out and about, he was writing letters, recommending this fellow for sponsorship and telling that one what political stance to take. He had views to expound on the administration of the church and the defence of the province. And he was apt to distribute copies of his sermons far and wide or to offer up his thoughts on higher education, with poetry attached, to a distant dignitary. Indeed, packed into the five-foot, six-inch frame of John Strachan there was as great a passion for involvement and leadership as existed in just about anyone else at York.

Later in the nineteenth century, historians looked back on these early days of Upper Canada with rose-tinted glasses and promoted the idea that the settlers, Loyalists and others alike "kept as clear as possible from causes of discord.... [and] [t]he consequence was that harmony and good progress marked the early career of the province."[34] This was quite inaccurate, of course, because Upper Canada was no closer to being an idyllic haven than any other community was. From the first days of Simcoe's administration up to Isaac Brock's dealings with the Legislative Assembly, the province had known one set of controversies after another. And York, being home to so many of the principal citizens of the colony, probably saw more scandals and conflicts than most.

Among the incidents of adulterous conduct and pistols fired at ten paces that startled the citizens of Little York was a controversy in 1810 involving one of the town's leading men. Alexander Wood was born in Scotland in 1772 and emigrated to Canada at the age of twenty-one, quickly joining the ranks of the industrious young men sometimes snidely referred to as the "scotch Pedlars."[35] After jointly owning a brewery at Kingston, he moved to York in 1797, formed a partnership with William Allan and then opened his own store in the old town at the corner of King and Frederick streets, specializing in high quality imports. Wood moved easily among the influential people of the colony and became close friends with William Powell, John Strachan and the military commissary

The Episcopal Church at York. As one of the first structures erected in the "civic square" between the old and new towns, the church, which did not become known as St. James' until 1827, was a plain frame building. Public subscriptions funded the church, which was first used in 1807; construction was completed during the next couple of years. (TRL, T35212)

George Crookshank, another of the old Loyalists. As proof of his acceptance among the elite, Wood became a militia lieutenant in 1798, a magistrate in 1800 and a commissioner for the Court of Requests in 1805 and had numerous other public positions, including a directorship on the library board.

It was in the execution of his duties as a magistrate in June 1810 that Wood committed a fateful indiscretion. A Mrs. Mitchell complained to him that a man had attempted to rape her, but that she had fought him off with a pair of scissors and cut him in the groin. She could not name her assailant, so Wood summoned a number of young men of the town to his home, explained the accusation and ordered them to remove their trousers so that he could see if they bore any wounds on their genitals. Some of the men were so intimidated by the circumstance that they quickly complied with Wood's request to clear themselves of blame, but James Ross, a married man with children, hesitated and requested that Dr. James Glennon be present. Wood rejected this suggestion and dismissed Ross, but by this time the news was out and the snickering about Wood's apparent interest in men's genitals had spread to such an extent that he was being chastised on the street and labelled as the "Inspector General of Private Accounts."[36]

The matter was brought to the attention of Justice Powell, who asked his friend for an explanation. All Wood would say was that he had "laid himself open to ridicule and malevolence."[37] Powell was devastated and angered by what he perceived to be Wood's admission of guilt and scolded his friend, telling him that he had betrayed the public trust and was destined to be fined and incarcerated, as an example against such overtly perverted behaviour. Powell moved quickly, however, to stifle any further investigation on the condition that Wood leave the colony immediately. Putting his business matters into the hands of an associate, Wood departed for Scotland, abandoning the judge to public censure for having used his powers to protect a man already deemed guilty in the court of public opinion. Acting in one of her favourite roles as self-appointed protector of local mores, Anne Powell vowed that if Alexander Wood ever came back to York he would certainly not be welcome in her home. When Wood took the risk of facing public humiliation anew by returning from Scotland in 1812 to continue his commercial enterprises at York, Mrs. Powell was true to her word and shunned him.

Of greater significance to the development of Upper Canada than the sordid affairs that unravelled at York was the growing unrest among the inhabitants about the way the province was being administered. The complaints ran back to the earliest days when tools and farming implements brought to the province for distribution among the settlers by Simcoe were locked up in the blockhouses on Gibraltar Point and left there, without explanation. Twenty years later people were still complaining that "The authorities would not allow these to be given out except to favourites."[38] Bigger issues of contention concerned the wastage of public funds, the selection of "favourites" for public posts and the way in which land reserved for the Church of England and the government or granted to the United Empire Loyalists was left undeveloped, much to the detriment of the

Alexander Wood (1772-1844). Wood enjoyed a place among the leading citizens of York before his troubles in 1810, as reflected in a comment made by Anne Powell in a letter to her brother in 1807: "We are got into our new Church, it is a good building and we have decidedly the best Pew in it – our Friend Wood was the purchaser."[3] (*The York Pioneer*, 54, 1959, 26)

settlers who lived in between the unimproved tracts of forest and swamp. The Late Loyalists might have received land for free but it was often located in out of-the-way places and had survey and lease fees attached to it which took strug- gling families years to pay off.

The various issues heated up especially during the administration of Lieu- tenant-Governor Francis Gore between 1806 and 1811 when "radicals" openly opposed to the government won seats in the Legislative Assembly. Their success was largely owing, in the opinion of leading officials of the province, to the great influx of settlers from the United States who had no allegiance to the Crown. One of the Crown's own appointees who ardently supported the opposition was the Irish-born Robert Thorpe, who was sent to Upper Canada to serve as a judge on the King's Bench in 1806. Thorpe immediately began exposing the many faults in the government system and was soon joined by John Mills Jackson, a land owner with friends in high places in Britain who arrived to settle near York in 1806 also.[39] The two men, and their close acquaintances, saw eye to eye on the problems of the province and were outspoken about their discontent with the government. At a private dinner party one time, Jackson shocked some of his neighbours by railing against "that damned Scotch faction, with the Gover- nor at their head [who] are striving to bear down all before them.... Damn the Governor and the Government."[40] Thorpe was suspended from office in 1807 and Jackson returned to England at the same time, where he published a pam- phlet bitterly condemning the government. Thanks to influence of his friends, however, Jackson was never taken to task for his views. Despite his opposition to government policies, he returned to York in 1811 and set up a store three miles up Yonge Street, ready to voice his radical views to anyone who would listen.

The suspected "disaffection" of a large portion of the province became Isaac Brock's problem when he took on the responsibilities as administrator of the province after Francis Gore returned to England on leave in 1811. It affected di- rectly his preparations for what seemed to be the imminent declaration of war by the United States. Without an adequate number of soldiers from the British regular regiments posted in the province, Brock knew he would have to rely on the men of the colony to take up muskets. But the general had been in Canada for ten years and he realized that no effective training program for the militia had ever been put in place and that the ranks of the citizen soldiers would be filled by what he termed "many doubtful characters."[41]

According to the province's militia law, every male between the ages of six- teen and sixty was required to show up for the annual muster and give his name, age and place of residence, or pay a fine of 10 shillings.[42] Exempt from duty were the Quakers, Mennonites and Tunkers, who paid 20 shillings annually in lieu of their service. Nearly all the government officials, from the justices, magistrates and sheriffs down to school masters, ferry men and even one worker at each grist mill, were likewise exempt from militia duty, without penalty. The purpose of this roll call was to have an accurate record of those men who could be called to defend town, district or province in time of insurrection or war. But there had never been funds for properly arming and drilling the 13,300 men on the militia lists across the province in 1812. As a result, the annual training day was more likely to devolve into a party, as Ely Playter, who took his service seriously, revealed in a June 1802 diary entry.

> Hurried to the allarm Post to join the Company. The men attended pretty generally, and we march'd into Town and joined the Battalion in the Park. The Men look'd very well we went throgh no exercise only formed the Line. The Captains gave in their returns to the Colonell and he disismiss'd us offering a Bever Hatt to the best marksman with the smooth board guns and another to the best with their Riffles we fired at the Target by Turns in the Companys – Mr. Hale got the first Hatt and Mr. P. Mills the other … The Town of Course was full of People, and a great number drunk, whare was restling, Jumping, Boxing and the like all the evening.[43]

As the threat of war with the United States grew through the early months of 1812, Brock attempted to better prepare the militia for active duty by having the Legislative Assembly make changes to the Militia Act. These included the formation of "flank" or "elite" companies for each of the province's regiments. They were to be composed of selected volunteers between the ages of sixteen and forty-five who could at least be fully outfitted with muskets and ammunition, if not uniforms and the normal infantry equipment. This sharp alteration in normal procedures heightened the awareness at York of a looming war and excited the aspirations of patriotic young men. "I am to be promoted to a Lieutenancy in the Grenadier Company," wrote twenty-one-year-old George Ridout, "which is a Flank Compy. composed of picked men nearly of a size and who are tolerably well-disciplined."[44]

The announcement that flank companies would soon be organized was coupled with a reorganization of the militia at York. Two regiments had formed over the years, the 1st Regiment of York Militia centred in the town and the 2nd York in the western townships. Due to the rise in population, the 1st York had grown to more than 1,100 officers and men, and so Brock decided to split it into two units. The new 1st York would be composed of men from the northern part of York Township and its environs, whereas individuals in the town and the settlements to the east would make up the 3rd York Regiment. Militia preparations escalated and Ely Playter, now possessing a commission as lieutenant, wrote that the 3rd Regiment assembled for drill on 24 April with six companies present the next day. They numbered 256 rank and file content to serve in the battalion companies and another 131 "volunteers" hoping to be picked for the flank companies. At the annual muster on 4 June, Playter noted, "Went to Town by 9 O'Clock – 8 Companies of Militia [the two flank companies had been picked on 4 May] met Drilled till past 2 O'Clock, the officers held a Court Martial on a Man for refusing to obey orders fined him 10/. the Col. forgave him the fine – Officers Dined at Jordan's about 25 in number all very agreeable."[45]

The urgent preparations were not wasted. Lately promoted Lieutenant George Ridout wrote to his brother on Saturday, 27 June: "an Express has come here announcing to us that *War is declared* – every one is in motion Genl. Brock went to Niagara last night … I do not know what we will do with our large family."[46]

No one at York knew how a war with the United States would affect life in their town, but as in every community along the opposing lake and river shores, they were about to find out.

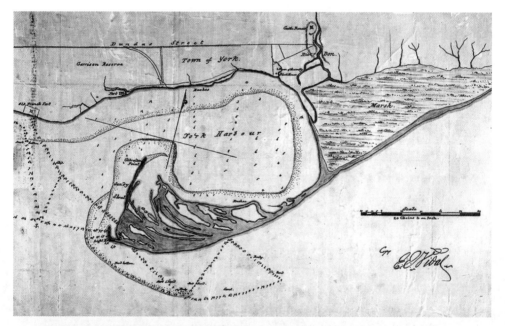

Plan of York Harbour. The navigational chart done in 1815 shows the townsite and military land, the post-battle garrison to the west of Garrison Creek. the location of the Parliament Buildings at the eastern end of town and where the Town Blockhouse had stood. The marshlands to the east were almost as large as the bay itself. (LAC, v30/440/ Toronto/1815, NMC 19400)

CHAPTER 2

"Worthy of being at the head of affairs"[1]

THE DEFENCE OF UPPER CANADA

The town of York and how it would fare in a war with the United States was but one item on a long list of responsibilities faced by the governor-in-chief of British North America, Lieutenant General Sir George Prevost. From his headquarters in Château St. Louis at Quebec, Sir George had to anticipate how the Americans would wage war and then decide how best to defend Britain's possessions.

Prevost was well suited to his task. He had been born into a military family in 1767 and joined his father's regiment with a commission as an ensign at the age of twelve, soon entering the fight against the American rebels.[2] Over the next thirty years, helped in no small way by patronage, he proved himself on the battlefield in the fever-infested islands of the West Indies, rising through the ranks and earning a number of civil posts and honours. He was the lieutenant-governor of Nova Scotia in 1811 when he received his most prestigious appointment – to civil and military command of the British colonies in North America. His jurisdiction was a large one, encompassing the provinces of Upper and Lower Canada, Nova Scotia, Cape Breton Island, New Brunswick and Prince Edward Island, as well as Bermuda and the fishing station at Newfoundland.

Prevost was small in stature – "this tiny, light, gossamer man," as an admirer once described him – but no less brave.[3] He knew what it was to be wounded in battle, to fight a tough rear-guard action, to oversee a complex amphibious operation. His fluency in French and courteous manner enhanced his talents for compromise and conciliation, especially in light of the French-Canadian element in his new command. He was devoted to the service and highly professional, cheerful and good-natured in temperament: "a quiet man, good, without prejudices," one observer wrote of him.[4]

Sir George Prevost (1767-1816). In April 1812 Lieutenant General Prevost had yet to visit Upper Canada, but reports had convinced him that Kingston was "a very exposed and unfit situation for our vessels" and he proposed "the removal of the naval establishment by degrees to York."[4] (LAC, C6152)

Sir George took command at Quebec on 14 September 1811 just as diplomatic tensions between Great Britain and the United States were reaching a boiling point. The Americans were making no headway in their attempts to persuade the British government to lift trade sanctions against France and its allies that seriously damaged American commerce. And the Royal Navy continued to impress American sailors from merchant vessels without regard for their rights. Some newly elected legislators were about to join the "War Hawks" already in the U.S. House of Representatives and the Senate, where they would renew their proclamations of outrage about impressment and trade interference as well as the threat posed to the western frontier by aboriginal nations with close links to the British. This threat of an impending war with the United States presented Prevost with his first critical challenge and eventually monopolized his entire term as governor-in-chief. Perfectly aware of the dire situation, Prevost began familiarizing himself with his new command as soon as he reached Quebec, determining how well it could withstand aggression from the south. As there was only enough time that autumn for him to make a quick inspection of posts as far west as Montreal, he relied heavily on Major General Isaac Brock and other advisors for information about Upper Canada, where it was expected the Americans would make their first major thrust.[5]

The reports from Upper Canada were not encouraging since none of the fortifications was considered strong enough to repel a concentrated attack and no safe depot for war materiel had ever been developed. Kingston, for instance, the key transshipment point at the head of the St. Lawrence River, was within 20 miles of the American shore with only a small garrison to defend it. There was a lack of funds to pay for improvements, shortages in provisions and armaments and not enough military or civil officers to handle all the work. The militia would have to play a key role in defending the province, but the presence of so many former Americans living in Upper Canada made the province's leading citizens wonder just how loyal the people would be in the event of invasion. Then there was the "radical" element in the Legislative Assembly, which was expected to oppose new legislation to put the province on a proper war footing.[6]

Prevost knew at least that he could rely on Major General Isaac Brock to implement the best possible defence of Upper Canada, despite the limited resources at hand. Brock's situation was indeed a difficult one. In the spring of 1812 he had just over 1,200 British regulars under his command, spread out along the 800-mile border from St. Joseph Island in northern Lake Huron to Fort Amherstburg on the Detroit River, Forts Erie and George on the Niagara River, York, Kingston, and smaller posts such as Prescott 70 miles down the St. Lawrence River. As well as employing the doubtful militia to bolster his military strength, Brock would also to have to form alliances with the aboriginal nations, although he believed them to be anything but dependable.[7] Fearing what would happen if the Americans were allowed to mass their troops for an invasion, Brock petitioned Prevost for reinforcements in December 1811 and suggested making pre-emptive strikes across the frontier at Detroit and Fort Mackinac to weaken the Americans before they even began mobilizing for war.

One of the few advantages that Brock enjoyed was that he could move men and supplies on the lakes with virtual impunity. The British operated two squadrons of armed vessels, one on Lake Ontario and the other on Lake Erie and the waters above. This was the Provincial Marine, which had been founded in the 1770s and administered by the quarter master general's department of the British army at Quebec. Although a handful of its officers and seamen were ex-Royal Navy men, the Marine Department, as it was also known, was completely independent of Britain's senior service. There had been several plans over the years to develop it into a fully equipped naval force but they had come to nothing because of the expense. Instead, the freshwater navy had evolved into a loosely run transport service for men, munitions and private cargo. A report prepared for Prevost in January 1812 clearly indicated the deficient state of the

THE WAR OF 1812
THE NORTHERN THEATRE

0   50   100 miles
0   50   100   150   km

■ fort   ● battle site or town/village

Lake Superior

St. Joseph I.

■ Fort Mackinac

Lake Michigan

Lake Huron

Georgian Bay

Nottawasaga Bay

Penetanguishene

Nottawasaga R.

L. Simcoe

Bay of Quinte

UPPER   CANADA

York

Lake Ontario

MICHIGAN TERRITORY

Stoney Creek

Burlington Bay

Fort Niagara

Charlotte

Sodus

Ft. George
Queenston

Grand R.

Niagara R.

St. Clair R.

Thames R.   ● Moraviantown

Port Dover

Ft. Erie ■ Black Rock
● Buffalo

Genesee R.

Detroit ●

Detroit R.

Sandwich

Malden (Fort Amherstburg)

Raisin R.

Frenchtown

Long Point

Lake Erie

Erie ●

Put-in-Bay

PENNSYLVANIA

Fort Miami ■

Fort Meigs ■

Maumee River

Sandusky R.

Cleveland ●

Fort Stephenson

■ Fort Defiance

BLACK SWAMP

Allegheny River

OHIO

● Urbana

● Dayton

● Pittsburgh

Ohio River

VA.   VA.

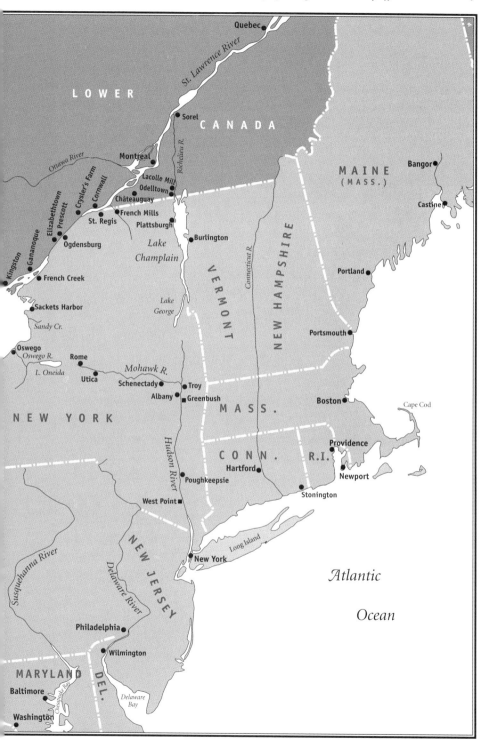

warships and their officers and of the facilities and support staff ashore, but the very existence of the squadrons was a valuable asset for the British. By force of numbers alone, the Provincial Marine was more than a match for the American presence on the lakes, which consisted of one U.S. Navy brig on Lake Ontario and an army vessel at Detroit.[8]

After listening to his closest advisors and reading the reports written by Brock and others, Governor-in-Chief Prevost devised his strategy for the defence of Canada. Not surprisingly, his priority was the preservation of the stronghold at Quebec, the same approach taken by the French during the Seven Years' War (1756-1763) and by the British during the early stage of the American War of Independence (1775-1783). Isaac Brock could not have been surprised by Prevost's decision, since he had made a similar one during the war scare of 1807 while he was the senior commander at Quebec. The humiliation of the U.S. Frigate *Chesapeake* by HMS *Leopard* during an incident involving British deserters in June of that year had caused such a diplomatic controversy that war seemed about to erupt any day. Petitioned for reinforcements by a subordinate officer in Upper Canada, Brock had answered, "every consideration of prudence and policy ought to determine me to keep in Quebec a sufficient force to se-cure its safety."[9] Prevost used similar language when he laid out his strategy for his superiors in England. "Quebec," he wrote on 18 May 1812, "is the key to the Whole and must be maintained…. If the Americans are determined to attack Canada it would be in vain the General should flatter himself with the hopes of making an effectual defence of the open country, unless powerfully assisted from Home." Any steps taken against the enemy, he added, must be done with care so "that the resources, for a future exertion, the defence of Quebec, may be unexhausted."[10] With that in mind, Prevost only increased Brock's strength to about 1,650 officers and men before the Americans made their declaration of war on 18 June while he kept a force of 5,550 in Lower Canada, about half of them at Quebec.

In assuming this line of reasoning, Prevost had the full approval of Prime Minister Lord Liverpool's Tory government and of the Crown.[11] The British government's overwhelming concern was the war against Napoleon and his allies in Europe and abroad, which strained the nation's resources nearly to the breaking point. There was little in the way of men and materiel to spare for a war in North America and Prevost was warned "not [to] expect that the Forces under your command can receive any considerable addition by the detachment of troops from home."[12] As well, heavy demands on British finances meant that Prevost's budget was tight and he was advised to take steps "adequate" to defend the provinces "without making any considerable demand upon the Treasury of this Country."[13]

Prevost hoped to avoid war altogether, and to this end he strictly forbade Brock from undertaking any aggressive actions along the American frontier for fear of handing President James Madison and his cohorts a controversy they could use to solidify the nation's enmity toward Britain. During his tenure at Halifax, Prevost had seen how the merchants of New England opposed the coming war for fear of what would happen to their profits, and since arriving at Quebec he had learned how prevalent anti-war sentiments were across the United States. His decision to hold Brock back from pre-emptive expeditions was also fully sanctioned by the home government. "You should cautiously avoid," his instructions read, "any act which can have the effect of irritating the Government or the People of the United States or can tend in any way whatever to accelerate the resort to actual hostility against this country."[14]

While hoping for a lasting peace, Sir George began making improvements to the defences of Upper Canada. He activated the long-discussed plan to raise the Glengarry Regiment of Fencibles for employment there and sent up most of the Royal Newfoundland Regiment of Fencibles to serve aboard the Provincial Marine vessels. He also ordered a new schooner for each squadron, forwarded arms and munitions, augmented staffs in the various departments, and approved the repair and improvement of fortifications. Soon after the declaration of war, the 1st Battalion of the 1st Regiment of Foot and the 103rd Foot arrived at Quebec, intended to replace the 41st in Upper Canada and the 49th Foot in the lower province. But Prevost kept the latter regiments, assigning the 49th to the upper province, while the new units remained in Lower Canada along with the 100th Foot, originally scheduled to be sent to Halifax.[15]

In Upper Canada, the defence of the capital, York, was a particular concern and led Brock and his advisors to develop a scheme similar to the vision Lieutenant-Governor John Graves Simcoe had formed. They proposed moving the headquarters of the Provincial Marine from Kingston to York, creating a fully equipped dockyard there and significantly improving its fortifications and storehouse space. Prevost liked the idea, and when he first summarized the plans for his superiors in London early in March 1812, he explained that the end result would be "a Citadel and a deposit for Military Stores for the Land and Lake Service."[16] Constrained by his fiscal limitations, however, Prevost did not set the ambitious project in motion, wisely anticipating the government's response, which eventually advised him that there was insufficient capital for "a measure of this description."[17] In the meantime, Prevost had authorized improvements at the capital to be made in stages, which resulted in the new Lake

GREAT ADVANTAGES,
to those who enlift for
Capt. LIDDELL's Company of the
GLENGARY
LIGHT INFANTRY FENCIBLES.

EVERY Young Man who afpires to ferve His Majefty in this fine Regiment now raifing, will do well to confider without delay, the very advantageous terms on which he enlifts. He is to receive FIVE GUINEAS BOUNTY, and is only required to ferve in the *Canadas* for *Three Years*, or *during the War*, which probably may not laft fo long, when he will, beyond a doubt, receive the Reward of his Services, by obtaining an allotment of the rich and fertile Lands of Upper Canada, or Lower Canada, if more convenient. This important Grant will make every Soldier of the Corps an Independant Man, at the expiration of his Service; enabled thereby to settle comfortably on his own Farm, in a fhort time he will have every Luxury of Life about him : he will be able to take his Wife and Family to Church or Market in his own Cariole, and if he has not a Wife, it will be the fure means of getting him a good one, for Fortune always favors the Brave, and flinty muft be the heart of that Damfel, and vain her pretenfions to tafte, who could refift a *Light Bob of the Glengary's* when equipped in his new *Green Uniform*, which will unqueftionably be the *neatest in the Service.*

Look around you! See how many rich and refpectable Inhabitants of Canada, who were formerly Soldiers, that are now enjoying the reward of their Services, and who date their Profperity from the time when they received their Grants of Land on being difcharged. The fame advantages will be yours. Such of you, on the réduction of the Corps, as are not then Officers, and who prefer the tranquil Pleafures of a Rural Life, may, by induftry and good management, hope to reach the higheft honours which the Province can beftow. In this happy Country, Merit and Ability muft ever lead to Preferment, and the Man poffeffed of thefe qualities, may have it in his power to chufe whether he will be a Colonel of Militia, a Juftice of the Peace, or a Member of the Houfe of Affembly. Brave Countrymen ! you muft be quick in your acceptance of fuch Offers as thefe, or you will certainly mifs the Golden Opportunity ; terms fo evidently advantageous muft foon complete the Regiment, and thofe who are too late, will have caufe all their lives to reproach themfelves for being fo blind to their own intereft. No deception is intended ; for the affurance of General SIR GEORGE PREVOST, as certified by *Colonel Baynes*, Adjutant General, muft convince the moft incredulous, that His Royal Highnefs the PRINCE REGENT will gracioufly attend to His Excellency's Recommendation, by beftowing a Grant of Lands upon every Soldier who has faithfully ferved for the stipulated period.

N. B. A few Taylors, Shoemakers, Carpenters and Black Smiths, will meet with great encouragement in the Corps ; a Serjeant Armourer Quarter Mafter Serjeant, Serjeant Major, Bugle Major, Paymafter's Clerk and Ten Pay Serjeants will be wanted, and fuch men as are qualified for these Offices, will see the neceffity of an early application.

Glengarry Regiment enlistment poster. Although recruiting began in Glengarry County, Upper Canada, it soon spread to the other provinces as the need arose for a full-sized regular regiment.

Ontario schooner *Prince Regent* being built at York. The first steps in laying out new fortifications were also to be undertaken and it was decided to moor all the warships at York during the coming winter, where they would be out of reach of the Americans and better protected.

G iven the restrictions in resources and the strict non-aggression policy under which the British began the war, events turned out surprisingly well, at first. Captain Charles Roberts and a motley force captured Fort Mackinac without a struggle on 17 July. The American general William Hull had already crossed into Canada earlier in the month but soon retreated to Detroit, where Brock, Tecumseh, British regulars, Canadian militia and aboriginal allies forced his ignominious surrender in August. It was the first battlefield victory of Isaac Brock's career and won him universal fame at the same time as it abruptly raised the patriotic spirits of people across the province. By now, however, news had arrived that Britain was ending the trade restrictions that had infuriated American commercial interests and helped bring about the war. In the wake of this report, representa-

The *Prince Regent*. This schooner-rigged warship measured 71 feet, 9 inches long and 21 feet wide on the upper deck and was typical of the Provincial Marine vessels that had cruised the lakes for decades. A handful of men could sail it but a full compliment of 70 officers and seamen was necessary to make it an efficient warship. (TRL, 15218)

20 Dollars Bounty,
will be paid to able SEAMEN,
AND
12 Dollars Bounty
will be given to ordinary SEA-
MEN, on entering for the Marine
Service for Three Years.　Apply
to Lieutenant FISH.
Marine Department.
York, May 21, 1812.

Provincial Marine recruitment notice.
Lieutenant William Fish of the Provincial
Marine was stationed at York during the
construction of the schooner *Prince Regent* in
the spring of 1812 and had this announcement
published in the *York Gazette* to raise a crew
for the new warship. (LAC, C107049)

tives of Governor-in-Chief Prevost and Major General Henry Dearborn negotiated an informal armistice to allow President Madison and his cabinet time to
rethink their declaration of war. For several weeks a return to peace seemed possible, but the Madison government would not change its mind and September
saw an energetic build-up of their troops, especially along the Niagara River.

The Americans launched their next invasion across the Niagara River at
Queenston on the miserably cold morning of Tuesday, 13 October. Brock raced
there from the town of Niagara and was killed leading a hasty charge against the
invaders shortly after dawn. The man who was considered the saviour of Upper
Canada for his defeat of Hull, and who had roused the populace, was suddenly
and irrevocably removed from the equation.

Into Isaac Brock's place stepped Major General Roger Hale Sheaffe. Although
the Battle of Queenston Heights would forever be linked with the name of the
fallen Brock, it was Sheaffe who took command after his death and engineered
the subsequent victory.[18] Instead of rushing forward to repeat the mistake of
Brock's charge, Sheaffe acted thoughtfully and with prudence. He was at Fort
George when he learned of Brock's death and immediately sent a half battery
of Royal Artillery with a screen of light infantry and a party of Grand River Six
Nations warriors to Queenston to keep the invaders under fire. Then he rode up
to examine the situation, established a staging point outside the village where
the troops from Fort George soon arrived and sent to Chippawa for reinforcements. He consolidated his force, marched to the Heights well beyond the range
of even the American skirmishers, met his Chippawa troops and confronted the
enemy around mid-afternoon. The attack was launched and the battle quickly
won, with 925 Americans in captivity. Roger Sheaffe had achieved what every
general dreamed of, indisputable success on the field of battle.

The victory at Queenston Heights lifted Sheaffe to the pinnacle of his career
and placed him in a position to directly influence the flow of the war through
the subsequent winter and spring. Histories of the period have generally given
him short shrift, but since he plays a pivotal role in this story, the events of his
life and career deserve a fuller treatment.

He was forty-nine years old in 1812, having been born in Boston, Massachusetts, in 1763, the third son of William Sheaffe, deputy collector of customs, and his wife, Susannah. It seems that Mrs. Sheaffe was the driving force in the household, determined to use connections to promote her family's interest; perhaps it was she who suggested naming the infant after Roger Hale, the Crown's customs collector and William's boss. Criticized for being too self-assertive, Susannah once wrote to her brother, "People are more disposed to do for those they know, and as Mr. Sheaffe is of so backward a disposition, I am bound to exert myself more than I otherwise should do. I know there are persons who think we might live more obscure, but we shall not be governed by their opinions, as we owe them nothing."[19]

William Sheaffe died in 1771, leaving his family with little. The resourceful widow moved into a house owned by her father at Columbia and Essex streets and turned it into a place of hired lodgings. In 1774 Colonel Hugh Percy of the 5th Regiment of Foot arrived at Boston and rented rooms in the Sheaffe house.[20] His family had great wealth and influence and was part of King George III's inner circle. Destined to inherit his father's title of Duke of Northumberland in 1776, Percy had proven himself as a valiant and capable officer whose popularity among the troops was due to his magnanimity. This quality showed itself when he developed a sympathy for the Sheaffes' situation and took young Roger under his wing, steering him toward a career in the King's forces. For a brief period, Percy placed Roger in the British fleet at Boston but then withdrew him and sent him to England to attend Lochee's Academy, where, it is said, he was a classmate to George Prevost, four years his junior. Percy, now the Second Duke of Northumberland, purchased an ensign's commission in the 5th Foot for Roger in May 1778 and a lieutenancy in December 1780. The boy remained in England, waiting to join the regiment after it returned to Ireland from the West Indies.

In 1787 the 5th Foot went to Canada and over the next years Sheaffe learned about the frontier wilderness while posted at Detroit and Fort Niagara, which were still in British hands at that time. He served under Simcoe and won his esteem as a "Gentleman of great discretion, incapable of any intemperate or uncivil conduct."[21] During this period Sheaffe also became acquainted with some of the other officials who were shaping the new province, men such as the judge William Dummer Powell and the military officers John McGill, Prideaux Selby and Æneas Shaw. In 1795, with Northumberland's direct assistance and encouragement, Sheaffe purchased a captaincy in the 5th and two years later, after returning to England, he acquired a majority in the 81st Foot. He held that rank for four months before purchasing his way as lieutenant colonel into the 49th Foot, in March 1798, where he was junior to Lieutenant Colonel Isaac Brock. The two men led their regiment during the unsuccessful campaign against the

The Brock Memorial in St. Paul's Cathedral. The popularity of Isaac Brock and the heroic nature of his death overshadowed the efforts of all the subsequent commanders in Upper Canada during the war. Richard Westmacott designed this military monument in St. Paul's Cathedral in London. (Photograph by Robert Malcomson)

French in Holland in the autumn of 1799 and were on board the British warships at Copenhagen, in preparation for an amphibious assault, when Lord Nelson won his startling victory against the Danish fleet on 2 April 1801. As with Brock, these two expeditions were the only experiences Sheaffe had under fire from the enemy before meeting the Americans in Upper Canada.

Orders arrived in 1802 for the 49th to go to Canada and Sheaffe returned to familiar territory, where he remained until the war broke out, with the exception of visits to his family in Boston. Besides maintaining his connections to friends and family in Boston and Britain, Sheaffe also renewed his acquaintances with William Powell, John McGill, Prideaux Selby and Æneas Shaw, all of whom held senior civil appointments. In 1808 he was promoted to colonel and in January 1810, at the age of forty-six years, he married Margaret Coffin, his thirty-year-old cousin and the daughter of John Coffin, a well connected businessman in Quebec who held a number of civil posts.[22] Although there is no evidence of Sheaffe having done anything of commendable notice during his second tour in Canada, he was promoted to major general in the block promotion that gave Brock the same rank on 4 June 1811. The Duke of Northumberland was nearly seventy years old by this time, but he had remained active and had widened his own influence, developing firm connections to the British cabinet and the Prince of Wales, and it is not unreasonable to suggest that the Duke continued to influence Sheaffe's advancement.[23] As he waited for a staff appointment, Sheaffe and his wife took up house at Quebec, where Julia, their first child, was born early in 1811. His brother William died in Ireland about the same time and Sheaffe assumed the support and guidance of his children, eventually steering two nephews towards military careers.[24]

In the Sheaffe family history there are references to Roger's concern over his lack of dispensable income, especially around 1811, but the facts indicate otherwise.[25] He had Northumberland's continuing support and that of his wife's family as well as his own military income. The record also shows that he outfitted himself with new and splendidly tailored uniforms and the other trappings of a general's office. Indicative of his affluence was one of his most prized possessions, an exquisite musical snuff box made of gold. It was probably one of the Swiss devices first fashioned during the late 1700s and, being barely four inches long, could easily slip into a pocket. It had two compartments, the lower one housing a clockwork motor and the delicate musical combs and drum, the upper one holding snuff. Sheaffe's little treasure, estimated by one source to be worth $500 at the time, was said to have been capable of playing more than one tune, activated by the wind-up mechanism. And, if the box was placed across the rim of a glass tumbler, the sound of the music was amplified enough to delight a roomful of listeners. Perhaps the music box was a gift from Mrs. Sheaffe, one that the general used to remember her when he was away from home. He brought it with him to Niagara and never suspected where it would end up or whose ears it would eventually please.[26]

The remembrances of family and friends paint an attractive picture of Roger Sheaffe. "He is tall, well-made, and reckoned handsome," wrote one, "very lively, yet prudent and steady in matters of consequence." Another who knew him

Roger Hale Sheaffe (1763-1851). Sheaffe sat for his photograph late in life, from which this widely used print was made. As a young man he was devoted to his mother and siblings, most of whom lived out their lives in Boston. Sending them gifts in 1809, he assured his mother that they proved "I am in a state that does not justify the maternal apprehensions which appear to have taken possession of your heart."[5] (LAC, C-111307)

both as a youth and an old man described him as "the idol of family and friends. His heart was as tender and affectionate as a woman's, joined to the noblest principles of honor and generosity. His disposition was cheerful, and his manner often playful. He was of middling stature, and his person was well-formed. His face was fine, his eyes of the deepest blue, full and prominent; and his teeth were of the purest white, regular and even."[27]

In sharp contrast to Roger Sheaffe's charming appearance and pleasant social life was the evidence of his lacking as an officer. The first reference to it came after the Holland expedition, when the 49th went into garrison on the island of Jersey in the English Channel. Sheaffe was the senior officer present and his administration was so harsh and unjustifiable that the troops on parade cheered when Brock arrived to resume command. Embarrassed as much for Sheaffe as for himself, Brock marched the lot into the privacy of the barracks square, "severely rebuked them for their unmilitary like conduct, and confined them to their barracks for a week."[28]

A much more serious imbroglio unfolded at Fort George in 1803, where Sheaffe was the garrison commander. Once more, his manner with the men was too strict and callous, even for men accustomed to enduring unforgiving reprimands and brutal lashings. Indignation rose among the sergeants and corporals, who could never be sharp enough in their dress, their punctuality, performance or anticipation of orders to please the lieutenant colonel. He berated them in what Brock later described as a "rude manner of speaking," reducing them to the ranks and replacing them with men who were unfit to hold any responsibility; Sheaffe had "little knowledge of mankind," Brock explained. Nor did he know when to let up on the parade ground, drilling the men relentlessly until they "became disgusted with what they should have taken delight to practice." The outcome was a near-mutiny that Brock only just managed to avoid by quick and commanding action and which led to the eventual execution of the main perpetrators. In reporting on the incident, Brock praised Sheaffe's "private character," his expert "knowledge of the duties of his profession" and his great "zeal, judgment and capacity," but there was no denying that he had many enemies among the men, who spread malicious stories about "his disagreeable ways."[29] His discharge from the army was considered as one solution to the problem, but he ended up with a private reprimand and temporary relocation to the less demanding post at York.

Sheaffe and Brock and their regiment spent the next years cycling through tours of duty in both provinces. When Sir George Prevost arrived at Quebec in September 1811, both of them had been promoted to major general, which made them eligible for the command of Upper Canada during Lieutenant-Governor

William Dummer Powell (1755-1834). Powell sat for this portrait just before his death. He was one of the elite citizens at York who counted Roger Sheaffe among their friends. Late in 1812 Sheaffe closed a letter to Powell with, "Thanks for your friendly hints, the benefit of which I trust will never be withheld."[6] (TRL, T13769)

Francis Gore's leave of absence. As it turned out, the post was nearly given to Sheaffe instead of Brock. The latter had requested permission to return home and seek employment with the army in Europe, and, with Brock's query in mind, Colonel Henry Torrens, military secretary at the Horse Guards, the army headquarters in London, advised Prevost in October 1811 to use his own discretion about filling Gore's vacancy with Sheaffe. By this time, however, Prevost had already given the post to Brock, who ultimately chose to remain in Canada, leaving Sheaffe to look on without the appointment he was clearly expecting. He revealed this in a letter to a cousin in Boston at this time, writing, "The expectations of my friends here that I should be placed on the Staff (that is, be employed as a Major-General) has not been realized; for, to their surprise and my mortification, a younger officer at home has been appointed."[30] To whom Sheaffe referred is uncertain, although during this period he saw the forty-one-year-old Brock appointed to Upper Canada and the thirty-nine-year-old Major General Gordon Drummond sent from the staff at Quebec back to England and eventually to the command of a district in Ireland. It must have been a frustrating time for him as the war clouds grew and then burst and he still waited at Quebec for employment.

Even before the Americans declared war, Brock had petitioned Prevost to send additional officers to join his staff and assist with the demanding administrative tasks. The governor-in-chief met this request, in part, in July 1812 when he sent Sheaffe to Upper Canada to act as Brock's second-in-command. There is nothing to be found in Brock's subsequent correspondence to suggest that he genuinely welcomed Sheaffe's arrival. The only indication of his thoughts on the matter was in a letter to his brothers in which wrote, "General Sheaffe has lately been sent to me," and immediately lamented his situation by adding, "There never was an individual so miserably off for the necessary assistance."[31] It was a private comment intended only for the eyes of his family and implied that, even with a man of Sheaffe's rank and experience present, he was still very much in need of competent support.

Nevertheless, it was Roger Sheaffe who picked up the pieces dropped by Brock and won the Battle of Queenston Heights, earning well deserved praise. The Executive Council, composed of his old friends at York, applauded his "coolness, intrepidity and Judgment" and Lieutenant John Beverley Robinson of the York militia mentioned Sheaffe's "determined and vigorous conduct."[32] The *Kingston Gazette* declared that he had "proved himself worthy to fill that important, tho' difficult and dangerous situation" and the native allies soon stepped forward to vow their "readiness to support him to the last."[33] But the pall of mourning that shrouded the province in the wake of Brock's death muted any loud peels of celebration that might have reached Sheaffe's ears under different circumstances. No one was about to name him the new "saviour of Upper Canada," since the late lamented Brock remained on a pedestal, remembered with such epithets as "the only man worthy of being at the head of affairs."[34]

Still, Sheaffe was not left unrewarded. He made a quick visit to York to have himself sworn in as the new president and administrator of the province, gratefully assuming this prestigious position and the annual stipend of £1,000 that went with it. Prevost was quick to send his approval of the army's conduct under Sheaffe's leadership at Queenston and relayed the details to England. The home government greeted the news with regret at the loss of Brock and praise for the efforts of his successor. Furthermore, Prince George Augustus, acting as Prince Regent during the illness of King George III, expressed "his entire approbation of the distinguished Services of that officer [Sheaffe] on this occasion" and conferred upon him the title of baronet of the United Kingdom.[35] The announcement of this honour would not reach the general until five months after the battle, finally allowing him the additional pleasure of being addressed as "Sir Roger".

Command on the active war front involved so much more than winning battles, however. Battles came as sporadic explosions of activity and emotion in what was otherwise a long, drawn-out campaign marked by the gruelling burdens of preparation, maintenance and endless problem-solving and personnel management. This was the reality of Roger Sheaffe's experience as the new commander-in-chief in Upper Canada and the smoke had barely cleared from the Niagara River when he came face to face with his first challenge.

Late on the afternoon of 13 October, after the American prisoners had been marched to Fort George, Captain William Derenzy, 41st Foot, offered to lead a detachment of his regulars across the river to destroy Fort Niagara. There were plenty of militiamen eager to join him, but Sheaffe forbade it since he was already arranging an armistice with his opposite number. Three days later both sides agreed to extend the armistice, which angered British soldiers and civilians alike, especially when they began to see enemy officers sent home on parole, carrying the side arms they had given up after the battle.[36] Nearly all the New York militiamen and a few of the regulars officers were allowed to cross the Niagara River to safety with parole certificates. They were now bound by honour not to take up arms again, until representatives of the warring nations arranged for them to be exchanged for paroled British and Canadian men of similar rank. Although it was an unpopular decision, Sheaffe used the paroles to rid himself of hundreds of men for whom he would otherwise have had to provide food, shelter and medical treatment.

At the same time, the gossip was spreading that Sheaffe had nearly bungled the attack on the Heights by marching his column onto the battlefield in the wrong order. Since the success of an attack depended largely on having the different units lined up the way they had been drilled on the parade ground, the British line was thrown into confusion and took nearly an hour to sort out. When the order finally came to advance, the militia was left without clear instructions, prompting Captain James Crooks of one of the Lincoln Militia regiments to write years later that the attack was "oddly managed."[37] Crooks remembered his surprise at seeing Sheaffe following along behind his advancing lines "with a stick in his hand," rather than leading them as the lionized Brock would have done.

The locals were not the only ones already having doubts about Sheaffe. When Prevost learned that the general had allowed the armistice to be extended, he criticized Sheaffe for "the extensive liberality" he had shown the Americans.[38] The governor-in-chief also bluntly reminded him that such a decision should not have been made "without having had a previous communication with me on this subject who alone in this Country can decide on the policy and propriety of such a measure."

In answer to the reprimand, Sheaffe simply wrote, "it mortifies me extremely that my conduct with regard to the Prisoners … is not approved of by Your Excellency."[39] He did not rebut Prevost's criticism by explaining in detail how badly the outcome of the battle had stretched his resources. He might have pointed out to his superior that there were still regiments of American soldiers posing a threat in the camps near Buffalo and that his own numbers had been reduced by the fighting and the necessity of sending detachments to guard the 400 enemy regulars being transported to the lower province. Or he might have defended himself by citing Prevost's repeated instructions to Brock, namely to maintain a "system of forbearance."[40] Instead, Sheaffe explained that he had been "encouraged by motives of duty" and would end the armistice as soon as it no longer benefitted his situation.[41] This marked the first of several incidents where, confronted by criticism, the general avoided a dispute by saying little and carrying on with the work at hand.

The challenges facing the new commander-in-chief in Upper Canada were large ones. Because Prevost still kept the majority of his armed forces in Lower Canada, Sheaffe was hamstrung by a shortage of staff officers, just as Brock had been. Luckily, most of the men on station were twenty-year veterans with proven competence and energy.[42] They included Brigade Major Thomas Evans, Captain John Glegg, Brock's former aide-de-camp from the 49th Foot, Deputy Quarter Master General Lieutenant Colonel Christopher Myers, Lieutenant Colonel Cecil Bisshopp and Captain Robert Loring, who would soon join as an expert administrative assistant and aide-de-camp. On the Detroit River, Sheaffe depended on Colonel Henry Procter, 41st Foot, while Lieutenant Colonel John Vincent, another of the general's colleagues in the 49th, commanded at Kingston. Key among the local officers who performed staff duties were Lieutenant Colonel Robert Nichol, the quarter master general for the Upper Canada militia, and Major James Givins, a superintendent in the Indian Department who travelled to Niagara from York to act as a liaison with the native allies and a provincial aide-de-camp. Less active because of his advanced years, but indispensable for his knowledge of the province's regiments, was Major General Æneas Shaw, who performed the duties of militia adjutant general in Upper Canada.[43]

Last on the list was Sheaffe's provincial aide-de-camp, Ensign Nathaniel Coffin, his brother-in-law.[44] A forty-six-year-old bachelor and lifelong resident of Lower Canada, Coffin was a surveyor and land agent and had held several civil posts, but lacked any military training except for a very brief commission in the 40th Foot during the early 1780s. He accompanied Sheaffe to Niagara and was promoted to lieutenant colonel following the battle at Queenston.

The logistical demands of keeping an effective army in the field and constantly on the alert weighed heavily on Sheaffe and his staff. In particular, the shaky, makeshift organization of the militia seemed about to collapse as the weather worsened through October and November. "The Militia," Lieutenant William Hamilton Merritt, a Lincoln County militiaman, wrote, "were kept out in masse, doing nothing, consequently most them went home, as their property was suffering, and [there was] no appearance of their being wanted on the frontier."[45] Sheaffe attempted to remedy the situation by discharging portions of the regiments, reshuffling the remaining companies, activating others and ordering all the commanders to submit their lists of needs.[46] He wrote to Prevost on 2 November, hoping that the armistice would not end "before the arrival of vessels with the supplies for the militia, many of whom are in a very destitute state with respect to clothing ... bedding and barrack comforts in general."[47] But when the Provincial Marine vessels *Earl of Moira* and *Governor Simcoe* reached Niagara, it was found that the quantity of shoes and shoe leather was far short of the need and some of the "clothing" existed only as bolts of fabric, with shirts and trousers still needing to be cut out and sewn.[48] Sheaffe and his staff worked feverishly to distribute the supplies as quickly as possible to the detachments that needed them the most. As compensation for their hardships, and to entice some of the deserters to return to the line, Sheaffe allowed each man a pair of grey trousers, a pair of shoes and a jacket or waistcoat, free of charge. Flannel shirts and stockings were offered at reduced rates and blankets and greatcoats were distributed on loan.[49]

During the second week of December the citizens of York stepped up to help by delivering 184 flannel shirts, plus mittens, stockings, socks and leather for shoes. Led by the Reverend John Strachan and Chief Justice Thomas Scott, a group of citizens had developed the idea and their wives and daughters quickly volunteered their skills as seamstresses. The success of the undertaking prompted the headmen at York to form the Loyal and Patriotic Society for the alleviation of the hardships of the men in the field and the families who had suffered due to war casualties and losses; Prideaux Selby, one of the committee members, attributed the origins of the society to his daughter Elizabeth.[50] Before the year was out, the committee began to raise funds through subscription, and Major General Sheaffe, no doubt pleased to receive such support, pledged £200, far exceeding any other individual in his generosity.

The need for basic clothing paralleled other shortages in everything from accommodations to firewood, forage and straw, and the situation was aggravated by gaping arrears in the payment of wages.[51] These matters fell within the jurisdiction of the commissariat and quarter master general's departments, whose confused and overlapping bureaucracies appear to have retarded the best of intentions. To make matters worse, there were not enough competent officers in Upper Canada to oversee the acquisition and distribution of supplies. Edward Couche was in charge of the commissariat in the province and his unwavering adherence to the recently revised rules of the department provoked more problems. In the opinion of Captain Glegg, Couche was "only anxious to stand well in the opinion of some stripling Lord of the Treasury for his saving knowledge, he has completely succeeded in drawing upon himself the odium and indignation of all the gentlemen who were formerly in the habit of furnishing supplies for the use of the King's service."[52] At the distribution end of the process, Lieutenant Colonel Nichol struggled with the obstacles put in the way of his duties as quarter master general on the front lines and declared, "Couche should be hanged."[53]

It was not just Couche's fault, however, nor was it Prevost's for concentrating his resources in Lower Canada. Avoidable mistakes had been made in preparations for the war which aggravated the situation after it began, and only one officer ever put quill to paper to express how they had happened. There were, claimed Brigade Major Thomas Evans, senior officers in the militia, the barracks department and the commissariat who "never have been nor are they now possessed of the necessary information or energy to render them competent."[54] Evans and Lieutenant Colonel Christopher Myers, and others, had warned their former commander, and friend, about these individuals but "Poor General Brock's high spirit would never descend to particulars, trifles I may say in the abstract, but ultimately essentials." As a result, Brock's staff had to work harder and "by stealth" to get anything done properly. The price of Brock's alleged lack of concern for the details was paid in the weeks and months after his death, one small example of which concerned the payment of officers in the western counties. Several of them were put on active duty by Brock himself as he hurried to form the expedition that eventually captured Detroit. But the general gave his orders verbally and apparently without written confirmation so that when Robert Nichol presented their claims for their salaries to the commissariat, they were rejected. Such incidents as this, Major Evans explained to his correspondent, "are not the results of any fault in General S[heaffe], tho' I plainly see he will have to bear the blame."[55]

All the logistical problems and the grumbling they evoked dominated the daily business of Roger Sheaffe and his cadre of officers. Long before winter blew in, however, the sharper edge of warfare made itself felt. The post-battle armistice was still in effect during the first week of November when word began to spread that the Americans were close to challenging the British for control of Lake Ontario. A detachment from the U.S. Navy had arrived at Sackets Harbor, where, the rumours said, "the keel of a 36-gun ship is laid … and they are working very rapidly to have her ready for the spring."[56] Hearing these reports, General Sheaffe ordered an inquiry into what was needed to improve the Provincial Marine "in order to counter-act the efforts of the Enemy."[57] Sheaffe's initiative was well-founded, although he did not discover how important it was until days later when more disturbing news arrived. The U.S. Navy had already sailed and had effectively severed his vital supply route to Kingston.

This single success gave the Americans a vital advantage and set events in motion that would shape the course of the campaign in the spring of 1813. The new commander-in-chief of Upper Canada had yet to face his greatest challenge.

CHAPTER 3

"We have now the command of the lake."[1]

ISAAC CHAUNCEY'S 1812 CAMPAIGN

The War of 1812 had begun poorly for the United States. Generals had been disgraced, armies captured and not one square foot of Canadian soil seized and held. The first year of hostilities would have been a complete loss had it not been for the unprecedented success achieved by the U.S. Navy in battles on the open ocean. Startling to everyone, except the officers and men who sailed them, the nation's warships captured one Royal Navy prize after another in classic ship-to-ship actions. Although the British took nearly as many American navy vessels in 1812, they did not balance the effect of the U.S. Frigate *Constitution*'s destruction of HMS *Guerriere* on 19 August south of Newfoundland. When word reached the eastern seaboard that David Porter's *Essex* had seized the British sloop *Alert* and Stephen Decatur's *United States* had taken HMS *Macedonian*, there were new rounds of jubilation and renewed hope that mighty Britain could be humbled. And there would be more good news to come after William Bainbridge steered the *Constitution* to success against HMS *Java* as the year ended.

Almost lost among the celebrations and outbursts of national pride was a brief but significant naval campaign on the fresh waters to the north. There were no thunderous broadsides from heavy frigates and British masts going by the board, but the November cruises of the U.S. squadron on Lake Ontario achieved a strategic victory that had a far greater impact on the tide of the war than anything accomplished on salt water.

The United States entered the war with one clearly defined strategic goal: capture the Canadian provinces.[2] President James Madison and his chief advisors believed this could be done by sending invasion forces across the Detroit River and at some point, or points, on the St. Lawrence, while an active demonstration

The U.S. Frigate *United States* vs HMS *Macedonian*. The second major frigate action of the war took place on 25 October 1812 500 miles west of the Canary Islands and brought a glorious victory for Captain Stephen Decatur. Not only did the Americans win the battle, but they also sailed the crippled *Macedonian* home as a prize. (LAC, C004847)

on the Niagara River would distract and diffuse the British defences. Former President Thomas Jefferson's oft-quoted prediction that "the acquisition of Canada as far as the neighborhood of Quebec, will be a mere matter of marching and give us experience for the attack on Halifax the next" might have given some patriots faith in such a plan but those in the know recognized Jefferson's words as pure rhetoric.[3] The U.S. Army was under-strength, ill-equipped and widely dispersed, and pre-war legislation passed in the U.S. Congress did little to remedy the situation before hostilities began. Still, Madison's administration ordered armies to be hurriedly assembled and marched toward Canada.

The weakness of the American land force was aggravated by the lack of naval support. Warships, with their ability to quickly transport men and materiel and to cover an exposed flank, were essential to any campaign waged on the shores of the Great Lakes. This was clearly demonstrated when Major General Brock supplied and reinforced his garrison at Fort Amherstburg by water without fear of attack from American warships on Lake Erie and soon forced the capture of Brigadier General William Hull's army.[4]

It was not as if the Madison administration had not been advised to establish squadrons on the lakes. Hull himself had suggested it in 1807 and later claimed to have raised the point with Madison and his cabinet early in 1812. About the same time John Armstrong, a veteran of the War of Independence, a statesman and recognized military expert, advised that "no time should be lost in getting a naval ascendancy on both [the lakes and rivers] for ... the belligerent who is the first to obtain this advantage will (miracles excepted) win the game."[5] Even on the brink of war, the lone naval commander on the lakes, Lieutenant Melancthon Woolsey, wrote from Sackets Harbor on Lake Ontario to emphasize how dependent the northern frontier was on a strong naval defence.

While Sir George Prevost added to his naval force by having the schooner *Prince Regent* launched on Lake Ontario and another one on Lake Erie in the spring of 1812, the Madison administration did nothing. By August when the glaring hole in the strategic planning became obvious, the President claimed that there had been "some mistake" and even alleged later that he and his cabinet "were misled by a reliance authorized by [Hull]."[6] Finally acknowledging their misunderstanding about the reality of war on the northern frontier, Madison and his men decided at the end of August to make gaining command of the lakes a priority. To effect the task, they turned to one of their most experienced and competent naval officers.

Captain Isaac Chauncey was forty years old when orders arrived from Secretary of the Navy Paul Hamilton to take command on the Great Lakes.[7] He had been born in 1772 on the shores of Long Island Sound at Fairfield, Connecticut, and early on showed an interest in life afloat. By the age of nineteen he had accrued enough experience at sea to become the master of a vessel owned by a large New York City shipping firm. Seven years later he was among the

James Madison (1751-1836). Within four months of signing the declaration of war, President Madison realized his administration's error in strategy. "The command of the lakes," he wrote early in October, "by a superior force on the water, ought to have been a fundamental point in the national policy, from the time the peace [the Treaty of Paris, 1783] took place."[7] (U.S. Naval Historical Center, NH48407)

Isaac Chauncey (1772-1840).
As devoted an officer as any
in the armed forces, Chauncey
assured Secretary of the Navy
Paul Hamilton in October 1812,
"No exertions on my part shall be
wanting to accomplish the wishes
of the government before the
winter sets in."[8] (TRL, T15206)

ambitious American mariners who offered their services to the newly created
Department of the Navy and, in recognition of his experience and abilities, as
well as his good connections, he was immediately ranked as a lieutenant, his
commission dating from 17 September 1798.

Chauncey saw nearly continuous service during the Quasi-War with France
(1798-1800) and the Tripolitan War (1801-1805). Although opportunities did not
present themselves for him to demonstrate bravery under fire and acquire the
sort of adulation that Stephen Decatur enjoyed, Chauncey proved his worth
and won promotion to master commandant and then to captain in April 1806.
By now, the navy was in a period of reduction, with no wars to fight and few
chances to win fame and fortune. Some officers, Chauncey included, took furloughs from the service and returned to the merchant trade. In 1807 he was
appointed to command the U.S. Navy Yard at New York City, and over the
next five years he established himself as one of the senior officers to whom the
department looked for advice. When war with Britain came in 1812, commissions to the nation's frigates went to other men and Chauncey remained at the
New York yard until he was selected to solve the problem of naval control on
the Great Lakes. This was going to be a massive undertaking and Chauncey's
proven skill as an effective administrator made him a perfect choice for the
challenge. As proof of his status within the navy, Chauncey was officially addressed thereafter as "commodore," an honorific which the secretaries of the
navy only used on a consistent basis with three of Chauncey's contemporaries
during this period.[8]

Melancthon Woolsey (1780-1838).
Before the war, Woolsey launched the
brig *Oneida,* the first U.S. Navy vessel
on the lakes, at Oswego, established
a base at Sackets Harbor and began
enforcing customs laws. He seized the
British schooner *Lord Nelson* on 3 June
1812 on suspicion of smuggling. It
was later converted for war use as the
Scourge. (U.S. Naval Historical Center,
NRL11122)

Isaac Chauncey was large in stature, "a brave and enterprising man," devoted
to the service and his nation and an expert in all things to do with warships,
their construction and operation.[9] He mobilized hundreds of seamen, marines
and artificers in September 1812, sending them along with masses of naval equipment to Lake Ontario by the water route that linked New York City and Oswego.
He reached the lake himself on 6 October, where he capitalized on the efforts
already undertaken by Lieutenant Woolsey and soon had the equally energetic
and competent master shipwright Henry Eckford building a 24-gun man-of-
war at Sackets Harbor. Chauncey's responsibilities also included the upper lakes
and he initiated activities there by sending officers to open a dockyard at Black
Rock near Buffalo on the Niagara River. But difficulties in transportation and
military setbacks in that region soon led the commodore to focus his attention
on the Lake Ontario squadron. He bought merchant vessels and oversaw the
shipping from Oswego to Sackets of guns, ammunition, ship fittings, rigging,
sails and all the myriad other equipment he needed at his new base to create a
force that could oppose the British Provincial Marine.

Within four weeks of his arrival on the lakes, Commodore Chauncey was
ready to begin testing his enemy's strength. Late on Monday, 2 November, word
reached the Harbor that a strange vessel was reconnoitering the post, and,
thinking that the British meant to cut off the schooner *Julia,* which was carrying much-needed ordnance from Oswego to Sackets, Chauncey determined to
set sail and chase off any interlopers. This he did in the U.S. Brig *Oneida.* The
vessel was a far cry from the likes of a heavily armed frigate, measuring barely 85

feet on the upper deck and armed with eighteen 32-pounder carronades, good for in-close fighting only. Nevertheless, the *Oneida* was the most powerful U.S. Navy vessel on Lake Ontario, or any of the other lakes for that matter, and the one in which Chauncey proudly raised his commodore's pendant.[10]

The last quarter of the moon was disappearing above a ceiling of cloud as the crew of the *Oneida* spread its canvas and the brig began to crawl away from its anchorage. Through the night, squalls of rain swept across the eastern end of Lake Ontario as Chauncey's sailing master, Augustus Ford, and pilot, William Eadus, men well-familiar with the channel out of Black River Bay, pointed out the safest course to deep water.[11] Dawn on Tuesday revealed that the Americans had travelled 35 miles northward and were approaching the Lower Gap of Kingston Channel, between Amherst Island and Simcoe Island. Kingston itself was about six miles to the northeast. This was Chauncey's first opportunity to examine the Canadian shoreline at close range and it is easy to imagine him standing on the brig's quarterdeck with a telescope to his eye as Ford and Eadus and probably Sailing Master William Vaughan, another old hand on the lake, pointed out the key landmarks and navigation perils.[12] In an age when charts of even friendly shores were scarce, this was vital information for the commodore, who knew that he was fated to become familiar with Kingston and its approaches.[13]

Sightseeing soon took a back seat, however, as the mist hanging over the lake dissipated and revealed three enemy vessels at anchor 5 miles to windward. The warships were the main part of the British Provincial Marine squadron and Chauncey immediately took them to be the flagship *Royal George* and the schooners *Prince Regent* and *Duke of Gloucester*. The man in charge of the squadron was Master and Commander Hugh Earl, a twenty-year veteran in the lake service and a resident of Kingston.[14] Earl had probably left Kingston on Monday afternoon bound for Niagara or York, gained the lake just before sunset and, with bad weather closing in, had anchored in the shallow bank just south of Amherst Island. He must have been as surprised as Chauncey was to see his enemy lying close at hand. To boot, with the wind blowing out of the southwest, as it was, Earl had the advantage of sailing downwind to meet the *Oneida*, the tactical advantage known among mariners as "having the wind gauge." The odds were in his favour, although the schooner Chauncey assumed was the *Duke of Gloucester* was actually a merchantman and not cut out for a fight. Nevertheless, given Earl's strength of position, in nearly any other naval setting the outcome of these circumstances would have been certain.

But the British did not man their guns and sail down to capture the *Oneida*. Instead, they remained immobile while the Americans bore up as close as they could on the starboard tack and passed the outcroppings of Wolfe Island to fetch the shores of New York and then lay a course toward Oswego in search of the *Julia*. For four hours the British remained in view, which left Chauncey mystified by his adversary's inaction, since Lieutenant Woolsey had informed him that the British force was formidable. The *Royal George* was reputed to carry twenty-six guns and a crew of 250 men while the *Prince Regent* was thought to have sixteen guns and the *Duke of Gloucester* fourteen, with 150 and 80 men respectively.[15] Puzzled, but no less grateful for having not been forced to fight, Chauncey speculated that Earl must have confused the *Oneida* with one of the British vessels. But this was as nonsensical as the rumours of the British strength because, even at a distance of five miles, there was no mistaking the American brig. On Lake Ontario no other vessel was built and rigged like the *Oneida* or so heavily armed and well-handled by a large and skilful crew.

The fact that Hugh Earl did nothing to make contact with the *Oneida* was proof of his squadron's true capabilities, its history and mission.[16] American reports of its firepower were greatly exaggerated. The *Royal George* mounted only twenty 32-pounder carronades and had but fifty seamen aboard. A detachment of sixty-five soldiers from the Royal Newfoundland Regiment of Fencibles supplemented the crew but did not make it much of a fighting ship; in 1813 it would take 130 experienced officers and men of the Royal Navy to sail the *Royal George* into battle effectively. As for the schooners, the *Prince Regent* never carried more than twelve guns during its service and in 1812 had a crew of perhaps thirty men, whereas the *Gloucester* carried six small guns and was so badly decayed that it had been taken out of service in October and used as a prison hulk at York.[17]

Since the end of the American War of Independence, the Provincial Marine had operated as a transport service without any opportunities to develop the tactics of a fighting navy, let alone the trained officers and crew, guns and equipment necessary to create and maintain such ability. When Earl's lookouts reported the presence of the American brig on 3 November, there was no efficient routine aboard the *Royal George* and its consorts to beat to quarters and manoeuvre in unison to cut off the *Oneida* and put a quick end to Chauncey's Great Lakes command. Earl had attempted to act like a fighting commodore on 19 July by threatening Sackets Harbor, but the attack was half-hearted and soon aborted. The squadron managed to capture one small merchantman in a raid at Charlotte, New York, early in October, but then resumed its transportation role. By November Earl's vessels were committed to making as many supply trips to Niagara as possible before the winter set in, and there was no time (or predilection) for offensive activities. The plan was that all the Provincial Marine vessels would end the sailing season with one final trip to York, where they would be moored for the winter, safely removed from a possible American raid over the ice at Kingston.[18]

Whatever Hugh Earl's reasoning was, the adversaries did not meet in battle on Tuesday, 3 November, and Commodore Chauncey was free to return to Sackets Harbor, feeling confident that he could face the British. The *Julia* had arrived safely in his absence and its cargo of heavy guns was soon being mounted in one or more of the merchantmen he had purchased into the service. The necessary adaptations for the first half dozen schooners were just about finished, and enough seamen and U.S. Marines had arrived to man them, so the commodore decided to sail out in force and challenge the Provincial Marine for the control of Lake Ontario.

November is a nasty month for sailing on the Great Lakes, and Commodore Chauncey might have been content to establish his bases and build warships all winter if he had not encountered Hugh Earl's passive Provincial Marine on 3 November. "I have determined to proceed with the force I have ready in quest of the Enemy," he informed Secretary Hamilton three days later. "The officers and men under my Command are all extremely anxious to meet the Enemy. We cannot command success, but we will endeavour to deserve it."[19]

On Saturday, 7 November 1812 the largest American naval force ever to cruise on the Great Lakes worked its way out from Sackets Harbor and Black River Bay, following a zig-zag course as it tacked against the prevailing westerly winds. The squadron consisted of the brig *Oneida* and six schooners, former merchantmen lately refitted to assume their new roles as warships. They were the *Julia* and *Pert*, each mounting a 32-pdr. long gun on a pivoting carriage (often referred to as a "circle" or "traverse") amidship and a 6-pdr. long gun on each broadside, the *Growler* and *Conquest*, one pivoting 32-pdr. each, the *Governor Tompkins* with two pivot guns, a 32- and 24-pdr. and four 32-pdr. carronades, and the *Diana*, just renamed the *Hamilton*, with five 18-pdr. carronades on each side and a pivoting 24-pdr. long gun. Although not all of the seamen detached for lake service had reached Sackets yet, there were enough on hand for Chauncey to fully man each vessel.[20]

From the quarterdeck of the *Oneida* Chauncey exercised command as squadron leader for the first time in his career, signalling his little flock to keep in its prescribed order, and quickly discovering that their uneven sailing abilities were going to make this difficult. His brig was not the best of sailers either. Lieutenant Woolsey had once boasted, understandably, that the *Oneida* was "the handsomest vessel in the Navy," but handsome or not, it earned the scorn of some of the experienced hands.[21] Ned Myers had been among the seamen who volunteered to join Chauncey's force at New York and was assigned to the schooner *Lord*

Nelson, renamed the *Scourge*, but it was not ready for service yet and so he went with his mates on board the *Oneida*. He considered it a "warm little brig … but as dull as a transport." Built to draw as little water as possible so that it could pass over sandbars at Oswego and elsewhere, Myers added, it "would not travel to windward," meaning that the more it was forced to sail into the wind, the more it tended to drift downwind.[22] He made a similar observation about the unseaworthiness of the schooners, overburdened as they were with guns and large crews, "scarcely fit for the duty on which they were employed."[23]

Chauncey proceeded slowly on this shakedown cruise, giving the officers time to work with their men and establish the many requisite routines. Sunday afternoon found him in the vicinity of the islands known as the Ducks, about 30 miles due west of Sackets. He probably kept a station north of the islands, his lookouts ordered to watch for the *Royal George* and the schooners returning from York. Chauncey's speculation proved nearly perfect because the Provincial Marine flagship appeared, probably in the gap between the Ducks and the shoals extending out from the southeast tip of the Prince Edward Peninsula, bound for Kingston. A signal promptly flew up the *Oneida*'s halliard to make chase.[24]

Seeing his direct route to Kingston cut off, Earl turned north and made for the passage into the Bay of Quinte between Amherst Island and the northeast end of the Prince Edward Peninsula. Chauncey followed but the *Royal George* was a better sailer than any of the American craft, and even with an under-sized crew, Master and Commander Earl outpaced his foe. Sunset came, and the Americans lost their prey in the dark.

The American squadron ended up at anchor between Amherst Island and the mainland, in the north channel of the Bay of Quinte. Earl must have done the same because at first light Chauncey's lookouts again announced "Sail ho" to the east and the pursuit was renewed, this time under the faintest of breezes. As he approached Collins Bay, six and a half miles west of Kingston, the commodore sent the *Hamilton* to capture a small schooner docked at the village of Amherst-view; lacking time to outfit it for sea, the landing party set fire to the vessel after removing any useable gear.

From late Sunday the Canadians living along the mainland had been watching the enemy's actions and sounding the alarm. Lieutenant Colonel John Vincent of the 49th Regiment of Foot held command at Kingston, with about 450 regulars and up to 600 militia. He sent detachments to man the batteries on the several points around the harbour while others assembled to oppose a landing if that was what the Americans had in mind. They waited past midday and into the afternoon as the *Royal George* crawled toward the harbour.

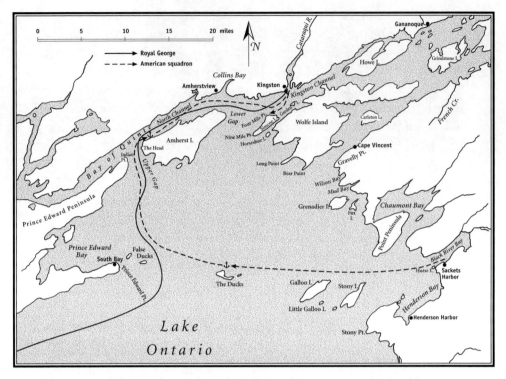

The course of Chauncey's squadron. The U.S. Squadron encounters the *Royal George* near the False Ducks on 9 November 1812 and pursues it through the North Channel of the Bay of Quinte to Kingston. (Map from Malcomson, *Lords of the Lake: The Naval War on Lake Ontario, 1812-1814*)

The protracted chase left the Americans strung out in a straggling line, each commanding officer endeavouring to make the best speed possible. Lieutenant Jesse Elliott led the way in the *Conquest* and opened fire around 3:00 P.M. with his long 32-pdr.[25] The *Royal George* had no guns that would bear, but the seven 6-pdrs., some of them brass field guns, mounted in the shore batteries at Points Murney, Mississauga and Frederick did their best to cover the ship as soon as the *Conquest*, then the *Julia*, *Pert*, *Growler* and the others came into range.

Earl hauled onto the larboard tack and the *Royal George* turned northward into Kingston Harbour, briefly exposing his guns to the enemy. If he fired a broadside at this point, it must have been a ragged one since his short-handed crew was busy shifting the sails, unlashing the anchors, ranging up their cables from below and watching ahead to make sure they evaded the shoals on either side of the channel. Earl proceeded about halfway into the harbour, and ordered one of the anchors to be let go, then the other, and the sails hurriedly taken in. Next he had a hawser passed through one of the aft gunports on the side facing away from the harbour's mouth, which was passed up to the anchor cable on that side and fastened to it. He sent his men to the capstan and as they walked it around, they hauled the hawser tight, using it as a "spring," and the *Royal George* slowly turned to confront the oncoming foe. Now, Earl could fight to save his ship. The ten 32-pdr. carronades were soon blasting away at the Americans as they came into the harbour one after another.

Lieutenant Elliott still led the pack in the *Conquest*. As he and the others had done since leaving Sackets Harbor, he was sailing into unfamiliar waters, so risky a situation that even the handful of pilots in the squadron, men who were familiar with the lake and its ports, refused to take responsibility for conning the vessels. The navy pressed on, however, with lookouts aloft watching for shoals, and a dependable hand or two heaving the lead-lines to gauge the water's depth. All this time the *Conquest* was the target of the shore batteries and Earl's broadside, but, unintimidated, Elliott kept his gun crew firing until he began to run out of room, whereupon he wore around onto the starboard tack and headed for the mouth of the harbour.

Next came the *Julia*, then the *Pert*, the *Growler* and finally the *Oneida* and the *Hamilton*, each of them following Elliott's course. The *Governor Tompkins*, temporarily ordered off on an errand, was recalled but proved to be such a slow, balky sailer that it never caught up to the others and missed the action altogether. For nearly two hours the schooners and the brig engaged the *Royal George* and the shore batteries, making two, maybe three, circuits of the harbour. Their attack was strong enough to prompt Earl to lift his anchors off the bottom and let the ship drift deeper into the harbour. Chauncey toyed with the idea of running the *Oneida* alongside the British ship and boarding it, but decided against it. He believed the batteries and the volleys of musketry on shore and reinforcements seen to join the *Royal George* made it too risky a situation. With darkness approaching and the wind rising, he withdrew his force, expecting to renew the battle next day. On the way out the *Growler* intercepted the little British schooner *Mary Hatt* downbound from Fort George and made it the first captive of the season.[26]

That night the Americans anchored near Four Mile Point on Simcoe Island, within clear view of Kingston. They had time to tend to their casualties, although there were few of these. British fire had killed one seaman on the *Oneida* and wounded three others, while one man was wounded on the *Julia*. It was the bursting of the 32-pdr. on the *Pert* during its entry into the harbour that caused its four casualties, one of whom was its commander, Sailing Master Robert Arundel; stunned by his injury, Arundel failed to get out of the way of the schooner's main boom during a tack and was knocked overboard, sinking out of view before anyone could reach him. Damage to the squadron had been similarly light: a couple of guns dismounted, a cable cut, sails holed, and several shot between wind and water. The only dependable British report of the action showed one man killed and the *Royal George*'s rigging cut up.

During the night the wind rose and brought rain, prompting Isaac Chauncey to abandon the idea of renewing the attack on the *Royal George* the next morning. He ordered the squadron to follow him onto the lake to avoid being trapped in Kingston Channel by a southwesterly gale. By 10:00 A.M. on Tuesday he had nearly accomplished this goal when one of the largest British merchant schooners on the lake, the *Governor Simcoe*, hove into view, making for Kingston, having just delivered stores to Fort George and picked up cargo at York. A new chase was undertaken and alarms sounded on the Canadian shore again as everyone watched the *Simcoe* flying before its pursuers. Chauncey had heard that the schooner was armed with twelve guns and manned by a crew of seventy, but there was no mention of resistance in any of the accounts of the incident.[27] Instead, the schooner's master ran into shoaly water, hoping the Americans would not follow. They did not, but a ledge of rock tore a hole in *Simcoe*'s hull and it sank as it took up its mooring.

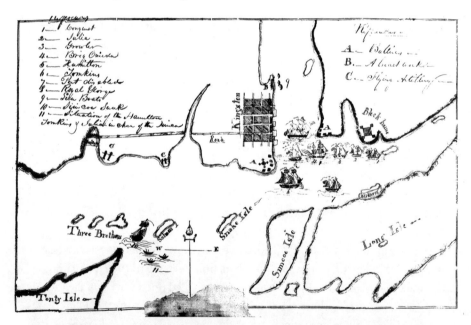

Attack on Kingston, 10 November 1812. This rare view of Chauncey's attack at Kingston provides details about the warships and defensive positions on shore. It gives the wrong impression that the schooner *Governor Simcoe* sank long before it reached safety at a wharf in the harbour. (Jefferson County Historical Society, Watertown, New York)

Pursuit of *Simcoe*. A contemporary portrayal of American naval vessels chasing the merchantman *Governor Simcoe* towards Kingston provides information on their rig and deployment pattern. (Courtesy of Sackets Harbor State Historic Site)

Chauncey gathered his force again and returned to open water as conditions worsened, and his pilots advised him to make for Sackets; he reached port on 12 November. The next day, Thursday, Sailing Master Mervin Mix in the *Growler* arrived with news. Since the captured *Mary Hatt* could not make its way to windward with the rest of the squadron, Chauncey had sent Mix to sail around the east end of Wolfe Island and back up the St. Lawrence River by the south channel. Upon reaching the lake on Wednesday, Mix spotted the *Earl of Moira* near the Ducks en route from York with the merchant sloop *Elizabeth*.[28] Seeing a new opportunity for glory, and additional prize money, he easily corralled the sloop, which was well separated from the *Moira*, and brought it into port.

Chauncey quickly decided to sail in search of the *Moira* and headed out from Sackets with the squadron late Thursday afternoon. After a horrendous night of fighting against northwest winds and very nearly losing half his schooners on the rocky coast of Galloo Island, Chauncey succeeded in reaching Kingston Channel on Friday morning in time to see the British ship just coming to anchor at Kingston. Conditions had deteriorated in the meantime, with snow driven by gale-force winds and "ice making so fast on the Slides of our Carronades that we could not have made use of them," as Chauncey reported later to navy secretary

Paul Hamilton.[29] The Americans returned to Sackets but tried again on 19 November to patrol the Canadian shore only to be forced back by wind and wave and ice. The commodore kept one or more of his more seaworthy craft on the lookout over the next couple of weeks, but there was nothing to report as none of the British dared make another cruise. He learned later that the British vessels were loaded with munitions and supplies for delivery to Fort George but would not risk an encounter with the Americans in open water.[30]

In describing these events to Secretary Hamilton, Isaac Chauncey confidently wrote, "I think I can say with great propriety that we have now the command of the Lake and that we can transport Troops and Stores to any part of it without any risk of an attack from the Enemy."[31] This was true. He had chased the flagship of the Provincial Marine squadron off the lake, taken three prizes, burned another at its dock, nearly captured the *Simcoe* and had seen the *Earl of Moira* hurry into harbour rather than come out with the *Royal George* to regain some of their lost pride. At least two other Provincial Marine vessels were probably at York and there was no sign that they would try to return to Kingston. The rest of the American seamen and marines soon reached Sackets and the shipwrights finished converting three more schooners. Under builder Eckford's watchful eye, a 24-gun ship, the *Madison,* rose in record time in the dockyard and slid down the ways on 26 November. Only the early arrival of bitter winter weather kept Chauncey from embarking a military force and striking at some point on the Canadian shore, plans for which he discussed with Colonel Alexander Macomb, who arrived with about 400 men of his Third U.S. Regiment of Artillery.[32]

Henry Eckford (1775-1832). Eckford was born in Scotland and began his apprenticeship in a shipyard at Quebec. After moving to New York in 1796, he became one of the most prominent and innovative master shipwrights in the United States. (U.S. Naval Historical Center, NH66615)

Worthy of note, and indicative of things to come, was the fact that the commodore did not revise his previous statements about the enemy's naval strength. At one point he had explained to Secretary Hamilton that his adversary had six vessels armed with 108 guns and 890 men, which was "double our force in guns and men."[33] But Chauncey's actual experience with Hugh Earl's squadron, the way the ships were handled and how frantically they avoided action, should have made it possible for him to see past the rumours. As a further inflation of his opponent's firepower, Chauncey reported that "all the officers in the squadron" believed the British "had more than 30 guns mounted" on shore at Kingston, whereas the evidence shows that the British batteries consisted of only seven light pieces of artillery.[34] There were between 1,000 and 1,500 men in arms at Kingston during the attack on the *Royal George*, Chauncey explained to Hamilton on 22 November; when the prisoners taken in the *Mary Hatt* were subsequently returned to Kingston under a flag of truce, allowing Sailing Master Vaughan to talk with his Canadian friends, Chauncey revised these numbers to 600 regulars, with 500 more on the way, and another 2,000 militia within a day's march.[35] Accepting this word-of-mouth intelligence at face value, Chauncey consistently exaggerated the strength of the British in the reports he sent to Washington. These misleading figures added to the flow of information that President Madison and his cabinet contemplated as they made their plans for the upcoming campaign.

With the enemy in port for the winter and the relevant despatches couriered to the navy department, Isaac Chauncey continued to work with the same determination and industry he had shown since receiving his orders in September. Before ice could seal off the 30-acre basin that formed the harbour at Sackets, he had the *Oneida* and the schooners hauled in and prepared for winter. This involved stripping down their sails and running rigging so that they could be dried, inspected, repaired and stored on board or in one of the storehouses being built. The vessels remained armed and ready to fight, and Chauncey had them moored in a line with one of them placed across each end to offer protection on the flanks. The *Madison* was with them but unarmed as there was still much work for Eckford's joiners to complete in its inner furnishings and for the riggers preparing its mast and spars. Nearby the prizes lay waiting to be assessed; Chauncey hoped to have them eventually bought into the service.[36]

The slipway where the *Madison* had stood was now empty but the commodore soon had a new project started. He was probably hoping to build another warship similar to or larger than the *Madison*, but as he waited for permission to undertake such expensive work, he had Eckford draft and begin the cutting out of the timbers for a schooner. This vessel was to have the sleek lines of the speedy little pilot schooners that operated in New York's harbour and Chauncey expected to use it for quick communications in the upcoming campaign.

On shore Colonel Macomb was demonstrating the competence that would earn him praise in years to come as he and Chauncey laid out plans for improving the post during the winter. Two lines of barracks were soon under construction near the north shore overlooking Black River Bay, next to the battery that Lieutenant Woolsey had erected in the summer. This battery was enlarged and strengthened and became known as Fort Tompkins. Nearby was to be a blockhouse for Chauncey's marines and others and on the point of land that created the basin more barracks were soon to spring up. A second fort, named Fort Volunteer, was begun at the foot of the harbour, formed by a rough square of earthen ramparts with embrasures for heavy guns. There was a need for storehouses as well, and when the necessary space could not be constructed fast enough, local barns and outbuildings were rented to hold the massive amount of military and naval gear accumulating in what had barely months before been a quiet lakeside village.[37]

Winter at Sackets Harbor proved to be the final season for a great many unlucky soldiers, marines and seamen. The terrible conditions there broke the health of many of the men who filled the rank and file or the shipboard watches. They suffered from dysentery and the various "fevers" that yellowed their skin and racked their heads and backs and limbs with pain. The maladies were caused by unsanitary conditions in camp, bad water, and bread made from dirty flour ground from unripe and diseased wheat. One surgeon later pointed out that the bake house was situated "on a stagnant part of the lake and [because of] the numerous privies which surround it, … the water thereabouts is impregnated with … excrementious matter."[38] As the men weakened they contracted pleurisy and pneumonia and ended up in a deplorably filthy makeshift hospital. They died in disturbing numbers, particularly in December and January, with the grim total soaring to 500 by spring, according to one source.

For some, however, the winter proved not to be too much of a misery. Ned Myers was one of those who "made good times of it." "We often went after wood," he recollected, "and occasionally we knocked over a deer. We had a target out on the lake, and this we practised on, making ourselves expert cannoneers."[39] Keeping the men well-fed and busily employed were two ways of ensuring their good health.

After petitioning Major General Henry Dearborn, who commanded the northern army from his headquarters at Albany, for more men to help defend Sackets in case of an attack, and giving his officers clear instructions about what needed to be done in the vessels and on shore, Chauncey set out on an overland journey with Henry Eckford to the dockyard at Black Rock. They arrived on 21 December and inspected five merchantmen being refitted as gunboats and then proceeded to Erie, Pennsylvania, where work had just begun to build four schooners. Chauncey was back at Buffalo on 5 January and off to Sackets five days later.[40]

The commodore returned to Sackets Harbor on 19 January and was disappointed to discover that Dearborn had ordered no other troops to the lake. Some progress had been made in the various construction projects and his new second-in-command, Master Commandant James Leonard, slated to be Chauncey's flag captain in the *Madison* in the spring, had reached the post. Chauncey pushed the preparations of the *Madison* forward, ordered the conversion of the prize vessels when they were bought into the service and attended to the endless other matters that wanted his attention. Of critical concern to the commodore was the news brought over by British deserters of a frigate being built at Kingston and two other warships rising in the shipyard at York. This prompted him to recommend to the navy secretary that another large ship be laid down at Sackets and to propose a combined navy and army attack to destroy the shipping at Kingston as soon in the spring as possible. Rather than wait for official approval to arrive from Washington, Chauncey left orders for the cutting and moulding of timber for the hull of a vessel about the size of the *Madison* and then set off for Albany around 5 February to confer with General Dearborn.[41]

It had been five months nearly to the day since he had received his orders to take command on the Great Lakes, and through that time Isaac Chauncey had barely stopped. Except for the few days he would soon enjoy with his family in New York, this would be the order of business for the commodore for many months to come.

James Leonard (1778-1832). Master Commandant Leonard joined the U.S. Navy in 1799 and served during the Quasi-War with France and the Tripolitan War. He was nearly killed in a duel in 1807 and spent from 1809 to 1811 on furlough in the merchant service. He commanded the gunboat flotilla at New York when he received his appointment to the newly launched *Madison* at Sackets Harbor. (USNA, 428-KM-10896)

Seat of war. This detail is taken from the "Map of the Seat of War in North America," published in *A Military and Topographical Atlas of the United States* in 1813 by John Melish. He was a former teacher turned cartographer whose map-making company in Philadelphia was the first of its kind in the United States. Melish's work enjoyed great popularity at a time when few accurate and dependable maps existed. (LAC, NMC 6760)

PART TWO

Strategies and Armed Camps

I hope we shall regain the command of the Lakes so shamefully lost, but to me it appears doubtful, for I do not like the Idea of having our Navy at different Ports.

DONALD MCLEAN, JANUARY 1813

The President has been pleased to express his approbation of the general outline … to attack and carry the Town of York; and after the capture and destruction of shipping and stores there, proceed directly to Fort George and carry it by assault.

WILLIAM JONES, APRIL 1813

CHAPTER 4

"Totally incompetent for the purpose"[1]

WINTER PLANS FOR UPPER CANADA

When the news of Chauncey's attack on Kingston reached York, there was an outburst of alarm. "Our navy is worse than nothing," protested the Reverend John Strachan, "the Officers are the greatest cowards that ever lived, and would fly from a single Batteau."[2] Merchant Alexander Wood, who had returned recently from his brief exile in Scotland, bemoaned the loss of goods which he had consigned to the *Governor Simcoe* only to have them ruined when the schooner sank at dockside after eluding the Americans. "Navigation was altogether shut to us," he wrote, "as nothing would venture again on the lake, the Americans having a Superior force, more able Officers and better Seamen."[3]

The Executive Council of the province's government expressed its deep concern about the turn of events to Major General Roger Sheaffe. "By Land our success has exceeded our Hopes, not so in our warfare on the Lakes," the message read, "[and] if faith is to be given to Report … our Enemies are using every effort to strengthen their Marine…. The consequences that will necessarily follow from the Command of the Lakes being in the power of the United States would be distressing in the extreme to this Province. We speak from the strongest conviction. We believe it would be fatal."[4]

Roger Sheaffe already knew how critical the situation was. He had heard the rumours himself and then received despatches from Lieutenant Colonel John Vincent at Kingston. Paymaster James Brock, 49th Foot, had been captured on the schooner *Mary Hatt* but allowed to return on parole to Kingston, where he detailed everything he had seen at Sackets Harbor. In the same way that American officers accepted word-of-mouth information as fact, the British accepted much of what they heard at face value. Sheaffe, for instance, described what he had learned about the *Madison*: "A frigate of 32-guns – keep it to yourself – was nearly ready to be launched," he wrote to one of his correspondents. "It was said that it would take place on the 17th – a rapid fire progress!"[5] To Sir George Prevost, Sheaffe openly expressed his anxieties about the American efforts to take control of the lakes. "It will require exertions of the most energetic kind to enable us to contend with them in the spring," he wrote.[6] As it was, the winter would provide anxious moments since the *Royal George* and *Earl of Moira* remained at Kingston, unable to join the *Prince Regent* and *Duke of Gloucester* at York as planned, and were in easy striking distance for the Americans across the ice of the St. Lawrence.

The British were not caught totally unprepared for a strong naval thrust by the Americans. Sheaffe already had Lieutenant Colonel Christopher Myers inquiring into what would be needed to strengthen the Provincial Marine, and Prevost had written in October to Secretary for War and the Colonies Lord Bathurst in London for a strong detachment of experienced Royal Navy officers and men. Sir George reiterated the plea to Bathurst later in the month and again on 5 November. After learning about the attack on Kingston, he upped the ante, informing Bathurst on 21 November, "I have given directions for the Construction, during the Winter, of two more armed Vessels on Lake Ontario, to carry each Eighteen 32 Pound Carronades."[7] To put this project in motion, Prevost ordered Captain Andrew Gray of the Nova Scotia Fencibles, who had been responsible for improving the Marine Department for the past year, to take a post in Upper Canada where he could direct the work in person. In the meantime, Prevost inquired locally for shipwrights willing to work in the upper province and for an experienced official to supervise them. Midway through December he wrote to Admiral Sir John Borlase Warren, commanding at Halifax, for assistance in manning and outfitting the new ships in the spring.

As the weather worsened with the gales and snow out of the northwest that kept Chauncey from active campaigning, the land war resumed. Brigadier General Alexander Smyth, the new commander of the American army on the Niagara Frontier, announced his decision to end the armistice on 20 November in a note to the British commander at Fort Erie. "The time is at hand," he proclaimed to his troops, "when you will cross the streams of Niagara to conquer Canada and to secure the peace of the American frontier."[8] Before Smyth could launch his invasion, however, Sheaffe took the initiative and at dawn on 21 November the batteries in and around Fort George opened up on Fort Niagara and its external works. The Americans responded in kind and the two forces kept up a cannonade that lasted until sunset. Both forts suffered damage, as did houses and other buildings near by, but there were relatively few casualties.

Anticipating a move by Smyth on the upper Niagara River, Sheaffe had ordered the artillery into action as a diversion, leaving it in the charge of Lieutenant Colonel Myers while he and his suite rode up to Chippawa, where he established his temporary headquarters.

Despite his blustering and hubris, Brigadier General Smyth had trouble getting his invasion moving. After a false start on 25 November, he managed to push two detachments of regulars and U.S. Navy personnel across the Niagara under an artillery barrage in the late hours of Saturday, 28 November. The Americans overran one battery, nearly captured a second, destroyed a bridge and threatened to establish a beachhead between Fort Erie and Frenchman's Creek. Sheaffe had just placed Lieutenant Colonel Cecil Bisshopp in charge of the district from Chippawa to Fort Erie, and after the initial setbacks in the fight Bisshopp and his senior officers were able to rally their troops, numbering about 300 regulars, several companies of militia and a party of native warriors under Major James Givins. After some intense combat, the Americans withdrew, and a larger force making for the Canadian shore turned back; the casualties and captured for both sides amounted to nearly 200.[9]

Around one o'clock the next afternoon, Smyth sent a flag of truce to Bisshopp with a note demanding that he surrender Fort Erie since Smyth believed it had fallen into his hands, despite the fact that his troops had withdrawn. Sheaffe had ridden up from Chippawa with reinforcements, but whether he was with Bisshopp when the note arrived is uncertain. At some point during these proceedings, Sheaffe is alleged to have remarked, half jokingly, that "it might be proper to give up Fort Erie as a sop to the Americans, who were so tired of the war that they only wanted the report of a single success to withdraw."[10] In the meantime Bisshopp refused Smyth's suggestion and began refitting the batteries and rebuilding the bridge as Sheaffe rode back toward Chippawa, unaware that tongues were already wagging about his commitment to the cause.

On the day when the armistice ended, Sheaffe had issued orders to his commanding officers detailing the tactics he preferred to see used against a large invading force. "The men are not on any occasion to be uselessly exposed to a cannonade," Sheaffe stated.[11] If the enemy approached *en masse*, musket fire was to be restrained until the invaders were well within range. If they gained the shore, they were "to be attacked at the point of the bayonet with the most determined resolution." In the event that resistance failed, the commander on the ground was to retreat in an orderly fashion, covering his flanks and making sure that he had destroyed all ammunition and provisions left behind. Sheaffe's tactics were not without precedent. Isaac Brock had issued a nearly identical set of instructions shortly before his death. The late hero had emphasized, "The possession of and

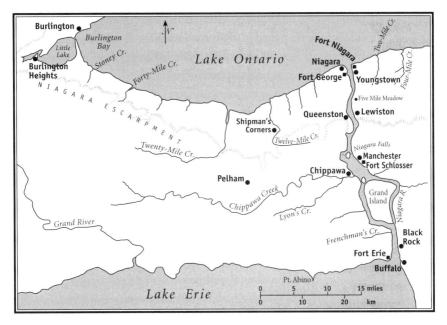

The Niagara Peninsula. Although completely surveyed long before 1812, the Niagara Peninsula was thinly settled except for the margin of land along the waterways and near the towns and villages. It saw more active land warfare than any other region on either side of the border. (Map from Malcomson, *A Very Brilliant Affair: The Battle of Queenston Heights, 1812*)

safety of Chippawa must be considered a primary object," and it was at this post that Sheaffe established his headquarters in the face of Smyth's threat.[12]

On Monday, 30 November, the Americans could be seen gathering for a large-scale assault. Unsure about their intended landing place, Sheaffe kept most of the 350 regulars at Chippawa where they were, rather then sending them all to stand with Bisshopp. Instead, he wrote a note to Bisshopp advising him that his force "ought not to be exposed incessantly" and to consider the "measures best adapted for a retreat if your force be inadequate."[13] This was essentially what his instructions of 20 November had said.

Within hours the general received a sharp reply to his note signed by six of Bisshopp's officers: Major Adam Ormsby, 49th Foot, and Captain Peter Chambers, 41st Foot, Major James Givins and three other militia officers, Lieutenant Colonels Thomas Clark and Robert Nichol and Major Richard Hatt. They did not, they stated, "under existing circumstances, consider retreat at all necessary, nor do we consider it a measure which ought to be looked forward to…. [A] small reinforcement would enable us to gain a decided advantage over any force the enemy has in its power to bring against us."[14]

It is difficult to imagine a similar group of officers sending such a note to Isaac Brock questioning his orders, but here they were, overtly challenging Sheaffe; there must have been something in his manner that prompted them to take this sort of liberty with him. Perhaps they already knew that Sheaffe would shrug off the note rather than viewing it as an act of insolence as Brock probably would have done. Sheaffe did not reprimand his subordinates and sometime later wrote that his intention had been to free Bisshopp and the others "from responsibility if it were decided to retreat."[15] This line of reasoning was clearly not apparent to many other observers of the incident. In fact some of these men began spreading the story around, taking any opportunity that presented itself to criticize Sheaffe's leadership.

There seems to have been another story circulating about the general at this time, a particularly prejudicial allegation that he was unwilling to act aggressively against the Americans because he was himself American-born. Sheaffe was said to have admitted this aversion to fighting his countrymen one night over dinner while entertaining some of his staff and several American officers captured at the Battle of Queenston Heights. Among the prisoners was Winfield Scott, then a lieutenant colonel in the Second U.S. Regiment of Artillery, who included the tale in the autobiography he produced in 1864. "At table," Scott wrote, "[I] learned from General Sheaffe himself, that he was a native of Boston ... [and] although he had never owed allegiance to the United States, yet [he was] anxious to avoid engaging in hostilities with Americans, his countrymen by birth, ... [and] had early requested to be sent to some other theatre of war."[16] Removed by half a century from the events of the day, Scott's recollection of the War of 1812 was peppered with flaws, but this story about Sheaffe is one that historians have repeated as one explanation for his failure to engage his enemy more energetically.

There is nothing in the record of Roger Sheaffe's military career to indicate that he was anything other than loyal to his King and Country. He may not have been the most active and charismatic officer who ever donned scarlet felt and golden braid, but there is nothing to show that he refused an appointment, or once in command, hesitated to perform his duty to the best of his abilities. Whether he made the remarks about his American roots with sincerity, as Scott reported, or as an offhand half-joke cannot be verified. But, if the general did express such feelings so candidly in front of local officers, they were probably repeated and added to the growing disapproval of his leadership. Certainly, Brock would never have uttered such a thing, and it was Brock's glorified shadow that helped to cloud Sheaffe's term as commander-in-chief of Upper Canada.

The large-scale assault that Brigadier General Smyth attempted on 30

November 1812 came to nothing and he was soon riding away from the Niagara Frontier in disgrace. Sheaffe returned to the town of Niagara, where a few days later his leadership was again questioned. Just before the armistice ended, he and his staff had developed a plan to attack and destroy the batteries in and around Fort Niagara and then lay waste to all the homes and buildings in its vicinity. This was supposed to have been done in conjunction with the artillery barrage on 21 November, but Sheaffe had gone to Chippawa instead. Even when he returned and the Americans were known to be in chaos, nothing was done. "For some reason or other the General abandoned the land enterprise," explained Major Thomas Evans to Justice William Powell at York, admitting that even as a staff member he did not know what his commander's plans were.[17] Still, Evans did not want to leave his post: "We are all in spirits here," he added without another word about the general. "Myers and Bisshopp are looked up to from all quarters."

Lieutenant Colonel Nichol, who bore heavy responsibilities as the militia's quarter master general, had dealt with the day-to-day stress of trying to outfit the militia from the inadequate provisions. The desertion rate rose and living conditions worsened to the point where nearly all the militia were discharged. "We are no longer commanded by Brock," Nichol complained to his friend Colonel Thomas Talbot, "and our situation is most materially changed for the worse."[18] The devotion and sacrifices of the regulars and the militia were being wasted due to *"bad management and despondency in those who are at our head and who ought to be better qualified to fill energetically the high and important situations they hold."* His script, underlined for emphasis, was a transparent reference to Sheaffe and to Prevost, but that was as far as Nichol would go: "I dare not trust myself to write you all," he added.

Captain Andrew Gray arrived at Sheaffe's headquarters in Niagara on 14 December. Little is known about Gray's background other than he joined the 87th Regiment of Foot in 1805 as an ensign and a year later moved as lieutenant into the Royal Staff Corps. This latter unit of the army served as a supplement to the undermanned Corps of Engineers and was composed of volunteers who had the breadth of education and the technical skills necessary to act as engineers. Gray remained with the corps until he obtained a captaincy in the Nova Scotia Fencibles in 1811. By the end of that year he was appointed acting deputy quarter master general at Quebec and was soon off to Upper Canada, where he wrote several reports on the nature of its fortifications and the state of the Provincial Marine. One officer who met Gray described him as "a Half-horse, half-Alligator sort of soldier, sailor, carpenter, etc." And a man mature enough in years to have a son with an ensign's commission in the 104th Foot.[19]

Gray passed through Kingston and York on his way to Niagara and made thorough inspections of the facilities and vessels at both places. By the time he met Sheaffe and his staff at Niagara he had already formed his ideas about what was needed, which led to a decision for augmenting Prevost's order. They would build one 20-gun ship, based on the design of the *Royal George,* at Kingston and a 30-gun frigate at York; initially a schooner was ordered to be constructed at Amherstburg but this was soon altered to be another of the *Royal George* class.

The plan, favoured by Brock, Prevost and others, to make York the head-quarters for the Provincial Marine had been frustrated when the *Royal George* and *Earl of Moira* could not escape from Kingston because of Commodore Chauncey's squadron, and so building the frigate at York presented another way to facilitate the transition. Building two ships at once on Lake Ontario, however, would require additional labourers, from axemen to shipwrights, and they would have to be split between the two dockyards. The list of materials needed to construct the vessels and the third at Amherstburg was daunting. Blocks and tackle, miles of rigging, iron fittings, sails, stoves and mess utensils, ammunition, small arms and seventy guns, all would have to be delivered up the St. Lawrence River supply line within sight of American troops and to three different places. The undertaking was ambitious in the extreme. And although some fresh enlistments were found among the sailors at Quebec, the ultimate success of the ships required the arrival in the early spring of a large detach-ment of experienced Royal Navy men from Britain to sail and fight them. In the meantime both Kingston and York needed their defences strengthened and Gray and Sheaffe advised Prevost that some heavy guns would have to be sent up from Quebec. "At Kingston," warned Gray, "there is little protection afforded the vessels from the works on shore. Here [at York] there is none."[20]

Captain Gray also championed a second method for dealing with the sudden escalation in American naval power and this was "to recover at a blow what we have lost" by attacking Sackets Harbor.[21] His informants had reported that the place was lightly and poorly defended and he conceived that a regiment, trained to march in snowshoes, could cross the St. Lawrence on the ice with a few small pieces of artillery at the end of January and destroy Chauncey's squadron. It was an idea that had become a popular topic of discussion and appeared in the cor-respondence of private citizens during this time. The Reverend John Strachan, for instance, wrote to his wife's former father-in-law late in November, "An ex-pedition against Sackets Harbor is now indispensable, if we mean to keep the Country. Could this expedition have been sent this fall we might have carried off all their vessels and naval Stores, and particularly, the large Frigate which they are just finishing."[22] Donald McLean, one of the magistrates at York and the clerk of the Legislative Assembly, favoured a raid and believed that "the population of the Country would Volunteer for such a service [and if] joined by a few of your Veteran Troops, Canadians and Indians on Snow Shoes, [and] commanded by a determined leader (such as the immortal Brock) [they all] would insure success."[23] There were others who voiced similar opinions, but Sir George was unwilling to commit a regiment and more to such a risky venture and the idea lapsed, although the suggestion was not forgotten.

Captain Gray left Niagara on 16 December for York, where he directed the few officers present, including Lieutenant William Fish of the *Prince Regent* and Major Alexander Clerk, the local officer for the quarter master general's department, to start building the large ship on the edge of the bay. Right from the outset, however, there was difficulty in finding a suitable site for constructing and launching a 30-gun man-of-war.[24] In all likelihood the *Prince Regent* had been built at the merchants' dockyard at the eastern end of the bay, but, even for a vessel that drew as little as nine feet of water, the water there was too shallow and it had taken several days of greasing and wedging to get the schooner down the slipway and afloat. This was a significant impediment to shipbuilding at York and why knowledgeable men such as Isaac Brock and Andrew Gray had promoted the idea of developing a shipyard there is puzzling. The shoreline was choked with rushes and deepened at a very slight grade. Even when merchant William Allan built the town's first wharf in 1801 it had to be extended 600 feet out into the bay before deep enough water could be found for schooners similar to the *Prince Regent* to tie up. The decision to build such a large ship at York, with a probable draft of 12 feet or so, did not go unnoticed by men who had spent their adult lives on this frontier. More than one foresaw problems with the project and there were others who doubted the wisdom of splitting the Marine Department's resources, but they kept their views to themselves or shared them in private conversations with their friends.[25]

Gray, Clerk and Fish surveyed the bay and found what they considered a suitable location for a slipway about half a mile east of the garrison. Even here the water was too shallow, but the officers came up with a novel solution. They suggested the construction of a building stage that would descend from the 25-foot bank out into the bay. A vast ramp, it would be 100 feet wide and 800 feet long.[26] Even Allan's 600-foot wharf was small in comparison to this structure, which might well have become the largest man-made feature in Upper Canada at the time.

The fabrication of the building stage was going to be a monumental project in itself, but, curiously, Captain Gray made no mention of it when he reported

Ironwork for the two Lake Ontario ships. This requisition represents only a small portion of the iron fittings needed for building the new ships in Upper Canada during the early months of 1813, all of which material had to be transported from Quebec, unless suitable parts could be salvaged from old lake vessels. (LAC, C138972)

Guns for *Brock*. The *Sir Isaac Brock* was intended to be armed with twenty-six 32-pdr. carronades on its broadsides and one pair of 18-pdr. long guns at the bow and a second pair at the stern. The long guns would be used as chase guns, but could also be employed for broadside fire. (LAC, C138973) to Prevost from Kingston on 31 December. He did note, however, that thirty militiamen were already employed as axe men in the woods a mile from the water and a dozen teams were hauling the felled timber to the construction site. They had been ordered to work as fast as they could, selecting fir and any other suitable trees that were close at hand. The frigate was going to have to be put together fast; "all idea of neatness in the work must be given up," Gray advised.[27] At the work site, carpenters were busily erecting barracks for the labourers and workshops so that the cutting out of the frame pieces and the forging of iron fittings could be started as soon as the skilled hands arrived.

Captain Gray hurried back along the winter road to Kingston, where he discovered 112 shipwrights, eight sawyers and eight smiths had arrived with a new man to supervise them. This was Thomas James Plucknett, said to have once been "the principle officer of His Majesty's Dock Yard at Deptford [England]."[28] His new role was that of "Superintendent and Storekeeper" of the dockyard at York and he had orders to build two 18-gun brigs there. Plucknett's instructions allowed him the same rations and barrack allowances as a captain in the army and required him to "obey all such instructions as you may receive thro' the officers of [the quarter master general's] department."[29] Gray ordered him to lay the new keel at Kingston first and then to head for York with about eighty of the shipwrights. Within a few days Gray received a despatch from Sir George approving the plans that had been made in Upper Canada and promising every effort to supply the dockyards with men, materiel and the extra guns needed to defend them. Presumably, before Plucknett left Kingston, Gray informed him that he was to build a 30-gun frigate at York rather than the two smaller brigs.

Andrew Gray's devotion to duty certainly demonstrated itself during the late fall of 1812 and the subsequent winter months. But, unfortunately for his reputation and that of Major General Sheaffe, his efforts were not restricted to promoting the public good alone – unless he believed that maligning his local commander-in-chief would somehow help the cause.

During his brief layover at the town of Niagara, Gray found time to listen to the indignant complaints of regular and militia officers about Sheaffe's alleged comments and conduct during Smyth's failed invasion on the upper Niagara River. Someone had made a copy of the note that Sheaffe sent to Bisshopp on 30 November advising him to retreat if needed, and within weeks there were other copies circulating through the Niagara region, accompanied by a repetition of Sheaffe's supposed offhand remark about giving up Fort Erie as a sop to the victory-hungry Americans. The offended officers do not appear to have confronted the general face-to-face with their grievance, and if Sheaffe learned of the intensity of their indignation during the first two weeks of December, he did nothing about it. The dissatisfaction grew until there were murmurs that some sort of action should be taken to replace Sheaffe and it was this invective which Andrew Gray heard at Niagara. In a blatant demonstration of professional indiscretion, Gray repeated the details of the controversy when he reached York, suggesting that a "combination" was forming on the Niagara line to remove Sheaffe from command.[30] He thoughtlessly made such comments in the company of William Powell and others of the York elite and then went on to Kingston, where he repeated them to Lieutenant Colonel John Vincent.

Powell, a long-time acquaintance and close correspondent of Sheaffe's, was so dismayed by Captain Gray's story that he wrote to the general to warn him and then to Captain John Glegg, one of Sheaffe's aides, for an explanation. Glegg returned to Niagara from a mission to Montreal at the end of December, only to discover a situation that left him wishing he had never left the lower province. He was outraged by the way that "Captain Gray's progress from here to Kingston has been marked with the most persecuting calumny that ever proceeded from the mouth of man."[31] Powell had heard that Lieutenant Colonel Myers, who had fallen ill during December, was involved in the conspiracy but Glegg assured him that this was a fabrication. On the contrary, Myers had confronted the critics and warned them "of the dangerous tendencies of their proceedings" and then had gone directly to Sheaffe with the information.[32] When Lieutenant Colonel Vincent heard Gray's accusations, he concluded a cabal was forming to oust the general, who was his regimental colleague and friend, and wrote to Glegg that he would hurry to Niagara, if the situation was urgent enough, to put down any "combination" and preserve the province's "honour" and "security."

Vincent was not needed at Niagara, however. Winter settled in during the first days of 1813, shutting down communications between the posts for days at a time and possibly cooling the passions of any conspirators. Word that Captain Gray was broadcasting their discontent far and wide may also have tempered their protests and raised their apprehensions about the repercussions such news might bring from headquarters at Quebec. Warned by Powell and Myers about how deep the anger ran among some of his subordinates, Sheaffe had a letter sent on 20 December to John Beverley Robinson, whom the general had recently appointed as attorney general at Powell's suggestion. It was meant "to take the necessary steps," Sheaffe explained to Powell, adding, "for I really have so much to do that I cannot do anything well."[33] A month later he informed Powell that Myers had shown him a letter from Gray in which the captain asserted that he had only criticized Sheaffe's refusal to reinforce Bisshopp, but "never uttered anything personal of me...." "Too much publicity has been given to this matter," wrote Sheaffe. "It is a pity that Lt.-Colonel B[isshopp] did not keep my official

Long gun. The 12-pdr. long gun, mounted on the U.S. Brig *Niagara* at Erie, Pennsylvania, has been outfitted with the tackle, quoin and canvas-covered trucks typically seen in 1812. Its basic range of fire of about 1,000 yards could be improved by withdrawing the quoin enough to allow the base of the gun to drop, increasing the weapon's elevation.

Carronade. Lighter in weight than long guns, carronades were commonly mounted on slides that could be swivelled by means of a pin in the gunport sill and trucks at the rear of the carriage. Even at full elevation of 5 degrees, a 32-pdr. carronade had a maximum range of about 1,000 yards. (Photographs by Robert Malcomson)

letter to himself."[34] Then, as if hoping to be rid of the matter, Sheaffe went on to note the latest news from Europe, his receipt of letters from his wife and to wish Powell the best.

About this time, Captain Glegg reported to Justice Powell that the general "is much changed of late. There appears at times an irresistible melancholy on his mind, which is most distressing."[35] Late in January Major General Sheaffe, under the stress of demands from all directions, took sick, forcing the cancellation of a trip to York to open the new legislative session. His condition worsened and he was confined to bed, incapable of performing his military or civil duties. "Too much confinement and anxiety of mind have nearly proven fatal," wrote Glegg.[36] "I fear," Major Evans reported to Colonel Procter at Amherstburg, "he finds his situation an arduous one and perhaps his mind is ill at ease from the treasonous and ill natured reports which he cannot but be otherwise aware of."[37] Nearly two weeks passed before Sheaffe was well enough to describe his malady: "I am advised to abstain as much as possible from business … [but] neither my head nor my hand is in a state to enter more largely into these [military] subjects."[38] The general's aide Nathaniel Coffin gradually began taking him out in a sleigh to visit the nearby posts and by 11 February Sheaffe was sitting up and laughing with the others by the hearth, though he continued to complain, "I am teased with a pain in my head and recover but slowly."[39] The visit to York was again put off for weeks.

By the time Sheaffe began to come out from under his illness another major crisis was brewing, this time over the frigate at York; Thomas Plucknett had refused to lay the keel and was threatening to return to Quebec. He believed the vast building stage proposed by Gray and others, and currently under construction, was not only impractical but outright dangerous, and he refused to follow the plan. Instead, he conducted his own survey of the shoreline and selected a place a mile further down the bay and just west of the foot of Bay Street where there was sufficient water within 300 feet of the shore. He planned to put a slipway down into the water and ordered the labourers to begin cutting an opening into the bank to gain access to the shoreline and create space for the foundation of the works.[40]

Major Clerk wrote to Gray about the problem immediately and received a quick reply, ordering Plucknett to go back to the original site.[41] At this point the disgruntled builder stopped everything, with timber strewn between both places, and the labourers and shipwrights put down their tools to wait for instructions. His conduct was a clear-cut failure to obey orders. Luckily, one of the most experienced and renowned British officers in Canada appeared on the scene on 23 January and took matters in hand. He was Ralph Bruyeres, the senior

Royal Engineer in the Canadian command, a man of proven competence and sound knowledge of the frontier posts. After listening to both sides, he arranged for the shipwrights to go back to work cutting and shaping parts for the keel and ribs of the frigate and then headed for Sheaffe's headquarters with Plucknett.

At Niagara Sheaffe was too sick to see anyone, but Lieutenant Colonel Myers conducted the meeting and effectively resolved the problem, giving Plucknett permission to build where he thought best. Myers was careful to record that since the superintendent had rejected the officially chosen site, it was understood that he was responsible should the project be delayed because of his preferences. He also let it be known that he would write directly to the governor-in-chief to determine the scope of Plucknett's authority since the superintendent seemed to think he could frivolously ignore orders.[42] Content with the decision, Plucknett returned to York while Bruyeres remained at Niagara to complete his other business.

The trained eyes of Ralph Bruyeres had seen something else at York that he did not like and, knowing that he commanded Prevost's respect, he did not hesitate to tell him. As he finished his report about the building-site disagreement on 28 January, the forty-seven-year-old engineer wrote, "York may undoubtedly in time of Peace be made an excellent Harbour and Dock yard much preferable to Kingston, but under present circumstances it is totally incompetent for the purpose." He added, "this Country is so totally deprived of the resources of means within itself that the distance becomes a very serious obstacle" since everything had to be sent from Quebec. Regretfully, Bruyeres told his commander, "I must candidly observe … that I have a much more unfavorable opinion of the possibility of obtaining an ascendancy on this lake (than I did when I was in Kingston)."[43] His comments were nearly identical to the views of the knowledgeable private citizens who were standing back and shaking their heads at the government's decisions.

Bruyeres repeated his thoughts about York, with added emphasis, after he passed through the town on his way to Lower Canada during the second week of February. "It is much too remote and distant a Post to obtain the necessary resources to carry on any great undertaking…. Everything must be created which will require considerable time and expense."[44] Christopher Myers was with Bruyeres at York and also expressed growing concerns, but they centred on Thomas Plucknett's competence. Even with approval to build the ship where he wanted, the superintendent made little progress. "Whether Mr. Plucknett is a regular professional ship builder or not," Myers wrote to Prevost's secretary, "it is not in my power to determine, but that he wants system and arrangement I feel no hesitation in asserting."[45] Myers went so far as to suggest that a replacement be found for him and added that Bruyeres intended to describe the troubling circumstances to Prevost when he saw him.

In relief of these gloomy circumstance, there soon came good news of more military successes. The previous November, during the time that General Smyth failed in his attempt to invade Upper Canada and Major General Henry Dearborn's intended invasion of Lower Canada fizzled after a skirmish at La Colle, a third army led by William Henry Harrison was attempting to reclaim what Hull had lost at Detroit. This last campaign suffered a severe setback on 22 January when Brigadier General Henry Procter marched his force from Amherstburg to attack, kill and capture nearly 900 Americans under Brigadier General James Winchester, Harrison's vanguard, at Frenchtown, in the Michigan Terrritory. Procter suffered heavy losses and his native allies murdered some of their captives, but once more hundreds of prisoners marched through Upper Canada and the defeated Winchester and his officers were on view at Niagara.

In late February a British expedition launched a surprise attack on Ogdensburg, New York, across the St. Lawrence River and routed the militia and a company of the U.S. Regiment of Rifles stationed there. It largely removed the threat of American attacks on British settlements along the river and made the transportation of materiel and provisions less risky. This victory and the one at Frenchtown raised spirits across the province. To celebrate such tidings and to keep morale up, some of the officers made an effort to gather people together for social events. William Hamilton Merritt, the young militiaman at Niagara, wrote to his future wife, Catherine Prendergast, "We had a splendid assembly last night, given by Col. Myers." He then added, "I never saw so many slays in all my life as this winter. Brigades of 50 or 60 every week from Lower Canada with stores and troops."[46]

Not known to Merritt, or many people at all, was the fact that a cavalcade of singular importance was approaching Upper Canada in comet-like fashion. On 17 February 1813 Sir George Prevost left Quebec in a brigade of sleighs and mounted riders for the upper province. Reports like Bruyeres's and rumours of dangerous intrigue had prompted the governor-in-chief to make a personal investigation of the situation before it got any worse. His route, post horses and accommodations were planned in detail to allow him to make the best possible speed on the well-formed winter roads and this goal was achieved.[47] By 21 February he had traversed the 240 miles to Prescott, Upper Canada, and about four days later he reached the town of Niagara, 550 miles from Quebec, averaging nearly 70 miles per day.

Somewhere in the last couple of days of Prevost's trek, he crossed paths with Roger Sheaffe, who had recovered well enough from his illness to head for York

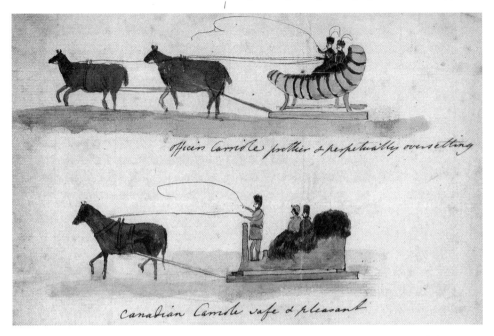

Officer's Carriole prettier & perpetually oversetting

Canadian Carriole safe & pleasant

Carrioles. The severe winter of 1812-13 turned the primitive roads of Upper Canada into convenient highways for the brigades of sleds that carried materiel from Lower Canada into the upper province. Sir George Prevost's sled may have resembled one of these traditional French-Canadian carrioles. (AO, F 47-11-1-0-18)

and open the long-delayed legislative session. The general knew that his chief was on the way, having been informed by him that he did not want "to interfere in the civil administration … [and that Sheaffe should] consider my visit as solely directed to researches regarding objects of a military nature."[48] Their likely meeting place was the King's Head Inn, which the government had built in the time of Simcoe at the southern end of the strip of beach stretching between Burlington Bay and Little Lake (today's Hamilton Harbour). Here the horses could be changed and time taken for a meal and a private discussion before the two men raced off to their separate destinations.

Prevost arrived at Niagara about 25 February but took little time to rest. The next day he headed up the river to observe the British posts and their opposite numbers across the frozen waterway, travelling as far as Fort Erie before hurrying back to Fort George. From there Prevost reported his journey to Lord Bathurst, explaining more openly than he did to Sheaffe that he had gone there not just to observe the military situation but "to check a disposition that had manifested itself in [the] province to cabal against the person administering the government of it, and [for the purpose of] restoring order to its militia force."[49]

King's Head Inn. Also known as "Government House," the King's Head Inn stood at the southern end of the strip of land that today encloses Hamilton Harbour at the extreme west end of Lake Ontario. It was erected in 1794 to serve as a depot and comprised a large, two-storey residence with two wings and various outbuildings. Elizabeth Simcoe visited the place and made this sketch. (AO, F 47-11-1-0-223)

He had already dealt with Andrew Gray, severely censuring him for his conduct, and, either during his tour of the river or later at Fort George, it is likely that he held some candid conversations with the likes of Cecil Bisshopp, Major Ormsby and Captain Chambers, and militiamen such as Lieutenant Colonels Robert Nichol and Thomas Clark. The documents of the period leave no traces of such discussions, other than Sir George's later assertion to Lord Bathurst that "a proper understanding is restored in that Province by the extinction of the cabal."[50] Sure enough, long before winter ended, all threat of a conspiracy in Upper Canada vanished.

From his temporary headquarters at Niagara overlooking the rim of ice on the shores of Lake Ontario, Sir George Prevost gained a first-hand understanding of the situation in Upper Canada, to which he responded immediately and decisively with a series of general orders. Since January Sheaffe had been proposing changes to the organization of the militia, but they were suddenly put into effect as Prevost ordered the formation of a troop of Provincial Artillery Drivers, a company of Provincial Artificers, and a troop of Provincial Light Cavalry. He also moved several officers into new posts, with special attention paid to the quarter master general's department.[51]

Meanwhile Sheaffe directed that all "the [militia] arms, accoutrements, blankets, greatcoats, packs, haversacks, canteens, etc., in possession of those not on duty" were to be immediately collected and sent to the various Niagara posts, where they would be inspected, recorded, and stored.[52] In the provincial assembly, Sheaffe succeeded in having several significant laws passed and others revised. The old system of calling up flank companies from county militia regiments was replaced with the creation of an "Incorporated Militia" that would draw volunteers from across the province to serve in battalions for eighteen months, unless the war ended sooner. Improvements were made to the pensions for disabled or killed militiamen and their families, with the province paying the bill. At the same time, in hope of avoiding the shortages that had made it so difficult to properly supply the troops, it became illegal to export grain (or use it for distilling) and other provisions.

Prevost arrived back at York about 3 March and took time to inspect the ship, which he had lately named the *Sir Isaac Brock.* He knew about the bad start to the project and now he saw for himself that it was making very slow headway. From Superintendent Plucknett the governor-in-chief heard that the lack of progress was due to an insufficient number of shipwrights and the incompetence of John Dennis, the master shipwright in charge of the actual building. After listening to Plucknett's complaints, Prevost ordered Major Clerk to get rid of Dennis, but the major begged the general's pardon and argued against the idea.[53] Plucknett, Clerk claimed, carried on each day without any organization or care for efficiency and had even refused to show Dennis the complete set of plans for the ship, making Dennis's job impossible. Clerk explained that Dennis, a resident of York, had proven his abilities in government shipyards for years and would have been farther along if he had been left to his own devices. Much to his credit, Prevost found more to believe in Clerk's words than those of the superintendent's, and left orders requiring Dennis to receive all the information and immediate assistance he needed to send up the ship. As for the evidence of Plucknett's ineptitude, Prevost said nothing for the record.

On a more positive note, at York the magistrates and other leading citizens gathered to express their appreciation for Prevost's visit to the province and his efforts in helping to defend it. They thanked him for approving of their militia's role in defending the province, for providing the troops with suitable clothing and motivating them to press on with their honourable service. They were also "particularly gratified" by his efforts to improve and strengthen the Provincial Marine, which reassured them that Prevost was "fully convinced that to maintain a superiority on the lakes is an object of the first importance to this Province."[54] After hearing these words of approval, Prevost bid farewell and good luck to Roger Sheaffe and his staff. His presence had solved a few problems and improved the overall outlook. And with those effects left behind, Prevost's cavalcade whisked away eastward over the hard-packed winter roads.

Sir George was pleased with what he had achieved during his lightning trip to Upper Canada. When he returned to Quebec, he described his journey to Lord Bathurst and how he had ensured that Sheaffe's command and the stability of the province were on a solid footing once more. He detailed the steps he had taken to send reinforcements to the upper province and significantly strengthen the naval force. He prided himself on "defending with all the means at my disposal the frontier of the Canadas," adding, in contradiction of his original policy, that in regard to that defence he had done more than his predecessor, Sir James Craig, "whose sole object appears to have been directed to the concentration of his force at Quebec, the only post … considered capable of a protracted resistance."[55] Clearly, the victories of the first year's campaign, capped by more success during the winter months and a productive tour of Upper Canada, had modified the governor-in-chief's thinking.

What Prevost did not mention to Bathurst were the reports he had received from Bruyeres about York, its virtual lack of defences, poor natural assets and the difficulty in transporting the necessary resources there while keeping Kingston's dockyard supplied at the same time. Nor did he write anything about the controversy continuing to swirl around Superintendent Plucknett and his dubious abilities. Any apprehension he may have felt after seeing Major General Sheaffe in command, or observing the lack of defensive works at Kingston and York, he kept to himself. He had done what he could, for the time being anyway, and could now take a few weeks to mull things over, before the coming of spring brought a renewal of active warfare on the Lake Ontario front.

CHAPTER 5

"A secondary, but still important object"[1]

AMERICAN CAMPAIGN GOALS FOR 1813

Even brilliant frigate victories at sea and Commodore Isaac Chauncey's late-season campaign on Lake Ontario were not enough to hide the bitter truth from the American public that the first campaign season against Britain had been a woeful failure. Fingers pointed in all directions, but ultimately the blame settled on the shoulders of Secretary of War William Eustis and Secretary of the Navy Paul Hamilton. Both men were considered lacking in the ability to handle the press of administrative business in their departments and to develop coherent war plans. Eustis resigned on 3 December and Hamilton followed at the end of the month.[2]

James Madison was sixty-one years old in December 1812 and was hardly the figure of a dynamic leader, being pale, slender and short in stature and frequently the victim of "my bilious visitor" or some other incapacitating malady.[3] Critics believed him unfit for the task, since he lacked what one observer considered "those commanding talents, which are necessary to controul those about him. He allows devision in his cabinet."[4] Still, Madison proceeded with business in a reserved and systematic manner, eschewing any overt display of emotion (which he considered inconsistent with effective leadership), but not at the expense of being gracious and attentive to others. One military officer described a twenty-minute private meeting he had with the president, remarking how Madison's "mild and agreeable manner brought me instantly at home" as they covered the issues at hand, point by point, quickly and with satisfaction.[5] With the same sort of steadfastness, the president was determined to prevail over the British or arrange a favourable settlement with them. He made this clear in his annual message to Congress on 4 November 1812, acknowledging the disappointments of the year, but also stressing the nation's many blessings and great potential, and recommending the kind of legislation needed to better prepare the army and the navy for another season of war.

After the resignations of Eustis and Hamilton, Madison's cabinet consisted of Secretary of State James Monroe, Secretary of the Treasury Albert Gallatin and Attorney General William Pinkney. Monroe was the president's first choice for the war department as he had repeatedly shown interest in the portfolio. But the secretary of state also had his eye sharply focused on being elected to the presidency in 1816 and, when his confidantes advised him that the war department might create more problems for him than it was worth, he only agreed to head up the department temporarily and retained his current post.[6] Nevertheless, Monroe worked energetically to advise and assist the congressional committees as they developed Madison's suggestions into legislation, and he began preparations for an ambitious campaign into Canada in 1813. Albert Gallatin played a key role in this process as well, providing critical input about what the nation's treasury could afford to devote to waging war.

While Monroe dealt with war department business, Madison looked for a replacement for Eustis, offering the job first to Senator William Crawford of Georgia and then Major General Henry Dearborn, but both men turned it down. As a fourth and reluctant choice, the president turned to John Armstrong. Like Madison, he was an alumnus of Princeton, but whereas Madison's frail health kept him off the battlefield during the War of Independence, Armstrong took up arms and competently served on the staff of General Horatio Gates, rising to the rank of major. As the war ended, a bitter dispute erupted when the government hesitated to quickly settle the arrears in army pay. Armstrong stepped into the centre of it by penning a series of letters which suggested that the military might eventually take up arms against the government to resolve the issue. Although the controversy did not end with an insurrection, Armstrong's part in writing what became known as the Newburgh letters scarred him with a notoriety he never escaped.

In 1784 Armstrong took a civil post in Pennsylvania and became a prominent militia officer before marrying Alida Livingston in 1789 and moving to the Hudson River Valley in New York State. The Livingstons were influential members of the state's Republican elite and Armstrong willingly joined their ranks and became a prosperous farmer and land owner. He was a leading figure in state politics, ending up as one of its federal senators during Jefferson's first administration. From 1804 until 1810 Armstrong was the ambassador to France, a post he came to dislike in part because of his opposition to some of Jefferson's and Madison's policies. By the time he returned to New York, he had firmly

John Armstrong (1758-1843). In January 1812 John Armstrong wrote to then-Secretary of War William Eustis, "No time should be lost in getting a naval ascendancy [on the lakes] ... the first to obtain this advantage will (miracles excepted) win the game."[9] (USNA, 111-SC-94151)

established his reputation as a cantankerous individual with a sharp tongue and no friend to the Madison administration. Armstrong would likely have backed the president's opponent in the 1812 election had Madison not secured his support by approving his prestigious appointment as brigadier general in charge of the defences of New York City.

Armstrong was more than twenty years out of army service when the war started but, notwithstanding his crusty persona, he was considered an expert in things military. His views on how to march armies into Canada, which he expounded in a long letter of advice to Secretary Eustis just before the war, contributed directly to the strategy of the 1812 campaign. And his practical knowledge of army life was revealed in a book he published in 1812 on procedures and tactics entitled *Hints to Young Generals*. In the absence of better candidates, Armstrong's military reputation helped make him an appropriate choice for secretary of war, but it was his affiliation with the New York State Republicans and the support that the Madison administration would gain by his selection that was his most important asset. After weighing the pros and cons of bringing Armstrong into the cabinet, the president finally decided to offer the war department to Armstrong, who quickly accepted it in the first week of January. The matter did not end there, however, since the nomination provoked a debate in the Senate and was only approved by a close vote of 18 to 15. Armstrong formally took up his duties on 5 February, knowing that he was not well-liked and faced a difficult challenge. "The office to which I am destined is full of drudgery and environed by perils," he wrote to a friend. "I have to execute other men's

William Jones (1760-1831). Secretary of the Navy Jones assured Commodore Chauncey that "the success of the ensuing campaign will depend absolutely on our superiority on all the lakes."[10] His heightened concern for gaining control on the upper lakes directly influenced Chauncey's operational plans. (U.S. Naval Historical Center, NH66633)

plans and fight with other men's weapons ... to rescue our arms from their present fallen condition."[7]

President Madison found it less difficult, or contentious, to fill the navy vacancy. His choice was William Jones, a fifty-two-year-old shipping merchant from Philadelphia. Jones had fought on land and the sea during the War of Independence and spent time in the merchant marine before establishing his commercial interests. He was a loyal Republican and had already been considered for appointments as commissary general in the army and superintendent for building warships on Lake Erie. Jones had misgivings about the impact a federal position in Washington would have on his private enterprises, but he accepted Madison's offer and the Senate confirmed it without debate on 12 January 1813.[8]

By the time the new secretaries undertook their duties, some of the necessary changes in the organization of the army and navy were already in motion.[9] Legislation had passed to improve the pay of non-commissioned officers and the rank and file as well as the incentives for new recruits and officers in charge of enlisting them. More ships would be added to the navy and twenty regular regiments raised for one-year terms while the existing regiments would be slightly augmented. Other bills under consideration would allow for the appointment of additional general officers, a more effectively administered supply system, the establishment of a set of regulations for the army and an expanded general staff to supervise the army in nine military districts across the nation.

At the end of January Madison's administration was stunned when news arrived of Brigadier General James Winchester's defeat at Frenchtown in the Michigan Territory. The setback caused Major General William Henry Harrison to halt plans for an early advance into Canada while he consolidated his force at the newly built Fort Meigs on the Maumee River to wait for spring. Reports also reached Washington about reinforcements on their way from Britain to Canada and ambitious efforts by the British on Lake Ontario to regain naval superiority there. Two warships were said to be under construction at Little York with one source claiming they would each carry forty guns. From Kingston came various accounts of 150 shipwrights arriving from Quebec and a 36-gun frigate on the stocks.[10] This news, combined with Commodore Chauncey's exaggerated representation of the strength of the Provincial Marine, raised concerns that the British might succeed in regaining command of Lake Ontario in the spring. Madison now considered this an issue of the greatest importance. "The command of those waters is the hinge on which the war will essentially turn," he wrote on 6 February. "If they build two ships, we should build four. If they build thirty or 40 guns ships, we should build them of 50 or 60 guns."[11] To this end one of the first things Secretary Jones did was to give Chauncey permission to build a new warship at Sackets Harbor at the same time as he approved construction of a second brig at Erie, Pennsylvania, where four schooners and a brig were already underway. On top of the demands of its naval stations on the seaboard, the government was now sending builders, seamen, ship fittings, weapons and ammunition to two quite separate posts on the lakes.

Creating strong naval establishments at Sackets and Erie was essential for success in the war, but Secretary Jones showed early in his term that he placed greater emphasis on the Lake Erie squadron. "This force would facilitate beyond calculation the operations of Genl. Harrisons [sic] Army," Jones explained to Chauncey on 27 January 1813," and in the event of the fall of Malden and Detroit, would enable you to detach a part of your force to Lake Huron."[12] The secretary's goals went beyond the invasion of Upper Canada and recapture of Fort Mackinac (a post at the entrance to Lake Michigan that the British had captured in the early days of the war), however, as he wanted U.S. Navy vessels eventually "to take post at the mouth of the French River on the N.E. Side of Lake Huron … [and] intercept the supplies for the western Indians." In this way, Jones argued, with the obvious approval of the president and the other cabinet members, British influence on the aboriginal nations would be greatly reduced; unspoken was the fact that American fur trading interests would also be secured once again. Secretary Jones assured Chauncey that "The command of Lake Ontario is no less important," but his greater interest in gaining control of the upper lakes was unmistakable.[13] This theme pervaded his correspondence with Chauncey in the weeks that led up to the opening of the spring campaign and had a significant effect on the shape of the eventual campaign.

During the early days of February, Madison's cabinet sat down to chart its military campaign for the spring. It was a plan that was as ambitious as the one Jones had explained to Chauncey, except that it went in the opposite direction. The idea that Thomas Jefferson had promoted of conquering the Canadian provinces and marching on to Halifax was still the guiding principle, despite the humiliating defeats on the battlefield suffered since the declaration of war. Late in December 1812, for instance, James Monroe gamely asserted, "Before this time next year ... the British forces [must] be driven into Quebec and Halifax, and taken there if possible."[14] However, some mature assessment of the logistics involved in raising and training enough men to accomplish such heady objectives had tempered this grand scheme. Treasurer Gallatin played the key role of portraying the reality of the situation, namely, that the government would not have the funds to pay the wages of such a force in the spring, let alone acquire and ship the arms and provisions needed, or house them in depots that did not yet exist.

John Armstrong was fully apprised of this situation when he was asked to present a strategy for 1813 to the cabinet in the first week of February. He began by proposing an invasion of Lower Canada via the Lake Champlain valley, based on the ideas Monroe put together in December. Armstrong then rejected it, pointing out that there were not enough men at Plattsburgh, New York, and Burlington, Vermont, to form the expedition and little chance that enough recruits could be enlisted and trained in time to be effective. "It then remains," Armstrong argued, "to choose between a course of entire inaction ... or one having a secondary, but still important object."[15]

Armstrong's secondary option was the "reduction" of Upper Canada between Prescott and Lake Erie. He estimated that the British defences were considerably stronger in Lower Canada than in the upper province and that a thrust against Upper Canada which employed the forces already in the field, trained as they were and in some cases battle-experienced, had a good chance of succeeding. The regiments could be marched immediately from their winter camps to congregate at Sackets Harbor and Buffalo and then sent against three specific targets. "Kingston and Prescott, and the destruction of the British ships at the former would present the first object," Armstrong explained; "York and the frigates said to be building there, the second; [Forts] George and Erie, the third."[16] British reinforcements from Lower Canada would be delayed, he reasoned, by the fact that the St. Lawrence River remained choked with ice until mid-May (according to Armstrong's sources), whereas Lake Ontario was open by 1 April, making it possible for Chauncey's squadron to operate and transport the army to the enemy shores.

Henry Dearborn (1751-1829).
Dearborn's appointment as commander-in-chief of the northern land forces indicated the shortage of experienced senior U.S. Army officers who were still young and energetic enough to bring the war to the British with the boldness demonstrated by the likes of forty-three-year-old Isaac Brock. (LAC, C10925)

The record does not show if the cabinet discussed such contingencies as the state of the weather or whether the Provincial Marine would immediately challenge Chauncey for control of the lake, and Armstrong presented his ideas without any reference to Harrison's army in the Northwest or Jones's high expectations for control of the upper lakes. He had been much more decisive than his predecessor and was confident of achieving success with the available means. The cabinet members liked what they heard, especially since it meant the armed forces could strike the British hard and fast early in the season and gain much-needed momentum. It has even been suggested that the administration hoped a quick victory would raise support for the war in New York State and help Republican Governor Daniel Tompkins win another term in the April elections.[17] In fairly short order, Madison and the others approved Armstrong's Lake Ontario-based strategy and two days later the secretary of war began issuing his orders to put the scheme into motion.

Major General Henry Dearborn was at his headquarters in Albany when he received Armstrong's instructions. Like many other prominent Americans, he had earned his first laurels as a Patriot, seeing action in several important engagements as a regimental leader and then a member of George Washington's staff in the 1770s and 80s. After the War of Independence, he settled in Kennebec County in Maine, which was still a part of Massachusetts, served two terms as a congressman and became a major general in the state's militia. From 1801 until 1809 Dearborn was the secretary of war in Jefferson's administration and he was well-familiar with Madison and Gallatin, who were also in the cabinet. Although the army was reduced during that period, Dearborn proved a competent administrator and, as his longevity in the office indicated, a compatible associate for the president and his men. After Madison's inauguration, Dearborn moved to Boston, where he took up the lucrative post of collector of customs with his son as his assistant. He also held two other influential positions, one as the financial manager for the Boston Marine Hospital and the other as superintendent of lighthouses in Massachusetts.

As the preliminary war legislation was moving through Congress in January 1812, President Madison invited Dearborn to return to military service as the senior major general in the U.S. Army. By this time Dearborn was comfortably set up in life and could look forward to years of prosperity, but he answered the president's call, travelled to Washington and played a leading role in planning the first campaign against the Canadas, strongly endorsing the popular idea of capturing Quebec.[18] He then went to Albany, where he established his headquarters and was near to the new cantonment across the Hudson River at Greenbush, where the regiments were collecting to be outfitted and trained.

To one young officer who saw him during this period, Dearborn appeared as "a large man, rather corpulent, about 60 years old I should judge, has a brave open countenance, walks on foot as smart as any man his age and size."[19] About the same time the *Boston Chronicle* claimed that "No man was ever more popular in the district in which he resided ... than general Dearborn."[20] But once he took on his new and very public post, it became evident that the years had taken their toll. His robust strength had given way to flab and age. Grief over the recent death of his second wife, Dorcas, and periodic illness had diminished his youthful zeal. The general was aware of his own decline as he admitted to Thomas Jefferson in March 1812: "I am neither so vain as to think my self as well-qualified as I ought to be, or so ambitious as to covet, at this time of life, a place that requires superior tallents, with all the ardour and vigour of youth."[21]

Dearborn's want of drive revealed itself soon after he reached Albany. He remained there less than two weeks before returning to Boston, where he promoted recruitment in New England and tried to get disgruntled Federalist governors in the region to conform with mobilization requests from Washington. Only repeated letters from Secretary Eustis, and one from the president, prompted him to return to Albany five weeks after the war started.[22] The general explained that he had not realized the army on the Niagara Frontier was under his command and that he was to have been working in conjunction with

Brigadier General Hull; this, despite the fact that he was the senior officer in the north and a leading architect of the first campaign. After Detroit fell, Dearborn sent men and munitions to Niagara but left the inexperienced militia general Stephen Van Rensselaer in charge of the army there, urging him to launch an invasion but refusing to go and take command himself. The dismal defeat at Queenston Heights in October was the result. Dearborn's only campaigning involved a late and slow march from Plattsburgh to the border of Lower Canada to fight one small skirmish and then to leave his army to the hardships of the winter camps at Plattsburgh and Burlington, while he returned to Albany.

Dearborn's conduct in 1812 gave British and American satirists opportunities for exercising their wit. One produced an ode lampooning "Granny Dearborn [who] held command o'er all the grannies of the land," while another published a cartoon of a ragged American army led by officers "in gold and silver lace and laurel." The image featured Dearborn on horseback, his sword stuck, not so subtly, in a knot hole in the bottom of a nearby cart "as the general is devouring a huge apple pie, which he holds in both hands and eats with great satisfaction."[23] Criticisms were also being voiced on a more influential level. "General Dearborn is a good man …," wrote one of President Madison's correspondents. "[But] I very much doubt if he is qualified for that station. Courage and Heels are absolutely necessary in a soldier [;] the former he may have but the lat[t]er from his age he cannot, complete victories are never obtained but by the Army who posseses [sic] both."[24]

Dearborn understood that he was open to criticism. In December he wrote to the president: "I fear that the close of our campaign will occasion some uneasiness, and probably much censure. I must expect my full share of it."[25] He was uncertain whether he should remain in command and admitted to Madison, "It will be equally agreeable to me to imploy such moderate talents as I possess in the service of my Country, or be permitted to retire to the shade of private life." James Monroe was also doubtful about Dearborn remaining in command and privately recommended his replacement. Monroe himself had been lobbying for a command in the field from the early days of the war and by December 1812 he believed he could lead the northern army more effectively than Dearborn could. When Congress approved the appointment of new major generals, Monroe's name was at the head of the proposed list, but Secretary Armstrong's intention was to assign him to the northern army as a subordinate to Dearborn. On the day the list was to be sent to the Senate, Madison called Monroe to his office to discuss the matter. The secretary of state suspected that Armstrong, who was known to have presidential aspirations as well, was purposely putting his potential rival in an undesirable situation. With Madison's approval, Monroe declined the appointment, suggesting that it would be indelicate to remove Dearborn and that his presence as second-in-command might actually reduce the old general's effectiveness.[26]

Dearborn was probably unaware of how close he came to being replaced. He had been expected to visit Washington once winter set in, but chose instead to submit his recommendations about improvements from his headquarters at Albany.[27] He kept himself busy with the maintenance of the winter camps and trying to implement a more effective recruitment system across the northern states, only to have it replaced by the new military district organization. From British deserters and other sources, he learned that a considerable number of regulars had gone from Kingston to Little York and Niagara, leaving about 1,000 men to garrison the port.

In the second week of February Commodore Chauncey passed through Albany on his way to New York and met with Dearborn. He confirmed what the general had heard about the British strength at Kingston and then discussed the plan for striking at Kingston that he had submitted to Secretary Jones on 21 January. As soon as the ice in the harbours and the lake broke up in April, Chauncey wanted to embark 1,000 men from the army in the squadron, slip

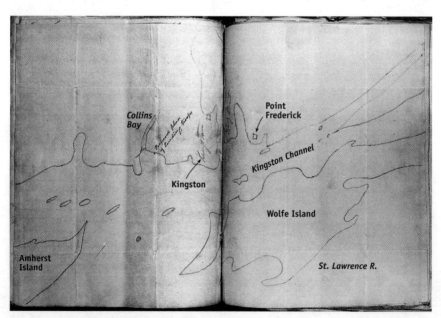

Chauncey's plan for attacking Kingston. Dependable charts of the lakes were virtually non-existent in 1812. The commodore relied on a rough sketch of the Canadian shore to identify for his superiors where he could disembark an invading land force for a combined attack on Kingston. (USNA, RG 45, M 125, 26:29)

across the lake, land the infantry and artillery three miles west of Kingston, and as they marched to assault the town, his squadron would attack the Provincial Marine vessels and the land batteries. "I have no doubt," he assured Jones, "but that we should succeed in taking or destroying their ships and Forts and of course preserve our ascendancy upon this Lake."[28] Dearborn seems to have liked Chauncey's proposal well enough, but soon after the commodore departed for New York, he drew up his own plan for an assault on Kingston across the ice of the St. Lawrence around the first of March, instead of waiting for later, and sent it off to Armstrong on 14 February. He wrote to President Madison the same day and confidently predicted, "I have very little doubt but we shall command Lake Ontario whether we attack Kingston on the ice or not, but if we can make a successful attack before the ice breaks up our command of the Lake will be insured."[29]

On 17 February Secretary of War Armstrong's orders for the spring campaign reached Dearborn, laying out the plan of action that began with an amphibious attack on Kingston in April, along the same lines as Chauncey's submission to William Jones.[30] There followed a brief period of confusion as Dearborn and Armstrong's letters and replies to each other crossed in the post, but it ended with Dearborn issuing instructions to his brigade commanders to start their units on the march from their winter camps toward Sackets Harbor and Buffalo in advance of the big push into Canada.

Armstrong's initial instructions also advised Dearborn to keep the campaign goals secret and to cover the movement of troops towards Lake Ontario by spreading it around that he was anticipating an attack on Sackets.[31] Unwittingly, the British complied with this subterfuge when they sprang their well-organized raid from Prescott across the ice of the St. Lawrence against Ogdensburg on 22 February, the day after Governor-in-Chief Prevost left there on his way to Niagara. Rumours soon reached Dearborn that Prevost had made a lightning advance from Quebec at the head of several thousand men with the clear intention of attacking Sackets Harbor. Rather than wait any longer for Chauncey to join him at Albany, Dearborn headed west on the turnpike and then north from Utica to Sackets, arriving there in fifty-two hours on 2 March.

This was Henry Dearborn's first visit to Sackets Harbor. Under the command of Colonel Alexander Macomb and Chauncey and his subordinates, the men at the post had made some significant structural improvements during the winter. Freshly built barracks stretched in two lines to the west just outside the palisade around Fort Tompkins, which now dominated the height of land overlooking the lake near the head of the harbour. New officers quarters, barracks and batteries stood behind it and along Navy Point. At the foot of the harbour was a

Oliver Hazard Perry (1785-1819). Master Commandant Perry petitioned Commodore Chauncey for an appointment on the Great Lakes on 1 January 1813, an offer which the commodore enthusiastically accepted and put into motion with a letter to Secretary Jones. (Courtesy of the Flagship Niagara League)

new blockhouse and 600 yards east of it were the earthen ramparts and battery at Fort Volunteer. In the shipyard the sleek little schooner laid down in December stood nearly ready to launch, and nearby were the stockpiles of timber being readied for a new vessel. The station was on constant alert, and when Dearborn's procession of sleighs arrived, sentries could be seen perched on platforms in the tallest of the trees, where they scoured the horizon of ice and forest for the faintest sign of trouble approaching.[32]

Commodore Chauncey reached Sackets on 3 March in company with Master Commandant Oliver Hazard Perry, whom he had met at Albany and who was slated for the command on Lake Erie. The latest rumours had it that the British force at Kingston had increased to 8,000 effectives and that an attack from that quarter was imminent. This threat hung over the Harbor for the better part of two weeks until Dearborn admitted to Secretary Armstrong that he believed Prevost had decided it was too late to send an expedition across the ice. In truth, given Armstrong's advice to explain the sudden movement of troops by "creating" an alarm, the whole uproar might have been a ruse. On 14 March the general certainly seemed convinced that the force at Kingston could not be as large as previously stated. "We are probably just strong enough on each side to defend; but not in sufficient force to hazard an offensive movement," he explained to Armstrong.[33] Chauncey had already made that assumption. He had doubted the reality of the threat, concluding that the apparent flurry of activity on the north shores had been a diversion in favour of a movement against Major General Harrison's army in the Northwest and he discounted the claims about thousands of British regulars on the march. "The people on the other side," he wrote to Jones, "are as credulous as our own countrymen, … they magnify a few sleighs loaded with stores and accompanied by guards into a brigade of regular troops."[34]

On Monday, 15 March 1813, Major General Dearborn convened a council of war at Sackets Harbor to discuss the upcoming campaign. It was apparently a small gathering, consisting of only the general, Chauncey and Colonel Macomb, and the details and decisions were guarded with "the most scrupulous silence," as the commodore explained to Secretary Jones.[35] Under their immediate review was the primary objective of a combined naval and military attack on Kingston. Secretary Armstrong's original scheme had been based on Lake Ontario losing its ice around the first of April, but the winter had been a hard one and at mid-March there was no sign of a break-up anytime soon. Putting this circumstance alongside the uncertain strength of the force at the British port, Dearborn and Chauncey began to question the wisdom of commencing the spring campaign at Kingston.

They turned to York as an enticing alternative for the first attack. There was little information about the strength of its defences, but because of its position on the lake, the prevailing wind would help sweep away the ice at York sooner than at Kingston, where floes would gather in the narrows at the opening to the St. Lawrence River. Furthermore, as a newly developed naval centre, York offered similar targets to those at Kingston; Chauncey's sources had informed him that there were "two brigs building [at York], calculated to carry 18 guns each," and that Provincial Marine schooners *Prince Regent* and *Duke of Gloucester* had wintered there. He continue to assert that the latter warships carried 18 and 16 guns respectively, still accepting all reports at face value and not seeing the irony in his complaints about the locals who "magnif[ied] a few sleighs loaded with stores … into a brigade of regular troops."[36] Chauncey utilized this unchallenged information along with stories about a vast supply of naval goods in the dockyard at York to strengthen his case for an expedition there. "By possessing ourselves of these vessels," he later explained to Secretary Jones, "and taking or destroying all the public stores and munitions of war at York … [we will have] a decided advantage in the commencement of the campaign."[37] Dearborn and Macomb found Chauncey's argument convincing and so the plan of operations changed, with York becoming the primary goal. It was also agreed that the army and navy would combine to attack Fort George next at the same time as the force at Buffalo took Fort Erie. After that they would proceed to Kingston.

When he described the alteration in the campaign to Secretary William Jones, Chauncey referred to the scheme as "my plan," suggesting that he had led the discussion during the council. The leadership might have naturally fallen to the commodore since he had shown himself to be considerably more ambitious and energetic than Dearborn, but Chauncey was also trying to meet Jones's expectations. There had been no mistaking the secretary's concern with capturing control on the upper lakes, and the full campaign that the commodore envisioned derived directly from that imperative. Once Little York fell, he explained to Jones on 18 March, and the British were suppressed at Niagara long enough to allow a handful of converted merchantmen to sail from Black Rock to Erie, Pennsylvania, the commodore intended to send his squadron to blockade Kingston. He would then take command on Lake Erie, overrun the Provincial Marine on that water, work in conjunction with Harrison to "attack and take Malden and Detroit and proceed into Lake Huron and attack and carry Michilimackinac *at all hazards*."[38] This was almost exactly what Jones had advised in January. As further proof of Chauncey's determination, he wrote out orders on the day of the council for Master Commandant Perry to go to Lake Erie and have "the vessels at Erie ready for service by the 1st of June at which time I hope to join you with such a force as will ensure us success against the enemy."[39]

How much Dearborn knew about Chauncey's grand scheme is unknown as the general's brief messages to Secretary Armstrong about the change in plans only mentioned attacks at York, Fort George and Kingston, in that order. Dearborn departed from Sackets on 18 March. In Washington Madison's cabinet received the revised campaign strategy and accepted it, with few questions. Jones's reply to the commodore suggested that the shifted order of operations was discussed openly at the cabinet table, earning President Madison's approval of "the general outline" and "satisfaction with [Chauncey's] judicious and zealous execution of the preparatory arrangements."[40] The secretary of war viewed the decision to make Kingston "the last object ... to be necessary, or at least proper," but he did not allude to action on the upper lakes.[41] He was concerned that the largest possible military force be carried to York and Niagara in Chauncey's squadron to guarantee success, even if it left Sackets without proper defence. "If our first step in the campaign and in the quarter from which most is expected, should fail," he stressed to Dearborn, "the disgrace of our arms will be complete. The public will lose all confidence in us, and we shall even cease to have any in ourselves."[42] The fact that Chauncey and Dearborn were about to deviate from the original campaign strategy was not an issue among the senior officials, who believed the commanders in the field were the best judges of what to do and when, based upon their circumstances. What mattered most was that they achieve a clear-cut victory early in the spring, and whether it was won at Kingston or York was immaterial at the time.

Through March and April, Sackets Harbor and the neighbourhood filled up with troops, thousands of them. A much smaller number of seamen arrived, but Commodore Chauncey was expecting more and also hoping for a reinforcement for the very depleted contingent of marines.[43] On 5 April he ordered the ice at the base of the slipway cut out and the next day launched the new schooner, which he named *Lady of the Lake*. It was soon rigged and equipped with a single 9-pdr. long gun. He named the former prizes *Raven* (*Mary Hatt*) and *Asp* (*Elizabeth*) and completed their arming. Then, on 8 April, Henry Eckford's managerial skills and the hard work of his shipwrights were demonstrated once again when they brought to the extended slipway the massive white oak timbers that would form the keel of the new warship. They had spent weeks cutting and shaping a wood lot of timber into all the many curving pieces of the ship's frame. So well organized and so industrious were these New York builders that in two weeks the hull was entirely framed and planking was already creeping up its sides.

The contrast between the productivity of the shipyard at Sackets Harbor and the state of affairs in the yard at York was beyond anything the American officers could have imagined. In fact, had they known the real situation in the Canadian dockyard, they might never have dropped the plan to attack Kingston first.

CHAPTER 6

"*Never more secure*"[1]

FORTIFYING YORK

The winter of 1812-1813 brought changes to the town of York that foreshadowed events to come. It had always been a garrison town, but the increased pace of military and naval activities warned the residents that the war with the United States was bound to arrive at their doorstep, and sooner rather than later.

The militia turned out in numbers and remained at the post for months on end. The order had been issued in October 1812 for the nearly 1,000 men of the 1st and 3rd York Regiments and some from the 1st Durham Regiment to muster at the capital. But military service intruded sharply on the daily occupations and responsibilities of the farmers, merchants and labourers whose names were on the lists, and many were reluctant to answer the call. Fully aware of the problem, the regimental leaders sent their officers through the countryside to remind everyone of his public duty. It could be a frustrating task. Lieutenant Ely Playter of the 3rd York, for instance, rode east of the town to Whitby and found that the people "kept out of the way," which left him "much vexed at this conduct," as he recorded in his diary.[2]

Nevertheless, there was a fairly good representation from the regiments on hand in October when a lottery, or draft, was held to determine who would stay for duty in the garrison. Viewing such service as their social responsibility or as a way to pick up additional income, some men stepped forward to volunteer whereas others joined the ranks only after the officers drew their names from the lottery drum. The requisite numbers were attained and between October 1812 and the following spring, between 190 and 240 officers and men from the three regiments were stationed at the garrison at one time or another, the numbers fluctuating from day to day as men fell sick and went home or left without permission. Ely Playter served continuously through this period, usually returning to his home near the Don River each night. The farmer and distiller John Lyon and the recent immigrant from England Isaac Wilson, both privates in the 3rd, were also there over the months. Wilson adapted to army life well and was soon advanced to corporal. He found sentry duty especially hard on frigid nights but the beds were comfortable and the food certainly filled him up. "When I was in the garrison at York," he later wrote to his family in England, "I got so fat that I couldn't get my clothes on that I brought from home without altering them."[3]

For most of this period there was little change in the number of regular troops at York. Lieutenant Colonel William Shortt, 41st Foot, was in command of several dozen men from each of the 41st and 49th Regiments of Foot and a handful of gunners from the Royal Regiment of Artillery.[4] There was a constant train of officers passing through with despatches or in charge of detachments, but only a few arrived to take up appointments at the post. These included Major Alexander Clerk of the Royal Newfoundland Regiment of Fencibles, who was assigned to the quarter master general's department, and Lieutenant Philip Ingouville of the same regiment, who served as an engineer.[5]

Major General Roger Sheaffe and his staff reached the capital from Niagara during the third week of February and moved into Government House, the lieutenant governor's home across Garrison Creek from the garrison, his presence announced by the Royal Standard flying at the peak of the flag pole nearby. His days were occupied with the demanding tasks of directing the military and naval forces at all the posts in Upper Canada (and the captured area around Detroit) as well as with the administrative business of the province's government.[6]

The militia spent part of its time in learning the manual of arms on the drill ground or standing guard, but its primary employment was the improvement of the fortifications at the garrison. The weather was often too cold and snowy to allow for more than the cutting, hauling and squaring of timber or preparation of other building supplies, but by April 1813 the men had advanced the projects begun during the fall and had noticeably strengthened the defences. Lieutenant Ingouville directed this work, following a plan prepared by Royal Engineer Captain Henry Vigoureux and approved by the late Major General Brock.[7]

Four batteries, in various stages of construction, stood on the lakeshore west of the garrison. One was in the ravine at the mouth of Garrison Creek, a second was adjacent to the lieutenant governor's house, a third, named the Half Moon Battery, was placed within 400 yards west of the governor's house and the fourth, the Western Battery, was situated another 300 yards farther on.[8] The scant details about their construction show that they consisted of parapets shaped out of piles of earth and lined on the outward side with sod. Each had two or more embra-

Muster roll and pay list, York militia. The surviving militia records of 1812 and 1813 reveal much about the organization and service of the individual companies. This muster roll shows Captain John Beverley Robinson, 3rd York Militia, in command of a company that Captain Thomas Hamilton had commanded until March 1813. Among the men who were paid for service that month, and for several preceding months, were Lieutenant Ely Playter and Private John Lyon. The latter's name appears as "Lyons," one of the spellings used to identify him in public documents. (LAC, RG 9, IB7, 18:437)

Effective men, fit for duty. This return of Robinson's company (although credited to Hamilton's command) clearly shows how many men were present for armed duty on 4 April and why others were absent. Those "in the King's Works" were employed in building one of the batteries or a similar project, while the single man "On Command" had been sent to a post outside York. (LAC, RG 9, IB7, 17: 24A)

9-pdr. battery. A battery at Fort George National Historic Site at Niagara-on-the-Lake, Ontario contains a functioning 9-pdr. long gun shown here on a garrison carriage with its block and tackle fixed to the inner face of the battery. A ramrod and other equipment lies on the floor while the embrasure opens onto the field of fire. (Photograph by Robert Malcomson)

sures, or gun ports, cut into it; one account mentioned that the Government House Battery had room for five guns. These openings and the interior faces of the batteries were lined with timber, and floors were laid down over heavy beams, tilting slightly toward the inner face of the works as a check on the recoiling guns.[9] The batteries differed in appearance and strength, with the Western Battery being the largest. It was on the edge of a deep ravine that marked the western limit of the wide swath of land that had long ago been cleared around the garrison. The thick virgin forest still covered the ravine and spread westwards along the shore to the clearing where the overgrown ramparts of Fort Rouillé sat. Nothing was done to refurbish the ruins and there is no evidence of any improvements on Gibraltar Point to guard the entrance to the bay.

The main garrison on the east side of the creek remained more or less as it had been, a two-storey blockhouse and twenty or so other buildings surrounded by a gated, wooden stockade that extended down to the shoreline. A change was underway, however, on the raised, roughly triangular piece of ground west of the creek where stood Government House, now Sheaffe's headquarters. In the spring of 1812 Brock and his advisors had debated whether to erect a "regular," or symmetrical, fort on this spot or to create an "irregular" design that conformed to the topography.[10] They chose the latter approach and Lieutenant Ingouville supervised the work at the same time as the batteries were being put up. By April 1813, the crews had excavated a wide, shallow ditch on a north-south line nearly connecting the creek ravine with the embankment above the lake about 50 yards west of Government House. The clay they removed was heaped up to form a seven-foot-high curtain on the eastern edge of the ditch, all but hiding the residence from anyone standing out near the Half Moon Battery. The road along the lake curved around the southern end of the curtain, passed the residence, dipped down across Garrison Creek and up through the gates at either side of the main garrison. The plans called for a line of picketing to be erected along the top of the embankment on either flank of the Government House Battery, but whether this work was done is uncertain.

These projects gave a more formidable appearance to the western approaches to York but heavy artillery was required in the batteries to put some punch behind that promise. General Sheaffe and Captain Andrew Gray had both advised Governor-in-Chief Sir George Prevost in December 1812 that at least a dozen 12- and 18-pdr. guns were wanted to protect the harbours at York and Kingston. Although the arsenal at Quebec housed more than forty guns of such calibres and dozens of 24- and 32-pdrs., only nine long guns and short-range carronades were sent up the St. Lawrence for use in the forts during the winter. Of these, two long 12-pdrs. reached York, prompting the effort to make the best of the ordnance on hand.[11] The half dozen 6-pdrs. taken out of the *Duke of Gloucester* in the fall were put into the batteries and a brigade of sleighs brought eight 18-pdr. carronades over from Fort George on the winter roads.[12] Apart from a pair of light, brass 6-pdrs. mounted on field carriages, there was no other artillery at York, except for the long guns and carronades that Lieutenant Governor Simcoe had collected there in the 1790s.

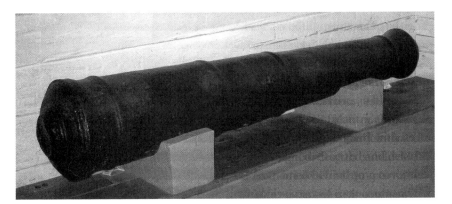

A Simcoe gun. Displayed at Historic Fort York in Toronto is this 18-pdr. long gun cast in England in the 1650s, was one of the guns transported to York by Lieutenant Governor John Simcoe and used during the battle. Its trunnions and cascabel were broken off to render it useless, but it was pressed into service out of the need for heavy artillery. (Photograph by Robert Malcomson)

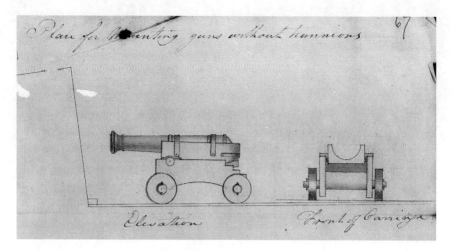

Carriage for a trunnion-less, obsolete gun. A plan drawn *circa* 1812 reveals one way to mount, or "block," one of the obsolete "Simcoe guns," using brackets and a cradle. This particular design has new trunnions attached to the cradle so that the gun may be elevated. This type of elevation adaptation was not apparently used on the guns in April 1813 as the record shows they could not be elevated. (TRL, Jarvis Papers, S126.B65/67)

Of the old "Simcoe guns" in storage, the heaviest pieces were two long 18-pdrs. and a single long 12-pdr. One of the 18-pdrs., (properly termed a "culverin drake") had been manufactured in England around 1657 during Oliver Cromwell's Commonwealth. It was used at Oswego and Fort Niagara during the Seven Years' War and at Carleton Island at the entrance to the St. Lawrence River during the American War of Independence. Brought to York in 1793, the gun was mounted in the Gibraltar Point redoubt, where it remained until 1807 when it was declared obsolete and rendered unusable by having its trunnions and cascabel broken off. The same thing was done to the other two guns, but early in 1813 all three were brought out of "retirement" and the artificers at the garrison adapted carriages that would hold them in place, if not allow them to be elevated as easily as other guns were.[13]

The large-grained black powder and ammunition required for the guns at York exceeded the capacity of the "small wooden shed not sixty yards from the King's house" that had served as a magazine for some years."[14] Since an arsenal for the province was also included as part of the plan to turn York into a key military centre, a more substantial building was ordered to be built, a project that appears to have begun in the autumn of 1812 and continued through the winter. Numerous plans for magazines of the period exist, all showing structures with thick stone walls, vaulted ceilings, heavily-timbered roofs, ventilation systems (to keep the powder dry), shifting rooms and double-doored vestibules, but no engineer's plan for the new grand magazine at York has come to light. It is known to have been built on the shore of the lake near the spot where the "wooden shed" stood and it was large enough to contain more than 325 barrels of powder, nearly 40,000 musket rounds in barrels, and crates containing up to 750 explosive shells by the end of March 1813.[15]

The most detailed description of the grand magazine at York may be the account given by American surgeon Amasa Trowbridge, who served with the New York State militia and who helped treat the wounded at York in the garrison for several days after the battle in April. Forty years later he wrote this remembrance of what he had learned from the locals and sent it to a historian who was preparing a book about the War of 1812.

[A] little farther west [from the Government House Battery] stood their principal magazine, being about Thirty feet [in size] with solid mason work and stone, 30 feet deep in the earth and [with] an entrance at the bottom from the lake. Over this stood a large stone building with apparatus for elevating military stores from the bottoms, different apartments were formed and arranged for the reception of military and naval stores. It was admitted that … there were five hundred barrels of powder on the first floor and the other rooms filled with fixed ammunition and the stone Arsenal above well-filled with the same material. All of an explosive character.[16]

The building in Trowbridge's account more closely resembles a storehouse or blockhouse than a typical free-standing grand magazine. It was not uncommon, however, for engineers to locate a magazine with a vaulted ceiling and a connecting room where cartridges could be prepared safely in the lower portion of a large blockhouse and to use adjoining space for an arsenal and storerooms. There is certainly ample evidence from other sources that the building at York was a sizeable structure mainly constructed of stone, brick and heavy timbers, which supports Trowbridge's recollection.[17] It was built in a hollow adjacent to the shore of the lake that must have been deepened and widened, leaving a thick embankment on the lakeside that hid the building almost completely from view in that direction. Enclosing a magazine in a depression in the ground was conventional practice to protect it from the enemy's direct fire and reduce immediate lateral damage in the event of an accidental detonation. Placing it outside a fort and close to the lake where ice and changing water levels could imperil it was not the norm. The magazine at York contained close to 30,000 pounds of highly flammable powder alone, so its destructive potential was enormous and something to worry about.

Interior of a grand magazine. The restoration of the magazine at Fort George National Historic Site depicts the storage of powder kegs in racks. Since keeping the powder dry was essential to its effectiveness, the chamber was fitted with openings for ventilation such as the one in the wall beneath the vaulted stone ceiling. (Photograph by Robert Malcomson)

The defensive preparations around the garrison were paralleled by the activity at the dockyard near the foot of Bay Street where the frigate *Sir Isaac Brock* was rising in the stocks. To at least one observer, the project seemed well in hand and progressing rapidly. He was William Baldwin, who lived at the corner of Front and Bay streets and had a perfect view of the shipyard. Baldwin had immigrated to York from Ireland with his father and siblings in 1799 and laboured industriously to make a life for himself.[18] He had been trained to be a physician, but by 1802 when he bought a home in the town, there were already several other doctors and not enough patients to make a medical practice profitable. Baldwin's attempt to run a school also failed to generate enough income so he studied law and was admitted to the bar in 1803. This career proved more successful and in time he was chosen to be a magistrate and district court judge. His marriage to Phoebe Willcocks in 1803 had produced four sons, and by the time the war came William's ambitions were producing a good life for his family at the same time as he rose in status in his community.

In the spring of 1812 William Baldwin risked everything he enjoyed when he challenged John Macdonell, another up-and-coming lawyer, to a duel over the issue of slanderous courtroom statements. The matter was settled without bloodshed and proved beyond any doubt that Baldwin was willing to stand up for his beliefs. He was ready to state his strong views whether others agreed or not, and this was seen in his comments on the *Sir Isaac Brock* and the man in charge of building it. "We have a large ship of 28 or 30 guns on the stock just by my door," he wrote to a correspondent. "She is building under the superintendence of Mr. Plucknett … a man well-qualified for the office and attentive to his duties from morning till night…. I know him well and he is often with me…. I hear from others great rumours of his delays, etc., etc., which are entirely without foundation."[19]

When he declared his support for Thomas Plucknett, lawyer Baldwin was arguing the minority opinion because no one working directly with the builder had anything good to say about his expertise and efforts. Quarter Master Major Alexander Clerk was still complaining about Plucknett at the end of March as he had all winter. "[He] may be a scientific man and a good draughtsman," Clerk declared to Captain Andrew Gray at Kingston, "[but] … he does not appear to have any method in regard to the workmen or their distribution…. [He] is in the habit of disobeying or at least of evading every order he gets…. [and] to him alone is ascribed the woeful state of the new ship."[20]

And the ship was in a woeful state. The first work on the project had started in the middle of December and up to eighty shipwrights and other tradesman reached the yard later that month or soon after, joining men hired locally.[21] The dispute in January about the building site slowed things down but it was quickly settled and the project should have moved ahead at full speed. At the end of March, however, the ship was still an incomplete skeleton. Its oak stem, stern and main frames were up but the five pieces of heavy timber that would form the keelson and fit over the inward ends of the frames, securing them to the keel, had yet to be inserted.[22] Shipwrights were setting up the last of the "filling" frames on the larboard side while others were bolting the first strakes of oak planking to the starboard side. The hull would require at least twenty strakes of planking to the level of the deck, two dozen or more heavy beams athwart the ship to support each of its decks, plus all the secondary supports and braces, the decks themselves, bulwarks, gun ports, cabins, storerooms, a magazine, the steering mechanism and a nearly endless list of other essential structural parts. In short, very little had actually been accomplished in the construction of the hull.

Work on the embankment above the ship showed signs of better progress. The component parts of the three lower masts, from 70 to nearly 90 feet long, were being assembled while shipwrights were busy squaring and tapering the other masts and the spars. Nearby in a workshop, the sailmaker and his mates were sewing the fore and main topsails. And across from them the blacksmiths had produced nearly all the iron work, from bolts to boom hoops. The boatwrights had just begun to work on the ship's launch and the two or three other small boats it would carry, laying out their keels and frames while some of the other hands constructed batteaux.

In the merchants' dockyard between the Town Blockhouse and the mouth of the Don River the *Duke of Gloucester* lay dismantled and not even close to being ready for service, and the merchant sloop *Mary Ann*, which Sheaffe had recently bought for military use, was also awaiting work.[23] Only on the schooner *Prince Regent* was there any sign of activity, where a few men slowly went about the myriad tasks needed to get it ready to sail.

The lack of progress in the naval establishment was due, Major Clerk asserted, not only to Thomas Plucknett's reluctance to obey orders, but to his refusal to give clear direction to Master Shipwright John Dennis and the foremen, and his own preoccupation with personal matters.[24] Operating under the assumption that his appointment as storekeeper and superintendent of the dockyard at York made him virtually autonomous, Plucknett continually gave orders where he had no authority and fancied himself a commissioned officer, parading around town with a pair of bright gold epaulettes on his coat. He requisitioned materials from the shipyard for use in the renovation of a house he rented and expropriated 100 man-days of labour from the shipyard carpenters to get the job done. He interfered with the payroll clerk's accounts and tried to have a personal servant he had brought from Montreal put on the dockyard books, first as a servant and then as an artificer and then, by his own appointment, as assistant storekeeper. Major Clerk and his superior, Christopher Myers (recently promoted to the rank of colonel), opposed Plucknett at every turn. Myers laughed at his audacity, wrote out specific instructions for him to follow and repeated his earlier criticisms of the man to Lieutenant Noah Freer, Prevost's secretary. But it made little difference, and Captain Gray, reading and hearing about all this at Kingston, was exasperated by what he termed "this man's folly." "If I had been at York," he asserted, "I should have had the ship *here by this time*."[25]

Major General Sheaffe was at York during this time and could not have helped but be aware of the obvious problems in the dockyard, but he did not use his unquestionable authority to reassign Plucknett to some other post or order him out of York altogether. His only censure of the superintendent was putting a halt to his pay until he could account for the expenditure of funds given to him in December.[26] Otherwise, Clerk and Myers appear to have been left on their own to make the best of the situation and they finally chose to ignore Plucknett and deal directly with Dennis. This tactic produced some good results, but as to when the *Sir Isaac Brock* would finally float free of the land, the estimates suggested May or June or later than that.

There was another significant obstacle that threatened to keep the *Sir Isaac Brock* from becoming the heavily armed frigate the British needed on Lake Ontario. The ship had originally been designed to carry twenty-six 32-pdr. carronades and four long 18-pdrs., but early in February Noah Freer informed Captain Gray that "the ordnance required for the vessels building at Kingston, York and Amherstburg not being able to be procured in this Country, the necessary application has some time since been transmitted to England, that the same may be sent to Quebec as early as possible in the Spring."[27] A set of 18-pdr. carronades was located at Quebec for the ship at Kingston that would be launched as the *Wolfe*, but the *Brock*'s guns and the sixteen 24-pdr. carronades and four long 12s meant for the *Detroit*, building at Amherstburg, were not to be found.

The first convoy of transports from England would reach Quebec as soon as ice conditions in the St. Lawrence allowed, probably in early May, and then it would take weeks for all the necessary guns to be transported to the lakes. It was the sort of dilemma that Colonel Ralph Bruyeres had warned Sir George about

HMS *Detroit* on the stocks. Late in the summer of 1813, the 20-gun ship *Detroit* was painted and ready for launch on the bank of the Detroit River at Amherstburg. It had been hoped that the *Sir Isaac Brock* would stand like this on the shore at York the previous spring. (Historic Fort Malden)

in January when he criticized York as the new headquarters for the Provincial Marine. "The distance," he had written, "becomes a very serious obstacle particularly as the armaments for the new ships must entirely come from Lower Canada and ought if possible to be sent complete during the winter for the Enemy are fully prepared to commence their Naval operations immediately on the opening of navigation."[28] With no alternative, the officers at York put together a plan for arming the *Sir Isaac Brock* as soon as they could launch it. They would take guns out of the batteries and the other Provincial Marine vessels on hand and put them into the frigate and then sail quickly for Kingston, where the ship could be kept until its proper guns arrived.[29]

All the activity around the garrison and at the dockyard produced benefits for the people at York. The merchants, especially Quetton St. George and William Allan, made tidy profits on the provisions and materials they supplied to the army services through the commissary general's office.[30] Local men found employment with the army, either in the militia drafts or by working as teamsters hauling building supplies to the construction sites or as clerks in one of the offices. Ely Playter, for instance, received 4 shillings and 8 pence a day as "overseer" of the militia artificers from December through February, at the same time as he drew his militia pay. William Stanton and Thomas Gibbs Ridout picked up jobs as clerks in the commissary while Hugh Heward worked there, too, as an issuer of goods.

Stephen Jarvis, an old ex-Queen's Ranger who arrived at York in 1809 and made his living as a government clerk and part-time merchant in 1812, was appointed acting adjutant general for the militia, which gave him a captain's wage and rations for a horse and a small daily allowance to hire an assistant. His fifteen-year-old son, George, was one of several adolescents at York who sought commissions in the British army by enlisting as "gentleman volunteers" and learning the army's ways among the rank and file until they were deemed ready to fill a vacancy among the commissioned officers.[31]

Justice William Powell's son Grant also joined the army late in 1812. He had been trained as a physician in England but had never been able to establish a successful practice. He and his wife and daughter were struggling to make ends meet in Montreal in the spring of 1812 when their long-time family friend Roger Sheaffe put Grant's name forward as a surgeon for the military. Prevost and Brock approved and Powell joined the Provincial Marine late in the year with an annual salary of £182. He moved his family to York, where he tended to the sick in the garrison and dockyard through the winter while his mother, Anne Powell, watched over the couple to make sure they did not live beyond their means, which she believed was at the root of their financial difficulties.[32]

Despite the increase in business, there was actually a shortage of specie in Upper Canada to pay bills and wages. Prevost remedied the problem by obtaining permission from the Lower Canada legislature to issue Army Bills, paper money backed by the Home Government. Soon entrepreneurs and investment associations began producing their own bills, leading a York merchant named Alexander Legg to claim later that the war caused "immense sums of money to be spent in the Country, and it consequently became a plentiful commodity, amongst the People, which enabled them to lay it out more liberally."[33] At least there was an abundance of cash available to those in the profitable loop caused by the boom; residents outside the war-driven marketplace struggled to keep up as inflation drove prices higher and the military's demands made some commodities scarce.

There was a handful of families who struggled with problems of a different kind through the spring of 1813. Although there had been no battles at York, veterans returned from the front lines changed forever by their war experiences. Private Thomas Kennedy lost a leg at the Battle of Queenston Heights and the same 18-pdr. round shot that nearly killed him rendered his friend Thomas Major a cripple. Neither man could resume his livelihood and both were hoping to qualify for a government pension. Isaac Devins was also wounded at Queenston and, after lingering for months, died and left his aged father without support. For the family of Thomas Smith, the impact of war and the quirks of fate were even worse. Smith was accidentally hatcheted to death at Queenston by a Six Nations warrior fighting for the British; few militiamen on either side wore uniforms and the warrior did not stop to ask about Smith's loyalties. Smith left his wife, Hannah, with two children, but in February she died giving birth to twins, prompting family and friends to step in and adopt the four orphans.

In the presence of such misery, there was at least some consolation to be found at York. The Loyal and Patriotic Society had been formed late in 1812 to provide relief for such situations, and during the winter and spring the society's headmen met to discuss these cases and grant immediate financial support to the needy. The amounts were small: £10 to help old Mr. Devins; £2 per week to Kennedy and Major until their pensions began; a £10 one-time sum for each of the Smith newborns and £8 for each of the older children, who at least had the clothes on their backs to take to their new families.[34]

In another, and very different, display of community spirit, the young women of York, reportedly led by twenty-one-year-old Mary Warren Baldwin, the doctor's sister, finally got the chance to present a banner they had made in the summer of 1812 to the 3rd Regiment of York Militia.[35] The flag, or regimental colour, was made of green wool with a yellow fringe around the edge.

Colours for the 3rd York Militia. This replica of the regimental colour presented to the 3rd York in March 1813 bears the slogan "Deeds Speak," a reference to the regiment's good conduct at the capture of Detroit and the Battle of Queenston Heights. (Toronto Culture, Fort York Collection)

It bore several embroidered motifs, the largest being a crown in the very centre with the letters "G" and "R" on either side of it standing for *Georgius Rex* – King George. Beneath it was a laurel branch above "3rd Regiment York Militia" and a scroll announcing the motto "Deeds Speak." The long-delayed ceremony took place on Tuesday, 23 March, in front of the church with the regiment assembled and Major General Sheaffe and his suite looking on. Major William Allan commanded the regiment that afternoon, since a death in Lieutenant Colonel William Chewett's family prevented him from being present.

The ceremony began with the Reverend Dr. Strachan reading a service and delivering a sermon after which he consecrated what was described as "the Regimental Colors, and the Standard," referring to the pair of flags that made up a regiment's "colours"; presumably a Union Jack accompanied the homemade regimental banner. One of the Powells' daughters, probably twenty-six-year-old Anne, made a short speech, asking the men to accept "this Ensign of Union, as a token of our lasting esteem and the harbinger of increasing glory."[36] On behalf of the regiment, Major Allan accepted the gifts and declared that the flags "shall animate us with a courage which may through divine assistance completely shield you from every danger."

General Sheaffe spoke next, congratulating the militia on the gift of "these honorable, these sacred Banners." He expressed his firm belief that "when you shall be called to rally around them, to defend not only them, but all besides that is precious to you, I am confident that you will give new proofs of your courage and patriotism, that you will reap fresh Laurels." After Sheaffe had withdrawn, Allan addressed the regiment. He reminded them of how the women depended on their "conduct and courage," predicting that the enemy "will wreak the bitterest vengeance upon us should they prove victorious," but that such a turn of events would never come to pass "while we are united." "On the contrary," he proclaimed, "they shall continue daily to receive bloody proofs that a country is never more secure, than when defended by its faithful, loyal and industrious inhabitants." As the band played "The British Grenadiers," the 3rd York marched off behind their brilliant new symbols to see them deposited at Allan's quarters.

The militia were not to be left entirely on their own in the struggle, however, because by the time of the colours ceremony about 160 officers and men of the Royal Newfoundland Regiment of Fencibles under the command of Major Rowland Heathcote had arrived at the garrison. They had been sent from Kingston to establish regimental headquarters at York as part of the larger objective to relocate the Provincial Marine there. Although a "fencible" unit, and therefore recruited in Canada for service only in North America, the Royal Newfoundland Regiment was in every other way a regular regiment of the British army. Men of the island first acted as volunteers with the British during the Seven Years' War (1756-1763), but their formal organization into a "Royal" regiment of fencibles did not come until 1795. The regiment was raised mainly in Newfoundland and

Sergeant, Royal Newfoundland Regiment of Fencibles. Late in March 1813 Sergeant Emmanuel Mitchell of the Newfoundland Fencibles was assigned to act as the sergeant major for the militia at York garrison. A short pike, or halbert, a sash, a sword and the chevrons on his arm were symbols of his authority.[11] (J.C.H. Forster, Toronto Culture, Fort York Collection)

remained there until it was disbanded in 1802, only to be reformed the next year and then sent to Nova Scotia in 1805 and on to Quebec in 1807.[37]

From the beginning of the war, the regiment, which mustered 478 officers and men in April 1813, had been widely dispersed with a large portion employed as marines in the Provincial Marine squadrons. Sir George Prevost believed this was a good fit since, as he wrote, the soldiers were "men accustomed to boats and vessels," although recruitment had certainly diluted the purely Newfound-lander-nature of the regiment.[38] The winter of 1812/13 found about 220 from five different companies at Kingston, some of whom had served in the *Royal George* and *Earl of Moira* the previous autumn. When the order came to head for York, men from the different companies were assigned to these vessels and the new ones under construction at Kingston and the rest departed with Heathcote.[39]

Wives and children of some of the officers and men accompanied them to York. British army regulations allowed twelve men out of every hundred pri-vates and non-commissioned officers to have their families live in the barracks and receive rations at a rate of half a man's portion per woman and one third of a ration per child; this number was normally reduced to six wives and their offspring while the regiment was on the march.[40] The officers made their own ar-rangements for their families, and among the Royal Newfoundland officers who preferred to have his loved ones with him was Quarter Master Bryan Finan, who had joined the regiment only the year before. Unwittingly, his decision led to the creation of a rare first-person account by a boy who followed his father to war.

Only ever identified as "P. Finan," Bryan Finan's son, a lad of ten or twelve years, took note of everything he saw and heard, and years later wrote a mem-oir of his experience as part of a larger religious tract. He remembered hearing about the orders to go to York and the journey there in a caravan of sleighs, at points passing along narrow tracks between great ridges of snow. The prosper-ous, inhabited stretches of land through which they travelled surprised him, as did the sight of native people "living in a settled, cultivated manner, on farms, and, in some instances, having spirits and other articles for sale."[41] One rainy night the Finans stopped in a less flourishing area and took shelter in a dreary little hovel, the home of a family of new settlers who owned barely enough flour to make some bread for the travellers and no other beverage but a sort of tea made from hemlock bark. Between the settlements were expanses of wilderness frozen in "solemn silence … not a sound being heard but the echo of the horses' hoofs prancing along the road."[42]

The snows were rapidly melting by the time the Finan family and the rest of the regiment reached York. Major General Sheaffe appointed Heathcote gar-rison commander and thereafter referred to him as "lieutenant colonel," apparently giving him a local promotion to a rank more appropriate to his station and duties. The rank and file moved into the cottage-barracks at the garrison much to the displeasure of two companies of militia who were evicted from their winter quarters and sent to the Town Blockhouse at the other end of the town. Heathcote and his officers took up accommodations either at Government House or Elmsley House or other hired quarters in town. Over the next few days they got acquainted with their new post and undertook their various duties. On the whole, the officer corps of the Newfoundland detachment was long in the tooth.[43] Heathcote was among the younger men, having received his commission in 1793, whereas Captain Charles Blaskowitz had entered the army in 1778 and Lieutenant John de Koven, at sixty-eight years of age, must have been the oldest line officer present. Captain François Tito Lelièvre was sixty but still possessed of energy and competence, which he would need since he was taking over from Major Clerk as deputy assistant quarter master general and would have to deal with all the dockyard problems.

About this time, General Sheaffe received some good news from England. Despatches had reached Quebec early in March via the overland route from Saint John, New Brunswick, and among them was the announcement that his grateful Sovereign, the Prince Regent, had approved Sheaffe's appointment as a baronet of the United Kingdom in recognition of his victory at Queenston Heights. He was now entitled to be addressed as "Sir" and would be allowed to pass the distinction to his heirs. Moved by the receipt of such an honour, Sheaffe quickly wrote to Secretary for War and the Colonies Lord Bathurst "to express the sentiments which swell my heart at receiving such a token of the approbation of my Prince."[44]

The story was soon told among family members of how Margaret Sheaffe first heard about her husband's achievement. She was living in Quebec with their daughter, Julia, and one day "She was met by a gentleman in the street, as she was going to church, who hardly passed her, before he turned about and accosted her by the title of 'Lady Sheaffe.'" Taken aback by the man's words, Margaret stood with a puzzled expression until the fellow "put a letter in her hand from the Duke of Northumberland, addressed to 'Lady Sheaffe,' which she received with her usual equanimity."[45]

Sheaffe was hoping to return to Niagara and Fort George toward the end of March and made suggestions to Prevost about senior officers who could take charge of the district around York. While he waited for a senior officer to arrive and assume command, Sir Roger tended to his many administrative tasks and oversaw preparation of the new defensive works near his residence. As he explained to Lord Bathurst during the first week of April, "I wish particularly

The Government House Rampart. During late 1812 and the spring of 1813 artificers excavated a wide, shallow ditch 50 yards to the west of Government House, heaping up the soil to create a rampart. This "curtain" ran on a roughly north-south line from the edge of the Garrison Creek ravine to the embankment above the lake (near where the grand magazine stood). There was no gate in the rampart and the roadway ran around the southern end of it. The photo above was taken at Historic Fort York from the edge of the portal later opened halfway along the rampart and shows the southern portion,

to see this place put into a more respectable state of defence before my departure, as I think it probable that the enemy may make some attempt on it in the spring."[46]

Popular opinion agreed with Sheaffe's prediction. "We are beginning to be in daily expectation," wrote Doctor Baldwin on 6 April, "of an attack on this place by the Enemy's force at Sackets Harbor."[47] And the reason for the American interest in York was clearly understood; namely, that building the largest warship on the lakes at the town and stockpiling loads of military and naval stores there made York a prime target for the Americans early in the spring, especially since it was obvious that the British would be unable to contest the U.S. Navy's control of Lake Ontario.

Only a handful of officers knew, however, that Sir George Prevost had changed his mind about making York the headquarters for the Provincial Marine. During his February-March trip into Upper Canada, he had seen for himself the

which has been altered considerably since 1813. The Gardiner Expressway rises where
the lake used to lap the shore and the Tip Top Tailors building stands in the distance,
one of the many structures constructed over the centuries on the landfill.

The second photo shows how the rampart hid the inside of the fort from view,
protecting the structures within and providing a place for the British to situate their
defensive line during a battle. (Photographs by Robert Malcomson)

problems endemic to building a frigate at a remote, poorly defended, resource-
strapped place like York and he had read the advice of such competent senior
officers as Ralph Bruyeres who pointed out the many liabilities of the plan. A
few weeks after returning to Château St. Louis at Quebec, Sir George quietly
altered his policy and had Lieutenant Freer inform Sheaffe that Captain Gray
was being sent to Kingston from Montreal for the purpose of affording "every
possible aid in the concentration of the Naval force on Lake Ontario at Kingston."[48] There would be a return to *status quo ante* – the previously existing state
of affairs – and York would no longer be built up to serve as the central naval
and military arsenal and dockyard.

At Sackets Harbor, of course, nobody knew about Prevost's change of mind,
and even if they did, the rumours of overflowing storehouses and more than
one warship rising on the stocks at York still made the place an enticing plum,
ripe for early harvest.

CHAPTER 7

"Be always ready."[1]

THE ARMY GATHERS AT SACKETS HARBOR

Zealous was a term scarcely strong enough to describe Zebulon Mont-gomery Pike's devotion to the service of his country. He was as eager to lead his troops into Canada as anyone ever could be and, borrowing from a well-known Shakespeare soliloquy, he declared to one of his friends, "You will hear of my fame or of my death – for I am determined to seek the 'Bubble' even in the cannon's mouth."[2]

He was born at Lamberton, New Jersey, in January 1779, the son of Zebulon Sr., who rose to the rank of major in the U.S. Army and brought his son into his regiment as a young cadet.[3] After receiving his first commission in 1799, Second Lieutenant Pike spent several years with detachments of the First U.S. Regiment of Infantry stationed at frontier posts west of the Appalachians. While on duty in Kentucky, he met Clarissa Brown of Cincinnati and married her in March 1801. Their daughter Clarissa was born in February 1803, the only one of their several offspring who survived infancy. It was evident even in his early twenties that Pike, who often signed himself as "Montgomery," was a fellow who took himself rather seriously. Lacking a thorough schooling, he went about reading every-thing he could find, learning the complexities of mathematical and scientific thought and teaching himself how to speak French, Spanish and Latin. He kept with him at all times a copy of Robert Dodsley's *The Economy of Human Life*, a popular collection of moral maxims published in 1784, and was apt to record in it private reflections on how a man should conduct himself. One passage he cop-ied out in hopes that it would someday provide guidance to a son was: "Preserve your honour free from blemish. Be always ready to die for your country. The sod which covers the brave shall be moistened by the tears of love and friendship."[4]

Zebulon Montgomery Pike (1779-1813). Pike's biographers barely restrain their effusions of praise for his "lofty spirit of honour, and iron constitution, ... no imperfect resemblance of one of the cavaliers of the sixteenth century."[12] (TRL, T15207)

Pike, the explorer. Pike is better remembered in the United States for his explorations than for his military accomplishments in the war. This romantic portrayal of his approach to the mountain that would later be known as Pikes Peak is typical of the glorification of his arduous, and dubiously successful, travels. (Colorado Springs Pioneers Museum)

It was not on a battlefield that Lieutenant Pike distinguished himself for the first time, but in the wilderness of the American frontier. In 1805 Brigadier General James Wilkinson, who was the senior ranking officer in the army at the time, selected him to command an expedition to find the source of the Mississippi. Enduring all nature of hardships, Pike completed his mission successfully and, although it was later shown that he had not located the true source of the great river, his management of the expedition and obvious competence as a commander earned him the chance to make another trek into the wilds at Wilkinson's request. The goals for this 1806 exploration were to reach the upper reaches of the Red and Arkansas rivers and investigate Spanish settlements in the territory that is now the state of New Mexico. While making what turned into a long and extremely arduous journey, Pike's party failed in an attempt to climb to the summit of a mountain in modern-day Colorado, never imagining that someday it would be named after the officer-explorer. It was the trip into Spanish territory that drew the most attention and resulted in Pike's detention by Spanish officials, who questioned him about the motive of his travels. Pike convinced them of his peaceful intentions, although they confiscated his papers and escorted him back to Louisiana. Returning to New Orleans to report his findings, Pike abruptly found himself embroiled in the scandal erupting around Wilkinson's alleged scheme with Aaron Burr to build an empire in the southwest. After inquiring into the matter, then-Secretary of War Henry Dearborn concluded that Pike was innocent of involvement. He had been promoted to captain in 1806 and was made a major in the Sixth Regiment of Infantry in 1808 and lieutenant colonel of the Fourth Infantry the next year.

In the spring of 1812 Zebulon Pike joined the Department of War as the deputy quarter master general. By now he had become closely acquainted with influential members of the military and political hierarchy and moved comfortably in their society. He had formed strong opinions about the army and the people who ran it. Secretary Eustis he considered "a Gentleman who I highly respected" but not suited "to be at the head of the W[ar] Department."[5] Pike believed John Armstrong or his own patron James Wilkinson better suited for the job and, as for some of the men chosen to lead the army at the outbreak of war, Pike observed to a friend, "The generals we have are all generals of the Cabinet, and it is only after several of us who have some knowledge of military business are sacrificed, that men will be placed to lead who are now in the ranks, or in obscurity. You shall then see our cabinet generals retire and fighting generals brought forward."[6]

On 6 July 1812, Pike accepted the promotion to colonel of the newly formed Fifteenth Infantry. Officers who had been in the army as long as he had were usually reluctant to move into the new regiments for fear that the war might end quickly and the regiments be disbanded before seeing action. But Pike was eager to take command of the Fifteenth, in part because he was going to be able to fill it up with recruits from his home state of New Jersey. Enlistments went well and by the middle of August the regiment marched from New Jersey to board sloops at New York and sail up the Hudson River to Albany. They disembarked on the bank across from the city and marched two miles to the new military cantonment being developed at Greenbush. Several regiments were already encamped there, comprising thousands of raw recruits undergoing the first steps in their rigorous training.

The Fifteenth numbered over 700 rank and file, commanded by a corps of officers that included only a handful of veterans, such as Major Ephraim Whitlock, who had fought during the War of Independence, and Major William King, who had joined during the army expansion of 1808.[7] Nearly every one of the other officers was new to the service and had left his civilian pastime to follow Pike to war. Among them were Donald Fraser, John Hoppock, Moses Bloomfield, Abraham PerLee, Jeremiah Hayden and John Scott. Of this band of young and ambitious gentlemen, Captain Scott became the unofficial regimental chronicler as he described his adventures in a series of letters to his friend David Thompson in Morristown, New Jersey. "What kind of figure they will make at the walls of Quebec I cannot say," admitted Scott of the men under his command, "but I think they will not disgrace the country from which they came."[8]

The regiment remained at Greenbush only long enough for some basic training and then headed for Plattsburgh, where it arrived on 11 September and pitched its tents beside the Saranac River three miles south of the town. The troops received their winter uniforms shortly afterward and were otherwise properly supplied, leading Scott to chastise "those who think the army is ill-provided for … [because] I do assert that no army on Earth was better fed, clothed and paid than ours has been thus far."[9] The disgraced Brigadier General William Hull passed through Plattsburgh about this time on his way to New York, having been paroled by the British. He was entertained at dinner by senior officers, and Colonel Pike had a long discussion with him about his experience with the British, but by and large no one had anything but contempt for his "dam'd cowardly action" at Detroit.[10]

The camps at Plattsburgh grew in size as other regiments arrived through September and October. They spent their days training in preparation for the expected invasion of Lower Canada via the Richelieu River valley. Henry Dearborn travelled from Albany to head the army, which comprised about 5,000 men in two brigades and set off for Canada on 16 November. It took three days to cover the 24 miles to the border and on the fourth day, 20 November, Colonel Pike led a detachment in an assault on the armed post at La Colle. This resulted in a confusing tramp through swamp and forest and an indecisive skirmish with the British. Pike withdrew to rejoin Dearborn, who signalled an end to the expedition and ordered the disgruntled force back to Plattsburgh. Pike took command of the First Brigade, which went into winter camp on the Saranac, while Brigadier General John Chandler transported the Second Brigade across Lake Champlain to winter quarters at Burlington, Vermont.[11]

Freezing temperatures and blasts of snow arrived late in November and found Pike's brigade still constructing its winter quarters while the men continued to seek shelter in their tents. Months of exposure to the elements had begun to take their toll among the regiments by this time, causing sick-rates to soar and the burial parties to trudge out to the cemetery daily.

It was amidst the epidemic-like conditions at the Saranac camp that a young physician destined to achieve international acclaim faced the first great challenge of his career. Twenty-seven-year-old William Beaumont was a resident of Champlain, New York, who had studied medicine for three years under local surgeons before accepting an appointment in the Sixth Regiment of Infantry as a surgeon's mate in September 1812. Beaumont was with his regiment at Plattsburgh through the fall and early winter under conditions he described as "wretched and deplorable" with so many men sick that "the very woods ring with coughing and groanings."[12] He tended to their ills, learning the practical applications of his profession from experiment as much as from his medical books. Doses of opium helped to relieve dysentery and intermittent fever, although he discovered that the root of the ipecacunha shrub provoked vomiting which also proved effective. Cases of pleurisy and pneumonia required bleeding followed by quantities of opium or digitalis, made from dried foxglove leaves, which stimulated the heart muscle. Too often the disease would turn to typhus and bring about a miserable end. "Behold the *gasping* Mortals how they die," Beaumont wrote in December, "from two to five in a day! Twenty-six in the course of two weeks out of four hundred."[13]

Colonel Pike was well suited to handle the dire situation at Plattsburgh. His explorations in the west had taught him the sort of discipline needed to survive under difficult circumstances and he used a firm hand to show the rank and file how to marshal themselves to assure order and cleanliness of their camps. When he was not relentlessly inspecting and drilling them, sometimes in snowshoes, he was directing the building of proper barracks and the supply of adequate food and fuel. It was said that Pike "was a severe disciplinarian but had the felicity to make his soldiers assured that *his* strictness had for its object *their* glory

– *their* ease – *their* preservation and safety."[14] In January he was felled by pleurisy but, unlike the other unfortunates who had no access to tender treatment, he was slowly nursed back to health by his wife, Clarissa, who had accompanied him on the campaign.

By the end of February, when Major General Dearborn's orders for the Lake Champlain brigades to march to Sackets Harbor reached Pike's headquarters, the regiments had recovered their health for the most part and were ready for active service. Pike made a plan for his brigade to march in stages by detachments and led the way by setting out on the 176-mile trek to Lake Ontario on 4 March with 500 of the fittest men from his Fifteenth Infantry.[15] They travelled in a cavalcade of 130 sleighs, passing through a countryside that lay three feet deep in snow with the mercury dropping so low in the thermometers that the men got out of the sleighs to warm themselves up by walking. Pike had provided them with snowshoes which proved to be useful during the trek. A small detachment of the Third Artillery under Lieutenant Alexander Fanning accompanied the infantry, but had such difficulty hauling the field guns, limbers and caissons through the snow that Pike gave Fanning the option of turning back; the determined lieutenant pressed on nevertheless.

The column averaged about 20 miles a day, as it moved from village to village where officers in the quarter master general's department had arranged for transportation, food and shelter. The latter often consisted of lean-to's open to the weather or tents of thin canvas where the men wrapped themselves in their blankets and crowded together for warmth; frostbite was common and as many as three men froze to death. It was not only the army that suffered because of the march, but also the locals whose horses and sleighs were pressed into service under threat of violence if compliance was not fast in coming. "The road from Plattsburgh to Sacketts harbor is completely strewed with dead and tired horses and broken sleighs," wrote one merchant whose business was completely disrupted.[16] "Many a poor farmer that has been forced into this expedition has left his body on the road," he added, some of them uttering, "the most bitter exclamations against their oppressors to their last breath." Such was the way the war affected people far from the front lines, provoking bitter and lasting resentment.

On 13 March the men in Pike's detachment removed their weapons and knapsacks from the sleighs and marched the last 8 miles to a camp just outside Sackets. Here they found three-sided huts resembling cow sheds, their temporary lodging until a proper set of barracks was completed near Fort Volunteer, afterward to be known as the Pike Cantonment. Following five days behind Pike came 300 of the Sixteenth Infantry and then four companies of the Sixth. More of the Third Artillery arrived, and in the meantime Pike ordered Major Whit-lock to muster anyone at the Saranac cantonment who could walk and carry a weapon and bring them to Sackets.[17]

As it did at Little York, the war changed Sackets Harbor, but in a much more dramatic fashion.[18] It had grown into a fairly active port in the years before the war, but its population did not exceed 250 and there were no more than forty homes overlooking the water or lining the several streets behind it. Militia de-tachments had pitched their tents there from the spring of 1812 and the arrival of Commodore Isaac Chauncey's naval detachment and the first of the U.S. Army units sharply heightened the pace of activity in and around the village through the autumn and winter. But in March 1813 the village's population suddenly increased twenty-fold. Pike's First Brigade included elements of the Sixth, Thir-teenth, Fourteenth, Fifteenth and Sixteenth Regiments of Infantry, plus some of the Regiment of Rifles. Brigadier General Chandler's Second Brigade comprised most of the Ninth, Eleventh, Twenty-first, Twenty-third and Twenty-fifth In-fantries. The two brigades totalled about 4,000 "bayonets," as the fighting men were sometimes referred to, and the rest of the land force included detachments of the First, Third and Light Artillery Regiments, troops from both the First and Second Regiments of Light Dragoons, several hundred local militia and some companies of federal volunteers.[19]

Any semblance of the Harbor's former daily life disappeared under the con-stant din of activity that rang in the streets from dawn to dusk and sometimes through the night. The place was alive with the rumble of heavily loaded wag-ons, the rhythmic tread of marching troops, the choruses of scratching saws and rapping hammers on new constructions, and the bawling of livestock on the way to the slaughterhouse. There was employment for anyone who wanted it and profits waiting to be made at every corner. The arrival of the army in such numbers meant than any kitchen could become a bakery and a single whiskey-producing still might turn a farmer into a tavern-keeper. Every empty room or squalid outbuilding was hired out for accommodations. Gardens became camp-grounds and barns turned into barracks. A flood of mail overflowed the post office and demand drove prices skyward in the handful of stores.

Samuel Hooker was the most prominent merchant in the village and lived with his wife and six children on Main Street in a two-storey frame home built in the classic Federal style.[20] He first conducted business at the village in 1808 and took up residence there two years later after he saw how lucrative the trade could be. The commerce produced by the war, however, exceeded even his ex-pectations. Between November 1812 and the following April, the navy, on just one list of vouchers alone, paid Hooker more than $15,000 to stock Chauncey's

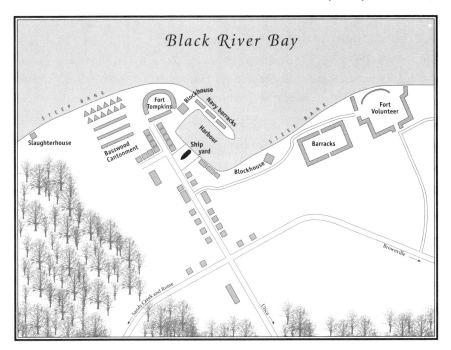

Sackets Harbor, 1813. During the early months of 1813 the Americans built fortifications, barracks and storehouses to prepare their vital lakeside post for the coming
campaign. Not shown here are the streets and lanes off the main roads where the 250 or
so residents had their homes, shops and farms. (Map from Malcomson, *Lords of the Lake*)

squadron with provisions and to equip the after-cabins with everything from a
$2 soup tureen for the schooner *Hamilton* to a teapot and six tumblers worth
$3.75 for the *Governor Tompkins* and mustard pot and pepperbox for the *Lady
of the Lake* costing $0.38. Other local merchants profited from the sudden rise
in business by selling all nature of necessities from axes and shovels to barrels of
beef. The boom times extended to the mill owners who supplied flour and sawn
plank and to the farmers who collected the going daily rate as teamsters.

Not surprisingly, the mass of men and materiel that engulfed Sackets Harbor
in March 1813 quickly overtaxed the village's resources. Colonel Pike realized
this as soon as he arrived there on the 13th and quickly wrote to Plattsburgh to
have any equipment left behind forwarded to Sackets immediately. "Although
we have Six Thousand men," he wrote, "we have not one Blacksmith Shop, nor
anything to work with – in fact you never saw such a scene of Confusion with
Militia, Volunteers, and regular irregulars."[21]

The changing weather aggravated the situation. As the snow melted and
showers of rain began to fall, the roads turned to mud and so did the camp-

grounds. The sanitation problems posed by an army of men and all the animals used to transport and feed it produced an atmosphere more rank than any barnyard. Drainage ditches overflowed and clean fresh water was no longer taken for granted. One visitor to Sackets Harbor during this period included this description of the place in his memoirs.

[Sackets was] one of the most filthy mud-holes I ever was compelled to wallow through, covered with dilapidated barracks, swarming with ruffians, under the appellation of common soldiers; the common dwellings of the inhabitants not much better than the barracks, weather-beaten, old, and dirty in the extreme, and, with very few exceptions the inmates equally as rough and uncivilized as the soldiers, lost to every feeling of common humanity and common courtesy, possessing nothing, scarcely, in common with the civilized world except physical formation.[22]

Two days after Pike and the vanguard of his brigade reached their campground near Sackets Harbor, Major General Dearborn, Commodore Chauncey and Colonel Alexander Macomb held the council of war in which they decided to make York the first target of the spring campaign. Dearborn did not mention in his letters of the period that he shared this information with Pike, nor does a trace of it appear in the latter's correspondence. The two men respected each other, however, and when Dearborn departed from Sackets on 18 March he left Pike in overall command until Chandler arrived. The colonel was honoured to have Dearborn's confidence and wrote to a friend that the reason why Sir George Prevost had not made the expected attack on the Harbor was because "the name of Genl. D[earborn] as Comdr. In Chief intimidated him."[23] Pike knew that Congress had increased the number of generals in the army and he was expecting to be advanced to brigadier; he had even been soliciting support for his nomination through the winter. The good news arrived on 6 April, and the colonel put the Fifteenth Regiment in the hands of Major King and formally assumed command of the brigade.

Major General Dearborn returned to Albany to deal with the paperwork generated by the latest round of changes in the organization of the army and to direct the movement and supply of the various brigades. There was a shortage of staff officers to assist him and the work was demanding to the point that he informed Chauncey at the end of March that "imperious instances may prevent my being with you previous to the sailing of the Expedition we mutually agreed on before I left you."[24] He made a similar remark about missing the first expedition to President Madison a week later after explaining how difficult his administrative tasks were because of the new regulations. But there was another issue up for consideration, as he had confided to the president even before leaving Sackets Harbor. Given the list of lately appointed major generals, Dearborn suggested, he understood that one of them might be more suitable for the leadership post he now held. "To be relieved from my present command by such an officer as may be considered better qualified for the duties of an active Campaign," he wrote, "would not be displeasing to me. A situation requiring less activity would at my time of life be desirable."[25] Hoping to remove any question of protocol that would prevent his removal, Dearborn informed Madison in plain language, "I have no desire for any particular command." This was the second time in three months that Dearborn offered to step down, again showing that, although the epithet of "Granny" was harsh, the old soldier had plainly lost his fighting spirit.

Whatever energy his commander-in-chief lacked, Brigadier General Pike more than made up for it in his efforts to prepare his brigade for the spring campaign. It was a daunting challenge and, like his superior, Pike lacked a coterie of experienced officers upon whom he could rely as he tried to prepare his brigade for war at the same time as he strove to make sense of all the confusion at Sackets Harbor. Majors Whitlock and King were men he could count on, however, and so were two other career officers present on station. Major Ninian Pinkney, Fifth Infantry, had been in the army nearly as long as Pike had and held the appointment of deputy adjutant general, while Major William Swan, Second Infantry, with the same length of service, was the deputy quarter master general.[26] To help with organization and communications, Pike brought three recently commissioned officers into his fold as aides-de-camp: Lieutenant Donald Fraser of the Fifteenth, Captain Charles Jones, Twenty-ninth Infantry, and Captain Benjamin Nicholson of the Fourteenth.

The lack of military experience extended through the entire brigade from the rank and file to the regimental commanders and was complicated by the mixture of regulars with federal volunteers and militia and recent changes in the enlistment periods.[27] The situation troubled Pike and he wondered how anyone could "bring into the field an army to act with effect against a well-organized enemy out of such a heterogeneous mass as the American forces [are]."[28] He doubted the value of enlisting men for a year or eighteen months when it took so long for recruits to learn their drill and duties and become accustomed to military life. Nevertheless, it was the men in front of him that Pike had to shape into an effective corps, and quickly, because the spring campaign was only weeks away. Nine out of ten of them were native-born Americans, and more than half came from New York, New England, Pennsylvania and New Jersey; foreign-born enlistments were predominantly Irish. Most of the men signed up at a recruitment rendezvous located in a city rather than a village or a rural setting. They were nearly all Caucasian – about two per hundred being Afro-American – and on average they were about twenty-seven years old, stood about five feet, seven inches tall, were well-built, with dark hair and, most likely, eyes of blue or grey.[29]

There is little evidence to suggest that the recruits came from the ranks of the permanently unemployed and destitute. About 40 per cent of the men had backgrounds in farming, while nearly as many others said they were trades-men, that is, shoemakers, carpenters, blacksmiths and tailors; a much smaller number had been labourers or seamen. Joining the army provided them with an opportunity to advance themselves in life. It seems most likely that the men had failed, for one reason or another, to establish themselves in agriculture or a trade, and were looking to acquire the enlistment bounties (which included free land in some instances) and regular pay they could later use to outfit a small farm or shop. With this distant dream in mind, these young Americans became the privates and corporals, sergeants and musicians of the rank and file and the first line of defence for their nation.

Their senior officers came from the elite of society.[30] They were the pros-perous land owners, merchants, lawyers and politicians, some of whom were veterans of the War of Independence or held commissions in their state mili-tias. They and their up-and-coming sons saw military service as an extension of the influential roles they played in their communities and states. Many were well educated and nearly all were devoted supporters of the Republican party. Such a man was Eleazar Ripley, a thirty-one-year-old Republican lawyer from Portland, Maine, and a member of the Massachusetts legislature, who had no military experience but willingly accepted a commission as lieutenant colonel of the Twenty-first Infantry in March 1812 and rose to be its colonel a year later. Cromwell Pearce, colonel of the Sixteenth Regiment, had been raised on a farm in Chester County, Pennsylvania, and given only the most basic of educations. He was a militia captain by 1793, joined the U.S. Army as a lieutenant in 1799 and was honourably discharged during the reduction of 1800. He had gained promotion to major general in the Pennsylvania Militia when he entered the federal service again by taking command of the newly-legislated Sixteenth In-fantry in April 1812 and doing the recruitment in his state to fill it up. Standing six feet, two inches tall, stout and powerfully built, Pearce took great pride in his regiment.

The captains, lieutenants and ensigns were generally young men from com-fortable circumstances. Most of them were as raw as their recruits, although

Eleazar Ripley (1782-1839). With no practical knowledge of military life, Ripley is said to have spent the winter nights of 1812/13 studying the business of war and then holding classes to instruct his officers, "which led his regiment to its subsequent fame, and made it the model of the army."[13] (Hood Museum of Art, Dartmouth College, NH)

there were a few individuals in Pike's First Brigade who had received a formal military education. They had completed the three-year program at the U.S. Military Academy at West Point, New York, and graduated with commissions as lieutenants, the majority of them accepting appointments in the artillery. Henry Hobart had been with the Light Artillery since early 1811 and George Washington Hight joined the regiment the next year about the same time that another graduate, Alexander Fanning, took up with the Third Artillery. Lieutenant Alexander Thompson of the Sixth Infantry was one of the smaller number of West Point men who went into the infantry. Captain Andrew McDowell's education was of a more practical nature. A native of New Hampshire, he enlisted as a private in the artillery in 1805 and subsequently rose to sergeant. Few men in the ranks could ever hope for more than that, but in June 1808, when the Regiment of Light Artillery was created, McDowell was granted a commission as second lieutenant.[31] His competence outweighed his humble start in the service and he attained his captaincy in the spring of 1812. His company was at Sackets the next year and former-cadets Hobart and Hight were under his command.

The first year of war brought the new officers face to face with the realities of military service, which proved more than some had bargained for. Captain John Scott of the Fifteenth Infantry remarked, for instance, on the conduct of Lieutenant Philip Whitehead, who lost his composure during the skirmish at La Colle. "Some officers say they found him behind a tree when we were firing," wrote Scott; Whitehead resigned on the first day of 1813.[32] After watching some young men lose their romantic notions about the quest for glory when the going got tough, Colonel Pearce condemned "the ruinous and disgraceful practice of officers obtaining furloughs, immediately on the army entering winter quarters, in order that they might spend the remainder of the winter in the cities."[33] Captain Scott had another view on furloughs, noting that "Ensign [Jacob] Dickerson has obtained leave of absence or *rather is ordered* on recruiting ... and has never done but very little duty except at the table where I *think when you see him you will say he is industrious....* [H]e will never join the Regt. again when he once more enjoys the comforts of a feather bed with his wife."[34]

The junior officers criticized their superiors too. In the first week of April, for instance, Ensign Joseph Dwight of the Thirteenth Infantry arrived at Sackets with a detachment of men he had recruited during the winter. He was untried in battle but not hesitant to pass quick judgement on staff officers. "Gen. C[handler] appears to be a man of very ordinary abilities," Dwight wrote in his diary, "and totally unfit for the command of an army."[35] Even Pike, who commanded respect among his peers and followers, was subject to slander. Captain John Walworth, Sixth Infantry, who had just days before praised Pike, passed this snide observation to his father-in-law, Jonas Simonds, who was the colonel of the Sixth and Walworth's patron: "The officers of his command almost detest him," wrote Walworth on the announcement of Pike's promotion. "None of them call to see him except one or two Sap Heads."[36] Granny Dearborn drew enough criticism in camp to provoke Lieutenant Christopher Van de Venter of the Light Artillery to write directly to Secretary of War Armstrong. He had heard a rumour that Dearborn had decided not to attack Kingston or the St. Lawrence first and warned the secretary about the "continuing wavering of the commanding General." Pike and all "the best officers," he insisted, were certain "that our country is again doomed to defeat if the operations now meditated by the General are attempted to be accomplished."[37]

One officer who did not fit the common mould was Major Benjamin Forsyth, commander of a company of the U.S. Regiment of Riflemen.[38] Little is known about his early life other than he was born in North Carolina around 1760 and joined the Sixth U.S. Infantry as a second lieutenant in April 1800, only to be discharged two months later when the army was reduced. In July 1808 Forsyth received a captain's commission in the newly formed Regiment of Riflemen, which he filled up with backwoodsmen from his native state who had learned their marksmanship fighting native warriors on the frontier. In camp, Forsyth is said to have kept very much to himself and could be found lounging by his quarters in the company of a few friends and subordinates. Unlike his peers in other regiments, he had a relaxed attitude about training, as an officer who met him in 1813 revealed: "When out of action, [Forsyth] exacted almost nothing from [his men], leaving them mostly at free quarters, free will and without any restraint, saving always that, when they heard the sound of his bugle … they should come at once to his tent."[39]

On the battlefield Benjamin Forsyth lost all his retiring demeanour. He was a heavy-set man, standing over six feet tall, and wore a broad-brimmed black hat and a long green coat (the regiment was outfitted in traditional riflemen green), which he left open to expose a white vest as if presenting a target to the foe. Carrying only a light sword, he usually took up a position just behind his men and moved back and forth without overt concern for his own safety, urging them on, directing their fire. The Rifles made their reputation as an effective fighting force in a series of raids on Canadian communities along the St. Lawrence River during the autumn of 1812 and the following winter. Once a skirmish was over, Forsyth felt no compulsion to restrain his men from grabbing whatever loot they could carry, private or public. This was their just reward for hard fighting and their commander apparently turned a blind eye to a practice that other officers were loathe to permit.

Forsyth was promoted to major late in January 1813 and then breveted to lieutenant colonel a few weeks later, although he was consistently referred to as "major" for months afterwards; his first lieutenant, William Smith, rose to captain and their company grew to nearly 200-strong. Major General Dearborn considered Forsyth "an excellent officer" but he had warned him about going too far and inciting a retaliatory attack by the British. Forsyth would not be restrained, however.[40] He attacked and seized Brockville briefly on 7 February and two weeks later the British assaulted and overran his headquarters at Ogdensburg, ending his independent campaign. The Rifles suffered heavy casualties and loss of pride, which left them rankled and looking for revenge.

Major Forsyth's reputation had spread by the time he joined Pike's brigade in March. William Thomson, a resident of the nearby village of Champion, heard the stories and related them to his brother. Forsyth, he wrote, was "a man whom the war hawks in this country call a second Washington without doubt he is a brave officer, but his bravery is such as a Washington would despise. To call him a man-killing idiot would perhaps be an unwarrantable assertion against his character but his conduct has been such as every honest man must condemn."[41]

There were other riflemen at Sackets Harbor who fancied themselves to be among the fighting elite of the nation, although they had done little, if anything, to prove themselves yet. They were volunteers, a hybrid unit, half way between the militia and the regular army that was created by the Volunteer Military Corps Act passed by Congress in February 1812.[42] The law's intention was to put a large number of temporary units into the field for one year, which the legislators in Washington believed would be cheaper than further increasing the regular army. They were to be raised in the individual states with their governors' approval and then the federal government would pay, arm, feed and equip them and give each man a $16 bounty in lieu of a uniform. As with many of the other initiatives in the winter and spring of 1812, the program fell far short of the mark, due to poor communication between Washington and the state capitals, a lack of money and munitions, and the fact that state governors were either opposed to the scheme or too busy dealing with their own war-related issues to do anything effective.

New York State provided a relatively large number of twelve-month volunteer companies and regiments.[43] One of the units was headed by Francis McClure, an Irish-born resident of New York City who had commanded a battalion of militia riflemen known as the "Greens" because of their uniforms and their Irish backgrounds. When he failed to obtain a commission in the U.S. Army during the spring of 1812, the hotheaded McClure decided to quit military life altogether, but Governor Daniel Tompkins convinced him to accept promotion from major to lieutenant colonel of a full regiment of militia rifles. This was not enough for McClure, however, and he pursued and obtained permission to assemble a regiment under the Volunteer Act. Drawing together four companies at New York, he received orders in September to march to the village of Onondaga, 100 miles west of Albany, where he was joined by the Republican Albany Greens, another company of twelve-month men.

The Albany Greens appear to have been among the numerous elite militia companies in New York that had specialized in light infantry tactics for years before successfully applying to the governor to become a rifle company.[44] The model of rifle used by the men is unknown, but they dressed themselves in the standard New York State rifleman's uniform, which consisted of a green frock and pantaloons with yellow fringes and buttons, black gaiters, a black round hat with yellow buttons, black loops and a short green feather. Captain James Maher is said by one source to have been a prominent wholesale grocer and there is no doubt that he was a devoted Republican, a supporter of Governor Tompkins and the war effort. His sub-unit was sometimes referred to as the Irish Greens, so it is likely that his blood, and that of many of his men, ran as true to the Emerald Isle as McClure's. General Dearborn ordered the regiment to Buffalo on 21 October and they arrived there by the end of the month.

Late in November another independent company of twelve-month men came under McClure's command at Black Rock. This was the Baltimore Volunteers, which had formed in the summer of 1812 and was equipped with the help of $15,000 raised through a local subscription. "They were fitted out in the most substantial manner by the munificent patriotism of the people of Baltimore," read one newspaper account. "[A]nd were besides presented with an elegant flag by the patriotic ladies of the seventh ward."[45] Captain Stephen H. Moore, a member of the local masonic lodge, was the captain of the company, one of his lieutenants being Baptist Irvine, the fiery Republican editor of the *Baltimore Whig*.

The Volunteers' ensign, Thomas Warner, left a record of some of their adventures in a handful of letters he sent home to his wife, Mary Ann, while on campaign. As a thirty-two-year-old silversmith, watch-case maker and assayer, Warner must have enjoyed a relatively comfortable home with his wife and son, but the fervour to defend his nation's rights was so strong in him and his friends that he left his life behind and went to war. Indeed, when the order came to march on 28 September, Warner chose not to ride the 8 miles into the city from the company's camp to bid farewell to Mary Ann, who was pregnant with their second child. With an unbecoming display of self-absorption, he explained his lack of a farewell ten days later by admitting that "The trial would have been too great for me to bear."[46]

Moore's volunteers left Baltimore with orders to join the army on the Niagara River. Their march north proved easier to tolerate than the farewell Warner had avoided and he happily, though without much tact, informed Mary Ann, "our men were in the highest spirits singing and joking [with] each other…. For my part, I never was healthier in my life, in high spirits."[47] They reached the Niagara just as Brigadier General Alexander Smyth was making his grand proclamations and plans were afoot for the invasion of Upper Canada. Some of the Baltimore Volunteers did not wait until the expedition to get their noses bloodied. When a tavern owner at Buffalo named Pomeroy was too free with his views on President Madison's ill-conceived war, they decided to teach him a lesson in respect. On 25 November a band of more than forty of them, including some of the Irish Greens from Albany, broke into Pomeroy's establishment, destroyed the furnishings and set the place on fire. Several locals managed to put out the flames and engaged the Volunteers in a tangled, hand-to-hand melee. This resulted in casualties to both sides but did not stop the vandalism. Some of the officers, including McClure and Maher, arrived at the scene and helped quell the disturbance, although it ultimately took a bayonet charge by a body of regulars to clear out the intruders and preserve Pomeroy's tavern.

One resident who was wounded during the fracas described the hooligans "as the same miscreants who were in the Baltimore riot," referring to the vicious attacks on a Federalist newspaper office during the summer.[48] He pointed out Lieutenant Irvine as having been a ringleader at Pomeroy's and among those

John Scott to David Thompson, 16 March 1813. This excerpt from Scott's letter reveals his speculation about the upcoming campaign and his confidence that the *Madison,* "once alongside of the Royal George," would quickly capture the British ship. (Scott Letters, New Jersey Historical Society)

who claimed they would tear down every Federalist home in Buffalo. Reports of the riot were widely published with Irvine and the Baltimore Volunteers named as the culprits, except in the pages of Baltimore's *Weekly Register,* which informed its readership that only five or six of the men from "that elegant corps that marched hence to sustain their country's honor" were involved.[49] The incident might have led to the death of one private and the desertion of several others over the next two weeks, as company records reveal.

McClure's Volunteers remained at Black Rock through January and then marched for Utica, where the officers received a favourable notice in the local newspaper for brilliantly illuminating their quarters in honour of George Washington's birthday. Most of the regiment was soon off for Sackets, called in because of the expectation of an attack from Kingston. Some of the sick had been left at Buffalo, others stayed behind at Utica and some, as Ensign Warner did, only reached the Harbor in the third week of April, after what he described as "a disagreeable journey blocked by ice, snow, etc."[50] Though convalescing,

Warner's *esprit de corps* still ran high and he proudly informed his wife "the British call us the Baltimore Blood hounds," neglecting to tell her that their only action had been in and around a tavern at Buffalo.

The volunteers and the regulars in Pike's brigade were certain that they would soon have the opportunity to test their mettle against the British. "I am in hopes you will hear of me in His Majesty's Dominions in less than three weeks," wrote Captain Walworth of the Sixth Infantry to his father-in-law.[51] Confident about the outcome of the coming expedition, Captain John Scott assured his friend, "Only give us man for man with their regular troops or two of their militia and I do not fear the result."[52]

Their brigadier was also sure of what his men could accomplish, but he nevertheless used every available minute in March and April to prepare them for battle, repeating the drill and disciplined manoeuvres they would need to perform like automatons under all nature of circumstances, even some that might be worse than anything they could ever anticipate.

Surgeon Amasa Trowbridge's sketch. Surgeon Trowbridge identified items on his sketch with a legend that needs explanation, and, in some cases, correction. He first numbers the American vessels, showing: the *Madison* (1); *Oneida* (2); one anchored schooner offshore and four at the mouth of the bay (3) to represent the eleven armed vessels; and the "store ship" *Gold Hunter* (6) on the right.

The second list of items is: the lighthouse (1); "Buildings for indian presents," the storehouse on Gibraltar Point (2); "point covered with trees and shrubbery," the peninsula (3); "there Marine Ship Gloucester" at the foot of the bay (4); "New Ship on the Stocks," the *Isaac Brock* (5); "Parliament House," more likely Elmsley House, which was used for government business (6); "Fort and Barracks," placed far too close to the town (7); the grand magazine, to the left of the fort (8); "Redoubt in which Pike was Killed," the Half Moon Battery (9); "American Troops," in column perpendicular to the shore, to the left of the Half Moon Battery (10); "Woods and Forests" surrounding the town and garrison common (11); "old site of Fort Toronto" (12). (Library of Congress)

136

PART THREE

The Battle

From the time we came within musket shot the enemy with whom the bank and wood was lined commenced and kept up a heavy fire upon us.

JOHN SCOTT, 17 MAY 1813

I came up with some other officers to the Barracks, and we got each of us a Musket as everyone expected a severe attack upon the enemy when they advanced from the Woods.

ELY PLAYTER, 27 APRIL 1813

CHAPTER 8

"Dashing evolutions"[1]

THE WAYS OF WAR IN 1813

The military forces assembling at opposite ends of Lake Ontario used the longer hours of daylight in the early weeks of spring 1813 to train for battle. On the garrison common at York the officers and sergeants of the Royal Newfoundland Regiment of Fencibles put their own men and the militia through their paces. As the redoubts along the shore were completed well enough to receive guns, other regulars trained the local men in how to serve their artillery pieces. Meanwhile, at Sackets Harbor Brigadier General Pike viewed the solid ice on Black River Bay as the ideal parade ground and marched his brigade onto it for sessions of drill that lasted up to six hours each. "We was manoeuvring on it yesterday," he exuberantly wrote to Major General Dearborn on 26 March about his icy drill square, "with Cavalry, Artillery and Riflemen."[2]

There was much in common between the preparations of the opposing armies. The chief objective of their training was to perfect their ability to overwhelm the enemy through the effective employment of firepower and strength of numbers and to do so in the most controlled and orderly fashion possible. To achieve this outcome, both armies had three branches, or arms: the infantry, artillery and cavalry. Artillery brought "destructive power of firearms" to the battlefield equation and cavalry had mobility and the ability for close-in fighting, but the infantry could combine power, movement and hand-to-hand combat in just about any situation and, not surprisingly, played the leading role in the events of April 1813.[3]

The men who saluted the Union Flag differed somewhat from those who made up Pike's brigade.[4] Like their counterparts, they had accepted the recruiters' bounties and the promise of regular food, clothing, shelter and pay of the service, but their enlistment periods were longer. In the past soldiers in the British army had signed on for life, unless discharged due to wounds or illness or because their regiment was reduced after a war, but new regulations in 1806 changed this to a minimum of seven years in the infantry, ten in the cavalry and twelve in the artillery. The 1812 height restriction for men intended to serve "in the line" was 5′4″, although some regiments only took bigger recruits. They were all supposed to be younger than thirty-five years old, with lads of eighteen who were 5′3″ and seventeen-year-old boys standing 5′2″ also being accepted into the line; shorter men of up to forty years were enlisted for "general" service only as were smaller lads and boys.

By contrast, the U.S. Army minimum height was 5′6″ and because the longest enlistment period was five years, and so many of the regiments in 1812 were new, the American force tended to have a larger percentage of young men, their average age being about twenty-seven years. The British army naturally preferred younger and more fit recruits, but there were plenty of older men among the ranks. Data for one detachment of the Royal Newfoundland Regiment of Fencibles in 1813 reflects this difference in the two forces, with the average man being thirty-years old and standing 5′6″ tall.

Just as the American rank and file came from the lower echelons of society, so did the British, although the majority of them had been labourers rather than farm workers prior to enlistment and fewer of them had been tradesmen. Another important difference was that Britain had been at war nearly continuously in the two decades before 1812 and the freshest and most patriotic of young men had long since been scooped up into the regiments. There were some who entered eagerly, as sixteen-year-old John Cooper did in 1803. He was thrilled to be issued a sword and practised his cuts and jabs on a field of innocent thistles that he imagined was a host of Frenchmen falling before him. But there were many more who enlisted out of desperation or while drunk at the expense of the recruiter's coin or who preferred a term in a regiment to a jail sentence.

The greatest British general of the period, the Duke of Wellington, once commented that the "scum of the earth, the mere scum of the earth" filled up his ranks and files, a criticism that was well supported. The army, Private Cooper discovered, "was composed of the lowest orders. Many, if not the most of them, were ignorant, idle and drunken."[5] Another dispirited but literate fellow, who joined when his plans to become an actor failed on his first stage, lamented, "I could not associate with the common soldiers; their habits made me shudder. I feared an oath – they never spoke without one: I could not drink – they loved liquor…. Thus I was a solitary individual among hundreds. They lost no opportunity of teasing me, [calling me] 'Saucy Tom,' or 'The distressed Methodist.'"[6]

Despite such disparaging comments about the nature of the British troops, a battalion of fresh recruits was not necessarily a despicable thing to see, and, as Wellington also stated, the "scum" could be moulded into "fine fellows" in the end. When several transport-loads of new men for the 41st Regiment of Foot arrived at Quebec in the fall of 1811, suffering from dysentery after sixteen difficult weeks at sea, officials rightly referred to them as "poor devils." But since they otherwise appeared to be "very fine young men," it was expected that they would make "a noble battalion ... when brought together."[7] After years of training and campaigning under efficient officers, a regiment could make an impressive appearance on the parade ground, just as the 8th Foot did when it landed at Quebec in 1810. "A finer looking regiment we do not recollect to have seen," reported the *Quebec Mercury*. "The men all appear hale, in the prime and vigour of manhood, and remarkably well-matched in size. The regiment ... will add life to the garrison, particularly as it has an excellent band of music."[8]

As with their opposite numbers in the American forces, the British officers came from what could be termed the middle and upper classes of society, were well educated for the times and conducted themselves, in theory at least, as "gentlemen."[9] A much larger percentage of them had extensive and recent experience on the battlefield since Britain had been at war for so long. Many infantry and cavalry officers had entered the service by purchasing a commission, something unknown in British artillery units and the engineer corps as well as the U.S. Army. The purchase system had long been subject to abuse, one of its deficits being that numerous under-aged and/or incompetent individuals, assisted by patronage, used it to reach as high as the rank of lieutenant colonel. But the system had advantages since it involved a tangible commitment to the army and provided an officer with the potential to sell his place and get out of the service with some money in hand; there were no pensions to encourage worn-out or incompetent officers to retire. Salaries were barely adequate to meet the needs of an officer, so private financial backing was essential and the purchased commission was part of the fiscal package. The old system was passing out of favour by 1812 and in the past ten years casualty rates had created so many vacancies that the number of men who received promotion without purchase had increased dramatically. In fact, the need for officers to fill out new regiments, such as the Glengarry Regiment of Light Infantry Fencibles, and to take the place of recently promoted ensigns in the old regiments nearly exceeded the supply. Even teenaged boys, such as George Jarvis and Allan MacNab at York, who offered their services as gentlemen volunteers advanced quickly. On the recommendation of an experienced officer, they were accepted into a regiment to learn their facings and steps among the rank and file while living with the officers and waiting for a vacancy, which in some cases came quickly.

There was a range of competence and effective leadership in the officer corps, with some men earning admiration while others became known as relentless martinets; Roger Sheaffe had been so branded while a lieutenant colonel in the 49th Foot. At the Battle of Waterloo in June 1815 a "notorious character" in the ranks watched a round shot take off the head of his captain and observed sarcastically, "Hullo, there goes my best friend." Stepping up to take command, and missing the point completely, a lieutenant attempted to console the dour private with, "Never mind I will be as good a friend to you as your captain." To which the fellow answered, "I hope not, sir."[10]

Other more charismatic men won the esteem of their people by leading the way with consistent discipline and humanity. "Captain Percy was beloved by his company," remembered John Cooper. "As a man, he was handsome; as an officer, kind; and as a soldier, brave and adventurous."[11] While officers had the leisure to enjoy their hounds and horses, their banquets and access to the best homes and the women in them, they were just as likely to suffer the same privations as their men during hard campaigns. "I have seen," remembered Saucy Tom, "officers of the Guards, and others, worth thousands, with pieces of old blankets wrapt around their feet and legs; the men pointing at them, with malicious satisfaction, saying, 'There goes three thousand a year;' or, 'There goes the prodigal son, on his return to his father, cured of his wanderings.'"[12] Yet, in the end, on battlefield after battlefield, the British officers and their troops combined to present a stalwart and intimidating presence. Contrasting the way French officers yelled and cheered their men to the attack with the conduct of his own superiors, Tom remained in awe of how they restrained their troops and kept them "still as death" until the perfect moment to attack. "'Steady, lads, steady,' is all your hear," he wrote, "and that in an undertone."[13]

To begin the process that would bring men like Saucy Tom to such a level of fighting efficiency, new recruits to the British army were outfitted in a splendid set of clothing which hid their rough edges behind the facade of a smart, military bearing.[14] This consisted of a black felt hat, or cap, (the typical "shako" of the period), a woollen coat with short tails, a vest and shirt, a leather stock around his neck, a pair of trousers, socks and shoes and a pair of gaiters, or leggings, that buttoned around the ankles and lay over the tops of the shoes in the hope of keeping the stones out during a march. While their officers might sport brilliant scarlet coats, the infantry rank and file wore coats of dull red that took on a brownish shade over time; woollen or cotton trousers commonly came in grey, white or black. Each regiment had its own coloured and styled "facings,"

British infantryman. The thin red line was made up of men dressed in nearly identical uniforms which, by their colours and shining brass buttons, buckles and shako plates, were intended to create an impression of well-disciplined efficiency and inspire awe among their opponents.

Glengarry Fencible. The green uniform of the Glengarry Regiment was based on the one worn by the renowned British rifle regiment, the 95th Regiment of Foot. This re-enactor is outfitted in grey rather than green pants. (Photographs by Robert Malcomson)

the cuffs, collar and trim around the bottom holes and shoulder flaps or tufts, as well as brass buttons, cross-belt buckles and shako plates engraved with the regiment's number. The facings of the Royal Newfoundland Fencibles, for instance, were blue, since it was a "Royal" regiment, and its lace trim had two red lines on either side of a blue line on a white background. The Glengarry Light Infantry Regiment of Fencibles cut quite a different appearance, their coats and trousers being a distinctive dark green with black facings and lace, modelled after those of the illustrious 95th Regiment of Rifles. The Royal Artillery had its easily recognizable blue coats and white pants, their collars and cuffs being faced with red and edged in yellow.

The men were usually given extra shirts, socks and shoes and even round jackets (short forage coats) and small felt caps for fatigue duty, but campaigning was hard on clothing and the longer a unit was in the field, the faster its appearance deteriorated; the replacement of any lost or ruined clothing came out of a man's pay so they made do until a shipment of new suits arrived. The irregularity of the men's appearance was not an issue during the Peninsular War since Wellington was more interested in making sure each soldier had good arms and ammunition than in what colour trousers he wore. In Canada, during Sir George Prevost's administration, however, maintaining dress standards was a priority and in November 1812 Prevost's office reminded infantry officers on foot that they were to wear black gaiters at all times, while those who were mounted must carry regulation swords and all officers were "to wear their Hats straight when on Duties or Parade."[15]

The American soldier's kit closely resembled that of his adversary, except that his trousers were actually overalls and he was not issued a waistcoat.[16] The British variations in colour and trim were absent as nearly all the American units were traditionally clothed in blue wool coats (cotton in warmer climes) with short tails, scarlet facings and very little in the way of specially designed lace; trousers were blue or white wool or cotton. The Rifle Regiment's green uniforms made them unique among the infantry, but this situation changed in 1812 when shortages in blue wool and blue dye forced a different look upon many

U.S. Infantry. The traditional uniform of the U.S. Army, featuring a dark blue coatee with red cuffs and collars, was still being worn in 1813, although some features were about to change. Contrary to the British style, the regiments were not differentiated by individually coloured lace or numbered buttons and shako plates. (Photograph by Robert Malcomson)

Alternative U.S. infantry uniform.
A shortage of blue fabric led to the issue of U.S. Army uniforms of various shades, including black, light brown, grey and drab, or dull brown. A similar shortage in Canada caused the distribution of green, rather than red, coatees to the Upper Canada Militia in the spring of 1813. (Photograph by Robert Malcomson)

of the new regiments. To fill the demand for clothing, the U.S. Army resorted to distributing coats of various colours. Of the units in Pike's brigade, for instance, the Fourteenth Infantry had received brown or "drab" coats and trousers, the Fifteenth had "mixed" grey and the Sixteenth wore black, while at least one group of new recruits must have looked like a patchwork quilt in formation since they had received coats of different shades. At Quebec a similar problem was encountered when Sir George Prevost ordered uniforms for the militia of Upper Canada.[17] He wanted them to have the traditional scarlet coats, but a lack of red wool required the militia to be issued with deep green coats with red collars and cuffs and white lace. They also received black felt shakos and blue trousers, but had to make their own gaiters. The first of the shipments did not reach the province until April 1813.

Dressing them up like soldiers did not turn new recruits into an effective fighting force, of course. This transition was accomplished by means of rigid regulation and stone-hard discipline and the tried and true teaching methods of the period, namely, rote, repetition and punishment for mistakes. "[We were] forced from bed at five o'clock each morning, to get all things ready for drill," wrote Saucy Tom, "then drilled for three hours with the most unfeeling rigour, and often beat by the sergeant for the faults of others."[18] The training was progressive, beginning with the instruction of small groups who were then combined and combined again until an entire brigade was in motion. Jarvis Hanks, a teenaged infantry drummer from Pittsford, New York, described the process perfectly: "In the morning after breakfast, every sergeant exercises his squad of from twelve to twenty men, in the various evolutions, for one hour. Captains drilled their companies from 11 to 12. And at 1 or 2 o'clock P.M., the whole brigade, with all its officers, musicians and privates, … were drilled from three to four hours."[19]

The constant drill was only part of the soldier's day that was otherwise taken up with patrols, sentry and fatigue duties, the carefully supervised cleaning and maintenance of their uniforms, equipment and accommodations and stringent adherence to mess and barracks rules. There were some who found this daily regime unbearable and who violated a regulation, left a boot unpolished, refused an order or, worse, ran from army life altogether. Both armies used vicious forms of corporal punishment to control such conduct, including execution by hanging or by firing squad for the most serious crimes.

The British army was known for flogging for delinquent behaviour in a formal ceremony with all the troops watching, so they could see what would happen to them if they did not conform. A young lieutenant with the 104th Foot named John Le Couteur remembered watching a stout private receive 300 lashes, the force of which soon "lacerated his back speedily and the blood flowed freely." Le Couteur felt each blow the man received and admitted that when "the Drummer, in swinging his Cat of Nine Tails, switched a quantity of [the soldier's] blood on my Face and Belts … I fainted away like a Sick girl…. The Officers laughed at me but the men did not."[20]

The U.S. Army suspended flogging but substituted branding with a red-hot poker and "picketing," wherein a bare-footed man was required to stand on a sharpened stake. Drummer Hanks described seeing a deserter run the gauntlet between two rows of fifty men each. The soldiers in the gauntlet were to strike the delinquent on his bare back with switches, and to make sure the offender did not miss a single blow two soldiers prodded him from behind with bayonets while two others walked backwards in front of him using bayonet points to slow him down. "The poor wretch could neither run nor escape," wrote Hanks, "but was compelled to bear his torture without remedy. The blood ran down his back in streams … and presented a spectacle to melt the heart of a stone."[21] The prisoner was then manacled to an 8-foot length of chain fixed to a 24-pdr. shot and sent off to do five years of incarceration and hard labour.

The daily drills and threat of brutal discipline formed the recruits into automatons who moved as one with their mates at the bark of an order and in time with the beat of the tunes played by the musicians on their fifes and drums. They learned which way to face and how to turn, how to step in any direction and how many steps to take per minute, according to the situation. It became second nature for them to stand facing forward with their elbows gently touching those of the adjacent men and to maintain an unwavering line, or rank, with one or two men standing behind them, forming the file. From this position they could wheel around by platoon or company to the right or left, with the inside men as pivots taking the smallest steps and the outside men taking long strides, and everyone between working in unison to maintain the alignment of the rank. They could then march as a column, with open spaces between the sections or closed up, reducing the width of the column to pass over a narrow bridge, if need be, and then fill it out again. They could proceed onto a field and deploy back into the two- or three-rank formation, presenting a wide front toward an enemy, dressing their ranks and files with little side-to-side and back-and-forth steps until perfection was achieved. All of this happened more or less in silence, except for the shouting of commands and the periodic accompaniment of drums and fifes. And when they were commanded to "support arms," the men brought their muskets into play.

The nature of the smooth-bore flintlock musket itself determined how the men were trained to move and operate. In other words, the musket, or firelock, as it was sometimes called, dictated the tactics of the time.[22] There were two main types of muskets used during this period, the English and French versions, both of which existed in numerous models. The bore of the British weapon, the well-known "Brown Bess," measured 0.75 inches in diameter. It fired a lead ball with a diameter of 0.68 inch, weighing just over an ounce, whereas a French musket had a 0.69-inch bore and fired a 0.63-inch ball, weighing just less than an ounce. The English Short Land Pattern musket had been a popular model for decades and there were many of them in Canada and the United States, although the British army had been equipping its infantry with the cheaper, but durable, India Pattern musket from the mid-1790s. The U.S. Army favoured models based

Musket firing mechanism. The "hammer" of a musket featured the flintlock, a vise that gripped a piece of flint. The steel frizzen is shown here in the open position. During loading it was closed to cover the priming powder in the pan and was forced open when the trigger was squeezed and the flintlock snapped forward, striking sparks against the frizzen which ignited the priming. The pan below the frizzen on this musket is hidden from view by a brass plate attached to cover the outward side of the pan. (Photograph by Robert Malcomson)

on the French Charleville pattern, versions of which were to be found in Canada as well. Both weapons used pre-packaged, finger-length paper tubes filled with fine black powder and a ball. American cartridges customarily contained two or three buckshot as well, each about one tenth the size of the ball. A bayonet, generally measuring 15 inches in length, was attached to the muzzle via a socket and lug, giving the weapon an overall length of more than 6 feet.

The inaccuracy of the smooth bore musket is legendary. Because it was spherical, the bullet lacked a tendency to fly straight, which was exacerbated by the fact that it did not fit tightly into the barrel and, after caroming ever so slightly as it passed up the smooth bore, it might fly off at an angle. It was also not unknown for some of the mass-produced barrels to have small distortions in them that would defy straight shooting. As a result, when trying to strike a man 200 yards down range, one observer remarked, "you might as well fire at the moon and have the same hope of hitting your object."[23] Numerous tests were conducted to determine the truth of such statements, one of which tests had "trained" and "ordinary" soldiers in Europe fire at a target representing a line of charging cavalry. At 100 yards, the trained men struck somewhere on the target 53 per cent of the time, while the others had 40 per cent accuracy. At 200 yards, this dropped to 30 per cent and 18 per cent respectively. These findings were supported in a "shoot out" conducted in November 1812 on the frontier of Lower Canada between men in the 103rd Regiment of Foot and a grenadier company of militia. Aiming at a target of unstated proportions, erected 150 yards away, fifty-five men from each unit took six shots each, with the British regulars hitting the mark 28 per cent of the time compared to the 20 per cent accuracy rate of the Canadians.

Although shooting with accuracy was obviously desirable, muskets were not generally fitted with a sighting bead near the muzzle. More important than precise aiming, which became very difficult when clouds of smoke created by the discharge of volleys on the battlefield hid one enemy from the other, was the shock-and-awe effect of mass volleys. To this end, the infantry was trained to level their weapons toward the enemy and fire together by platoon or company, often one group after the other from right to left, or in some other sequence. Achieving such controlled fire required the men to work in unison as closely as they did when they marched and manoeuvred, and so they were trained to load their weapons step by step maintaining an identical pace, man for man. The number of individual movements in this "manual of arms" favoured by the British and American varied slightly, but essentially they employed the following routine.

The soldier wore leather belts, slung over his shoulders and fastened with a regimental badge on his chest, which held a bayonet in a scabbard on his left hip and a leather box holding up to sixty cartridges on his right.[24] Before firing, he might first go through several motions to draw and fix his bayonet. Then he would cradle the musket at his waist with his left hand and remove a cartridge from the box with his right, tear it open with his teeth and pour a small amount of the powder into a pan on the right side of the barrel just above the trigger. He then pulled down a hinged cap called the frizzen to cover this "priming"pan, put the heel of the musket's stock on the ground and poured the rest of the powder down the barrel, followed by the ball, still wrapped in the paper. He tamped it all home using a ramrod which was carried in brackets beneath the barrel. The soldier next lifted the weapon to a vertical position on his left side and pulled the firelock, or the "hammer," located just below the level of his shoulder, to full cock with his right hand. The firelock was a mechanism that literally locked a piece of flint into a slender, hammer-like vise. The soldier made ready by pointing the weapon forward from his right shoulder. When the order came to fire, he squeezed the trigger, which caused the firelock to snap forward, forcing the frizzen open as it struck flint against steel and created sparks that fell into the powder in the pan. This detonated the priming, the flash of which passed through a narrow vent in the base of the barrel, igniting the main charge which propelled the ball.

It was a dangerous business, made riskier as the number of arms in use increased, and many were the "friendly" wounds suffered through ignition flashes, accidental firings and careless handling of pointed steel. Much more often – 15 to 25 per cent of the time – the muskets would misfire due to black powder debris that clogged the vents and barrels or because of damp powder or high wind that made priming the pan more difficult. Trained infantrymen could get off four rounds per minute and, under battlefield conditions, often needed only the simple commands of "Load," "Present," "Fire," to maintain their uniformity. Such a rate of fire was rare, however, as it fouled the pieces quickly and used up ammunition too fast. Even after a long day of fighting the French in Portugal during May 1811, Saucy Tom recollected, "My shoulder was as black as a coal, from the recoil of my musket; for this day I had fired 107 round of ball-cartridge. Sore as I was, I slept as sound as a top."[25]

Despite its inaccuracy, the musket was a deadly weapon. At close range, the soft metal ball punched a narrow path through a body, creating a shock wave that magnified the damage done directly to soft tissue and bone. Bullets could kill at 200 yards or more, as Jarvis Hanks witnessed one day when a group of men standing behind a rampart watched a skirmish at some distance from their position, thinking they were safe. "A musket ball, however," wrote Hanks, "reached this soldier [next to me], and hit him in the forehead. It split in two; half of it penetrating his brain and half falling at his feet. He lived only a day

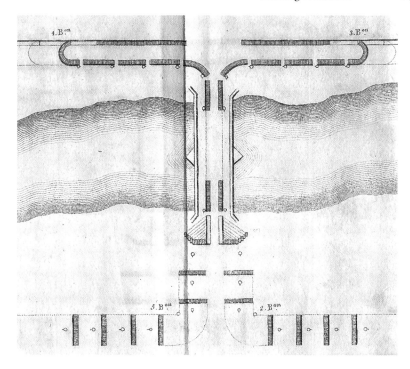

Bridge crossing. It was no simple matter to manage hundreds, or thousands, of infantrymen on a battlefield, let alone march them to the battle over broken terrain and across streams. Their order of march had to be strictly controlled so that they could be brought into battle formation at a moment's notice. This diagram shows how a regiment in line of battle formation with its back to a bridge crosses the obstacle by marching off by companies in files from both flanks, reforms into ranks and, after gaining the opposite bank, wheels around to face across the stream, regaining its previous formation. (Alexander Smyth's *Regulations,* 1812)

or two, before the wound proved fatal."[26] Even if "spent," the ball could knock a man down, as our Tom discovered while engaging the French near Toulouse in April 1814. "I had just risen to run behind my file," he wrote, "when a spent shot struck me on the groin and took the breath from me. 'God receive my soul' I said and sat down resigned.... I laid my musket down and gasped for breath.... I looked to my thigh and, seeing no blood, took resolution to put my hand to the part to feel the wound. My hand was unstained with blood; but the part was so painful that I could not touch it."[27]

In 1812 both armies had designated training manuals, but universal implementation was not easy to achieve.[28] The British army had suffered from a lack of uniformity in how brigades drilled in the 1790s, owing to too many guidebooks and too few officers who felt it their duty to study them and properly instruct their men. One solution to these problems came with the selection of Major General Sir David Dundas's *Principles of Military Movements* for use in all infantry units. It appeared from the 1790s in numerous editions and supplements, and as its use spread, the performance level of the army improved. The U.S. Army had similar inconsistencies in 1812, which the Department of War tried to alleviate with a new drill book, adapted by Brigadier General Alexander Smyth from the French *Règlement* of 1791. It was poorly received, as was its replacement the next year. Consequently, the Americans entered the second year of war with officers instructing their infantry from a variety of manuals – the *Règlement*, Smyth's adaptation of it, Baron Von Steuben's *Regulations* or even Dundas's book.

It is uncertain which manual Brigadier General Pike preferred, but he clearly believed that he had the freedom not only to train but to also equip his troops in whatever manner he felt was the best. The various guidebooks used by the Americans favoured a three-rank formation; Dundas recommended this also, but by 1812 the British army was generally using two ranks as a means of widening the frontage of a regiment. As colonel of the Fifteenth Infantry, Pike diverged from his contemporaries by equipping each man in the third rank with a shortened musket, the barrel of which was cut off 18 inches from the muzzle. This made the weapon easier to handle and then sling over the back so that the soldier could bring his pike into action. The pike was about 12 feet long and consisted of an ash staff capped by a 13-inch iron spearhead with a crosspiece at its base to prevent over-penetration. During their training, the third-rank men learned how to extend them between the men in the front ranks and beyond their bayonets during the final stages of a charge or as a defensive measure. These pikemen also had swords instead of bayonets for use during hand-to-hand combat.

Pike's employment of pikes was a virtually unique experiment in tactics during the Napoleonic period.[29] Sergeants often used pikes or other similar pole-arms (spontoons or halberds) to dress, or more perfectly align, the ranks in

Pikes. Zebulon Pike's decision to incorporate pikes into his infantry tactics was a cross between innovation and a throwback to ancient times. The on-the-ground conditions at York in April 1813 revealed how practical Pike's ideas were. (William Duane's *American Military Library,* 1809)

formation and for close-in fighting. But with the exception of a volunteer unit of rifles in Maine, some Sea Fencibles at Boston and temporary use by forces in Russia and Portugal, no other infantry commander appears to have gone to the trouble and expense that Pike did to equip his regiment in this way. How Pike integrated this unique tactic into brigade manoeuvres on the icy parade ground at Sackets Harbor is not clear, but Captain John Scott of the Fifteenth seemed to think that his regiment was formidable. "I should like to meet," he wrote, "with our Regt., as small as it is, the 49th British Regt. on some plain. I think we should have a pretty hard fight … [and] I think the Jersey troops … will prove themselves worthy."[30] Pike also equipped his regiment with snowshoes and some rifles, which were not widely seen in most infantry units.

The rifle was generally restricted for use by select regiments in both armies.[31] Rifles were originally used for hunting and did not appear on battlefields until the mid-1700s. Muskets were cheaper to manufacture and easier for men to learn how to handle so the role of the rifle in the infantry was limited until the American Patriots proved their effectiveness during the War of Independence. Having relied on foreign companies of riflemen (mainly from Germany) in the past, the British army developed its first homegrown companies of rifles in 1800, while the U.S. Regiment of Rifles was created in 1808.[32] Rifles were widespread among militia units in the United States and Canada who equipped themselves. Captain Peter Robinson of the 1st York Militia Regiment commanded a company of rifles in 1812, although it was not identified as such the following year, and native warriors often carried rifles as well.

Since it required more time to load than a musket, the rifle was not well-suited to the conventional linear fire-by-volley tactics. It was, however, perfect for employment in a branch of the infantry that specialized in independent movement, the light infantry.[33] Originating during the mid-1700s in both Europe and North America, the light infantry was an essential element of every army by 1812. Nearly all regiments had "light" companies and entire regiments of light infantry had been created, of which the U.S. Rifles and the Glengarry Fencibles were two examples. The soldiers were equipped in a manner almost identical to their peers (and most of them carried muskets rather than rifles), but their role on the battlefield was quite different. Instead of being kept in rigid ranks and files, the "light bobs" as they were sometimes known, operated in small groups or in pairs. Their job was to move ahead of a marching column or a line of battle preparing for an engagement and to pester the enemy, feeling out his strengths and weaknesses, or drawing him back toward the main body. They were sometimes called "skirmishers" because of the many small actions they waged as they fanned out in a "chain" beyond the periphery of the main body. Soldiers capable of such stealth had to be smart, fit and experienced enough to read a situation and respond appropriately to threat or opportunity, as well as attending to the instructions relayed to them by their commanding officer, who signalled them by means of a series of whistle- or bugle-calls.

Exercising the brigades at Sackets Harbor and York, then, involved perfecting the coordinated movements of the infantry *en masse,* while the skirmishers moved ahead or covered the flanks and rear. Native warriors were added to the mix at York, but more as a shadowy presence than anything else. There were families of the Mississauga-Ojibway nations and others of the Chippawa "encamped on the skirts of the woods back of the town," as Thomas Gibbs Ridout noted in January 1813. "They keep us alive with their war dances and make the dark cedar woods echo with many savage yells."[34] There is no evidence of how, or even if, Major General Sheaffe integrated the native fighters into whatever brigade evolutions he directed during the winter and spring. Their traditional tactics made them more suitable for use as light infantry than standing as part of the line, but they did not continuously train as the army did. Native warriors could be shockingly effective as hit-and-run raiders, as they had shown at the Battle of Queenston Heights under John Norton, although even on that day many of the warriors refused to either enter the fray or remain in it as the casualty count rose, despite Norton's commanding presence. Each individual had personal goals to achieve in battle and, as a group, they would not throw lives away in some "forlorn hope" attack, since their numbers were relatively small anyway. As a result, the reliability of the native forces, whether on the attack or in defence, was uncertain at best.

In addition to the infantry, the cavalry and artillery were also involved in the preparations for battle. There were only a few militia dragoons at York in the spring of 1813, their mission being mainly to carry messages, so their part in the training was minimal. Several troops of the First and Second U.S. Regiments of Dragoons had reached Sackets, some of them without horses and forced to participate as infantry, but they were not fated to become part of the first expedition of the season.[35] The artillery, however, would see battle and have a chance to add the lessons of practical experience to its endless drill.

The artillery branch of an army was essential to success because of its ability to augment the firepower of the infantry with the intensity of its own, but it was more limited in its movement, which could influence the overall mobility of its accompanying infantry. The guns of the period worked in a manner very similar to muskets. They were smooth-bored, with a muzzle and priming vent, black powder and shot, a ramrod and a strict series of steps for loading that could be abbreviated by skilled hands under duress. It generally took a crew of five men to serve an artillery piece, supported by others who carried ammunition and helped move the equipment.[36] The gun captain, or "Number One," gave the orders while "Number Two" handled the ramrod, pushing each round into place at the base of the bore and damp-sponging the bore clean after each firing. The third man loaded the cartridge and shot, either separately or as pre-packaged fixed ammunition, and the fourth man finished the process by inserting a brass prick into the vent to puncture the bag of powder and then placing a fuse in the vent. The captain next aimed the gun by means of an elevating screw or wooden wedge known as a quoin and by shifting its lateral position with handspikes, usually with help from the extras. When the senior officer in charge ordered the gun to be fired, the captain repeated the command and "Number Five" ignited the fuse by touching it with the lighted end of a length of slow match held in either a linstock or a portfire. The gun went off, spitting its shot out with a deafening concussion of sound and a dense cloud of white smoke.

There were different types of artillery. Long guns and carronades operated on a "direct fire" basis only; that is, they were used against visible targets.[37] Their range varied according to the elevation of the piece with 1,000 yards being easily attainable and most practical since it was difficult to observe the effect of the shot beyond that distance, especially if smoke was obscuring the field. At that distance a 6-pdr. round shot, which measured about 3.7 inches in diameter, had a velocity of 450 feet per second while the 5.3-inch 18-pdr. shot was traveling at about 840 feet per second. Since the trajectory was relatively flat, the ball that encountered no obstacle skipped across the field like a flat stone on water, extending its deadly range for hundreds of yard. Long guns grew ponderous as their calibre increased, requiring more muscle-power to move them, whereas even a 32-pdr. carronade needed but a handful of men, though it was less effective over long ranges that its bigger cousin.

Howitzers and mortars had the ability to deliver their rounds over obstacles, owing to the high arcing trajectory attainable by the way the pieces were mounted. Their short, stubby barrels could fire the same round shot used in the other weapons but were more likely to be loaded with explosive shells, or bombs. These projectiles, sometimes referred to as "common shell," were hollow iron balls filled with powder and fitted with a wooden plug in which was embedded a fuse that was ignited by the gun's blast. A bombardier would estimate how long he wanted the fuse to burn and trim it accordingly, his intention being to detonate the shell over the heads of the enemy or in their midst. The British also had a shell, known as spherical case, which contained lead bullets – up to 85 in a 6-pdr. round – making it more lethal. The British more often used spherical case in their long guns, and both armies used canister or regular "case shot," which

U.S. field artillery. The 6-pdr. field gun seen above has been detached from
its limber, which has yet to be withdrawn to a suitable distance along with the
ammunition box. A bucket of water, the ramrod and sponge are in place.

The half field battery below consists of a 3-pdr. on the left and two howitzers.
The guns were usually spaced farther apart than shown here and, because of
reduced charges used during re-enactor events, the cloud of smoke is thinner than
seen on an actual battlefield. (Photographs by Robert Malcomson)

was literally a tin can that fit the bore of the gun and contained iron balls which burst out of the can on exiting the muzzle, spreading in a conical pattern. Heavy 6-pdr. case contained 41 bullets weighing 3.25 ounces each while the lighter shot held 85 1.5-ounce bullets. Grape shot was another type of bursting projectile. It consisted of nine heavy balls secured around an iron spindle on a circular iron plate within a thick canvas shroud and, although often mentioned in battlefield memoirs, was employed almost exclusively on warships.

When mounted in fortifications, guns were fixed to heavily-built wooden carriages which rolled on small wheels of iron or wood known as trucks and they were tightly secured to the ramparts with blocks and tackle. On occasion, these carriage guns were set up on traverses *en barbette,* that is, on a raised platform that could be swivelled allowing the gun to fire over the top of the rampart and widen the field of fire. Because of the great weight of large-calibre iron guns, it was only rarely that pieces larger than 12-pdrs. were mounted on lighter carriages with large wheels for ease of transportation. Such field guns were often made of brass, which made them lighter and easier to move.

On the battlefield, a brigade commander gave his artillery officers direct orders, as he did with any of his subordinates, on the placement of the guns, but he also depended upon their advice to select the best possible positions and then make subsequent recommendations about their movement. In most cases the officers commanding the American artillery and their counterparts in the Royal Regiment of Artillery were well-educated in their craft.[38] As with the corps of engineers, British artillery officers were not administered by the British army but by the Board of Ordnance and differed from their colleagues in the field in a number of ways. None of their commissions were purchased, promotion was by seniority alone and every officer was a graduate of the Royal Military Academy at Woolwich, whereas few officers belonging to the "army" had attended classes there or at the Royal Military College at Sandhurst.

The artillery battery commander sent to support the infantry in the field looked for a raised position on either flank of the main force which allowed the longest practical view of the enemy's position. Generally, a battery, or division, of guns comprised six pieces set up about 15 yards apart, with their limbers (two-wheeled carts to which the guns were hooked for transportation) 25 yards to the rear and the ammunition wagons, or caissons, at 50 yards. The Royal Artillery equipped a typical 6-pdr. field gun with 8 rounds in a box on the gun's carriage, 42 in the gun limber, 40 in the wagon limber and 90 in the wagon itself.[39] At a rate of two pounds of powder for each round, the one 6-pdr. required 360 pounds of propellant to discharge its full supply. Because of the destructive potential of such a large supply of powder, it was kept well away from the gun and extreme caution had to be taken with the movement and handling of the cartridges. Only in extreme situations were cartridges ever stacked up near a working piece. Still, enemy rounds had a way of finding limbers, and gunners were careless with their portfires, and devastation was the result.

One way to avoid accidents was to follow a slow and methodical firing pattern, about one shot per minute or more, which also served to conserve ammunition and keep the guns from getting too hot. But even in the warmest of actions, the number of rounds fired per gun was surprisingly low. At the Battle of Salamanca in July 1812, for instance, which lasted about five hours, one British battery of six guns fired a total of 492 rounds, 82 per piece on average, and even at the Waterloo, the average was less than 130 rounds per gun.[40]

In the face of an enemy attack, guns in the field opened fire at a range of about 1,100 yards. The Americans began with round shot, while the British threw round shot and spherical case, until the line closed to within 600 yards after which the Americans switched to heavy canister and then to light canister within 250 yards. The British added common shell to their barrage at about 600 yards, saving the heavy case for within 350 yards and light case for 250 yards. While the enemy regiments were the main target of the guns, opposing batteries often engaged each other in counterbattery fire, a practice Wellington forbade late in the Peninsular War, since he believed the guns were most effective against massed infantry and cavalry.

As with so many other things, Wellington was right because artillery fire did have withering effects on the large masses on men. A British officer recorded that during one advance, "there came a shot from a 24-pdr ... and twelve men sank together with a groan that would have shook to the soul the nerves of the oldest soldier.... I believe ten of them never rose again, the nearest was within a foot of me, the farthest not four yards off. It swept like a besom all within its range."[41] Another artillery officer wrote of how the persistent French "advanced within range of our canister, which, however, it was impossible for them to stand, and they fell by hundreds."[42] Jarvis Hanks was watching men line up one day to be shaved by a corporal when a British round shot sliced off the barber's razor hand and the head of the sergeant whose beard he was trimming, "throwing blood, brains, hair, fragments of flesh and bones ... upon the clothing of several spectators of the horrible scene."[43] Not too surprisingly, it was a given that "a young soldier is much more alarmed at a nine pounder shot passing within 4 yrds. of his head than he is of a bullet at a distance of as many inches, although one would settle him as effectively as the other."[44]

Despite the endless drill, the threat of punishments and the horrors of the battlefield, most recruits adapted successfully to life in the army. They survived

Single-rank formation with colours. Strapped for numbers, the commanding officer here formed his group of British re-enactors in a single rank. A regimental flag (on the right) and a Union Jack form the colours at the centre of the formation. (Photograph by Robert Malcomson)

the discomforts of miserable accommodations in the field and the footsore marches with as much as fifty-five pounds of equipment, clothing, bedding and "necessaries" hanging on their shoulders and they did so with a spirit of camaraderie. Lieutenant George Hennell had this recollection of his men on the march.

> They marched off and … commenced their wit upon each other with grossness and sometimes point hardly to be exceeded. As they grow tired they begin to swear at the country and the inhabitants. As they get more so, at soldiering and the commissaries and when nearly exhausted there is little said except now and then a faint dispute about distance, etc. But when they arrive, if they can get wine, all their troubles are instantly forgotten and songs and hoarse laughs resound through the place.[45]

Under the best conditions, a well-trained unit also developed an intangible characteristic which was essential for success: fighting morale or *esprit de corps*.[46] It came as a result of consistently maintained high standards in appearance and conduct of the individual and pride in belonging to the company and battalion. Discipline and drill were integral to the process, but it also took a skilful and wise commander to foster such self-confidence and group cohesion. Isaac Brock had been such a man and was seen by his followers as "active, brave, gallant. He had a peculiar faculty of attaching all parties and people to his person: in short, he infused the most unbounded confidence in all ranks and descriptions of men under his command."[47] Zebulon Pike aspired to cut the same sort of figure in his quest to emulate the Shakespearian soldiering ideal and "seek the 'Bubble' even in the cannon's mouth," and so set the standard for boldness for all to see.[48] The trappings of a regiment helped inculcate its *esprit de corps,* and a ceremony such as the one held at York on 23 March 1813 when a homemade banner was presented to the 3rd Regiment of York Militia was not an idle affair. And words such as those spoken by Major William Allan – "a country is never more secure, than when defended by its faithful, loyal and industrious inhabitants" – served to cement a feeling of patriotism in the ranks.[49] Lastly, a company or battalion of men who had been bloodied and lived to hold their heads high acquired a tradition of answering the call and zealously facing the enemy's steel. Enlistment in the regiment meant acceptance of the responsibility that tradition carried but also reliance on it as a rule for proper conduct. "I heard," wrote Saucy Tom on the day he first faced the enemy's fire, "an old soldier answer, to a youth like myself, who inquired what he should do during the battle, 'Do your duty.'"[50]

After long days of drill and manoeuvres, of fatigue duties and patrols, the barracks and camps at Sackets Harbor and York undoubtedly echoed with the sounds of laughter and loud talk about battles to be fought. By the middle of April, everyone knew that a renewal of the war was just around the corner. As an American surgeon remembered years later, "The trains of Battalions, the dashing evolutions of the Artillery and the mimic charges all served to increase the expectation and led to the conclusion that a great enterprise or struggle of no ordinary might was at hand."[51] "There are many conjectures relative to our Destination," Captain John Walworth of the Sixth U.S. Infantry wrote to his father-in-law. "Whither it is for Niagara, Little York, Kingston or some place on the River below is uncertain."[52] There was little uncertainty, however, about the eagerness to meet the enemy and put long months of training and hardship to the test, as Ensign Thomas Warner from Baltimore expressed to his wife, Mary Ann. He wrote to her on 19 April that the Volunteers were about to "embark for some secret expedition" and, referring to one of the family's aging fathers, asked Mary Ann to "give my love … to old seventisixer and tell him I have not forgot what he suffered for my liberties neither will I part with them until I suffer full as much."[53]

His chance would come soon enough.

CHAPTER 9

"Forebodings of an attack"[1]

THE DAY APPROACHES

Sir Roger Hale Sheaffe was pleased to welcome an old friend to his table at Government House at York during the third week of April 1813. This was John Norton, alternately known as the Snipe, or Teyoninhokarawen, war chief of the Grand River Six Nations.[2] Norton was Scottish by birth, the product of the marriage of a Scottish woman and a Cherokee man who was an orphan of war raised in England. Norton and Sheaffe probably met in Canada around 1790 when Norton entered the fur trade and before he was hired as an interpreter in the British Indian Department. He became a follower of the illustrious Joseph Brant, influential native ally of the British during the period, and rose quickly in status among Brant's Six Nations people on the Grand River of Upper Canada, all the while maintaining good relations with the British army. Through Brant he became known to the Duke of Northumberland and won his patronage, just as Sheaffe had done early in his life. At the Battle of Queenston Heights, it was to Norton that Sheaffe turned when he needed a detachment of warriors to harass the Americans while he organized his reinforcements. In recognition of Norton's effective leadership that day, Sheaffe subsequently appointed him "Captain of the Confederate Indians." "He is the only leader of the Indians that I can repose confidence in," the general wrote.[3]

It is obvious from the notes in Norton's memoirs that he admired Roger Sheaffe and the way he was preparing for the spring campaign by "mounting every Gun [at York] that could be found, hastening the Building of a Ship then on the Stocks and forwarding the Troops as they came up to the Niagara Frontier."[4] While discussing the strategic situation in the province, Sheaffe confided in his friend "that he was fully assured from information which he had received,

John Norton (1770-ca. 1830). Fed up with the politics of the Grand River reserve, Norton was preparing to leave Upper Canada early in 1812 when Isaac Brock persuaded him to remain. He proved to be one of the most consistent native allies for the British throughout the war. (LAC, C123481)

that either York, Niagara or Kingston would be attacked, that he was anxious to get the Ship upon the Stocks completed as soon as possible." The general would have preferred to keep a man of Norton's talents with him at York, but the chief was needed elsewhere and stayed but a few days. "I parted with my good friend Sir Roger H. Sheaffe," he recalled, "in hopes that his forebodings of an attack would not take place, – till I should have rejoined him, or till he had received reinforcements sufficiently powerful to repel any attempt of the Enemy."

There was an increase in the military might at York about the time of Norton's visit, albeit a small one. Captain Daniel McPherson's company of Glengarry Light Infantry Fencibles, numbering sixty-nine officers and men, marched into town from Kingston on Wednesday, 14 April.[5] McPherson had been in the army since 1798 when, at the age of nineteen, he joined a Scottish regiment of fencibles, raised for duty at home. Seven years later he became the adjutant for the Glasgow Trades Volunteers, which was manned by the Incorporation of the Skinners and Glovers House, one of the craft guilds in Glasgow.[6] In 1806 McPherson obtained a commission as ensign in the 8th Foot and two years later gained his lieutenancy, both advancements being made through promotion rather than by purchase. He arrived at Quebec with the 8th Foot in 1810 and in February 1812 he was appointed to open a recruiting station near Cornwall, Upper Canada, to enlist men for the recently created Glengarry Fencibles. So quickly did re-cruits answer his call that McPherson was rewarded with a captaincy in the Glengarries. The early weeks of 1813 found his company on its way to Kingston; they just missed the opportunity to join with others of their regiment in the

22 February raid on Major Benjamin Forsyth's Rifles at Ogdensburg. Although they had yet to meet the Americans in battle, McPherson's Light Infantry Fencibles cut quite the distinctive figure in their dark green coats and trousers as they tramped through York on the way to the garrison. Whereas other similar detachments had passed through the town, Sheaffe picked this company to remain at the capital to strengthen the garrison.

The arrival of the Glengarries hardly balanced the departure of other men. Nearly a dozen officers of the Provincial Marine had been at York through the winter but several of them, and about twenty seamen, had headed for Amherstburg by the third week of April. Others left York on board the *Prince Regent* when it sailed about the fifteenth for Kingston.[7] Lieutenant William Fish had set out as soon the ice opened enough to allow his passage out of the bay, in accordance with orders that Governor-in-Chief Prevost had issued near the end of March for the Provincial Marine vessels to be concentrated at Kingston instead of York.[8] It also appears that a portion of Lieutenant Colonel Rowland Heathcote's Royal Newfoundland Fencibles was on board to fill out the crew. There had been a plan to transfer some of the *Prince Regent*'s guns to the *Sir Isaac Brock* for its maiden voyage, but the schooner sailed with its full battery of ten 12-pdr. carronades and two long 6s. In the next few days the merchant sloop

Glengarry Light Infantry officer. Armed with a sabre, this officer is awaiting action, probably while he watches his men deploy in skirmish formation. Note the whistle fastened by a lanyard to his cross belt by which he would signal his orders to his far-flung men. (J.C.H. Forster, Toronto Culture, Fort York Collection)

The *Sir Isaac Brock* on the stocks. This fanciful drawing of the *Brock* at the time of the American attack fails to show the staging that would have enclosed its hull so that the shipwrights could complete the planking. The preparation of heavy timbers for insertion into the hull would not have been done so closely underfoot and it is highly unlikely that any cannon were cluttering the worksite. (Detail from painting by Owen Staples, TRL, T15211))

Mary Ann, which Sheaffe had purchased, also left York. Although work was underway to outfit the previously condemned *Duke of Gloucester* for another season on the lake, its repairs were incomplete and it remained behind under the care of Lieutenant François Gauvreau and a small group of officers.

The *Sir Isaac Brock* was also far from being ready for launch.[9] Even with Captain Tito Lelièvre bypassing the inefficient Superintendent Thomas Plucknett and giving his orders directly to Master Shipwright John Dennis, it would be many weeks before the little frigate would be ready to swim. Its starboard side was barely half-planked and only the first few strakes of oak had been bent and fastened around its ribs on the larboard side. The lower masts were fully assembled on shore and two large sails were ready, as was most of the ironwork, and the ship's boats had been framed, but all the inner structures of the ship needed to be put in place, followed by its armament, equipment, masts and rigging. At Kingston, the ship to be named the *Wolfe*, begun about the same time as the *Brock*, was within days of making its plunge. A new project to build a schooner like the *Prince Regent* was well underway and the merchantman *Governor*

Simcoe was being converted for war use. The contrast in production between the two yards was striking.

Norton's assertion that Sheaffe was "mounting every Gun that could be found" must have been shaded by his friendship with the general, because the evidence shows that only some of the artillery pieces at York were prepared for use.[10] There were three dozen or more guns at York, including the half-dozen pieces from the *Duke of Gloucester,* others sent from Fort George and Kingston and even the weapons ordered to York by Simcoe in the 1790s. But, there were not enough men at the capital to operate all of them at once, let alone leave any reasonable force to act as infantry. As well, there were not enough places to mount the guns. Work still continued to finish the four batteries near the garrison where between twelve and fifteen of the long guns and carronades were eventually mounted. This meant that the rest of the weapons were left in storage or perhaps lying on the ground at the garrison. Near two of the batteries, the artificers had constructed shot ovens, probably of brick. Also known as "furnaces," their purpose was to "bake" iron cannon balls until they were so hot that they would ignite any wooden object with which they came in contact; hot shot could be fatal to wooden warships.

It was a lack of time and manpower that prevented the building of further fortifications, and even the old battery on Gibraltar Point remained in a derelict state.[11] Bad weather complicated everything, trying the patience and endurance of Lieutenant Philip Ingouville, who, as acting engineer, directed the labour parties of militia and regulars. At least Ingouville was able to share the burdens of his duties with an expert senior officer when Lieutenant Colonel Philip Hughes of the Royal Engineers arrived on 11 April, having been instructed to take command of engineering activities in Upper Canada. Even Hughes was unable to begin the erection of additional fortifications, however. The only new project of any size was the removal of the bridges across the channels in the mouth of the Don River that gave the town easy access to the peninsula.

A less obvious sign of the preparations for a battle at York was that the government began its move out of town. The province was just past twenty years old, yet an immense quantity of documents had been generated covering the wide-ranging government business from land surveys and grants to court records, legislative matters and finances. In March Surveyor General Thomas Ridout had raised the question of what would happen to the government paperwork "should this place be attacked."[12] His office was in Elmsley House, within a mile of the fort, and Ridout was concerned that he would not be able to get there in time from his home in the old town and save all the documents before the Americans landed. As his clerks were busy with their militia duty and could not help in an emergency, Ridout asked Major General Sheaffe for permission to remove the contents of his office to his home between Duke and Duchess streets at the east end of town.

It took three weeks for Sheaffe to officially attend to the matter, but finally on 10 April his acting secretary, Lieutenant Edward McMahon, 3rd York, sent Ridout permission to make the move, but to a spot farther out of town; the materials were packed and sent to George Playter Sr.'s home up the Don River. McMahon also instructed John Small, clerk of the Executive Council, to relocate all the records in his office "to such place of safety, distant not less than a mile from the Town of York, as you may find convenient and Secure them there to remain until further orders."[13] A similar order was made to William Jarvis, who had been the province's secretary and registrar since its inception, and to Prideaux Selby, the auditor general. But John McGill, the inspector general of public accounts, did not receive such instructions, and when he heard about the transfers, he mentioned that Selby had not been told to find shelter for the accounts and records of the receiver general's office, which he also administered. Somehow these two important departments of the government had been overlooked; presumably Sheaffe issued the appropriate orders.

The removal of the provincial papers was common knowledge in the town and helped to reinforce the widespread belief that an attack was imminent. Rumours had spread that the American army near Fort Niagara was weak while the force at Sackets Harbor was strong and it was from that direction that the enemy would come. William Baldwin reflected the public mood when he wrote in April to a friend in England about the good health enjoyed by his large family and added, "but [we] are not quite at our ease as you may suppose from our exposed situation to the enemy – However batteries are preparing and it is hoped that we shall have a force of abt 1000 men – militia, regulars and Indians – it has just occurred to me that perhaps this is the last letter I may ever write you for we must all stand forth in the hour of Danger."[14]

Just as winter finally released its grip on the bay at York, so it did at Sackets Harbor, but in dramatic fashion. On the night of 12 April, ice floes swept the new flagship *Madison* from its anchorage and carried it, wallowing and out of control, towards open water.

The culprit was a blast of wind and rain out of the south, but the blame fell on the shoulders of Master Commandant James Leonard.[15] On orders from the Department of the Navy, Leonard had arrived at Sackets in December to take command of the *Madison*, as sweet a plum as any aspiring officer could hope for in a navy that did not yet have twenty well-armed warships afloat. He had

Jesse Elliott (1782-1845). Elliott was among the first naval officers sent to the lakes by Commodore Chauncey in September 1812 and was active in the brief November campaign. His subsequent naval career, however, was marked by a controversy arising from his participation in the Battle of Put-in-Bay in September 1813. (U.S. Naval Institute)

done a good job of supervising the last of its construction, its care over the winter and its arming, rigging and fitting out in the spring, but he allowed himself to be distracted by the allures of a woman he had brought with him from New York City. Commodore Chauncey knew of her presence and warned Leonard about the local gossip, advising him to send her away. Leonard did so, but she came back, and late on 11 April when he should have settled into his berth on the *Madison*, as per the commodore's standing order, Leonard went on shore to a more comfortable bed.

An alarm before dawn sent Chauncey speeding through the pans of ice in his gig to the *Madison,* where he was outraged to discover only junior officers in charge. He assumed command and signalled the squadron to bring the additional anchors and ballast needed to steady the ship and, after several hours of heavy labour, made it safe and secure again. The absent master commandant did not reach the flagship until nearly noon, at which point Chauncey had him arrested. Leonard's subsequent complaints to Secretary of the Navy William Jones and the drawn-out court martial process proved to be a bitter annoyance to the commodore through the rest of the year, just as a series of similar, though less extreme, disputes among the officers at Sackets took up Chauncey's time and exhausted his patience.

There was one spin-off of the Leonard affair, however, that became a minor controversy the commodore could have avoided. In replacing Leonard, Chauncey selected Lieutenant Jesse Elliott to command the *Madison*. Such an appointment, even a temporary one, was a prestigious post that might suddenly lead to promotion through some turn of events, and there were two other officers in the squadron who might have expected to be given the opportunity. Melancthon Woolsey and Thomas Brown both had three years more of seniority as lieutenants than Elliott did, and Woolsey had more practical experience on Lake Ontario than any other officer, yet Chauncey left them in the brig *Oneida* and the schooner *Governor Tompkins* respectively. Nothing appears to have been said publicly at the time, but the issue of Elliott's seniority would soon arise.[16]

The sight of the U.S. Navy squadron at Sackets Harbor was impressive enough in itself to obscure interpersonal problems in the wardrooms and between decks. The warming weather allowed the warships to spread their wings on Black River Bay and they found plenty of admirers on shore. Ensign Thomas Warner of the Baltimore Volunteers looked out at the squadron and wrote, "the beauty of our little fleet surpasses anything I ever saw I think they can flog twice their number without any difficulty."[17]

The squadron had doubled in size since Chauncey's attack at Kingston in November.[18] Where only the *Oneida* and six former merchantmen had sailed originally from Sackets Harbor, there was now the *Madison*, the recently launched *Lady of the Lake*, three other converted schooners and two former British prizes, armed and ready to meet the enemy. They carried a total of 40 long guns and 46 carronades, their crews numbering about 800 men. Illness had depleted the force, especially the contingent of U.S. Marines, but 150 seamen had followed Master Commandant Oliver Perry to Sackets from Rhode Island and remained while he went on to Lake Erie. Another 50 officers and men had arrived from New York with Lieutenant Wolcott Chauncey, the commodore's brother.

The crews had been drilled through the winter in the operation of the long guns and carronades and in hand-to-hand fighting with cutlass, pistol and pike. For the most part, the seamen were experienced in the work of sailing a vessel, some of them being expert old hands, so the matter of setting out on a voyage was nothing new. Functioning as part of a squadron was, however. Whereas the brigades had practised their evolutions throughout the winter, the time for learning to coordinate the manoeuvres of the squadron would only come when it reached open water. Knowing that his subordinate commanders were going to be learning on the job, the commodore laid out his plans for them simply and clearly.[19] He detailed the order of sailing, whether the squadron was in a single line ahead or abreast or in parallel lines, noting that a space of one cable, about 200 yards, should be kept between adjacent vessels. There were not enough signal books to go around, so the commanders were to follow their commodore's lead as he tacked or wore through the day, and to watch and listen during the night for one gun and two lights to signal such routine course changes. Anyone who got lost was to sail for Fort Niagara and await the arrival of the squadron.

With the water open and the warships ready, it was time to get the long-awaited expedition to Canada underway. Brigadier Generals Pike and Chandler and their staffs met with Chauncey and his senior officers to work out the details of embarking the men and material necessary for the operation. Chauncey ordered five weeks of stores for his crews and set up a system for transporting men and munitions from shore to ship as efficiently as possible.[20] No military officer received credit for working out the logistics of the lift from the land side of the process, but Brigade Major Charles Hunter signed the embarkation order and Pike's aides, Donald Fraser, Charles Jones and Benjamin Nicholson, were probably busy carrying messages to the officers whose troops and equipment were being queued up, ready to go on board the squadron.

Right from the first discussions about the spring campaign, American officials had been concerned about the size of the force involved. Secretary of War John Armstrong had argued that the largest possible number of men be taken to ensure success, even suggesting that a portion of the troops could be put into large batteaux and hauled across the lake by the individual vessels.[21] In answer to this, Major General Dearborn explained that the lake was too dangerous for carrying men across large stretches of open water in batteaux and that he believed 1,200 effectives would be enough to get the job done. With the intent of putting as many soldiers aboard as possible, the embarkation began on Tuesday, 20 April.

It was a prodigious task. Elements of at least two companies of artillery went on board with a total of eight field guns, limbers and caissons, all of which needed to be dismantled, lugged by brute force into the boats, rowed out to the anchorage and then hauled onto the vessels. The heavy equipment had to be tightly secured on deck and ammunition covered to protect it from rain and spray and accidental detonation. The soldiers went out in platoons, each man fully equipped with musket, bayonet, cartridge box, canteen, greatcoat, haversack and knapsack, in which he had stored his extra clothing, necessaries, a blanket and several days of pre-cooked food; one third of the Fifteenth Infantry also carried their unwieldy pikes. No single regiment or company went aboard with its full roster, as each one had left a trail of sick and furloughed, deserted and detached at various posts on the way to Sackets. Some remained behind to recover their health and to garrison the place, and so it was only a part of each company, and only some of the officers, that climbed into the ships' boats and batteaux used to ferry the men. Officers and men from six companies of the Fifteenth made their way to the anchorage, followed by parts of four companies from the Sixth and three from the Sixteenth Regiment, a company or more from the Twenty-first and one company of the Fourteenth with Ensign Joseph Dwight's new recruits for the Thirteenth attached. Major Benjamin Forsyth's Rifle battalion also embarked, as did the Baltimore Volunteers and Albany Greens from Lieutenant Colonel Francis McClure's regiment of twelve-month federal volunteers.

Bad weather slowed the process, which took three days to complete.[22] The *Lady of the Lake* would not be part of the expedition as it was ordered to sail for Fort Niagara to deliver a crew of riggers needed at the Black Rock shipyard. The *Growler*, which had been on patrol, came in from the lake on Thursday and the merchantman *Gold Hunter* (seized by the customs collector at Oswego in February 1812 for import violations) arrived from Oswego. Final detachments, numbering 150 men, were sent out to the new arrivals. No precise list of the soldiers on the expedition appears to have been made and estimates of their numbers varied considerably, with the most likely total amounting to nearly 1,800. Combined with the 800 or so officers and men of the U.S. Navy, the assault force headed for York had a strength of about 2,600 in thirteen warships and the *Gold Hunter*.[23]

On the first day of the embarkation, the harbour thundered to the sounds of a seventeen-gun salute in honour of Major General Henry Dearborn as he rolled into town.[24] President Madison had refused Dearborn's offer to stand down from his command so that a younger and more active general could take his place. The president had even asked Secretary Armstrong to order Dearborn to command the York operation in person. The general and his staff went out to the *Madison* and shared its tight quarters with Pike and his people and Chauncey and the ship's officers. Senior military men, such as Colonel Cromwell Pearce and Lieutenant Colonel Eleazar Ripley, were accommodated with their regiments in other vessels, as were a number of volunteers. Lieutenant Colonel George Mitchell of the Third U.S. Artillery, for instance, had offered his services, since a command suitable to his rank was not available in the expedition, and other officers, such as Captain Horatio Gates Armstrong of the Twenty-third Infantry (and the son of the secretary of war), did the same.[25] Surgeon Amasa Trowbridge was there by invitation as a volunteer. He was stationed with the New York Militia, but Pike and Chauncey arranged with Brigadier General Jacob Brown for him to be lent to the army for the first venture in the campaign.

Finally, on Friday, 23 April, the squadron pulled its anchors at mid-morning and headed for the mouth of Black River Bay. The weather had been bad and promised so obviously to get worse soon that Commodore Chauncey advised Dearborn against setting out but the general was insistent. A storm of rain and wind soon descended and at 2:00 P.M., when the squadron was suffering badly with broken spars and hulls straining under their heavy loads, with no more than half the seamen or soldiers able to get below deck at any one time, the general relented and Chauncey reversed course to find calmer water and a safe anchorage at the Harbor.

By now, some of the soldiers had been on board for four days, exposed to the weather in unbelievably crowded conditions. There were 600 seamen and soldiers on the *Madison* alone. The open area of the upper deck of the ship, excluding the space taken up with gun carriages, masts, bitts, hatchways, rigging, stores, munitions and baggage, measured less than 3,500 square feet. The single deck below was smaller, and no doubt stacked in places from deck to beams with munitions and stores. How the crew managed to work the ship with so little elbow room in the rough seas is difficult to imagine. The preparation of food, arrangement for sleeping and management of basic sanitary needs must have pushed everyone's endurance to the limit. There was no exaggeration in Commodore Chauncey's report of the situation to Secretary Jones. "I am particularly anxious," he wrote early on 24 April, "to get the Troops to the place of their destination as soon as possible for crowded as they are now on board of the different vessels, they as well as my own Men, will very Soon become Sickly."[26]

The bad weather finally abated and on 25 April the squadron set sail at 8:00 A.M., this time reaching the lake and shaping a course to the west.[27] Even the least experienced of the men soon realized that Kingston was not to be their object. It would be at Niagara or Little York that they would splash ashore to commence the spring campaign.

At Quebec on 21 April, Governor-in-Chief Sir George Prevost composed a despatch for Lord Bathurst to share with the prime minister and cabinet in London. It was one in a list of messages that grew longer with each passing day and in which he detailed the many issues of his command, explaining his decisions and asking for more men and munitions. Prevost's letter concerned the situation in Upper Canada and how he hoped the government and the Prince Regent would continue to approve of the measures he had taken to defend it. He had heard that Royal Navy officers were travelling to Quebec overland from New Brunswick and he intended to send them immediately to Kingston to take command of naval matters. Without admitting that the Lake Ontario squadron was not ready to face Commodore Chauncey, he pointed out that American supremacy on the lake would "expose Upper Canada to devastation and insult."[28] Prevost repeated how he had attempted to improve the defence of the province by sending detachments of regulars to the upper province and approving the creation of the Incorporated Militia. And then he baldly expressed his lack of faith in Sheaffe's leadership.

After the affair of Queenston Sir R. H. Sheaffe lost a glorious opportunity of crossing the Niagara River during the confusion and dismay which then prevailed, for the purpose of destroying Fort Niagara, by which the command of the Niagara River would have been secured to us during the war, and Niagara, like Ogdensburg, would have ceased to be an object of disquietude. But the eminent military talents of Sir Isaac Brock having ceased to animate the little army, the advantage of that day was not sufficiently improved.[29]

Sir George did not elaborate on why he waited nearly six months to inform the home government of his disappointment with Sheaffe's conduct after the action at Queenston. In the aftermath of the battle, he had criticized Sheaffe for allowing the New York Militia to be paroled but had said nothing about Fort Niagara.[30] His assertion that its capture would have relieved Niagara from further threats from the enemy shore was disingenuous and played upon the lack of knowledge possessed by Bathurst and his colleagues about the American positions on the Niagara River compared to the area around Ogdensburg; events in 1814 would reveal the absurdity of his contention. What Prevost also failed to reveal was that he had recently given orders for the concentration of the naval force on Lake Ontario at Kingston and that he had essentially abandoned his plan to make York the centre of operations. During his winter visit to the upper province, he had seen how Sheaffe struggled as a commander-in-chief and the many deficits of the dockyard and fortifications at York, but he waited weeks before he commented on Sheaffe's leadership and did not mention the problems at York. Like nearly everyone else in Canada, he knew full well that Chauncey would rule the waves in the spring and that an early attack somewhere in Upper Canada was a certainty, and, after listing all he had done to defend the province, Prevost informed his superiors that Sheaffe lacked "eminent military talents." It was as if he expected a disaster to occur and was setting up Sheaffe as the object of blame.

Commander Robert Barclay, RN, reached Quebec on the day before Prevost wrote his despatch to Bathurst. He carried correspondence from Halifax and the news that two other commanders and four lieutenants were on the road behind him and that a handful of others were travelling with a shipment of carronades by sea. Barclay's stay at Quebec was brief. He headed up the St. Lawrence River to Kingston, where he arrived around the end of the month and, on Prevost's instructions, took command of the squadron anchored there. He received a letter from the governor-in-chief in which Prevost wrote, "I hope you found the King's Vessels on Lake Ontario Concentrated at Kingston Har-

Robert Barclay (1785-1837). Commander Barclay, pictured here as a young lieutenant, was a seasoned naval officer by the time he arrived to take command at Kingston late in April 1813. He had fought in the Battle of Trafalgar in 1805 and lost his left arm during a shipboard action in 1808. When Commodore James Yeo reached Kingston in May, Barclay was sent to take command at Amherstburg. (TRL, T15258)

bour on your arrival at Kingston and the New Ship Ready to Launch."[31] Barclay replied that most of the warships were there and that he was already hard at work, making improvements in the strength of the squadron and the efficiency of the dockyard.

The grenadier company of the 1st Battalion of the 8th Regiment of Foot marched into York on Sunday, 25 April, en route to Fort George. The unit traced its lineage to 1685 when it had been formed as the Princess Anne of Denmark's Regiment of Foot, a name which was changed in 1716 to the King's Regiment in honour of George I. Known after 1751 as the 8th, but often referred to simply as "the King's," the regiment had tramped across numerous battlefields and won the honour of having a Sphinx with "Egypt" emblazoned on its regimental colours for distinguished service there in 1801.[32] A second battalion of the regiment was raised and trained in England from 1804 while the 1st Battalion was involved in expeditions in northern Europe before being sent to Halifax in 1808. From there it took part in the campaign against Martinique, in which Prevost was a senior officer, and added that place to its colours. The 1st Battalion went to Quebec in 1810 and remained there until the arrival of reinforcements from abroad allowed Prevost to send it into Upper Canada in 1813. It was fully manned, numbering 35 commissioned officers and 975 non commissioned officers, musicians and privates.

The grenadier company in any regiment was made up of the biggest and strongest soldiers and, along with the light company, was considered the "elite," taking its place at the right of the formation and, therefore, the head of any marching column; the "light bobs" took the leftmost position. The King's grenadiers numbered over 120 officers and men and were led by Captain Neal McNeale.[33] The record of his career is thin, showing only that he was Scottish and entered the British army as an ensign in 1800 with the 72nd Foot, a highlander regiment, transferred into the 48th with a lieutenancy three years later and joined the 8th as a captain in 1805. He was almost certainly involved in the Martinique expedition and eventually earned an influential enough place in the battalion to rise to command of the number one company.

One day behind the grenadiers was Captain James Eustace's company, number three in the battalion.[34] It comprised seventy-eight officers and men, but there were also several dozen other foot soldiers accompanying Eustace, men from the sixth, seventh and ninth companies. Eustace and his men had been involved in the attack on Ogdensburg and earned mention in despatches for having "nobly supported" the advance with bayonets fixed. Sergeant James Commins of Eustace's company recalled that the Americans who did not flee "fired upon our men from their windows, but they suffered for their Temerity every one was bayoneted."[35]

It appears that Eustace's company took up quarters with the militia in the Town Blockhouse and the nearby legislative building, which was being used for

Captain, 8th Regiment of Foot. One of the oldest and most highly decorated of the British regiments, the 8th Foot was also known as the "King's Regiment," and documents of the time often referred to them by that name. This drawing of the captain of a grenadier company of the King's gives a fair impression of how Neal McNeale would have looked early on the morning of the battle. (J.C.H. Forster, Toronto Culture, Fort York Collection)

housing the passing troops. As with the grenadiers, their stay at York was only to be temporary since they were bound for Fort George and were themselves being followed by 8th's light company. The layover at the capital allowed the men time to relax and reconstitute themselves. Sergeant Commins and his mates had heard a rumour that the Americans had been "reinforced from France with gunners and artificers, and their army was better organized under more subordination, as they endeavoured to adopt all our plans."[36] The 8th knew they were in for hard duty ahead.

The fair winds that propelled the American squadron away from Sackets Harbor on Sunday, 25 April, turned foul later in the day. A heavy swell was soon rocking the vessels as they followed Commodore Chauncey's signals to tack and tack again, struggling to make way to westward. On board the schooner *Julia* Surgeon's Mate William Beaumont and others of the Sixth Infantry turned green with sea sickness and retched in misery over the lee rails; Ensign Dwight remarked that many of his men suffered the same malady on the *Governor Tompkins*.[37] On Monday conditions calmed and Chauncey seemed to be heading for a landing at Fort Niagara, even passing the mouth of the Niagara River late in the afternoon, when, to everyone's surprise, the *Madison* signalled an abrupt change of course and the squadron turned to steer north toward Little York.

The flagship signalled again, this time summoning all senior officers to attend a council of war. With the sun going down and the enemy's capital in sight, boats gathered around the *Madison*, and the wardroom, the largest "private" space in the ship, soon became crowded with gold braid. Chauncey hosted the affair, welcoming Lieutenant Colonels Cromwell Pearce, Eleazar Ripley and George Mitchell. Lieutenant Colonel Francis McClure of the twelve-month volunteers and Majors William King, William Swan and Abraham Eustis found places around the table as did Major Benjamin Forsyth, whose height made it necessary for him to navigate the deck beams with care until he could lower his hulking frame into a seat. Zebulon Pike had a prominent place, surrounded by his aides Fraser, Jones and Nicholson. Some of the senior naval officers were likely present as well: Lieutenants Jesse Elliott, Melancthon Woolsey, Thomas Brown, Wolcott Chauncey and others. It was cramped quarters to be sure and Chauncey's seamen/servants circulated deftly, finding the necessary elbow room to tend to the beverage preferences of the officers.

When all had assembled, a word from the commodore sent the servants out the door, where marine privates stood guard, and a hush fell as Major General Dearborn, overfilling one of the chairs with his ponderous girth, called the

U.S. squadron, Lake Ontario. U.S. Midshipman Peter Spicer sketched this view of part of Chauncey's squadron in 1813. The vessels (left to right) are: the *Fair American, Oneida, Governor Tompkins, Ontario, Madison* and *Lady of the Lake.* (U.S. Naval Historical Center, NH75734)

council to order and announced that General Pike would explain the details of the impending expedition ashore. Pike was well organized and went over in detail the plan he had issued in advance for the landing and march on the British positions. Forsyth's rifles would be the vanguard, gaining the beachhead and then forming a "chain" to cover the first wave of infantry. This would comprise elements from each regiment of Pike's brigade and be followed by a battery of Third Artillery with infantry support. Next would come a reserve of platoons under Swan's command and then Eustis and his artillery, McClure's volunteers and finally Ripley's men from the Twenty-first Infantry. When everyone was on shore and the expedition had formed into a column, with the rifle units covering the flanks, it would begin the march toward the fortifications.

Pike wanted the platoon leaders to "pay the greatest attention to the coolness and aim of their men" and warned that "any man firing or quitting his post without orders must be put to death, as an example may be necessary."[38] Pike foresaw an eventual bayonet charge, "thus letting the enemy see we can meet them with their own weapons," and called for "humanity after victory" despite "whatever examples the savage allies of our enemy have given us." The general insisted upon honourable and courteous conduct after the battle, especially in regards to "the unoffending citizens." "Their property," he ordered, "... must be held sacred, and any soldier who shall ... be guilty of plundering the inhabitants, shall, if convicted, be punished with death."

Chauncey had formed a similar, but much shorter, set of instructions stating the order in which the troops would be landed from the various vessels.[39] After questions and comments and even a few motivational words from Dearborn, the officers likely raised their glasses in a toast to victory before the meeting ended and they returned to their vessels in the twilight. There must have been some who wondered if Dearborn himself would command in the morning or leave the job to Pike, because nothing had been said to confirm one or the other.

General Pike was one of the very few who found privacy enough in the final hours on Monday to sharpen a quill and record his thoughts on the coming event. He addressed a letter to his wife: "My dear Clara, we are now standing on and off the harbor of York, which we shall attack at daylight in the morning: I shall dedicate these last moments to you, my love, and tomorrow throw all other ideas but my country to the wind."[40] He mentioned that he still did not know what Dearborn's intentions were regarding who would lead the assault, but allowed that "he has acted honorably so far, and I feel great gratitude to the old gentleman: My sword and pen shall both be exerted to do him honor." He left his wife with no new requests but wanted her to know that if fate meant him to meet his end on the morrow's battlefield, he would die aspiring "to deeds worthy of your husband." He asked to be remembered "with a father's love, a father's care, to our daughter," ended with "warmest sentiments of love and friendship" and signed it "Montgomery."

Early Monday evening Quarter Master Bryan Finan of the Royal Newfoundland Fencibles and his son were walking back to the garrison from the town when Captain McNeale caught up to them. The boy remembered the "brave and elegant Captain McNeill" talking about arrangements he had made for setting out the next morning and that he "spoke as confidently of being in Fort George … on a certain day, as if no untoward circumstance could intervene."[41]

As the trio walked along, guns began to fire at the fort to signal an alarm.[42] A rider from the lookout post on the Scarborough Bluffs, ten miles east of the town, had reined his steaming horse to a stop at the garrison and hurried to tell Sheaffe that the sails of at least ten vessels had been spotted; it was between 5:00 and 6:00 P.M., less than two hours before the sun would set. By that time the news must have been confirmed by the small party of soldiers at the lighthouse on the peninsula, who raised a Union Jack to telegraph that the enemy was approaching from the east.

The regulars and militia in the garrison were promptly called to arms and presumably the militia at the Town Blockhouse formed up there alongside Eustace's men. The Finan boy remembered that "the greatest activity prevailed in making the necessary dispositions for the defence of the place."[43] Lieutenant Ely Playter had been on his way home when he received word that Major William Allan wanted to see him. He rode to the fort with his brother George and saw "the Troops and Militia were all prepairing [and] Patrols and Guard [were] sent out every direction."[44] There was uncertainty about where the Americans intended to land, so the detachments at the garrison and Town Blockhouse were kept where they were to guard each flank while patrols were sent out to spread the alarm and keep an eye out for the enemy. One rider headed along the Kingston Road to find the light company of the 8th Foot, which was known to be approaching York, and give their captain Sheaffe's order to press forward as fast as possible.

There is no record of Sir Roger Sheaffe calling his senior officers together to discuss the situation at this point. Lieutenant Colonel Heathcote, the senior officers of the Royal Newfoundland Regiment, Captains McPherson, McNeale and Eustace were all close at hand. So were Lieutenant Colonel Chewett and Major Allan, Sheaffe's aides Robert Loring, Nathan Coffin and James Givins, and Lieutenant Colonel Hughes of the engineers, but if the general summoned them to a council of war to discuss his plan for defending York, no one made note of it. In fact, once the initial alarm was over and the express riders had been sent to relay the news, the troops were apparently dismissed to their quarters for the night and any sense of urgency settled down along with the sun. The calm left an impression on the Finan boy, who remembered that "little apprehension was entertained for [York's] safety which was rather surprising."[45]

Justice William Powell visited the general's quarters and later wrote "Sheaffe appeared to have given the requisite instructions to the officers under his command, as at 8 o'clock he was found at a table smoking his cigar and conversing on indifferent topics with his Adjt.-Genl. Of Militia [Stephen Jarvis] and [the] Surgeon of Marine [Grant Powell]."[46] Powell also wrote that either at Sheaffe's or somewhere else "in the evening there was much discussion as to the probable point of attack. The major opinion was that it would be above and below the town."[47] There were others at York who expected the Americans to make one main landing on the narrowest part of the peninsula, close to the Don River, since the last views of the squadron revealed them steering in that direction.

Major Allan had ordered Lieutenant Playter to find Major James Givins and gather some of the native warriors together. Playter heard Givins was at the general's residence and went there to pass on Allan's request, but nothing was done about it. "The Genl.," Playter wrote, "thought I need not go till near Daylight." Playter lay down on the dining room floor and eventually fell asleep. [48]

If General Sheaffe was calm and nonchalant about the approaching fleet,

Elizabeth Derenzy was certainly not. She was the former Elizabeth Selby, daughter of Prideaux Selby, who had married Captain William Derenzy of the 41st Foot in a ceremony performed by the Reverend Strachan on 8 February. Her father had taken seriously ill and Elizabeth found herself looking after his affairs, namely the offices of the receiver general and auditor general. In this capacity he had been in charge of provincial funds and therefore had nearly £2,500 locked up in a large iron chest at his home on Frederick Street just south of King Street. Someone must have alerted Sheaffe to the presence of so much money and, knowing that Selby was incapacitated, he asked Powell and Chief Justice Thomas Scott to visit Mrs. Derenzy and make arrangements for safe removal of the funds.

They discovered that there was a second amount of money on hand, about $600 in army bills, which Elizabeth put into a bag and packed into a small iron case along with some of the office papers. With Scott and Powell's approval, this box was sent for safekeeping to the home of Donald McLean, the magistrate and clerk of the assembly. What was done with the larger amount of money is unclear, although one popular story has it that Selby's clerk, William Roe, was disguised as an elderly lady, so as to avoid attracting attention, and took the money in a strong box by wagon out of town and buried it east of the Don River near the property of Peter Robinson.[49]

In his private study that evening the Reverend Dr. John Strachan sat as he so often did, quill in hand, writing a letter to one of his innumerable correspondents, in this instance Professor James Brown of the University of Glasgow. Strachan began briefly with news of the war, lamenting the loss of command on Lake Ontario and hoping that a detachment of the Royal Navy would soon arrive to regain supremacy. Then he mentioned the death of a daughter of one of Kingston's prominent merchants, the sad loss of his own infant daughter the previous fall and the hard news that his mother had passed away in Scotland. He turned to Brown's theories in mathematics and his sermons, praising them highly, urging his former teacher to publish his work.

Abruptly, Strachan broke his line of thought. "I am interrupted," he wrote, "an express has come in to tell us the [Americans are] within a few miles steering for this place. [A]ll is hurry, and confusion, and I do not know when I shall be able to finish this."[50] Before he blotted the ink and put the letter aside, the Reverend Strachan hinted at his anticipation of what was about to unfold. "I am not afraid," he wrote, "but our Commandant is weak."

Strachan soon retired to his bed but was up at 4:00 A.M. and getting his horse ready. He was among the first to hear the alarm spread afresh.

CHAPTER 10

"Disagreeable presages"[1]

THE AMERICANS LAND

T he moon was halfway through its last quarter in the early hours of Tuesday, 27 April 1813. Even if the sky was clear, the movements of the American squadron would have been virtually invisible to weary eyes peering into the darkness from the Scarborough Bluffs or any other point between there and the lighthouse on the peninsula opposite York.[2] Commodore Isaac Chauncey probably ordered the night watches in the *Madison* to lead the squadron through a long triangular course, tacking and wearing under easy sail so that the first glimmer of dawn would see them in the right place to begin their advance on the Canadian shore.

The sky first lightened east of the town at 4:45 and found the people up and scanning the horizon for the Americans. A cluster of sails came into view shortly after 5:00, approaching through the mist from the east, prompting some to declare that they had been right in predicting the enemy would land on the peninsula near the bottom of the bay. There were sixteen ships, Major General Sheaffe later reported, although most people correctly counted fourteen.[3] They came on under the press of a steady breeze, passing the point at which an easterly attack could be launched, gliding beyond the lighthouse and the garrison until, about 6:00, they were nearly opposite the clearing where the ruins of old Fort Rouillé were.[4]

The Reverend John Strachan awoke before dawn and rode to the garrison just as the sun touched the horizon and then along the lakeshore to get a better view of the warships.[5] He passed groups of officers and others who had risen early to see what the Americans were about. They sat on horseback or stood on the bank above the lake, the military men wrapped in their slate-coloured greatcoats against the chill of the morning, focusing telescopes and passing them around.

It is not difficult to imagine the indefatigable chaplain seeking out the knot of men where Major General Sheaffe stood and going to greet him and ask him his thoughts. Sir Roger would have been easy to spot even in a huddle of grey coats, white trousers and black boots. Only the lofty bicorn of a major general was trimmed with ostrich feathers, the accompanying red and white plume and black cockade with a golden loop.[6] Besides, his group would have been the largest, with his aides and the senior regular and militia officers present to await his orders.

This was a defining moment for Sir Roger Sheaffe. He was forty-nine years old and at the zenith of his career. His victory at Queenston had earned him the baronetcy and appointment as military commander of the province and head administrator of its government. The day that lay before him offered a new harvest of glory, or its opposite. It was a test of what he had learned in thirty-five years in the British army and how he could read the hand that the gods of war would deal him. He must have taken a long hard look at the American squadron, trying to anticipate his enemy's intent.

Even without the aid of a telescope, anyone could see that the Americans were preparing to anchor.[7] Crewmen were hurrying aloft to take in square sails,

Gibraltar Point Lighthouse. The lighthouse located at the southwest corner of the peninsula began its operation in September 1808. It stood 52 feet tall, was built of Queenston limestone and used sperm whale oil to fuel lamps that burned a white light which was amplified by reflectors. John Paul Rademüller was the keeper during the war and a small militia detachment was stationed there to telegraph the appearance of approaching vessels to the garrison and town. Raising a red ensign, as shown here, indicated sails to the west, while a Union Jack meant sails to the east. (TRL, T10274)

while others got the anchors off the bows. Cables had probably been left bent to the anchors for the short cruise up the lake, but great lengths of the stout hempen lines had to be ranged up from below and laid out in "flakes," long serpentine loops, on the decks, no simple task with deck space crowded with soldiers. The commodore signalled the squadron to anchor and, at his own choosing, each individual master ordered "Helm down," his vessel turned into the wind, and just as it lost the last of its forward motion came the command, "Let go!" A man cast off the ring stopper, which held the anchor suspended from the cathead, and down it plunged into the depths. The breeze pushed the vessel back, its helm amidship, as the cable snaked out through the hawse until it was stoppered, forcing the anchor to bite; some forecastle hand fixed a buoy to the cable, while his mates brailed up or hauled down the last of the fore and aft sails and the waves began their rhythmic chop against the vessel's bows as it rose and fell, straining on the cable. In this way, one after another, the warships came to anchor in a widely spread pattern about one and half miles southwest of the garrison shortly after 6:00 A.M.

So the mystery of where the Americans would land was solved as the sun peeked above the horizon and it was time for Sheaffe to execute his plan of defence. The night before, when only ten of the warships had been visible in the distance, there were those at the British post who believed their own numbers were strong enough to oppose a force carried in a squadron of that size.[8] Now with the crowded decks of the American vessels clearly in view, some of the confidence in the British and Canadian ranks shrank and later estimates were made that the enemy had up to 3,000 soldier ready to land. The general returned to his headquarters to issue his orders.

How strong *was* the force under Roger Sheaffe's command at York that morning? The general officially reported having "about six hundred, including militia and dockyard men" in one of his versions of events.[9] Besides Sheaffe, only a handful of British and Canadian observers commented on how many men under arms were present, their estimates ranging from just over 500 to nearly 700. Justice William Powell for instance, wrote that there were "two companies of the King's ... 2 weak companies of the Newfoundland Regt, 40 of the Glengarry Regt., and about 45 Indians, in all 365, [and] to them may be added in numbers 250 militia and 40 art[ificers]: 290."[10] As events evolved, there was never a point during the day when Sheaffe assembled all the regulars, militia, volunteers and natives in one place so no one ever viewed his army as a whole.

Surviving data from the regimental musters, the casualty lists and the subsequent military claims for losses reveal that Sheaffe commanded more men than has previously been noted, most likely between 1,000 and 1,100.[11] This total included approximately 104 officers and men in the detachment of Royal New-foundland Fencibles, 62 of the Glengarry Fencibles, 203 of the 8th Foot, 16 of the Royal Artillery, 24 of the 49th Foot and 4 of the 41st Foot. There had been three companies from each of the 1st and 3rd Regiments of York Militia and one of the 1st Durham Militia on duty at York in April and more joined the ranks on Tuesday morning, bringing the sedentary militia force to over 400. One company of infantry and one of artillery belonging to the newly raised Incorporated Militia were on hand, adding another 50 men. Estimates of how many warriors of the Mississauga, Ojibwa and Chippawa nations gathered around Major James Givins that morning ranged from as low as 40 to as high as 100. Early in the month Sheaffe had given orders for arms to be distributed to the dockyard men, and so, with Thomas Plucknett at their head, 70 or more shipwrights and crafts-men were available to fight, along with a handful of Provincial Marine personnel. Sheaffe had also instructed magistrates and other officials who were exempt from militia duty to be equipped, and this call was answered when at least ten individuals came forward, including Magistrate Alexander Wood, Sheriff John Beikie and Clerk of the Legislative Assembly Donald McLean.

As commander-in-chief on the spot, it was Sir Roger's responsibility to make the most efficient use of this force. But when the time came for him to issue orders, he appears to have solicited the opinions of others rather than executing

Native warriors. Major Givins commanded a mixed group of Ojibwa, Mississauga and Chippawa warriors on 27 April. This illustration, made around 1807, shows the mix of fabric and leather that they usually wore. The men have returned from a hunting party where they have used their long rifles to pick off some waterfowl. (LAC, C012781)

preconceived decisions. His friend Justice Powell revealed this when he wrote that before any deployments were made "some difference of opinion existed on opposing or admitting the landing."[12] Sheaffe was presumably at the centre of such a debate, but Powell left no details about who voiced which opinions.

It was not as if Sheaffe had been without advice on how to conduct the spring campaign, at least in the larger context. At the end of March Governor-in-Chief Prevost had written to remind him of that the "fatal effects of dividing and dissipating a force by attempting to support too many points have been so frequently illustrated of late."[13] Sir George did not clarify the points to which he was referring, unless he meant his own decision to divide and dissipate the naval resources on Lake Ontario and make York a vulnerable target for the Americans. Apparently without any sense of the irony in his words, Prevost advised Sheaffe, "it is by concentrated means alone that adequate effects can ever be produced." In the face of an overwhelming invasion, however, Prevost directed Sheaffe "to act with such caution as would enable you to husband your resources for future exertion."

In the face of the imminent American landing on that Tuesday morning, Sir Roger implemented aspects of a plan of defence similar to what he had outlined for Lieutenant Colonel Cecil Bisshopp the previous November when Brigadier General Alexander Smyth seemed about to cross the Upper Niagara River. Paralleling a set of instructions issued earlier by Major General Brock, Sheaffe's orders on that occasion read:

> if the enemy attempts to cross the water he is not to be opposed by musquetry until he is well within its range, and if he perserveres in endeavouring to gain the shore he is to be attacked at the point of the bayonet…. If in spite of every exertion any portion of the troops should be forced by great superiority of numbers to retire, the best possible order is to be preserved, covering the retreat by a steady and well-directed fire…. If necessity should arise for abandoning a post all ammunition, provisions and other articles that may be useful to an enemy are to be destroyed, timely preparations for which having been previously made.[14]

On 27 April vital minutes slipped by before Sheaffe finally gave his first orders of the day. He directed Major James Givins to hurry forward at the head of the warriors and oppose the landing. They set off at a trot across the open ground between the Half Moon and Western batteries and along the lakeshore road that sliced through the woods to the site of Fort Rouillé.

They were soon followed, if not preceded, by detachments who went to man the guns in the four batteries. Bombardier William Needham and some of his

Æneas Shaw (d. 1814). A leading citizen in Upper Canada from its inauguration, Shaw was in semi-retirement when, in 1811, he was promoted to major general in the British army and appointed adjutant general of the province's militia to supervise its training. Sheaffe's orders to him on the morning of the battle led to a confusion in the deployment of the militia and the Glengarry Light Infantry. (AO, 605017)

gunners were posted to the Western Battery while the rest of the Royal Artillery was probably distributed among the other batteries. They were reinforced by militia and regulars; as many as twenty-two of the Glengarries appear to have been with Needham, for instance.[15]

More minutes passed before Sheaffe gave his next command, this time to Captain Daniel McPherson of the Glengarries, ordering him to march forward and oppose the landing too. The men were to leave their greatcoats, knapsacks and other "necessaries" behind at the garrison so that they would not be encumbered. While the Glengarries stowed their belongings, Sheaffe asked Major General Æneas Shaw to take a portion of the militia mustered at the garrison and one of the field guns and occupy a position "on a road at the back of the woods to watch our rear." The road, the western extension of Lot Street, which was roughly parallel to the lakeshore about half a mile north of the lake, ran all the way to Humber Bay.[16]

Æneas Shaw was a senior members of York's elite citizens, probably in his sixties, and had not seen any military action since fighting as one of Simcoe's Queen's Rangers in the American War of Independence, yet Sheaffe saw fit to put him in command of a detachment. The choice promptly proved regrettable because, for some unexplained reason, Shaw convinced Captain McPherson to follow him. Although the Glengarries had been in the town for nearly two weeks and McPherson presumably had some knowledge of the local topography, he refrained from challenging Shaw's advice and followed the militia on a path that actually took him away from where the Americans would soon be landing. If Sheaffe or any of his staff who were present noticed where the Glengarries were going, they said nothing to stop them.

Sir Roger now paused again to observe the American squadron. Lieutenant Colonel Rowland Heathcote's Newfoundland Fencibles had fallen in at their barracks in the garrison. They marched through its western gate, down to Garrison Creek, crossing its narrow bridge and forming up in the flats just behind and below the garden next to Sheaffe's residence. The grenadier company of the 8th Foot soon joined them, led by Captain Neal McNeale. Like Heathcote and McPherson's men, the King's had been ordered to leave their greatcoats and other belongings at the garrison. Heathcote had even ordered seven of his drummers to lay their instruments aside and arm themselves.[17] With these regulars were the two dozen members of the 49th Foot and the handful of men from the 41st, unless they had been sent to work in the batteries. All the members of the 1st and 3rd York and possibly even Captain John Burn's company of the 1st Durham company, who had been at the garrison, had marched off with Æneas Shaw, but Lieutenant Colonel William Chewett had been instructed to gather others of the militia at the market area between the old and new quarters of the town and he soon appeared with them. Major William Allan seems to have carried orders to Captain James Eustace at the Town Blockhouse to bring his detachment of the 8th up to the garrison, so they were on a quick march along Palace Street to where it angled off to follow the shoreline and become Front Street.

The rampart above the dry ditch provided a good view of the American squadron and perhaps the next thing General Sheaffe did was to walk up there to watch his enemy. He too may have shrugged off his heavy woollen coat so that the brilliant scarlet of his uniform was revealed. There had been new regulations and a major general no longer wore plush epaulets, but was distinguishable by the aiguillette, a series of looping, braided golden cords on his right shoulder. Again, Sheaffe lifted his telescope to his eye to study his foe.

Only on the quarterdeck of the flagship *Madison* would there have been men with enough idle time to sweep their glasses along the Canadian shore, noting the activity, speculating on whether or not it was Sheaffe they could see watching them in return. Everyone else was busily securing the rig, hoisting the ships' boats off their chocks amidship and swinging them over the side, hauling up the empty batteaux that had been trailing astern. Or keeping out of the way of the seamen, whose low curses revealed their frustration with the tangle of lubbers who made even the simplest task impossible, disrupted the routine of the watches, fouled the decks and never shut up. A schooner crewed by fifty officers and seamen was a crowded place; insert a hundred foot soldiers with nothing to do but gawk and squawk into such a society and tensions soared. "I never was more disappointed in men, than I was in the soldiers," recalled seaman Ned Myers in the *Scourge*. "They were mostly tall, pale-looking Yankees, half dead with sickness and the bad weather – so mealy, indeed, that half of them could not take their grog, which by this time, I had got to think a bad sign."[18]

On Tuesday morning, however, the soldiers came to life. The galleys in the squadron had been bustling well before sun-up, so the seamen at least could have something warm in their bellies at the beginning of a day that would most certainly depart from the routine. To simplify things, it was probably standard naval fare that a cook and his mates boiled up in the coppers, the huge pots heating on the stoves. Burgoo, a thick soup of oatmeal and water, would stick to ribs and was maybe supplemented on this day with cheese and butter and an extra portion of loaf bread for later.[19] There may have been tea or Scottish coffee, which was made from burnt toast boiled in water and sweetened with sugar. More than a few whistles were wet with a tot of rum secretly put aside for rousing the spirit. The soldiers would have boarded with their pre-cooked meals with them, but many of them had been on the ships for seven days and their rations had run out, and by now they were being fed by harried naval cooks and their mates.

The call came to fall in, and once the men had been inspected, they did what soldiers had always done, which was to stand and wait. The scene was repeated on the decks of the fourteen vessels, because, ready or not, there would be no mass landing since the rate of disembarkation depended on the space available

Infantry kit. Besides arms, ammunition and his basic uniform, a soldier's kit included his knapsack, a haversack, a canteen and belt, mess tin, blanket, greatcoat, spare shirts, shoes and stockings, brushes, a comb, pipe clay, chalk and even tent pegs. Sergeants and corporals also carried their written records. The regulars at York, outfitted like the Glengarry re-enactor in this photograph, were ordered to leave their baggage at the garrison when they marched to confront the Americans. (Photograph by Robert Malcomson)

in the boats. A typical batteau measured about 40 feet in length and could carry about thirty passengers, while the cutters and longboats of the warships varied in size from 16 to 32 feet and had proportionately less capacity. Not surprisingly, one officer stated that only about 300 men could be landed in each wave of the attack. Brigadier General Zebulon Pike had specified the order in which the force would go ashore and Commodore Chauncey had listed the order in which the vessels should be emptied.[20] In accordance with their instructions, then, the extra ships' boats began to gather around the schooners *Conquest* and *Ontario*, the flagship and the *Governor Tompkins*. The squadron had not come to anchor in a close pack, but was spread out over a half mile of water at least, some of the vessels nearly a mile offshore from the old French fort. It was a hard pull for the boat crews to get to their assigned places, but when signal flags on the *Madison* announced the go-ahead, the disembarkation began as planned.

It was just about 7:00 when Major Benjamin Forsyth heaved his heavy frame over the side of the *Conquest* and stepped down into one of the largest of the batteaux. He was followed by maybe three dozen of his men, but scarcely more than that because even a big boat could only hold so many. Besides, the seamen who had volunteered to row them ashore under the command of their boatswains or midshipmen needed leg and elbow room. Some of the riflemen may have stood to make room for others, but the wind was rising out of the east and whipping up a chop and they would soon have discovered how hard it was to keep their footing. Knowing full well that it took only a moment's mishap to upset a boat in such conditions, the seamen probably warned the troops to sit still on the floor boards and keep the centre of gravity low.

Everyone saw the Rifle Regiment getting underway and anxiously watched their progress. Some observers recalled that they went ashore in two large batteaux, but Forsyth's force numbered about 170 so that they must have formed a flotilla of five or six boats.[21] It soon became obvious that the easterly wind was pushing them off course for a landing at Fort Rouillé, and when they got within 200 yards of the shore, the enemy warriors whom they could clearly see among the trees and bushes on the bank began to fire at them independently. Now Forsyth displayed some of his tactical savvy as he asked for the sailors to rest on their oars. He signalled the others to do the same, and as the helmsmen kept the boats broadside to the wind, giving the riflemen time to load their weapons, the flotilla drifted westward. On shore the natives followed their progress, stretching out in a line beyond the clearing where the old fort stood. Perched in the stern of his batteau, wrapped in his long green coat, Forsyth stared out from under the wide brim of his dark hat and studied the shoreline, waiting for the right time to make a dash for the beach.

During this time, General Sheaffe continued to watch the Americans and then decided to make his next move. He summoned Captain McNeale and ordered him to advance along the road by the lake and meet the enemy as they landed. The distance from the governor's residence to Fort Rouillé was a few yards longer than a mile but that was not too great a challenge for McNeale's grenadiers. They were the biggest and best of the regiment with battle experience and a reputation to maintain. About 120 officers and men stood at ease in their double ranks, dressed in their red coatees, with the deep blue facings and shoulder wings trimmed with white, woollen fringes. They were accustomed to turning out at dawn and going some hours before breakfast, but McNeale knew well that this day would write its own timetable. In all accounts, the captain was portrayed as an ideal officer and gentlemen, "valiant" and "beloved by his men," and no doubt as attentive to their needs as he was to their discipline.[22] Even in the disorder of the garrison that morning, he probably had milk and bread, two breakfast staples, distributed to the ranks along with whatever cheese or bits of cooked ham or beef were available. At nearly 7:00 they filed around the southern end of the earthen rampart behind Government House and when they were clear of it began a quick march, maintaining a well-practised rate of 108 steps, about 270 feet, in a minute. At that speed, they could cover the mile to the clearing in about twenty minutes.[23]

Sir Roger had now deployed four parts of his force separately. James Givins's warriors were just beginning to engage the enemy. The Glengarries were still following Æneas Shaw's militia through the woods away from the lake. And McNeale's grenadiers were heading for the landing place. Lieutenant Colonel Heathcote's Newfoundland Fencibles were still waiting for orders and within a few minutes Captain Eustace's detachment of the 8th Foot came quick-stepping up to the garrison.

There was confusion about the militia, who were soon at the garrison in numbers.[24] Major Allan arrived back from town to discover that men from the 3rd York had been sent off with Shaw. He sought out the general to ask where they were, but Sheaffe sent him to see Lieutenant Colonel Heathcote for instructions. It appears Eustace's 8th came up next with Lieutenant Colonel Chewett and a contingent of militia on their heels. Thomas Plucknett also reached the garrison with his shipwrights and others about this time. Though armed, they were certainly the least prepared for battle and must have made a motley sight. At least for Superintendent Plucknett it was his first chance to show off his dazzling epaulettes on some genuinely martial service. A portion of the artificers were put under the command of Daniel Daverne, a clerk in the quarter master general's department. Captain William Jarvie was there too, having just returned to York with three batteaux full of militia uniforms and medical supplies. He took command of his company of Incorporated Militia from his lieutenant, Thomas Humberstone.

And the volunteers turned out, some of whom did not wait for orders. Donald McLean, though no youngster and with no known military background, was there and immediately attached himself to McNeale's grenadiers. So, it seems, did sixteen-year-old George Jarvis, militia adjutant general Stephen Jarvis's son. Seeking a commission as a "gentleman volunteer" in the British army, he had fought at Queenston Heights, witnessing Brock's death, and ending up briefly as a prisoner of war. His father later said that he was at home at York in April and that Sheaffe himself assigned a section of McNeale's grenadiers to young Jarvis's personal command. This is highly unlikely, but does suggest that he too hurried along with them. And so did Sheriff John Beikie and his son Donald. Alexander Wood arrived, armed and ready to defend the town. It was reputed that fifteen-year-old Allan Napier MacNab and his father also turned out with arms as did Quetton St. George and two other young gentlemen volunteers, Donald McDonell and John Mathewson.[25]

As the grenadiers and volunteers marched off to oppose the landing, the guns in the batteries prepared for action. There was little chance of even the old 18-pdrs. in the Western Battery having any effect, since the nearest warship and the boats crawling towards shore were at least 1,200 yards further west and the uncut forest

Upper Canada militia. Only a portion of the militia uniforms ordered during the winter reached York by 27 April, so most of the citizen-soldiers went into battle dressed in their workaday clothing. Many of the officers had probably outfitted themselves suitably and some of the rank and file may have worn, old uniforms handed down from the regular regiments. (Parks Canada)

covered them. Whether Sheaffe thought of it, or someone made the suggestion, a third condemned gun, an ancient 12-pdr., was hauled out on its improvised carriage about this time.[26] Where it was put into action was never specified; maybe it ended up at an empty embrasure in the Government House Battery.

After another pause, the general gave his next orders, which were for everyone on hand to form up in column, ready for the advance. There were between 300 and 400 men under arms and they were slowly moved into place and halted, waiting for the others. Lieutenant Colonel Heathcote and his Royal Newfoundland corps formed the van, followed by Eustace's 8th, then Chewett and Allan with whatever parts of the 1st and 3rd York and 1st Durham were present, Jarvie's Incorporated infantry, Plucknett's artificers and the rest of volunteers. The one remaining 6-pdr. was finally rolled out as part of the column, possibly under the hands of Lieutenant William Jarvis's Incorporated Artillery (not surprisingly, accounts of the battle would forever confuse the two officers with nearly identical names, Jarvie and Jarvis).

By the time Sheaffe led the column past the Half Moon Battery, the sounds of scattered musketry up the shore had been heard for more than half an hour. Now the rattle of shots increased in tempo, interspersed with the thuds of a few controlled volleys. The battle was on and the main strength of the British/Canadian force was only just beginning its advance.

The American seamen in the batteaux carrying Benjamin Forsyth's riflemen ashore lay on their oars long enough for the first boats that had taken elements of the Fifteenth Infantry off the *Madison* to get within 200 yards of shore also. The rifle flotilla had drifted half a mile or more west of the old fort and Major Givins's warriors darted along the bank to keep up with them.

Finally, Forsyth felt the time was right and asked the oarsmen to dig in deep and reach shore as fast as possible. It took only minutes and in the meantime, as the North Carolinian sharpshooters reckoned themselves close enough to hit their marks, they began their independent and deliberate shooting from the boats. Walnut stock against jaw, eye squinting along the barrel to the bead, seeking a target in the brush, waiting for the roll of the boat, smooth squeeze on trigger … *cr-ack!* Given their tight quarters, they probably worked in pairs, one man loading, while the other methodically made his shot count, then exchanging weapons. And when they felt the boat scrape against gravel and grind to a stop, they sprang over the gunwales, scampered up the bank and disappeared into the foliage overlooking the eastern rim of Humber Bay. They spread out in what one of the officers described as a "wood which was a very thick growth of young timber."[27]

190 CAPITAL IN FLAMES

The vanguard of General Sheaffe's defence was Givins's group of Mississauga, Ojibwa and Chippawa warriors. Although they shot at the Americans with muskets and even a few rifles, they were instantly recognized as "Indians" by their mode of dress and style of fighting.[28] With an April chill in the morning air, they probably wore long buckskin coats over buckskin leggings and breechcloths, cotton shirts, colourful sashes and moccasins. Their greased hair was spiked up or cut to leave a narrow swath known as a "roach" and adorned with feathers or wrapped in an embroidered band bearing silver brooches. Loops and other ornaments hung from their ears and gaudy necklaces lay over their coat fronts. They wore rings on their fingers and bands of silver around their arms. Their heads and faces and bodies were painted according to each individual's taste and they appeared as savage as their reputations. Of all the men involved in the battle, the natives fought in the least regular manner.[29] They had no rank and file, no facings and steps, depending instead on their time-worn skills of pursuing a prey and getting within range for a sure kill. Major Givins led them to the fray, but his control of the force was tenuous at best for the warriors viewed battle as a highly individual affair.

The natives were up against a foe on 27 April who blended a warrior's natural-born skill in the forest with the determination of the best light infantry in any regular army. Armed with their Harper's Ferry rifles, Forsyth's men rapidly deployed in a scattered formation among the bushes, trees and forest waste, penetrating inland rather than sticking to the edge of the beach. Their green coats with black facings, green pants and black hats topped by green feathers merged with the pine and balsam and went almost undetected behind the thin veil of broad leaves that were just beginning to open in this late-arriving spring.[30] The yellow cord and plate on a shako might have caught an eye, but only briefly as the wearer dodged behind cover, silently exchanging signals with his nearby mates.

In the accounts of the day, the action between the men under Forsyth and Givins received little notice. And it appears that only one native memoir of the incident was recorded, this being recited by a man named John York, who died in 1916 at the age of ninety-seven on the Rama Reserve near Lake Simcoe. "All our men got ready on the shore and they could see the American boats coming towards where they were," York said, repeating the words of his grandfather, who had been there as one of the warriors.[31] "When the boats came in close our men began to shoot and kept up a hot fire all day long, and killed many." As his remembrance of the duration of the fight revealed, the decades had altered the facts in his grandfather's tale, which also had native warriors attacking under the American flag in place of the riflemen. They surrounded Givins's warriors

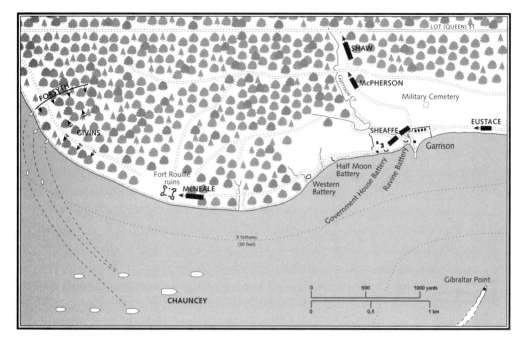

The Battle of York, Tuesday, 27 April 1813, 7:00 a.m.

1. The first wave of American troops heads for shore and is blown off course, landing west of Fort Rouillé. Givins's warriors engage them. Forsyth's Rifles engage the natives.
2. Sheaffe sends Shaw and some militia to guard Lot Street and McPherson's Glengarries follow.
3. McNeale leads his grenadiers toward the scene of action.
4. Sheaffe remains at the garrison while reinforcements march to join him.

and shot one of their chiefs, whose men gave him a *coup de grace* to prevent him falling into enemy hands. Others discovered a dead American soldier and dragged him back to their camp, where they butchered him and ate his flesh, according to John York's oral history.

What actually happened resembled parts of John York's tale. Forsyth's people outnumbered the Mississauga, Ojibwa and Chippawa and began to inflict casualties on them, gradually pushing them back toward Fort Rouillé. It was a murderous game of hide and seek among the trees, and as the minutes went by, the warriors' resolve slackened and then dissolved. One of their chiefs did indeed fall, mortally wounded, while another of the lead men and six or eight others were wounded or killed. None of their names were recorded except that of a warrior called Yellowhead, who was said to have received a mortal wound and was buried at a point up on Yonge Street. The fighting got too severe for the natives to stand

and, as one account discreetly reported, they "retreated through the woods."[32] John York's grandfather sadly admitted that, finding themselves surrounded, "they all ran away for their lives."[33] Sheriff Beikie's version of the retreat was blunter and slanted by bitter prejudice: "the Indians took fright ran way and never stopt 'till they got to Matchedash [on Georgian Bay]."[34] Nevertheless, the first skirmish in the woods lasted long enough for the next elements of the contest to converge.

Having discharged their military passengers, Sailing Masters Francis Mallaby in the *Conquest* and Joseph Stevens in the *Ontario* were now free to provide some support for the men on shore; at some point during the battle Mallaby gave up command to Lieutenant Jesse Elliott, who obtained permission from Chauncey to leave the *Madison,* and take a more active role in the battle.[35] They could have slipped their cables, leaving them fastened to buoys for later retrieval, but both men knew they would need the hooks, so their forecastle men worked hard to get them aweigh, while others made sail and prepared the heavy guns for action. The *Conquest* mounted long guns on circles, a 6-pdr. and two 24-pdrs., while the *Ontario* had a 12-pdr. and 32-pdr. The schooners got underway, fell to the westward a little and then began to crawl back inshore against the headwind out of the east to a place where they could see the enemy on the road above the bank. Down dropped the bowers again, with perhaps stream anchors paid out to stabilize the vessels. The guns were veered around to face the shore, and when all was ready, the crews began blasting salvoes of grape shot toward the shore.

Zebulon Pike's former regiment, the Fifteenth, was to back up the Rifles and so it did, in sections, pulling for the land and coming under fire. Captain John Scott claimed that his boat, carrying between thirty and forty men, was the second one to strike the Canadian shore at a point between 300 and 400 yards west of the clearing.[36] By that time Scott's company had already experienced the startling realities of warfare. Two men in their boat were hit and fell overboard. Lieutenant Alexander PerLee and five others were wounded.

Ned Myers, seaman on the *Scourge,* was in the middle of it, having volunteered to handle an oar. "I confess frankly I did not like the work at all," he recounted. "It is no fun to pull in under a sharp fire, with one's back to his enemy and nothing but an oar to amuse himself with. The shot flew pretty thick, and two of our oars were split."[37] At least the soldiers whom he had considered less than inspiring up to this point earned his respect. "They became wide awake, pointed out to each other where to aim, and many of them actually jumped into the water, to get the sooner to shore."

More platoons of the Fifteenth joined Scott's men, each boat grounding at a different spot, owing to the wind, the waves, the frantic last moments. The one carrying the party under Captain John Hoppock landed right after Scott's, but

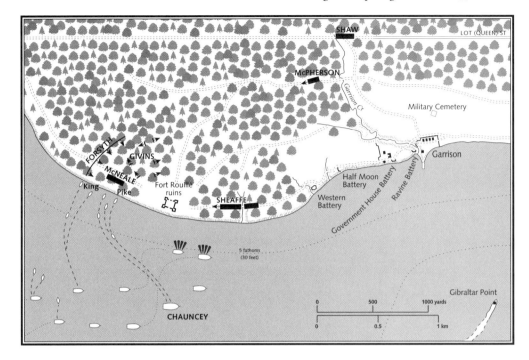

The Battle of York, 7:20 a.m.

1. Americans continue to land in waves. Forsyth's Rifles engage McNeale's grenadiers. Givins's warriors withdraw.
2. Sheaffe gathers militia and regulars and marches toward the scene of action.
3. Chauncey's schooners enter the action by firing at British troops.
4. McPherson leaves Shaw and marches toward the sound of battle.

the captain had been badly wounded in the thigh and slumped down in the stern. Hoppock's lieutenant, also named John Scott, abruptly found himself in command of the company. Major William King arrived and took charge on the beach, where some of Captain Henry Van Delsen's men were soon wading ashore.

When the Fifteenth tried to mount the bank, they discovered what Captain Scott described as "the woods filled with Regulars, Militia and Indians."[38] He was mistaken, for no one but Neal McNeale's 8th Foot and the town volunteers had joined the fight at this point. After their hurried march up the lake road through the forest, past Rouillé and into the forest again, the grenadiers had little time to compose themselves before they were hotly engaged. Some of the warriors may have come back past their position, pursued by the relentless riflemen, whose fingernail-sized bullets promptly began seeking out the red coats of the grenadiers. Almost immediately Neal McNeale was shot through the head and died on the spot.[39]

From the quarterdeck of the *Madison*, General Pike watched the Rifle Regiment go ashore and then the first of the Fifteenth, who landed under a hail of fire. The rest of the regiment was still disembarking from the flagship when Pike announced, "By God, I can't stay here any longer!" And turning to his staff officers, he said, "Come. Jump into the boat!"[40] Captains Jones and Nicholson stepped forward and so did Lieutenant Donald Fraser, following Pike over the side and down into the boat Chauncey had delegated for his express use. Henry Dearborn and his aide, Lieutenant Colonel Samuel Conner, did not join them.[41] At some point that morning the old general had let the young general know that he would hold command of the expedition on shore while his superior observed his progress from the ship. As Dearborn later explained to Secretary of War John Armstrong, he put the attack in Pike's hands "from a conviction that he fully expected it, and would be much mortified at being deprived of the honour, which he highly appreciated."[42]

Pike and his staff went off to battle in high spirits. As their boat closed with the beach, "the balls whistled gloriously; probably their number was owing to seeing so many officers in the boat," recalled Lieutenant Fraser, "but we laughed at their clumsy efforts as we pressed forward with well-pulled oars."[43]

It was the grenadiers of the 8th Foot who fired the volleys at Pike's boat and the others crawling to shore. They appear to have been formed on the roadway and near the edge of the bank overlooking the narrow beach, and by this time were fighting a desperate action on two fronts. Forsyth's Rifles were coming into range, if not into sight, to the west and north and the Fifteenth was landing to the south. There were no reinforcements anywhere close behind them. Robert Beveridge, the sergeant major of the company, and probably the best foot soldier of this elite group, was shot and killed right after McNeale went down.[44] Others were falling too, at a shocking rate. Having advanced so willingly with the grenadiers, Donald McLean realized he was in a situation for which he had no training whatsoever. He must have struggled to load and fire with the others until, suddenly, some invisible force knocked him off his feet. McLean lay there, struggling for breath, the green world spinning above him, the numbness swallowing him up, and he died. Patrick Hartney, a resident of the town and barrack master at the garrison, had joined the grenadiers also and barely eluded McLean's fate. One ball perforated his right leg, while another drove into his right thigh and a third tore the skin off his other thigh. He collapsed in agony.[45]

As they were instructed, the Fifteenth Infantry went ashore with bayonets fixed and pikes in hand. They had been told not to load their muskets, or the rifles carried by a small portion of the regiment (some of the men in the Sixteenth also had rifles). Once there were enough of the men on the beach to form

Donald McLean (d. 1813). McLean was a long-time resident of York and was both a magistrate and the clerk of the Legislative Assembly. He believed the successful defence of Upper Canada in 1812 had been "owing to the Mutual confidence the Militia and the regular Forces have in each other."[14] (TRL, T31590)

up into platoons, Captain Scott and the other officers, under the direction of Major Swan, ordered them to climb up the bank and charge the enemy with bayonets and pikes levelled. This they did with their officers leading the way only to come face to face with the grenadiers, who fired a volley and surged forward with pointed steel. Scott later wrote, "we fell back below the bank, to the brink of which they advanced and fired a volley at, or rather, over us for I do not know that they killed anyone at the time."[46] Some British bullets had found their mark, however. Lieutenant Moses Bloomfield had been shot in the head as he climbed the bank and was dying in a crumpled heap on the shore. Five others of the Fifteenth were killed outright, while some, such as Captain Hoppock, would succumb to their wounds in a short time.

Swan called for everyone to load their muskets and, when they were ready, it was back up the bank again, but this time with a different tactic in mind. "We just raised our heads over the brink and took deliberate aim," John Scott explained. "The balls flew as thick as Large Drops of rain at the commencement of a Shower."[47] Further down the beach, Pike had arrived and taken command of those around him. He had them form in platoons, load their pieces, climb up to the woods and get back into their platoons, ready for fire by volley and advance with bayonet and pike.

By then the toll had risen too high. The grenadiers were being cut to ribbons and Forsyth's riflemen had done most of the damage. The story was told afterwards that among the first of the fourteen men in the Rifle Regiment killed that morning was the company's armourer, a man respected for his talent with rifles and loved for his nature. With all the cunning of the clever leader he was,

Panorama. This panorama of the Battle of York, painted by Owen Staples, distorts distance, proportion and the number of vessels in Chauncey's squadron, but still presents a striking impression of the flow of the battle on land and lake. (TRL, T10271)

Forsyth turned his rage, and that of his men, to advantage. The major "continued, through the action, to move to and fro, armed only with a light sword, immediately in the rear of his men, pointing with an earnest solemnity that partook both of sorrow and anger, to one rifleman after another, some one of the enemy, and exclaiming that he was the man who had killed the favourite armorer."[48]

With one end of their skirmishing line anchored at a point to the west of where the grenadiers stood, the green-coated woodsmen from North Carolina spread out to the north and west with the intent of cutting off the British escape route, while keeping up a continuous and unrelenting fire. It was too much for the grenadiers to bear. Their casualties were literally outnumbering the men who were unhurt. No subaltern ever received credit for ordering a retreat. Lieutenants Edward Finch, Henry Hill and George Nuttall were all present at York that day but events seem to have devolved out of their control. As the surviving grenadiers tried to hold their position and protect their wounded, Forsyth's men moved in so close and were so effective in their fire that the unheard-of happened. The best company in the 1st Battalion of the 8th Foot lost its composure. The men broke ranks and they fled.[49]

All during the engagement in the woods the air had been filled with the constant rattle of small arms, the shouts of men, the war cries of Givins's party and the blare of Forsyth's trumpet as he directed the movement of his men. As the grenadiers turned their backs and ran, Forsyth peeled out a measure of victory and the spirits of his comrades rose to a higher notch. The riflemen pressed forward along with the Fifteenth and the handful of the Sixteenth Infantry who had made it to shore.[50] Meanwhile more waves of attackers arrived. Lieutenant Alexander Fanning's company of Third Artillery was wrestling two field guns onto the beach and looking for a way to get them up the bank. Major Abraham Eustis and men of the Light Artillery arrived, equipped to fight as infantry. And the others followed in what was evolving into a nearly letter-perfect amphibious assault.

It was at this point that the van of Sheaffe's column entered the fray. It emerged from the woods into the clearing by Fort Rouillé and the general ordered the companies to deploy into a line formation. The Newfoundland Fencibles were in the centre, Eustace's 8th was on the left by the lake, and, presumably, some of the militia, artificers and volunteers were on the right or in the rear; for some reason Sheaffe had left two dozen or more of the militia to guard the entrance to the woods near the Western Battery. When the general gave the word to advance, Rowland Heathcote led his men across the 30-acre clearing, around the mounds of the old fort and toward the sound of battle. Whether they penetrated the forest on the other side of the clearing or not, they soon beheld the grenadiers struggling toward them and let them pass through their ranks. By then the Fencibles were under fire from Pike's infantry and Forsyth's overpowering sharpshooters. The British fired back, but when their casualties began to mount at a surprising rate, Heathcote ordered a withdrawal.

The Newfoundland Fencibles fell back across the clearing. General Sheaffe stepped up and rallied them, urging them to renew their attack. They stopped, collected themselves and moved forward again. About this time Captain McPherson and his Glengarries arrived on the scene.[51] He had finally given up on the insistence of old General Shaw about a better route to the beach and had retraced his steps and let the sound of battle guide him. His green-coated lights joined the line.

Eustace's detachment had marched forward with Heathcote, covering the left flank. Here they were exposed to blasts of grape shot from one of the schooners, although rough lake conditions made it difficult to fire with much accuracy. Positioned as they were, the men of the 8th were soon exchanging fire with a party of American infantry proceeding along the lakeshore under cover of the embankment. Intent on outflanking the British, the Americans were stopped in their tracks by Eustace's volleys and backed off to safety.[52] It was a small victory for the British, one of very few that day.

Meanwhile the Rifle Regiment was gathering near the edge of woods at the clearing and the Fifteenth was coming on in style. One of the last boatloads carried the regiment's colours and Major King had them unfurled and told the musicians to do their best. Led by what was probably a cream-coloured regimental flag, simply decorated with the unit's name, and a deep blue banner, the National Standard, bearing the soaring eagle and a constellation of stars, the Fifteenth stepped forward to a rousing version of *Yankee Doodle*. Such pageantry only made the American fire more intense and once more the British regulars withered and began to slowly retrace their steps eastward across the clearing.

Again Sheaffe tried to press his men forward but without effect.[53] They had been stunned by the force of the American attack and had left their dead, dying and wounded behind, dozens of them. Some of the wounded were helped off the field; sixty-eight-year-old Lieutenant John de Koven of the Royal Newfoundland was one of these, shot through the foot. The Glengarries probably remained in skirmish formation, covering the main body.

The role of the militia in this stage of the fighting appears to have been minimal, although they were bloodied too. Captain William Jarvie was close to the action and unlucky enough to have a bullet slice through the joint of his right

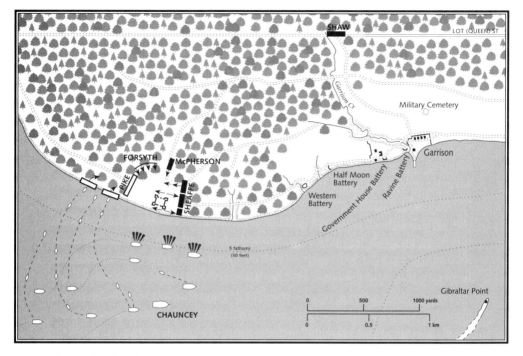

The Battle of York, 7:40 a.m.

1. Americans continue to land in waves.
2. Pike and Forsyth engage Sheaffe's force, which attacks across the clearing at Fort Rouillé.
3. McPherson's Glengarries arrive on the battlefield.

wrist while he suffered another wound to his leg.[54] He fell to his knees and someone had the presence of mind to strip off his coat, tear open his sleeve and apply a tourniquet quickly enough to save him from bleeding to death. Private Daniel Murray and at least two of Plucknett's men were said to have received their mortal wounds in action, and they may have occurred at this time, just as Private Andrew Borland may have received his six wounds in the clearing. Otherwise, there were few, if any, other casualties among the militia as none but a handful of them got close enough to the Americans to suffer as the regulars did.[55] Meanwhile, half a mile to the north, a portion of the militia was listening to the roar of battle and staying put with Æneas Shaw, who never saw fit to rush forward and who, it appears, was never summoned to the action by General Sheaffe.

Sir Roger ordered a retreat and the column formed up and proceeded back down the roadway through the thousand-yard span of forest between the clearing and the Western Battery. It was said that Sheaffe and Loring, his aide, were the last to leave the field.[56]

John Strachan had a different view of events. He had gone home, where he could leave his horse in safe surroundings, and then returned to the garrison and from there to the Western Battery. The enemy vessels and the small boats were either out of range or out of sight completely from that post and he mused on how poorly the battery had been located. Then he saw the first of the wounded and their mates struggling down the forest road and went to help them get to the garrison and the hospital quarters there. He stayed to assist the surgeons and then went out again to find out what was happening.

Strachan beheld the troops retreating out of the forest, some of them gathering around the distant battery. And then he noticed "the General in front," which later prompted him to record his thoughts in two words, "disagreeable presages."[57]

The chaplain hurried forward to find out what had happened.

Above **The landing place today.** The American landing place was near the intersection of Dowling Avenue and Lakeshore Boulevard, just west of the Canadian National Exhibition grounds. The fiercest fighting of the day happened here and continued toward the clearing around Fort Rouillé. The wind turbine on the right is adjacent to where the clearing was. The western edge of the town was about where the CN Tower, in the distance on the left, stands today.

Fort Rouillé. Erected in the 1880s near the west end of the CNE grounds, this monument marks the location of Fort Rouillé. (Photographs by Robert Malcomson)

CHAPTER 11

"The Stars are going up!"[1]

MARCH TO THE GARRISON

Major General Henry Dearborn remained on the U.S. Ship *Madison*, watching and listening to the battle raging on the wooded embankment along the shore that someone later called "the hill." It had started around 7:00 A.M. and the last of the steady firing had ended by 8:00. He saw the British retreat from the clearing at Fort Rouillé and Major Benjamin Forsyth's Rifles scurry across the opening to spread out on the edge of the woods nearer the British position. He could hear the fifes and drums of the Fifteenth U.S. Infantry following the regiment's colours towards the ruins of the old fort and perhaps he even picked out Brigadier General Zebulon Pike and his staff. The view prompted Dearborn to lend his expertise to the expedition and he scribbled a note, advising Pike not to advance past the clearing until his entire force was on shore and ready for battle.[2] He sent his instructions in the hands of his aide-de-camp, Lieutenant Colonel Samuel Conner. Dearborn's advice made good sense. After such a fierce firefight and an apparently successful landing, a young commander like Pike might have been tempted to rush on after his foe. And who knew what the British might have waiting for him in that next long stretch of forest?

It was a major undertaking to land nearly 1,800 men and all their equipment and provisions. Given that eight field guns went ashore along with the necessary ammunition wagons and accessories, it probably took seven or eight "lifts" to complete the task. The movements of the boats, their loading and unloading had to be carefully marshalled, but the officers of the two services who played this vital role in the operation went more of less unnoticed. Only Brigade Major Charles Hunter received credit for organizing the troops as they came ashore and sending them to form up in the marching order laid out in advance by Pike.[3]

Rarely was it ever mentioned afterward that this was the first-ever combined operation of the U.S. Army and U.S. Navy.

The late-comers to the beach did not have to face the savage yells of the aboriginal warriors or the stalwart defence of Captain Neal McNeale's grenadiers. Perhaps they took heart when they saw the bodies of their enemy strewn among the trees or at the edge of the road where they had been dragged. Some must have felt pity for the battered redcoats groaning in agony and appealing for help, and maybe offered them sips of water from their canteens. Many probably tried to ignore the sight and talked with their mates about what they themselves would soon be facing. There was plenty of time for such speculations as the last of the troops, the federal volunteers under Lieutenant Colonel Francis McClure, did not appear until after 9:00. Unlike the others who arrived in the later waves, they were bloodied, or at least one of them was. This was Lieutenant Baptist Irvine, the ardent Republican editor of the *Baltimore Whig* and proud second-in-command to Captain Stephen Moore of the Baltimore Volunteers.[4] Either he had stumbled in getting out of the boat, or one of the infantrymen near him had, because somehow a bayonet sliced upward into his armpit and out at his collar bone when the closest enemy was nearly a mile in the distance. He bled profusely and fainted dead away.

The time that it took for the Americans to assemble allowed the regulars and militia under Major General Sir Roger Sheaffe to complete their withdrawal to safer ground. They came out of the forest at a spot near the Western Battery where the road climbed up from the creek bed. The two obsolete 18-pdr. long guns, and perhaps a carronade, were mounted there, the long guns, *en barbette*, that is on raised platforms that could be traversed or swivelled in a wide arc of fire above the rampart. The soldiers passed the battery, some of them struggling on toward the hospital at the garrison, others coming to a stop, a number simply walking away.

The Reverend John Strachan strode into the midst of the men, curious to know what had occurred at the landing point, why the shooting had stopped, what was going to happen next. What he heard eventually ended up on paper in staccato point form: "They had no orders – no plan of attack – Capt. M [McPherson?] declared there was no plan – no future point of resistance mentioned."[5]

Strachan helped some of the wounded to the hospital at the garrison. Ready and waiting to treat the wounded were Surgeons William Hackett of the 8th Foot and Grant Powell of the Provincial Marine; William Lee, the hospital mate was also on hand. They had been joined by William Baldwin, who came forth to offer his medical skills, as did Dr. Eleazer Aspinwall, a shopkeeper in the town.

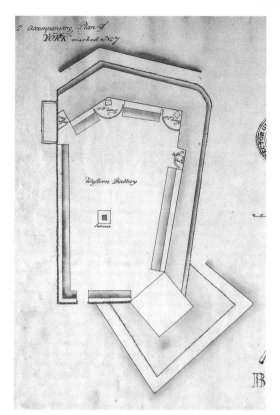

The Western Battery.
Following the battle, the Western Battery was enlarged and strengthened. The plan for these improvements suggests the arrangement of guns during the battle: two long guns and one carronade on traversing platforms. Note the later location of a furnace for heating shot in the centre behind the guns and the addition of a stationary field magazine in the top left corner. (LAC, NMC 5431)

Apothecary Joseph Cawthra also arrived to help the surgeons.[6] Their operating equipment, the knives, saws, forceps, tourniquets, splints, lint, bandages and medicines would soon be in urgent service.

Word spread about the confusion at the battle scene. Sheriff John Beikie and his son Donald had been with the grenadiers and escaped with their lives back to where Sheaffe had assembled the regulars and militia in the clearing. After this force was repulsed by the Americans, Beikie somehow missed the order to withdraw and came upon Major James Givins, who advised him to move away for fear of being captured. "Everyone fled the best way he could," remembered Beikie. "I got safe to the Government House battery."[7] It was there that the sheriff noticed that a rifle bullet had passed through the cape of his coat.

Corporal Isaac Wilson had spent the first hours of the morning waiting with part of Samuel Ridout's company, 3rd York, at the Town Blockhouse. The order for them to come to the scene of the action arrived some time after Captain Eustace's 8th Foot had left, and as they hurried through the town they saw the flashes of the guns in the American schooners that had closed in on the shore. They met men heading away from the front who told them quickly about the engagement at the landing, and then they encountered "the wounded men, some [going] one way and some another, such a bloody sight made me wish for the first time that I was safe at 'Birkbank' again."[8]

Lieutenant Ely Playter, 3rd York, arrived at the garrison about the same time. As per Sheaffe's orders of the night before, he had ridden out at dawn with a party to check on the sentries on the Scarborough Bluffs. When they got there and learned that there was no sign of any enemy movement to the east, Playter and the others climbed into their saddles again and rushed back to the town. "We came back double-Quick near all the way and was not a little wearied when we came to the Garrison," he wrote in his diary.[9] Like Wilson, Playter listened to what had happened, saw the wounded and then "I came with some other officers to the Barracks, and we got each of us a Musket, as every one expected a severe attack upon the enemy when they advanced from the Woods." This was not routine conduct because a commissioned officer, even in the militia, traditionally went into battle armed only with his sword. Taking up firearms as they did showed that Playter and the others fully expected that a desperate fight was about to be waged and they intended to be a part of it.

Some of the militia who had advanced under Chewett and Allan with Sheaffe's column had drifted from the scene, but others were taking their places. The alarm spread since Monday night was answered and militiamen who had not been on duty at the garrison arrived there during the battle. Major Samuel Wilmot and Captain James Fenwick of the 1st York, for instance, do not appear to have served at the fort during the winter, but the record shows that they were present on 27 April, just as the record shows that dozens of other officers and rank and file rallied to the cause. No one made a list of them at the time, nor was this possible in the chaos of the moment, but their presence was confirmed and they counted among those who joined the likes of Ely Playter and prepared to oppose the enemy with everything they had.[10]

It was nearly 10:00 and at least six of the American schooners had found positions opposite the four batteries and were firing away at them with round shot and grape. The British and Canadians were returning the fire, although the consensus was that their handful of 6- and 12-pdr. long guns and their short-range 18-pdr. carronades were a poor match for the heavy naval 24s and 32s that opposed them.[11] Only the long 18-pdrs. in the Western Battery seemed capable of inflicting much hurt on the ships. The two shot furnaces were in operation, the only advantage that the British artillery had over their enemy.

Most of the regulars and some of the militia assumed that the Western Battery was a rallying place and so they gathered near it. A number of them also crowded into the battery or stood up on the breastwork to watch the fall of the

Shot oven. This portable shot oven and its equipment, on display at Historic Fort York, date to a period after the War of 1812. The two shot ovens, or "furnaces," used in the fortifications at York during the battle were stationary structures probably fashioned of bricks manufactured at the town. (Photograph by Robert Malcomson)

shot. There appears to have been no one there with commanding authority, and sufficient knowledge, to keep the place clear so that the gunners could do their work without hindrance. Such an officer would certainly have prevented a second fatal error. A limber was wheeled up and the box of cartridges taken down and placed adjacent to one of the guns; the reason for this nearly unheard-of break with protocol was never explained. Perhaps someone thought that if the limber stayed at its regular position, fifty or so yards behind the battery, it might be hit by a lucky shot from one of the schooners. Such would have been much preferable to what actually took place.

About this incident, nearly all accounts agree.[12] The Number Five gunner for one of the guns allowed the port-fire he used to ignite the charge in the vent to come in contact with the box of cartridges. He either threw it aside or held it behind his back without realizing, in the crowded conditions, what was sitting there. To make it worse, the box was open and in an instant its contents exploded with such force that anyone standing on the breastwork was sent flying and one of the massive 18-pdrs. was knocked over on its side. Ten or more men were killed outright, their dismembered corpses presenting a horrid spectacle, while twice that number were shattered and burned black.

In the shock of the aftermath, men picked themselves up and tried to figure out what had happened. One of these was Alexander Wood, who had made it back from the fight at the landing only to narrowly miss a violent death again.[13] The blast threw him onto Donald Beikie, who suffered a few scratches on his

York garrison, 1804. In 1813, the garrison at York, not yet known as "Fort York," had changed very little from 1804 when Lieutenant Sempronius Stretton painted this view showing the blockhouse, cottage-like barracks, stockade and interior parade ground. Note the Union Jack on the flag pole. (LAC, C014905)

hands, while William Jarvis, the lieutenant commanding the Incorporated Artillery, was hit in the right eye by debris. The deaths that day of three men from the Royal Artillery and two others who were wounded were probably due to the explosion. One poor suffering fellow was carted to the hospital in a wheelbarrow, his limbs dangling over the sides as if every bone in them had been broken. Others staggered forward, dazed and deafened, smoke rising off their coats, their skin charred and hair scorched into frizzy mops.

After the explosion in the battery, it was widely noticed that the ranks of the militia began to thin as men left the scene without comment. Although some expected a stand to be made at the ravine just beyond the battery, many of the farmers, millers and shopkeepers who formed the York regiments (and Durham militia who were present) were no longer willing to fight. No officer stepped forward at this time to rally them or order them to stand their ground. They did not all leave, however. Isaac Wilson was curious about the enemy and ventured into the wood to examine the warships more carefully.[14] It almost cost him his life because he soon spied a number of green uniforms moving among the trees and realized they were the riflemen he had heard about. Wilson's interest in the navy vanished and he fled while rifle bullets whacked into the trees around him. He did not stop until he had reached the safety of the Government House Battery.

The regulars had no choice in the matter. Without orders to the contrary, they remained where they were. Lieutenant Colonel Philip Hughes of the Royal Engineers and Lieutenant Philip Ingouville of the Newfoundland Fencibles took charge of the battery. They had the dead and wounded removed and went about getting the guns back into action. Perhaps Captain McPherson took the initiative to spread his men on the verge of the woods as a protective screen. Lieutenant Colonel Heathcote kept his thinned ranks in place, probably restocking their cartridge boxes.

The surviving grenadiers were taken into the detachment under Captain Eustace, dismayed to realize how many familiar faces were not among them anymore. Little did this brave bunch know that their fatal clash with the Americans would someday be twisted into a legend. A story would be created that their company suffered its extraordinary losses when it plunged through the ice of a pond while retreating from battle, despite the fact that there was no ice on nearby ponds in late April 1813 and the legendary body of water was two miles west of the battlefield. Still, they would be linked to Grenadier Pond, lying in today's High Park and surrounded by a vast metropolis that would rise on the ground they had fought to hold.[15]

About this time, Quarter Master Bryan Finan of the Newfoundland Regiment advised his wife that she should take their children and leave the barracks.[16] This she did, going with the other women of the regiment to the house of one of the militia officers just north of the town. Young "P. Finan" had been witness to the retreat and the condition of survivors of the explosion in the battery and he was not satisfied to remain with his mother. As soon as she was distracted, he slipped away and headed back for the garrison.

A general exodus of the women, the young, the old and the infirm from York had begun. When William Baldwin went to the garrison to help in the hospital, his wife, Phoebe, organized a retreat from their home overlooking the dockyard.[17] She and the family's close friend Elizabeth Russell decided to combine their efforts and within a short time they had Russell's phaeton, a four-wheeled carriage, loaded with necessities until there was no room left for anyone to ride in it. As a result, Phoebe and her four sons, the youngest a two-year-old riding on the back of Mary-Warren Baldwin, her sister-in-law, set out on foot. With them went one of Phoebe's sisters, the invalid Major Fuller who had been staying with them, and Dr. Baldwin's seventy-two-year-old father, Robert, who had insisted on loading his musket and hurrying off to join the ranks earlier. Someone had been sent to bring him home and he reluctantly joined the cavalcade with the spinster Russell and her servants. Just two weeks away from his ninth birthday, the future politician Robert Baldwin trekked along with his family; if he had any remembrance of the event, it went unrecorded. They headed north toward a farm on Yonge Street owned by a close acquaintance, the old German Frederick von Horn, commonly known as "Baron de Hoen."

Grant Powell's wife, Elizabeth, quickly packed some belongings in their two-storey home on Duke Street, locked it and left with their six-year-old daughter, Anne Jane, and a servant. They walked about half a mile to John McGill's "cottage" a large residence on one of the park lots just to the west of modern Church Street.[18] There they were joined by Ann Strachan and her son, James. The chaplain had discovered her panicking at their home and had given her quick instructions to flee before he rushed back to the garrison.

James Givins's wife, Angelique, at her house almost a mile north of where the fighting had occurred, found herself the host to a number of the warriors whom the major had led into battle. The men were wounded and sought medical attention from her, leaving legendary blood stains on the dining room floor. Elizabeth Derenzy remained in her home too, refusing to abandon her ailing father, Prideaux Selby, whose mind was wandering in and out of consciousness. Penelope Beikie also stayed behind, not willing to leave "with my two poor fellows in the heat of the battle."[19] She prayed with earnest conviction, repeating a favourite psalm and believing that "He who strengthens the weak gave me more strength and fortitude than all the other females of York put together; for I kept my Castle when all the rest fled."

The formation of Pike's column took nearly an hour and a half and during this interval Commodore Isaac Chauncey decided to get in on the action. The *Madison* drew too much water to risk an approach close to the Canadian shore, and so to get a better look at his enemy's batteries he ordered up his gig's crew and left the ship. Under the direction of the commodore's coxswain, the seamen dug in with their long sweeps and drove the sleek craft through the water at a brisk rate, despite having to steer into the easterly headwind.

On the *Scourge* Ned Myers and his mates were having some "sharp work with the batteries, keeping up a steady fire."[20] They had returned to the schooner after dropping off the last of the troops on the beach trip and had then joined the line of vessels bombarding the British post, taking up an anchorage third from the front of the line. Several of the seamen had been killed or wounded during the landing operation and the battle with the British guns cost others their mess numbers. Midshipman John Hatfield was one of these. He was working the guns on the *Conquest* when a shot tore inboard from the Western Battery and sliced through his right thigh. Nothing could be done for him, and Lieutenant Jesse Elliott, who had left the flagship to command his former schooner, later wrote that young Hatfield lasted only twelve minutes and died without a groan.

Myers was in just as vulnerable a situation. He was a gun captain posted on the larboard side of the cramped quarterdeck and commanded "five negroes, strapping fellows, and as strong as jackasses."[21] Their piece was either a 4-pdr. or a 6-pdr. they had nicknamed the "Black Joke." When the cartridge box in the Western Battery blew up, everyone on the *Scourge* gave three cheers, thinking that a shot from one of the schooners had done the damage.

They had just returned to work when they heard more cheering from the vessels astern and turned to see Chauncey approaching in his gig. Though stout, Chauncey climbed nimbly aboard the schooner and received three cheers from the crew as Sailing Master Joseph Osgood greeted him. Moments later a hot shot glanced off the gunport near the stern just yards from where Chauncey and Osgood stood, carried away the rear trucks of the Black Joke's carriage and crashed through a stand of boarding pikes, which knocked down a seaman named Lemuel Bryant, whose clothes instantly caught fire. The flames were doused and he was passed below. Determined to stay in the fight, Myers's men pushed the damaged gun out of the way, unhooked its mate in the starboard port, picked it up and lugged it across to the fighting side of the schooner. In no time they had the tackles and breeching in place and renewed their firing, "That is quick work, my lads!"[22] Chauncey called out. The commodore remained on the *Scourge* for a short time and when he left Myers watched him go, later remembering, "the old man, he pulled through the fire as coolly as if it were a snow-balling scrape."

The American column began to move sometime around 10:00, the musicians setting the rhythm for an easy pace. Forsyth's riflemen were scattered among the trees ahead and on the left flank to guard against surprise, and behind them McClure's Volunteers were doing the same. It was a long procession, comprising more than 1,700 men, six field guns, all their auxiliary limbers and caissons and wagons for infantry ammunition as well, everything hauled by hand in the absence of horses. The column, marching in open order (with spaces between companies and guns), stretched more than a quarter of a mile.[23]

The Americans proceeded slowly along the lake road through the forest and met no opposition.[24] The road itself was difficult enough to travel on as it rose and fell through several ravines and what one officer described as swampy ground. The British had hurriedly destroyed the short bridges, but active hands soon wrestled fallen timber into place as improvised bridges so the guns and wagons could cross. To the right and ahead could be heard the heavy concussions of the cannonade between ship and shore, but in the woods only *Yankee Doodle* resonated among the maples and beech, the fir and spruce.

I n the Western Battery Hughes and Ingouville had given up trying to right the overturned gun; its platform and the timber floor upon which it sat were too badly damaged. Instead, they had the gunners who remained swivel the second 18-pdr. as far to the west as it would go when that necessity came.[25] In this way it could at least cover the road to the old fort. In the meantime, they turned it back to engage the U.S. Navy.

Only the regulars were left near the battery now. All the militia had melted away. Major William Allan ordered Lieutenant Playter to gather up what militia he could at the garrison.[26] Here, they were exposed to the naval grape and round shot that were knocking holes in the blockhouse, the barracks and stockade, prompting Playter to draw his men down beside the Garrison Creek behind the battery of 6-pdrs.

General Sheaffe was neither at the battery nor the garrison, but some place in between with only his aides, walking back and forth on a roadway said to be half a mile away from the troops. One officer after another approached him or one of his aides or messengers for instructions, but none were forthcoming. Sir Roger's longtime friend Justice William Powell wrote that he had given orders earlier "with his usual coolness," but about his lack of leadership at this point in the affair, he said nothing.[27] Others were less hesitant to criticize Sheaffe, asserting that he "kept too far from his troops after retreating from the woods, never cheered or animated them, nor showed by his personal conduct that he was hearty in the cause."[28]

Time slipped by as the general pondered his predicament. His initial attempt to stop the Americans had failed miserably. This day was not to be a replication of his attack on the undersized, worn-out American force at Queenston, which fired barely a volley before retreating in disarray. The well trained Americans under Pike, especially the murderously effective Rifle Regiment, had already sharply reduced Sheaffe's strength.

Perhaps Sir Roger saw an error of omission as he looked at the woods through which he knew the Americans were marching and wondered why no one had thought to block that road by felling the trees that surrounded it. And why had the trees in the ravine below the Western Battery and on its western bank not been cleared. Some of that timber might have been used to barricade the eastern lip of the ravine. A stand against the Americans might have been made there, with the battery securing the vulnerable left flank. In fact, Sheaffe might have collected his main body at that point in the first place while the natives and Glengarries harassed the Americans at the landing and as they advanced through the woods; the British skirmishers might have then retreated to the barricade. Then the enemy would have had to cross open ground, descend into the stream bed

William Chewett (1753-1849).
Lieutenant Colonel Chewett was fifty-nine years old at the time of the battle. One biographical sketch claims that, along with Captain Robert Loring, he was badly wounded during the explosion of the grand magazine, but the records of the day do not support this. The same sketch stated that his son, Lieutenant James Chewett, 3rd York, helped detonate the magazine.[15] (TRL, T17010)

and try to scale its other side in the face of mass fire from hundreds of regulars, militia and natives. A second line of defence might have been formed at the rampart behind Government House. But there is no evidence that any thought had been given to such tactics, nor the underlying principle that a wise general carefully chose the ground upon which he intended to meet the enemy.[29]

One of the many anecdotes that emerged days later came from Major General Æneas Shaw, who had gone with the garrison militia at Sheaffe's command to guard a road half a mile inland and apparently never returned to the garrison.[30] Shaw spread it around that Sir Roger had talked first thing that morning about retreating with his staff and leaving the troops under Shaw's command. Shaw claimed to have answered that he did not have the authority for it and that Sheaffe should take them with him. If such a thought had crossed Sheaffe's mind at dawn, then it returned as he contemplated his situation in veritable isolation. He does not seem to have made his final decision at this point, but he did issue some orders. As with everything else that day, however, he did so in piecemeal fashion, with little coordination and no clear evidence of careful forethought.

"We expected to have been ordered up to attack near [the] Batteries," Lieutenant Playter wrote in his diary, expressing what seemed to be the logical next step.[31] He and his men and other militia had moved into "the hollow" a short way up Garrison Creek where there were storehouses and there they waited for orders. Instead of being sent ahead they were surprised to hear around 12:00 that the regulars were falling back from the Western Battery. The militia stood there and watched the red-, green- and blue-coated soldiers march past Government House, down into the bed of Garrison Creek, across the bridge and up through

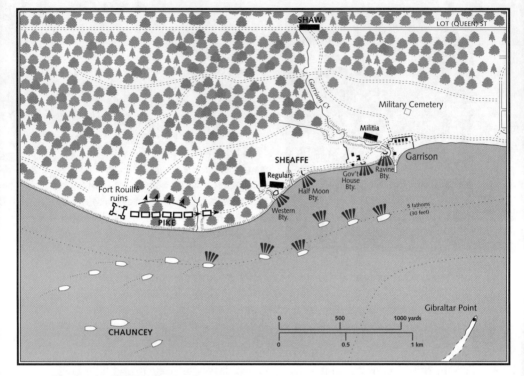

The Battle of York, 10:30 a.m.

1. Sheaffe has withdrawn from the battlefield. His regulars remain near the batteries. The remaining militia collect in Garrison Creek ravine.
2. Pike has assembled his line of march and proceeds towards the batteries.
3. The batteries and American schooners exchange fire.

the garrison without stopping to pick up any of their greatcoats, knapsacks or other belongings. Lieutenant Colonel Chewett or Major Allan attempted to form the militia into a column and follow, but once more there was confusion in the ranks and men drifted off, heedless of their officers.

Meanwhile the batteries had continued to exchange fire with the schooners, although the men in the Western Battery soon had to direct their attention elsewhere. The music of the American column was growing more distinct and its vanguard appeared coming down the road. The crew swivelled the old gun around on its platform and let fly with round shot, having no canister on hand and but a small supply of grape in the arsenal.[32] They had little effect on their enemy, who reported that nothing but a few pikes and bayonets were snapped off when the 18-pdr. balls ripped through the air overhead. Because of the way the gun was secured to its carriage, the gunners could not adjust its elevation and had to hope for some divine intervention to make a shot tell.

On the road Brigadier General Pike called a halt around 11:00 and asked his aide Fraser to go with one of the sergeants and make a reconnaissance of the Western Battery. Fraser reported that it was lightly manned, so Pike directed Captain John Walworth of the Sixth Infantry to assault the battery and carry it. This task Walworth eagerly accepted and he moved forward, deploying his men to make the attack. He later remembered that the British fired "two charges of canister and grape" as his company approached within 50 yards of the battery, but when they made the final dash down into the ravine and up the other side to climb the rampart and circle around behind it, they found no one there except four wounded men.[33] The others had cut and run. They had abandoned their mates, but had taken the time to push gunners' spikes into the vents of the weapons and bend them over in place with a couple of strong thrusts of the ramrod, rendering the guns inoperable.

When Pike received word that Walworth had secured the battery, he resumed the march and came into view of the garrison about 700 yards ahead across open ground. He could see a second battery, the Half Moon Battery, smaller in size than the first and situated on a slight rise of ground, its guns pointing toward the road over another small ravine. A second reconnaissance revealed that this position was also abandoned, and so the column took up its march again, advancing slowly until the van reached the Half Moon Battery.

The Americans were now within 400 yards of the curtain wall and, as Lieutenant Fraser recollected, "a fire was opened upon us of round and cannister."[34] The British regulars had taken the 6-pdr. field gun with them so this was almost certainly coming from the Government House Battery, where at least one embrasure opened to the west to allow one of the 12-pdrs. to fire along the edge of the common.

Since the first fire fight, events had unfolded very slowly. Noon came and went as it took nearly three hours for Pike's column to advance from the clearing to the garrison common. The procession halted again and Pike ordered Major Eustis to bring up his guns. Lieutenant Alexander Fanning already had a pair of Third Artillery field guns at the front of the column, but Pike had work for Eustis's heavier 12s. From where he stood, the general could see the Government House Battery on the edge of the embankment overlooking the lake, as well as the curtain wall and the roofs of Government House and the buildings adjacent to it. Angling northwards from the wall, the ground seemed to fall away (into Garrison Creek). There were two flags flying, one of them being the Royal Standard, the symbol of Sheaffe's headquarters, probably on a lofty pole next to Government House. A Union Jack flapped on a staff near the blockhouse in the garrison.[35]

Pike had no way of knowing what his enemy was doing and he took his time determining what next to do. There was every reason to suspect that the British general had massed his men behind the curtain and in the ravine and was just waiting for the Americans to get close enough. Sheaffe might have used the time since the first major action at the landing to arm and supply his force, readied to make a determined resistance at the rampart. Or perhaps he was keeping them concealed so as to spring a sudden, desperate charge.

It was indicative of Pike's competence that he decided to feel out his enemy's strength by asking Major Eustis to open fire on the garrison blockhouse. Eustis proposed that the lay of the land would allow him to "reverse the battery and fire under cover of it into the fort and block-house," meaning he would place his guns in front of the breastwork and direct his shots over it.[36] Pike agreed to the idea, and while the Light Artillery set up, he seems to have sent a reconnaissance party ahead as well. The rest of the infantrymen in the van he ordered "to lie close," stretching out on the ground to be less of a target for the British gun in the Government House Battery.[37] These men, and probably those of any party that went to reconnoitre, formed the four companies of Sixth Infantry and right behind them was the detachment of the Sixteenth. The detachments of the Fourteenth (with the small portion of the Thirteenth) and Twenty-first were further back. The Fifteenth had seen some hard going at the landing and had been placed at the end of the column while their brothers-in-arms got their chance to face the enemy. Forsyth's Rifles were also some distance to the rear, no doubt taking a break to eat and prepare for what they probably thought was going to be another bloody engagement.

Zebulon Pike selected a spot from which he could view the artillery at work and see its effects on the enemy. He sat down on the stump of a tree with his staff gathered around him. The tall and heavy-set Colonel Cromwell Pearce came up to watch the action and sat down on another stump fifteen paces away from the general.[38] They had time to discuss the situation briefly, speculating about what the British had in mind.

Chewett's militia in the Garrison Creek hollow had followed the British regulars down the road to town, but, as had been the case throughout the morning, there was a lack of order to the movement. Lieutenant Playter left the line to go to the barracks and get his greatcoat. Corporal Wilson hung back too, as did Private Joseph Shepherd, 3rd York, who may have been with Private Matthias Saunders, 1st York, one of the men who had answered the call to arms and had joined the gun crew at the Government House Battery. Captain Robert Loring had ridden back to Sheaffe's residence in a hurry to gather up whatever money and important papers he could lay his hands on. Sir Roger, it seems, had finally made a stark decision, and at the last moment without adequate thought about the inevitable results of it.

Among Sheaffe's hurried instructions was an order to Captain Tito LeLièvre of the Royal Newfoundland Regiment to blow up the grand magazine.[39] As the rear of the militia column left the garrison LeLièvre ran along the lakeshore below the Government House Battery, probably in company with a couple of trustworthy hands, one of whom may have been Ensign James Robins of the Glengarries. Theirs was a task fraught with extreme hazard, but which had to be done quickly because the enemy was in sight and obviously preparing to attack. And then there were the shots being fired from the American schooners standing off shore, any one of which might ricochet and hit the magazine at the right angle to strike a spark that would be fatal for the captain and his men.

The orders that Sheaffe had issued at Niagara the previous November had suggested that arrangements be made in advance to destroy arms and ammunition should a retreat be necessary, but, given the lack of planning that characterized almost everything else that morning, it is likely that LeLièvre had to improvise on the spot. Under ideal conditions, he would have been equipped with a *saucisson*, a long pipe made of heavy fabric with a diameter of about one and a half inches and packed with half a pound of powder per foot.[40] The record says nothing about how the British prepared the magazine for detonation, but in the absence of a *saucisson*, LeLièvre and his men probably opened casks of powder in the magazine, spilled their contents on to the floor and then laid a thick train of powder out the door and along the path. When LeLièvre determined the course of powder was long enough to give his men and him time to get under cover, he told the others to run and began making sparks by striking a piece of flint against steel or "snapping" an unloaded pistol above the powder. When a spark caught and the powder ignited and the flame went hissing away toward the magazine, the sixty-year-old captain took to his heels as fast as any man of that vintage could go.

Major Eustis's guns had fired their second round at the garrison when some riflemen approached. The evidence suggests they were Captain Stephen Moore with Corporal Thomas Hazelton and half a dozen privates, bringing up a British sergeant they had captured in the woods for interrogation by the general.[41] Lieutenant Fraser and Captains Benjamin Nicholson and Charles Jones, the other aides-de-camp, stood with Pike and began to ask the captive questions.

Captain Loring raced out of Government House with whatever money and papers he had been able to grab and climbed hurriedly into his saddle.

Eustis's 12s fired and sent rounds tearing eastward through the air. The wind blew the vast cloud of white smoke away.

Ely Playter encountered Mrs. Chapman, the woman who cooked for the officers, and anxiously advised her to follow the others in retreat.

Private Saunders and his friends hurriedly abandoned their gun and began hauling the ammunition wagon away.

Pike sat on the tree stump and listened to the sergeant's answers.

Playter left his quarters and passed through the garrison gate.

The hour had swung past 1:00 P.M.[42]

The powder train ran sparking through the door of the magazine.

In an instant 300 barrels of black powder were vaporized and transformed into a yellow-orange-red ball of flame that erupted through the upper storey, roof and sides of the magazine, blooming up into the air like some nightmarish mushroom.[43] It folded back down and into itself and up and out again, expanding further. And then the fireball was consumed by a pitch-black cloud of smoke that climbed up and around it, boiled out from its curves and stretched up into the sky. Stone, brick and clay, pulverized into dust, soared aloft in reddish brown and white sheets. Out of the fulminating mass flew rocks and pieces of timber streaking on a thousand different trajectories. These tendrils emerged from the billowing plume like rockets with tails of white and black.

The survivors later described the sight.

"It was more horrible, more awful, at the same time, more sublime, than my pen can portray."

"As it rose in a majestic manner it assumed the shape of a vast balloon."

"The noise of the explosion was tremendous. The earth shook and the sun was darkened, while the crashing of the rocks, high in the air … rendered it one of the most awful sights in nature."

"It seemed that the heaven and earth were coming together."

Some of the Americans had long enough to form the thought that their enemy had sprung a mine under them.[44] The idea passed through their brains as they turned and involuntarily crouched and raised hands to shield their eyes, grimacing and squinting at the explosion.

"They had hardly time to trace up the eruption through its rapid parabola, instinctively watching its direction, ere the heavy fragments came booming down."

"A most shocking scene ensued, the stones falling thick as hail in all directions."

"At first the air was darkened with stones, rafters and clay… the infernal shower descended and dealt destruction to our column."

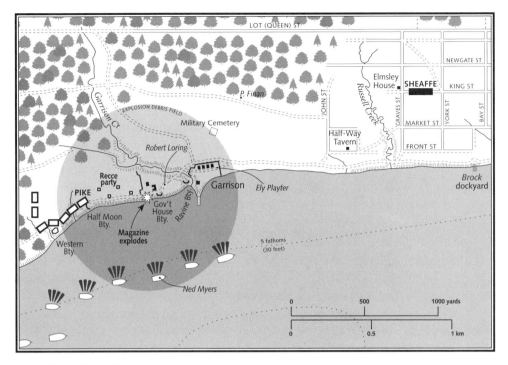

The Battle of York, 1:00 p.m.

1. Sheaffe has withdrawn nearly all his remaining force to Elmsley House on King Street.
2. Pike's column has advanced to within 400 yards of Sheaffe's residence and the grand magazine.
3. Pike orders field guns to fire at the British garrison while an infantry detachment conducts a reconnaissance. Pike observes the situation from the Half Moon Battery.
4. Chauncey's schooners continue their attack on the land batteries.
5. The grand magazine explodes, witnessed by such individuals as Ely Playter, P. Finan and Ned Myers, scattering debris beyond a radius of 500 yards.

"Cart loads of stone, and an immense quantity of iron, shell and shot ... the column was raked from front to rear."

The violence of the explosion of the grand magazine at York was unprecedented in the history of Upper Canada. It created "a tremulous motion in the earth resembling the shock of an earthquake" and produced a shock wave that rattled the windows in the forts at the mouth of the Niagara River 28 miles across the lake, where it sounded like "rolling thunder."[45] The stone magazine served to confine the ignition and chemical reaction of the black powder for only a moment, as the heat of it instantly rose to 1650°C and the release of energy immediately blew the structure to smithereens, leaving only a gaping crater behind. Debris fell more than 500 yards from the site, raining death on the troops and punching holes into the buildings in the garrison. By modern reckonings, the blast had the power produced by about seven tons of TNT.

A large fragment of stone knocked Zebulon Pike to the ground, crushing his spine. Nicholson was similarly bowled over and thrown down, insensible, as was Jones. The captive sergeant was killed on the spot, his corpulent body landing on Fraser. Moore's left foot and ankle were smashed and down he went in agony. Hazelton too was gravely wounded and two of the privates were killed by the debris.[46]

Others were quick-witted enough to try to save themselves. One artillery officer bent double along the underside of his gun's barrel "and escaped with only a few rents in those parts of his garments, which projected beyond the cover."[47] A second dived headlong into an empty cask "leaving his nether man to bide the pelting of the pitiless storm."[48] For him, time came to a standstill as "the falling stones beat a tattoo on the bilge of the barrel, which he thought was to put him to sleep forever."

For dozens of Americans, the blast did bring eternal sleep, while among the more than 200 wounded were some who wished it had. Of the others, wrote Major Eustis, "hardly a man escaped without a bruise."[49] Men like Donald Fraser, who crawled out from under the bloody body of the British prisoner, stood up to find themselves alive and in the middle of a scene they could not have imagined. There were dead and wounded "strewed around in every direction," some of them "crushed down, and even into, the earth," their wounds "of the worst kind, comp'd fractures of the *legs, thighs and arms, fractures of Sculls.*"[50]

The Sixth Infantry, being farthest forward, suffered the worst, with 13 men killed and 104 wounded, according to one count.[51] The totals for the artillery units, the Fourteenth, Sixteenth and Twenty-first amounted to 13 dead and 83 wounded, while there were no casualties from the explosion in the ranks of the Fifteenth, only two in Forsyth's Rifles and that small group of Moore's Volunteers.

The head of the column had recoiled 20 yards in the face of the overpowering explosion. The cries of the wounded began to fill the air. Men asked, "What happened?" "A mine," offered some, but most soon concluded that the British had blown up their magazine, and a few voices even suggested the thing had been purposely constructed to loft as much stone as possible at an invading force.[52]

Officers who could stand thought to get their men in order and then looked to the head of the column for instructions. It was instantly realized that Pike, who was gasping for breath on the ground with Fraser beside him, was unable to continue and the senior surviving officers quickly decided to try to keep his fall secret from the men.[53] By seniority, Colonel Cromwell Pearce, Sixteenth Infantry, who had also been slightly wounded, assumed command of the army

The general falls. Artists produced several versions of Pike's fall at York. Here stone blocks and timbers rain down upon the American column, but Pike has collapsed into the arms of his apparently uninjured aides while standing next to the Half Moon Battery which was actually constructed of earth and sod, not stone. (LAC, C7434)

and began giving orders, sending forward the first squad of men he could find ready to see what the enemy was doing. Captain Charles Hunter, the brigade master, and Lieutenant Colonel George Mitchell took it upon themselves to get the companies up and prepared to fight because there seemed a very strong likelihood that the British and Canadians would now launch an all-out attack upon their dishevelled enemy.

It was said afterwards, with maybe a tinge of exaggeration, that the American column was ready to march on York within five minutes of the explosion. To their credit, the units did not fall apart after the startling disaster that had killed or wounded one man in seven. They carried on with their mission and, as more than one observer mentioned, "Our troops gave three cheers in the midst of this dreadful scene.... [which] seemed to add vigor to their strength."[54] At the word for advance, they proceeded across the field of death toward the rampart at Government House.

While destruction rained down on the Americans, Ely Playter realized he was "in a Horrid-situation, the stone falling thick as Hail and large one's sinking into the very earth."[55] He looked through the gate and witnessed a block of stone strike and kill Captain Loring's horse, sending the rider tumbling to the earth. Stunned, Loring picked himself up and fled.

Isaac Wilson was in similar peril. "The air seemed full of stones," he remem-

Mangled bayonet. This artefact, on display at Historic Fort York, was recovered during archeological excavation on the garrison property and is believed to have been damaged during the detonation of the grand magazine. (Photograph by Robert Malcomson)

bered, "some large ones came near me but I got under a tree that was fallen down."[56] Privates Shepherd and Saunders were not so lucky. Both men were hit by stone or timber and left on the ground with ghastly wounds to their legs. John Bassell, a court official, was among the volunteers still at the garrison and was struck senseless by a chunk of stone. Ensign Robins was wounded at this time too, perhaps as he fled with LeLièvre's party.

Although some Americans declared that the explosion killed as many of the enemy as their own, only a handful of British and Canadians seem to have been present and most of them escaped. They fled toward the town as fast as they could go. Playter stopped to take a look back and saw some Americans running out through the garrison gate.[57] They paused to shoot at him, but the lieutenant was already in flight.

A new round of spirited huzzas rang along the American column as Donald Fraser and a party of soldiers lifted the ashen-faced Pike onto an improvised stretcher. The extent of the general's wounds was immediately recognized as serious and even he had bravely asserted, "I am mortally wounded – my ribs and back are stove in."[58] Attended by surgeons who had accompanied the column, Pike, Nicholson and Jones were carried toward the shore to be taken out to the squadron. One officer in the column remembered passing the general and hearing him call out, "Push on my brave fellows and avenge your general."[59] When Pike heard cheering, he asked its reason and a sergeant helping to transport him answered, "The British union jack is coming down, general, the Stars are going up!"[60]

Bryan Finan's boy had approached close enough to the garrison to witness the incredible explosion, but still at a distance that saved him from its deadly effects. Transfixed by the sight, he walked forward slowly, gazing at the vast round cloud of black smoke that rose slowly into the heavens and then dissipated to the west. He stopped and noticed the British regulars and some of the militia off to his left by Russell Creek. He turned back and beheld "what I have never witnessed upon any former occasion and what I had little anticipated on this."[61] It was the flag staff in the garrison, miraculously still standing after the blast, that caught his attention and left him incredulous. "I saw the 'meteor flag' of England bow by impious traitorous hands to the then triumphant 'star-spangled' banner of America." One account claimed it was the flag presented to Moore's Volunteers by the ladies of Baltimore that was hauled up over the ruined garrison.

The boy turned tail and raced back to where his mother and siblings had taken refuge, not bothering, when he recorded his adventure later in life, to mention whether his mother cuffed his ears for running off.

Major General Sir Roger Hale Sheaffe had led his retreating column east to King Street, passing down into the wide ravine at Russell's Creek and back up to where Elmsley House stood on the corner of Graves Street. Here, nearly one mile from the fort, he called a halt.[62] By this time few of the men entertained any notion of offering further resistance to the Americans. Most of the militia who remained now deserted without hesitation, heading into town for food and drink. Sheaffe called an impromptu meeting of the senior officers and briefly described the situation, perhaps mentioning the points he eventually made in his official report, that turning to fight the enemy would only worsen the day's losses and that some of the schooners appeared to be heading for the bay, where they could continue to assist the advancing column. Sheaffe asked for reactions but only Lieutenant Colonel Heathcote had time to speak, urging his general to stand and fight.

Sir Roger, however, had made up his mind; having destroyed the grand magazine, he resolved to preserve as many of his regulars as possible by retreating. He advised militia officers Lieutenant Colonel Chewett and Major Allan to negotiate terms of capitulation with the Americans. If Æneas Shaw's anecdote about Sheaffe's earlier consideration of retreat was true, the general's actions showed that he had not contemplated the logistics of a full retreat in any depth. Otherwise, Sheaffe would have allowed his men to stop at the garrison, albeit briefly, to snatch up their greatcoats and knapsacks and other essentials. But he had marched them past the blockhouse and barracks without a pause and now doomed them to a 150-mile slog back to Kingston with nothing but their battle-stained uniforms to shield them from the chilly spring weather. The officers must have had to speak quickly and sternly to stifle the muttering that undoubtedly ran up and down the column.

Some of the militia followed the regulars, while others stood and watched them go, trailing the two 6-pdr. field guns behind them. Sheriff Beikie was there and summed up rather succinctly the general attitude about the way that Roger Sheaffe abandoned York and its people. "The General with his troops," wrote Beikie, "pushed on for Kingston and left us all standing in the street like a parcel of sheep."[63]

Princes' Gates. The site of the Western Battery was a short distance inside the Princes' Gates at the eastern end of the CNE Grounds. The gates were named for Edward, Prince of Wales, and Prince George, who opened them in 1927. In this view looking west, the wind turbine in the distance stands adjacent to where the clearing around Fort Rouillé was and near the American landing point.

Location of the grand magazine. A sugar maple was planted at Historic Fort York in 1968 to commemorate the 150th anniversary of the Rush-Bagot Treaty. The grand magazine was adjacent to the tree, just outside the rampart. (Photographs by Robert Malcomson)

CHAPTER **12**

"Almost as bad as none"[1]

THE CAPITULATION

It was after 1:30 on Tuesday afternoon when Lieutenant Colonel William Chewett and Major William Allan of the 3rd Regiment of York Militia assumed command of the situation at York. Other commissioned militia officers were with them at Elmsley House on King Street and the Reverend John Strachan soon joined the group. There must have an air of disbelief about what had happened since dawn and a sense of apprehension about what was to come, especially after Sir Roger Sheaffe retreated with the surviving regulars, and the militia rank and file were reduced to all but the last few stalwarts.

Having been ordered by Sheaffe to arrange a capitulation of the town, Chewett and Allan had no option but to improvise a flag of surrender and go in search of their enemy; Captain John Beverley Robinson is said to have gone with them.[2] They walked down into the Russell Creek ravine on the roadway that angled southwest and when they came up on the other side at Front Street they could see that the American column had halted a few hundred steps on the town side of the garrison stockade and that a group was out ahead of it walking toward them.

Colonel Cromwell Pearce had taken command of the expedition after Pike's fall and marched his men to the garrison, passing the scores of dead and wounded lying amid the stones and debris from the explosion on the fort common. A party of skirmishers had ensured that there was no British trap waiting to be sprung, and so the column picked its way around the end of the curtain wall, taking a quick look at the vast smoking crater produced by the detonation of the magazine, and then crossed the property of the damaged Government House. It went down into Garrison Creek and up into the stockaded grounds, emerging from the garrison's east gate, where everyone could see the wide stretch of open land leading toward the town. Minutes later Pearce called a stop and ordered Captain White Youngs to take some men ahead and seek a parley with the enemy.[3]

The Canadian and American representatives met in the roadway in front of a large white frame building, the home of George Crookshank, the assistant deputy commissary general.[4] After introductions, Youngs asked about the intentions of the British commander and Chewett explained that Major General Sheaffe had retreated with the regulars, leaving him and the others to negotiate the surrender of York. Youngs replied that he would take this information to his chief and that a meeting to discuss terms could probably begin in about fifteen minutes.

Chewett and his companions returned to Elmsley House to tell the others that the Americans seemed willing to treat for peace. With the fate of the day now in their hands, the other militia officers and men present decided to head into town to find some food and drink, leaving Chewett and Allan to settle the terms. Strachan, who had been back and forth between his home and the garrison all day, now saw a task ahead that was appropriate to his calling and offered to join the negotiators. Off they tramped to Crookshank's place.

Elmsley House. Chief Justice John Elmsley owned an estate near the intersection of modern King and Simcoe streets. After his death in 1805, the government rented space there for offices and then bought the house during the war. Intruders vandalized the residence after the battle, stealing its furnishings and fittings and a large portion of the lending library. (TRL, T11867)

The banner made by the ladies of York for the 3rd Militia made its appearance about this time at the McGill home on Lot Street; according to one story, Captain Archibald McLean walked up with it wrapped around his body. So that it would not fall into the hands of the enemy, he had taken it from Ensigns Edward Thompson and George Denison, who had carried the regiment's colours into battle. Upon McLean's entrance, one of the women who had taken refuge at McGill's asked contemptuously if the men had sent the flag back for them to protect. McLean was all for rushing back to confront the Americans rather than bear such an insinuation, but was convinced instead to make his escape; he went out behind the house and buried the flag in the orchard. The anecdote, repeated eighty years later, made no mention of the Union Jack that was the second part of the regiment's colours.[5]

Not all of the other militia ended up quenching their thirst as quickly as they planned because they had not gone far when a party of redcoats appeared, hurrying toward them. As Lieutenant Playter remembered, "We came on towards the town, [but] met Captn Lealeaver returning and [he] desired assistance to set fire to the Marine Store and the New ship."[6] This was, of course, Captain Tito LeLièvre of the Royal Newfoundland Regiment of Fencibles, who, along with a handful of volunteers, had blown up the grand magazine and escaped its deluge before joining the regulars on their retreat. At what point he made his report to General Sheaffe is not known, but here he was running back into town to destroy the dockyard facilities and the *Sir Isaac Brock.* Clearly, Sir Roger had not thought to issue instructions for this to happen at the time he commenced his retreat. In fact, it seems likely that he had nearly left the town when he ordered LeLièvre back.

With the enemy in sight, the work in the dockyard had to be done quickly. It is not an easy task to kindle a large enough fire to consume the partially planked hull of a ship that must have measured close to 130 feet in length, and the prepared wood and ironwork around it, the nearby workshops and storehouses, the tools, the wagons, the stockpiles of goods. The British worked frantically with the help of Playter and his friends. Thomas Plucknett, the superintendent of the dockyard, later claimed responsibility for the destruction of the *Brock* and the dockyard resources. He may well have been there, but it is unlikely that LeLièvre would have bowed to the authority of a man who was universally condemned by the army officers for the abysmal manner in which he had supervised the project. After twenty or thirty minutes, the job was done as well as time would allow, the flames were licking up around the frames and some of the surrounding shops and stores and a great cloud of black smoke was churning up into the air and drifting westward under the force of the wind that had prevailed all day.

Crookshank residence. George Crookshank was the commissary general for Upper Canada from the time of Simcoe. His home, on the extreme left, overlooked the bay at Front Street on the westernmost edge of the "new" town, near the modern intersection with Blue Jays Way (Peter Street). John and Penelope Beikie lived in the two-storey frame house next door. The Half-Way Tavern was just down the road and opposite the commissary dock. (TRL, T12567)

Once more, LeLièvre and his men hurried away and, as he attested, "narrowly escaped from being taken prisoner."[7] An attempt to burn the *Duke of Gloucester*, still under repair at the end of the bay, was aborted.

In the meantime, Chewett's party had met Lieutenant Colonel George Mitchell and Major William King, the senior American officers appointed by Pearce to conduct the negotiations. After an exchange of introductions, the Americans opened the conference by stating their displeasure with having to deal with militia officers. That General Sheaffe had admitted defeat by seeking a capitulation and then retreated with his regular forces was repugnant to them, but Chewett and Allan were able to convince their opposites that they now represented York and in that capacity could come to terms. At length, the men sat down in Crookshank's house to begin the negotiation, with Strachan and Robinson looking on, offering their views.

By this time, Sir Roger's column had stopped near the bridge over the Don River. John McGill, the inspector general of public accounts, and his brother-in-law, the commissary George Crookshank, had joined the march, fearing that they would be captured and detained in the United States. Major James Givins and Major General Æneas Shaw were there too, as were Surgeons William Hackett and Grant Powell and Hospital Mate William Lee. Major Samuel Wilmot, 1st

York, arrived with Captain James Fenwick of the same unit and five sergeants and ten privates, some of whom had joined them from other companies in the regiment. The families of some of the regulars came up, included Bryan Finan's wife and children, having been summoned from the local homes where they had taken refuge in the morning. Wagons had probably been appropriated for carrying the badly wounded and the women and children and, perhaps because of a lack of horses, Sheaffe decided to abandon the two 6-pdr. field guns in the roadway.

The order to advance finally came around 2:00 and the procession rumbled across the Don River bridge, joined at the last minute by Captain LeLièvre's party; no one took time to destroy the bridge. Bryan Finan's son later described the dire condition in which the retreat was commenced. "We brought no clothing with us more than we wore at the moment, and consequently left York … to commence a journey of 200 miles through the woods of America without an outside garment of any description or a second pair of shoes."[8] Their fathers and husbands and their cohorts were in the same situation, having left all of their greatcoats and "necessaries" at the garrison by order. Only worse off were the

Death of General Pike. Without regard for the actual landscape at York, one artist depicted Pike's heroic fatal wound happening outside the walls of a stone fortress and within sight of a lofty steeple the likes of which would not be built there for years. A captured flag was brought to Pike just before he died on board the U.S. Ship *Madison*. (Brackenridge, *History of the Late War,* 1818)

wounded, whose suffering was aggravated by the endless jarring motion of the wagons rolling along the rutted road.

Out on the lake at the western extremes of the town Surgeon Walter Buchanan was struggling at that moment to relieve the sufferings of the gravely wounded Brigadier General Zebulon Pike. The general had been taken by boat to the schooner *Pert* and from there to the *Madison* in the hope that the senior physician in the squadron might be able to do something for him. His wounds, however, were beyond the limits of Buchanan's skills, though Pike was still coherent enough to ask Lieutenant Donald Fraser to write to his friend William Duane, editor of the *Aurora* of Philadelphia, and to his wife. Major General Henry Dearborn and Commodore Isaac Chauncey visited with Pike as his strength ebbed and presented him with a flag that had been brought to the ship from the British garrison. One source reported that having the trophy as his pillow eased the general's sufferings and he whispered, "I die contented."[9] Another officer claimed that as Pike rested his head on the flag "an inexpressible serenity beamed upon his countenance, and he expired without a sigh."[10] Buchanan later wrote that his friend literally died in his arms.

At the Crookshank house, negotiations were proceeding through the matters of captives and arms, paroles, public stores and private property, when an American officer interrupted the meeting and asked to speak with Major King. He went outside, returning promptly to tell the others that the dockyard was on fire. Everyone went to look and beheld a vast column of black smoke rising from the lakeshore in town and blowing towards them. Mitchell and King erupted in protest that a fire would be set after the negotiations had begun. It was in their view unconscionable and they were livid about it. Chewett, Allan and the others could do nothing but plead ignorance, vowing that someone beyond their control had started the fire because they had certainly not ordered it.

At that point the American column started moving forward and it was only a frantic effort on King's part that convinced Colonel Pearce to halt the advance so the terms could be completed. This was effected quickly and the officers added their signatures to the original and two copies, agreeing that all British and Canadians under arms would surrender, the wounded would be cared for, and all private property respected while public property and papers would be subject to seizure. It was a roughly scripted document of five paragraphs, crediting the navy first and army second for the capture of the town and naming Pearce as the commanding officer; it was subject to the approval of the senior officers. Strachan considered the arrangement "almost as bad as none, but situated as matters then were, better could not be obtained."[11]

The tone of negotiations had been unpleasant from the start but the sight of the dockyard going up in flames worsened the situation. King took two copies of the agreement and went to have it approved by Pearce. This involved some time and served to heighten the impatience of the American officers and men, who were waiting to march into town and complete their victory. Major Abraham Eustis believed Pearce's decision to stop for a parley cost the army a great opportunity. "Had [Pike] lived, it would have been indeed a victory," he wrote, "for I am sure we should have secured Sheaffe and every one who was under arms with him."[12] There were others in the column who felt the same way and the murmurs of their complaints may have reached Pearce's ears because when he produced his account of the engagement he subtly altered the events. He noted that he did not send Mitchell and King to negotiate terms until the dockyard had been torched and "the dense volumes of smoke which blew violently in our faces rendered it impossible to proceed for some minutes."[13]

The truth was that if Cromwell Pearce had pressed forward, ignoring the militia officers or asking them to wait while he secured the town, he might well have interrupted Captain LeLièvre's party and seized the *Sir Isaac Brock* before it could be destroyed. He might even have caught up to Sheaffe's regulars and taken them easily in their vulnerable state. The hour lost in discussing terms cost the Americans mightily.

Evidence of discord among the victors revealed itself when Major King failed to return with a confirmation of agreement. Instead, another officer approached Crookshank's and told William Allan that Colonel Pearce was requesting him to hand over his sword and proceed under guard into town. William Chewett must have left the house by now, making Allan the senior man on the spot, but John Strachan was still present and he joined with the major in protesting such an indignity. Protected by the honour of a flag of truce, it was unheard of for an officer to be deprived of his sword, but the American insisted and Allan relented. He was brought forward and made to stand within the column, which was then ordered to march. Strachan walked alongside, to watch over his friend and to bear witness to the situation.

The Americans marched through York until they reached its eastern limits. As they went they instructed any likely militiaman they encountered to fall in under guard, probably with Allan's reluctant agreement. Some of these appear to have been men who had heard the alarm some distance from York and had hurried forth to help in its defence. Ely Playter remembered seeing groups of militia from the outlying country arriving too late to see action, but probably not too late to be rounded up.[14] By and large, however, it appears a considerable number of men who might have been picked up as the enemy took possession of the town simply stayed indoors or fled and escaped being apprehended. All attempts to keep the militia companies together had long been abandoned and it was, essentially, every man for himself. Playter, for instance, finally made it to Jordan's Hotel, where he met friends, some of whom had heard that he had been killed. After some refreshment, he left in company with his brother George, Captain Samuel Ridout and the militia paymaster Andrew Mercer; they had so far evaded capture. They headed to his father's home up the Don River, where Ely was reunited with his wife, Sophia, and their children. Several families from the town had taken refuge there; among them was Ferusha Detlor and most of her nine children, wondering if Playter had heard anything about her husband, John.

Meanwhile the Americans completed their sweep of the town. Colonel Pearce took note of the public buildings and storehouses and posted guards at them. A party of sentries was left at the bridge over the Don River, where the army picked up the abandoned field guns and dragged them along on the march back to the garrison. It was about now that Major General Henry Dearborn made his appearance. He and his aide, Lieutenant Colonel Samuel Conner, and Commodore Chauncey all remarked that he went ashore from the *Madison* and assumed command as soon as he learned about Pike's wound.[15] But it was not until 3:00 or so that he caught up to his force, and once there he had little to say. As Pearce recalled the scene, "Colonel Pearce was engaged in superintending the removal of the public stores when General Dearborn rode up and asked Colonel Pearce what had been done. The colonel delivered to him the terms of capitulation and the General immediately rode off without speaking or issuing an order that day."[16] Captain John Scott of the Fifteenth Infantry and Major Eustis were in Pearce's column and confirmed his remembrance of Dearborn's late arrival and lack of involvement in matters. Perhaps the general's attention had been distracted, or his temper aroused, when he read the clause in the agreement that credited Pearce with command of the army at the time of signing.[17]

The conquering army marched back to the garrison, where the captured rank and file of the militia were locked up in the damaged blockhouse while commissioned officers were allowed parole or freedom to return to their homes with the understanding they would return to the garrison the next day. The troops then appear to have moved into the barrack cabins and whatever other shelter they could find, organizing some form of camp where they could eat and sleep. Pearce arranged with the other officers for a protective perimeter to be established and a regular rotation of sentries.[18] He had already made sure the town was under guard, giving this assignment to the portion of the landing force that had played such a significant role in the early stages of the battle, Major Benjamin Forsyth's Regiment of Rifles.

The easterly wind that had blown all day lived up to its threat by sweeping in deep layers of dark clouds that opened up just before sunset and drenched the town and its environs. Exhausted from an extraordinary day of exertions, the soldiers who were free to eat and bed down fell deeply asleep while their comrades on guard quickly improvised ways to keep dry and alert at their posts. They were not the only ones for whom sleep would have been a blessing.

In the manner of the day, there was no system in place for tending to the wounded on a battlefield immediately and efficiently. A friend might assist a mate to find where the surgeon had laid out his instruments, or a wife might find her bleeding husband and try to make him comfortable while begging for someone to help. But more likely a man struck down by ball or the blast of the magazine lay unattended until the fighting had stopped and the site was secured. And so it was that an American officer who had marched into town and back and arranged for what he termed "comfortable quarters" for himself and his men, decided around 5:30 to go and have another look at the scene of the action, west of the garrison.[19] Here he saw "a vast number of wounded who were not assisted by a single surgeon, but left to groan and bleed to death from their wounds." He immediately ordered a detachment of his company to bring the survivors to the garrison, where the army doctors and their assistants established their field hospital and undertook their grisly work.

Surgeon's Mate William Beaumont, who had treated the many ills of camp life during the previous winter, now had his first experience with battlefield casualties. It was, in his words, "a most distressing scene."[20] There were more than thirty men suffering from gunshot wounds and over 220 who had been injured as a result of the grand magazine's explosion. But Beaumont was not alone in the task since Hospital Surgeon James Mann of the Ninth Military District was on hand, as were Surgeons Thomas Lawson (Beaumont's superior in the Sixth Infantry), Samuel Gilliland (Fifteenth Infantry), Amasa Trowbridge and probably a number of surgeons' mates. As well, there was Buchanan on the *Madison* and Surgeon's Mate William Caton on the *Oneida* to deal with the naval casualties and wounded soldiers who had been returned to the squadron during the landing phase.

The American doctors discovered that their British counterparts were already hard at work at the garrison hospital. The exact location of the building is uncertain, but it was close enough to Government House to have been pelted by the debris of the explosion. William Baldwin had been tending to one of the wounded when he became aware "of a strange sensation – it was too great to be called a sound – and he found a shower of stones falling all around him, but he was quite unhurt."[21] The number of casualties had soon filled the main

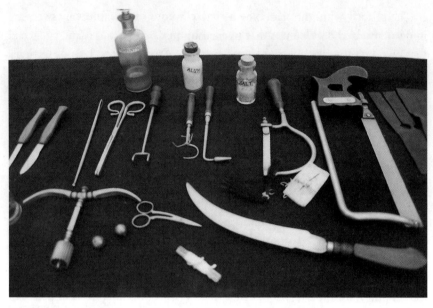

Surgical instruments. Resembling a set of carpenter's tools, this assortment of surgical instruments is similar to those used by the surgeons at York. The corkscrew-like device on the left is a trephine, used for opening the skull, a surgical procedure dating back to 2000 BC. (Photograph by Robert Malcomson)

building and probably overflowed into the cottage-like barracks. It was here that Beaumont and the others met the British medical staff, reduced to only Baldwin and the chemist Joseph Cawthra. General Sheaffe had taken Surgeons Hackett and Powell and hospital mate Lee with him, which provoked one of the first instances of public disgust for his conduct.[22] Their departure had been so quick that they had grabbed as much of the medicines as they could carry and had mistakenly taken the surgical instruments belonging to Dr. Eleazar Aspinwall, a shopkeeper in the town who had come forward to offer his skills. Aspinwall rode off to catch up with the regulars and retrieve the tools of his trade. They would be much needed as there were fifty or more men under British care, many of whom had yet to receive treatment, and others still to be brought in from the field.

Gunshot wounds had to be probed so that the balls and bits of fabric they carried through bone and tissue could be extracted.[23] Ligatures were applied to seeping arteries, the skin sewn shut, and lint laid over it and wrapped tightly with bandages. A number of the British suffered serious burns in the accident in the Western Battery while the majority of American wounds were contusions and lacerations from the grand magazine's explosion. Many of these received poultices before being wrapped up, while the simple fractures were set, splinted and bound. Irreparable damage to limbs required quick and efficient amputation, while the worst of the head wounds involved cautious trepanning in which the affected portion of skull was cut out and removed to take pressure off the brain. In many cases, suspicious injuries were treated and bandaged for later inspection and possibly further and more drastic treatment.

Some surgeons selected their patients according to the severity of their wounds, while others simply took whoever was brought in next. Officers generally received preferential treatment, being seen first and recovering in more private and quieter surroundings, with some personal attention and maybe a tincture of laudanum, a liquid form of opium, to dull the senses. For the rank and file, it was hurried treatment and then removal to crowded, nightmarish conditions in whatever space was available.

This dark aspect of the battle at York was conducted amid "the Groans of the wounded and the agonies of the Dying," as William Beaumont recorded in his diary.[24] "The Surgeons, [were] wading in blood, cutting off arms, legs and trepanning heads to rescue their fellow creatures from untimely deaths." All the while they could hear the pitiful calls of the men who had waited for hours for some care and attention or those for whom treatment had brought no end to pain. "Oh, Dear! Oh Dear! Oh my God! my God!" they cried. "Do, Doctor, Doctor! Do cut off my leg! my arm! my head! to relieve me from misery!" Hoarse throats sobbed, "I can't live! I can't live!"

Through a night without end the surgeons stood and dealt with one case after another at the centre of a chaotic, stinking scene of human desperation, the likes of which none of them had ever witnessed. If they took time to step out in search of fresh air, they would have seen the hellish glow reflecting off the clouds over the town as the last of the fires in the dockyard were finally quenched by the heavy rain.

Underneath that glow the looting began. There is no clear chronology of whose home or shop suffered first, but it appears that as soon as the last responsible senior American officer left the town, the prowlers went to work. Penelope Beikie had remained in her two-storey frame house next to George Crookshank's place and proudly asserted, "I had the temerity to frighten, and even to threaten, some of the enemy, though they had the place and me in their power."[25] Her husband reported that, despite his presence, the American soldiers snatched up all his poultry and walked away with anything else they could lay their hands on. Others broke into Grant Powell's residence and, since no one was home, were at liberty to ransack the place. John Hunter, the messenger for the Legislative Assembly who lived in one of the buildings adjacent to it, returned to find it broken into and some of his belongings missing, including clothing and a chest in which he had kept $150 in army bills. The patrols posted to the outskirts of town did not miss out on the plunder, the isolation of Major James Givins's house making it one place that was ripe for plunder. The major had retreated with Sheaffe, but his wife, Angelique, was there and could do nothing to stop the intruders, except get out of their way for fear for her life and those of her nine children. They stole carpets, curtains, sheets, knives and forks, clothing, a saddle and double set of harness.

The men of the Rifle Regiment were blamed for the intrusions into the dwellings of the citizens of York on the night after the battle.[26] This was not unwarranted, given their reputation for plundering private property during their winter raids across the St. Lawrence River and Benjamin Forsyth's indifferent attitude toward their conduct once the fighting was over. Some of them also audaciously made it known that they were exacting vengeance for the drubbing the British had given them during the raid on Ogdensburg and the plunder taken afterwards. But there were others who joined in the looting, possibly some of the riflemen from the Baltimore Volunteers, who had shown a tendency for vandalism at Buffalo the previous autumn. About the only individual to publicly admit his guilt, however, was Ned Myers of the U.S. Schooner *Scourge*.

At the time that Pearce's column took possession of the garrison, Sailing Master Joseph Osgood went on shore from the *Scourge* so that he could see what was happening. Myers was a member of the boat crew and shortly found himself entering General Sheaffe's residence, where the Americans discovered "tables set and eggs in the cups."[27] While poking around in the pantry, Myers came upon an older woman, a servant, hiding in the potato locker. He helped her out and assured her that she had nothing to worry about and, true to his word, Ned and the others made no trouble since they had been ordered not to disturb or take anything. That is, until they found casks containing liquor, which they instantly uncorked and drank as fast as they could. This frivolity was soon stopped when some officers came in and chased the men out, staving in the barrels so that no one could enjoy them.

"The pull I got in the grocery just made me ripe for mischief," Myers recollected, and when Osgood returned to the *Scourge*, Ned told his gun crew about his adventure and they soon all settled on launching an expedition after dark.[28] With the approval of one of the petty officers, they climbed into a canoe and paddled up the bay toward the town, where they tied up at a wharf and went to see what they could find. At the foot of the wharf was a store and through a window they could see by the light of a lamp inside that a man was sitting in a chair with his musket across his lap and his head on the store counter, fast asleep. The

Americans opened the window and one of the black seamen quietly entered and seized the weary watchman. Shocked at his sudden predicament, the man explained that he was only trying to protect the shop, but they assured him he did not have to fear for his life. It was liquor and luxuries the looters were after and they promptly grabbed as much as they could carry – Ned remembered stealing some coffee and sugar – took it down to the canoe and then returned for more. By now, the seamen had drunk enough to be noticed by their loud voices and antics, and just as Myers was deciding it was time to head back to the *Scourge,* "some riflemen came in" to join the fun.[29] After the exchange of a few words, the sailors departed and slipped down the bay to the schooner, where they lugged their booty aboard, most of it consisting of whisky. They had taken a sizeable risk, considering Pike's pre-battle warning about respecting private property, but Myers and his friends considered the adventure a lark. "For myself," he explained, "I was influenced more by the love of mischief and a weak desire to have it said I was foremost in such an exploit, than from any mercenary motive."[30]

Wednesday morning dawned beneath a continuing shower of rain. William Allan, who had been set free the night before, met with William Chewett, John Strachan and other militia officers, and they were on their way to the garrison when they encountered Major King. Strachan immediately demanded to know why King had not returned to Crookshank's with a confirmation of the terms of capitulation and why Allan had been taken prisoner so ignobly. He angrily alleged "that the whole appeared a deception."[31] King seemed at a loss to explain what had happened and asked the men to accompany him to the garrison, where the problems could be resolved.

The dim light of day revealed the "dismal" state of the garrison, which had been "rent by the Balls and the explosion of the Magazine," every building either scarred or literally torn to pieces.[32] The party met with Colonel Pearce in his makeshift headquarters – probably Government House – but he admitted there was nothing he could do to answer their questions, since he had given the terms to General Dearborn, who had ridden off with them without a word. Strachan and the others pointed out that the militia who had been rounded up and locked in the blockhouse were still in there, along with some of the wounded, and had received no food; Pearce gave orders to feed the prisoners and have a surgeon attend to them as needed.

A new delegation of negotiators now appeared at the garrison: Dearborn's aide-de-camp Lieutenant Colonel Samuel Conner and Lieutenant Jesse Elliott, acting commander of the *Madison.* They had fresh orders to review and confirm the conditions of surrender because General Dearborn had found them unsatisfactory. The first issue raised was that the *Sir Isaac Brock* and the naval stores had been destroyed after surrender discussions had started. To this complaint, Allan and Chewett could only profess their ignorance of the circumstances, which prompted Conner and Elliott to offer disparaging remarks about Roger Sheaffe's honour, threatening that it was impossible to come to an agreement under such conditions. The British agreed with the "impropriety" of Sheaffe's actions, trying to get the Americans past this issue so that the captive militia could be freed. They offered to ensure that every participant would be paroled, which meant they would not take up arms again until formally exchanged, but were told that General Dearborn had "expressly reserved it for his own decision."[33]

Hours were spent haggling over the circumstances and issues. Parts of the original text were struck out, putting the army's role in the attack ahead of the navy's and replacing Pearce's name with Dearborn's, and then it was decided to clarify all the statements by rewriting them.[34] Finally, Strachan's patience reached its limits and he said that, being at liberty to come and go as he pleased, he wanted the Americans to provide him with a boat and crew so that he could go to the *Madison* and get a quick resolution from the commanding general in person. He charged off to the garrison wharf with some of the others in tow and abruptly came face to face with his adversary.

The lethargic old general had finally roused himself enough to deal with matters on shore, but he had no interest in the protests of the belligerent Scot whether he wore a chaplain's collar or not. He paused long enough to make a cursory review of the capitulation agreement Strachan thrust into his hands and then gave it back without comment. Strachan demanded to know when Dearborn would approve the paroles and allow the British and Canadian wounded to be properly cared for. The American met the clergyman's scowl with one of his own and harshly answered that the British people "had given a false return of officers." When Strachan challenged him on this point, Dearborn told him "to keep off [and] not to follow him as he has business of more importance to attend to."[35] Dearborn turned and continued on his way to the garrison.

Chauncey had ferried the general to shore in his gig and he now received Strachan's broadside of complaints. "If the capitulation [is] not signed … we [will] not receive it," he vowed. "The delay [is] a deception calculated to give the riflemen time to plunder."[36] After the town was stripped, Strachan continued, the Americans would then settle on terms and make it look as if they had honoured private property. But he, Allan, Chewett and the others "were determined that this should not be the case and that [the Americans] would not have it in their power to say that they respected private property after it had been robbed."

King and Elliott had accompanied Strachan to the wharf and now interrupted him to explain the situation to the commodore. Contrary to Dearborn's style, Chauncey listened attentively and discussed the problems in reasonable tones, expressing his view on the need to reach a settlement. The other officers agreed but could give no definite answers as to when or how it could be finalized. Still disgruntled, Strachan returned to the barracks and told his friends that things were still up in the air.

The time was about 11:00 Wednesday morning and, as far as he understood, Cromwell Pearce continued to be the nominal head of operations on land. So he was surprised to suddenly hear drums roll to call the garrison to arms and hurried outside to demand an explanation. There he found one of Dearborn's aides, who confessed that he had given the order since he had heard that the British were advancing. "Let them come," Pearce answered. "We are ready."[37] He instructed the drums to stop and the aide ran off, only to return a few minutes later with Dearborn's direct order that the force be paraded.

There was no disobeying the general's order, especially since, as Pearce pointed out in his version of events, "This was the first order given by General Dearborn, after the arrival of the army in Canada."[38] A column comprising those parts of the brigade that were still at the garrison proceeded down the road to town with Dearborn striding along in the rear, his hands clasped behind his back and attended by his staff officers. It did not advance far before the call was made to halt. Pearce went to consult with his superior, suggesting that it did not seem as if the enemy was even in sight, let alone posing a threat. Dearborn concurred and the column returned to the garrison.

In the next few minutes the terms for capitulation of the town were suddenly completed and ratified. Having established himself as commander of the operation, Dearborn entered the meeting room and gave his approval to the list of conditions in a most amiable fashion. The new document was signed by the officers who had conducted the negotiations and by Lieutenant François Gauvreau of the Provincial Marine, who, along with several other marine officers, had somehow failed to join Sheaffe's retreat. The agreement consisted of the same basic statements as the original plan, but would now list the officers and men under parole.[39]

Strachan and the others quickly freed the men penned up in the fetid conditions of the blockhouse, although none were at liberty to leave until they had formally signed their paroles and received passes, a system that required the rest of the day to organize. Meanwhile Allan, Chewett, Strachan and the others helped the surgeons with the casualties. Their immediate plan was to remove the wounded men from the overcrowded garrison, but there was no single place in town big enough and suitable, so they struck upon the scheme of billeting them with citizens. To do this they needed wagons and teams, and that proved difficult since the Americans had appropriated all the wagons they could find to move public stores and munitions down to the wharves. Through the afternoon, led by the energetic Dr. Strachan, the men hurried to make the many necessary arrangements, no doubt assisted by the other leading town fathers, William Powell, Duncan Cameron and Alexander Wood included.

While the long negotiation to settle terms went on, the business of burying the dead was completed. Some, such as Lieutenant Moses Bloomfield, had already been committed to the lake, but on Wednesday morning, Captain Jeremiah Hayden, Fifteenth Infantry, commanded the fatigue party assigned to the gruesome task on land, and it was joined by seamen who brought bodies to shore from the squadron. The grave of only one young officer was recorded at the time. Lieutenant Jesse Elliott wrote to the parents of Midshipman John Hatfield to praise his "distinguished gallantry and merit" and inform them that he had overseen his burial "within a few yards from the battery from whence the ball [that killed him] was discharged."[40] Captains John Hoppock and Thomas Lyon, who had died of their wounds, and the remaining dead were likely gathered in groups to be laid to rest in hurriedly dug individual and mass graves near Hatfield at the Western Battery or in the clearing at the old French fort, while some of the British and Canadians may have been taken to the cemetery located just northeast of the garrison.

Only Zebulon Pike's earthly remains received special attention. His body was stripped and cleansed and placed into a cask filled with rum or whatever strong liquor would preserve it long enough so that it could be taken to Sackets Harbor for interment. "I have lost my best friend," lamented Donald Fraser, who consoled himself with the memory that Pike had "conducted himself like a General, and that he died like a Soldier."[41]

It was a thought that would cross many a brow in the days and weeks to come.

Burning the Don Bridge. This widely published illustration, painted in the 1860s, depicts a party of British soldiers setting fire to the main span of the bridge over the Don River as a well marshalled column begins the retreat to Kingston. The contemporary evidence suggests that the bridge was left standing and kept under guard by the American occupation force and that Sheaffe's retreat lacked such perfect military precision. (LAC, C6147)

PART FOUR

Repercussions

We send you an authentic narrative of the affair at York with some General reflexions … signed by the principal Militia Officers, Magistrates and inhabitants of this disgraced city.

JOHN STRACHAN, 10 MAY 1813

In your late affair I have thought (perhaps erroneously) that had the descent been made between the town and the barracks things might have turned out better.

JOHN ARMSTRONG, 15 MAY 1813

CHAPTER 13

"This disgraced city"[1]

THE OCCUPATION OF YORK

The Reverend John Strachan's accusation about American soldiers plundering the town fell on deaf ears.[2] But there was no doubting that there was evidence everywhere on Wednesday morning of empty houses that had been forcibly entered, looted and vandalized. Parties of American soldiers and sailors roamed the streets, some of them assigned to move materiel to the wharves, but others seemingly at liberty to do what they wanted.

Grant Powell's wife, Elizabeth, returned to their home to discover her family was a victim of crime. The place was ransacked; furniture, a bed, linen, dinnerware, kitchen utensils, her clothing, her daughter's clothing, books and groceries, gone. And there was a lanky American infantryman slouching at the doorway to the pantry, nonchalantly eating pieces from a cone of sugar. Bessy Walters, the Powells' servant, could not tolerate this affront and immediately challenged the intruder, telling him he had no right to steal the family's belongings, rudely asking why he did not just go home.

"I guess I wish I could," the young man replied.[3]

"Where is your home?" inquired Mrs. Powell.

"Down to Stillwater, New York," he answered. "I've one of Major Bleecker's farms."

"Oh my," Elizabeth gasped, "Major Bleecker is my father." And as six-year-old Ann Powell looked on, the two strangers lost their enmity for each other and exchanged news of people they both knew from the vicinity of New York City, where her father, a respected patriot of the War of Independence, had gained prominence and wealth.

The common link between some of the townsfolk and the invaders did little to reduce the indignation over the vandalism and theft that had taken place Tuesday night after the battle. Someone had gone through the Crookshank home, others broke into John Small's house, and one or more groups had invaded the residence of Æneas Shaw's eldest son, William, and carried off silver dinnerware, earrings, silk shawls and eight yards of lace, among other things. William Allan was devastated to discover on Wednesday that while he had been at the garrison, vandals had pried open the locks on his store and carried off Jamaican rum, soap, glass and a supply of expensive copperas, the high-quality fixative for dyes. Word of these incidents and the losses of the Beikies, the Givinses and John Hunter reached the ears of Strachan, Alexander Wood and the town's other headmen as they began trying to arrange for the billeting of the wounded. Late in the day William Powell took it upon himself to address a note to Henry Dearborn. He wanted to know why, if the terms of capitulation meant anything, he had been forced to resist intruders at his home and why his neighbours were living in fear of who would come knocking next.[4] Powell received no immediate answer.

The feeling of uncertainty and apprehension was felt in all quarters of York and the outlying area. Ely Playter woke up early on Wednesday at his father's house and greeted Joel Beman, who had driven down in his wagon from Newmarket, having also heard the rumour of his friend's death. Playter and his wife gathered up some of their belongings from their home and loaded them in Beman's wagon before he set off back to Newmarket, taking Sophia and the children with him. Ely, his brother George and Andrew Mercer decided to go and have a look about in town, but when they got there, Ely did not think it wise to get too nosey and hung back while the other two continued. He snooped around the rear of the town and came upon Ferusha Detlor's son George, whose face betrayed the grievous news he was carrying back to his mother.[5] She had sent the eighteen-year-old to the garrison to inquire about his father, and there he learned that his father had died a short time after the doctors had amputated the leg so badly crushed by debris from the explosion of the grand magazine.

Playter stayed out of the town and eventually met his brother, who had also heard about Detlor. They soon encountered Thomas Gibb Ridout, who had retreated with Sheaffe but was sent back to York along with some others. Together they all returned to the elder Playter's farm, where more people had gathered. Among them was Daniel Brooke, who had gone to the garrison to sign for his parole, saying that "the Yankees [had] used them well" and that the explosion had killed the general commanding the attack, a fellow named Pike.[6] Elsewhere through the town and its environs, rumours spread, leaving everyone wondering what was going to happen and what was the wisest thing to do in the meantime.

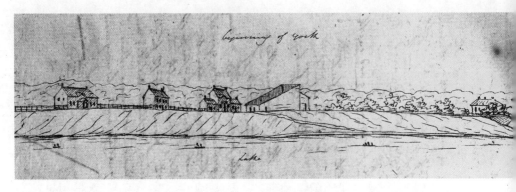

Shoreline of the town. Lieutenant Sempronius Stretton made this sketch of the waterfront as it appeared in 1806. The buildings on the left are the homes of George Crookshank and John Beikie, the Half-Way Tavern and a large storehouse, probably one burned by the Americans. Also burned were the Town Blockhouse (note the flag, probably a Union Jack, at its peak) and the nearby Parliament Buildings. (LAC, C1806)

For the doctors and the wounded, Wednesday was another day of torment. The surgeons had worked through the night, dealing with the hundreds of cases and then starting over again as those who had been treated needed further attention. William Beaumont found time at 10:00 Wednesday morning to make a note in his diary, eat something and sleep briefly before he returned "to the bloody scene of distress to continue dressing, Amputating and Trepanning."[7] That day Beaumont treated fifty patients, removing two limbs, opening a fractured skull, and dealing with an endless array of contusions and compound fractures before he collapsed from exhaustion around midnight.

William Baldwin was equally busy, trying to save John Detlor and then losing him, amputating Matthias Saunders's leg, inspecting William Jarvie's wrist that had been shattered by a ball and deciding that an amputation was not yet called for, easing the sufferings of John de Koven, whose wounded foot was causing him considerable pain and suffering. Like their American colleagues, Baldwin, Eleazar Aspinwall and the druggist Joseph Cawthra laboured through a second day of treatment until fatigue finally, and fittingly, overtook them.

On Thursday the Reverend Strachan and his friends eased the British doctors' workload by moving the rest of the wounded into the town, where residents could give the men closer care. It was raining, cold and windy, making the work difficult, and this was compounded by the shortage of wagons and medical supplies and the occasional refusal of townspeople to take in the wounded. John Jordan, the proprietor of the popular Jordan's Hotel, for instance, would not allow Alexander Wood to billet two wounded men with him, claiming that all his rooms were full.[8] Wood explained that it was his civic duty and that his

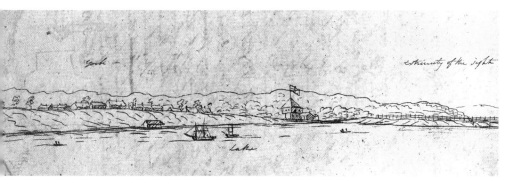

fellow tavern keepers were doing their share, but Jordan would hear nothing of it and rebuffed Wood rudely. Despite such opposition, Strachan's party managed to get all of the casualties out of the garrison and billeted by nightfall.

The Americans had by then discovered the extent of the munitions and stores they had captured. Even though the *Sir Isaac Brock* and some of the nearby buildings and sheds had been consumed by fire, there was still "about one million of public stores and property," wrote one officer, while another declared the value at "a million and half."[9] They believed they had seized "the grand depot of Upper Canada," an amount of military and naval materiel and provisions so great that they would never be able to carry it all away.[10] The list included the *Duke of Gloucester*, the private sloop *Governor Hunter*, dozens of artillery pieces and their equipment. There were uncounted batteaux, both used and newly constructed, ten anchors, two cabooses (naval cooking stoves), artificers' tools, tons of rigging, hundreds of casks of nails and spikes, lengths of iron rod and sheets of lead. Cases of fixed ammunition, shells and shot, labelled to be sent to Niagara and Amherstburg, survived the fires. At the barracks were the knapsacks and "necessaries" left behind by the regulars and in storehouses there were the uniforms and arms belonging to the Royal Newfoundland Fencibles crewing Provincial Marine vessels, as well as the new militia uniforms and medical supplies. In addition there were countless barrels of flour, salt meat and other provisions, and when the Americans opened the old blockhouses on Gibraltar Point, they discovered the hoard of farming implements and sundry items that had been sent to Upper Canada during the Simcoe years and never distributed.

Besides the military, naval and public material that fell into American hands there were the personal effects of all the regular officers, including nearly everything that General Sheaffe had with him at York. The value and quality of Sir Roger's possessions excited some genuine interest among the American officers. Surgeon Beaumont later saw his dress uniform coatee and declared it "the most

Musical snuff box. Roger Sheaffe's treasured music box may have resembled the one shown here. Such Swiss-made devices were exquisitely precise in construction and beautifully decorated. Besides the musical works and the compartment for snuff, there was also a slot for storing the key used to wind up the mechanism. (Courtesy of Kim. J. Bunker)

elegant thing I ever saw … embroidered in Gold and of the finest quality."[11] More important, from a military point of view, was the seizure of the general's correspondence, with all the details of the British plans and projects dating back to the previous October. The letter books and other documents were laid before Henry Dearborn for his inspection, but he was in no hurry to relay their contents to Secretary of War John Armstrong. Nearly a week after the battle he wrote to the secretary, "Sheaffe's baggage and papers fell into our hands. The papers are a valuable acquisition. I have not had time for a full examination of them."[12] Dearborn was, however, fascinated by a most singular prize found among Sir Roger's belongings. This was the general's musical snuff box, and when Dearborn saw it, he offered to pay the soldier who showed it to him $100 for it. It was said that "Granny" greatly enjoyed the wonders of the box's music and movements and helped himself freely to his adversary's snuff.

Commodore Chauncey ordered his schooners to move into the bay and moor at the wharves, where the process of shipping the goods began. Overcrowded as they already were with the troops and their equipment, there was not a great deal of room in the vessels, which led to the decision to distribute some of the goods to the people of the town. As a result, the shortage of wagons that had hampered Strachan's efforts to billet the wounded was not only due to the Americans, but also to the fact that citizens of the town, joined by men from the outlying regions, were driving their wagons to the waterside depots and loading up with whatever the Americans would give them. Even the thought of the British and Canadian blood that had been shed to defend the place did not diminish the rush to take advantage of this windfall. And some particularly callous sorts even went so far as to help the Americans load provisions and equipment from Elmsley House and barns belonging to Quetton St. George and the Boulton family and drive them down to the wharves.[13]

The fraternization of conquerors and conquered netted unexpected gains for the Americans. In casual conversation with the locals, American officers soon learned that there were other caches of public papers besides General Sheaffe's to be found, and that officials had hidden the provincial and military money when the American squadron first appeared on Monday evening. The sanctity of some of the papers, such as those belonging to the office of Surveyor General Thomas Ridout, was protected by the terms of capitulation, and General Dearborn made a further guarantee of this. But the money was another matter and Major William King asked the town's representatives to hand it over; a story even spread that the Americans threatened to burn York to the ground if it was not produced, with the harshest threats being attributed to Lieutenant Jesse Elliott.

A delegation went to visit Elizabeth Derenzy, who had remained to look after her dying father, Prideaux Selby, in the family home. William Roe, Selby's clerk in the receiver general's office, was then summoned and told to fetch the funds from where he had hidden them the night before the battle. This he did and, with Mrs. Derenzy looking on, William Chewett and William Allan gave the money to Strachan, who delivered it to Captain Horatio Gates Armstrong, Twenty-third Infantry. Armstrong, who like Colonel Mitchell appears to have volunteered to join the expedition, gave Strachan a receipt for "the Sum of Eight thousand, five hundred and Seventy Eight Dollars, one shilling and four pence, principal and interest in Army Bills."[14] But this was only the money buried near Peter Robinson's home east of the Don River. The bag of army bills, estimated at about $600 in worth, that Roe had secreted at the home of the late Donald McLean was gone, and so was the strongbox in which it had been stowed. The Americans accepted Roe's story and, at the advice of William Powell and his colleagues, Mrs. Derenzy offered a $50 reward for its return; someone eventually found the chest and brought it back, empty. Obviously, one group of looters had gotten away with a tidy sum of cash.

It was on the third night of the American occupation of York that one of the best known incidents of that momentous week took place. After dark on Thursday the town continued to be a dangerous place, as men moved stealthily through the shadows intent on plunder. At some point in the early hours of Friday, the vandalism suddenly escalated when someone set fire to the Parliament Buildings near the Town Blockhouse at the eastern end of York. The two houses of government, one of which had been used lately as a barracks, had already been broken into on the night of the battle, as John Hunter, the messenger of the assembly, reported. But this time, the intruders, by design or accident, kindled a fire in one or both of the structures, which were so quickly engulfed in flames

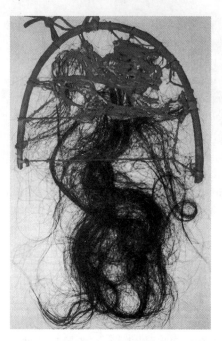

A preserved scalp. The scalp discovered at York may have resembled this pre-1815 artefact, comprising skin and hair removed from someone's head (probably after the victim had died). Both whites and natives took scalps in the War of 1812. Many aboriginal people believed scalps held much of the spiritual power of their opponents. Thus a scalp could strengthen the spiritual well-being of a family that received it as well as symbolize that a past offence against them had been avenged. (Toronto Culture, Fort York Collection)

that no one could do anything to save them. When the last of the fires burned out, only the brick walls and some charred timbers were left standing.[15]

No one undertook an immediate investigation of the fire nor were any suspects apprehended. The earliest and most intensive look into events took place years later while Robert Gourlay was assembling his study of Upper Canada and asked the townspeople what had happened.[16] They pointed the finger at American seamen, although Gourlay also learned that Captain Joseph Grafton, Twenty-first Infantry, who was doing the rounds of sentries posted in the town, claimed that there were no Americans present as the buildings burned, only residents. Grafton speculated that some disaffected locals had done the deed, but Gourlay thought the sailors were the likely suspects, because of the story that had spread about the scalp.

A human scalp became the most bizarre trophy of war taken at York. Some said intruders discovered it hanging beside the ceremonial mace next to the speaker's chair and were so mortified that the British would display such a gruesome trophy of war in their legislature that they decided to burn the place down. While a few observers have suggested that this item was only the speaker's peruke, comments made by Chauncey and Dearborn left little doubt as to what it was. The commodore sent one of the captured British flags and a carved wooden lion that had stood atop the speaker's chair to the navy department along with "the Mace over which was hanging a human *scalp*, these articles was taken from the Parliament House by one of my officers and presented to me – the scalp I caused to be presented to General Dearborn."[17] This the general confirmed: "A scalp was found in the Executive and Legislative Council chamber, *suspended near* the *Speaker's chair*, in company with the mace and other emblems of royalty."[18] Chauncey's admission that someone in his squadron had the scalp first directs blame for the fire toward the navy, but it is by no means conclusive; one account claimed that Major Forsyth of the Rifle Regiment found the scalp.

There is a good possibility that Captain Grafton's suggestion that local citizens set the blaze is correct, since the Americans had opened up the jail shortly after the capitulation and let the prisoners loose. And by Friday, 30 April, it was obvious that men from the town and the outlying region were guilty of looting and vandalism.[19] William Smith, for instance, a soap and candle maker in the town, was apprehended in Elmsley House removing locks and hinges from the doors and lead weights from the sashes of broken windows. Duncan Cameron, acting in his role as magistrate, came upon Benjamin Thrall from Markham loading his wagon with iron fittings from a stash of stolen materiel on the grounds of Jesse Ketchum's tannery at Yonge and Newgate Streets. Cameron ordered the men with him to remove the iron from Thrall's wagon, whereupon Thrall told him that the Americans had given it to him and, if Cameron preferred, they could row out to the *Madison* and have the deal confirmed.

An incident with the potential for violence took place in the home of William Knott, who lived at York with a family of ten.[20] On 30 April William Howard from nearby Whitchurch broke into their residence and grabbed Knott by the collar, ordering him to hand over his boots. Knott struggled with Howard and told him to stop for fear of trampling the wounded soldiers who had been billeted there and were lying on the floor. Howard warned him that he had a party of men outside and if Knott did not give up his boots, they would cut his head

The Parliamentary Mace. Traditionally used as weapons, maces became symbols of the authority of parliaments and their speakers. This mace was carried into the legislative assembly of Upper Canada at York by the sergeant-at-arms and displayed on a table in front of the speaker throughout each day's session until April 1813. It is made of gilded wood and measures 4 feet, 8 inches long (142 cm). President Franklin Roosevelt ordered its return to Ontario in 1934. (Legislative Assembly of Ontario)

The British Lion. Least well known among government symbols plundered at York is the golden lion that adorned the speaker's chair in the Legislative Assembly, probably atop its canopy. Carved of wood, the lion is 4 feet long (122 cm) and still remains in the custody of the U.S. Navy. (U.S.N.A. Museum)

off. The situation might have had tragic results if a platoon of American soldiers had not interceded and taken Howard into custody, saying he was one of their deserters.

Besides stealing public and private belongings, some of the locals took advantage of the American occupation to show their true colours without restraint.[21] A particularly notorious individual was William Peters, a thirty-nine-year-old lawyer who had recently opened an office in the town and who resided with friends on Yonge Street. He lived on military half pay and a pension earned for his years in Simcoe's Queen's Rangers, but he had run afoul of the law himself and was imprisoned at the garrison when the Americans attacked. Liberated by them, this "wretch," as William Powell described him, paraded around York with a couple of soldiers in tow, celebrating the American victory and calling for the British to be run out of the country. Similar comments were heard on the lips of Timothy Wheeler and Gideon Orton, while Alfred Barrett was seen to drink to the success of the enemy fleet and the Baptist minister, Elijah Bentley, urged anyone who would listen to him to reject loyalty to the British and help the Americans take over the province.

John Lyon, the miller from Markham, had mustered with William Jarvis's company of Incorporated Artillery just days before the battle.[22] The record does not show if he was present at the battle, captured and given a parole chit, but it certainly reveals his willingness to fraternize with the invaders. Lyon appeared in town in the days after the battle and left with an ox cart containing a pair of wheels for a field gun carriage and two iron trucks from a garrison carriage, a hundredweight of iron and some sort of bathing machine. He later claimed that General Dearborn gave them to him and he had no scruples about keeping them.

Disloyalty of a different kind had also become rampant. Chewett and Allan and their captains advised any of the militiamen who had stood with them on Tuesday and who had avoided being taken prisoner to give themselves up at the garrison and obtain their paroles. But there were others who spread the word through the countryside that every militiaman should surrender to the Americans and attain his parole whether he had borne arms that day or not. John Mills Jackson, the well known radical who owned the farm where William Peters resided and who had published an anti-government tract in 1809, was among the men named, as were his two sons, and a butcher named Ludden. Men prompted

The Royal Standard. Such flags are symbols of royal authority, and Sir Roger Sheaffe flew one at his headquarters at York as the lieutenant-governor of Upper Canada and servant of the Crown. This standard is held by the U.S. Naval Academy Museum in Annapolis, Maryland, and despite popular belief it is not the flag brought to Zebulon Pike as he lay dying. That flag, probably a Union Jack, was destroyed in a fire in the 1840s. (U.S.N.A. Museum)

by such encouragement or the supposition that they could never be called to duty if they held a parole certificate hurried into the town, a sight that merchant Stephen Jarvis remembered with disgust. "[O]ld men of seventy and boys of twelve years of age," he wrote, "[t]o the everlasting disgrace of the Country … were hourly coming in and giving themselves to Major-General Dearborn as Prisoners."[23] The seventy-year-old to whom Jarvis referred was probably Jacob De Long, Sr., who "had been dismissed [from duty with the 3rd York] as being incapable of doing any service in Garrison." But he was an exception as most of the voluntary prisoners of war were hale and hearty. As it was, even old De Long drew criticism from Lieutenant Colonel Chewett, who puzzled over how "a man of his stump who can hardly move, comes forward from the distance of 10 or 11 miles where the Enemy has not penetrated to give himself up."[24] For the Americans, it was not a case of puzzlement but one of delight, and they eagerly recorded names and gave out notes of parole all week Their estimates of how many parolees they accepted ranged from 500 to 1,000 and beyond.

The evidence of disloyalty, the burning of the legislative buildings and the disheartening discovery on Friday morning that even the church and the library in Elmsley House had been pillaged brought matters to a head for the leading citizens of at York, and on that morning they convened a meeting to discuss the situation. Present were Chief Justice Thomas Scott and William Powell, the magistrates Thomas Ridout and Duncan Cameron, and John Strachan. After some deliberation, they wrote a formal request to General Dearborn that the magistrates and sheriffs resume their roles as keepers of the peace so that the lawlessness in the town could be brought under control. The general was in a more accommodating mood than he had been the day after the battle. He told them that he had already ordered Lieutenant Colonel Eleazar Ripley to send a detachment of his Twenty-first Infantry to act as sentries in the town in response to the note Justice Powell had sent him on Wednesday. Dearborn also issued a general order stating that he expected his troops to "support the civil authority when properly exercised."[25] One thing Dearborn was not willing to do, however, was to return General Sheaffe's baggage as Powell had requested, making an effort to regain his old friend's belongings. Dearborn believed that Sir Roger had "not acted honourably in relation to the capitulation" and so his possessions, public and private, were "detained on public account for future disposition."[26]

Ripley's Twenty-first made a good account of itself among the people of York, as had some officers throughout the week. Sheriff Beikie expressed his gratitude for the way Captain White Youngs, Fifteenth Infantry, and Lieutenant William Sumter, Light Artillery, had offered their assistance on Tuesday and then stayed around to chase off some men who tried to break into his house. The Beikies recognized Major William Swan, the quarter master general with the expedition, who also helped the family and even stayed over one night. "Should he fall into our hands [in battle]," Mrs. Beikie wrote later, "I hope it will not be forgotten of him."[27] Lieutenant Peter Pelham of Ripley's unit was another young gentleman who made a good impression and there was more than one family who felt they owed him a debt for helping to preserve their safety during the difficult times.

Dearborn's attempt to guard the town was too little and too late for some people. On Thursday Ely Playter, with his brother George, had watched from the safety of the woods while American soldiers broke down the door of his home and carted off as much as they could carry.[28] The army seemed to be everywhere, visiting the farms in the outlying region – as often on legitimate patrols as not – and guarding the Don River bridge on the road to Kingston. On Friday Playter decided to risk a visit to town to see General Dearborn about the damage done to his place and went into York with Andrew Mercer. There they met William Allan, who assured them that it was not improper for them to add their names to the list of prisoners and accept parole notes, so this he and Mercer did. They looked around at the damaged garrison and found out that two of their friends, Patrick Hartney and Andrew Borland, had been billeted with the Higgins family and walked over to see them. Both men appeared to be making good progress despite the fact that Borland had suffered six wounds and Hartney three. After some conversation Playter went back to the garrison to plead his case with General Dearborn. The general expressed his deep regret, informed Playter about the formal posting of guards in the town and assured him that he would find out who was responsible for the break-in and punish them.

The next morning, Saturday, the first of May, when John Strachan brought a distraught Angelique Givins to Dearborn to explain that her house had been vandalized repeatedly, the general was at first not very sympathetic.[29] He admitted that there was little he could do for anyone connected with the native warriors. But Strachan added the tale of the widow of Henry Brown, messenger to the lieutenant governor, whose home, also located outside the town, had been pillaged, with two chests of drawers, a bedstead, women's clothing, tools, silverware, carded wool, candle sticks, crockery and a table cloth all pilfered. There were other sad stories to tell and Strachan even had his own experience to recount. Dearborn had given him fifty barrels of flour to distribute among the needy, and the pastor had hurried away to find a wagon, only to discover when he drove back to the depot that nearly every one of the fifty barrels had vanished.

In response to this latest petition for help, Dearborn declared "that he had issued the strictest orders to the contrary, but it was evident that the great degree

The Givins house. James Givins owned a park lot at the modern intersection of Queen and Givins streets and was a neighbour to Æneas Shaw, who lived on a lot just to the east. He built a substantial house in the 1790s that stood until 1891. (TRL, T11234)

of insubordination that prevailed among his troops rendered such orders of no effect."[30] Repeating his regrets and promising to do something to alleviate the situation, the general bid good-day to his visitors and shortly afterward issued orders for the embarkation of the American force. Chauncey had been expecting to be under sail within two days of the battle, the original plan having been to take York and then quickly combine with the force at Fort Niagara to attack Fort George. But the shock of so many casualties, the mountain of materiel and stores captured at York, bad weather and worse management had changed the timetable.

The evacuation of the wounded began Saturday morning. Some of them had already been sent on board the vessels on Thursday and then returned to shore in a frustrating reversal of orders that led to unnecessary suffering. Now they were again bundled up and carried out to the *Asp* and *Gold Hunter*, which had been delegated to serve as hospital ships. The cask containing Zebulon Pike's remains was also sent over to the *Asp* along with Chauncey's despatches, and the commodore ordered Lieutenant Smith on the *Asp* to take the *Gold Hunter* under tow and head immediately for Sackets Harbor. There were too many casualties for the two vessels, however, so the others were spread around the squadron along with their attendants; William Beaumont ended up on the schooner *Julia.*

Eleazar Aspinwall, the storekeeper and part-time doctor from the town who had laboured so tirelessly to treat the British wounded after the battle, also embarked in one of the vessels. A native of Massachusetts with neither wife nor children at York, he had accepted the enticements of the army officers to join their service. Despite his defection to the enemy, Aspinwall's former neighbours praised his "exertions" on the behalf of the troops. His departure was unfortunate for William Baldwin, who had to do the rounds of all the wounded by himself until William Hackett, the surgeon of the 8th Foot, returned to York, and Surgeon Robert Kerr from Forty Mile Creek and another medico named Sumner came to town nine days after the battle.[31]

While the troops began the long process of transferring out to the squadron, Chauncey's crews took on the last of the public and military goods. About this time Lieutenant Magno Leos Green of the Provincial Marine was escorted out to the *Madison*, becoming the only prisoner of war taken from York. The Americans lacked room on the warships to carry off any other prisoners of war and so left several hundred combatants behind, bound by honour not to take up arms until exchanged for captured Americans. As for Green, whose naval career had only lately begun and who had yet to serve afloat, Chauncey intended to exchange him for one of his recently captured naval officers. All the American vessels were weighed down under the captured goods "as deep as they could swim," as one observer wrote.[32] Mrs. Beikie heard that the Americans "so loaded their vessels with the spirits of this place, that I am told they have thrown quantities of pork and flour into the lake."[33] They had given much of the surplus foodstuff to the inhabitants, even to the point of being "ordered to roll barrels of salt meat and barrels of bread to their doors," as seaman Ned Myers recollected.[34]

The Americans also loaded stores into the *Duke of Gloucester,* which would be sailing with the squadron. The British had almost finished refitting the badly decayed schooner as a transport and U.S. Navy personnel completed the jobs of caulking and rigging so it would be seaworthy.[35] The same could not be done for the *Governor Hunter,* which was awash by the shore, and so the sloop was burned. General Dearborn used part of the funds collected from Prideaux Selby's office to compensate its owner, Joseph Kendrick, with army bills worth £300.

As the last of the army and navy left the town and garrison, parties of soldiers set fire to the Town Blockhouse, the blockhouse in the garrison, a barracks built for the naval artificers, another used by the army and Government House; they also broke the town's only printing press and scattered the print into the bay. They had already dismantled the batteries, transporting their guns and equipment and any other ordnance they could find to the squadron, where some of them were unceremoniously dumped overboard. The discarded weapons appear to have been the old condemned guns because one officer wrote "the battering ordnance were all spiked and sunk in the Lake, on our evacuation of the place."[36] Such "battering ordnance" usually referred to the heaviest calibre of guns used during sieges, but since the old 12-pdr. and pair of 18-pdrs. were the heaviest weapons at York and were useless to the navy without trunnions, they were the most likely to be tipped over the side. Captain John Scott also noted the disposal of some of the guns and Ned Myers remembered, "we sunk many guns in the lake," which might suggest that some of the other ancient ordnance brought to York by Lieutenant Governor Simcoe had been discovered and deemed unusable.[37] The guns that were kept were probably the two 12-pdr. and six 6-pdr. long guns, the eight 18-pdr. carronades and the two brass 6-pdr. field guns abandoned by Sheaffe. This last pair may have ended up on the *Scourge* as Myers also recounted how the crew "got two small brass guns at York, four-pounders, I believe, which Mr. [Joseph] Osgood clapped into our two spare ports forward."[38] Whatever naval service the brass guns performed, it was brief, as the schooner was outfitted with two iron guns on its forecastle within the next few weeks.

The embarkation was nearly completed late Saturday night beneath a glow reflected off the cloud cover from the burning blockhouses, barracks and storehouses, resembling the aftermath on the day of the battle. The next morning one of the officers came on shore again with a patrol to collect a group of stragglers who had spent the night in one of the taverns.[39] By Sunday afternoon the squadron had left the bay but the wind had been blowing strongly on shore all day, making it impossible for the squadron to claw its way off the land and gain a seaway, so Chauncey ordered his captains to anchor and wait for more favourable conditions. The weather had been foul for days and had even forced Lieutenant Smith in the *Asp* with the *Gold Hunter* in tow to return from the lake and join the others after more than a day of trying to break free of the land.

The *Lady of the Lake* had joined the squadron by now after delivering Master Shipwright Henry Eckford and a crew of artificers to Niagara to join Master Commandant Oliver Perry, who was hurriedly fitting out several converted merchantmen at Black Rock near Buffalo.[40] The schooner easily outsailed the other small craft, which lumbered under their weight of guns, men and captured goods, and Chauncey transferred over to it along with Dearborn, his staff and some of the wounded. They made a quick passage across the lake and landed at Four Mile Creek, just east of Fort Niagara, late Sunday afternoon.

The concussion caused by the exploding grand magazine on Tuesday had rattled the windows at Fort Niagara at 1:30 P.M. on Tuesday, and later that night officers on Lewiston Heights could make out a red glow to the north. It was assumed that the town of York was in flames, but this notion only lasted until Sailing Master Mervin Mix arrived in the *Growler* on Wednesday with Chauncey and Dearborn's first reports about the battle. By the time Mix upped anchor that afternoon to return to York, word was already spreading of the great victory, the death of Pike, the escape of Sheaffe and the mountain of captured stores.[41]

As soon as the *Lady of the Lake* dropped its hooks off Four Mile Creek on Sunday, Chauncey went on land with Dearborn and they were soon in consultation with Major General Morgan Lewis, who commanded in that sector.[42] After some explanations about the battle at York, the officers turned to the next step in the campaign, the attack on Fort George. In the end they decided to delay the assault until the army could be brought over from York and more reinforcements could be assembled. Leaving Dearborn behind, Chauncey returned to the schooner on Monday to retrace his route to York.

The American squadron remained pinned in Humber Bay by an unrelenting wind that threw sheets of rain at the warships through Sunday and Monday and into Tuesday. Living conditions became intolerable, since there was less room in the vessels than during the voyage from Sackets, owing to the heaps of captured cargo, and the soldiers and sailors were forced to remain on deck while they waited their turn to spend a few hours below out of the elements. They put up with the situation for a couple of days, but the bad weather would not let up and by Wednesday Surgeon Beaumont was recording how the men were getting sick and could find little relief in the crowded and stinking conditions below decks. Dysentery and diarrhea soon became rampant and tempers turned foul. Neither officers nor men knew what was going on – whether it was just the wind or some other campaign objective that was keeping them at anchor. It was only known that Dearborn had left the anchorage and not returned, and this matter became a focus for the pent-up frustrations and misery. Captain Scott explained to his friend, "We never saw him again until the 10th [of May]. What his object could have been for keeping the men on Board crammed in heaps on each other During 7 days of rain and storm … I cannot conceive."[43]

Commodore Chauncey's temper showed too when he finally managed to return to the squadron on Tuesday, 4 May. He noticed right away that there was a commodore's broad pendant flying at the truck of the *Oneida*'s main mast and he did not delay in scribbling a note to Lieutenant Melancthon Woolsey demanding "to know by what authority you have assumed the command of the Squadron at this anchorage."[44] In the U.S. Navy, the title "commodore" was an honorific rather than an authorized rank, used by the department to highlight the command status of only a handful of senior officers. It had become a popular practice, however, for the senior officer on a station to raise a broad pendant without official approval, and this is what Woolsey did as soon as the *Lady of the Lake* departed on Sunday. In Chauncey's absence, he was the senior ranking officer, and even though Chauncey had left his pendant flying in the *Madison* and given Lieutenant Elliott permission to issue orders, Woolsey assumed a place he believed was rightly his and subsequently ignored any signal sent from the *Madison*.

This was a clear example of the ever-simmering controversy about rank among commissioned officers afloat and on shore. In this instance a grievance had probably been fermenting from the day that Woolsey and the other lieutenants in the squadron were bypassed for command of the flagship after the arrest of Master Commandant James Leonard. Woolsey and his fellows watched Elliott get the post and then act as a special delegate at York, conceivably another slight to their seniority of service. Woolsey apparently did not reveal such issues to Chauncey when he replied in writing to him, although he did mention that some of the other officers sanctioned his assumption of temporary command. To this Chauncey curtly replied, "it is a matter of indifference to me what their opinions are."[45] He made himself clear: "My pendant was my representative and as long as that was flying on board of this ship, every Signal made from her ought to have been obeyed, and hereafter *Shall* be obeyed." Case closed, but wounds left unhealed.

The expedition suffered for three more days in Humber Bay as the unprecedented stormy weather continued with high winds and heavy rains; locals said they had never seen a season like it. The vessels tossed about at their moorings, "with two anchors ahead and lower Yards and Top Gallant Masts down," the commodore reported, adding, "[The] Troops are becoming Sickley ... [and] are not only exposed to the rain, but the Sea makes a fair break over them."[46] Chauncey had the *Asp* try again on Tuesday to get away with the wounded, this time heading for Four Mile Creek instead of Sackets. He ordered the *Fair American* to pass a tow cable to the *Gold Hunter* and head across the lake as well, and the *Lady of the Lake* also left with some of the wounded. Finally, on Saturday, 8 May, the weather broke, the rain stopped and the wind shifted and the squadron quickly weighed anchor and slipped over to Four Mile Creek, where the tedious process of transferring everyone to land began. It was too late for one poor soul whom William Beaumont found dead in the hold of the *Julia*. The man had been recovering from a slight contusion on his back, inflicted during the devastating explosion, when he succumbed to suffocation in the dank and airless conditions of the bilge. At least he was spared the next set of hardships his former messmates would face on shore.

At York the week of steady rain brought a matter of extreme unpleasantness into plain view. The nearly continuous downpour soaked the ground and washed away the soil, eroding rivulets across the cleared land beyond the burned-out garrison and around the old French fort, revealing how little effort Captain Jeremiah Hayden's fatigue party had put into burying the dead. Anyone who went to the garrison to see what the Americans had left behind was horror-struck at the sight of exposed corpses. Ely Playter was one of the witnesses to the macabre spectacle and noted in his diary, "The Yankies had buried all the Dead and I perceived they had done it very ill."[47] When the rain stopped, John Strachan stepped forward once more to perform his civic duty by enlisting a group of men who were willing to go with him and complete the grisly task. They dug proper graves and put the fallen soldiers to rest again, the pastor praying over them for salvation and peace.

While the American squadron still pitched and swayed at its anchors in Humber Bay, the people of York began to assess the impact of the attack on their town. Some held the same God-fearing opinion as Penelope Beikie, who declared, "I really attribute this visit to the vengeance of heaven on this place."[48] The government heads had invoked the wrath of God, she explained, by refusing to distribute the stores and equipment that had been kept in storage since the time of Simcoe. "I think we deserve all we have got," she added. Some people were impressed with how the invaders had distributed so much of the captured goods to the locals, prompting Isaac Wilson to write, "They used the people with great civility…. [and] were praised for their good conduct."[49] Nobody was killed during the occupation, no one complained of having been physically molested and the widespread looting by the soldiers and seamen seemed to be largely forgotten. Even the town's leaders agreed that the Americans "behaved much better than we expected."[50] The gentlemanly conduct of such young officers as Peter Pelham and William King left a lasting impression, and it was even suggested that if the British had not been so destructive in their attack on Ogdensburg in February, "there would have been little or no depredations committed here."[51]

Blame for what had happened to "this disgraced city," as John Strachan described York, turned inward.[52] The authorities issued a notice on 3 May stating that law had been restored and that acts of treason against His Majesty's government would be subject to punishment. The traitorous behavior of local men who sought their parole without ever taking up arms aroused disgust and the process began to identify exactly who they were. As a result, those who had looted their neighbours and fraternized with the enemy found their names on lists and the magistrates at their doors. But the lion's share of resentment for what had happened to the town was reserved for one man.

Even Justice William Powell had to admit that "the universal reproach of every man and woman" was directed at his friend Roger Sheaffe.[53] There had been murmurs about his conduct on the day of the battle and they increased throughout the week. Such "impeachments and idle boastings of the ignorant were beneath notice," Powell wrote, given the dire straits of the town, but when he heard the senior militia officers repeating the complaints, he determined to make a record of what had happened and what their opinions were.[54] He wrote two accounts of the day and the subsequent events without overtly criticizing the general's decisions, but he also made a point of mentioning accusations made by Major Allan and Lieutenant Colonel Chewett on how the engagement had been directed. In the end Powell admitted that Sheaffe had failed to support Major Givins's warriors adequately in the morning and missed a chance to counter-attack after the explosion of the grand magazine left the enemy stunned and disordered.

Powell's accounts were mild compared to a long narrative composed by a committee of York's most influential men on Saturday, 8 May. Dr. Baldwin, Alexander Wood, Duncan Cameron, Allan, Chewett, Thomas Ridout and a magistrate from the township named Samuel Smith sat down to read over and revise a document that John Strachan had drawn up. It detailed the situation from Monday night through to the embarkation of the Americans and the re-establishment of civil authority a week later. The manuscript followed the events of the battle in chronological order, the tactics employed by each side, the advantages won by the Americans and the accidents suffered by the British. Tribute was paid to the "greatest courage and intrepidity" of the grenadiers of the 8th Foot and to "the vigour and courage" of Lieutenant Colonel Philip Hughes and Lieutenant Philip Ingouville, but the evidence of "indecision and want of energy" in the commander, the lack of orders, the lost opportunities and the failure to make a stand were also noticed.[55] The last portion came to the regrettable conclusion that the loss of York was largely due to Roger Sheaffe's inept generalship. His inadequate preparations for the impending attack, his "ill calculated" tactics, his failure to rouse the troops "by his personal conduct that he was hearty in the cause," his abrupt retreat, abandonment of the field guns and decision to take the medical staff and supplies with him were all reasons for his censure. There was no doubt that he had "lost entirely the confidence of the regulars and militia, and his very name is odious to all ranks of people."

But the committee did not stop there. They endorsed Strachan's second key point of criticism, one he and others had been making for half a year, that the "true cause of our defeat" was Governor-in-Chief Prevost's policy of "forbearance." The governor was not specifically named, but there was a clear reference to his failure to take the war to the Americans, especially with an attack on Sackets Harbor. This had led to the loss of command on Lake Ontario and the fall of York was the outcome. "In the capture of York," they agreed, "behold the first fruits of that imbecility which prevented a vigorous attack upon Sacketts Harbour, an attack which … would have secured this Province during the whole war."

The circle of head men did not haggle over the manuscript for long, finally making only a few revisions to the original copy. To them, as they sat in the middle of war-ravaged York, the answers seemed simple. Sheaffe was incompetent. Prevost's strategy was misguided and, as the condition of their town showed, ultimately self-destructive. Everyone signed, except for Thomas Ridout, which aroused some ill will afterwards, and they agreed that Strachan should send the account to John Richardson, a successful merchant and elected official in Montreal. Richardson was to show it around to his acquaintances and to Prevost, and then, perhaps, have it published "in the form of a pamphlet."[56] The truth about what happened at York would then be public knowledge.

Location of the Parliament Buildings. The Parliament Buildings stood on the lot to the left at the intersection of Front Street and Parliament Street. This was the eastern limit of the town in 1813, while the westernmost streets were about where the CN Tower now stands. This view looks westward along Front Street toward downtown Toronto. (Photograph by Robert Malcomson)

CHAPTER 14

"Great men in little things and little men in great things"[1]

CAMPAIGN CONSEQUENCES

Sir Roger Hale Sheaffe's retreat to Kingston was a dismal affair. The column had gone but a few miles when it met the light company of the 8th Regiment of Foot coming on at a brisk pace. The general had sent a rider the night before with orders for the light bobs to push forward, but they had arrived too late for the action and now could only form a rearguard and undertake the depressing task of retracing their steps to Kingston. By sunset it began to rain and, since the soldiers from York had left their greatcoats at the garrison along with their knapsacks, blankets and spare clothing, they were soon soaked through. Fatigued and in shock after their defeat in battle and the loss of their comrades, the men trudged through the mud to put distance between themselves and the enemy, who could be close on their heels for all they knew. The easterly wind drove the cold April rain into their faces, deepening their misery, sapping their strength. They were, as one military expert described such a demoralized body of men, "like burned-out cinders."[2]

The main body moved ahead, leaving a few officers behind with some of the walking wounded and the women and children. Quarter Master Bryan Finan of the Royal Newfoundland Fencibles and his family were in this group and years later his son faithfully recorded their experiences. They took shelter that first night in a cottage 8 miles east of York, where their only meal was mutton and bread left over from breakfast. They all crowded into the small dwelling and spent the night amid "the piteous cries and groans of the wounded, the squalling of children, and lamentations of the women."[3]

Next morning the officers procured a wagon hauled by a team of oxen, in which the women and children rode while the men walked. The rain continued hard before turning to drizzle and the road was so bad that they managed to cover about a mile per hour. They came upon another house, where they obtained food for breakfast, and Mrs. Finan and Lieutenant Robin Cook's wife bought two blankets, at the steep price of 10 shillings each, to provide some covering and warmth for the shivering children. The homeowners were eager to see their visitors off, warning them that they had heard the American army was coming and that they feared reprisal for offering help to the party. The sad procession managed only 5 miles that day, ending up in what appears to have been a squalid barn with only tea to warm their innards and filthy straw to soothe their aching limbs.

And so the march continued day after day with the hardships piling up. Not only were the inhabitants reluctant to help them but some blatantly stated how pleased they were to hear of the American victory. Added to this was the fact that the main body of the retreat had already seized any available resources – food, horses, wagons – and had left the more severely wounded behind in twos and threes. Bryan Finan's temper finally broke one morning when he asked a farmer for help and received only a shrug in return. Exasperated by the entire situation, Finan threatened to have the man charged with treason and all his property confiscated, whereupon the intimidated settler admitted to knowing where there might be a pair of wagons. In short order he rolled them out of the woods where they had been hidden.

The main body of the column broke into several segments so they could advance from point to point in stages, with Thomas Plucknett's artificers bringing up the rear, just ahead of Finan's people.[4] The handful of militia under Major Samuel Wilmot who had joined the retreat went as far as the town of Hamilton (today's Cobourg) and were then sent back. Surgeon William Hackett turned around too and made the muddy trek back to York, checking on the wounded as he met them. For some of the casualties the march was their last as they succumbed to their wounds.

It was a miserable corps of soldiers that trudged along the Kingston Road, and the dissatisfaction with their circumstances showed itself in at least two incidents. The first was recorded by an anonymous "gentleman of high respectability" and printed in the newspapers.[5] He trumpeted the bravery of a sergeant who had retreated with Sheaffe, "but (I suppose) not liking his company," embarked in a leaky batteau with four of his mates and rowed back to York. Once there, they sneaked past the American guards and gathered up a large number of the knapsacks and personal effects that had been left behind and set out on their return voyage. The batteau leaked so badly that the sergeant's party soon beached it and went back to York, where they found and made off in a large

Jabez Lynde house. Built during the War of 1812, the Lynde house in Whitby was a frequent rest stop on the road from York to Kingston; Lynde's tavern was in an adjacent log building. The home was preserved through the years and moved to its present location at Cullen Park on Taunton Road in Whitby in 1986. (Whitby Historical Society)

boat that General Brock had been accustomed to using. In this craft, they rowed to their batteau, moved the stores from it into the other boat, and some days later caught up with their regiment. The Kingston scribe identified the energetic leader of the salvage party as "Sergeant Derby" of the 8th Foot, but this must have a pseudonym meant to protect the fellow because no non-commissioned officer with that name appeared in any of the relevant regimental books. Perhaps the writer was simply adding his spin to a tale that had grown in proportion to the number of tongues that told it.

The second incident took a more violent path and was probably caused by the privations suffered by the troops, the absence of officers and the "disaffected" inhabitants they had encountered during the retreat. It occurred on the Whitby property of Jabez Lynde, one of the members of Captain John Button's "cavalry" attached to the 1st York.[6] His family lived in what was said to be one of the finest dwellings between York and Kingston and a frequent resting place for travellers. As Sheaffe's troops moved through the area, some of the wounded were left with Lynde while others stayed briefly at his home and took refreshment in the tavern he operated. When Grant Powell and William Lee were there, they told him not to let the soldiers have access to his liquor, but when Lynde announced this to the next detachment, the men took exception and broke into his house and tavern, making off with 18 gallons of spirits. It may have been the consumption of part of this brew that prompted the men also to ransack the place, stealing clothing, dinnerware, a watch, a clock and $68 in army bills. Lynde was quick to submit his claim for damages to army headquarters.

Major General Sheaffe and his staff moved ahead of the rest of the column, avoiding the crowded conditions and slim pickings that the others knew. Between the difficulties posed by travel through the nearly continuous rain and the need to make arrangements for those who followed, the general did not find time until Friday, 30 April, to write his first despatch to Governor-in-Chief Prevost about the defeat at York. This he did at the home of Major David Rogers of the Northumberland Militia, who had helped him find provisions for the rest of his sodden army. Sheaffe had time only to inform his chief that the Americans had attacked with "a force too powerful to resist with success," that Captain McNeale had been killed, the grand magazine blown up and the *Sir Isaac Brock* probably reduced to ashes.[7] He promised to submit a full report when he reached Kingston.

The general rode into town late on Sunday, 2 May.[8] The launch of the new warship *Wolfe* had taken place the week before and Commander Robert Barclay, RN, had arrived and taken over the naval station. Sheaffe occupied himself with matters of immediate concern and waited for another three days before he sat down to compose his official report about the battle at York. He described the approach of the American squadron, the assembly of his force, the detachment of its parts and the mistaken distraction of the Glengarry Light Infantry by Æneas Shaw. He referred to his own force as "our handful of troops" and failed to mention that he sent them into battle piecemeal rather than leading them as a consolidated whole.[9] Sheaffe gave full credit to Givins and McNeale, Heathcote, Eustace and Ingouville and described the accidental detonation of the Western Battery in some detail. But he stated that he only had the condemned guns and a pair of 12-pdrs. to contend with the 32-pdrs. of the squadron and did not mention that, once the first major skirmish of the battle was over, at about 8:00 A.M., he allowed his regulars and militia to wait around for hours without orders and never formed them up again to oppose the advancing Americans. Sheaffe explained his decisions to detonate the grand magazine and then retreat, "it being too apparent that a further opposition would but render the result more disastrous." There was no acknowledgment of leaving the militia officers to surrender the town, and although he noted the destruction of the *Sir Isaac Brock*, he omitted any reference to the timing of these events. He reported the enemy's strength as between 1,900 and 3,000 but gave no precise tally of his own. He complimented the units under his command as "of so superior a description, and their disposition so good, that, under less unfavourable circumstances, we might have repulsed the Enemy in spite of his numbers." To conclude his report, Sheaffe wrote a long explanation of why he had still been at York, expecting as he was to leave the post in the command of an officer of field rank.

The general's report appears to have been an amplification of a shorter despatch he wrote earlier in the day, in which he gave his strength as 600, noted that he asked Lieutenant Colonel Chewett and Major Allan to settle the terms of capitulation and that the battle had lasted for nearly eight hours, information not contained in the longer letter.[10] Sheaffe sent off both explanations to Prevost by the next express rider, together with a list of casualties, and the surrender terms, a copy of which had by now reached him from York.

The official return of dead, wounded and missing prepared at Kingston on 10 May only concerned the regular units and made no reference to the ten battle casualties among the militia and town volunteers, nor to the losses among Plucknett's artificers. It also omitted a list of the native warriors who had fallen; Sheaffe mentioned that "a few" of them were wounded and killed, the latter of whom included two chiefs.[11] More than one copy of the official report was prepared, the more widely repeated list showing that the butcher's bill among the regulars was 62 killed, 77 wounded (of whom 43 were prisoners), 10 non-wounded prisoners and 7 missing. Data in the regimental records, however, eventually showed a steeper count of 71 killed in action, 78 wounded (including 47 prisoners), 12 uninjured prisoners and 5 missing. Since the total number of regulars present at the engagement may have been as many as 413, the second set of figures revealed the high casualty rate for killed and wounded of 36 per cent.[12] Just over 50 per cent of the officers and men in the 8th Foot were killed or wounded, the 42 killed and 37 wounded among McNeale's grenadiers accounting for 65 per cent of that company's strength. By comparison the Royal Newfoundland Fencibles took nearly 32 per cent casualties and the Glengarry Infantry suffered about 10 per cent.

The capitulation papers included a return of the prisoners of war totalling 293 officers and men from regulars and irregulars alike, but this tally was also incomplete.[13] The list named 37 militia officers, but the 19 sergeants, 4 corporals and 204 privates were not identified; it was also a number far below the hundreds who were said to have surrendered after the battle without having had a part in it. In addition to the militia were William Dunbar of the Field Train Department, 7 officers of the Provincial Marine, 15 artificers, Lieutenant de Koven and 5 other regulars. A later parole list showed that there were 40 regular non-coms and rank and file who had been left wounded or sick at York most of whom were not referenced in the return which the Americans and British published widely with the terms of capitulation. At least one contemporary source shows that the capitulation tally was based on the recent muster lists as it was impossible to determine exactly how many militiamen were captured

On Saturday, 8 May, Sheaffe wrote again to Prevost, this time to describe at length a rumour he had heard that Tecumseh had captured Major General William Harrison in an action on the Maumee River in Ohio. He also passed along copies of reports he had received from York, including the information that the Americans "did not expect half the resistance they met with, … that the possession of York had cost them dearly [and] they were very much mortified at my escaping from them."[14] The general mentioned the work of Commander Barclay and his cohorts, an impending court martial and that he had informed the engineer, Lieutenant Colonel Philip Hughes, of the governor-in-chief's displeasure with the tardy manner in which he had journeyed to his new post in Upper Canada. "I have repeated my endeavours," Sheaffe wrote, "to rouse him to a sense of the necessity for the utmost diligence and activity in his department."

Sir Roger remained at Kingston awaiting orders from Prevost. In the meantime he turned to provincial matters, and because he needed members of the Executive Council to authorize any public business, he summoned Chief Justice Thomas Scott and Puisne Justice Powell to join him and John McGill at Kingston.[15] He also wrote directly to Secretary for War and the Colonies Lord Bathurst about the American seizure of provincial funds, the increase in provincial expenses and the settlement of an account dealing with the purchase of Elmsley House for use as government offices. Sir Roger did not, however, send a report about the battle immediately to Brigadier Generals John Vincent and Henry Procter nor instructions on how to conduct themselves, an omission that Vincent, for one, found surprising. Only word of mouth carried the news of battle westward at first, prompting one officer to regret that "all my accounts of the disastrous and I fear disgraceful proceedings attending the capture have been by fragments."[16] Another officer wondered if Sheaffe had been taken prisoner, while elsewhere it was thought that he had only retreated to the Don River. Hearing that the provincial papers had been destroyed, Colonel Thomas Talbot wrote, "The *Governing Heads* must have been in a state of torpor not to have made [proper] arrangements."[17] The newspaper in Buffalo even reported that Sheaffe had arrived at Fort George with a large reinforcement. At Fort George, Vincent watched the comings and goings of the American squadron and wondered when and where they would follow up their victory at York, while at Amherstburg Procter heard about the battle after returning from an unsuccessful siege of Fort Meigs and realized that his pleas for additional support would be even harder to fill.

On 13 May Sheaffe released a brief district general order about the battle, lamenting the loss of so many brave men and the unprecedented result of the action. Without offering any details, he attributed the outcome to "accidental circumstances ... the enemy's vast superiority ... [and the] inadequate aid" provided by York's defences.[18] The death of Captain McNeale and the volunteer Donald McLean received respectful notice as did the efforts of other volunteers such as Alexander Wood and John Beikie. In all, the announcement stated, the British defenders suffered 130 killed and wounded, but the *Sir Isaac Brock* and the naval stores had been destroyed to avoid capture even though the Americans landed 2,500 men. Under such circumstances, he declared, "It was not disgraceful for 200 to retire from such a force." This memorandum was soon sent on its way down the St. Lawrence for the attention of the governor-in-chief at Quebec.

Unknown to Roger Sheaffe, Sir George was on the move. The Royal Navy detachment from England reached Quebec on 5 May, about the same time as news of the fall of York.[19] Prevost met with Commodore Sir James Lucas Yeo, commander of the 465 officers and men who had crossed the Atlantic Ocean in the old troopship *Woolwich*, and the next morning they were off by boat up the St. Lawrence with the first division of the naval corps. They arrived at Kingston ten days later. Along the way all of Sheaffe's despatches and other relevant reports reached the governor-in-chief's hands, and so he was well apprised of the situation by the time he met Sir Roger at Kingston. Prevost was an experienced military man and knew not only how to write a battle report but also how to interpret one, and he could read between the lines of the several versions Sheaffe had prepared, as well as appreciate the significance of the casualty return, even if it was understated. Added to these were unofficial verbal accounts that came to his ears, and it is even possible that he had received a copy of the narrative written by the Reverend John Strachan and the headmen of York.

As soon as he learned of the fall of York, Prevost had sent word to Brigadier Generals Vincent and Procter to keep up their "best exertions for repelling any attack of the Enemy" and promising to send them reinforcements, but as for the overall situation in Upper Canada he made no immediate decisions.[20] A record of his day-to-day activities at Kingston is lacking, although he no doubt interviewed Sheaffe in detail and discussed the battle with Lieutenant Colonel Heathcote and the other officers who had been present. Powell and Scott arrived at Kingston and, along with John McGill, certainly met with Prevost and shared their insights, which were made more legitimate by their long residence and high status in the province; Powell may even have submitted his two accounts of events to the governor.

If Prevost wrote any private thoughts during the three days, they have not come to light, and he revealed little when he composed his official despatch to Bathurst on 18 May. He enclosed a copy of one of Sheaffe's reports about the battle and added only that he hoped Bathurst would give a favourable explanation to the Prince Regent about "the gallant efforts made by a handful of British troops … against the numerous force" of the enemy.[21] There was not a word in the letter about Sheaffe's conduct, nor an admission that his own decision to divide the operations of the Marine Department between Kingston and York had unnecessarily stretched his resources for defence and supply. Instead, Prevost attributed the loss to "the small proportion of regular force yet at my disposal," the American efforts to gain superiority on Lake Ontario and the fact that Admiral Warren had not sent him "a timely reinforcement of seamen" from Halifax. In other despatches he wrote that day for Bathurst, Prevost mentioned Yeo's arrival, some speculations about what the Americans intended to do next and his hope that he would soon "be enabled to prevent the enemy from availing themselves of any advantage or footing they may gain."[22]

Lieutenant Magno Leos Green, the Provincial Marine prisoner of war taken from York, was paroled by the Americans at Sackets Harbor about this time and sent to Kingston in exchange for an American officer. With Green were two seamen captured the previous November and the three of them provided as much information as they had about the fortifications and dockyard at Sackets. Prevost was keen to hear these reports and other information about the American base as it seems clear that he was awaiting an opportunity to shift the balance in the spring campaign as soon as possible.

The American army that disembarked from the squadron at Four Mile Creek on Saturday 8 May was just about as worn-out as their dejected adversaries trudging through the mud on their way back to Kingston. They had been so long exposed to bad weather, Commodore Chauncey explained to Secretary of the Navy William Jones, without the chance to get out of their wet clothes, and under unbearably crowded conditions, that fever was sweeping through them, leaving fewer than 1,000 soldiers fit for duty and more than 100 seamen on the sick lists.[23] Once on land the misery continued. It had been expected that Major General Dearborn, who had reached Niagara six days before, would make preparations for their reception, but such was not the case.

"We were ordered in[to] a huge piece of woods," wrote Captain John Scott, Fifteenth Infantry, "without a single tent in the whole Brigade and not one axe to 200 men [facing] a Rainey Wet Night to shift for Ourselves without any thing to Eat or Drink and the Ground Very Wet from the Rain of 8 or 10 successive

Days previous to our landing."[24] The wounded who had been landed earlier in the week had not fared much better. They had been taken to Fort Niagara, where, as one officer noted, "they were put into the large mess house which had no roof, the rain fell in torrents and the poor fellows lying cold and wet with their broken legs and arms undressed since they were wounded."[25] Over the next few days conditions improved for the troops, even if the weather did not, and tents soon arrived along with all the other equipment necessary for establishing camps at Four Mile and Two Mile creeks, while a portion of the force was housed in and around Fort Niagara.

A complaint, about the treatment of the wounded eventually landed on Secretary of War John Armstrong's desk and he fired off a terse order to Dearborn to make a full investigation into the matter. Indignant at the criticism, the general wrote back to acknowledge the unpleasant conditions suffered while the squadron lay wind-bound near York and the regrettable circumstances under which the army landed at Niagara. In his defence, he explained that he had ordered a well equipped camp to be set up on dry ground, had visited the sick daily and could offer nothing but praise for his medical staff. Given the situation "where so great a proportion of wounded men were so shockingly mangled" and the efforts to attend to their needs, Dearborn believed they had been as "humanely treated as any reasonable man could expect."[26] He also had some thoughts to share with Armstrong about the source of his information. "We have many scribblers in the Army," he wrote, "who view all subjects on the dark side and who appear to embrace with pleasure every opportunity of grumbling and finding fault ... to the real injury of the Service."

There *was* a fair deal of discontent in the army. Captain Scott, for one, put the blame for everyone's misery on "Granny Dearborn." Scott was with the group of officers who headed for Fort Niagara to find food and equipment for their men the morning after landing at Four Mile Creek. They got as far as the home of Joseph West, the garrison surgeon, where the general had taken up residence, and were ordered back to their camp. "The Genl has got himself in comfortable quarters," reported Scott to his friend David Thompson, "where he has wine aplenty with which he was furnished in abundance at York."[27] Scott was also one of the individuals who spread what he had heard about Dearborn's fascination with General Sheaffe's musical snuff box. "Their [sic] are some Great men in Little things," Scott added, vowing to drop the subject thereafter, "and Little men in Great things."

Captain John Walworth, Sixth Infantry, was not too pleased with Old Granny either. He was concerned that he and his company would not get the public notice he felt was deserved for capturing the Western Battery. "General Dearborn

… was on board during the whole of the action and … seldom rewards those entitled to it," he complained to his father-in-law. "It is sufficient to say that he is the most unpopular man with that part of the army that I know of."[28] Colonel Cromwell Pearce was watching to see what credit he would reap for having assumed command after Brigadier General Pike was wounded, while others were noting that Pike's death left a need for aggressive leadership which neither Pearce nor Dearborn filled. One of the anonymous "scribblers," almost certainly Baptist Irvine of the Baltimore Volunteers, who was recovering from his accidental bayonet wound, revealed to his own newspaper, the *Baltimore Whig*, "I do assure you there appeared no generalship. Had we landed *before* day light, and attacked the enemy *at* day break, it is almost certain we could have made all the British regulars prisoners, with Sheaffe into the bargain."[29]

It was not all doom and gloom that filled the letters and informal reports about the battle. Irvine's captain, Stephen Moore, who had been felled at Pike's side in the explosion of the grand magazine, announced that the "descent on the Canadian shore … has been victorious and glorious to the American arms."[30] This despite the fact that his wound had taken a bad turn after he was transported to Fort Niagara, prompting the surgeons to amputate his left leg below the knee. Surgeon Amasa Trowbridge, who had been up to his elbows in blood, eventually passed along "information which must be pleasing to every person who will be pleased with the success of American arms over our enemies."[31] Dearborn's aide-de-camp Lieutenant Colonel Samuel Conner proudly asserted that the victory "decides the command of the Lakes … [and] evinces the firmness, intrepidity and discipline of the American Troops under trying circumstances."[32] And even the grumblers took pride in their accomplishments and adopted informal badges to signify their membership in that band of brothers who had been bloodied at York, as one officer who arrived on the scene at this time noted. "The heroes of York," he wrote, "assumed the privilege of wearing their caps more on one side, of giving greater latitude to their whiskers, and particularly of cultivating large mustachios…. Many of the Yorkers were in the habit of carrying a naked [sword] on all occasions, with no scabbards at the belt, as if it had been thrown away as a useless incumbrance, at the opening of the campaign."[33]

The official reporting of the battle took several forms. Dearborn penned a brief note to Secretary of War John Armstrong on 27 April, announcing the victory and lamenting Pike's death, and then took time the next day to compose a longer account. To Major Benjamin Forsyth, and his riflemen, the general gave full credit for gaining the beach-head against what he stated were 700 regulars and militia and 100 warriors led by General Sheaffe "in person."[34] He described how Pike led the next wave ashore and forced the British to withdraw at the cost of about fifty killed and wounded, but he did not mention the time and organization that went into landing the rest of the force and all the artillery. Instead, he commented briefly on the taking of the Western Battery and described the detonation of the grand magazine and its disastrous effects. "Our loss by the explosion must I fear exceed one hundred," he admitted. But Dearborn also asserted that the British lost forty men at the same time, an error that Colonel Pearce later alleged was due to the general's distant vantage point and foggy knowledge of the earlier explosion in the Western Battery. The general praised the efforts of Commodore Chauncey and his squadron in subduing the enemy batteries but had to acknowledge the enemy's destruction of the *Sir Isaac Brock* and the absence of any other warships (omitting notice of the *Duke of Gloucester*).

Two further reports to the secretary supplemented Dearborn's original despatch. The general wrote again on 3 May when he reached Fort Niagara to provide more details about the casualties and the privations suffered by the troops because of the horrid weather conditions. The British had lost 100 killed and 200 wounded, he announced, 300 taken prisoner and upwards of 500 militia left on parole, "York was the principal depot for Niagara and Detroit" and more material and provisions had been captured than the squadron could carry away.[35] Trophies of war about which Dearborn made special mention were the scalp, the speaker's mace "and other emblems of royalty."

Lieutenant Colonel Conner also submitted a summary of the action to the secretary on the general's behalf. He included details about the units involved and some of the individuals, but as Pearce and Scott, Walworth and others had feared, their personal conduct received neither recognition nor praise in either Conner's or Dearborn's despatches.[36] Beyond Benjamin Forsyth, the only officers Conner mentioned were his friend Colonel Eleazar Ripley and Lieutenant Colonel Francis McClure, whose volunteers had not been involved in the fighting at all.

Commodore Chauncey's reports to Secretary Jones repeated the facts as presented in the other despatches, with the exception that he filled in some of the navy-related details, mentioning, for instance, that his schooners "took a position within about Six hundred yards of their principal fort and opened a heavy carronade upon the Enemy which did great execution and very much contributed to their final destruction."[37] He emphasized the amount of ordnance and provisions captured by the expedition and predicted that "the loss of stores at this place will be an irreparable one to the enemy, for, independent of the difficulty in transportation, the articles cannot be replaced in this country."[38]

If the official despatches were vague or offered only round figures, the returns of killed and wounded revealed the stark details of the price paid to seize

Little York. Of the several lists that were eventually published, the official report prepared by Brigade Major Charles Hunter and attached to Dearborn's letter to Armstrong on 3 May was the most informative.[39] It showed a total of 308 officers and men killed and wounded, about 17 per cent of the 1,800 army personnel said to have been in the expedition. Hunter's return broke the casualties down into those inflicted by gunshot versus the explosion. The former group included men from only the Rifle Regiment and the Fifteenth Infantry, which suffered 8 killed, 23 wounded and 6 killed, 8 wounded, respectively. Casualties in the other units were shown to have been a result of the explosion, the tallies revealing their positions in Pike's column at the time of the explosion, with those in the rear or on the flank nearly out of range of the deluge of debris. The Sixth Infantry suffered the worst, with 13 killed and 104 wounded, followed by the artillery units (6, 34), the Sixteenth (5, 33), the Fifteenth (9, 25), the Twenty-first (1, 14), McClure's Volunteers (2, 6), the Fourteenth (1, 4), and the Rifles (1, 1). One captain and one lieutenant were killed on the spot during the engagement, while 8 captains and 9 lieutenants and ensigns were wounded, some fatally. Most of Pike's staff fell at his side and Colonels Pearce and Ripley both stated they were wounded, although this was not shown on Hunter's return.

One of the unrecorded military "casualties" of the battle was Pike's pikes. The general's unique plan for confronting the enemy with pointy steel had proven to be cumbersome and ineffective. As Cromwell Pearce discreetly put it, they were "found not to answer the purpose intended," and the Fifteenth Infantry never carried pikes into battle again.[40]

Commodore Chauncey does not appear to have submitted a list of his casualties. He mentioned only the loss of Midshipmen John Hatfield and Benjamin Thompson and several seamen, while published reports showed between one and four seamen killed and between eight and eleven wounded.[41] The squadron, however, suffered from the sickness that spread after the long forced anchorage off York and some of the more than 100 men who were on the sick list died, including two sailing masters, one of whom was Frederick Leonard (brother of the former commander of the *Madison*).

Casualties and illness had so weakened Dearborn's force that an immediate attack on Fort George was out of the question.[42] The general blamed the delay on the lack of preparations Major General Morgan Lewis had made at Fort Niagara, but, given the long sick lists, it was clear that reinforcements were needed to launch the assault. To this end, most of the squadron sailed on 9 May to Sackets Harbor, leaving three of the schooners behind to keep an eye on enemy movements.

C hauncey arrived at his base on Tuesday, 11 May, and began the laborious task of unloading all the materiel and provisions captured at York.[43] The larger part of it went so quickly into the storehouses at the shipyard that no one made a detailed list. The wounded and sick, including soldiers who had not been disembarked at Niagara, were transferred to the hospital. Luckily for the commodore, 150 officers and seamen had just arrived from Boston and they soon helped fill in the vacancies on the watch bills. As soon as the warships were emptied and cleaned out, Brigadier General John Chandler began the embarkation of his brigade, numbering roughly 1,000 officers and men.

During all this activity there was one solemn transfer from ship to shore that probably brought everything to a silent and reverent halt. The cask containing the body of Zebulon Pike, which had been moved from the *Gold Hunter* to the *Duke of Gloucester*, was opened and the remains were placed in a suitable casket and taken on shore. If Ned Myers of the *Scourge* is to be believed, this was actually the second time the cask had been opened. Somehow Myers had heard that it was Isaac Brock's corpse that was being preserved and he witnessed it being transferred to a fresh cask and then added the macabre anecdote, "I am ashamed to say that some of our men were inclined to drink the old rum."[44]

In contrast to Myers's remembrance, the records showed that full military honours were rightly bestowed upon the fallen general. His remains were placed in an iron casket, said to have a glass panel in the lid and filled with alcohol for preservation purposes. His widow, Clarissa, ventured to Sackets from her quarters in Watertown to grieve over her dead Montgomery and then to attend the dignified procession that laid the general to rest in a grave adjacent to Fort Tompkins on 13 May. He was joined in eternity by his aide-de-camp Captain Benjamin Nicholson, who had died earlier that day from complications following the amputation of the leg that had been crushed at the moment Pike received his fatal wound. Two days later Isaac Chauncey sent the flag he had placed beneath the hero's head on board the *Madison* to Widow Pike "as a memento of the first victory gained over the Enemy in Canada."[45] He wrote a second note the same day, this one acknowledging "that military men are not the most provident in their pecuniary arrangements."[46] "Madam," he explained, "if you will ... do me the honor to accept the loan of any sum of money that you may require to meet the expenses of your journey, I shall feel extremely flattered by such a mark of your confidence." As Clarissa made her journey to her family in Ohio, she was to hear of other tributes to her husband. Newspapers would lament the loss of the valiant soldier. Between acts of a play in a theatre in Baltimore, the curtain would rise to reveal "that elegant actress, Mrs *Green*," costumed as *Columbia*, kneeling before an obelisk engraved with an epitaph to the fallen hero, to which the audi-

Battle of Fort George, 27 May 1813. The second combined operation of American naval and military forces took place at the town of Niagara one month after the attack at York. Weather conditions allowed scores of batteaux to transport men the short distance from the American shores near Fort Niagara while Chauncey's squadron efficiently bombarded the British batteries and troops. (LAC, C40819)

ence would reply with deferential silence and then spontaneous applause.[47] In June, at President Madison's request, the powerful warship rising in the stocks at Sackets Harbor would be launched and christened *General Pike*.

During the third week of May the commodore's squadron moved men and materiel from Sackets to Four Mile Creek near Fort Niagara, and by the time he arrived there in the *Madison* with the last of the reinforcements, an army of 4,000 had been assembled and the bombardment of Fort George had begun. The assault was launched early on 27 May with the warships playing a crucial role in subduing the British batteries while a large flotilla of batteaux landed the force in waves. As at York, Dearborn took a back seat, leaving Major General Lewis in command, with brigades under Chandler and Brigadier General John Boyd, but it was the personal leadership of Colonel Winfield Scott and the aggressive energy and skill of Benjamin Forsyth's rifles that gained the beach-head. Brigadier General John Vincent directed a much better organized resistance than Sheaffe had done at York, but the weight of the American assault was too strong and he was forced to withdraw. A plan to cut off his escape route failed and, in a repetition of Sheaffe's retreat, although with far less ignominy, Vincent preserved the larger part of his division and began a march toward Stoney Creek.

The assault on Fort George brought another victory for the combined forces of the United States, and a less costly one than they had won the month before. But thanks to Vincent's successful retreat, there was business left undone, and it was to this end that Dearborn, Chauncey and the other senior officers were planning a third combined operation at Burlington Bay when startling news reached Niagara from Sackets Harbor. The British had appeared in force off the port with the obvious intention to land. Without hesitating, Chauncey withdrew his squadron from any part in the pursuit of Vincent and set sail immediately for Sackets.[48]

At Kingston Sir George Prevost had met with his senior military and naval officers to deliberate over the reports made by Lieutenant Green and the two captured seamen sent on parole from Sackets. They discussed the defences of the place and the new ship in the dockyard and the logistics involved in launching an attack that would serve as a reprisal for the defeat at York and create a diversion in support of Brigadier General Vincent's army at Fort George. There is the likelihood that Prevost had also heard the rising criticism about his failure to launch an assault on Chauncey's base during the winter, the omission which the headmen at York had bluntly represented as "that imbecility," and wanted to do something to refute such claims.[49] Chauncey's departure for Niagara was known at Kingston on 22 May and four days later a large part of the garrison at the place embarked in Yeo's squadron, which weighed its anchors and headed for the American shore. Captain Daniel McPherson and his Glengarries and some of the 8th Foot who had returned from York were in the brigade, but none of the other officers appear to have joined it, including Sheaffe.

The British attack on Sackets Harbor illustrated the difficulties inherent in amphibious operations and the sort of unpredictable circumstances that armchair generals such as John Strachan and others, who had advocated this type of expedition, had failed to understand. Bad weather postponed the initial assault on 28 May, eliminating the advantage of surprise. The Americans hit the British hard as they approached the shore the next day, and in the light wind conditions Yeo was unable to get his warships in close enough to support the British troops. The first line of American defenders, mainly local militia, fled when the British surged forward to make their landing, but the redcoats were slowed down by having to tramp through woods, and when they finally charged the fortifications the Americans repelled them with unexpected vigour and effectiveness. British casualties mounted quickly, prompting the commander of the operation, Colonel Edward Baynes, to reappraise the situation. He turned for advice to Prevost, who was present, and the two agreed to call off the attack. Most of

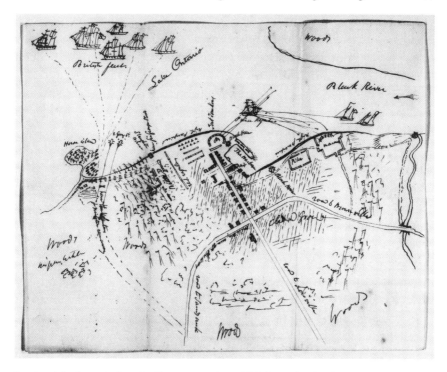

Battle of Sackets Harbor, 29 May 1813. The British force that landed at Sackets Harbor came within yards of overrunning American fortifications and Chauncey's shipyard. Prevost and Baynes's decision to call off the attack saved the Americans from a disastrous setback. (LOC, 400434)

military and naval officers received this order with disbelief, since they felt that victory was within their grasp. "Highly mystified and looking very sheepish at one another," wrote Sergeant James Commins of the 8th Foot, one of the York survivors who fought at Sackets, "you would hardly have heard a whisper until that powerful stimulant grog was served out when the Tower of Babel was nothing like it, everyone blaming another."[50]

Prevost had little choice but to characterize the affair at Sackets as "not being attended with the complete success which was expected from it" when he wrote to Lord Bathurst on 1 June.[51] Unknown to him at the time were two critical outcomes of the battle. Due to lack of effective leadership and confused orders, the U.S. Navy detachment left at the Harbor prematurely and needlessly set fire to the storehouses to prevent their capture by the British. The new ship was saved from being destroyed, but the nearby storehouses went up in flame and smoke and took with them nearly all the equipment and stores captured at York as well as the sails, rigging and fittings on hand for the new ship; the responsibility for this mistake was widely attributed to Lieutenant Wolcott Chauncey, the commodore's brother. Furthermore, when Isaac Chauncey returned from Niagara, he saw how close he had come to losing his base and was ever afterward hesitant to leave unless there was an adequate military force on hand to defend it. This took effect immediately, as he remained at Sackets through June and into July, allowing Yeo a free hand to support Vincent's force near Burlington Bay and to raid the New York State shoreline.

But in the first week of June Sir George Prevost did not know the full implications of his aborted expedition against Sackets Harbor. Almost as soon as he returned to Kingston, news arrived of the American capture of Fort George and Vincent's retreat, so it was in the context of a perilous military situation that Prevost was making his decisions and one of them directly involved Sir Roger Sheaffe.

There were plenty of questions being asked privately about the decision to divide the resources of the Provincial Marine by building the *Sir Isaac Brock* at York. "As York was not a place of defence," John Askin, one of the province's more prosperous merchants, wrote on 3 June, "I was rather astonished that a vessel was building there which could not be protected."[52] "There was not a man in the country," declared John McGillivray, another merchant, "... that did not predict that [the *Brock*] would be burnt at the opening of navigation, and ... had it not been burnt it was next to certain there was not enough water to launch it or soil to support the ways."[53] A senior militia officer from Port Talbot on the Lake Erie shore commented, "I am glad to hear that Sir G. P. is a little aroused for the security of the Province."[54]

The public forum of the *Quebec Mercury*, one of the handful of newspapers in the provinces, raised the same questions. After describing York as "a town of small note ... a place of no natural strength, and [which] art had done little for it," the editors added, "It is astonishing how a large ship came to be laid down at a place of this description, where no protection could be afforded her when the enemy ventured upon the Lake? Circumstances have proved Kingston the fittest situation for our naval depot."[55]

The fingers of blame were pointing more or less at Prevost, but since it was neither the predominant leadership style of the day, nor in Prevost's nature, for him to accept responsibility for what had happened at York, someone else had to be found culpable for the downturn of British fortunes in the spring. Prevost's choice was obvious, and not just to him. "The business of York," observed John McGillivray, "has given such a disgust to General Sheaffe that he can never have the least influence in that Province."[56] While William Powell was in Kingston, his wife, Anne, kept him well informed about the situation at York. At one point there was a rumour of Sheaffe's intention to return to the capital and Anne wrote, "I think and for his sake *hope it will not be; –* the indignation against him does not subside and *surely it is not* a moment to oppose the wishes of the majority *of every class of people.*"[57]

Sir Roger was well aware of the things being said about him, and, to Grant Powell's eyes, "seemed hurt at the silence of his York Friends."[58] The general sent a newsy sort of letter to Æneas Shaw and, remarking briefly on his situation, wrote, "Slander has been busy, I am told, but truth, though a slow, is generally a sure antidote for its poison."[59] Sheaffe expanded this notion of his own inculpability and the misunderstandings that prevailed when he penned a long letter to his close friend, Bishop Jacob Mountain at Quebec, during the fourth week of May.

> My Dear Lord
>
> ….
>
> You will probably have heard, my Lord, ere this reach[es] you, that a popular outcry has been raised against me – it is quite in the natural order of things: those who join in it are too violent to be just – the event which has given rise to it everybody expected, yet, having happened, and being the first serious disaster, the public mind is highly irritated and I am selected as the object of its indignation. I who would not have been found by the Enemy at York but for my desire to do everything that our means could afford to avert such a result – for I had expected an attempt on York and by staying there so long I had brought forward means much greater that those which the Commander of the Forces had placed at my disposal for its defence – … but this devotion, and the facts that occurred on the 27th of April seem to be forgot at least some of the facts – such as a contest maintained nearly eight hours – though there was a combination of force so greatly superior brought against us, and those accidents, to which military operations are liable, were in favour of the Enemy: – our own loss great, that of the Enemy much greater; what he most desired possession of not allowed to fall into his hands – the efficient part of the regular troops withdrawn to act against him elsewhere. Two twelve pounds and two field sixes were furnished for the defence of an open untenable town, affording no local advantages to aid an inferior number in its defence.[60]

Sheaffe was obviously well reinforced by his own fatalistic attitude and his distorted view of such basic truths as the artillery he commanded at York or the length of time he kept his infantry actively fighting off the attack. It was from this position of incontestable self-assurance that he already had discussed the situation with Prevost and calmly listened to and accepted his commander's decisions, as he explained to Bishop Mountain.

> Sir George Prevost calls the popular clamour unjust, though he seems to think it necessary to yield to it – he says, too, that they cannot substantiate one of their accusations, and that his good opinion of me is not in the smallest degree impaired: I presume that some mode of publishing these sentiments will be resorted to: – an investigation, he tells me, must be deferred as incompatible at present with the public service.
>
> I fear that the excellent Wife, whom I received from your Lordship's hands will suffer much uneasiness from what she may hear on this subject through some channels, but I trust that from you, my Lord, and from her kind friends or your family as well as from a few others she will have soothing and comfort.
>
> … this is a critical period for these provinces.

The governor-in-chief had actually decided on how to quell "the public clamour" before the attack on Sackets Harbor as he announced it to Lord Bathurst on 26 May. "It is my intention," he wrote, " to place the civil administration and military command of Upper Canada in the hands of Major General De Rottenburg, and Major General Sir R. Sheaffe will return to Lower Canada, where he will remain, (for reasons which shall be hereafter detailed for your Lordship)."[61] Sheaffe appears to have accepted the news without protest or a formal request to have his conduct examined by a court martial, whether it was "incompatible … with the public service" or not. His warped view of what had happened at York made it easier for Prevost to convince him of "his good opinion," a confidence he expressed on a later occasion when he assured the general, "in order to relieve you from command …, I made a sacrifice of my private feelings to my public duty, and my own opinion yielded to the General clamour."[62]

Prevost was being less than truthful with Sheaffe, as his despatches to England showed. To Bathurst on 24 June he wrote about "Finding upon arriving at [Kingston] that Major General Sir Roger Sheaffe had altogether lost the confidence of the Province by the measures he had pursued for its defence."[63] And about the same time in a despatch to the Duke of York, the commander-in-chief of the British army, he wrote about "an insufficiency on the part of Major General Sir R. H. Sheaffe to [conduct] the arduous task of defending Upper Canada."[64] Prevost was right: Sheaffe was not competent enough to handle the challenges of command, but Prevost's own strategic decisions had made those challenges more difficult. He made no candid admissions along that line to Bathurst or York, however, choosing instead to make Sheaffe the scapegoat for the recent setbacks at the same time as he privately assured the general of his personal support. It was not the first time, nor the last, that Prevost would obscure the truth about Sheaffe and the events at York.

A general order issued on 6 June announced the appointment of Francis, Baron de Rottenburg, as military commander and head administrator of Upper Canada.[65] De Rottenburg was Polish by birth and an experienced military man who had gained some renown in the British army for his expertise in light infantry tactics. He had been in Canada since 1810 and had lately handled the civil administration of the lower province. The order required him to hand over this responsibility to Major General George Glasgow and proceed to Kingston. Sheaffe's demotion was further emphasized by the public notice of his reassignment as commander of the district around Montreal.

There was little else for Sir Roger to do in Upper Canada. At Prevost's direction, he and the Executive Council issued a proclamation on 4 June reminding the citizens of Upper Canada (particularly those at York) that any public property given to them by the Americans was to be returned. It was illegal to keep such a "pretended gift from the enemy" and "the army of Genl. Vincent was in want of many of the articles of public property so possessed."[66] A few days later Sheaffe sent an order for all commanding officers in the province to complete and submit returns of their detachments, arms, stores and accommodations, which appears to have been his last official act. One of the final public communications he received while commanding in Upper Canada was a statement of appreciation from the Executive Council. Scott, McGill and Powell wrote on 16 June to thank Sheaffe for the "candour, justice and impartiality" he had displayed during his term and to extend their best wishes for his "health and prosperity."[67] Sheaffe replied with gratitude, assuring the councillors that he valued their support and that they could depend upon "the lively interest I shall always feel in your welfare."[68]

The formal transfer of appointments between Sheaffe and de Rottenburg took place at Kingston on 19 June.[69] Afterwards Sir Roger began his final journey down the St. Lawrence River and out of Upper Canada, seemingly immune to the pangs of humiliation that another officer would have felt under such circumstances. If it mattered to him at all, events would soon show that he was not the only senior officer to be relieved of his command in the wake of the battle at York.

CHAPTER 15

"*A true account of our proceedings*"[1]

LEGACIES OF THE BATTLE OF YORK

The news of the victory at York spread across American newspapers in May and June and stories continued to appear through the summer. It arrived first as rumours: the army's departure in Chauncey's squadron for an attack against Canada; the capture of the *Earl of Moira*, armed with twenty-one guns, and the *Prince Regent* with eighteen; a landing on the Niagara Peninsula, the taking of Fort George, the occupation of Queenston Heights.[2] And then it was trumpeted as "the brilliant affair at Little York" and a "Great Victory." "The first blow is struck," read one article, "and will be followed without relaxation till the whole of the upper country is subdued." The casualties were thought at first to be "comparatively trifling" but were soon confirmed as "heavy and distressing" as the lists of dead and wounded filled the columns, along with the official reports and terms of capitulation and names of British and Canadian prisoners. There was exultation in "the glory of our arms" and assurances that "the consequences of this victory are all important."

The victory came too late to affect the New York State elections since the voters went to the polls on the day of the battle and the returns were published on the same pages where the first rumours and accounts appeared. As it turned out, Governor Daniel Tompkins narrowly defeated his Federalist rival Stephen Van Rensselaer, while the Federalists ended up with control of the Legislative Assembly and the Republicans held onto a majority in the upper house. Tompkins's friends celebrated their success at a dinner held at the village of Sandy Hill, 35 miles north of Albany. The toasts led off with accolades for Tompkins, "the friend of America," and saluted, among others, the president and federal departments, the army and the navy before arriving at Zebulon Pike.[3] They drank silently to his memory, agreeing that "Though slain, he lives in the warm regions of the hearts of his countrymen." Six cheers followed the toast to Dearborn and Chauncey: "Ever glorious and hallowed be that day that announced them victors of the British force at Little York."

The battle was soon portrayed at the Lion's Den, a theatre in Philadelphia, in a five-part bill of entertainment on Saturday, 5 June 1813. There was the farce *Of Age Tomorrow* and a line of Cossack Dancers, a "Grand Combat" between "two amateurs mounted on ten-toed machines" and a play entitled *The Honey Moon.*[4] And cleverly added to the play was a newly composed musical interlude called "The Capture of Little York." In fine voice, three regulars amused the audience with their ballad, the part of General Dearborn sung by a Mr. Phillipths, while an actor known as Great Boxer took General Sheaffe's place and Mr. Thia Rantail assumed the role of Lieutenant O'Carrothead.

Elsewhere a Scottish "feddler" of some fame named Georgi Paw More pleased his listeners with a verse of his own construction which he sang *a cappella* while he rosined his bow.

> Aw roond my head, my country's pride I tweine
> Sa sud a scottish baird be croon'd
> Sa sud a Yaunkee chaif be sung
> To Grawnny Derburn noo weill rraise the sang
>
> That late in Cawnada, befoor the ark,
>   Danc'd, like a wuld theng in his sark;
> Wheil the Bretish lawsses,
> 'tis with sham I speck it'
> Au heedless o' his mairtial train
>   kecked, an lawgh'd
>   An lawgh'd and keck'd
> An lawgh'd and keck'd again,
> Scarce could they keep their water at the seight
> Sa well auld Derburn did their eyne delight.[5]

Naturally, "delight" was not universal, and it was more than just the scribblers in the general's camp who raised doubts about the outcome of the battle. Federalist newspapers such as the *New-York Evening Post* questioned the "'Grand Victory' at Little York," noting that "it seemed a little mysterious, that, after having made good their landing in Canada, the grand object of all their hopes, and taken such a valuable fort [due to its vast supply of provisions and munitions], the conquerors should think of nothing but leaving it again as soon as possi-

Victory by
Gen. Dearborn.

Messenger Office, Canandaigua, May 1, 1813.

☞ The following letter from Gen. P. B. Porter, was sent by exprefs to John C. Spencer, Efq. of this village and received here this afternoon. We fincerely congratulate the readers of the Meffenger upon the gallant achievement it defcribes. While we exult in tne glory of our arms, we cannot but feel, deeply feel the lofs of the brave Gen. Pike.

Manchefter, (Niagara County) April 28, 1813, 6 o'clock P.M.

DEAR SIR,

"I have just returned from Fort Niagara, where I saw a Captain of the U. S. navy. He is just from Little York, the capital of U. Canada, and gives the following account, which is confirmed by official dispatches from Gen. Dearborn to Gen. Lewis, now here.

"On Tuesday, the 26th (April) at sunrise, Commodore Chauncey, with a squadron of 10 or 12 vessels, appeared before York, with Gen. Dearborn and near 3000 men. The infantry under Brig. Gen. Pike landed, attacked the town and batterries in the rear, while the squadron attacked them by water. At 2 P.M. they carried the place, taking a great number of Indians and militia prisoners, 1000 Indians being engaged.

"General Sheaffe, with a few regular troops, made their efcape. Gen. Pike with about 200 men were killed, by the blowing up of a magazine in one of their batteries, and in which they had a train of powder for the purpofe. About fifty of the Britifh artillerifts were killed by the fame explofion. The lofs on both fides is confiderable. Our army is now in poffeffion of the town and is expected here fhortly. Our troops behaved with the greateft gallantry. Immenfe quantities of military ftores and India goods were taken at York, which feems to have been the depot for thofe articles. The veffels of the fquadron are not fufficient to bring them away."

FURTHER PARTICULARS.

Altho' Gen. Porter does not mention the taking any Britifh veffels, yet we are well informed that a confiderable portion of the enemy's lake-navy, was lying at York, and the other part at Kingfton. It is therefore highly probable that our gallant tars have either deftroyed or obtained poffeffion of a fufficient number of the enemy's fhips, to enable us very foon to chafe the refidue from the lake.

By a gentleman direct from Sackett's harbor we learn that the force that failed from there on Sunday the 25th, confifted of Com. Chauncey and about 1000 failors; with Gen. Dearborn and Gen. Pike, who took with them the 6th, 16th, and 15th reg'ts, Col. M'Clure's regiment, consisting of the N.York, Albany and Baltimore Volunteers, and Capt. Forsyth's company, all of Infantry; and a detachment from Col. Macomb's regiment of artillery, in all about 2000 men.

[*Printed at the Salem Gazette Office—Price 12 cts.*]

Battle broadside. The *Gazette* in Salem, Massachusetts, published this broadside about the victory purportedly won by the favourite son of Massachusetts. It featured a reprint of the letter written by Peter Porter on 28 April 1813 after he heard a report of the battle from Sailing Master Mix at Fort Niagara. As the first unofficial report about the action, Porter's letter was published widely in the United States. (TRL Broadside Collection) ble."[6] "If the object of the government," asked the editor of the *Northern Whig* in Hudson, New York, "is the conquest of Canada, why were two or three hundred men sacrificed to obtain York, for the purpose of immediately abandoning it?"[7]

What none of the newspaper editors knew were the strategic goals of the 1813 campaign's first phase, which had been closely guarded by the Madison cabinet and the senior officers in the field. High on the list was the attainment of an early victory; "[the] first service should be a successful one," Secretary of War John Armstrong had explained to Dearborn at the end of March. "The good effect of this will be felt throughout the campaign."[8] After an exchange of views among the cabinet officials and with Dearborn and Chauncey as to where to make the initial strike, the commodore had conceived the notion of a rapid series of attacks against York, Fort George and Kingston. The two warships said to be building at York and their stores and guns made York attractive, as did the fact that the town was believed to be lightly defended. After taking the capital, the force would "proceed directly to Fort George, and carry it by assault."[9]

But the army that finally landed near Fort Niagara was so depleted by casualties and sickness that no quick attack on Fort George was feasible. And the only warship Chauncey had come away with was the worn-out *Duke of Gloucester* (renamed *York*), which soon proved to be of no immediate use except as a hulk for storing ammunition and later as a hospital, although it did fetch $2,500 for Chauncey and his followers when the government bought it in the prize court. The captured ordnance and the heaps of materiel and provisions would have earned more prize money, but most of the perishables went up in flames at Sackets Harbor a month later. Two weeks before this accident of war, Secretary Armstrong pointed out these deficits of the expedition in a private letter to Dearborn and then added another criticism "less apt to be noticed by ordinary critics."[10] This was the "vexatious" escape of Sheaffe and so many of his regulars, especially at a time when British forces were stretched so thinly. Admitting his lack of knowledge of the topography of York, Armstrong still questioned why a two-pronged attack had not been made to prevent Sheaffe's unchallenged withdrawal. He candidly explained to Dearborn that his remarks would read like "an official censure" in a public despatch, but that he made them privately out of regard for the general and his reputation. "In the affair before you," Armstrong stated plainly, referring to the impending attack on Fort George, "nothing will be omitted … with regard to the [British] garrison in particular [and] it will not be permitted to escape today that it may fight us tomorrow." Whether he said anything about it at the time is uncertain, but years later Armstrong identified another of Dearborn's mistakes at York: "Had the command-in-chief … been on the field of battle, or near it, or had he made Colonel Pierce acquainted with the orders given to Pike (as he ought to have done), the unnecessary delay made in the pursuit of the enemy would not have occurred; and … Sheaffe and his followers would, in all probability, have been overtaken and captured."[11]

Armstrong's worst fears were realized when Brigadier General John Vincent eluded the Americans at Fort George and then stopped their advance at Stoney Creek on 6 June. By then Chauncey had withdrawn to Sackets Harbor, allowing Commodore Sir James Yeo to control Lake Ontario and assist Vincent in putting pressure on the Americans, who had pulled back to Fort George. Exasperated by the turn of events, Armstrong wrote to Dearborn, "There is, indeed, a strange fatality attending our efforts. Battles are not gained when an inferior or broken enemy is not destroyed. Nothing is done, while any thing that might have been done is omitted."[12]

The effects of the failing campaign showed themselves on Tuesday, 8 June, six weeks, nearly to the hour, after Chauncey's squadron had anchored off York. Just before dawn American drums rattled out "To Arms" at Fort George and the regiments marched to their assigned posts to repel what appeared to be a flotilla of British boats about to make a landing. It proved to be a false alarm and the units soon stood down, but it clearly demonstrated how the promise of success on that morning in April had been lost.[13]

The early speculation that the victory at York had given the U.S. Navy command of the Great Lakes, or at least that the British would soon be driven off the waters, proved to be incorrect.[14] It was eventually claimed, however, that one of the reasons why the British lost the Battle of Put-in-Bay on Lake Erie on 10 September 1813 was that the guns intended for the new ship (HMS *Detroit*) being built at Amherstburg, as well as its fittings, sails, rigging and stores, were destroyed or captured at York. A favourite source of support for this contention was seen in Chauncey's despatch to Secretary Jones on 7 May:

> We found at this place 28 Cannon of different calibre, from 32 to 6 pounders, a number of Muskets, large quantities of fixed ammunition-shot-shells and munitions of War of various kinds, a great deal of which was put up in boxes marked for Niagara and Malden…. The store which the Enemy burned was filled with Cables, Cordage, Canvass, Tools and Stores of every kind for the use of this Lake and Lake Erie, supposed to be worth $500,000.[15]

Additional support for the causal link between York and Put-in-Bay appeared in Governor-in-Chief Sir George Prevost's letter on 20 July 1813 to Secretary of War and the Colonies Lord Bathurst about the state of naval affairs on Lake Erie.

The Battle of Put-in-Bay, 10 September 1813. Master Commandant Perry gained a critical strategic advantage in the struggle for control of Lake Erie early in August 1813 when his squadron cut off the British supply line to Amherstburg. Because of the growing need for provisions at that post, Commander Robert Barclay challenged Perry to a battle a few weeks later and lost. (U.S. Naval Historical Center, NH902599)

The ordnance, ammunition and other stores for the service on Lake Erie had been deposited at York for the purpose of being transported to Amherstburg, but unfortunately were either destroyed or fell into the enemy's hands when York was taken by them, and the subsequent interruption to the communication by their occupation of Fort George has rendered it extremely difficult to [transport] the [necessary] supplies.[16]

Prevost's explanation stretched the facts to a breaking point. Through his military secretary, Prevost had informed Captain Andrew Gray at Kingston at the end of January that the guns for the new vessels at Kingston, York and Amherstburg would not reach Canada from England until the spring.[17] This had prompted the officers at York to form a plan for arming the *Sir Isaac Brock* with the best guns available at York for its first trip to Kingston. As it turned out, the only guns specifically intended for HMS *Detroit*, ten 24-pdr. carronades, were not unloaded at Burlington Bay for shipment overland to Lake Erie until late August or early September 1813. Furthermore, few guns were sent up from Quebec to York before the battle there and the collection of artillery on hand was a hodgepodge of calibres and some of it so old as to be nearly useless.

While Chauncey claimed to have captured twenty-eight pieces, some of these were sunk in the lake, and when he finally submitted his list of guns (and ships stores that had been saved from the fire at Sackets Harbor) the number had dropped to sixteen of various calibres, none of which were large enough to use in his squadron. No itemized list of these weapons appears to have been written, but in all likelihood they comprised the six 6-pdr. long guns for the *Duke of Gloucester*, the eight 18-pdr. carronades from Fort George and the two 12-pdrs. sent from Quebec; what became of the two brass 6-pdr. field guns abandoned by Sheaffe is unclear. All the captured guns may have ended up in the batteries that were later built at Sackets Harbor. When the prize court finished its deliberation in 1814, the guns were valued at nearly $29,000, of which about $2,200 went into the commodore's pocket.

Fact did not get in the way of myth-making, however. In 1818, British writer William James, basing his account of the Battle of York on hearsay and imagination, stated that "the guns [that] belonged to the ship that was building, ... lay on the ground partly covered with snow and frozen mud."[18] In his 1882 classic account of the naval war, Theodore Roosevelt noted that "the 24-gun ship was burned, her guns taken away," and in 1905 James Hannay put the "24-gun ship" into his *History of the War* with its "heavy carronades ... which might have been placed in the batteries ... thrown carelessly in the mud, where they lay covered with ice and snow."[19] The idea has been repeated in various forms until recent times with authorities claiming that the British "lost the guns intended for the Erie establishment when Chauncey and General Dearborn raided York in April 1813, and destroyed twenty-eight cannons ranging from 6- to 32-pounders together with a large amount of store intended to be forwarded to Amherstburg."[20] It is well established that stores were being collected at York so that it could serve as a depot for the whole province, including both lakes. Some of the materiel was shipped to Amherstburg before the attack on York, and shortages otherwise suffered there were certainly attributable to the April attack. The loss of the Lake Erie squadron at Put-in-Bay, however, had much more to do with a lack of experienced seamen and uniform ordnance, the vagaries of the wind and plain bad luck, than it did with a want of sails and rigging. The long-held notion that the guns taken at York contributed to that defeat is false.

Another legacy of the Battle of York took wing faster than the implications of captured ordnance did, namely that "when Washington was burned [in August 1814] the British were quick to justify their conduct by citing the destruction by our army of the public buildings at York."[21] There were differences in the circumstances of the fires, however, and a long string of conflagrations in between, making the connection thin at best.

The Burning of Washington, 24-25 August 1814. Following orders by Vice Admiral Sir Alexander Cochrane to exact a harsh penalty on the Americans for burning villages in Upper Canada, Rear Admiral George Cockburn and Major General Robert Ross ordered some of the public buildings in Washington to be torched. (USNA, 148-GW-478)

When asked by a congressional committee to explain what actually happened at York, Henry Dearborn took responsibility for ordering the two blockhouses, some storage sheds and the *Governor Hunter* set aflame. He stated that the explosion had badly damaged the garrison and Government House and that the British themselves had destroyed the *Sir Isaac Brock* and neighbouring storehouses. But he adamantly denied giving an order to burn the Parliament Buildings, and it was never proven whether American servicemen or Canadian residents caused the blaze.[22] As for the burnings at Washington, there was no doubt about what happened. Major General Robert Ross and Rear Admiral George Cockburn purposely selected certain public buildings for the torch (the president's mansion, the Capitol, the Departments of the Treasury and War, the naval yard) and never backed away from that decision.

The fires at York were among the first such acts to gain wide notice. The citizens were angered by the destruction, but when an American naval and military detachment landed on the beach at Burlington on 9 May and burned down the

King's Head Inn, the old "Government House" where Sheaffe and Prevost had probably met in February, the locals were outraged and the raid was condemned as "a wanton, ferocious and savage proceeding."²³ At the same time, detachments from the British fleet in Chesapeake Bay were raiding villages, burning public store houses and private vessels. Rear Admiral Cockburn led many of these expeditions, earning the hatred of most Americans, especially after he ordered the destruction on 3 May 1813 of most of the village of Havre de Grace, Maryland, when residents kept firing at his men after they had captured the place. In newspaper columns adjacent to reports about the American victory at Little York were such loud protests as, "We never before heard of such wanton violence – such horrid deviations from the rules and practices of civilized war."²⁴

The "deviations" continued through 1813 with the most notable acts of arson being the unauthorized American burning of the town of Niagara during severe winter conditions on 10-11 December and the authorized retaliatory torching by the British of every American settlement on the Niagara River later that month. The following April Vice Admiral Sir Alexander Cochrane instructed his commanders on the American coast to have the enemy's "Sea Port Towns laid in Ashes and the Country wasted … as a sort of retaliation for the savage Conduct in Canada; where they destroyed our Towns, in the most inclement Seasons of the Year; it is therefore but just, that Retaliation shall be made near to the Seat of their Government from whence those Orders emanated."²⁵ When an American raid in May 1814 resulted in burnings in and around Port Dover on Lake Erie, Sir George Prevost asked Cochrane to intensify the destruction, which the admiral agreeably ordered on 18 July. The flames roared in Washington less than a month later, probably more as a result of Niagara and Port Dover than the events at York.

Once again, fact did not inhibit the story tellers and it became popular knowledge that the British reaped their revenge at Washington for the burning of the Parliament Buildings at York. The American historian Milo Quaife took the historiography of this explanation to task in his pamphlet *The Yankees Capture Little York* and showed that it had never been proven that American personnel set the buildings afire and that Dearborn had never ordered their destruction. By tradition, however, the dastardly detonation of the grand magazine and the discovery of the scalp hanging above the Speaker's mace in the assembly were seen as justification on the American side for the arson at York.

The scalp, in particular, became an object of outrage and disgust, especially since its discovery came on the heels of the murder of wounded Americans by native warriors following the British victory at Frenchtown, Michigan, in January; Brigadier General James Winchester was even said at first to have been among the butchered. Linked to the mace, "the emblem of authority," as the editor of the *Weekly Register* of Baltimore reported, the scalp was seen as "truly symbolical of the *British* power in *Canada*."[26] "It is fact, horrible fact," the newspaper later alleged, "that the legislature of '*unoffending Canada*' did sanction (by hanging up in their hall, in evidence of their authority; a *human scalp*) the murders of our people by the savages."[27] Even though such claims were refuted as "false and ridiculous" by the likes of the Reverend John Strachan and others, they endured and were used to explain the destruction of the Parliament Buildings which became the motivation for burning Washington.[28] And so the story goes.

Despite its grisly presence, the scalp provided satirists with material upon which to practise their wit. Poking fun at exaggerated accounts about Frenchtown, an item in the *American Daily Advertiser* in Philadelphia on 29 May announced: "FOUND: by General Dearborn, in the Council Chamber, at York, the identical SCALP which General Winchester lost at the time he was 'killed, scalped and mangled, in the most shocking manner.'"[29] In the same vein, but in the metre of the muse, appeared the following:

> Said HARRISON to General SHEAFFE,
> With patriotic zeal,
> To let our *allies* scalp my men
> Is devilish ungenteel
>
> Says SHEAFFE to General HARRISON,
> (Quite calm about the matter),
> If we don't suit you, go *invade*
> Where you'll be treated better.[30]

Secretary of War Armstrong did not find the scalp amusing in the least. When Dearborn had it shipped to him, the only trophy of war he forwarded to the war department, the secretary immediately sent it back. Commodore Chauncey ended up with the other trophies, the mace, a carved wooden lion and the Royal Standard, all of which he sent to Secretary Jones, who said he would send them to "the National Archives."[31]

By the time Armstrong received the scalp he was in no mood for such trivialities. The situation of the army at Niagara was deteriorating in June and it was even uncertain on some days who held command, as Dearborn took ill with a fever of some kind that was accompanied by an occasional "violent spasmodic attack on his breast."[32] He would recover but, "on the least agitation of mind," suffer a relapse and give command to Major General Morgan Lewis and later to Brigadier General John Boyd.[33] Dearborn or his aide Lieutenant Colonel Samuel Conner wrote frequently to Armstrong about Dearborn's poor health, the general suggesting at one point that he might have to absent himself from his post so that he could regain his strength.

There were other reports reaching Washington at the same time that caused concern among the governing heads. Failure to be noticed in the public battle reports and disappointment and resentment caused by recent appointments and promotions had stirred the officer corps into a lather. A friend of Winfield Scott's wrote to warn him about a rumour being circulated at the war department "that the camp, where all would be united, in the one cause, is rent with quarrels, party jealousies and plots among its own officers."[34] Scott, himself, it was alleged, was involved in a bitter dispute with Colonel John Chrystie, Twenty-third Infantry, and Lieutenant Colonel Homer Milton, Fifth Infantry, and that the three of them had "pledged to shoot each other when the campaign is over." In his reply Scott expressed regrets about the tone of the rumours without denying his problems with Chrystie and Milton, and then he added fuel to the fire by mentioning a "cabal" he had learned about. It was directed at Dearborn with the supposed ringleaders being General Boyd, Chrystie, Baptist Irvine, who had been made the acting adjutant inspector general, and Lieutenant Donald Fraser, whom Boyd had taken as an aide. Irvine, Scott suggested, had been "provided with a desk ... for writing their puffs which have appeared in the public papers in favour of Boyd and the abuse of Genl Lewis and others."[35]

Concern in Washington grew to such an extent that Henry Clay and Charles Ingersoll, influential Republican congressmen, took the matter to James Monroe on behalf of their colleagues. Monroe then discussed the situation with the president and, presumably, Secretary Armstrong, after which Madison gave his approval for Dearborn's recall. Armstrong, who later revealed how critical he was about "Granny's" handling of the campaign, did nothing to cushion the blow, tersely informing the general on 6 July, "I have the President's orders to express to you his decision that you retire from command of district No. 9, and of the troops within the same, until your health be re-established, and until further orders."[36]

The general took the news badly when it arrived on 15 July, but immediately began preparing to leave the front. Word of his imminent departure spread through the camp at Fort George and was confirmed by a general order which promptly evoked an outpouring of regret. It was expressed in a long "solicitation" to Dearborn to postpone his time of leaving and "continue in the exercise of that command which you have already holden with honor to yourself and country, and with what is of less consequence, the approbation of those who now address you."[37] The criticisms of the old man seem to have been forgotten as most, if not all, of the officers of field rank added their signatures to the letter. Dearborn had no recourse in the matter and replied "with sentiments of grateful feeling … [for] your expressions of personal friendship and confidence."[38] He made it clear, however, that he was going and did not expect to return.

By mid-afternoon he left his headquarters and walked down to the wharf at the Niagara River with some of his staff to board his boat and cross over. The commissioned officers of the army followed him, a large assembly of the rank and file in their wake, and individually approached the general to wish him well. One of them recorded the scene.

> Respect and regret were apparent in almost every countenance that approached and a tear or two was seen to course down Pluto's iron cheek. He was habitually a man of sententious speech. Only one brief phrase seemed to have been prepared for this occasion – "You know how a father feels when separated from his children" – which he probably intended to have said only once, but which, as the groups approached in succession he had to repeat several times.[39]

The general climbed into the boat and as it pulled for the New York shore, he stood in the stern and raised his tricorn hat to the gathering on the bank below Fort George. At that point the guns of the fort began to pound out their farewell, not in a salute which signified celebration, nor in the minute-by-minute notice of mourning, but in an irregular pattern as if to make a statement of "regret … at the unmerited disgrace of an old officer, who had done the state much service."[40] It was as if all the complaints, all of Dearborn's reluctance to take active command of any operation, his dallying with Sheaffe's musical snuff box, his persistent illness, were forgotten. The next day, even Winfield Scott, who never minced his words, wrote compassionately about the general.

> His manner had always been rude and unpolished. I will go further to say that nature never designed him for *a great general*. His principal defect is yet to be stated – *his want of method*. With all these deductions, I am obliged to say, that he possessed … more energy, zeal and comprehension than any General with whom I have served *since* the war [began]. His courage, patriotism and devotedness to this country have never been impeached and are unimpeachable.[41]

H enry Dearborn stewed over his removal from command and on 24 July at Utica, New York, he wrote directly to President Madison to request a formal inquiry into his conduct. Madison answered back to declare his continuing "esteem and regard" for the general, but explained that such a process would have to wait until Congress could deal with it.[42] Dearborn appears to have pursued the matter later in the year, to which James Monroe responded with expressions of his "highest confidence in your integrity, attachment to free govt. and ability to command," but asserted that an inquiry would have to wait "until a time when it may be done without injury to the service."[43]

Dearborn returned to Boston, where he soon married the widow Sarah Bowdoin, his third wife. He was given command of New York City, which he held until the end of the war, and was honourably discharged from the army soon after; Congress rejected an attempt by Madison to have him made the secretary of war in the spring of 1815. Dearborn's last public service of note was his term as the American ambassador to Portugal between 1822 and 1824. He died at his estate at Roxbury, Massachusetts, on 6 June 1829 at the age of seventy-eight. The fates of the controversial scalp and Sheaffe's musical snuff box are unknown.

Many of the officers and men Dearborn left behind him at Niagara continued to serve through the war, some with accolades, some with censure. Isaac Chauncey never managed to win the decisive naval action he craved and was forever criticized for being too cautious after the near-loss of Sackets Harbor in May 1813. But he had the distinction of being the longest-serving senior American commander involved in the northern war and ended his days as one of the most highly respected officers in the U.S. Navy. Cromwell Pearce led his Sixteenth Infantry across one bloody battlefield after another, but never received the credit he felt was due to his men and him. He left the army with an honourable discharge in 1815 and returned to his home in Pennsylvania, where he eventually published an historical sketch of his regiment's exploits, hoping to win some well-deserved laurels. Eleazar Ripley also played an active role through the war, ending up as the temporary commander of the American army after the Battle of Lundy's Lane on 25 July 1814, where Major General Jacob Brown criticized him for not renewing the battle the next day. He remained in the army until 1820 and, after some dispute, finally received a gold medal from Congress for his war service in 1834. Benjamin Forsyth did not live to see the end of the conflict. He continued to skilfully deploy his riflemen as skirmishers until battlefield bravado caught up with him and he was shot to death during a minor action at Odelltown, Lower Canada, in June 1814.

At the camp at Niagara, Captain John Scott felt passed over for promotion and doomed "to remain a Stallatite [satellite] to Grace the Splendor of other military Constalations."[44] He found an excuse to resign his commission due to ill health in August 1813, returned to New Jersey and eventually became a banker. Thomas Warner's last extant letter to his wife was written at Fort Niagara in May, where he was suffering from dysentery. He had had his taste of war and when the one-year enlistment expired, he and the surviving Baltimore Volunteers gladly went home. The greeting Thomas received from his wife, Mary Ann, and their new child was not recorded. Joseph Dwight soon gained the lieutenancy he thought he deserved but resigned due to promotion issues, while John Walworth stuck it out and was raised to major in 1814, with an honourable discharge the next year. Peter Pelham was severely wounded and captured at the Battle of Crysler's Farm, 11 November 1813, but his good conduct towards the citizens of Little York paid off when they wrote to Sir George Prevost's office on his behalf and he was soon allowed to return to the United States on parole. He remained in the army until his death in 1826. Surgeon William Beaumont stayed in the service too and won international fame for his detailed examination in the 1820s of a severe gunshot wound to a man's stomach, eventually becoming known as the "Father of Gastric Physiology."

Jesse Elliott served his country for the rest of his life, but the controversy that arose over his conduct at the Battle of Put-in-Bay clouded his record, and the resulting feud with Oliver Hazard Perry and his deranged obsession with the matter only made things worse. Ned Myers barely survived the accidental sinking of the *Scourge* on 8 August 1813 and shortly thereafter was captured by the British. Freed after the war, he spent most of the rest of his life at sea until in 1843 he met with an old sea buddy, James Fenimore Cooper, who spent five months recording the events of Myers's life, creating one of the great first-person narratives of the age of sail.

William Beaumont (1785-1853). While stationed on Mackinac Island in 1822, Beaumont treated a French-Canadian voyageur named Alexis St. Martin for an accidental musket wound to his stomach. The wound did not fully heal and over the next eleven years, Beaumont observed the processes in St. Martin's stomach, eventually publishing his discoveries.

And then there were the thousands of virtually anonymous men who had landed at York and bore the scars of it for the rest of their lives. Among the long-forgotten soldiers were: Peter Myers, who was left disabled by a wound to his right wrist suffered during the explosion of the grand magazine and who, beginning in 1838, received a pension of $4 per month in compensation; Private Samuel Marshall, Sixth Infantry, who appealed for a pension because of a leg wound taken at the same time and was turned down; Robert Casey, Rifle Regiment, injured and left nearly deaf by the explosion, and given a grant of land in 1840.[45]

Clarissa Pike never remarried. She lived a frugal life at the family home near Cincinnati, Ohio, on her husband's "half pay" until it was cut five years after his death.[46] In the 1840s Mrs. Pike sought some form of pension for the general's service, even in recognition of his early explorations in the southwest. But tragedy struck again and in March 1845 the house where she and her grandchildren lived was completely destroyed by a fire and with it went every memento of Zebulon Pike's career, his letters, uniforms, sword and the British flag that cushioned his last moments. Men of influence stepped in to help and managed to obtain a one-time payment from the government of about $3,000 for the widow. Clarissa's "Montgomery" would have been proud of her perseverance in the face of adversity; she died in 1847. Had they enjoyed life together long enough, the two of them would certainly have gained some pleasure in seeing how the soldier's name spread across the nation. In time, there were ten counties, eighteen towns, two bays, three rivers, four lakes, a series of naval vessels and a mountain named in his memory, and a shelf-load of books written about his exploits.

In Canada newspapers were fewer and farther between and the reports about the action at York were relatively scarce. The first news reached Quebec by 4 May and had General Sheaffe taking a position eight miles from the capital, awaiting reinforcements, after which it was expected that the enemy would "have to pay dearly for their temerity."[47] Then there was admitted agitation of mind over the occupation of Canadian soil, which was balanced by the knowledge that "our gallant little band" of only "300" had held off many times that number in a fight lasting ten hours and that Sheaffe "acted as became an able and experienced commander." The next week brought bits and pieces of information about casualties, the explosion, plundering, Chauncey's dominant position on the lake and Sheaffe having been lucky to escape with as many men as he did. Before other events completely occupied column space in June, the Quebec Mercury warned: "Oh! Jonathan! Jonathan! With how little foresight didst thou calculate, when, not content with shewing and gnashing thy teeth,

LIEU꜠ GEN꜠ SIR GEORGE PROVOST
GOVERNOR OF CANADA.

Prevost in caricature. The notorious English artist, actor and caricaturist Robert Dighton made this hand-coloured etching and published it in November 1812 from his shop in Spring Gardens, Charing Cross, London. It was prophetic of the derogatory view of Prevost that would arise in Canada within two years. (TRL, T15460)

thou becamest bold enough to dare to attempt to fix them in the vitals of that potent animal, John Bull, and chase him into that mortal coil, which so dreadfully works thy calamity."

American newspapers that were carried into the provinces revealed more information than the few Canadian sheets did and offered criticisms of their government as well as personal anecdotes of their anonymous officers. Apart from the occasional question, such as the *Quebec Mercury* asking why the naval force on Lake Ontario was split, the battle at York was only lightly covered and assessed in Canada.[48] Readers had to make inferences about what really happened at York in the absence of a published official account apart from Sheaffe's brief general order of 13 May. They only had the anecdote about Sergeant Derby's retrieval of abandoned belongings to ponder and a copy of the testimonial from the Executive Council to General Sheaffe upon his departure from Upper Canada. The long narrative of the battle written by John Strachan and his friends, with its harsh indictments of Sheaffe and Prevost, does not appear to have been published, but by combining word-of-mouth and what they read in American sources, few men of reason could fail to conclude that even the temporary loss of York was a clear defeat and that the general's head had rolled because of it.

The commander-in-chief managed to keep his head firmly attached. In his despatches to the home government, Sir George Prevost had attributed the defeat at York to his lack of resources, the energetic American naval build-up, Admiral Warren's failure to send him a detachment sooner and Sheaffe's mismanagement of the province's defences.[49] He never mentioned to Lord Bathurst that he had decided late in March to abandon the idea of making York the naval headquarters and to keep it concentrated at Kingston instead, which would have involved admitting his strategic error of painting a bull's eye on an unfortified town in the first place. Bathurst did not notice the omission or, if he did, he ignored it, knowing well that Prevost had been left to run the war on a shoestring budget so anything less than a full invasion was also less than a complete disaster. And this deserved approval and praise, which is what Prevost soon received. Even before he read Prevost's May and June correspondence, Bathurst had learned about the outcome at York, probably through American newspapers, and the matter had been discussed in cabinet and with the Prince Regent. Bathurst informed Prevost on 1 July that "His Royal Majesty approves of the early measures which you took for strengthening the line of defence in Upper Canada ... and altho' ... the enemy ... obtain[ed] temporary possession of York, His Royal Majesty sees no reason to attribute that disaster to any want of proper precautions on your part or to any deficiency in the instructions furnished by you to Sir R. H. Sheaffe."[50]

The honeymoon was over for the governor-in-chief, however. Sir George had held command in British North America for nearly twenty months by the time of the attack on York and had managed the preparation for war and defence of the provinces successfully, especially with the early victories at Detroit and Queenston. But there had been rumblings through the autumn of 1812 about his lack of support of the upper province and the Battle of York gave them legitimacy. It was a turning point in his administration that was quickly followed by the loss of Fort George and the retreat from Sackets Harbor with its malignant rumours of his lack of "boldness" on the battlefield.[51] Commodore Yeo's efforts to win control of Lake Ontario would bring some reprieve from the pressure, but hard defeats would soon come on Lake Erie and at Amherstburg and then Moraviantown. Prevost's critics grew in number and the knives came out with such remarks as: "military foresight, anticipation, or counteraction of the possible or probable movements or designs of the enemy, formed no part of Sir George's system of operations."[52] The questions about his leadership would eventually lead to his recall just weeks before a peace treaty was signed at Ghent in 1814.

For Roger Sheaffe there was no expression of official approval for his role in the defence of York. Bathurst wrote to him on 10 July in anticipation of reading the general's account of the defeat and the amount of damage wrought by the Americans, even though he already knew many of the details and had absolved Prevost of culpability. Not yet informed about Prevost's reassignment of Sheaffe, Bathurst was also hoping to hear about what the general had done in the meantime "to repair the losses which the capture of the capital must have caused."[53] A month went by before Prevost's correspondence about York, Sackets Harbor, Fort George and Stoney Creek, the removal of Sheaffe from Upper Canada and his "insufficiency" reached Bathurst, along with Sir Roger's own despatches about the battle and subsequent matters. With those documents in hand, Bathurst once more communicated the Prince Regent's "entire approbation" for Prevost's administration on 11 August and extended further approval for Brigadier Generals Henry Procter (for his April-May campaign against Fort Meigs) and John Vincent, as well as for Edward Baynes's conduct at Sackets Harbor.[54] But there was not one word about Roger Sheaffe, whose fate had been decided the day before when the Duke of York signed a despatch for Prevost announcing Sheaffe's "return … to this country with a view to other employment."[55]

Whether Sir Roger had a notion that he was about to be recalled or not, there is no hint of it in his official correspondence during the summer and early autumn. He remained at Montreal, supervising the defence of that district of the lower province, apparently unruffled by his demotion. At one point in July he seems to have been too slow to attend to the inspection of a militia battalion and received a sharp reprimand from Prevost, who complained about "the indifference with which you discharge the important Duties now committed to you." "The difficulties of my situation," Sir George ranted, "require the active support of every individual holding a place of trust – you will I hope not again disappoint my expectations as regards yourself."[56] Sheaffe wrote back to assure his chief that "indifference" would be the last thing most people would accuse him of and "no one can be more sensible of the difficulties which you have to encounter, nor can any one be more desirous of affording you support to enable you to surmount them than me, My dear Sir George."[57]

Although he was instrumental in providing support for the British raid launched late in July from Isle aux Noix on the Richelieu River against American ports on Lake Champlain, Roger Sheaffe saw no further battlefield action. He was moved in September to command of a reserve force on the Richelieu where his duties were mainly routine. When the order arrived to return to England, probably in late October, Sheaffe made quick arrangements to take passage in the last of the ships going home before winter. Among his final acts in Canada was to submit a claim for the loss of baggage, effects and immoveable property of various descriptions at the Battle of York amounting to £550 British sterling.[58]

With Lady Sheaffe and two-year-old Julia in company, Sir Roger boarded HMS *Dover* at Quebec during the second week of November. If his pride had been further pricked by the recall from the Horse Guards, he did not show it in his correspondence. Saturday, 13 November, saw him contentedly writing a farewell letter to Prevost, to be taken ashore with the last of the mail when the pilot left the ship at the Brandy Pots, near Rivière-du-Loup. Sheaffe was full of news about the officers taking passage home (one of whom was Surgeon William Hackett of the 8th Foot) and the tight quarters of the between decks. His family had comfortable accommodations and were in good health. Word of American Major General James Wilkinson's expedition down the St. Lawrence River toward Montreal had reached Quebec just before their departure, prompting Sheaffe to write,

> The intelligence we have received since our departure from Quebec has created an anxiety which, probably, will not be relieved till some time after our arrival in England. May God grant you success in the result of the campaign, or at least in the operations which are about to terminate it. Accept, my dear Sir George, my best wishes for the welfare of Lady Prevost and of your family, and believe me
>
> Your very faithfully
devoted servant
R. H. Sheaffe[59]

There were some observers who defended General Sheaffe's term in Upper Canada and conduct at York. A contemporary critic of Prevost argued that "it must be evident that [Sheaffe] had not the means of making an effectual resistance [at York], against such a superiority, covered by a fleet."[60] Historians opined freely on the issue, some supporting the view that the general's reputation suffered from "many imputations, some thoughtless, many reckless – all equally unjust and ungenerous."[61] One modern authority has even made the case that "the reasons for Sheaffe's dismissal from the Canadas appear extremely flimsy."[62]

Certainly Prevost's defence of his own efforts, his fervent assertions and unchallenged omissions, made Sheaffe the scapegoat for the first defeats in Upper Canada. But there were many voices in the province who had questioned Prevost's strategic decisions, and if Roger Sheaffe had been more effective in making the best of a difficult decision, such critics of the governor-in-chief as the Reverend John Strachan would probably have praised Sheaffe as a means of underlining Prevost's faults. Voices might have risen to protest his removal from the province and then from Canada altogether. But the announcement of those decisions raised barely a whisper, because the truth was that Sir Roger had left very few admirers behind him.

Generally unpopular from the time he returned to Niagara in 1812, Sheaffe failed to win over his followers in the army or among the public. He showed himself to be slow to act, unwilling to confront his accusers (notably during the conspiracy forming late in 1812) and stressed by his command responsibilities to the point of illness. He might have done more with the time and limited resources available at York to prepare its defences thoroughly and he should have formed clear and definite plans for defending against an attack that was so widely anticipated. His eventual conduct during the battle revealed his lack of command and control, his indecisiveness and passive acceptance of defeat. In a classic example of a battle going badly, with all its disturbing and discouraging impressions, Sheaffe had been anything but steadfast and capable of rescuing anything other than destroying the grand magazine and saving a portion of his force by means of a straggling retreat.[63] Later, Sheaffe's "shrug" of acceptance was seen again when he did not demand an inquiry into his performance and quietly departed, all the while continuing to profess his support and devotion to Prevost. It was as if Roger Sheaffe let all his disappointments slide off his back,

John Beverley Robinson (1791-1863). Robinson was among the young men of York who rose to prominence in Upper Canada after the war. He owed his temporary appointment as attorney general in 1812 to Roger Sheaffe (on the advice of William Powell) and he was present at the Battle of York, but his personal papers and biographies are surprisingly silent about his role in the action or his thoughts on how events unfolded.(LAC, 111481)

with none of the resentment and passion another man would feel, aloof to insult, content to look ahead unperturbed.

By the time the Sheaffes reached England, Wellington and the British allies were close to forcing Napoleon's abdication, but although the campaigning was nearly complete, there was still a need for generals in the European posts. And generals were soon to be wanted when the British government escalated its commitment to the war against the United States in the spring of 1814, but Sir Roger did not get the call. He was briefly appointed to the military staff in England and then dropped. During a visit to London in 1816 John Beverley Robinson visited Sheaffe and found John Norton, the general's old friend, there too. Minutes later, William Derenzy of the 49th Foot arrived and the four of them reminisced about their days together. "We had a long talk about Canadian matters," wrote Robinson. "We talked over the unfortunate business at York, which he [Sheaffe] seems to like to dwell upon."[64] So the events of 27 April had not completely rolled off the general's back.

Sir Roger and Lady Sheaffe moved from Penzance to Worcester and then Edinburgh. Their family life was busy, as the general described in a long letter to Anne Powell in 1818, and despite Margaret Sheaffe's frequent illnesses, she and the general had produced four brothers and a sister for Julia by then and had another one on the way. Hugh Percy, Sheaffe's lifelong patron, died in 1817, but the general had been such a good family friend that Hugh Percy, Jr., the 3rd Duke of Northumberland, continued to keep Sir Roger's interests in mind. In 1829 it looked as if the duke was going to be able to come through with some sort of appropriate posting for Sheaffe, but the best he could arrange was a colonelcy of the 36th Regiment of Foot; by seniority, Sheaffe rose to lieutenant general in 1831 and general in 1838.

There were no more campaigns for Sheaffe, and he spent the years with his family, visiting friends, pursuing the life of a country gentleman. He enjoyed excellent health, but suffered the deaths of all his children; the longest surviving was Percy, named for his father's patron, who barely reached the age of twenty-one. Sir Roger was eighty-seven years old when he passed away on 17 July 1851 in Edinburgh and, because he had no direct heirs, his baronetcy became extinct. Lady Sheaffe died four years later and the last surviving member of their family was Captain William Sheaffe, 50th Foot, one of his brother's three children, whom Sheaffe had adopted. William had gone with his regiment to Australia in the 1830s, left the army in 1841 and settled in New South Wales, and it is in nearby Brisbane that his descendants honour his memory, and the general's, today.[65]

The record of what happened to the individuals in the regular units that fought at York is sparse.[66] Most of the Royal Newfoundland Fencibles who

Jack Canuck and Uncle Sam. Elisha Newton McConnell, an editorial cartoonist with the *Toronto Daily News,* produced this panel in 1913. Reflecting the strain in relations with the United States over trade issues, Jack assures Sam that, with Premier Sir James Whitney in charge of Ontario, burning the Provincial Parliament Buildings would not be accomplished as easily as it had been in 1813. (AO, C301, 1149)

returned to Kingston with Sheaffe embarked to serve as marines with Commodore Yeo on Lake Ontario. Few of the officers appear to have seen further action, not even the energetic Tito LeLièvre, who remained with the quarter master general's department and went on half pay in 1816; he died at Pointe-Claire, Lower Canada, in 1831, aged seventy-eight. Captain Daniel McPherson's company of Glengarries participated in the assault at Sackets Harbor, where a half dozen were killed, their captain taking a severe leg wound that ended his fighting days. He transferred into one of the Royal Veteran Battalions, retiring with full pay in 1821, and living out his last years in Edinburgh, where he died in 1856. Ensign James Robins of the Glengarries recovered from the wound suffered at York, saw considerable action on the Niagara Peninsula and was captured at the Battle of Lundy's Lane, 25 July 1814. He was detained with other British officers in Cheshire, Massachusetts, and died there the following September after some misadventure, "a victim of his own imprudence," as fellow captive William Merritt noted.[67] Robert Loring, who was left partially disabled by the injury to his right arm during the explosion of the grand magazine, was at Cheshire too, having also been taken prisoner at Lundy's Lane while serving as Lieutenant General Gordon Drummond's military secretary. After the war Loring remained in the army, stationed mainly in Canada, and died, a lieutenant colonel on half pay, at his home in Toronto in 1839. Sergeant James Commins had been in Captain James Eustace's company of the 8th Foot and so had avoided the slaughter suffered by McNeale's grenadiers at York. But he and his mates were at Sackets Harbor and were then transported to the Niagara Peninsula, where they fought in most of the major engagements through the rest of the war. Greatly depleted and quite worn out, the 8th was sent to England in 1815, where Commins recorded his adventures in a series of letters to an acquaintance. He described the battles, expressed his distaste for native warriors – "the most cowardly despicable characters I ever saw" – and regret at the loss of one "promising young man ... beloved by the men of his company" after another. He prided himself in giving "a true account of all our proceedings," but warned his reader that he had "been obliged to abridge some part of it as it would not be prudent to put in on paper," promising to tell all when they met.[68]

How many other young men thought of writing their accounts of the war, and of 27 April 1813 at York in particular, but never took up their quills or pencils? What deeper understandings were revealed across dinner tables or in smokey tavern corners, and were lost forever, except to those who heard them? All those soldiers and sailors, on both sides of the issue, with all their mutual and private experiences on the field at York; how would the story change if we knew what they knew?

CHAPTER **16**

"A place equal to this"[1]

YORK AFTER THE OCCUPATION

Life at York did not return to normal after the American squadron departed. Beyond the piles of ashes at the garrison and broken windows in Elmsley House, the looted homes and the scorched-brick remains of the Parliament Buildings, there were disruptions to nearly every aspect of normal affairs. More than one illusion had been erased and a sense of foreboding hung over the town.

"We are," wrote Anne Powell to her husband William on 10 May, "… leading a life of uncertainty without feeling it possible to form or pursue any plan even for a day."[2] The relief felt after the Americans left was replaced instantly with apprehensions about what they would do next. Ears were cocked southward for the sound of guns, and eyes scanned the horizon constantly for a return of hostile sails. There were false alarms that sent women scurrying to gather up their children and possessions and flee, while others tried to remain calm. Anne had her domestic duties to occupy her and these now included the care of several wounded soldiers. Dr. Robert Kerr told her that a diet of milk was good for them, so she resolved to send a kettle of milk broth daily to the garrison hospital, where the casualties were slowly being relocated. She also visited with her neighbours and friends, consoling Elizabeth Derenzy grief-stricken by the death of her father, Prideaux Selby, on 9 May and in fear of what would become of her husband, Captain William Derenzy, 49th Foot, stationed at Fort George. Anne kept in touch with Angelique Givins and Margaret Shaw, who were trying to put things back together in their looted homes. Penelope Beikie bent Anne's ear with her beliefs that the suffering of York was God's punishment for the government's refusal to properly distribute equipment sitting in the storehouses since Simcoe's time. And Ann Strachan, like so many others in town, was "very violent in her invective against Sir R[oger]."[3]

Anne Murray Powell (1755-1849).
Anne Powell lived at York/Toronto for the better part of fifty years, witnessing its remarkable development and many momentous events while suffering endless family problems. Her daughter Anne was mentally deranged and stalked John Beverley Robinson before dying in a shipwreck in 1822. One of her granddaughters gained notoriety in 1840 during Upper Canada's first divorce case. (TRL, T15180)

Despite the universal criticisms of Sheaffe, Anne Powell consistently supported him, at least in her letters to William (who remained at Kingston through May), agonizing over the "shocking things" that were being repeated and hoping that the general would "escape from the load of censure which must, in spite of appearances, oppress him."[4] Her disgust was reserved for the Americans, that "lawless mob," that "rabble," although she questioned why no one in the army or among the town's loyal citizens had thought to remove the Royal Standard before evacuating the garrison.[5] She hoped that each easterly breeze would bring the squadron from Kingston, and the reports about the arrival of Royal Navy officers partly relieved her fears, especially the rumour that Thomas Masterman Hardy, one of Lord Horatio Nelson's best-known captains and friends, led the detachment. Anne disbelieved the story that their son, Dr. Grant Powell, had retreated with Sheaffe by his own volition rather than being ordered to do so, and then, when it was confirmed, she expressed her dismay that he would leave his family and the town at a time of such desperate need. This did not stop her, however, from discussing with her closest acquaintances the possibility of Grant being appointed to one of the two positions held by the late Mr. Selby, thinking that this would help him and his wife get properly settled. Despite her anxieties and stresses, Anne Powell maintained a resolute outlook, assuring William that she was glad he was away from the chaos and cabal at York, and that she had things under control in their home as much as that was possible. In a trying hour, she could always count on "our excellent pastor" John Strachan, who visited daily and was ever ready to seek a solution to any of her woes.

Sophia Playter and her children had taken refuge in a little schoolhouse near

Newmarket and it was not until Wednesday, 12 May, that husband Ely was able to get his family back to their home by the Don River.[6] Over the next few days he repaired damage done by the looters and helped out at his father's place. He went into town several times, once to collect his militia pay from the commissary George Crookshank (who had returned from Kingston) and another day to attend the auction of Donald McLean's worldly goods. He probably heard during one of these visits that a party of men had gone into the woods to look for the buried colours of the 3rd York and that Sam Ridout had made the happy discovery.

Early on Tuesday, 25 May, Ely heard the unmistakable sound of booming guns across the lake and knew instantly that something was going on at Fort George. He wrote in his diary that "everyone was uneasy," but they were calmed the next day when word came that Fort George was safe. Then the cannonade began again, and more fiercely, at dawn on Thursday, and while he was down at Crookshank's arranging to have his militia company paid for their service, the noise of a magazine at Fort George exploding pounded over the water after which the steady din of battle stopped. Friday brought confirmation of everyone's fears, that Fort George had fallen, but that Brigadier General Vincent had managed to retreat back toward Stoney Creek. "All York was alarmed with the bad news," Playter noted.[7]

"Every hour seems pregnant with evil," Anne Powell wrote to William, and so it continued for a week, with the hourly expectation that Commodore Chauncey's squadron would appear on the horizon and land another force to outflank Vincent.[8] Then the tide turned, and the victory at Stoney Creek in the early hours of 6 June was announced, followed by sails out of the east, bringing Commodore Sir James Lucas Yeo to the fray. Fear and uncertainty still prevailed about the fighting on the Niagara Peninsula and the possibility that the Americans would attack Kingston while Yeo was supporting Vincent, but the overwhelming sense of vulnerability seemed to lift a little at York.

No regular units arrived to reestablish a post at York in May and June and none marched through town on their way to the front, since Yeo's squadron could now take them there directly. Detachments stopped briefly at the town while escorting Americans captured at Stoney Creek and Beaver Dams late in June to Kingston, but few others appeared except for couriers and officers, Nathaniel Coffin, Sheaffe's aide, being the most frequent visitor. The remnants of the militia formed the only permanent military presence during this period, with Lieutenant Colonel William Chewett and Major William Allan taking turns in command along with several staff officers, despite their having been paroled by the Americans.[9] The force in the town consisted of Lieutenant William Jarvis, a sergeant and two gunners of his artillery company of Incorporated Militia and a handful of the 1st York's cavalry, supervised by 3rd York officers, who carried messages between York and Whitby. There was also William Jarvie's company of Incorporated infantry, now commanded by Lieutenant Thomas Humberstone (the captain having suffered a disabling wound at the battle), comprising four non-coms and twenty-seven privates. Lists were made of the casualties and men who had fought and surrendered and those who had obtained paroles from the Americans without having borne arms on 27 April, but no action was taken against the latter group at this time. Chewett also ordered the captains to account for all the weapons in their companies and distribute them only to the most trustworthy of their men so "that precautions may be taken against robbers and incendiaries of whom there are but too many to the great annoyance of the public peace and safety."[10]

Public safety was a primary concern for the headmen of the town, and they began to look into laying charges for plundering and for affiliation with the enemy. The illegality of such conduct and the need for the loyalty of all citizens had been announced by Sheaffe and the Executive Council on 4 June and reiterated by Prevost in a proclamation of his own ten days later.[11] The task of dealing with the situation was left to local officials, however, and so the magistrates and constables at York followed up on word-of-mouth reports and paid visits to the homes of certain individuals, looking for stolen goods. John Lyon, the Markham miller and distiller, was one of the men who received such a visit and he protested vehemently when William Allan and several others repossessed items they knew to be public property, including an ox cart, wheels for artillery carriages, some iron and the "bathing machine." Others must have complained as loudly as Lyon did because militia detachments were called out on several occasions to form patrols and to back up the magistrates and Sheriff John Beikie and his constables in case they met with violent opposition or some sort of uprising.

In answer to a request from Governor-in-Chief Prevost late in June about the state of affairs at York, Justice William Powell complimented the efforts being made by William Allan, but he had reservations about Sheriff Beikie and others. Implying that there was a general hesitation to push the issue with the alleged plunderers, Powell wrote, "The Sheriff is a man of personal Intrepidity, but extremely cautious of responsibility – our police is weak as must be the Case where a numerous body of Individuals have an equal voice."[12] He recommended that the permanent placement of a body of regulars would help "in confirming the Loyal and over awing the disaffected." And Powell warned that if the Americans made a strong advance, local officials would have extreme difficulty in trying "to repress and keep down the Turbulence of the disaffected who are very

3rd York banner. The gift of the ladies of York to their favourite regiment was preserved through the centuries and exists in a discoloured, threadbare state. Long held in the archives of St. James' Cathedral, it has lately passed into the care of the City of Toronto Museums and Heritage Services for conservation. (Photograph by Robert Malcomson)

numerous." In answer to Powell's advice, Prevost ordered Lieutenant Colonel Francis Battersby, Glengarry Light Infantry Fencibles, on 7 July to take post at York with about 200 infantry, a handful of Royal Artillery with some field guns and a troop of the 19th Regiment of Light Dragoons; they arrived about the middle of the month.

Despite the talk about disloyal behaviour and fear of what it might develop into, little legal action appears to have been taken between May and July against any of the suspected miscreants.[13] At a special session of the Court of Quarter Sessions of the Peace in May, William Smith, who was being held in jail on the charge of vandalizing Elmsley House, was refused permission to leave on bail, but whether he was ever tried is not clear. On 10 June the court called John Jordan to atone for his refusal to billet wounded soldiers at his hotel after the battle, for which he contritely agreed to pay a fine of £2. Two days after this Nathaniel Hastings, a farmer on Yonge Street, was fined £10 for having in his possession a musket that he claimed he had purchased from a soldier in the 8th Foot; his option was to spend two months in jail, which is what he chose. A month later Major General Francis de Rottenburg, acting as lieutenant governor of the province, ordered the detention of five men from York, including the well-known tanner Jesse Ketchum and the belligerent lawyer William Peters, but no further steps were taken for want of incriminating evidence.

The return of the American squadron to York at the end of July provoked a new emergency for the townspeople and heightened concerns about the seditious sentiments spreading through the local population. The incident began when an express rider brought word to Lieutenant Colonel Battersby on 28 or 29 July that Commodore Chauncey was about to land a force at Burlington Bay and attack the British post at Burlington Heights.[14] Battersby quickly paraded all his regulars and set out from York to join other reinforcements converging at Burlington, but the Americans aborted their attack and early on 31 July set sail to the east. Battersby could only look on and wonder what they intended, not knowing that Chauncey, in consultation with Colonel Winfield Scott, who commanded the 300-man military detachment in the squadron, had decided to pay another visit to York. They arrived off York around 3:00 P.M., the larger vessels anchoring opposite the garrison while several schooners worked their way into the bay.

As soon as the American squadron was spotted, nearly all the men of York made a quick departure, having heard that the invaders on the Niagara Penin-sula had been kidnapping British sympathizers and sending them to confine-ment across the border. Before he left town, William Allan hurriedly managed to fill several batteaux with ammunition and the baggage and belongings of most of Battersby's force so that they could be taken away and hidden. This service was performed by the ever-present and dependable Ely and George Playter, who hauled the boats well up the Don River. In the meantime, Allan sought refuge, which turned out to be the better part of valour as he learned afterward that Colonel Scott had offered a $500 reward for his capture. The merchant, it seems, had earned himself a bad reputation among the Americans, either because of his belligerence while marching under guard with the conquering column on the afternoon of the battle in April, or because of his conduct toward them dur-ing the occupation.

There were but a few women and children left to defend their homes and the Reverend John Strachan, assisted by Dr. Grant Powell (who had returned from Kingston). These two met Scott and Chauncey and their officers at the garrison wharf and asked what their intentions were, asserting that the place was com-pletely without defence. Chauncey explained that they were only after public stores, that he meant to destroy any fortifications that had been made and that the landing was actually a form of retaliation for Commodore Yeo's activities along the New York State shoreline, particularly his burning of public buildings at Sodus in June. There was no plan to plunder and vandalize and in fact the commodore took the opportunity to express regret that the public library had been pillaged in April and explain that he was taking measures to collect the stolen books for their return.

The army marched into town, liberated the prisoners in the jail, paroled some of the sick and wounded in the various buildings where they lay conva-lescing and then began to look for public stores. They broke into William Allan's home and completely ransacked it and then removed flour and other goods from Allan's storehouse, including a stack of baggage belonging to Battersby's officers and others. When Strachan and Powell protested this destruction of private property, Scott explained that all the provisions and other material were public goods and ordered his men to give Quetton St. George's store the same treatment. They gave away some of the flour to townspeople who came forward, but most of it was packed into the schooners.

The Americans were going to leave that night, but certain individuals informed them about the batteaux Allan had tried to preserve, and early on 1 August five boats, loaded with infantry and flanked on shore by foot patrols, rowed up the Don River. Their search had been anticipated, however, and once more the Playter boys were active. Assisted by John Beverley Robinson and two other men, they removed all the ammunition and arms from the one batteau and either hid or sank it, while a party of dragoons who had returned grabbed their belongings from another boat. The Americans soon turned back to the squadron, the tally of material captured amounting to between one and five artillery pieces, some ammunition, eleven batteaux and 400 barrels of flour and bread. The night before they had set fire to the blockhouses and outbuildings on Gibraltar Point, having found no new fortifications to replace those destroyed in April.

The second American visit to York was certainly less traumatic for the people of York than the first, but it created a renewed alarm over the treacherous behaviour of what seemed to be an increasingly brazen set of unpatriotic vandals. William Peters, for instance, was seen meeting the Americans when they landed, shaking hands and offering his assistance. Nathaniel Hastings was one of the prisoners released from the jail and he later returned to steal carpets used as bedding there. John Lyon, with Timothy Wheeler, was also at the jail and, despite Jailer William Knott's protests, loaded his wagon with the items he had received from the Americans in April which had been reclaimed and locked up. Lyon was also seen helping the enemy carry provisions to their schooners, while elsewhere men celebrated the Americans' return and drank to their continued success.

Meeting as the Executive Council on 14 August, Thomas Scott, John McGill and William Powell described the situation in a letter to Francis de Rottenburg. They had convened at the general's request to offer suggestions on how to deal with such traitorous behaviour. They stated clearly that there were plenty of individuals who had boldly demonstrated their disloyalty, but that "the Police is too weak to act with effect in securing and detaining all the Persons suspected."[15] Furthermore, the sheriff and constables, the magistrates and the jailer were reluctant to act too aggressively for fear of "the threatened vengeance of an exasperated Banditti." One clear example of this came to light during this period, a note apparently signed by John Lyon stating, "We are five Hundred and fear not five Thousand. I mean to have William Graham's scalp, William Allan, Duncan Cameron, Samuel S. Wilmot and Micah Dyes and George Cutters scalp before one month in my Still House Hung up."[16] When confronted about the government property he had taken back, Lyon exploded in a rage, telling his accusers that Commodore Chauncey had given him a certificate for them and that he had even added other things to his stash. He warned off the constable who was investigating the matter, telling him that he could get support from the Americans to defend himself and anyone who challenged him could expect to be "beheaded and sent to Greenbush."[17] Furthermore, Lyon exclaimed, "I wish the American fleet would conquer and the British fleet sink to the bottom."

Even with such evidence, the councillors believed it would be hard to form a jury that would not include men sympathetic to those brought before the court. Their suggestion was to post a regular officer at York with the authority to seize suspects pointed out to him by local officials and enough infantry and dragoons to hunt the men down and arrest them. Then, these suspects should be sent to Lower Canada for detention until the war was over or Prevost approved their release.

Acting Attorney General John Beverley Robinson, who had only turned twenty-two years of age in July and had yet to be called to the bar, soon entered the debate and explained that it was illegal to arrest people without proper charges being laid and to hold them without trial, let alone send them out of the province for detention. Privately, however, he believed that "the Country must not be lost by a too scrupulous attention to form" and, given the situation, he felt that more extreme methods were justified.[18] Robinson suggested that de Rottenburg begin to collect information about seditious behaviour across the province, and to that end he submitted the first of several reports on individuals in the Home District. He and Thomas Ridout, John Strachan, William Allan, Duncan Cameron and Alexander Wood had already produced a list of suspects and pages of depositions given by men who had witnessed their wrongdoings. They continued their inquiries and submitted a summary of their findings late in September, although they had to admit that some of the testimonies were "mixed with prejudice and some with malice."[19] They had prepared warrants for the arrest of some men, but did not know how they would be apprehended and convicted or what alternative steps could be taken since de Rottenburg had not decided yet on how to suppress sedition.

In the end, little was done to punish the local men who had looted York and welcomed the American victory. Nathaniel Hastings was tried in the criminal assize held at York in October 1813 for larceny, presumably in regards to the rugs taken from the jail, and was acquitted.[20] The Baptist preacher Elijah Bentley appeared before the court in the same session, charged with sedition for having urged men to give themselves up to parole while praising Dearborn and his army and spreading lies. His case was held over until the next spring when the jury found him guilty and he was sentenced to six months imprisonment and required to give a surety bond of £200 to guarantee his good behaviour for five years. Of the thirty other men named by the committee at York in September 1813, only Gideon Orton was indicted for sedition, but apparently was never brought to trial. Even the notorious William Peters avoided punishment, and others, such as the radical John Mills Jackson, who was alleged to have urged non-combatant militia to give themselves up to the Americans, escaped notice altogether.

Charges were prepared for John Lyon, who was number one on the York committee's list, but he died at his home in Markham around the end of August. It appears to have been a sudden demise, with Lyon conscious enough to realize his imminent fate and to direct the hurried writing of "a will in distress."[21] The first copy of it was written in barely literate language by his friend Joseph Williams on the front of a blank British regimental pay roll; how such a document came to hand in an apparent emergency was never explained. A second copy, done on a blank sheet, corrected the bad spelling of the first while Lyon was still able to make his mark next to his name, which he insisted should be spelled "Lianss." He directed his mills and stills be sold for the support of his wife and family on their farm and he gave certain land-use permission to Williams, but as to the cause of his abrupt end, nothing was recorded, just as there is no trace of the reasons why a man who had served his militia duty through the winter had abruptly displayed such a sharp disgust for authority.

The measures that Attorney General Robinson and others believed were necessary to suppress looting and treason more or less came into effect in March 1814 after Lieutenant General Gordon Drummond had replaced de Rottenburg as the commander-in-chief in Upper Canada. Under Drummond's leadership a more aggressive approach was adopted for dealing with the problem, which led to the assize in Ancaster in the spring where traitors were tried and convicted. By now the worst of the disaffected had formed into mobs of banditti, the type that John Lyon would probably have joined, and were marauding through the western parts of Upper Canada, especially around the Grand River. None of the men blamed with plundering at York were among their numbers, which saved them the fate of imprisonment, expulsion or death at the end of a rope. When the nine men who were hanged at Ancaster had ceased their final struggles, their heads were cut off and put on display as public notice of the consequences of treachery in Upper Canada.[22]

The matter of misconduct by the militiamen at York (and others at Niagara following the capture of Fort George) received attention from Sir George Prevost in September 1813. An order went out on Saturday, the 26th, for all the men of the 1st and 3rd York Regiments to appear at York the next day. A large number of them came into town, formed up in their companies and were paraded in front of Major Samuel Wilmot, who read a proclamation from the commander-in-chief. It announced that "the novel and unjustifiable principle of making prisoners of war and paroling the unarmed peaceful citizens" was "not sanctioned by the usages of war amongst civilized nations" and, therefore, was illegal and not binding and the men who held such certificates from the Americans were required to continue in service.[23] Furthermore, those men who had been under arms and properly paroled could not take up arms against the enemy, but they were at liberty to perform other militia duties for the good of the public. Prevost warned that anyone who obtained a false parole, or refused his duties because of it, would be transported to the United States so he could be made a prisoner of war under that government's supervision. The next day the officers wrote out returns of all their men, and from that date forward, drafts of the men were summoned to the garrison as required.

A formal exchange of the prisoners of war was finalized in April 1814, and all men who had been captured were required to report to their units. This brought to light once again the illegitimacy of some of the paroles received by men at York in the days after the battle, and a board of three officers of the 3rd York convened on 4 July to examine the matter. They concluded that thirty-two men in the regiment were guilty of the offence and, as punishment, they were summoned for service in the garrison for the next three months.[24] The 1st York did not follow suit. A list of delinquent members of the 1st York had been made, but this evidence did not come out until January 1817 after former-sergeant George Cutter revealed to William Chewett that he had given a return of such men to Lieutenant Colonel William Graham shortly after the battle. Graham died later in the year, however, and nothing further was done with the information, despite the common knowledge of how the 3rd Regiment dealt with its offenders. Late in 1816 the regiments were about to be recombined and, concerned that undeserving individuals would get appointments and promotions, Cutter felt it his duty to bring the information into the open. He identified twenty-three men, adding that there were others who were guilty but he could not recollect all their names. As well, he claimed that Captain John Arnold had taken advantage of the invasion to join "in collusion with others in buying, selling and secreting the property of the Crown."[25]

About the same time, Sergeant John Stooks of the 1st York and at least two other men made complaints to Chewett about the conduct of some of their officers after the battle, notably alleging that Major Samuel Wilmot had fraternized with the enemy and acquired and sold public property. Chewett pursued the matter and ordered a court of inquiry in July 1817, which acquitted Arnold and Wilmot of the charges. Ensign Elijah Hawley was not so fortunate and, owing to Wilmot's statements, was found guilty of having given himself up to the Americans without a proper reason. He appears to have been the sole member of the regiment to be punished for such conduct; his penalty was to have his name put at the bottom of the ensigns' list, thereby restricting his chances of promotion.

In the same way that the 1st Regiment of York Militia seems to have turned a blind eye to the misconduct of its men, so did historians in the nineteenth century ignore the black marks on the militia's performance as they created what came to be known as the "militia myth." Typical of the portrayals of the militia's contribution to the war effort was the declaration in 1880 by Egerton Ryerson, one of the most influential men in nineteenth-century Ontario, that "The Spartan bands of Canadian Loyalist volunteers … maintained the virgin soil of Canada unpolluted by the foot of the plundering invader."[26] Truer representations of the facts have long since debunked the myth by showing that, at best, the militia only played a secondary role in the defence of Upper Canada. And, the regrettable conduct of some of its men at York was but one example of a phenomenon that occurred across the province throughout the war.

No one should have been surprised by the militia's poor performance, since it had been known before the war began that the militia included "many doubtful characters," as Isaac Brock put it, and that even loyal citizens were inadequately equipped and virtually untrained.[27] Only the most patriotic and zealous of their number were capable of overcoming such drawbacks and were willing to tolerate the privations inherent in war service, including the constant anxiety about how their families, farms and businesses were suffering in their absence. The notion that civilians could become efficient soldiers and would undertake the task willingly was unrealistic. To expect a common citizen to pick up a musket and perform well in a pitched battle against U.S. Army regiments made about as much sense as asking one of the British regular rank and file to lay down his weapon and immediately become an affluent farmer or merchant. Besides, the Upper Canada militia were not alone in this respect; their counterparts to the south rarely acquitted themselves well when it came to joining their own regulars on the field of battle. For the most part, Americans on the state militia rolls showed little interest in hard campaigning and were apt to shun a fight or take to their heels after a hurried volley or two.

The presence of some bad apples in the militia barrel, however, should not overshadow the fact that several hundred local men were on duty at York on 27 April and were joined by others who answered the alarm. They mustered on the parade ground at the garrison and were prepared to fight the enemy. What might have been the result had their general been a man who possessed the military acumen necessary to employ the militia as part of a concentrated defence of the town? What if Roger Sheaffe had rallied them after the first, and only, major skirmish that morning and by his own example and strength of character used the militia in concert with the remaining regulars to make a determined stand at the garrison? What if Sheaffe had stood as tall and resolutely as Andrew Jackson did late in 1814 when his defence of New Orleans rested heavily on his ability to sternly marshal and efficiently deploy a reluctant and disaffected citizenry.[28] Under such circumstances, the Canadian militia's legacy at York might have been different.

Although respectable citizens such as Stephen Jarvis complained that after the battle "[O]ld men of seventy and boys of twelve years of age,[t]o the everlasting disgrace of the Country ... were hourly coming in and giving themselves to Major-General Dearborn as Prisoners," their numbers were not large.[29] The available evidence suggests as many as 110 delinquents rather than the 500 to 1,200 claimed by American officers. Similiarly, when Attorney General Robinson's committee submitted its final report about disloyal conduct in September 1813, the list of miscreants included only thirty-two names, some of them shown to have illegal paroles as well. Such estimates reflect only a small fraction of the 559 members of the 1st Regiment of York Militia and the 495 men in the 3rd York and exclude men older than service age and those exempt from duty or belonging to other regiments.

There is no denying that the population in and around York contained numerous disgruntled individuals or that there were disturbing elements of disaffection in other parts of the province. Just after the Americans captured Fort George, for instance, the citizens of Chippawa appealed to enemy officers for protection against the "poor wretches about that part of the country ... [who] enrich themselves by plundering whatever Property they can lay their hands upon."[30] But such behaviour was not just an anomaly peculiar to Upper Canada. Federal and state officials fought a losing battle throughout the war against the citizens of New York and Vermont who profited by shipping foodstuff and timber to the British in Lower Canada. And when the British withdrew from Washington, D.C. in August 1814, having burned the president's mansion and other public buildings, a swarm of locals went on a looting rampage, to the shock and dismay of civic authorities. Radical political views and seditious intent may have spurred such individuals to extremes in any of these situations, but the vandals and profiteers probably ran shoulder to shoulder with as many selfish opportunists and deranged sociopaths bent on wreaking vengeance. The tendency of some people to take advantage of a temporary breakdown in the security of social institutions was certainly not restricted to Upper Canada, nor to the period of the War of 1812. And their numbers represent but a small part of the whole.

It has been argued that "those [citizens] who took an active part in the war were not typical Upper Canadians" and that such "voluntary service was aberrant behavior."[31] In direct challenge to such a position stood the examples of militiamen such as the steadfast William Allan and the likes of Alexander Wood who, though as a magistrate he was not beholden to bear arms, joined the regulars on the firing line. In the same manner Donald McLean, who had eked out a living as a public servant, paid for his loyalty with his life, while William Baldwin and Joseph Cawthra worked tirelessly to save lives. There is nothing aberrant to be found in the diary of Ely Playter or the letters of Isaac Wilson, two men who epitomized the best of pioneer ambition and who saw their militia service as a duty and an opportunity for advancement. Perhaps if John Detlor or Daniel Murray or Matthias Saunders had survived the wounds they suffered on 27 April and produced letters and diaries about their daily lives and motivations, an even stronger argument could be made for a more comprehensive and balanced characterization of the Upper Canada militia.

Through the summer and autumn of 1813 the people of York adapted to their changed circumstances. Many had sustained personal losses and none more so than the handful of families whose men were killed or disabled by wounds. The Loyal and Patriotic Society acted quickly to provide compensation to their kin.[32] Ferusha Detlor and Frances Murray each received $50, while Captain Matthias Saunders's wife, Elizabeth, received $100. Donald McLean was often said to have been a man without a family, but the Society granted $25 to his grown children. John Bassell's family was awarded $50. He had been the Keeper and Crier of the Court of General Sessions and suffered a severe concussion during the explosion of the grand magazine. He helped out at the hospital through the summer until, worn out by fatigue and the effects of his injury, he took ill and died. Andrew Borland, who survived his numerous wounds, received $60, partly in recognition of his service during the Detroit and Queenston engagements. Even elderly Jacob Miller, who lost a son on duty at Niagara to illness in 1812 and a second son who took ill after serving at York, received a bounty exceeding $100. The Society also reached out to the wives and families of two of the regular soldiers who died at York in the weeks following the battle, giving each of them money for the passage back to Lower Canada.

Some men, such as William Jarvis, Patrick Hartney, Joseph Shepherd and William Jarvie, who were all wounded at the battle, appear to have been missed when the Loyal and Patriotic Society gave out its grants, but they and others applied for pensions from the government. William Jarvie, for one, left York shortly after the engagement and returned to Scotland, where he joined his father and brothers in managing a rope works. He never recovered from the gunshot wound to his right wrist and when John Beverley Robinson met him in Glasgow in April 1817, he remarked, "Poor fellow, his arm is a useless burden to him, and another serious shot he received in his leg, when York was attacked …, has changed him much from the braw, sturdy chiel [fellow] he used to be."[33]

Another soldier who never returned to good health was Lieutenant John de Koven of the Royal Newfoundland Regiment. He remained at York, recovering from the bullet wound to his foot in the care of his wife, two children and a female servant. Considered no longer capable of regular service, de Koven was recommended for transfer into the Royal Battalion of Veterans, but this does not seem to have taken place, and he remained in the Fencibles until the unit was disbanded after the war. Thereafter he apparently lived off a paltry half pay allowance, with some additional stipends. During February 1814, while trying to help de Koven sort out his income difficulties, Alexander Wood wrote to a friend in exasperation, "he is a stupid old man but has certainly great cause for complaint."[34]

De Koven's reasons for upset increased because his foot healed slowly and was complicated by the sudden onset of violent spasms in the muscles around his left eye, accompanied by intolerable pain. The local garrison surgeon diagnosed the affliction as *tic douloureux* (trigeminal neuralgia) and attributed it to his injury in battle. The doctor prescribed different medicines that had no effect and finally resorted to performing surgery on de Koven's face to cut nerves above and below the eye. This was also ineffective and by 1818, at the age of seventy-two, de Koven was in Montreal with his family, petitioning the government for a pension and passage home to Great Britain. Medical boards had examined him and ruled that he was suffering from "a severe nervous attack" and that a return to a milder climate offered his only hope of recovery.[35] They were correct in describing *tic douloureux* as a "nervous" disorder, since it is a condition with only slim physical explanations that is brought on by stress, especially among the elderly, and is eased today with sedatives. How long John de Koven lived in such agony is not known. Only a nameless few witnessed how this virtually anonymous old soldier paid for his service on the battlefield at York.

The fortifications at York lay in ruins until late summer 1813 when work commenced to rebuild them.[36] The position on the east side of Garrison Creek was abandoned in favour of the irregular fort on the west side which had been started in 1812 on the advice of Isaac Brock. The Americans had failed to destroy stockpiles of timber intended for the slipway and a wharf for the *Sir Isaac Brock*, and much of this went into the construction of two large blockhouses adjacent to where the lieutenant general's residence had stood. A draft of 100 militia who paraded to hear Prevost's proclamation on 26 September 1813 formed the first major labour force and they hauled away the remains of the burned-out buildings and started on the new structures. Ramparts were thrown up around the perimeter and a gateway was cut through the west-facing curtain. Storehouses, a hospital, a magazine and other buildings eventually rose on and near the site, while Elmsley House was repaired for use as offices and a hospital ward, and buildings on the property were made into barracks. The remains of the batteries

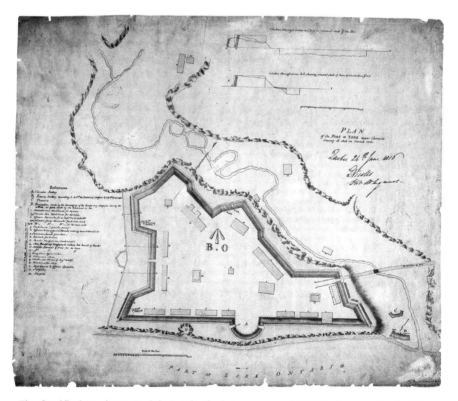

The fortified garrison. Work began in the late summer of 1813 to improve the fortifications at York. Engineers followed the basic plan laid out by Brock and his advisers in 1812, creating an irregular fortification on the west bank of Garrison Creek. The stockade and buildings on the east bank were demolished and removed. (LAC, NMC 23139)

that had stood in the ravine and next to the residence were rebuilt and strength-ened. Nothing was done to the Half Moon Battery but the Western Battery was repaired and improved and surrounded by a stockade of cedar pickets. A guard-house was erected at one corner of it and all the trees within 500 yards were felled. The sites on Gibraltar Point and at the Town Blockhouse were cleared and left without improvement. The burned-out shells of the Parliament Build-ings were hastily repaired as two-storey structures, serving as barracks through the rest of the war. At no point did anyone ever revive the misguided notion of developing a headquarters for the naval force at York.

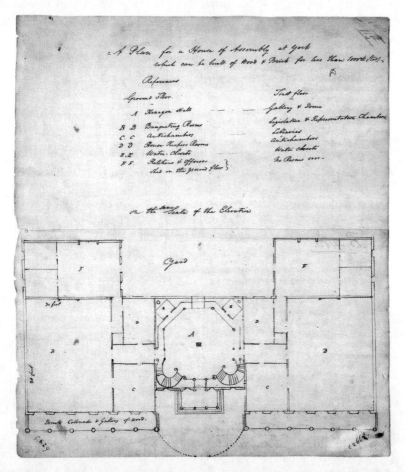

Parliament Building restoration plan. The burned-out shells of the Parliament Buildings were repaired and turned into barracks in 1814. Five years later plans were discussed for completing the original scheme of a governor's mansion with the meeting rooms as wings. This proposal shows one approach to adapting the old buildings ("B" on the diagram) into a new structure. (LAC, NMC 0542)

William Allan's "Moss Park." Allan acquired one of the 100-acre park lots on Queen Street west of Sherbourne Street in 1819 and began developing it into an estate. His Greek-revival mansion stood amidst gardens and orchards, indicative of his prosperity. (TRL, T11099)

The batteries were eventually armed and various regular army detachments took turns in garrison at York, but by the time the new constructions began, the garrison and the town had taken on the role as a medical depot where the sick and wounded from the forces on the Niagara Peninsula and the southwest of the province were transported for care and convalescence.[37] By November it was nearly impossible to find a public or private bed in town, and as the number of patients grew to over 400, the Reverend John Strachan lent the church for use as a temporary hospital. Apprehensions lingered that the Americans would come again and that Prevost "still thinks this place unworthy of protection," but never again did hostile sails come any closer than the horizon.[38] Only the *Lady of the Lake* anchored off York midway through November 1813 to deliver two boxes of books, the best that Commodore Chauncey could do, much to his mortification, to replace the texts stolen from the public library in April.

The merchants William Allan, Quetton St. George, Alexander Wood and others recovered from their losses and began to profit once again from the rush of public business and the rapid inflation in prices. Beef that had been 5 or 6 pence per pound late in 1811, cost 2 shillings by March 1814; butter rose from 1 shilling 6 pence a pound to 6 shillings; the same weight of cheese went from 1

Alexander Wood memorialized. Unveiled in May 2005, this bronze rendering of the merchant who shocked York in a lurid scandal in 1810 stands at the corner of Church and Alexander streets, where Wood owned property. It is a centrepiece of Toronto's Church and Wellesley gay village and includes a plaque that celebrates Wood's place in history as "militia officer, businessman, public servant, justice of the peace, gay pioneer." (Photograph by Robert Malcomson)

to 4 shillings.[39] Isaac Wilson wrote to his brother about one fellow he knew who had bought hundreds of dollars worth of merchandise at Montreal – in which currency he did not say – and sold it all for a 200 per cent markup, a profit margin that other entrepreneurs were enjoying too. When Lieutenant General Gordon Drummond tried to solve some of the problems of supply by imposing martial law on the acquisition of food and forage, the Home District magistrates held a special Quarter Session of the Peace and set a "going" rate for most staples, bringing their prices back down to prewar levels. Despite such controls, the leading merchants continued to do very well, as did the local farmers, whose crops and livestock were desperately needed to feed the increasing number of military and naval personnel in the province.

One incident that caused Alexander Wood some frustration was the final flurry of controversy provoked by an individual who had contributed to problems at York during the winter. This was Superintendent Thomas Plucknett, who retreated with Major General Sheaffe and reached Kingston in safety. By then Wood had retrieved his account books from where he had hidden them outside the town and reopened his business. On the books was a private debt owed by Plucknett for more than £36 and an unpaid bill for shoes he had taken on credit for the shipwrights. Knowing full well that the superintendent was "not very scrupulous," Wood wrote to Joseph Forsyth, an associate in Kingston, to call on Plucknett and collect the funds owing.[40] Forsyth did so and when Plucknett hesitated to pay up, he went to the local sheriff and had a writ prepared for Plucknett's arrest. Before this could be served, Plucknett left for Montreal, where Wood's next attempt to have friends catch up with him also failed; as compensation, Wood intended to seize some of the possessions Plunkett left behind.

Ever attendant to his own needs, Thomas Plucknett made a claim on the personal items he abandoned at York at the inquiry held at Kingston in May and received £60 for them and later an amount of back pay exceeding £120. This did not stop him, however, from reapplying for the same funds in 1816 and when they were refused, he sought half pay since he still considered himself equivalent to a military captain in rank. He asked Gordon Drummond to forward his petition to the Prince Regent and in October 1818 he wrote from Montreal to the Duke of Richmond, a prominent British politician who had just arrived at Quebec to assume the post of governor-in-chief. Plucknett admitted never having met the duke, but informed him that his father had served on a ship that once transported the duke's father on a campaign. It was a slender connection, to say the least, but the wily Plucknett counted on Richmond's appreciation for the plight of a loyal subject who had "succeeded in destroying the ship and stores" at York after the Americans landed and who lost several men and all his effects "while employed in this hazardous service."[41] He asked for the duke's protection, adding that he had "been left in this Country with a sick Family, without any support whatsoever." Staff officers dug out the receipts and warrants to show the duke that Plucknett had been properly compensated; the shipbuilder's paper chase for money appears to have ended there.

Men of greater virtue than Thomas Plucknett remained at York and by their consistent loyalty, and ambitious self-interest, gained a level of prominence during the war that put them on the path to become the leading citizens of their time. John Strachan was a sterling example of this. He had lived at York for only ten months by the time of the battle, and although he had already shown himself to be energetic and devoted, his conduct that day, and in the weeks and months afterwards, propelled him to the top echelon of local citizens. He was tireless in his service to his congregation, the troops and the town in general, involving himself in nearly every aspect of its daily life. He was zealous in his loyalty to the Crown, but not hesitant to openly censure the government and military heads when he felt they erred; he remained a sharp critic of Prevost, but eventually considered Commodore Yeo worse, a man of "pure perverseness."[42] Through his own dogged determination, and good connections, Strachan's fortunes rose and he joined the Executive Council as an honorary member in 1815, becoming a full

"John Toronto," The Honourable & Right Rev. John Strachan, D.D. Lord Bishop of Toronto. Strachan Avenue, running on a north-south line through the battlefield just west of Historic Fort York, is one of the ways in which Toronto honoured the memory of one of the most influential people in its history. Strachan worked consistently through his life to maintain the conservative polices upon which the province had been created. He believed that an education based on the principles of the Church of the England could act as a safeguard against American influences and he was a founder of the University of Toronto and its Trinity College. The library at Trinity College holds 3,600 volumes from his personal collection. Strachan, who signed official documents with the name "John Toronto," died on 1 November 1867, having lived long enough to witness the birth of the nation of Canada the previous July. (TRL)

member in 1817 and serving until 1836. He sat on the Legislative Council from 1820 to 1840, became a bishop of the Anglican Church in 1839 and until well into his eighties championed the interests of his faith and public education. He died in 1867 at the age of ninety, a giant in the early history of Toronto.

Although far less flamboyant and outspoken than Strachan, William Dummer Powell's steady service during the war helped him become one of the most influential senior government officials of the province's next decade.[43] He worked on a number of commissions, joined the Legislative Council and finally became the chief justice (upon Thomas Scott's retirement) in 1816. His uncompromising viewpoints led him eventually into numerous conflicts with governmental officials and private citizens, one of the worst instances involving Alexander Wood. Powell refused to approve his appointment to a war claims committee in 1823, revealing that his reason lay in his attitude toward Wood's conduct in the sordid sexual controversy of 1810; Wood sued his former friend for £120 in damages and won the case, but Powell never paid up. Powell left active public service in 1825 and died at the age of seventy-eight years in 1834, whereupon Wood humbly approached Anne Powell and forgave the outstanding debt. For his humanity, the dowager thereafter accepted Wood into her circle of friends. Anne lived on at York, renamed Toronto in 1834, until her death in 1849. One of her many disappointments had been her son Grant, who presented her with ten grandchildren but never learned how to manage his money properly despite the number of public appointments that came his way.

Among the merchants, Quetton St. George left York in 1815 for a visit to Europe and never returned.[44] Alexander Wood gave up his business in 1815 and returned to Scotland, intending to stay there, but a visit to York to settle his affairs in 1821 lasted until 1842, during which time he was successfully involved as an agent and with positions on boards and councils. He died, unmarried, in Scotland in 1844 without a will and no close relatives, his considerable fortune passing to a distant cousin. William Allan continued to pursue his commercial and political interests, and was a leader in both avenues of endeavour in his town and province until his death in 1853.

William Baldwin's star rose also.[45] After the war he continued to serve as a circuit judge while his law office flourished and his land holdings began to turn a nice profit. He was elected to the provincial assembly in 1820 and it was his involvement with this body that was recognized as his greatest accomplishment. He played a key role in bringing responsible government to the province after its troubles in the 1820s and 1830s, a task that his son Robert carried on to its maturity after William died in 1844.

Beyond these well recognized names in Canadian history were the hundreds of others dwelling in and around York on 27 April 1813 who lived out their days more or less in obscurity.[46] Once more Ely Playter's life stands as a fitting example. He returned to occasional militia duty after the battle, escorted some of the Americans captured at the Battle of Beaver Dams on their way to Kingston, returning home to cut wheat, helped out at his father's and his neighbours' farms, went to town to watch the opposing squadrons engage each other on the horizon, spent most Sundays with Sophia and their children visiting with friends, ploughed his fields, did his jury duty, bought his whiskey, went fishing with his brother George. In 1824 Ely stood for election and won a seat in the assembly,

York, 1828. This view across the peninsula toward the town gives an indication of how progress changed the frontier town. In 1834 when it was incorporated as a city and renamed Toronto, the population was 9,254. (TRL, T10339)

but two years later when he was charged with forgery, he abruptly moved his family to Buffalo to avoid trial. And there his story ends.

But not the story of the town where Playter and so many like him spent the most productive years of their lives and where they shared the common experience of the Battle of York. Some of them never found prosperity and happiness in the frontier community, but there were plenty of people who would have agreed with Isaac Wilson's view of the place. Writing home to his brother in December 1813, he declared, "I do not think there ever was a place equal to this for making money if a person be in any kind of trade or business whatever."[47] And possessed of a healthy portion of ambition and energy to boot. How awestruck they all would be to witness what unfailing enterprise has done with the place that even in their day was considered to be blossoming "as if by enchantment" in the middle of the Canadian wilderness.

A community is wanting in self-respect which does not take an interest in its own history and seek to preserve those records by which that history can be traced and authenticated.

GOVERNOR GENERAL, THE MARQUESS OF LANSDOWNE, 6 SEPTEMBER 1887, AT THE UNVEILING OF THE FORT ROUILLÉ MONUMENT

Toronto grew up in the shadow of Fort York and without the fort there would be no city. For the fort came first. Simcoe, the founder of Toronto, slept here and so did Brock, the general who saved Upper Canada. General Pike, of Pike's Peak, died here, storming the ramparts.

PIERRE BERTON, 6 JANUARY 1959

In ruins, 1926. The road to restoration was a long one for Historic Fort York. Visitors in the mid-1920s found only collapsing battlements to tell the story of the War of 1812. (City of Toronto Archives, Fonds 1244, William James family fonds, Item 1507)

Appendices

The Fort, the Graves, the Monuments

Lieutenant Governor John Graves Simcoe's dream of York as a military bastion for Upper Canada never came to fruition. Despite the passage of time, however, and at least two striking examples of the deadly potential of "friendly fire," the land first staked out for military purposes has survived with its heritage preserved.

Work to replace the burned buildings and improve the fortifications adjacent to Government House began in the late summer of 1813, while the old post on the east side of Garrison Creek was levelled. The north and south barracks, the officers' quarters and mess and the magazines now standing on the grounds of Historic Fort York were built over the next couple of years. By early 1816 there were eighteen structures at the garrison, which had been walled in by an earthen parapet; other buildings were constructed outside the fort. The Western Battery was enlarged and strengthened, as were the Government House and Ravine batteries. A new blockhouse rose on Gibraltar Point, and a second blockhouse, at what is now Trinity-Bellwoods Park at the intersection of Queen Street West and Strachan Avenue, was constructed to cover the flank about two-thirds of a mile (800 metres) northwest of the fort. The artificers also constructed earthworks at the Don River to guard Kingston Road. The various points were armed with long guns and carronades, at least two of which – a 9-pdr. and an 18-pdr. – were obsolete weapons from Simcoe's time. Such artillery might have been left behind by the Americans in 1813 or, possibly, the army salvaged them from where Chauncey's crews had discarded them in the lake.

The size of the force on station fluctuated over the years and the buildings gradually fell into disrepair. The Rebellions of 1837 and a concern that war might erupt with the United States prompted a mobilization of the militia and an influx of regulars from Britain, which in turn led to the call for the construction of a new and larger fort. It was built between 1840 and 1841 west of the Western Battery on the current grounds of the Canadian National Exhibition (CNE), but consisted only of limestone buildings surrounded by a heavily constructed stockade, with no gun emplacements. The military took up residence in the "New Fort," while the old fort continued its service as the main harbour defence, with its heaviest armed period being during the 1860s. In 1893 the new fort was named the Stanley Barracks to honour Governor General Lord Stanley, and the Canadian Army was still using the site until the 1940s. Between 1951 and 1953, all but one of the buildings of the Stanley Barracks were demolished in what Carl Benn of the City of Toronto Museums and Heritage Services appropriately declared was "an astonishing act of architectural vandalism."[1]

Two Assaults on Old Fort York

Long before the Stanley Barracks were reduced to rubble, the old fort had withstood a similar assault on its existence and another attempt on it lay just around the corner.

The fort continued as a functioning, if dilapidated, military post through the 1800s, during which time much of the surrounding garrison common was taken up for civic use. Its existence was endangered by these encroachments until 1889 when representatives from the City of Toronto met with federal officials to consider the idea of restoring the fort and opening it to the public. This suggestion was an off-shoot of a growing awareness among the people of Ontario, and across the other provinces, that honouring the new country's heritage had many advantages, not the least of which was the promotion of national pride. Nothing came of the initiative, however, apart from the erection of small marble plaques at the eastern and western entrances commemorating the fort's beginnings and capture by the Americans in 1813. At the same time, railway companies had applied unsuccessfully for permission essentially to level the fort in order to expand their lines.

The clash between the forces of restoration and obliteration came to a head in 1903, right after the city purchased most of the remaining garrison land from the Federal Department of Militia and Defence (later the Department of National Defence) for $200,000, with the agreement that the fort would be preserved.[2] Almost immediately, the city reneged on its promise and allowed the Park, Blackwell Packing Company to build a slaughterhouse at the east end of the fort, destroying some of its features. A more serious threat arose through 1904 as City Hall began planning a new streetcar line through the fort to facilitate access to the grounds of the CNE, seen by Mayor Thomas Urquhart and others as one of Toronto's greatest assets.

It took a letter to the editor of the *Globe* in October 1905 by a teacher and amateur historian named Miss Jean Earle Geeson to make the public aware that historic buildings would be taken down and the property disrupted by the streetcar service.[3] After Geeson's appeal, the Ontario Historical Society (OHS) got involved in the controversy and, led by the likes of Frederick Barlow Cumberland, William Rennie and Matilda Ridout, better know as Lady Edgar, the OHS waged a lengthy battle with City Hall to stop the project. It defeated an attempt to allow the Grand Trunk Railway to encroach on the northern edge of the grounds and raised enough votes to stifle a change in the bylaw that would have given City Hall permission to build the streetcar line. Undeterred, the city fathers ignored this result and kept on with their planning until 1909 when the OHS convinced Prime Minister Sir Wilfrid Laurier to step in and insert a clause into the grant effecting the transfer agreed on in 1903 that prohibited the proposed alterations to the property.

One of the outcomes of this battle with City Hall was that the OHS put together detailed plans for restoring the fort to a semblance of its earlier self. Making them a reality proved to be another difficult struggle and it was not until 24 May 1934 that the site was officially opened as Historic Fort York. Fittingly this was not just Queen Victoria's birthday but also the centenary celebration of the town of York being incorporated as a city and renamed Toronto.

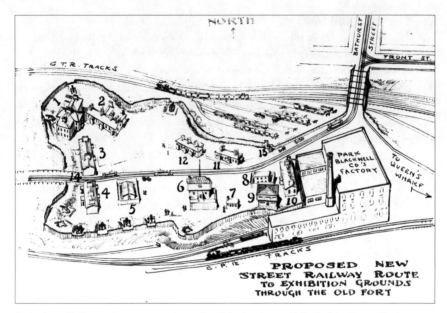

Early twentieth-century encroachments. This drawing, attributed to Owen Staples, revealed how rail lines and a slaughterhouse were already encroaching on Fort York in 1905 when a proposed streetcar line through the centre of the garrison would have cut it in half. (TRL, T14143)

The second potentially lethal assault on Fort York began in 1958, arising again over a matter of transportation.[4] The plans for the erection of an elevated throughway (the Frederick G. Gardiner Expressway) across the waterfront of the city were well advanced when people realized that its path lay over the cemetery opened in 1863 just east of Strachan Avenue on the fort common and over the southwest corner of the fort. To further complicate matters, one scheme showed Highway 400 slicing from north of Toronto straight through to the lake and linking up with the Gardiner in a truncated clover leaf between the fort and the cemetery. Members of the Toronto Civic Historical Committee joined with the OHS and the York Pioneer and Historical Society to oppose this intrusion on protected historic grounds and succeeded in having a change in the route of the highway proposed to avoid the encroachment.

The council for Metropolitan Toronto suggested dismantling Fort York and moving it closer to the lake, thereby saving a million dollars or more by not re-routing the Gardiner. Since the 1850s earth and debris from construction sites had been dumped along the lakeshore until no sign of its original beach remained. Whereas it had once stood overlooking the water, the fort was now 500 metres inland and it was argued that its rightful place was adjacent to the lake.

"The offer to move the fort at Metro's expense was made in a commendable spirit of compromise," argued the editors of the *Toronto Daily Star*. Besides, they insisted, "Fort York was blown up in the War of 1812 and all that was left were a few logs and piles of earth. It has been 'restored' twice and bears only a general resemblance to the original fortification. A member of the historical board … said he doesn't want 'a Madame Tussaud's replica.' Yet that is what it is today."[5] Elsewhere the *Star* editors asserted, "The importance of Fort York in Canadian history is largely a myth."[6] The *Globe and Mail* editors supported the suggestion "that the fort be moved from its present inland hemmed-in position to a site on the lakefront … [where] the flow of outside visitors would be multiplied many times."[7]

Opponents to the relocation of the fort raged back at such notions. "You can move buildings, but not battlefields," former Mayor Leslie Saunders argued.[8] "It is an act of bad faith … to violate the old fort by a noisy overshadowing expressway," wrote one *Star* reader.[9] "It is perhaps true," explained Pierre Berton in his column in the *Star*, "that the fort is inconveniently situated (though 50,000 people visited it last summer) but so is the Tower of London. Most historical sites are found in odd places. That is why they are historical."[10] The Canadian comedy team of Wayne and Shuster mused in their *Star* column that the trend to move historic buildings might catch on and result in "the Leaning Tower of Moose Jaw … the Pyramids along the banks of the Rideau."[11]

Early in 1959 Metro Toronto gave up its battle to relocate the fort, and the defenders of heritage celebrated their successful stand. The Gardiner Expressway was rerouted to jog around the property, although its shadow darkened the garrison and its din joined with the noise of the railway trains to further destroy any historic tranquility. The decades passed with continued struggles for funding and support which is sadly typical of historic sites everywhere. As the bicentennial of the War of 1812 approaches, the City of Toronto and the Friends of Fort York have plans underway to extend the fort's footprint and enhance its potential as a historic centrepiece.

The Graves
Nearly 140 men died during the fighting on 27 April 1813 and an uncounted number succumbed to their wounds over the following days and weeks, but the final resting places of only a handful of them can be identified with any certainty.

At the time of the battle the garrison cemetery was located about 300 metres northeast of the fort.[12] The parcel of land has been preserved as part of Victoria Memorial Square, just east of Bathurst Street at the intersection of Niagara and Portland streets. Some of the casualties must have been buried there, perhaps local men such as John Detlor and Matthias Saunders who died of their wounds after the fighting.

Bodies lying on the battlefield were interred in hurriedly dug single and mass graves near where they fell. Since the sharpest fire fight of the day happened west of Fort Rouillé, one likely site for American, British, Canadian and native graves was on the grounds of the CNE west of Dufferin Street and in the area of Alberta Circle and Yukon Place. Dozens of Americans were also knocked down by the exploding grand magazine and died on the common west of the fort. They were probably buried between the Half Moon Battery (located east of the intersection of Strachan Avenue and Fleet Street) and the Western Battery, which stood a short distance inside the modern Princes' Gate, the grand eastern entrance to the CNE. U.S. Navy Lieutenant Jesse Elliott alluded to this spot when he informed the parents of Midshipman John Hatfield that he had been buried "within a few yards from the battery from whence the ball [that killed him] was discharged."[13] Some of the Americans who died on board the squadron were committed to the depths of Lake Ontario. The story was repeated years later that the native warrior Yellowhead, who suffered a mortal wound, was buried at Clover Hill near where St. Basil's Church stands on St. Joseph Street just west of Bay Street and east of Queen's Park.[14]

Carried back to Sackets Harbor in a cask of spirits, Brigadier General Zebulon Pike was buried on a plot of ground near Fort Tompkins on 13 May 1813 as was his aide-de-camp, Captain Benjamin Nicholson. Others who died of their wounds, or illness (such as Sailing Master Frederick Leonard), were interred in the same place. Their remains were moved in 1818 to a cemetery on the other side of town beside the Madison Barracks and then moved again in 1909 to the Sackets Harbor Military Cemetery. In the vicinity of the grave is a granite marker comprising an artillery mortar and a plaque simply stating: "Brig. Gen'l Z.M. Pike U.S.A. and his officers killed in battle York Upper Canada. April 27 1813." The certainty of Pike having been buried on this spot has been frequently challenged, so town officials enlisted the help of specialists from nearby Fort Drum to solve the question in 2003. They conducted a survey of the site with ground-penetrating radar, looking for evidence of the iron casket in which Pike was said to have been buried, and obtained readings that suggested such a casket might be present. The general has been memorialized in numerous places across the western states in relation to his explorations. Descendants of Pike and officials at Colorado Springs, near Pikes Peak, have tried unsuccessfully on several occasions to retrieve his remains from Sackets for reburial in Colorado.[15]

The graves of others who fell at York were eventually disturbed by erosion and excavation. The first incident occurred in 1829 when wave action on the shoreline exposed the remains of Captain Neal McNeale, apparently identifiable by a grave marker.[16] On 9 May, to the accompaniment of the military band, a guard of honour

Pike's grave marker, Sackets Harbor. Who's buried beneath Pike's gravestone? Pike's remains and those of the men buried near him during the war were moved twice and there is doubt as to where exactly the famous explorer and fighting general lies. (Photograph by Robert Malcomson)

conveyed the captain to a new resting place in the garrison cemetery. The washing-out of bones along the lakeshore appears to have been a common occurrence, but other specific efforts made to rebury the remains went unnoticed.

Construction of a bridge on Bathurst Street, just east of the old fort, in August 1860 turned up bones from at least fifteen different men, identified as British and American soldiers by the adjacent coins and buttons. The remains were collected into one box and reinterred in the garrison cemetery.[17] In August 1888 workers came upon a gravesite near where Fort Rouillé had stood. Officials summoned Henry Scadding to the site to offer his explanation of who they could be. Scadding, a clergyman who had gained renown as an archeologist, antiquarian and author, declared that the remains were likely those of soldiers from the mid-1700s when the French occupied the site. His conclusion did not take into consideration that the bloodiest exchange of the Battle of York had happened near this spot and that the remains may have dated to that event. One brief mention of the bones in the *Globe* did not explain what was done with them.[18]

On 25 August 1894, during excavations for a factory, the well preserved skeleton of a large man was discovered under 11 feet of debris and dirt in a ravine behind the Berkeley Street Firehall (currently home of the Alumnae Theatre).[19] He was lying face down on what was later reasoned to be a litter of some sort, with a few scraps of his red coatee and blue trousers evident along with a number of buttons belonging to the 8th Regiment of Foot and a piece of a sword that marked him as an officer. A Colonel Hamilton of the local garrison concluded this had to be the body of Captain McNeale and arranged with the regiment's officers stationed at Halifax to have the bones promptly shipped there for burial. Henry Scadding was called in to examine the remains and pointed out that McNeale had been reburied at the other end of town sixty-five years before and that the fellow found behind the firehall had suffered an amputation of one of his forearms. Scadding speculated that the body was that of a sergeant in the grenadier company who had died of his wounds as General Sheaffe led his force along King Street in defeat. Sergeant Major Robert Beveridge died on 27 April as did Sergeants Joseph Lawson and Archibald Robinson and any one of them might have been quickly hidden away when Sheaffe's column paused before crossing the Don River. Newspaper stories mentioned that another skeleton had been found near the same spot seven or eight years before, but no record existed about what was done with it.

In October 1903 as the Park, Blackwell Packing Company began its city-approved excavations on the eastern end of the fort, the bones of five men came to light and were identified as Americans by the scattering of coins lying among them. A Lieutenant Colonel Gravely took the remains and presumably had them properly re-interred. Two years later, during the excavation of a ditch between the Stanley Barracks and Strachan Avenue, another scattering of bones, two pieces of pipe and a brass button were found and carried away with little notice.[20]

The graves of the men who fought that day and survived are scattered far and wide. Among the most prominent, the resting place of Sir Roger Hale Sheaffe's is marked by a crumbling tombstone in the New Carlton Cemetery in Edinburgh.[21]

The Monuments

Canadians were slow to erect monuments to honour the brave soldiers of the War of 1812. The Legislative Assembly of Upper Canada proposed in 1814 to raise a monument to Major General Sir Isaac Brock; the subsequent construction of a tower at Queenston Heights in the 1820s and its replacement in the 1850s were unique.[22] When work on the second one had begun and Brock and his aide-de-camp Lieutenant Colonel John Macdonell were laid to rest in its tomb on 13 October 1853, speakers proposed that markers should be built throughout the province in memory of the battles and the men who fought in them. The vast crowd roared its approval, but it took decades before any concerted effort to put the resolutions into effect produced results.

One of the first monuments related to the 1813 battlefield was erected to mark the location of Fort Rouillé.[23] While preparing a new site on the waterfront for the Ontario Provincial Exhibition (destined to become the grounds of the CNE) in 1878, labourers levelled the remnants of the ramparts in the old fort. Dr. Scadding and other influential local historians did not want the spot where the old fort had stood (near the current Alberta Circle and Yukon Place on the CNE grounds) to be forgotten and put together the monument project. On 24 September 1878 the Earl of Dufferin, Governor General of Canada, unveiled the monument shortly before officially opening the fair. The monument was a lofty stone cairn, topped by a massive round boulder dredged from the shipping channel. Its plaque referred to the original French trading post.

The Fort Rouillé cairn weathered badly and within half a dozen years it was decided to replace it. The new structure (see page 200) was begun in 1885 and finished in time for the celebration of Queen Victoria's fiftieth anniversary as sovereign. Again, a governor general was on hand, the Marquess of Lansdowne, to perform the official unveiling at the opening of the exhibition on 6 September 1887. The new pillar, made of Credit River sandstone, was a reference point used to identify the origins of the "French" skeletons found in its vicinity the next year. Archeological digs conducted on the site between 1979 and 1982 led to the laying of concrete walkways to mark the original shape and size of the fort; a second plaque explains this project.

On 1 July 1902 the Army and Navy Veterans' Association of Toronto sponsored a ceremony to lay the cornerstone of a monument to which they had devoted years of work.[24] The monument stood in Victoria Square, the site of the old garrison cemetery. It commemorated the estimated 400 servicemen who lay buried on the site and the sacrifice that they and their cohorts made for their country. The band of the Queen's Own Rifles led a procession from the 1894 armoury on University Avenue for the event. Mayor William Holmes Howland addressed the crowd and oversaw the placement of a glass jar containing coins, newspapers and documents inside the cornerstone before it was sealed. One of the four tablets placed on the sides of the 15-foot granite pedestal paid homage to the units that had fought on 27 April 1813, while the others concerned the fallen from that war and those who were later stationed at the fort. In January 1907, the Veterans completed their task when they had the figure of an old soldier mounted on top of the pedestal. Its designer was Walter Seymour Allward, who would create Canada's monument at Vimy Ridge years later.

Victoria Square Memorial. Completed in 1907, this monument to the men who served at the garrisons of York and Toronto stands in a quiet park surrounded by the bustling neighbourhood just northeast of the fort. Few visitors are aware that the park is the final resting place for hundreds of soldiers. (Photograph by Robert Malcomson)

Possibly, the busiest day in the history of landmarks and symbols at Fort York was Wednesday, 4 July 1934.[25] As part of the celebration of Toronto's 100th anniversary, Historic Fort York was officially opened in an international event that saw American and Canadian infantry occupy the grounds simultaneously for the first time in 121 years. Assisted by funds for public works, restoration of the fort proceeded quickly after 1930, during which time a cairn and plaque was raised on the parade ground. Thousands gathered around the cairn in 1934 for the grand opening, including Lieutenant Governor Herbert Bruce, W. D. Robbins, the United States Minister to Canada, city officials, the Toronto Regiment, a portion of the 28th U.S. Infantry from Fort Niagara and U.S. seamen and marines from the (unarmed) USN gunboat *Wilmington,* which had travelled from Toledo, Ohio, for the event. The Daughters of the Empire unveiled a plaque to the memory of Neal McNeale, Donald McLean and the others who "fell whilst defending York." The United States Daughters of 1812, with the permission of the city, dedicated a plaque in memory of Zebulon Pike and those who fell with him. And then Rear Admiral William D. Leahy handed over to the Canadians the mace taken by the Americans from the Provincial Legislative Assembly before it was burned in the days after the battle. President Franklin Roosevelt had approved the repatriation of the old symbol of democratic authority, which had been held by the U.S. Naval Academy in Annapolis. It was a fitting resolution to a long-ago conflict and a much-admired symbol of friendship between nations. It resides today in the Provincial Assembly at Queen's Park at the head of University Avenue in Toronto.

The Ontario Heritage Trust has erected numerous plaques recognizing events, sites and individuals connected to the battle, including: the battle itself, just inside the grounds of the fort; the second American visit, adjacent to the Princes' Gate; Stanley Barracks, on the CNE grounds; Gibraltar Point, next to the Hanlan's Point ferry dock; the first Parliament Buildings, near the intersection of Berkeley Street and the Esplanade; the church at York, on the grounds of St. James' Cathedral, Church Street at King Street East; Æneas Shaw, near the intersection of Strachan Avenue and Queen Street West; James Givins, at the corner of Givins and Bruce streets; and John Strachan, on a building at 150 Front Street West, the site of his home, the "Bishop's Palace."[26]

Less formal than an historic plaque is the sugar maple that flourishes within the perimeter of Historic Fort York adjacent to the place where the grand magazine stood in 1813. The tree was planted on 20 May 1968, a gift from the Buffalo and Erie County Historical Society to the Toronto Historical Board and a memorial for the 150th anniversary of the Rush-Bagot Agreement, which essentially de-militarized the Great Lakes. As the accompanying plaque still reads, it was given in "appreciation of our two countries who build not walls, but bridges."[27] When the cairn was taken down, two of its plaques were mounted on the wall beside the tree and a third was put into storage. Unnoticed amid the vast cityscape, the sugar maple marks the place of past conflict, a symbol of subsequent peace.

Hunting for Heritage

The street references in this section and through the book are intended to help historians, both amateur and professional, find the places that played a part in this story. Historic Fort York is situated in the shadow the Gardiner Expressway on Garrison Road, which enters onto Fleet Street just east of Strachan Avenue. The latter runs past the Princes' Gates at the east end of the CNE grounds, which visitors will find by proceeding east from the Queen Elizabeth Highway along the Lakeshore Boulevard or exiting off the eastbound lanes of the Gardiner at Jameson Avenue.

I advise interested readers to surf the internet, visiting the many worthwhile websites containing the most recent information about the roads, visitor hours and fees. In time, the internet will become as anachronistic as the telegraph, and its replacement will no doubt bring travellers to their destinations and help them make their discoveries with unimagined efficiency. Their explorations will turn up new facts and ideas, and the story will be refreshed and made more real. Good luck, time travellers.

Plaques by the sugar maple. Several plaques have been mounted next to the sugar maple on the masonry wall, built during the restoration of the fort in the 1930s, close to the site of the explosion of the grand magazine. (Photograph by Robert Malcomson)

Historic Fort York, 2007. This view of the fort was taken from the Bathurst Street Bridge, looking southwest, and shows the eastern gate. At the time of the battle, there were no fortifications along the western edge of Garrison Creek, which flowed in a stream bed in the foreground. Only Government House and the adjacent battery (located then on the other side of the large blockhouse in the centre of this view), some outbuildings, a garden and the western rampart stood on this stretch of ground in 1813. (Photograph by Robert Malcomson)

APPENDIX 2

The Explosion of the Grand Magazine

The violence of the explosion of the grand magazine at York was unprecedented in the history of Upper Canada. Standing a thousand yards or so away from the blast, Quarter Master Bryan Finan's son felt "a tremulous motion in the earth resembling the shock of an earthquake."[1] The concussion of it rattled the windows in the forts at the mouth of the Niagara River, twenty-eight miles across the lake, where it sounded like "rolling thunder."[2] In a matter of seconds, it killed and wounded more than 263 Americans and a handful of Canadians and British. Not since 31 October 1780 when 90 soldiers, sailors and passengers lost their lives as the British armed vessel *Ontario* sank in a storm near Oswego had such casualties been suffered so quickly in this region.

At the centre of the explosion was the grand magazine built between 1812 and 1813 to replace an old wooden structure. Little is known for certain about the appearance of the new building as no British plans for it have come to light. American Surgeon Amasa Trowbridge's description of it, as given in Chapter 6, puts the powder magazine in the lower part of a two-storey structure used to also house artillery projectiles and small arms. Colonel Cromwell Pearce described it as having been built "considerably below the surface of the ground … and lined to keep the powder dry and arched with large stones."[3] Like Trowbridge, Pearce must have heard this information from the locals during his stay at the garrison following the battle. Descriptions of the debris also substantiate the building's heavy construction and contents. "At first the air was darkened with stones, rafters and clay… . the infernal shower descended and dealt destruction to our column," wrote Major Abraham Eustis.[4] Lieutenant Colonel Samuel Conner reported, "Cart loads of stone, and an immense quantity of iron, shell and shot … the column was raked from front to rear."[5] Henry Dearborn believed, as did others, that the "immense magazine" had been constructed with detonation in mind since it "threw into the air such a quantity of stones … it [having] been so contrived as to discharge much of the greatest portion of stones in the direction our columns were advancing."[6]

Opinions varied as to how much powder the magazine contained. Lieutenant Colonel Conner, Ensign Joseph Dwight, Colonel Pearce and Surgeon Trowbridge claimed it held 500 barrels, while Surgeon William Beaumont mentioned 300 barrels and the York citizens committee headed by John Strachan said it contained only 200 kegs.[7]

Documentation about the ordnance supplies at York exists and provides insight into the likely contents of the magazine.[8] William Dunbar, the conductor of stores for the Field Train Department, prepared three reports on 31 March 1813 concerning the ordnance in Upper Canada. The reports dealt separately with mounted ordnance, field ordnance and small arms. Since the Americans took away several tons of shot and some kegs of powder (some of which must have been abandoned at or near the batteries), not all of the following materiel was in the magazine. Nevertheless, it appears to have been well stocked at the end of March and further deliveries of such materiel might have continued through April.

Powder

Type	No. of Barrels
large grain	314
fine grain	11

Projectiles

| | Calibre | | | | | | | |
Type	24-pdr.	18-pdr.	12-pdr.	9-pdr.	6-pdr.	3-pdr.	8-inch	4.4-inch
round shot	695	1606	3087	1340	3942	904	-	-
grape shot	0	10	194	0	400	0	-	-
common case	0	0	397	0	333	0	-	-
shells	-	-	-	-	-	-	204	543

Small Arms

Type	No.	Prepared Cartridges	Lead Balls
English muskets	321	5838	6260 lbs.
French muskets	6	33,656	3334 lbs.
rifles	0	0	0
pistols	30	-	0
swords	18	-	
pikes	24	-	
pole axes	30	-	
musket flints	10413	-	

The shot and shell alone amounted to roughly 74 tons of iron, while the powder for the guns and small arms, packed in kegs weighing between 90 and 100 pounds, added a further 15 or more tons. It is highly likely that a large portion of this ammunition was stored in the magazine at the time of the explosion. By way of comparison, the ordnance at Fort George comprised approximately 112 tons of shot and shell and about 10 tons of powder on 31 March.[9]

The powder was the critical ingredient in the explosion, of course. It consisted of a mixture of saltpetre, sulphur and charcoal in a ratio of 75:10:15, as preferred by British manufacturers.[10]

The experience of a town in Holland offers a reference point for judging the event at York.[11] A ship docked alongside a canal in the centre of Leiden and loaded with 369 barrels of black powder weighing 18.5 tons blew up accidentally on 12 January 1807. The explosion resulted in the death of more than 150 people and the injury of 2000 others. It destroyed 220 homes, flattening structures within 185 yards, damaging others up to 530 yards away and breaking windows at a distance of nearly 1700 yards. Most of the debris from the ship fell within 500 yards of the canal although an anchor landed nearly 1000 yards away. It is estimated that the fireball achieved a temperature of 1650 degrees Celsius and that the explosive force was equal to that produced by about 9 tons of TNT.

The best known accidental wartime explosion in Canadian history occurred on 6 December 1917 when a munitions ship blew up in Halifax Harbour.[12] It flattened or damaged about one square mile of the city, throwing a piece of an anchor three miles and resulting in the deaths of more than 2000 people.

At York American casualty records showed that 39 men were killed by the explosion and 224 others were wounded. Although some sources suggested high casualties among the locals and British regulars, only half a dozen or so occurred.[13]

Henry Dearborn provided the sole description of the size of the debris field, estimating that it was from "sixty to eighty rods" (330-440 yards) wide.[14] Ned Myers described "stones as big as my two fists" falling on and around the *Scourge* which was engaging the batteries at a range of at least 300 yards.[15] The Half Moon Battery, where Pike and others were mortally wounded, stood less than 400 yards from the magazine, but many casualties occurred in the front part of the American column so lethal debris probably fell 500 yards or more from the magazine.

No one reported damage in the town because of the explosion, not even to the buildings on the western boundary about 1000 yards from the magazine. Similarly, little detail was recorded about the condition of the garrison and Sheaffe's residence other than Major Eustis's remark that "The fort before us was in ruins," and Surgeon Beaumont's note about the later burning of "the ruins of the Government house."[16] On the night of the battle one American officer acquired what he termed "comfortable quarters" at the garrison.[17] Ely Playter made the most thorough description of the place after he went to the garrison on Friday, 30 April to obtain his parole and to complain to Dearborn about the looting of his home. "The appearance of the town and the garrison were dismal," he wrote in his diary, "the latter shattered and rent by the [artillery] balls and the explosion of the magazine, not a building but shewed some marks of it and some all torn to pieces."[18]

Playter also noted the next great explosion to take place in Upper Canada.[19] He and his neighbours clearly heard the cannonade that took place between Forts George and Niagara on 25 May and the battle that occurred there two days later. For the attentive ears at York, the end of the fighting that day was punctuated by the sound of a magazine at Fort George blowing up.

In the opinion of at least one resident at York, the detonations of the two magazines paled in comparison to what happened on 5 August 1814. Four British warships were stationed at Niagara through the summer ferrying men and materiel between there and York. One of them, the schooner *Magnet*, was making the run on the fifth when Commodore Chauncey's squadron appeared and gave chase. Realizing he could not outrun the Americans, the British commander drove his schooner ashore at 10 Mile Creek near Fort George and, after salvaging as much of its cargo as he could, set fire to it. The *Magnet* was loaded with powder and it blew up with astounding effect. At York, Thomas Ridout later wrote, "I felt a violent concussion of the air, and presently heard an explosion towards Niagara, much greater, than the explosion of our magazine – on looking over the Lake where the enemy's vessels were – I saw a prodigious cloud of smoke, rising to a great height – I then concluded and do now that one of the enemy's vessels has blown up."[20]

Credit for what was probably the most impressive explosion in the area, then, went to the *Magnet*. It had originally been named the *Governor Simcoe*, the oldest merchant vessel on Lake Ontario and the one in which merchant Alexander Wood lost a shipment of goods when the Americans chased it into Kingston in November 1812. Part of the British response to Chauncey's presence was to turn York into a naval centre and arsenal which, of course, led to the explosive events on 27 April 1813.

APPENDIX 3

British Artillery at York

One of the issues related to the Battle of York was the American capture of artillery pieces, long guns and carronades, and the impact their seizure (and the taking of a large supply of naval materiel and fittings) had on subsequent events, in particular Master Commandant Oliver Perry's victory on Lake Erie in September 1813. A close examination of the contemporary records reveals that the Americans only kept sixteen pieces of different calibres none of which had been intended for use by the British on Lake Erie. The details of this investigation are presented here.

The Guns of the *Sir Isaac Brock*
The *Sir Isaac Brock* was supposed to have been armed with twenty-six 32-pdr. carronades and four long 18-pdrs., but it became obvious during February 1813 that

such guns would not be available for it until late spring. British officers formed plans to mount guns from land batteries and the other vessels on the ship to provide some firepower for its expected first voyage to Kingston where it could be properly armed.[1]

The events at York prompted some Americans to claim that their victory "decides the command of the Lakes" and Commodore Chauncey initially announced the capture of twenty-eight guns.[2] Many of them were not considered worth keeping, however, and were dumped into the lake off York, and when Chauncey later put in a claim for prize money for the guns from York, he only mentioned sixteen of them.

Governor-in-Chief Sir George Prevost complicated the situation when he wrote to his superiors in England on 20 July 1813 that "the ordnance, ammunition and other stores for the service on Lake Erie had been deposited at York for the purpose of being transported to Amherstburg, but unfortunately were either destroyed or fell into the enemy's hands when York was taken by them."[3] Early historians combined the intended strength of the *Sir Isaac Brock*, Chauncey's first report and Prevost's misleading information to create an inaccurate picture of the outcome. William James, for instance, wrote in 1818 of "the guns [that] belonged to the ship that was building" lying in frozen mud under a thick cover of snow (despite it being the end of April).[4] Other writers took up this image and it has extended to modern times with authorities making such assertions as the destruction of "twenty-eight cannons ranging from 6- to 32-pounders together with a large amount of stores intended to be forwarded to Amherstburg" contributed to the British loss on Lake Erie.[5]

Had a clear statement of the artillery strength at York been made in the spring of 1813, these misunderstandings might have been avoided. The following explanation is intended to clarify this matter.

The Guns at York
At the time of the Battle of York, there were up to thirty-seven pieces of artillery available at York, including the following:

Field artillery
2 6-pdr. brass field guns (in the garrison from 1811, at least)

Garrison/ship guns
6 6-pdr. long guns (removed from the *Duke of Gloucester*, autumn1812)
2 12-pdr. long guns (sent from Lower Canada, via Kingston, winter1813)
1 9-pdr. long gun (brought by Simcoe, condemned)
1 12-pdr. long gun (brought by Simcoe, condemned)
2 18-pdr long guns (brought by Simcoe, condemned)

Carronades
8 18-pdr. carronades (sent from Fort George, winter1813)
5 18-pdr. carronades (brought by Simcoe)
10 12-pdr carronades (brought by Simcoe)

Lieutenant Governor John Graves Simcoe, intent on developing York into a well defended naval depot, had guns and carronades collected and sent to York where they were stored in the blockhouse at Gibraltar Point unless mounted at the garrison. They included two old 18-pdr. guns that had been sunk in the lake (presumably at

Kingston or Carleton Island) around 1783, a 12-pdr. brass long gun suited for use in a gunboat, five 18-pdr. carronades and ten 12-pdr. carronades. A 9-pdr. long gun, cast before 1754 was also taken to York and, along with the three heavier guns, was subsequently condemned and its trunnions and cascabels were broken off.[6]

The two brass field guns at York were noted in ordnance reports from at least 1811.[7] Two reports in December 1812 also noted the presence of six 6-pdrs., later said to have been taken out of the *Duke of Gloucester*, and they were mounted on garrison carriages in March 1813. There were four 12-pdr. carronades mounted in December, but not the following March, having apparently been returned to the *Prince Regent* before it sailed to Kingston.

The two 12-pdr. long guns were sent from Kingston during the winter, while eight 18-pdr. carronades were sent from Fort George about the same time. Both sets of guns were listed as being at York at the end of March.[8]

The Artillery Strength at York on 27 April 1813

Without a specific list of the artillery mounted for use in battle, conclusions about which guns were put in which battery are based on fragments of information in correspondence and memoirs.

Major General Sheaffe gave conflicting accounts of his artillery strength. On 7 April he remarked, "2 12prs mounted – 6 18prs and hope to have more ready in a few days."[9] In the two versions of the battle report dated 5 May he mentioned only two 12-pdrs., two condemned 18-pdrs., and one condemned 12-pdr. brought into use late in the action. In another letter written in late May he claimed that "two twelve pounds and two field sixes were furnished for the defence of an open untenable town."[10]

Other descriptions of the guns include: William Powell – two 6-pdrs., two 12-pdrs. and 18-pdrs.; Thomas Ridout – "only five guns"; Stephen Jarvis – "the British Troops … allowed two field pieces to be taken"; Abraham Eustis – three 18-pdrs. in the Western Battery; Cromwell Pearce – two long 18s in the Western Battery; Amasa Trowbridge – five pieces in the Government House Battery, 24-pdrs. in the Western Battery.[11] These sources verify the presence of the field guns and indicate the strength of the Western Battery and the Government House Battery. The other batteries were mentioned, but the guns in them were not specified. There was some indication, for instance, that the Half Moon Battery had no guns, but the weight of evidence suggests otherwise.[12]

It is safe to conclude that not all of the artillery available at York was mounted and put into action on 27 April. Where the other guns were was never explained, leaving the best speculation about the deployment of the pieces to be the following.

Presumably, many of the discarded guns were retrieved from the lake at some later time, which explains the presence of the condemned 18-pdr. and 9-pdr. on display at Fort York today.

Field Battery
2 6-pdr. brass field guns*

Western Battery
2 18-pdr. long guns (condemned)*
1 or more 18-pdr. carronade‡

Half Moon Battery
2 6-pdr. long guns‡
    or
2 18-pdr. carronades‡

Government House Battery
2 12-pdr. long guns*
1 12-pdr. long gun (condemned)†
2 6-pdr. long guns ‡

Ravine Battery
2 6-pdr. long guns†

* confirmed arrangement
† probable arrangement
‡ possible arrangement

Chauncey's Prize Guns

When Commodore Chauncey made his claim on 7 May that twenty-eight guns had been taken from the British, he also admitted that an accurate record of the items captured could not be made until they were landed as each vessel had loaded everything it could without keeping a tally.[13] So there might have been as many as thirty-seven pieces of artillery at York, as shown above. Many of them were found to be unserviceable (such as the condemned guns) and discarded at the anchorage off York. When the Americans returned to York at the end of July 1813, they confiscated one 24-pdr., according to Lieutenant Colonel Winfield Scott, while Chauncey stated that five guns were taken (without describing them) or destroyed along with shot, shells and ammunition. Whether these pieces of artillery were at York in April is unknown.

Chauncey only claimed prize money for "16 cannon of different calibres" which probably included the most serviceable of the weapons: six 6-pdr. and two 12-pdr. long guns and eight 18-pdr. carronades.[14] This leaves the two brass field guns out of the count, but Ned Myers claimed that they were taken on board the *Scourge*. Archeological evidence shows that the schooner carried only iron guns when it sank in August 1813, so perhaps the two brass pieces were exchanged for two of the long iron guns. This is speculation at best, but it seems a reasonable explanation for Chauncey's contradictory reports and suggests which guns Chauncey kept and which ones were dumped overboard into the lake.

British Order of Battle at York, 27 April 1813

The strength of the force under the command of Major General Sir Roger Hale Sheaffe at York on 27 April 1813 is estimated to have been 1,052 officers and men, a total which considerably exceeds tallies in earlier accounts of the action.

Previous accounts have relied on rough anecdotal estimates about the total strength of the force, including the following: Sir Roger Sheaffe – "about six hundred, including militia and dockyard men"; William Powell – "365 [regulars] to them may be added in numbers 250 militia and 40 art[ificers]" and "in all 600 men"; Thomas Ridout – "300 regulars and 208 militia"; John Strachan – "about 650 or 700" and "regulars – 360, militia – 350."[1]

The strength presented here is the result of an analysis of extant regimental records, casualty lists, the York Garrison Account Book for 1813 and contemporary correspondence. The force comprised the following units and contingents.

ORDER OF BATTLE

Major General Sheaffe did not muster his entire force in one place at one time, nor direct it as a coherent line of battle. The elements present and the artillery that supported them are summarized here. The numbers are taken from the muster and pay lists below

Staff and Departments		15
Upper Canada Militia		477
Staff	10	
1st York Regiment	159	
3rd York Regiment	236	
1st Durham Regiment	20	
Incorporated Regiment	52	
Town Volunteers		11
Native Warriors		50
QMGD/PM		86
British Regulars		413
Royal Artillery	16	
41st Foot	4	
49th Foot	24	
RNRF	104	
GRLIF	62	
8th Foot	203	
TOTAL		1052

ARTILLERY

The British artillery present at York is also a matter of contention and is described with full references in Appendix 3, British Artillery at York.

Field Battery
2 6-pdr. brass field guns*

Western Battery
2 18-pdr. long guns (condemned)*
1 or more 18-pdr. carronade‡

Half Moon Battery
2 6-pdr. long guns‡ or 2 18-pdr. carronades‡

Government House Battery
2 12-pdr. long guns*
1 12-pdr. long gun (condemned)†

Ravine Battery
2 6-pdr. long guns†

* confirmed as mounted
† probably mounted
‡ possibly mounted

Staff and Garrison Departments

There were at least 15 staff and department officers and officials present on 27 April 1813, excluding the two officers who are counted below with their regiment.

Major General Sir Roger Hale Sheaffe	Commander, British Forces in Upper Canada, Acting Administrator, Provincial Government
Captain Robert Loring, 104th Foot	Aide-de-camp
Lieutenant Colonel Nathaniel Coffin, 15th Foot	Provincial Aide-de-camp
Major James Givins	Provincial Aide-de-camp, Superintendent, Indian Department
Lieutenant Colonel Rowland Heathcote, RNRF*	Commander, York Garrison
Lieutenant Colonel Philip Hughes	Senior Royal Engineer, Upper Canada
Lieutenant Philip Ingouville, RNRF*	Assistant Engineer

Commissariat

George Crookshank	Acting Commissary General
John McGill	Assistant Deputy Commissary General
Edward Hartney	Clerk
T. G. Ridout	Clerk
Hugh Heward	Issuer

Others

John Strachan	Chaplain
William Lee	Hospital Mate
Patrick Hartney	Barrack Master
William Dunbar	Conductor of Stores, Field Train Department
J. P. Radelmiller	Lighthouse Keeper

* counted with his regiment below

Upper Canada Militia

There were 477 officers and men of the Upper Canada Militia present at York. The full report on the compositions of the regiments is presented in Appendix 5, Upper Canada Militia at the Battle of York.

Town Volunteers

There were 10 men and boys who came forward to volunteer their services during the battle. The Militia Law exempted certain individuals from militia service for a number of reasons, including age and appointment to civil offices. The following individuals were acknowledged to have rallied to the alarm and participated in the defence of York.[2]

John Bassell	John Mathewson	
John Beikie	Donald McDonell	
Duncan Beikie	Donald McLean	KIA
George S. B. Jarvis	Quetton St. George	
Allan MacNab, Sr.	Alexander Wood	
Allan MacNab, Jr.		

Native Warriors

No official tally was made of the native warriors who participated in the fighting at York. Based on anecdotal sources, the strength of the party of Mississauga, Ojibwa and Chippawa warriors at York is estimated to have been about 50.[3] Major James Givins was in command of them and has been placed above as one of the staff officers.

Quarter Master General's Office/Provincial Marine

The strength of the Quarter Master General's Department and the Provincial Marine at York is estimated to have been 86 officers and men, excluding Captain LeLièvre who is counted below with his regiment.

The QMGD oversaw the day to day management of the Provincial Marine, while the naval officers were in charge of their crews and the superintendent directed the work of the artificers in the yard.

QMGD Office[4]

Captain François Tito LeLièvre, RNRF*	Deputy Assistant Quarter Master General
Daniel Daverne	Clerk

Provincial Marine[5]
Lieutenant François Gauvreau
Lieutenant M. L Green
Midshipman Louis Beaupré
Midshipman John Ridout
Surgeon Grant Powell
Clerk and Steward James Langdon
1 boatswain
George Langley
Joseph Cloutier

Dockyard Personnel[6]

Thomas Plucknett	Superintendent of the Dockyard
John Dennis	Master Shipwright
Don McKay	Foreman
James Bennet	Blacksmith
Pierce Lonnegan	
William Patrick	
70 artificers	

Identified Artificers[7]
William Borland
Thomas Douglas
William Forfer†
Jesse Goodwin
Isaiah Hire
Joshua Leach†
William Livingstone
Peter McCallum
George Midday
Martin Midday

* counted with his regiment below
† member of Captain J. B. Robinson's 3rd York militia.

British Army Units

The total strength of the British army units present at the battle is estimated to have been 413. Based on extant records of the period, this figure is larger than previous accounts which have based their strength estimates on anecdotal records.

Anecdotal remarks about the strength of the British army unit included the following: Sir Roger Sheaffe – "a bombardier and twelve gunners of the Royal Artillery … two companies of the 8th (or King's) Regiment … about a company of the Royal Newfoundland Regiment and one of the Glengarry Light Infantry," and "a company of Glengarry Light Infantry … two companies of the 8th … Regiment and a company of the Royal Newfoundland Regiment"; William Powell – "two companies of the 8th, about 180 men, two weak companies of the Newfoundland, 40 of the Glengarry Regt…"; Thomas Ridout – "300 regulars"; John Strachan – "two companies of the eighth, and as many of the Newfoundland Regt…. and one company of the Glengarry Regt," and "Regulars, 360"; and an anonymous British witness – "two companies of the King's, two weak companies of the Newfoundland, forty men of the Glengarry sharpshooters, about 320 men."[8]

The extant records examined included regimental muster and pay lists and lists of dead, deserted and transferred, casualty lists and claims for losses. The nature of the records prevented a definitive conclusion as to the strength of the British army on 27 April. It is clear, however, that members of the 41st and 49th Regiments were present and that the detachments of the 8th and Royal Newfoundland Regiments each comprised elements of several companies. As shown below, the total strength (413) shown here represents a minimum estimate for the units. Given the uncertainties about how the records were tallied, it is possible that the true strength might have exceeded 500.

Strength of the British units present at the battle of York

4th Battalion, Royal Regiment of Artillery	16
1st Battalion, 41st Regiment of Foot	4
49th Regiment of Foot	24
Royal Newfoundland Regiment of Fencibles	104
Glengarry Regiment of Light Infantry Fencibles	62
1st Battalion, 8th Regiment of Foot	203
Total	**413**

Key
POW = Prisoner of War
KIA = Killed in action
WIA = Wounded in action
WIAd = Wounded in action, died
MIA = Missing in action

4th Battalion, Royal Regiment of Artillery[9]

The strength of the Royal Artillery detachment at York is estimated to have been 16 men, all detached from Captain William Holcroft's company, based on limited references in the casualty lists and regimental records. The inquiry into losses due to the battle included no claims from this detachment. The prisoner information enclosed with the Terms of Capitulation (transcribed in Appendix 8) included one bombardier and three gunners (unnamed).

Strength, according to muster, pay and casualty lists

Bdr.	Gr.	Dvr.	Total
1	14	1	16

Bombardier				
William Needham	POW	Thomas Hobroyd	MIA	
		John Isaac	KIA	
Gunners		William Jenkins	KIA	
John Bynon	MIA	James Lang	POW	
David Coulter		Thomas Manners		
Edward Dowler		Edward Murphy	KIA	
Robert Elder		Alexander Scott		
James Gower		William Terrall		
John Henny	MIA	William Timothy*	WIA/POW	

* Although listed as a casualty, William Timothy does not appear on any of the musters or pay lists for Holcroft's or other RA companies. The casualties reports identify him as a driver. He may have been part of the Royal Provincial Artillery Drivers (Car Brigade) raised in March 1813.

1st Battalion, 41st Regiment of Foot[10]

The only data available for the presence of members of the 41st Foot at York is in Lieutenant Colonel Heathcote's claim for the losses on behalf of a sergeant and three privates of that unit (no names).

Strength, according to claims for losses

Sgt.	Cp.	Mu.	Pr.	Total
1	0	0	3	4

49th Regiment of Foot[11]

The strength of the 49th Foot at York is estimated to have been 24 men, based on limited references in the casualty lists and regimental records. The inquiry into losses due to the battle included no claims from this detachment.

Strength, according to muster, pay and casualty lists

Sgt.	Cp.	Mu.	Pr.	Total
3	0	0	21	24

Sergeants (by company)
Patrick Jordan (8)
Barnard Kelly (8)
Daniel Sweeney (9)

Privates (Company 8)
Thomas Boyce   WIA/POW
Thomas Gilstein   POW
Richard Graham
Edward Green

John Green
Thomas Harding
John Harding
Michael Hendon
Dudley Kelly
Owen Kelly
William March
Hiram Pinder
Joseph Smith

Other Privates (by Company)
Thomas Reid (1)   WIA/POW
Thomas Porter (2)
Florence Leary (2)   POW
John McCann (3)   WIA/POW
John Brown (5)
William Meaton (6)
Patrick Gallaher (10)
James Jeffery (10)

Royal Newfoundland Regiment of Fencibles[12]

The strength of the Newfoundland Fencibles at York is estimated to have been about 104 officers and men. The number of individuals shown below amounts to 158. Most of these men were present at York, but some of them had either remained at Kingston or sailed there on the *Prince Regent* in the week before the battle. The regiment differentiated among men with identical names by adding 1st or 2nd.

The clearest indication of the detachment's strength is Heathcote's claim for the lost "necessaries" of 10 sergeants, 8 drummers and 77 rank and file, plus the claims of 7 officers from the regiment, and Ingouville and de Koven, for whom claims are not included, equaling a total of 104. Whether the lost necessaries of the 28 men who were KIA, WIA/POW and POW was included in this claim is uncertain. If they were not part of the claim, then the detachment's strength totalled 132 officers and men. Heathcote submitted a claim for 133 great coats, but the claim implies that some of them were in storage and not used on 27 April.

Strength, according to muster, pay and casualty lists

	Sgt.	Cp.	Mu.	Pr.	Total
Commissioned Officers	-	-	-	-	11
Company 1	2	2	1	25	30
Company 2	1	0	0	20	21
Company 3	3	2	1	30	36
Company 6	3	2	2	17	24
Company 9	0	0	1	0	1
Company 10	2	1	2	26	31
Others	4	-	-	-	4
Totals	**15**	**7**	**7**	**118**	**158**

Officers at York

Staff

Lieutenant Colonel Rowland Heathcote	Commander, York Garrison
Ensign Robert Cook	Adjutant and Pay Master
Bryan Finan	Regimental Quarter Master (counted here among commissioned officers)

Staff Sergeants (Companies)

James Barnard (1)	Sergeant Major
Michael Moran (1)	Second Master Sergeant
Joseph Willetts (1)	Pay Master Clerk
Thomas Kelly (10)	Drum Major, WIA/POW

Captains

Charles Blaskowitz	
Captain François LeLièvre	Dep. Asst. Quarter Master General

Lieutenants

John L.C. de Koven,	WIA/POW
Philip Ingouville	Assistant Engineer
Patrick Walsh	

Ensign

Charles W. Davis

Elias Pipon's #1 Company

Captain Elias Pipon

Sergeants
H. H. Withers
Joseph Morrisett

Corporals
Edward Power
Robert Foley

Musicians
Alexander Seaton   WIA

Privates
William Barlow
William Bartlett (2nd)
George Bell
Edward Brien   KIA
Thomas Casey   WIA/POW
B. Cookman
Pat Cooney
Carle Frederick
William Gardner (2nd)   POW
James Godfrey
Edward Howell
Christopher Hughes   POW
John Linstead
James Lovell
John McDonald
Charles McGarahan
John McGrath
John Parker
Thomas Price
Patrick Stafford
James Swartz
Thomas Thompson
John Thomy

Michael Walsh
John Wilcox

William Morris's #2 Company

Captain William Morris

Sergeants
Matthew Hennesey

Privates
Elf Anderson   KIA
James Bannen
George Bennett
William Boyde
Christian Christopher
William Dowling
Richard Duffy
John Gorman
John Grace (2nd)
James Hawkins   WIA
George Holliday
Michael Hutchinson
John Lewis
Matthew Moriarty   KIA
Emmanuel Murdan
Dennis Sheerson
Thomas Shurman .
John Sparrow   WIA/POW
John Stride
Robert Whelan

John Hierlihy's #3 Company

Captain John Hierlihy

Sergeants
William Campion WIA/POW
John Chesney   WIA/POW
William Simons   KIA

Corporals
James McDonaugh
John Fannen   KIA

Musicians
John Hickland

Privates
Claude Bellisle
Christopher Blackberry
Peter Blundell
Jonathan Bradin
Mark Britt
John Carrol
William Chuter
Thomas Clarke (1st) WIA/POW
Arthur Clarke   WIA
John Cripps
Cornelius Fieley   WIA/POW
John Foot
William Hartley
Stephen Head   KIA
Isaac Hunt
Peter Jackson
John B. Kelly
Joseph Lannigan   WIA/POW
Allan McDonald   WIA/POW
Alexander Miller
William Mitchell
James Moran
Edward Morgan   KIA
George Morin
John S. Nelson
William Payne
Brian Puzey
Francis Saunders
Edward Sponder
Thomas Stricker

John Evans's # 6 Company
Captain John Evans

Sergeants
Timothy McCarthy
Dennis McCarthy.
Daniel Wilcox

Corporals
Isaac Abbott
Patrick McCadden

Musicians
Thomas Hamilton
William Toogood   KIA

Privates
Peter Abbott
George Aldridge   WIA
Robert Chapman
William Coleman
Martin Conway
Ambrose Cook
T. C. Detzer
John Grace (1st)
James Isaacs
William King
T. F. Linanden

James Milner   KIA
Peter Styrban
Matthew Whelan
John Williams (1st)
Emanuel Williams

William Winter's # 9 Company
Captain William Winter

Musician
David Keeley   WIA/POW

Charles Blaskowitz's #10 Company
Captain Charles Blaskowitz

Sergeants
Hugh Coleman
Emmanuel Mitchell

Corporals
John Silvey

Musicians
John Menham
Bartholomew Richardson

Privates
Isaac Bartlett

Richard Beck   WIA/POW
John Beckey
William Berry.
Peter Bonair
William Brent
Thomas Deane
Thomas Gleeson   KIA
Nathaniel Hill   KIA
Patrick Hogan   WIAd
Samuel Hussey   KIA
Thomas Hussey.
Joseph Janny
John Jestin   KIA
Anthony Lally
Richard Lane
George Lore
Henry Loveland
Henry Lovell
William Maher   WIA/POW
Thomas Males
Frederick Robinson
Peter Rowe
John Walsh (1st)   KIA
John Walsh (2nd)   WIA
Thomas Whittle

Glengarry Regiment of Light Infantry Fencibles[13]

The strength of the Glengarry Fencibles at York is estimated to have been 62 officers and men. As with the other officers noted above, Captain McPherson submitted claims for items lost at York, including 59 great coats and 60 sets of necessaries (in knapsacks). When McPherson and Robins are included, the strength of 62 is attained. Whether McPherson included the 6 WIA/POWs, POWs and MIA in this total is unclear; if he did the total was 68. The list below includes 69 individuals, most of whom were present at York on 27 April 1813.

Strength, according to muster, pay and casualty lists

Capt.	Lt.	En.	Sgt.	Cp.	Mu.	Pr.	Total
1	0	1	3	3	2	59	69

Officers at York
Captain Daniel McPherson
Ensign James Robins   WIA

Daniel McPherson's #7 Company
Captain Daniel McPherson
Ensign James Robins   WIA

Sergeants
Alexander Macdonell
John Macdonell
Patrick Strange

Corporals
John Cronks
James Dulmage
Seth Marshall

Musicians
William Babcock
Peter Campbell

Privates
John Alguire
Thomas Barry
Benjamin Beckwith   POW
John Bedel   POW
Robert Blair
Charles Blanchard
John Bone
Jesse Brown   WIA
Ebenezer Buck
John Burke

Thomas Burke
Dougald Cameron
John Carroll
Archibald Carscallen*   MIA
Benjamin Cotton
James Fenton
Michael Gallinger   WIA
Joseph Gould   POW
Martin Graham
William Grant
David Hamilton
Joseph Hardy
William Harris*   WIAd
Joseph Hewitt
Ansill Hill

John Hillman
Joseph Hillman
John Hineman
Andrew Hoffman
John Hoover
Christopher Hossingrod
John Kerby[+]   POW
John Knapp
John LaForme
Joseph Lareaux
Samuel Leaking
Zechariah Leaking
Mathew Lower
Neil McLean
Joseph Mott
John Myers
Peter Norton

Peter Oman
John Patterson
William Patterson
Barthemew Peppan
Emanuel Peppan
Baptiste Poulin
Anthony Rafael
William Smith
Charles Spooner
Malcolm Stewart
David Studevant[*]   MIA
John Taylor
Samuel Taylor   WIA/POW
William Taylor
James Thompson
George Willbanks
David Wilcox

* Private Archibald Carscallen, listed on the casualty lists as MIA, was marked present on the musters through the spring and summer. Private William Harris, listed as KIA on the casualty lists, was shown to have died on 19 June 1813, presumably from wounds received at York. The spring muster remarks that Private David Studevant, listed on the casualty lists as KIA, was "not carried forward"; his name does not appear on the summer muster.

[+] Private John Kerby was identified as a member of Company 9 and a POW at York, the only non-member of McPherson's Company 7 apparently connected with the battle.

1st Battalion, 8th Regiment of Foot[14]

The strength of the 8th Foot at York is estimated to have been about 203 officers and men. According to regimental records, Captain McNeale's #1 company mustered 120 men (apart from commissioned officers) and Captain Eustaces #3 had 78. Five officers submitted claims for losses and the casualty lists showed men from companies #6, 7 and 9. These bare numbers total 214 officers and men, although the additional companies must have included more men.

As with the RNRF data above, the claims made subsequent to the battle shed a different but not unreasonable light on the subject. Among the claims Eustace submitted for losses after the battle was one for lost great coats, showing 109 lost by #1, 38 by #2, 23 by #7, 13 by "detachments" and 14 by #2 company (which company was not noted among the casualties). If taken at face value, this means that neither McNeale's nor Eustace's company was fully intact at the time of the battle, and that the detachments from the other companies varied in size. When combined with the six officers shown to be present, this gives the regiment's strength as 203, the amount used in this account.

Just as it is not clear if Lieutenant Colonel Heathcote included the 28 men of the RNRF who were dead or still at York in the claim, it is not clear if Eustace included the 86 KIAs, WIA/POWs and POWs in his tally. If he did, then 289 officers and men of the 8th Foot were at York, which seems like an inordinately large number.

The lists of men below, therefore, include men who were present at the battle as well as others who were not, and it omits some men who deserve recognition for their service.

Strength, according to muster, pay and casualty lists

	Sgt.	Cp.	Mu.	Pr.	Total
Commissioned Officers, etc.	-	-	-	-	6
Company #1	6	5	3	105	119
Company #3	5	5	3	64	77
Company #6	-	2	-	7	9*
Company #7	-	-	-	2	2*
Company #9	1	-	-	-	1*
Totals	12	12	6	178	214

* This figure represents casualties only

Officers at York
Captain James Hardy Eustace
Captain Neal McNeale   KIA
Lieutenant Edward Finch
Lieutenant Henry Palmer Hill
Lieutenant George Nuttall
Paymaster Nicholas Kingsley

Neal McNeale's #1 Company
Captain Neal McNeale   KIA
Sergeant Major Robert
   Beveridge   KIA

Sergeants
George Herne   WIA/POW
Joseph Rawson   KIA
Archibald Robinson   KIA
John Softly   WIA

Corporals
David Barry   WIA/POW
Daniel McIntosh
Donald McIntosh   WIA
Thomas Pemberton   KIA
Richard Totten   WIA/POW

Sergeant and Drum Major
William Ankers

Drummers and Fifers
James Hinds
John Smith
Joseph Taylor

Privates
Stephen Adams   WIA/POW
Squire Arkroyde   KIA
William Ayres   KIA
Patrick Barker   KIA
William Bennett   WIA
Edward Blakeman   KIA
Benjamin Bowe
Robert Boyd   KIA
Joseph Bradshaw   WIA
Henry Branwhite   WIA/POW
David Bridle   KIA
Nicholas Callaghan   KIA
Peter Campbell   WIA
John Carney
William Carter   KIA
Thomas Chapman
William Chapman
James Clark
William Clark
James Cowing   KIA
James Dale
Robert Darnell   KIA
Thomas Day   WIA/POW
George Dixon   WIA/POW
Thomas Downes   WIA/POW
Joseph Ellis   WIA/POW
William Fairburnie

Nicholas Furlong   WIA
Samuel Furnace   KIA
Joseph Giddons   KIA
William Golden
Joseph Gough   WIA
John Griffen
Joseph Groves
John Hamly   WIA/POW
James Hardy
Robert Hardy
John Harris
Benjamin Hayden   KIA
Hugh Healy   WIA
Martin Hebran   KIA
Thomas Henderson   KIA
Samuel Henshaw   WIA/POW
Martin Hessean   KIA
Richard Hewitt   WIA
James Higgins   KIA
James Hoyle   WIA/POW
James Humes
James Ireland   KIA
Robert Ireland   WIA/POW
Mark Kearnes   KIA
John Keegan
Patrick Keegan
John Kelly
James Knight
John Lee   WIA
John Leighton
Edward Lesney
John Lowden
James Martin   WIA/POW
William Martin   WIA/POW
Michael McGuire   KIA
Patrick McManus
Archibald McPhee
Robert Meighan   KIA
Reuben Miller   WIA/POW
Alexander Mills   KIA
James Mitchell   KIA
Alexander Mulloney   KIA
Michael Murphy   WIA/POW
William Nichol   WIA
George Pealing   KIA
Thomas Pope   WIA/POW
Andrew Pringle   KIA
John Purchase
Jonathan Radley   WIA
James Rudd   KIA
Wilcox Ruddock   KIA

Daniel Scary   WIA/POW
Thomas Sewell   KIA
John Smith
John Softly
John Steele
John Stewart
William Stowton
Edward Stratton
Thomas Stretch
Robert Sundey   KIA
Patrick Sutton   WIA
Christopher Tennant
James Thompson
James Tiffen   KIA
John Tuffley
James Vallely
Thomas Walker   WIA/POW
John Walters   WIA
Laskey Ward   KIA
John Ward   WIA
Joseph Weakly   KIA
Joseph Westbroom   KIA
Joseph Wheelton   WIA/POW
Joseph Willcock   KIA
John Williams   KIA
William Woodcock   KIA
William Yates   WIA

James Eustace's #3 Company
Captain James Eustace

Sergeants
James Commins
Andrew Dick
Robert Gray   WIA
Softly Monaghan
James Row

Corporals
Patrick Burnes
George Helroyde
John McLucky
Charles Ogden   WIA/POW
Henry Smith

Drummers and Fifers
William Ash
William Chandler
Thomas Mathews

Privates
Thomas Alligan
John Anderson

Alexander Armstrong
Joseph Arthurs   WIA/POW
William Badman
Robert Baillie
Tom Barber
Patrick Barker   KIA
William Bradshaw
David Carmount
Peter Carroll   KIA
John Carter
James Cartmill
John Cartwright
Thomas Cave
Thomas Clemett   KIA
William Collinet
Thomas Connell
Martin Cooke
Thomas Craits
John Cranny
William Crawford   WIA/POW
William Croke
Peter Daly   KIA
John Duffie
Thomas Eustace
John Fielding
Thomas Fletcher
Edward Gartland
James George
Edward Griffiths

James Halfpenny
William Harocks
John Healy   KIA
John Hemus
Thomas Hewitt
John Holmes
William Kerwin   WIA/POW
Barton Lepham   WIA/POW
Lawrence Lougham
Joseph Lucas
Patrick Lyons
William Mair
Thomas Marlow
Patrick McAlister
Patrick McDonnell
John McDonnell
Charles McKenny
Thomas McManus
George Moore
Henry Nowlan   KIA
Philip O'Brien
James O'Hare   WIA
Thomas Quinn   KIA
Joseph Rawson
Lewis Robert
William Shaw
Hugh Smith
John Smith
James Stephenson   WIA

James Sullivan
John Sweeney
John Tomlinson
Michael Tunny

James S. Tyeth's #6 Company

Corporals
William Lisk   KIA
Jacob Newton

Privates
Henry Orford   WIA/POW
Thomas Taylor WIA/POW/dead
Thomas Singleton   WIA/POW
Henry Hickman   KIA
Felix Donnelly   POW
Joseph Daig   POW
James Weakly   KIA

James Mundy's #7 Company

Privates
John Wale   WIA/POW
James Cartledge   KIA

Robert McDouall's #9 Company

Sergeant
William Shaw   KIA

APPENDIX 5

Upper Canada Militia at the Battle of York

The strength of the militia of Upper Canada at the battle of York is estimated to have been 477, comprising the following elements

Upper Canada Militia

Staff	10
1st York Regiment	159
3rd York Regiment	236
1st Durham Regiment	20
Incorporated Regiment	52
Total	**477**

Past accounts of the events of 27 April 1813 have provided little detail about the militia, its structure and actions, and have mainly relied upon anecdotal information. The following description results from a full analysis of extant records from the period and attempts to clarify what is a complex matter. Although the strength is estimated here as 477, there is reason to believe that the actual number exceeded 500.

Furthermore, it is estimated 58 men were later accused of voluntarily surrendering in the days after the battle in order to obtain paroles while 54 men were alleged to have shown disaffected behavior in one way or another.

The Organization and Strength of the Militia

Æneas Shaw held the rank of major general in the British army and acted as the senior officer for the militia of Upper Canada. Although his responsibility was wide ranging, he was present at York in the spring of 1813 and was supported by staff officers, as shown below.

There were three regiments of militia in the Home District during 1812 and early 1813. The 2nd Regiment of York militia was composed of men from the western part of the district. The 1st Regiment mustered men from the northern part of York Township and its environs while the 3rd Regiment was raised in York, the settlements just north and the region east of the town. These latter two regiments were directly involved in the defence of York. The best available (September 1813) quarterly return of the 1st York shows that it comprised 27 commissioned officers and 427 non commissioned officers and men. A similar return dated 24 March 1813 for the 3rd York gives its strength as 35 officers and 460 in the ranks.[1]

Detachments from the regiments served on the Niagara front, at York and other posts from the beginning of the war. When a call was made for a detachment or for a company to serve at a specific post, men volunteered to join and when that number did not match the required strength, others were chosen by the drawing of ballots.

As pertains to service at the York garrison, muster and pay lists show that companies were present from the first days of the war through to spring 1813. There was much coming and going of individuals, but the majority of the men served from one muster to the next. Some companies were present longer than others. For instance, Captain Thomas Hamilton's company of the 3rd York (later commanded by John Beverley Robinson) was on duty continuously from 25 November 1812 until the time of the battle; Lieutenant Ely Playter and Private John Lyon were among those paid for full service during that period. By way of comparison, the records show that Captain Thomas Selby's company of the 1st York mustered from 1 July 1812 until 24 October and 24 November to 25 December, but was then dismissed.

Muster and pay lists reveal that there were 284 officers and men at the York garrison on 24 April and others mustered on 27 April, as shown in Table One.

Table One

In total, there were 310 officers and men of the militia mustered at the York garrison on 24 and 27 April 1813.

Musters of		24 April	27 April
Staff		10	
1st York	Richardson	38	
	P. Robinson	35	
	J. Willson	33	
	Button	1	
	Fenwick/Pringle		16
	Wilmot/Fenwick		10

Musters of		24 April	27 April
3rd York	Cameron	28	
	Ridout	44	
	J. Robinson	26	
1st Durham	Burn	20	
Incorporated	Jarvie	27	
	Jarvis	22	
Totals		**284**	**26** **310**

Militia Strength on 27 April 1813

Anecdotal evidence in the documents of the period has been used in the past to estimate the strength of the militia at the battle, since no complete list of participants was made on the day of the battle. The following individuals gave the militia strength as: Thomas Ridout – 208; William Powell – 250; Sir Roger Sheaffe – 300 (including dockyard workers); and John Strachan – 350.[2] None of these anecdotes differentiated among the regiments. The dockyard workers formed an entirely separate contingent (see Appendix 4, British Order of Battle at York, 27 April 1813) and were not at all part of the Upper Canada Militia. Historians have used one or another of these figures to portray the militia strength without providing detail about the militia's organization and members.

There are several sets of data concerning the strength of the militia at the battle and in the days afterwards, including the muster and pay lists (M) mentioned above.[3] The terms of capitulation included a list of prisoners (C), which shows a tally of 263 officers and men from the militia, but provides only names for the commissioned officers. In 1814 the 1st and 3rd York Regiments produced lists totaling 287 individuals who were paroled properly after the battle (P).[4] These lists and others named 58 officers and men who were alleged to have improperly volunteered to surrender (VP).[5] Only one American list (POW) with 99 names came to light during this study, but due to probable misspellings and obvious omissions contributed little useful information.[6] Although none of the totals agree, overlapping information at least confirms the presence of numerous individuals.

A comparison of the capitulation list (C) and the combined parole lists (P and VP = 345) shows that the accounting made by the capitulation negotiators after the battle fell far short of what was later provided by Canadian sources.[7] And, these Canadian sources only concerned the York Regiments without reference to Captain John Burn's company from Durham or more than a handful of men from the two Incorporated Militia companies. In other words, the capitulation list is too short and the Canadian parole lists alone do not accurately represent the militia at the battle. Appendix 8 features a transcription and discussion of the 28 April Terms of Capitulation.

The muster and pay lists (M) from 24 and 27 April offer solid information about militia participation, but the names of many of the men do not appear on the York Regiment parole lists (P and VP) made in 1814 and later. It is not unreasonable to speculate, however, that the strength of the individual companies mustered at the garrison on 24 April changed very little before the alarm was sounded two days later. Most of these men had served continuously for months, the work to prepare defences was incomplete, training was ongoing and everyone expected an American attack at any moment. The fact that many of these mustered men were not on the 1814 York Regiment parole lists may be explained by evidence that control of the militia broke down during the day and men walked away from the battlefield and were not captured. Some even joined Sheaffe's retreat under Major Samuel Wilmot.

So, the 24 April tally of 284 is a reasonable representation of basic strength, but it is still too low because men who were not mustered on that date came forward after the alarm was given on 26 April. The York Regiment parole lists show men from such companies as John Fenwick's, John Denison's and Stephen Heward's who were credited with having been there. Evidence is also seen in the instance of Ensign John Pringle mustering a small group of Fenwick's men on 27 April and Major Wilmot's arrival on the scene and his decision to join Sheaffe's retreat, eventually making up a list of his detachment. An explanatory note regarding this matter was enclosed with the 28 April terms and is transcribed in Appendix 9.

If the figure of 284 officers and men mustered at the garrison on 24 April is used as a base and then increased by the two formal musters covering 27 April and any other militiamen named on the York Regiment parole lists who were not on one of the April musters (M plus any one else only on P), then the strength of the militia would equal 477 men. If those suspected of having surrendered voluntarily (VP) are added – some of them were never proven guilty of the charge – the number increases to 532.

In summary, contrary to other accounts, militia strength on 27 April was considerably greater than previously shown. The figure of 477 is used in this account, although it does not include any of the men who rejoined their companies in the garrison or who came to York at the sound of the alarm and never received credit for it. It is not illogical to suggest that more than 500 militia gathered at York at some time during the hectic events on 27 April 1813.

The figures used for this discussion appear in Tables Two and Three.

Table Two
The data from various lists show that up to 477 militia were present at York on 27 April 1813.

Sources	Strength
Capitulation terms list (C)	263
24 or 27 April musters (M)	310
1814 proper parole lists (P)	287
improper parole lists (VP)	58
M plus any others only on P	477
M plus only on P and VP	532

Table Three
Located closest to the garrison, the 3rd York had the highest participation in the battle.

Sources	Staff	1st York	3rd York	1st Dur.	Incorp.	Totals
24 or 27 April musters (M)	10	133	98	20	49	310
1814 proper parole lists (P)	5	102	174	-	6	287
Improper parole lists (VP)	-	5	51	-	2	58
M plus any others only on P	10	159	236	20	52	477
M plus only on P and VP	10	164	284	20	54	532

Voluntary Prisoners and the Disaffected

Some of the conquering Americans noted with pleasure that large numbers of the local inhabitants appeared to be giving themselves up for parole after the battle even though they had not been present on 27 April, their purpose being to avoid further militia service. Major General Henry Dearborn reported the number at 500 while Captain John Scott gave the figure of 1000 and Surgeon William Beaumont claimed there were 1200 such willing prisoners.[8] Very few historians have mentioned this conduct and the displays of disloyal behavior have similarly received little attention.

To determine the extent of the misconduct, the various lists and other material were examined and revealed that the largest number of identified individuals on the parole lists was (P plus VP) 345 and that, of these, only 58 were alleged to have given themselves up as prisoners improperly. Some of this latter group were also alleged to have been among the disaffected. Table Four shows this data.

Table Four
When compared to the nearly 1000 men on the two York Regiment militia rolls alone, the tally of voluntary surrenders and disaffected account for about 5% of the whole each.

	Staff	1st York	3rd York	1st Dur.	Incorp.	Others	Totals
Voluntarily surrendered (**VP**)	-	5	51	-	2	-	58
Identified as "disaffected" (**D**)	-	8	14	-	1	34	57
Named as both **VP** and **D**	-	-	5	-	-	-	5

Sedentary Militia

This section and the ones that follow present the lists of individuals who served in the regiments, based upon data available in extant muster and pay lists and other lists of the period. Seven companies of Sedentary Militia were mustered and paid at the garrison in the first months of 1813. The regular monthly record-keeping system was disrupted at the time of the battle. This set of lists differs from those that deal with the regular forces in that it includes every name found on musters and pay lists, even those noted as absent, ill, deserted, discharged or at another post. This was done to show a fuller picture of the militia companies, offering a notion of how many other men might have responded to the alarm on 26 April.

As above, the following codes were used to identify individuals' places on the various contemporary records.

M = mustered on 24 or 27 April 1813
C = listed as prisoner on terms of capitulation
P = on 1814 lists of paroled prisoners
VP = on 1814 lists as voluntarily surrendered, put themselves in the way of being made prisoners.
D = on 1813 lists of looting and disaffected suspects[9]
W = retreated with Major Samuel Wilmot[10]
POW = prisoner of war, American list

Militia Staff

Major General Æneas Shaw	Adjutant General, Commanding
Lieutenant Colonel William Graham	1st York, Commanding, not present
Major Samuel Wilmot	
Lieutenant Colonel William Chewett	3rd York, Commanding, **C P**
Major William Allan	**C P POW**
Captain Stephen Jarvis, 3rd York	Assistant Adjutant General, **C**
Captain Archibald McLean, 3rd York	Assistant Quarter Master General
Ensign Daniel Brooke, 3rd York	Adjutant, **C**
Ensign Andrew Mercer, 3rd York	Pay Master General, **C P**
Charles Baynes	Quarter Master, **C P**
Lieutenant Edward McMahon	Acting secretary to Major General Sheaffe, **C P**

1st Regiment of York Militia

The strength of the 1st York is estimated to have been 159 officers and men during the battle of York. Lieutenant Colonel William Graham, the commanding officer, was not present that day and was not paroled. Major Samuel Wilmot appears to have arrived and retreated with a small detachment and was not paroled.

1st York Company Strengths

Captains	R.R.	P.R.	J.W.	J.F./H.P.	S.W./J.F.	T.S.	J.B.	Others	Totals
Sources									
24 or 27 April musters (M)	38	35	33	16	10	-	1	-	133
1814 proper parole lists (P)	30	21	30	2	3	4	1	11	102
Improper parole lists (VP)	-	-	-	-	-	2	-	3	5
M plus any others only on P	43	35	39	16	10	4	1	11	159
M plus only on P and VP	43	35	39	16	10	6	1	14	164

Reuben Richardson's Company[11]

The muster roll and pay list for this company for the period of 25 March to 24 April 1813 listed these men.

Captain Reuben Richardson C P
Lieutenant George Mustard C P
Ensign Arad Smalley   C P

Sergeants
Valentine Fisher   P
Christopher Hilts   P
Lewis Kerby   P

Corporals
Henry Procter   P
Parnel Webb   P
Jacob Yeager   P W

Privates
John Cline   P
Ezra Clubine   P
Stephen Cornwall
James Crittendon   P
Amos Dexter
Samuel Fenton
John Finkner   P
Peter Harman
Peter La Point   P
John Leppard
Henry Line   P
Daniel Mann   P
Joseph Marr   P
Thomas McGuire   P
Mathew Mills
John Noir
Johon Ostrand
Jacob Rawn   P W
Henry Robbins   P
Richard Rooyen

Henry Rose
Mark Shell   P W
Jacob Spiker   P
Martine Stiles
Martin Warner   P
James Wells
Timothy Wheeler   P D
John Williams   POW P

Contractors, King's Works
Michael Foucard

OTHERS

On Duty, Whitchurch *
Whitfield Patterson

On another list for this company

Sergeant
Henry White   P

Privates
Ebenezer Cook   P
John Nigh   P
John Peterbaugh   P
John Stedmann   P

Deserted
George McCarty   POW

Discharged

Privates
William Barber, 11 April
Adam Caffer, 22 April
William Macklem, 11 April

Richardson – Summary
M = 38 C = 3 P =30 VP = 0
D = 1 W = 3 POW = 2
M + others on P = 43
M + others on P + VP = 43

* Whitchurch was about 20 miles north of York.

Peter Robinson's Company[12]

The muster roll and pay list for this company for the period of 25 March to 24 April 1813 listed these men.

Captain Peter Robinson   C P
Lieutenant Barnet Vanderburgh
                           C P

Sergeants
Andrew Borland   WIA
Reuben Kennedy

Corporals
Ephraim Dunham
Joshua Sprague

Privates
Antoine Arnaud
Francis Boileau   P
David Bridgeford   P W
Antoine Brueyn
Warren Clarkson
Joseph Davis   P
John Fordom   P
Sanders Goddaire   P
John Hannagan   W
Joseph Henry
John Hilts   P
William Kennedy
Jacob Kline   P
Joseph Le Belle   P
Louis Le Front   P
James Macklem   W
Thomas Macklem   W
James Malotte   P D
Moses Martin   P
Daniel Orton   P
John Rumahr
Peter Rush   P
William Rush

Francis Smyth   P
Henry Teal   P
Levy Van Kleck   P
Isaac Vanderburgh   P
Robert Wilkin   P
David Yeomans   P

In jail
Private Charles French

OTHERS

Deserted
Private Allen Perkins, 18 April

P. Robinson – Summary.
M = 35 C = 2 P = 21 VP = 0
D = 1 W = 4 POW = 0
M + others on P = 35
M + others on P + VP = 35

John Willson's Company[13]
The muster roll and pay list for this company for the period of 25 March to 24 April 1813 listed these men.

Captain John Willson   C P
Lieutenant John Shultz   C P
Ensign Andrew Thomson   C P

Sergeants
Benjamin Hoshel   P
John Pingle   P

Corporals
John Smeltser   P

Privates
Isaiah Booth   P
Jedadiah Britton   P
William Butterbough
Moses Butts   P
David Gohn   P
Hiram Harrison   P
Jeremiah Hilts
Isaac Johnson   P
Samuel Kenlough
Henry Lapp   P
Francis Laughlin
Joseph Minthorn   P
Isaac Morris
Conrad Orsmond   P
Jacob Papst
Francis Reneau   P
Matthias Saunders   WIAd
Aaron Sawyer   P
Peter Stiver   P
Rufus Wells   D
Gilbert Williams   P
Anthony Wunch   P

At Gilbratar Point

Privates
John Staggman

At the Island Telegraph

Privates
Peter Kuyser   P
William Piper   P
William Watson   P

At the Lighthouse
Private Michael Fisher   P

OTHERS

*On Command at Hamilton ***

Privates
Isaac Bens
Peter Brooks   P
James Daniels   P
Henry Summerfeldt
Jeduthan Williams

On Command at Kingston
Corporal Angus Vallier

Deserted

Privates
Leonard Klinck, 23 Feb.
Henry Shell, 17 April; joined
    Fenwick, see below

Absent without explanation

Corporals
Peter Matthews

Privates
Jeremiah Brown, joined Ridout,
    see below
Jacob Evers
John Fletcher
John Heckfield
Neal Holm
Orcleany Hudson
Philip Peck
William Sutter
Henry Vanderbrough
Jacob Wise

On another list for this company
Privates
John Dexter   P
Moses Hemingway   P POW
Peter Kuyser   P
George Summerfeldt   P

Willson – Summary
M = 33 C = 3 P = 30 VP = 0
D = 1 W = 0 POW = 1
M + others on P = 39
M + others on P + VP = 39

*Modern Cobourg, about 70 miles east of York, is the site of the 1813 village of Hamilton.

James Fenwick's Company[14]
The muster roll and pay list for this company for the period of 27 to 29 April 1813 listed these men, commanded by Henry Pringle.

Captain James Fenwick
Ensign Henry Pringle

Sergeant
John Pringle

Privates
Philip Eackhart
Jonas Lott
Joseph Lyon   P W
Abraham Norton   P
James Osburn
George Pringle
Jacob Pringle
George Reed
Henry Shell
Christian Smith
Francis Smith
John Stam
Todrick Steffins
William Wagnor

Summary – Fenwick/Pringle
M = 16 C = 0 P = 2 VP = 0
D = 0 W = 1 POW = 0
M + others on P = 16
M + others on P + VP = 16

Samuel Wilmot and Fenwick's detachment in retreat on 27 April 1813
There were actually 17 officers and men in Wilmot's detachment, but 7 of them, as noted below, have been identified with their proper companies.

Major Samuel Wilmot   W
Captain James Fenwick W C P

Sergeant Major
John C. Stooks   W P

Sergeants
Michael Dye   W
George Cutter   W

Privates
Willian Gurner   W
William Johnston   W
Edward Saunders   W
Richard Taylor   W
James Tomlinson   W

Joined the retreat from other companies

Sergeant
Jacob Rawn †

Privates
David Bridgeford *
John Hannagan   *
Joseph Lyon   ‡
James Macklem   *
Thomas Macklem *
Jacob Yeager   †

Not with the retreat
John Oyster   P

Summary – Wilmot/Fenwick
M = 10   C = 1   P = 3   VP = 0
D = 0   W = 10
M + others on P = 10
M + others on P + VP = 10

Notes
Pringle's detachment of Fenwick's company is the clearest example of a group of men, not on duty at the garrison, who mustered at the alarm given before the battle. It also shows how men who were present during the action never registered as paroled prisoners.

The muster of Wilmot's retreating party raises questions about how Fenwick and two of the men listed here and four others listed in their original companies retreated but were also on the 1814 parole list, and how Fenwick appeared as one of the captured officers on the capitulation agreement.

John Oyster was not part of the retreat, although he belonged to Fenwick's company and was on the 1814 parole list.

The men who joined from other companies were not in-

cluded in the statistics for this company.

* joined from Peter Robinson's company, see above
† joined from Reuben Richardson's company, see above
‡ joined from Pringle's detachment of Fenwick's company

Thomas Selby's Company[15]
Only men on the parole list are shown for this company as it does not appear to have been mustered at the garrison in April 1813.

Sergeant
John Kennedy   P

Privates
William Coopland   VP
Ransom Dexter   D
Richard Gerard   P
Jacob Hollingshead   VP
Daniel Kennedy   P
Austin Nobles   D
George Patterson   P

Summary – Selby
M = 0   C = 0   P = 4   VP = 2
D = 2   W = 0   POW = 0
M + others on P = 4
M + others on P + VP = 6

John Button's Company of "Cavalry"[16]
The muster roll and pay list for this company for the period of 25 March to 24 April 1813 listed these men. Although part of the 1st York, they were attached to the 3rd York. It is assumed that the five privates were at their assigned posts and not at the battle.

Captain John Button   C P

Privates
Silas Fletcher   D
Jabez Lynde, on duty at Whitby
Stephen Pherrill, on duty at Scarborough
George Post, on duty at Scarborough
Mathew Terwilliger, on duty at Whitby
Noadiah Woodroffe, on duty at Pickering

Summary – Button
M = 1   C = 1   P = 1   VP = 1
D = 1   W = 0   POW = 0
M + others on P = 1
M + others on P + VP = 1

Others
These officers and men of the 1st Regiment of York Militia do not appear on relevant 1812 and 1813 musters but were listed in 1814 as having been captured right after the battle.

Captain John Arnold[17]   C P
Captain James Mustard[18]   C P
Ensign Elijah Hawley[19]   VP

Privates
Calvin Aimes   P D
James Davies   P
Richard De Clute   P
Nathaniel Gage   P D
Phillip Gower   P
Isaac Griffin   VP
Richard Rod   P
Peter Reimers   P
John Remon   P
Hamilton Vanzant   P
Edmond Woodrough   VP

Summary – Others
M = 0   C = 2   P = 11   VP = 3
D = 2   W = 0   POW = 0
M + others on P = 11
M + others on P + VP = 14

3rd Regiment of York Militia

The strength of the 3rd York is estimated to have been 236 officers and men during the battle of York. Both Lieutenant Colonel William Chewett and Major William Allan were present and active throughout the day.

3rd York Company Strengths

Captains	D.C.	S.R.	J.R	J.D.	S.H.	D.T.	Others	Totals
Sources								
24 or 27 April musters (M)	27	44	26	-	-	-	1	98
1814 proper parole lists (P)	12	46	33	13	39	27	4	174
Improper parole lists (VP)	-	15	1	26	-	5	4	51
M plus any others only on P	35	67	50	13	39	27	5	236
M plus only on P and VP	35	81	51	37	39	32	9	284

Duncan Cameron's Company[20]

The muster roll and pay list for this company for the period of 25 March to 24 April 1813 listed these men.

Captain Duncan Cameron C P
Lieutenant Samuel P. Jarvis
Ensign Edward Thompson C P

QM Sergeant William Huntingdon
Sergeant Major William Mitchell

Sergeants
Ezak Benson
William Black
Charles Cameron
Peter Mathews

Corporals
Erastus Gilbert   P
Joseph Secord

Privates

James Anderson
James Conner
James Elliott
John Ellis
John Hays   POW
James Jones
James Lamoreaux
Selo Longsdon
Alexander Montgomery
John Palmer
Peter Pettier
Gabriel Sethfield
Joseph Shepherd   WIA P
John Staats
Thomas Tivey
Cornelius Van Ostrand
Stephen Whitney

Joined Ridout's company
Joseph Harrison

Joined J.B. Robinson's company
Private Nathaniel Hastings

Joined Denison's company

Privates
John Chapman
Oliver Prentice
William Stoughtenborough

Joined Heward's company
Norris Lawrence
Ephraim Post, 18 April .

On POW List of 1814
These men were on the 1814 lists, but not shown on the March-April 1813 muster.

Lieutenant
George Ridout   C P

Sergeant
John Merchison   P

Privates
William Hands   P
John Jordan   P
William Roe   P
James Ross   P
William Shaw   P
William Smith   P

OTHERS
These men appeared on January and/or February 1813 lists but not on the March-April list.

Discharged
James Couvillion, 19 March
Samuel Kennedy, 19 March

Joined Jarvie's Incorporated Militia
Sergeant George Smallman

Privates
Francis Brock

David Henry
Russell Hoag, Jr.
Jonathan Hutchinson
Daniel Kemp
David Mitchell
James Parker
John Sterns
Henry Stoner
Thomas Tyrer

Absent without leave

Privates
Isaac Groff
James Kendrick

Absent without explanation

Privates
William Cornell
Barnard Glennon
William Halley
Lyman Herrick
Francis Lee, see Jarvie below
James Macdonough
Thomas McCrany
Henry Smith
John Stoner
John Truman
Abraham Work

Summary – Cameron
M = 27 C = 3 P = 12 VP = 0
D = 0 W = 0 POW = 0
M + others on P = 35
M + others on P + VP = 35

Samuel Ridout's Company[21]

The muster roll and pay list for this company for the period of 25 March to 24 April 1813 listed these men.

Captain Samuel Ridout   C P
Ensign George Kuck   C P

Sergeants

George Denison	C P
Jacob Snyder	P

Corporals

Thomas Hollingshead	P
Isaac Wilson	P

Privates

Elias Anderson	POW
James Ashley	POW
William Burkholder	
Thomas B. Carey	P
Henry Carpenter	P
Martin Chapman	
Peter Christy	
John Crawford	
Daniel Commer	P
Benjamin Delong	
Levy Devans	
John Divar	
James Everson	P
Samuel Finch	P
George Goldthorpe	
Richard Heron	P
William Hollingshead	P
John Huff	POW P D
Joseph Johnson	P
Thomas Johnson	POW P
Benjamin Lewis	P
John Mathews	
Alexander McIntosh	P
Jacob McKay	
David Miller	P
Jonathan Montgomery	P
Eliezar Norton	
John Peeler	
James Penny	P
Arrable Pereau	.
Jacob Phillips	VP
Samuel Rummerfield	
Justus Seeley	
Daniel Trimper	
James Ward	
John Wilson	P
Joseph Wixon	
Jonathan Woolcot	P

In hospital

Private James Grandford, 9 April

Joined J. B. Robinson's company

Private Jacob Nell, 15 April

Joined Denison's company

Privates

William Muttice
Edward Phillips
Benjamin Reynolds
James Wyant

Joined Incorporated Militia Artillery

Private Thomas Armsworth,
　9 April

On command at Hamilton*

Sergeant Benjamin Slater	P
Private William Hill	P

Absent without leave

Private Samuel Mercer	P

Deserted

Privates

William Gray, 16 April	P
Thomas Mercer, 19 April	P
Ira White, 12 April	

Discharged

Private

John Giles, 9 April	
David Hill, 31 March	POW

On POW List of 1814

These men were on the 1814 lists, but not shown on the March-April 1813 muster.

Sergeants

Adam Everson	P
Nathaniel Finch	VP
Laughlin McIntosh	POW P

Privates

James Anderson	P
Leonard Ashley	P
Alfred Barrett	VP D
Benjamin Barrett	VP
Jeremiah Brown	P D
James Burns	VP
Patrick Burns	P
Jeremiah De Cloot	P
George Gary	P
Jonathan Hale	VP D
Joseph Harrison	P
Joseph Huff	POW VP
William Huff	POW P
Jonathan Hule	VP
John Lawrence	VP
Leonard Marshm	VP
William Marsh, Sr.	POW VP
William Marsh, Jr.	POW VP
Jacob Miller	POW VP
Peter Miller	POW VP
Alexander Montgomery	P
William Moore	P
Jacob Papts	P
Phillip Phillips	VP
Angus Valier	P
Cornelius Vanostrand	P
Robert Wells	P
Isaac White	P

Leduthan Williams	P

OTHERS

These men appeared on January and/or February 1813 lists but not on the March-April list.

Joined Jarvie's Incorporated Militia

Private James O'Hara

Deserted

Privates

James Davidson, 26 Feb.
Henry Johnson, 12 March
John Mallory, 27 Feb.; see Jarvie

Discharged

Joseph Heron, 10 March

Absent without explanation

Private William Fraser	POW

Summary – Ridout

M = 44　C = 3　P = 46　VP = 15
D = 4　W = 0　POW = 13
M + others on P = 67
M + others on P + VP = 81

*Modern Cobourg, about 70 miles east of York, is the site of the 1813 village of Hamilton.

J. B. Robinson's Company[22]

The muster roll and pay list for this company for the period of 25 March to 24 April 1813 listed these men.

Captain John Beverley Robin-son†	C P
Lieutenant Ely Playter	C P

Sergeants

Andrew Johnston
John Johnston

Privates

Lardner Bostwick	P
Daniel Carley	P
William Devenish	
Henry Ernest	
John Evans	
Thomas Forfer	P
William Forfer	P
Lewis Hamley	
Obediah Huff	POW P
Mathias Mackay	
James McClure	P
Daniel Murray	WIAd
Jacob Nell	
Asa Patrick	
John Richardson	
John Sheeler,	

Joseph Shoveaux
Jonathan Stevens

At the King's Works

Privates
Andrew Bingham, contractor
Joseph Burton, teamster
Robert Johnson, with the
    engineers
Joshua Leach   P D

On Command at Hamilton*

Privates
Jacob Dehart
Joseph Smith

Joined Incorporated Militia Artillery
Sergeant Daniel Wallis, 31 March

Privates
Thomas Ellice, 31 March
Anthony Gilgary, 4 April
Richard Graham, 31 March
Joseph La Compte, 8 April
John Lyon, 31 March
Timothy McPherson, 31 March
Sam Mills, 11 April
William Myers, 31 March
Andrew Piereau, 8 April
Daniel Snyder, 19 April
Andrew Thompson, 31 March
James Thompson, 31 March
Thomas Wood, Jr., 31 March

Discharged
Private John Henry, 14 April
                           POW

Deserted
John Dehart, 16 April
Joseph Farnum, 17 April
Daniel Herrick, 23 April POW
John Hutchinson, 19 April

Absent without leave

Privates
Isaac Lameraux
Joshua Lameraux

On POW List of 1814
These men were on the 1814 list, but not shown on the March-April 1813 muster.

Captain
Thomas Hamilton‡   C P

Sergeant
William Knott   P

Privates
John Ashbridge	P
Philip Clinger	P
John Coveys	P
Calvin Davis	P
Thomas Deary	P
Goerge Gasner	P
Isaac Groff	P
Nathaniel Hastings	POW P D
John Higgins	POW P
Caleb Humphreys	POW P
James Kenrick	P
John Kerr	P
Jesse Ketchum	P D
Bradwick McMurray	P
Parker Mills	POW P
William Norday	P
George Shelden	P
Thomas Simson	P
William Taylor	P
John Taylor	P
Thomas Tivey	P
John Vanzante	VP
William Waters	P

OTHERS
These men appeared on January and/or February 1813 lists but not on the March-April list.

Transferred to Heward's company

Privates
John Edgell
John McBeth
Samuel Whitesides

Absent without explanation

Privates
John Clawson
Francis Delisle
Thomas Jobbett
John Murphy, see Jarvie below
Francis Rolo, see Heward below

† Robinson took command of the company on 25 March 1813.
‡ Thomas Hamilton commanded the company until 24 March 1813.
*Modern Cobourg, about 70 miles east of York, is the site of the 1813 village of Hamilton.

Summary – Robinson
M = 26 C = 3 P = 33 VP = 1
D = 2 W = 0 POW = 7
M + others on P = 50
M + others on P + VP = 51

John Denison's Company[23]
Only men on the parole list are shown for this company as it does not appear to have been mustered at the garrison in April 1813.

Captain John Denison	VP
Lieutenant John Endicott	VP
Ensign Charles Denison	C P

Sergeants
John Cameron	P
Moses Dewar	P
Alex Thompson	P

Privates
Hynes Bennet	VP
John Berry	P
Joe Brundige	VP
John Brundige	VP
John Chapman	VP
John Giles	P
Conrad Clock	VP
Jacob Clock	VP D
John Clock	VP
Benjamin Davis	VP D
Benjamin De Long	VP
Jacob De Long, Sr.	VP
Jacob De Long, Jr.	VP
John Diver	VP
John Dixon	VP
George Goldthorpe	P
Robert Gray	P
Henry Jackson	POW P
George Johnston	POW VP
William Mattice	VP
Jacob McKay	VP
Caleb Peck	VP
Oliver Prentice	VP D
John Peeler	P
Edward Phillips	P D
Benjamin Reynolds	VP
Luke Stoughtenborough	VP
Martin Stoughtenborough	VP
Wm. Stoughtenborough	POW VP
Philip Waynes	P
Isaac Wilcocks	P
Richard Wilson	P
Jacob Winters	VP
James Wynant	VP

Summary – Denison
M = 0 C = 1 P = 13 VP = 26
D = 4 W = 0 POW = 3
M + others on P = 13
M + others on P + VP = 37

Stephen Heward's Company[24]

Only men on the parole list are shown for this company as it does not appear to have been mustered at the garrison in April 1813.

Captain Stephen Heward, not present

Lieutenants

Archibald McLean, not present

Robert Stanton   C P

Sergeants

John Bush	P
Isaac Pilkington	P
John Thompson	P

Privates

Ezekiel Benson	P
Thomas Bingle	P
John Bright	P
Robert Bright	P
Henry Cawthorn	P
Osborn Cox	P
Benjamin Cozens	P
Elisha Dexter, Jr.	D
William Forrest	P
John Edgell	P
Peter Ernest	P
Henry Ernest	P
John Evans	P
Harvey Gilbert	P
Gill Hamilton	P D
John Henry	P
Hugh Heward	P
Willian Hurley	P
Charles Joler	P
Robert Lackey	P
Frederick Lawrence	P
Norris Lawrence	P
Alexander Legg	P
Aaron Leonard	P
John McBeth	P
James McIntosh	P
John McIntosh	POW P
Thomas Mosely	POW P
Andrew O'Keefe, Sr.	P
Andrew O'Keefe, Jr.	P
Jordan Post	P
Ephraim Post	P

Francis Rollo	P
Joseph Shaw	P
Amasa Stebins	P D
Samuel Whitesides	P

Summary – Heward

M = 0 C = 1 P = 39 VP = 0
D = 3 W = 0 POW = 2
M + others on P = 39
M + others on P + VP = 39

David Thompson's Company[25]

Only men on the parole list are shown for this company as it does not appear to have been mustered at the garrison in April 1813.

Captain David Thompson   C P
Lieutenant William Smith   C P
Ensign Edward Thompson   C P

Sergeants

Colin Drummond	P
Andrew Johnstone	P
William Knowles	VP
Andrew Thompson	P
Daniel Willis	P

Privates

Thomas Adams	P
Levy Annis	POW VP
William Devinish	P
John Ellice	P
Thomas Ellice	P
James Elliott	P
John Hurtshorn	P
Robert Johnstone	P
James Jones	P
Thomas Kennedy	P
James Palmer	VP
John Palmer	P
Asa Patrick	P
Reuben Patrick	P
Peter Pelkic	P
John Procter	VP
John Richardson	P
James Stephens	P
Alexander Thompson	P
Archibald Thompson	P
Archibald Thompson, Sr.	P
Archibald Thompson, Jr.	P

James Thompson	P
Gad Willer	VP

Summary – Thompson

M = 0 C = 3 P = 27 VP = 5
D = 0 W = 0 POW = 1
M + others on P = 27
M + others on P + VP = 32

Others

Only men on the parole list are shown for these companies as they do not appear to have been mustered at the garrison in April 1813.

John Playter's Company[26]

Only men on the parole list are shown

Captain John Playter	VP
Lieutenant John Wilson	C P
Ensign D'Arcy Boulton	C P
Ensign John Detlor	WIAd

Yonge Street Company[28]

Lieutenant John Scarlett   VP

Town Company[29]

Lieutenant Edward McMahon, see Staff above

Ensign James Chewett   C P

Whitby Company[30]

Lieutenant

Donald McArthur	C P
George Duggan	VP

Ensigns

Charles Baynes, see Staff above
Thomas Denison   VP

Summary – Others

M = 1 C = 4 P = 4 VP = 4
D = 0 W = 0 POW = 0
M + others on P = 5
M + others on P + VP = 9

Detlor was added to the M data to reflect his presence.

1st Regiment of Durham Militia

The strength of the 1st Durham is estimated to have been 20 officers and men during the battle of York, with Captain John Burn as the senior officer.

John Burn's Company[31]
Captain John Burn   C
Lieutenant James Bates

Sergeants
Garner Gifford
Benjamin Reston

Corporals
James Caldwell

Privates
John Barber
Adna Bates
Hiram Bedford
Joel Byrnes
Elijah Franklin
Thomas Gage

Jacob Miller
Clement Neff
John Payne
William Pickle
William Ralph
William Reston
Waterman Spencer
George Stevens
Daniel Wright

On Command at Clarke*
Private Adna Bates

Absent without leave
Private Daniel Lightheart, 22 April

Note
These figures based upon Muster Roll and Pay List of Captain John Burn's Company of the 1st Regiment of Durham Militia, 25 March to 24 April 1813, LAC, RG 9, IB7, 18:434-5.

Summary – Burn
M = 20 C = 1 P = 0 VP = 0
D = 0 W = 0 POW = 0
M + others on P = 20
M + others on P + VP = 20

*The Township of Clarke was located about 60 miles east of York in Durham County, District of Newcastle.

Incorporated Militia

The strength of the Incorporated Militia at York, including one company of infantry and one company of artillery, is estimated to have been 52 officers and men.

Incorporated Militia Company Strengths

Captains	Jarvie	Jarvis	Totals
Sources			
24 or 27 April musters (M)	27	22	49
1814 proper parole lists (P)	3	3	6
improper parole lists (VP)	2	-	2
M plus any others only on P	30	22	52
M plus only on P and VP	32	22	54

William Jarvie's Company[32]
Captain William Jarvie C WIA
Lieutenant Thomas Humberstone

Sergeants
David Mitchell

Corporals
Edward Hamilton   POW
Francis Lee
Thomas McCraney

Privates
George Anderson
William Brock
Patrick Burns
Jonathan Cameron, Jr.
Jonathan Cameron, Sr.
George Chace
George Clunis
James Davidson

Jacob Fisher
John Freeman
David Henry
Jeremiah Hills
Daniel Moore
George Moore
John Murphy   POW
James O'Hara   POW
Jonathan Starkweather
Henry Stoner
Lewis Storshaw
John Tipp
Jacob Vice

On Command at Hamilton*

Sergeants
George Smallman

Privates
Francis Brock
Moses Clendenning

Andrew Davidson
Russell Hoag, Jr.
Jonathan Hutchinson
William Perkins
John Shaver
William Suter

On Command at Niagara
Private Richard Mills

Deserted (n.d.)

Privates
Jacob Axley
Jeremiah Chapman
Daniel Clunis
Allan Gerow
Miles Herrick
Daniel Kemp
James Parker
John Tyrer
John Scott

On POW List of 1814
These men were on the 1814 list, but not shown on the March-April 1813 muster.

Privates

Jacob Crawford	P
John Mallory	VP
William McCartin	P
Abraham Townsend	VP
John Wixon	P

*Modern Cobourg, about 70 miles east of York, is the site of the 1813 village of Hamilton.

Summary – Jarvie
M = 27 C =14 P = 3 VP = 2
D = 0 W = 0 POW = 0
M + others on P = 30
M + others on P + VP = 9

William Jarvis's Artillery[33]

2nd Lieutenant, Commanding

William M. Jarvis	C WIA

Sergeant
Daniel Wallace

Corporals
Thomas Ellice
Andrew Thompson

Bombardier
Edward McBride

Gunners
Thomas Armsworth
John Belcher
Elias Benjamin
John Deetsman
Joseph Freeman
Anthony Gilgary

Richard Graham	
Joseph La Compte	
John Lyon	D
Sam Mills	POW P
William Myers	P
David O'Flynn	
Andrew Piereau	
Daniel Snyder	
James Thomson	
Thomas Wood, Jr.	P
Abraham Wurts	

Discharged
Private Timothy McPherson, 15 April   POW

Summary – Jarvis
M = 22 C = 1 P = 3 VP =04
D = 1 W = 0 POW = 1
M + others on P = 22
M + others on P + VP = 22

The Disaffected

The following individuals were among those identified after the battle as having fraternized with the Americans, accepted the gift of British public property from them and/or committed looting, but their names do not appear on any of the muster and pay lists of the period.

Suspects in the 1813 investigations[34]
These 21 men (and some others grouped above with their companies) were among those listed as suspects during the investigation conducted in the summer of 1813 to identify disaffected subjects in the vicinity of York. These names could not be matched with individuals on the militia lists shown above.

Michael Cortz	D
Elijah Bentley	D
Sam Bentley	D
Moses Chilson	D
William Chilson	D
John Finch	D
Ira Gilbert	D
William Howard	D

John Mills Jackson	D
Jacob Lawrence	D
Simeon Morton	D
Stephen Nobel	POW D
Gideon Orton	D
Andrew Patterson	D
William Peters	D
James Stevens	D
Mr. Sudden	D
Benjamin Thrall	D
Samuel Utley	D
Calvin Wood	D
John Young	D

Alleged disaffected individuals[35]
Sergeant George Cutter, 1st York, named these 13 men (and some others grouped above with their companies) as having been on the list he prepared shortly af-

ter the battle for his commander, Lieutenant Colonel William Graham. These names could not be matched with individuals on the militia lists shown above.

Robert Briggs	D
William Culp	D
Elisha Dexter, Sr.	D
William Dunham	D
Garratt Lloyd	D
Samuel Lyons	D
Simon Martin	D
Reuben Smith	D
David Spragg	POW D
Silas Sutherland	POW D
Joseph Sutherland	D
Abraham Walker	D
Peter Wilder	D

American Order of Battle at York, 27 April 1813

The strength of the military force under the command of Major General Henry Dearborn at York on 27 April 1813 is estimated to have been nearly 1800 officers and men. Commodore Chauncey commanded about 800 officers, seamen and marines. The naval musters are presented in Appendix 7, United States Naval Squadron, April 1813.

The military estimate is based on an examination of extant musters and pay lists and anecdotal remarks made by such participants as the following: Commodore Isaac Chauncey – 1700 and 1800; Colonel Cromwell Pearce – 1700; Major General Henry Dearborn – 1750; Ensign Joseph Dwight – 1750; Surgeon's Mate William Beaumont – 1500; Major Abraham Eustis – 2000; Surgeon Amasa Trowbridge – 2370.[1]

Of the muster and pay lists examined for the British, Canadian and American forces in these appendices, the records for the U.S. Army proved to be the most difficult to analyze. The U.S. Army did not have a routine regimental-book system in place as the British did and which still exists as bound, comprehensive and legible volumes. The extant American records consist of regimental collections of individual sheets of varying sizes and organizations, some well preserved, others not and with only occasional comprehensive, chronological reports for individual companies. More standardization is seen in the 1814 records, but those for 1812 and 1813 have many gaps in information.

Using the names of unit officers mentioned in reports, correspondence and accounts as a starting point, a search was made of the U.S. Army records. The regiments and their companies shown below feature officers who were known to have been present and the men of their companies as mustered during April 1813 or the nearest relevant date. The company records are actually larger than shown here, but men identified as having been discharged for one reason or another or as having deserted, etc., have been omitted for this presentation. The depictions of the companies as shown should not be considered as definitive. They represent a "best guess" of which men and how many were part of the expedition.

As it turns out, the tally of all the men shown here is about 1788, which agrees with anecdotal sources. The data reveals a good indication of company and detachment sizes, and in a few cases, casualties taken by the companies. Anecdotal comments about the individual companies are included and in some ways substantiate the data found on the muster and pay lists.

Field and staff officers for some of the units are named also, but not all of them were present. To identify those known to be part of the expedition, their names have been marked with an asterisk.

ORDER OF BATTLE

The American force involved in the expedition to York included the following:

U.S. Army		1667
Field and Staff Officers	15	
Sixth Infantry	309	
Fourteenth infantry	125	
Fifteenth Infantry	458	
Sixteenth Infantry	291	
Twenty-first Infantry	133	
Rifle Regiment	176	
Third Artillery	80	
Light Artillery	80	
Twelve-Month Volunteers		**122**
Field and Staff	2	
"Albany Greens"	55	
"Baltimore Volunteers"	65	
Total U.S. Army		**1789**
U.S. Navy	**800**	

ARTILLERY[2]

Third Artillery
1 6-pdr. field gun
1 howitzer

Light Artillery
2 12-pdr. field guns
4 other field guns

85 long guns and carronades of various calibres

Key
KIA = Killed in action
WIA = Wounded in action
WIAd = Wounded in action, died
* = This officer known to have been present

Military Field and Staff Officers[3]

There were at least 10 field and staff officers and 5 officer-volunteers present on 27 April 1813.

Major General Henry Dearborn*	Commander, Ninth Military District
Lieutenant Colonel Samuel Conner, 13th Infantry*	Aide-de-camp
Major Ninian Pinkney, 5th Infantry*	Acting Deputy Adjutant General
Major William Swan, 2nd Infantry*	Deputy Quarter Master General
James Mann*	Hospital Surgeon
Brigadier General Zebulon Pike*	Commander, First Brigade, Ninth Division, WIAd
Lieutenant Donald Fraser, 15th Infantry*	Aide-de-camp, WIA
Captain Charles Jones, 29th Infantry*	Aide-de-camp, WIA
Captain Benjamin Nicholson, 14th Infantry*	Aide-de-camp, WIAd, 13 May
Captain Charles Hunter, 15th Infantry*	Brigade Major

Officer-Volunteers

Lieutenant Colonel George E. Mitchell	Third Artillery
Lieutenant Charles Macomb	Third Artillery
Lieutenant Benjamin Pierce	Third Artillery
Captain Horatio Armstrong	Twenty-third Infantry
Amasa Trowbridge	Surgeon, New York State Militia

U.S. ARMY UNITS

Sixth U.S. Regiment of Infantry[4]

Captain Walworth mentioned the four captains whose companies are listed here and Surgeon's Mate Beaumont wrote that all but Sadleir's company sailed on the U.S. Schooner *Julia*.[5] With Surgeon's Mate Beaumont included, the strength of the unit is 309 officers and men; this total does not include the four men at the end of Sadlier's company who may or may not have been casualties sent back to Sackets Harbor.

Jonas Simonds	Colonel
James Miller	Lieutenant Colonel
John Campbell	Major
Horatio Stark	Major
William Hazard	Lieutenant and Quarter Master
G. D. Smith	Lieutenant and Adjutant
R. McClelland	Lieutenant and Paymaster
William Beaumont*	Surgeon's Mate

Gad Humphreys's Company
Captain Gad Humphreys WIA
First Lieutenant James Bailey
Second Lieutenant Gerrard D. Smith

Sergeants
Charles Jotman
Benjamin Justin
Isaac Lloyd
Zachariah Pack

Corporals
Rudolph Bay
David Free   KIA
Richard Irvin
Thomas Lemarks
Harvey St. John
Henry Waite

Musicians
Elisha H. Gardner
Henry Spicer

Privates
George Anderson
Willet Arden
Nathaniel Baisley
Caleb Baker
John Baker
Thomas Bane
James Bartlett
Gilbert Berlew
David Blissan
David Boyle
Thomas Brookmier
Stephen Brown
James Brown
John Bunce
Joseph Carter   KIA
Peter Chambers
Sheldon Clarke
Alexander Coen
John Crabtree

William Curran
Christopher Decker
Thomas Denton
George Fisher
William Flick
George Frasier   KIA
Michael Gilligan
George Griner
James Gruett
John Hamilton   KIA
John Hanly
Christian Harry
John Hart
William Hartcliff
Samuel Haus
Phillip Higgins
Duncan Hire
James Holland
John Huggins
William Jordon
Charles King
David Ludlum   WIAd 16 May
Patrick Maham   d 23 May
Cornelius McCurdy
James McDaniel
Bernard McKee
James McMinn
Lodowick Miller
Israel Niffin
John Noggle
John O'Conner
James Orr
John Owens
Edward Perry
Daniel Phillips
Daniel Porter
John Prann   d 9 May
Daniel Reeves
William Saunders
Joshua C. Smith
Hugh Sterling   KIA
Herman Sullivan

William Swift
Levi Tarr
Samuel Thompson
John Van Allen
Isaac Williamson   KIA
James Willson

Peter Muhlenberg's Company
Captain Peter Muhlenberg WIA
Second Lieutenant David Vanderhyden

Sergeants
Daniel Ask
Louis Callame
John Gaffey
Hugh Johnston
William A. Smith
Nicholas Sylvian

Corporal
John Childers
David Fulton   KIA
Thomas Farden
Christian Wood

Musicians
Jacob Brown
William Parkinson

Privates
James Allen
John B. Laws
Jacob Barber
David Barry
William Bates
George Bingerman
Walter Boyd
Thomas Brotten
Seymour Brown
Henry Carkheiff
Elijah Cole
Jesse Crowfoot
Edward Dempsey
Aaron Dunham

William Farrington
John Gilchrist
John Green
Daniel Griffith
Elihu Henyon
Francis Higgins
John Hone   KIA
Robert Humphries
William Johnson
Isaac Kane
Isreal Keane
Edward Kelly
Michael Kelly
John Keysley
John McDonald
Malcolm McGregor
John McNally
Isaac Minton
Ransom Mix
John Moore
John Phillips
John Porterfield
Benow Privley   d 1 May
Jonathon Raveley   d 10 May
Samuel Raybold
Thomas Redman   KIA
Henry Right
Thomas Row
Robert Searl
Abram Sears
Nathan Sidney   WIAd 14 May
Jacob Stephen
Erastus Stephens
Collin Test
Elisha Thompson   d 7 May
John Tobin
John Tompkins   d 8 May
Stoats Vanackerson   d 16 may
Oliver Vanhoven
George Weirs
Warren Weldon
Andrews Williams
John Williams

Clement Sadleir's Company
Captain Clement Sadleir WIA
First Lieutenant John Chapman

Sergeants
Soloman Ensign
John Morrell
Andrew Nikinger
Henry Sellect
John Walker

Corporals)
William Burtis
John Galbreath
William Walters
Allen Wynance

Musicians
Lewis Hall
Thomas Graves

Privates
John Beals
Benjamin Bowman
John Canada
Nathaniel Carter
Isaac Case
Julian Clemier
John Cockran
Andrew Cole
Joseph Cole
Manus Cornyn
Charles Cres
Anthony Dailey
Abraham David
John Downey
Edward Duffery
Relief Ervine
Benjamin Estey
Stephen Flood
Samuel Foster
George Gibbs
Darrien Glaves
Edward Gormain
David Hall
William Happin   WIA
Thomas Hardwick
Georges Hughes
Jonathan Ireland
Christian Jastian
James Johnson
Joseph Kingsland
John Lafferts
John Laning
John Leach
Thomas Malarix
Edeard McCann
Michael McCurly
John McGee
John McLaghlen
John Monroe
John Morris
Randolph Moses
William Nation
Elias Overbaugh
William Parcel
Robert Penman
Stephen Penny
John Pike
Nicholas Rhoady
John Rice
Levi Simonds
Elias Squire
Ralph Stephenson
William Thompson
Henry Trowbridge

Robert Wade
William West
Elias Wheeler
John Willson
Alexander Willson
John Woolford
John Worden   WIAd.
Peter Wyngarden

Wounded at Sackets Harbor
James Allen
John Scarett
John Spence

Died at Sackets Harbor
Corporal Mahlon Whitearm n.d.

John Walworth's Company
Captain John Walworth WIA

First Lieutenants
Henry Shell   WIA
Alexander Ten Broeck
Alexander Thompson

Second Lieutenant
Henry Cooke   WI A

Sergeants
James Agnew
Samuel Airns
James Fulton
Cromwell Sprague
Elias Taylor   KIA

Corporals
John Clarke
John Colio
Oliver Everet
Samuel Marshall
John Roberts
Timothy Thompson
David Youngs

Musicians
John Daniels
Patrick McAlvey
Isaac Vosburgh

Privates
Martin Ambony
Josiah Arnold
Chauncey Babcock   KIA
Walter Beament
Edward Bowdry
David Brown
Francis Brown
Josiah Bullard
John Curtis
Benjamin Darby
Bernard Dodge
Thomas Donaldson
John Elliott

Benjamin Evertson
Elijah Evetts
Charles Fitch
Andrew Foy
John Goodcourage
John Grant
William Gruit
Philip Haight
James Hamilton
Henry Harris
Emanuel Haskins
Richard Hayman — KIA
David Haywood
Amos Headen
John Hinderer — KIA
Nicholas Hollanbeck
James Hunter
John Jackson
Samuel Jobe — KIA
Nathaniel Kingstand

Ira Knapp
Thomas Laird
William Lane
George LeCain
Joseph Lowe
Peter Manderville
Robert McGirhy
Thomas McKane
Peter McLaughlin
John Millard
Cookswain Milligan
Chauncey Miner
Christopher Morris
Alexander Moulton
Samuel Nash
Leonard Neymaster
James Oley
Eli Philmore
John Pierce
James Randolph

Daniel Riley
John Shoemaker
Michael Sickels
Peter Smith
Abraham Sprung
Benjamin Stevens
Charles Stewart
David Taylor
James Thompson
Ebenezer Tibbals
John Tiercy
John Van Allen
John Walker
Samuel Watson
Edward Wilborn
Charles Windsor
William Wood

Fourteenth U.S. Regiment of Infantry [6]

The strength of the Fourteenth Infantry with a detachment of the Thirteenth added to it is estimated at about 125 officers and men. They were transported across the lake in the *Governor Tompkins*, according to Ensign Joseph Dwight, Thirteenth Infantry.

Before joining Brigadier General Pike's staff, Captain Benjamin Nicholson temporarily commanded this company until Captain Grindage returned from a furlough on 22 April to resume command, as Dwight reported. Dwight's detachment of recruits from Captain Richard Malcom's company of the Thirteenth was attached to Grindage. No muster or payroll identifying this detachment was found, but Dwight said that it numbered 61 men at one point, only 21 of whom were present and fit for duty at Fort Niagara by 9 May. A return of the strength of the force at Sackets Harbor on 1 March showed 38 members of the Thirteenth Infantry present. [7]

Henry Grindage's Company
Captain Henry Grindage
First Lieutenant John Beckett
Second Lieutenant William
    Mills

Sergeants
Lymon Baggs
Mark Simpson
Stephen Taylor
Robert Watt

Corporal
William Kelly
John Pearl
William Ross
James Sweeting
Richard Taylor
Daniel Welch

Musicians
Azle Barnes
Joseph Boehm

Privates
John Adams
David Andrews
William Armstrong
John Barcus
George Batts
Mordecia Bloice
Zachariah Bloice
James Bouldin
James Carey
William Carr
Isaac Carroll
Samuel Christopher
Seth Cleaver
Dominick Connor
William Cook

David Daughtery
Lewis David
Shadrick Davis
Hugh Davis
George Deliquy
Robert Drummond
Constantine Gomley
Thomas Hall
John Hallue
Dennis Hargan
Caleb Heminger
James Herrow
George Hogg
Frederick Hood
Hugh Hubbert
Robert Humphries
William Hurst
John Hutson
Thomas Irwin

Moses Jackson	Benjamin Notter	Isaac Vanbibber
John James	John Paradise	Jeremiah Waggaman
Benjamin James	William Parsons	Benjamin Wagles
John Johnson	Thomas Patterson	Lewis Wagner
William Lamb	Job Price	Elisha Webb
John Larimore	John Purnell	Jacob Whiles
John Lawless	Allen Ritchie	William Whitton
Fletcher Littlejohn	Thomas Russell	William Wilkins
Elijah Lynch	Bennett Simms	James Wilkins
Stephen Macaraker	William Simpson	Elisha Wilkins
Thomas Marshall	Jacob Smith	John Williams
Joseph Matlock	Joseph Stacia	Alexander Willson
Cornelius McDevitt	George Stannigers	
Scarborough Melvin	Samuel Starkey	**Thirteenth U.S. Regiment of**
Samuel Miller	William Taylor	**Infantry**
James Miller KIA	Amos Thompson	Ensign Joseph Dwight
George Nooner	John Thompson	and about 40 men

Fifteenth U.S. Regiment of Infantry [8]

The Fifteenth Infantry formed the largest unit in the expedition to York, comprising six companies and about 458 officers and men.

Captain John Scott provided the most complete description of the unit, which was transported aboard the *Madison* and the *Governor Tompkins*. Excluding Captain Hunter who was with the Field and Staff Officers, there were 450 officers and men in the six companies. [9] The regiment's field and staff officers listed here were all shown to be at Niagara in June and it is speculated that, given the size of the detachment on the expedition, all of them accompanied the regiment (although verification is only attainable for King and Bloomfield), bringing the total to 458.

Field and Staff Officers

William King*	Major
Fenn Dening	Surgeon
Henry McMullen	Ensign and Adjutant
Moses Bloomfield*	Lieutenant and Quarter Master, KIA
Reuben Baker	Surgeon's Mate
Francis Walters	Sergeant Major
David Irwin	Quarter Master Sergeant
John Connelly	Drum Major

Charles Hunter's Company	John Kitrough	Jacob Cress
Captain Charles Hunter, brigade major	Callahan Quinlan KIA	Jacob Dallas
	Peter Vaughan	Soloman Dennis
First Lieutenant Joseph Scofield		Clayton Dodney
Second Lieutenant David Riddle	**Musicians**	Edward Dougherty
Ensign Charles Roberts	Vincent Lacore	George Edward
	George Smith	Stephen Field
Sergeants		James Fletcher
John Coulsen	**Privates**	David Flin
Jerimiah McDonald	James Atkinson	Jacob G. Smith
Robert McQuoir	Michael Beekly	John Gaddis
Christian Moses KIA	George Callihan	Benjamin Gardener
	Edward Carney	Barnabas Golden KIA
Corporals	Silas Chitester	Richard Halliday
John Adams	John Conklin	Thomas Hanlin
Elijah Albright	James Cooper	John Heeler
Hugh Hicks KIA	Joseph Cowell	

Jacob Hilyard
James Hunter
David Jackson   KIA
John Johnson
Tobias Kiker
Nicholas Lallaway
Cornelius Larney
Thomas Lewis
Manasah Logue
Peter Lush
William McCassel
John McCinny
Hugh McDermit
Dennis McDonald
Francis McDonald
John McGowen
Thomas McMuns
William Mead
William Miller
Thomas Moffit
James Mordon
James Morrison
Henry Muneys
Henry Pailin
John Patterson
John Plotts
Mark Shannon   KIA
George Sherry
Phillip Sigler
Hugh Skelly
Aaron Slate   KIA
William Stewart
James Stroud
Joseph Sutton
Samuel Thomas
William Thomas
John Thompson
Jonathan Tice
James Wilson

John Hoppock's Company
Captain John L. Hoppock   KIA
First Lieutenant William Barnet
Second Lieutenant John Scott

Sergeants
Thomas Dennis
John Knapp
Jacob Rusk
Alden Wolcott

Corporals
William Brooks
William Cozens
Isaac Hoffman   KIA
James McCann
Eli Robison

Musicians
John Connelley

John Goodrich

Privates
Andrew Aston
Stephen Beard
Peter Bell
George Biggs
Dann Bramble
Isaac Buck
Timothy Carrol
William Coburn
Arthur Courtney
John Craig
Daniel Cribbs
William Cross
James Dalton
David Davis
John Dearbourn
Stephen Decous
John Derby
Abraham Derevier
Benjamin Derrickson
James Dougherty
Dennis Ferry   KIA
William Forbes
Edward Gallagher
Michael Gallagher
Edward Grant
John Gregg
Imla Haines
Patrick Harkins
James Hendrick
John Hillerman
John Hilyard
William Jenkins
Thomas Kennedy
Zela Kenner
Moses Kent
Henry Kimble
John Kough
William Lloyd
Asa Lucas
Edward Mapes
John Mathews
Jacob Mathews
Daniel McDevitt
Thomas McMillen
George Moore
James Nichols
Michael O'Cain
John Pye
Joseph Rake
Isaac Reed
John Reever
Abner Rouse
John Russel
Andrew Scott
Alexander Shaw
Pelice Slocum

William Slocum
Jacob Smally
Daniel Sweeney
Nathaniel Thatcher
Ambrose Thompson
John Uber   KIA
Oakum Wilson
Joseph Wilson
John Wilson

Zachariah Rossell's Company
Captain Zachariah Rossell
First Lieutenant Jeremiah D.
    Hayden
Ensign John Collins

Sergeants
Richard Douglas
John Downing
John Shadiker
Alexis Simon

Corporal
Asa Daniels
Abraham Pike
William Spear

Musicians
William Jourdan
Samuel Norton

Privates
Samuel Aiman
Gregory Ayers
Sybarius Baker
William Beckner
Hugh Bradley
John Carr
Joseph Carter
Andrew Conner
Hudson Core
Edward Corey
Joseph Corrigan
Thomas Croshaw
Asa Danforth
Andrew Davis
Peter Deal
William Devon
John Duff
Samuel Eck
George Ernest
James Evans
Josiah Ferris
Caleb Foy
Ebenezer Francis
Peter Garriband
James Grant
John Hallock
Thomas Hamilton
Joseph Jacobs
Benjamin Jenkins

Adam Keinback
William Kemble
Victor Killon
Thomas Land
William Lawrence
William Lewis
Daniel Longstreet
Samuel Lovet
Patrick McEver
Joshua Mills, Sr.
William Mitchell
William Morris
Adrian Neimuler
Thomas Parent
Thomas Powell
Edward Reel
Daniel Reimer
Benjamin Rennie
Patrick Rourche
James Sayrey
John Scott   KIA
John Shaft
Anthony Smith
John Smith   KIA
Richard Smith
Dennis Snee
John Stevenson
Washington Still
Benjamin Thompson
George Thorpe
John Waters
William Williams
James Williamson   KIA
Peter Wood

John Scott's Company
Captain John Scott
First Lieutenant Abraham
    PerLee   WIA
Second Lieutenant Richard Edsall
Ensign Jacob Dickerson
Ensign William Coffee

Sergeants
William Conelly
Thomas Willis

Corporals
James Flood
Elezer Hiler
Benjamin Root
Robert Smith

Musicians
William Able
John Brown
Benjamin Perry
Elexis Tendre

Privates
Silas Abers

George Adams
William Baker
Humphrey Barber
George Barner
John Beaty
John Beleher
Peter Benson
William Boyd
Alexander Brown
Joseph Caston
Francis Clark
Israel Coleman
John Compton
Luther Connet
John Cunliff   d May 1813
John Devers
John Dougherty
Thomas Edsall
Charles Gain
James Gamble
Thomas Gilbreath
Samuel Glenny
John Graham
John Henry
Solomon Lewis
Stephen Lewis
Francis Losan
Amzy Lucky
William Lucky
Michael Maghan
John McGinnis   KIA
Hugh McNeal
Barthew Mecker
Abner Miller
James Parliament
Ebenezer Perry
James Petty
James Rickman
Levi Riker
Cyres Rodgers
Charles Rodman
Joel Russell
David Sample
Peter Seaman
Jacob Smith
James Smith
William Smith
D. W. Stickney
Hiram Terry
David Thomas
James Torrye
Cornelius Vandroof
Hal Wakeman
Peter Wallace
Henry Wright

Henry Van Delsem's Company
Captain Henry Van Delsem
First Lieutenant Samuel
    McDougal

Sergeants
John Lewis
John Logan
John Simonson
James Steward
Peter Willis

Corporals
John Caslo
Chillen Forster
John Houston
Jacob Post

Musicians
James Coward
James Punoe
John Reed

Private
William Abbot
David Allison
John Balm
Daniel Baron
Thomas Benger
Thomas Borden
William Bower
Henry Bowler
Gilbert Bowne
Samuel Brigham
Peter Burns
John Cadmus
John Cleft
John Craver
Peter Crumb
William Daniel
Jasper Degraw
Daniel Dowling
William Drake
Andrew Duffie
John Flanagan
Mathew Galaspie
Joseph Golden
James Gray
Zemire Gree
William Green
John Halfpenny
John Hamilton
John Harris
Joseph Hitchock
Bernard Hughes
Samuel Irvine
William Jones
James Kirkpatrick
John Kish
William Lyon

Marseilles Marseilles
Michael Mason
James Massacre
William McElven
John McGinness
James McKay
Thomas McKrahen
Alexander Morgan
Andrew Patton
Jeremiah Pearsels
Peter Piker
Luke Riley
Willaim Shippey
John Simonson
Mathias Spear
William Stanley
Alexander Stewart
William Stillman
John Story
Abraham Van Droof   KIA
Thomas Van Orden
George Walton
Amos Watson
Joseph Webb
Amos White

White Youngs's Company
Captain White Youngs
First Lieutenant George
    McGlassin

Sergeants
John Darr
Francis Dixey
Phineas Morse
Jesse Van Horne

Corporals
Robert Combs
Samuel Elliott
Justinian Fox   KIA
John Satterfield
Henry Shepherd

Musicians
Jerome Bremner
Francis LaForge

Privates
Philip Alesworth
Lewis Archer
James Ashmore
Anthony Benoit
Charles Bird
James Boggs
James Carlisle
Thomas Chapman
John Clark
Edward Clemmins
Stephen Cobb
Calvin Cook
Peter Cummings
Henry Dice
John Dixon
Anthony Dougherty
Daniel Egerter
William Elliston
Hugh Estes
James Ewin
Ezra Freeman
Russell Frisbee
James Gallagher
Daniel Hains
Jesse Harman

Joseph Heaton
Thomas Johnson
Jesse Jones
Humphrey Jones
Lawrence Justison
John Leister
William Levins
Obadiah Linkin
Henry Lynn
John Martin
Henry Mason
Thomas McCann
John McGonnigal
Hugh McGuire
Thomas McMenamy
Hiram Millington
Andrew Minihan   KIA
William Paisley
John Plumley, Sr.
John Plumley, Jr.
John Pope
Joseph Reed   KIA
John Scott
Robert Sharp
James Sofier
Jacob Steubert, Sr.
Jacob Steubert, Jr.   KIA
William Sullivan
George Thompson
James Trumble
William Wentworth
John Wise
David Wright
Thomas Wright

Sixteenth U.S. Regiment of Infantry[10]

The Sixteenth Infantry comprised three companies, which had 282 officers and men. Only Colonel Pearce's presence is verified, but since this was a large part of the regiment and the staff officers listed here were present, it is speculated that all nine were on the expedition, bringing the total to 291 officers and men.

Field and Staff Officers

Cromwell Pearce*	Colonel
William Cumming	Major, Belonging to the Eighth U.S. Infantry
Samuel Gilliland	Surgeon
Francis D. Cummings	First Lieutenant and Adjutant
Jonathan Aitken	First Lieutenant and Pay master
John Rahm	Quarter Master
William Smith	Sergeant Major
James White	Pay Master Sergeant
John Vorheis	Quarter Master Sergeant

George Steele's Company
Captain George G. Steele
First Lieutenant Peter Donelly
First Lieutenant John Machesney

Sergeants
James Doyle
Thomas Hogan
Joseph Land
William Middleton
William Rightmyer
Major Stone
John Summers
Peter Weiner

Corporals
John Barnet
John Bowers
Edward Ferril
German Henderson
David Hill
Alexander McCrea
John St. Clair
William Willson

Musicians
Thomas Downing
John Glaizer
David Kelly
Phililp Miller

Privates
JamesCraig
Thomas Adams
George Armstrong
Ben Balitz
John Beason   KIA
Smith Beasting
William Beasting
Samuel Bennett
Jacob Besser
John Betts
Robert Brady
William Brinton
William Brown   WIA
David Bryan
William Buck
Jacob Bumgard
Luther Butts
John Cameron
Ben Canby
James Cannon
Robert Carry
Samuel Chew
Thomas Clark
John Clemmons
John Colgin
Elisha Condit
John Craig
David Crites
John Davis

Patrick Donnelly
Anthony Dougherty
Jeremiah Dougherty
David Drum
Jacob Duck
Thomas Dugan
James Dwyer
John Edwards
George Ellis
George Frailey
John Fritz   KIA
James Garrison
Joseph Gibson
William Gillespie
James Gladding
George Golt   WIA
Andrew Gregg
Samuel Hackney
Jacob Hampton,   WIA
Christopher Hart
George Hicks
William Hill
Isaac Hoglan
John Hoover
James Howley
James Huffy
John J. Betts
William Jones
James Kelly
Anthony Lewis
William List
Jacob Lister   WIAd
Joseph Loyd
John Lynch
John Lynn
John Martin
Joel Mason
George Matsinger
John Matsinger
Richard McCloskey
Hugh McCoy   WIA
James McEvers
James McIntire   WIA
William McMains
Alex McMullen
Neil McMullen
Alex McMullen
Samuel Miller
Jacob Moneymaker
John Murphy   KIA
Benjamin Nanna
John Newman
Isaac O'Donnel
Grover Osborne
Bunyan Parker
Joel Parker
George Pawyer
William Pennington   WIA
Michael Pierre

John Pool
George Power
Daniel Pretzman
Isaiah Robbins
John Rowe
John Salter
William Saunderson
Richard Seaford
Frederick Seamers
Casper Sedinger
Bruno Sharks
Michael Sheets
Bernard Shriner
William Shriner
Michael Silvess
Nicholas Silvess
Stephen Singlewood   WIA
John Sloan
John Smith
Anthony Stall
Charles Steward
Daniel Stilwell
Abraham Swayne
Matthew Taylor
Thomas Thomson
Isaac Townsend
George Tracy
Greenburg Tucker
John Updike
Michael Viner
William Walker
James Wall
William Waln
John Weaver   KIA
John White   WIA
William Whitesides   KIA
William Wiatt
Daniel Witman
John Woomley
William Wyatt

Thomas Lyon's Company
Captain Thomas Lyon   KIA
Second Lieutenant Isaac Finch

Sergeants
John Luther
Thomas Lyon, Jr.
David Roe
Ebenezer Snow
James Thompson

Corporals
Charles Barden
Joseph Boyers
Abiel Case
John Farley
Frederick Myers
Joseph When

Musicians
Jesse Atkins
William Delany

Privates
Elisha Albin
James Anderson
James Andrews
John Baker
John Bee
James Beech
William Bell
Dominick Boyle
Frederick Campbell
James Canada
Thomas Catlin
Thomas Conley
George Dain
William Danford
William Delaney
Adam Detir
John Fairfield
William Fairfield
Thomas Gray
John Griffin
John Heaffer
William Johnson
Phillip Keeler
John Lawler
Jacob Likes
Lawrence Martin
Paul McCloskey
John McFeely
Hugh McGee
Henry Miller
John Mincher   KIA
Samuel Parker
John Pennel
William Pope
Thomas Quinton
Samuel Rusco
James Scott
Jeremiah Shearer
Archibald Stephans

John Stewart
Jacob Stillwaggon
Albert Taylor
Samuel Taylor
Clark Thayer
Elijah Tomlison
Joshua Ward
Robert Ward
William Weaver
Abraham Westbrook
Peter Wolf

Captain McEwen's Company
Captain Alexander McEwen
First Lieutenant Miles Greenwood
Second Lieutenant Thomas
    Horrell
Ensign Jacob Whistler   WIA

Sergeants
Charles Barden
Joseph Dawson
George Fuller
James Kelly
Richard Richman
William Zottman

Corporals
Reuben Brinton
Austin Foot
Joseph Jackson

Musicians
John Alexander

Privates
Samuel Ashton
Abner Bennett
George Bleeker   KIA
Christopher Byers
Thomas Carty
Theodore Cliflin
William Coleman
John Cooper
George Cronitt
John Crowly

Thomas Cunningham
John Deveraux
John Dunclebarger
Phillip Fair
Thomas Fell
George Fox
Cornelius Foy
Nathan Hanes
George Howell
George Isenprise
                       WIAd 29 April
Isaac Justison
Joseph Kellogg
Benjamin Lotter
Francis Ludenbek
James Mahan
Richard Maher
George McAllister
Francis McCan
George Menness
Jesse Milner
George Mitchell
James Moore
Thomas Noles
Francis O'Flagherty
Jacob Powell
Samuel Riau
Isiah Richards
George Roberts
Joshua Sage
George Scott
David Sheaffer
John Sickels
Oliver Smith
Jacob Stayley
Charles Steward
John Sweney
John Tait
Mahlon Thomas
Cornelius Van Ricker
Joseph Van Luving
James White
Samuel Witelsy
Michar Zimmers

Twenty-first U.S. Regiment of Infantry[11]

The evidence available shows that only one large company of the Twenty-first Infantry joined the expedition and the presence of only three staff officers can be verified, leading to the estimated size of this unit to have been 133 officers and men.

Field and Staff Officers

Eleazar Ripley*	Lieutenant Colonel, WIA
Azor Orne	First Lieutenant and Adjutant
Jonathan Eastman	First Lieutenant and Pay master
Peter Pelham*	First Lieutenant and Quarter Master
Ira White	Surgeon's Mate
William Thorndike	Surgeon's Mate

John Holding   Sergeant Major
Nathaniel Raynes   Pay Master Sergeant
Arthur Rawson   Quarter Master Seargeant
Newell Stone   Chief Musician

Joseph Grafton's Company
Captain Joseph Grafton
First Lieutenant Morrill
  Marston
Ensign Nathaniel Hall

Sergeants
David Buchan
Isaac Langley
Patetiah Liscomb
Josiah Peirce
Arthur Rawson   d 24 May
Aaron Stewart
Cyrenus Stone
John Stout

Corporals
Jesse Arminty
Robert Cox
Theophilus Frye
Isaac Ross
Samuel Smith
Nathan Underwood

Musicians
Bernard Pumfully
John Rainhart
Paul Williams

Privates
Joseph Abbott, waiter to Major
  Conner
Jeremiah Banker
James Bark
Jesse Barker
Rene Bellamore
William Berdsley
Jonathan Beverley
Ephraim Bixby
M. W. Blake
William Bridgeman
Edward Britton
Gilbert Brondson
John Brown
Peter Brown
William Brown
Nathaniel Bullard   KIA
Daniel Bursell
D. H. Buttman

Josiah Calkins
Joseph Camp
Isaac Campbell
Willing Campbell
David Camperniel
Joseph Cate
Daniel Chase
John Clark
Willey Clay
John Clough
Stephen Content
Nathaniel Cram
Abel Creasy
John Curtis
Able Dewey
B. W. Dewey
Elisha Dike
Caleb Dill
David Dodge
Seth Dow
George Drew
John Dunlap
Ralph Edez
Nathaniel Estes
Chester Fairbanks
Stephen Fletcher
Joseph Foster
Albert Fowles
Israel Frisby
Oliver Frye
George Gale
John Gardner
Abel Garlick
Adolphus Garlick
Josiah Gaylord
Peter Glaxun
Peter Gloyd
Joseph Goodill
Agnes Grant
Benjamin Graves
George Groves
Moses Hanson
John Hanson
James Hart
John Hawthorne
N. H. Hayes
Royal Heath

James Hill
Daniel Hoit
George Hooper
Asa Jackson
Jonathan Jacobs
James Johnson
John Johnson
Amos Jones
Levin Jones
Constant Jones
Jeremiah Jordan
Thomas Lethbridge
Joshua Lock
Simon Mandill
Chester McClenthan
Josiah McClenthan
Zebulon Meads
Ethen Melvin
E. Merrick
Cornelius Nye
Samuel Oakes
Joseph Osgood
John Palmer
Enoch Parsons
Abijah Petty
A. Rathborn
John Ross
N. H. Sanderson
John Stevens
George Stoking
Thomas Sullivan
John Swaney
Judah Swift
Ladock Thomas
Samuel Thompson
Oliver Thrall
William Traste
Joshua Trevis
Ezekiel Turner
George Wamack
John West
David Wharff
William White
Ebenzer Wood
Benajah Woodbury
Charles Wright

U.S. Regiment of Rifles[12]

Major Benjamin Forsyth had overall command of Captain Smith's large company, which appears to have had about 176 officers and men on the expedition. Anecdotal estimates of its size varied from 150 to 200 to 300.[13]

William Smyth's Company "Forsyth's Rifles"

Major Benjamin Forsyth
Captain William Smyth   WIA
First Lieutenant William Beard
Second Lieutenant John
   Hanson
Ensign Samuel Cobbs

Sergeants
Jon Carr
William Eaton
Horace Fish
Woodword James   KIA
John Johnston
William Matthews
Lindsay Milstead
George Rogers

Corporals
George Allen
John Blanchard
Richard Buchanan
James Chambers
William Hill
David James
James Lownes
Ephraim Marsh
William McCane
Robert Rogers
Reuben Stebbins
Mitchell Tate
George Wight
Thomas Zimmerman

Musicians
Charles Barber
Hugh McKay
Joshua Roach
Shadrach Snell
Asabell Storrs
William Wallace

Privates
Stephen Barker
Simon Barton Sr.
Simon Barton Jr.
Asa Bemis
Briggs Bennifield
Daniel Bevins
John Bigelow   KIA
Joshua Bond
James Bosworth
Joel Bowen
Nathaniel Boyd

John Brazell
John Briggs
Blacknel Brooks
Abraham Bross
Thomas Burke
Hirom Burlow
Salmon Burton
Caleb Butterfield
Guy Carpenter
John Cofer
Isaiah Cole
Thomas Conley
William Coppernol
John Coppernol
Amos Corlis
Jonathan Cray
Peter Curran
Benjamin Daniels
Stephen Danslord   d 13 May
John Delange
Justin Dickinson
Larken Diutt
Moses Dunham
John Evans
Adam Feslter
Joseph Fields
John Finney
Adiel Gleason
Miles Goforth
William Goslin
Robert Gray
Moses Green
Jacob Groves
James Hall
William Harn
John Harriss
Philip Henning
Daniel Holder
William Jackson
W. James
Hendrick Janes
Amaziah Johnston
William Johnston
Hendrick Jones
John Kenny
Ebenezer Kingsbury
Elisha Lacy
Francis Ledman
Charles Lewaller
David Lyttle
Parley Marsh
Timothy McGaffey

Edmund McKinney
Samuel Miller
A. Mitchell   d 23 May
Daniel Mitchell
Henry Mitchell
James Mitchell   d 23 May
James Moore
William Morgan   d 15 May
William Muir
Obadian Murray
Joseph Myers
Zebediah Nobles
James Norton
Amasa Payson   d 14 June
Benjamin Pearl
Silas Pearson
William Pearson
John Pelon
William Phillip
Hudson Pierce
Hezekiah Pierce
John Pills   KIA
William Pointer
John Puryear
John Raines
Bruce Redding
Truman Reynolds
Daniel Richards WIAd 27 May
Charles Richards
            WIAd, 30 April
Francis Richards   d 5 May
William Richardson
S. Robeson
Nicholas Robeson
Gideon Rockwell
            WIAd, 24 May
James Roell
Cornelius Romer
Robert Ross
Joseph Sampetan
Almond Sands   d 22 May
Aaron Sands
Salisbury Shearman
Charles Sheffield
Daniel Shippey
David Sigg
S. Simpkins
Nathan Skinner   KIA
B. Smith
Benjamin Smith
John Smith
Josiah Smith

Norman Smith	George Wagan	A. Wilbone
John Southenlin	Symon Wallace	Jeremiam Wilbore
Asa Stewart	Benjamin Warren	William Williams
Nathan Stone	David Warren	Turner Willsford
Samuel Thomas	Joseph Warren	John Wilsey
Guy Thompson	Thomas Washburn	Peter Woodcock
Ephraim Thornton	Isaac Webb	Allen Wooden
Martin Thurber	Benjamin White KIA	Silas Woods
Silas Town	Elizah White	William Wright
M. Victory	Joseph Whites	Francis Yates

Third U.S. Regiment of Artillery[14]

Lieutenant Fanning commanded part of Captain Alexander Brooks's company of Third Artillery which numbered about 80 officers and men, including Lieutenant Colonel Mitchell who joined the expedition as a volunteer. Brooks was not with the detachment.

Anecdotal references to the artillery in Pike's brigade are conflicting, although it seems clear that there was only one company of Third Artillery present. For a further discussion of this issue, see the notes under the Light Artillery.

Field and Staff Officers

Alexander Macomb	Colonel, absent
George E. Mitchell*	Lieutenant Colonel, volunteer
Samuel Nye	Major
Charles M. Macomb*	Second Lieutenant and Adjutant
Benjamin K. Pierce*	First Lieutenant and aide-de-camp
Joseph Eaton	Surgeon's Mate
George Mainwaring	Chief Musician
Jacob Robins	Musician
Porter Walker	Quarter Master Sergeant

Alexander Brooks's Company

First Lieutenant Alexander
    Charles Fanning   WIA
Second Lieutenant John
    Mountfort

Sergeants
Samuel Crabtree
Frederick House
Robert Orr
Jacob Thumb
Joel Wicker

Corporals
Dennis Weaver
Benjamin Pinkham
Daniel Bartlett
John Casey

Musicians
Charles Frost
Adam Bruman

Artificers
Allen Charles
John Johnson
Joshua Mathias

Joseph Tilden
William Warren

Privates
Francis Allen
Michael Baily
James Baker   KIA
James Bowen
William Brogan
Joseph Brownell
Jonathan Cabot
John Cade
David Calahan
William Cameron
Charles Chatteau   WIAd
Zachariah Clark
Lewis Cranston
Moses Davinson
John Dolph
David Erwin
Henry Everly
James Fagan
Thomas Ferrall
James Fitzgerald
Michael Fitzgerald

John Folts
William Folts
George Gallinger
James Giles
Stephen Gregg
Robert Hancock
William Hants   WIAd
Frederick Hartzes
Martin Hooper
James Howe
Jacob Johnson
John Legate
Paul Longbean
John Loyal
Phillip Marty
Michael McDormant
Abraham McKenzie
James Murphy
Martin Murphy
Henry Percy
Francis Quinn
John Ross
George Schuyler
Herman Segelken
John Segelken

Robert Simpson		William Steward		Joseph Wilbur
John Skayls	KIA	Thomas Swift		Liba Wilbur
John Smith	KIA	Joseph Vaquet		Daniel Wild
Thomas Smith		Thomas Wallace		John Wyman
Eli Stevenson		Vandermaas Wheeler		James Young

U.S. Regiment of Light Artillery[15]

The strength of the Light Artillery detachment was at least 80 officers and men.

Major Eustis did not identify the size of his detachment, nor the officers under him. Ensign Dwight, Thirteenth Infantry, mentioned three companies of artillery without further details. Colonel Pearce, Sixteenth Infantry, mentioned "one company of light artillery." Aide-de-camp Lieutenant Colonel Conner noted a detachment of light and heavy artillery, some of the light artillery men acting as infantry. Surgeon Beaumont, Sixth Infantry, referred only to the Light Artillery. One anonymous officer mentioned both but without numbers. Captain Scott, Fifteenth Infantry, remembered three Light Artillery companies, mistakenly including Fanning's with them. Pike's brigade order listed Fanning's two guns and Eustis train of artillery protected by his own infantry. In all likelihood, Eustis had more than one company under his command, but no contemporary muster or pay list could be found to identify it.[16]

Field and Staff Officers

Abraham Eustis   Major

Andrew McDowell's Company
Captain Andrew McDowell
                     WIA
First Lieutenant Henry Hobart

Second Lieutenants
John Gates
George Hight
George Morris

Sergeants
Ezeriah Bennett
Benjamin Henley
Job Nash
John White

Corporals
Jonathan Church
Israel Waters

Musicians
James Crocker
Matthew Van Everly

Artificers
Bezaleel Bennett
James Cady
John Fullerton
Brian Martin
Joshua Smith
Simeon Walker

Saddler
Reuben Hamlet   KIA

Privates
Ephraim Badges
William Bateman
Isaac Baxter
Gilbert Benson
Lewis Betts
Jesse Bishop
Nelson Boys
James Brice
William Davenport
Robert Day
Arthur Forester
William Fullerton
Peter Gilman
Michael Goddard
John Gorden
Nathaniel Griswald
Richard Guildenstone
William Hall
James Harkness
Richard Harrington
John Hart   WIAd, 10 June
Ezekiel Hazzard
John Holden
David Kemp
Harsham Kettle
William Law
Joseph Lawrence
Alfred Leonard
Henry Leonard

William McGowan
George McKendrick
John Medrick
Sylvenis Merchant
Jacob Moore
Andrew Morgan
Andrew Nichols
Mark Noe
William Norris
Herbert Owen
Thomas Payne
Valentine Reynick
Thomas Richards
Thomas Rollins
David Ross
John Schultz
Richard Serwen
David Simpson
Frederick Smeck
Asa Snow
Luther Stanley
David Stewart
Ephraim Talbot
Enoch Tally
David Weaver
John Weeks
Stephen Wilkinson
Solomon Willard
Alfred Willis

TWELVE-MONTH FEDERAL VOLUNTEERS

"McClure's Volunteers"

The strength of the Federal Volunteers from Francis McClure's Regiment amounted to about 122 officers and men.

McClure's Regiment comprised ten companies, nine of which were drawn from New York State of which only one, Maher's "Albany Greens," numbering about 55 effectives, was on the expedition. With desertions and deaths, etc. on the extant records removed, Moore's "Baltimore Volunteers" included the 93 officers and men listed here, but Ensign Warner wrote that only 65 of them were fit for duty on the eve of the embarkation.[17] It is speculated that at least one of the field and staff officers accompanied McClure, although only his presence is verified.

Field and Staff Officers[18]

Francis McClure*	Colonel
Darby Noon	Major
Samuel Swartout	Adjutant
Christopher Fonda	Surgeon's Mate
W. W. Quackenbush	Quarter Master
Daniel Adams	Pay Master
Adam Gamble	Sergeant Major
John Hurley	Quarter Master Sergeant

James Maher's Company [19]
The " Albany Greens"

Captain James Maher
First Lieutenant Thomas
   Dawson
Second Lieutenant Thomas
   Doyle
Ensign Patrick Coad

Sergeants
Jonathan Brown
John Clite, Jr.
James Kerr
George Waters

Corporals
James Collins
Michael McGrath
John McKelvry
James Smith

Musician
Daniel Campbell

Privates
Dan Aldrich
William Archer
Patrick Bannan
Joseph Bates
Abraham Burgess
Herbert Burk
Dennis Cahill
Henry Clemisher

Thomas Collins
William Collins
John Colten
James Cullens
Hiram Cummings
Andrew Donlevy
Samuel Fulsom
John Green
Thomas Hawthorne
James James
James Johnson
Cornelius Johnson   KIA
Henry Joslin
Dennis Kerney
Andrew McBride
Patrick McGuire
Thomas McHugh
John McKay
James McKelvey
Michael McMurray
Edward Morgan
Joseph Murphy   KIA
William Nelson
Thomas Russell
William Scott
John Skarrett
John W. Smith
Peter Starilaux
James Sturges
Adam Timple
Nathan Tomlinson

Wm. Van Duzen
Armstrong Waugh
James Woods

Stephen Moore's Company[20]
The "Baltimore Volunteers"

Captain Stephen H. Moore
              WIA
Lieutenant John Gill
Lieutenant Baptist Irvine WIA
Ensign Thomas Warner

Sergeants
George Craig
Joseph Crane
Aquilla Edwards
George Evans
Gregory Foy
William Jarvis
Robert McAllister.

Corporals
Christian Baker
James Cochrane
Thomas Hazelton   WIAd
William Maxwell
William Watkins
John Williams
Thomas Williams

Privates
Nathaniel Andrews
Joseph Armitage

David Armstrong
Henry Baker
Henry Bishop
Peter Borgese
Daniel Bowers
Edward Boyle
Jonathan Camper
Jonathan Chapman
John R. Caffrey
Levin Cook
John Daley
James Davis
Cornelius Day
John Deppish
Henry Dillchary
John Dixon
Joseph Dougherty
Peter Eichelberger
Edward Edwards   WIAd
Benjamin Elliott
Andrew Fife
Henry Fitch
Joseph Fondar
Daniel Forman
James Garroway

Peter Gardiner
Samuel Gardiner
Ezekiel George
Edward Haley
George Hayes
Nicholas Hayes
James Hilton
John Howard
Thomas Jones
William Keeves
Conrad Kellar
Patrick Kelly
Robert Kent
George Kelnor
John Kepner
George Kleinhand
George Knott
Benjamin Kohlsladt
Joseph Lawrence
John Maxwell
Frederick McComas
John McCracken
Isaac Melchior
Richard Merchant
John Myers

John Patterson
Henry Pearsall
John Penman
William Peregoy
William Peters
John Pike
Thomas Pocock
William Porter
Thomas Price
John Rattle
William Ryan
Joseph Sadler
Micajah Selby
Lewis Sherman
Francis Sinton
John Sinnard
John Small
Edward Speaks
Andrew Stoutsberger
Samuel Tufts
James Underwood
William Van Bergen
Moses Welch

APPENDIX 7

United States Navy Squadron, April 1813

The U.S. Navy squadron that carried the U.S. Army to York and supported its landing consisted of fourteen vessels, manned by nearly 800 men and mounting 39 long guns and 46 carronades.

No precise report was made of the American naval strength involved in the battle and anecdotal descriptions were rare. Surgeon Amasa Trowbridge, Twenty-first U.S. Regiment of Infantry, recalled one ship, one brig, eleven schooners, 200 marines and 700 seamen while his medical colleague, William Beaumont, noted the ship, the brig and twelve schooners. Although Major General Sir Roger Sheaffe reported sixteen warships, most other British observers agreed that there were only fourteen. The Reverend John Strachan estimated that there were 800 seamen and marines on board.[1]

Commodore Isaac Chauncey's correspondence shows that he planned to sail with thirteen vessels and that he had added the hired merchant schooner *Gold Hunter* for the voyage. He had sent the *Lady of the Lake* to Niagara before sailing for York with orders to join him there, bringing the squadron's strength to fifteen and then, with the addition of the *Duke of Gloucester* (which appears to have been towed to Sackets Harbor), sixteen. Chauncey had about 640 seamen and marines at Sackets by December

1812, of whom about 600 were still on the rolls in April. His force was strengthened by about 150 men brought from Rhode Island by Master Commandant Oliver Perry and 50 others who arrived from New York with Lieutenant Wolcott Chauncey.[2]

Vessels in the Squadron

The following vessels made up Commodore Chauncey's squadron, although the *Lady of the Lake* was not at York for the attack and its single gun has not been included in the armament total. The *Scourge* is shown as having only eight guns during the battle, to which Sailing Master Osgood is said to have added a pair of 6-pdrs. found at York. No dependable information was found regarding the *Gold Hunter*. Some crew sizes include seamen plus marines.[3]

Vessel	Commander	Crew Size	Total Guns	Carronades No. & Type	Long Guns No. & Type
Asp	Lt. Joseph Smith	38	2	0	1 12-pdr*, 1 24-pdr*
Conquest	S.M. Francis Mallaby	40+8	3	0	1 6-pdr*, 2 24-pdr*
Fair American	Lt. Wolcott Chauncey	58	2	0	1 24-pdr*, 1 32-pdr*
Gold Hunter	-	-	-	-	-
Governor Tompkins	Lt. Thomas Brown	58+18	6	2 24-pdrs	2 9-pdrs, 1 24-pdr*, 1 32-pdr*
Growler	S.M. Mervin Mix	33+7	5	0	4 4-pdrs, 1 32-pdr*
Hamilton	Lt. Joseph Macpherson	46	9	8 18-pdrs	1 12-pdr*
Julia	S.M. James Trant	35	2	0	1 12-pdr*, 1 32-pdr*
Lady of the Lake	S.M. Thomas Nichols	41	1	0	1 9-pdr*
Madison	Lt. Jesse Elliott Com. Isaac Chauncey	200	24	20 32-pdrs	4 12-pdrs
Oneida	Lt. Melancthon Woolsey	129+32	18	16 24-pdrs	2 6-pdrs
Ontario	S.M. Joseph Stevens	28	2	0	1 12-pdr*, 1 32-pdr*
Pert	Lt. Samuel Adams	27	3	0	2 6-pdr, 1 32-pdr*
Raven	S.M. Thomas Almy	28	1	0	1 18-pdr*
Scourge	S.M. Joseph Osgood	32	8	0	4 4-pdrs, 4 6-pdrs
Totals		**793+65**	**86**	**46**	**39**
		858	**Guns**	**Carronades**	**Long Guns**

* mounted on a swivelling carriage

The Squadron Crews

The musters and pay lists for all of the vessels in Chauncey's squadron for the spring of 1813 are extant and formed the basis of the lists presented below. Interpretation of the records, reading the handwriting and spelling made it impossible to create the definitive report of the strength of each vessel present at York. It is safe to assume, however, that *most* of the men listed here were present in the squadron during the expedition. The crew sizes for the various vessels are similar to those in a formal report Chauncey prepared in July 1813. There were probably more marines on board the vessels, but the musters and pay lists did not include them with any consistency; they are shown in the tally as added to the naval personnel count. Men killed on the day of the battle are identified as DD, 27 April, meaning "discharged, dead" on that date, as they are shown on the musters. Others marked "discharged, dead" in the weeks after the battle are also listed, reflecting men who died of wounds or illness suffered during the period. Some men were identified on the casualty lists as KIA or WIA, which has been repeated here. Men with identical names on vessels have been shown with ordinal numbers.[4]

Key
KIA = Killed in action
WIA = Wounded in action
WIAd = Wounded in action, died
DD = Discharged, dead

Asp [5]
Crew strength: 38 officers and men

Commanding Officer
Lieutenant Joseph E. Smith

Warrant Officers
Charles Caldwell, midshipman
Stephen Champlin, sailing
    master

Petty Officers
Joseph Bray, quarter gunner
Horace Flint, quarter gunner
Thomas Brownell, master's
    mate
Noah Gates, steward
John Vose, steward

Seamen
Robert Boatswain
John Clark, 2
Stephen Gallagher
Gardner Gaskell
Gilbert Norcott
Robert Peterson
James Smith
Joseph Southwick
Richard Trott
Mathew West

Ordinary Seamen
James Allen
Joseph Ballard
Robert Burges
Bernard Crandle
William Cranston
Benjamin Deering
Thomas Farrell
Ebenezer Freeman   DD 9 May
Cassius Jones
Daniel Manning
John Moreau
John Norton
Alexander Sickling
John Starr
Henry Thomas
John Welch
George Williams

Landsmen
Peter O'Donnell
Roger Sullivan

Boy
Edward Vanblarcom

Conquest [6]
Crew strength: 40 officers and men
and 8 marines

Commanding Officers
Sailing Master Francis Mallaby,
    to 3 May
Lieutenant John Pettigrew, from
    4 May

Commission Officer
James Garrison, surgeon's mate

Warrant Officers
John Hatfield, midshipman KIA
Robert H. Nichols, midshipman
Benjamin Quereau, sail maker
    WIAd 7 May

Petty Officers
Mustagh Glynn, steward
John Home, boatswain's mate
John Simpson, master's mate
Henry Smith, quarter gunner

Seamen
Samuel Aberdeen
Antonio Barbara
Samuel Beamer
Daniel Benjamin
Parcal Benjamin
Charles Brown
John Brown
Thomas Brown
Joseph Burbeck
John Burdette
John Ford
Joseph Hutchington DD 9 May
Henry Proger
John M. Pugh
John Segerstrom
Amos Shaw
William Smith
John Surline
William Tooky
Nathan Warrington
William Willis

Ordinary Seamen
John Amery
Anthony Carroll   DD 7 May
Robert Garner
Benjamin Garrett
Henry Hopkins
Lewis Matthews
Joseph Pellbrooke

Roger Welsh

Landsmen
Junis B. Kniffin
Jacob Townsend

U.S. Marines
– Stephenson, corporal

Privates
– Budeck
– Hanque
– Kelly
– McCormick
– Mitchell
– States
– Stockwell

Fair American [7]
Crew strength: 58 officers and men

Commanding Officer
Lieutenant Wolcott Chauncey

Commission Officer
Lieutenant Charles Skinner

Warrant Officers
James Mason, midshipman
John Sullivan, midshipman
Robert Tatem, midshipman
Benjamin Thompson,
    midshipman   KIA

Petty Officers
William Bedwell, master's mate
John Driscole, quarter gunner
Robert Dunn, master's mate
William Fengar, steward
William Jarboe, quarter gunner
David Johnson, boatswain's mate
John Johnson, pilot
Joseph Laza, master's mate
William Philips, quarter master
Peter Thompson, master's mate
John York, quarter gunner

Seaman
John Ackerman
John Bailey
William Blackston
William Burrows   DD 7 May
Michael Chauvel
John Clark
Martin Clause
Joseph Dent
Thomas Evans

John Goddard
David Hill
Samuel Hughes
George Hutton
Benjamin Lovell
Joshua Lunt
William McGee
John Mills
John Nulty
David Poor
John Simpson
Henry Spires
Alexander Stewart
Henry Stiles
Perry Trusty
George Wiggs

Ordinary Seaman
John Anderson
Samuel Andrews
Jesse Cadrone
Charles Connelly
John Denny
Alexander Dickson
Amos Harker
James Harland
Francis Lemie
Edward Lightfoot
William Pogue
Edward Price
John Richardson
William Thompson

Boy
John Sherman

Governor Tompkins [8]
Crew strength: 58 officers and men,
11 marines and 7 soldiers

Commanding Officer
Lieutenant Thomas Brown

Warrant Officers
St. Clair Elliott, sailing master
Richard Hubbard, midshipman

Petty Officers
Archibald Bates, steward
George Cherry, pilot
John Duncan, master's mate
Daniel Keiff, quarter gunners
Samuel Lolly, quarter gunners
Peter Mastin, quarter gunners
James Morrison, boatswain's
    mate
James Rowland, steward
John Scott, boatswain's mate
William Sweet, master's mate
James Weaver, master's mate

Seamen
Edmund Ames
Job Anderson
John Baptiste
Anthony Blanch
John Boldevan
James Bowen
James Brown
Timothy Claney
Maurice Collins
John Corry
George Davis
Peter Davis
Andrew Deas
John Downing
Joseph Elkins
James Evans
Francis Lawrence
Thomas Leach
John Malbone
James Miller
John Moody
John Mustra
Hans Osman
William Parker
Robert Paulis
William Russel
John Stephens
John Thomas
Robert Tyler
Willis Watkins
Jacob Watson
James Williams
John Williams 1st
John Williams 2nd

Ordinary Seamen
Levi Allen
Samuel Anderson
Archibald Bates
Francis Burns
John Caplet
Charles Cook
Caleb Hitchcock
Michael James
George Ricks

Landsmen
Dennis Summers

U.S. Marines
Jonathan Curtis, sergeant major

Privates
Edward Barr
Robert Hutchinson
Bradford Phillips
Jacob Kyser
Peter Hamerty
David Fitzgerald
John Sogue

Thomas Savage
Robert Adams
James Richmond

U.S. Army
7 soldiers

Gold Hunter
No relevant data was found to
identify the crew.

Growler [9]
Crew strength: 33 officers and men
and 7 marines

Commanding Officer
Sailing Master Mervin Mix

Petty Officers
Abel Armington, master's mate
Philip Baker, boatswain's mate
Jeremiah Buel, steward
Robert Huginen, pilot
Lewis Krutziger, quarter gunner
Samuel Osgood, master's mate
John Wells, master's mate
Calvin Williams, boatswain's
    mate

Seamen
Samuel Baker
William Dunn
Thomas Everett
Robert Harris
Paul Harvey
Thomas Mortimer
John Peterson
Joel Roberts
John Stimers   WIA
John Taylor
William Thornton
William Warren
David Watson
Peter Young

Ordinary Seamen
Thomas Brown
William Buckley
William Johnston
William Mallett
John McVoy
John Peirson   WIA
Thomas Thorning
Job Winslow
John Winslow

Landsman
Richard Page

U.S. Marines
7

Hamilton [10]

Crew strength: 46 officers and men

Commanding Officer
Lieutenant Joseph MacPherson

Warrant Officers
William Bonnell, midshipman
William Harper, midshipman
John Jackson, sailing master
Samuel Stiness, sailing master

Petty Officers
Thomas Burr, quarter gunner
William Clark, master's mate
Thomas Downs, quarter gunner
Roderick Olcott, steward
George Pocock, quarter gunner
John Smith, master's mate
Sylvester Wilcox, carpenter's mate
George Wilson, boatswain's mate

Seamen
John Adams
Nathaniel Alexander
John Barret
Richard Birch
Henry Bran
Samuel Brown
Enoch Chase
Dayton Crilly
William Cross
John Delahunt
John Emory
Herman Lewis
George Lewis   KIA
Paul Maloyle
Stephen Nowell
Edward Perrin
Thomas Stanfield
Phillip Vanvoorst
John Westbury
Merril Whitmore
Joseph Whitney
George Wilkinson

Ordinary Seamen
Joseph Le Brent
John Merril
William Scott
Daniel Sinclair
Aaron Stulphin
William Tice

Landsmen
William Ager
Joseph Blinker
Peter Trumane
Francis Udder

Boy
William Druxy

Julia [11]

Crew strength: 35 officers and men

Commanding Officer
Sailing Master James Trant

Warrant Officers
John Hutton, sailing master
Frederick Leonard, sg. master
                    DD 12 May

Petty Officers
Gerard Clausen, quarter gunner
Robert Dunn, master's mate
John Mallet, boatswain's mate
Gordon Palmer, quarter gunner
William Reed, carpenter's mate
Henry Williams, cook

Seamen
John Barnet
Samuel Blank
John Casey
James Cook
William Dowers
Thomas Fittock
John Gallison
Benjamin Halstead
Nathaniel Hossa
Martin Jones
Henry Price
Joseph Rhine
John Smith
John R. Smith
George Sprigg
Benjamin Tribe
William Wilcox
John Wildon

Ordinary Seamen
John Lorton
William Reynolds
Benjamin Williams

Landsmen
John C. Fanning
William Smith
William Palmer
James Patterson

Boy
John Phonix, boy

U.S. Marines
7 men

Lady of the Lake [12]

Crew strength: 41 officers and men

Commanding Officer
Sailing Master Thomas Nichols

Warrant Officers
John Campbell, boatswain
Wadsworth Loring, midshipman

Elliott Smith, gunner
James Young, midshipman

Petty Officers
Abel Armington, master's mate
William Atkins, quarter gunner
Denny Castanaugh, quarter
     gunner
Adoniram Chandler, steward
R. G. Thompson, master's mate
Robert Huginin, pilot
John Manella, boatswain's mate
James Morrison, boatswain's
     mate
Peter Thompson, master's mate
William White, quarter gunner

Seaman
John Barker
Joseph Buxton
Hugh Campbell
David Chubb
Anthonio Decruize
Lewis Donsett
Benjamin Halston
James Hatch
William Laportes
Joseph Lowe
Benjamin Morris
William Neezey
William Parker
John Reynolds
William Schuster
John Schwartz
David Talbot
Peter Young
William Zane

Ordinary Seaman
Henry Anderson
Henry Edwards
William Johnson
Joseph Johnston
William Reid

Boy
Francis Crane
Charles Greenidge

Madison [13]

Crew strength: 200 officers and men

Commodore
Isaac Chauncey

Commanding Officer
Lieutenant Jesse Elliott

Commission Officers
Francis Gregory, acting lieutenant
John Drury, acting lieutenant
Samuel Anderson, acting purser
Walter Buchanan, acting surgeon

Warrant Officers
Caleb Hayden, carpenter
William Lowe, master
John Nestley, boatswain
John Raburg, sailmaker

Midshipmen
Seth Alby
John Clarke
Thomas Freelon
Philip F. Livingston
John Montgomery
Joshua Sands
Charles Smith
Daniel Walker
Samuel Wardell Adams
John Wendell
William Wetmore

Petty Officers
John Carson, cooper
Thomas Hammond, armourer
John James, coxswain
Isaac Minnie, cook
Isaac Pelham, coxswain's mate
Simon Warn. captain's clerk

Master's Mates
John Cummings
Ezra Taylor

Quarter Masters
James Alford
John Blight
Daniel Brown
John Green
Amos Salsbury
William Wilds

Quarter Gunners
John Blight
Lewis Cruitzeiger
James Demorant
Christopher Garon
John Gibbs
Francis Helegan
Joshua Manchurn
James Mattison
John Mortanson
John Smith
John Wigmore
John Young

Boatswain's Mates
William Arnot
Thomas Clarke
William Davis
William Douglas
Lawrence Hansen
Thomas Harrison
James Hellan
Dennis MacHogan

William Miller

Carpenter's Mates
Solomon Hamilton
Charles Jordan
William Noales
Lemuel Palmer

Stewards
William Ralph
Charles Selding
John Steward
John Thomas

Seamen
Joshua Abbott
John Alfonse
Edmund Ames
Henry Antland
Henry Atkins
John Barnes
Lawrence Beckman
James Blake
John Bowree
Christian Brennan
Francis Brucbank
David Bunnel   WIA
John Campbell   WIA
Mondell Churchill
John Clarke
John Clay
Thomas Clews
John Coles
John Colston
William H Cortlin
Joseph Costans
Arthur Crepley
Anderson Custard
Thomas Davis
William Davis
Henry Dereck
Thomas Duffy
Peter Dunn
Abijah Eddy
James Evans
John Ferguson
Inman Franklin
Christian Freedings
Darius Gates
William Gibson
Nicholas Gravenstein
Justin Hamburg
James Hammond
Thomas Hanker
John Harkins
Henry Herman
Samuel Isabell
James Jackson
John James
James Johnson

Thomas Jones
James Kyne
Lewis Lane
Daniel Lewis
John Malbone
James McClure
James McCoy
Lucas McGlen
James Miller
Jacob Myers
John Myers
Philip Neajohn
Thomas Nelson
David Neware
Lemuel Oliver
Thomas Parker
William Perkins
Nelson Peters
William Phillips
Jeremiah Pritchard
Thomas Reginald
John Ridley
Dan Roberts
Joseph Roberts
Joseph Rue
Matthew Ruffard
John Saundery
James Smith
William Smith
Nathan Stanfield
Mathew Stark
James Stone
Edward Stone
Anthony Thadaux
William Thompson
Dennis Vanderhysen
James Wade
John Warren
Thomas Washburne
Benjamin Waters
Samuel Welsh
William White
Hercules Whiting
John Wilhelms
John Williams 1st
John Williams 2nd
John Williams 3rd
Thomas Williams
Thomas Williams 2nd
James Woodard

Ordinary Seamen
Joseph Andrews
John Clarke
John Craig
Moses Crapper
William Davis
Joseph Dent
John Freeman

Asa Gabriel
Joseph Grindstate
James Halpay
Richard Handy
Samuel Haskell
Joshua Hutchings
Solomon Jenkins
Christopher Johnson
Cassius Jones
James Katch
John Lane
Stephen Lantus
Joseph LeBrant
Amos Lines
John Lynn
William Meighen
Thomas Miller
James Morrison
George Ranigan
Henry Redford
John Rednick
Thomas Regin
Benjamin Smith
John Steed
William Stevenson
Joshua Sweet
Joseph Tucker
Richard Welch   WIA
John White
Henry Williams
Jesse Williams
William Williams
Zoshier Wood
Philip Wren

Boy
Samuel Dunn

Oneida [14]
Crew strength: 129 officers and
men, 14 marines and 18 soldiers

Commanding Officer
Lieutenant Melancthon Woolsey

Commission Officers
Henry Wells, lieutenant
Augustus Conkling, Lieutenant
William Caton, surgeon
Alexander Darragh, purser

Warrant Officers
Cadwallader Billlings, midshipman
Thomas Burr, sailmaker
Richard Caton, midshipman
John Fair, gunner
Augustus Ford, master
Thomas Hall, boatswain
Benedict Higden, midshipman
John Hill, gunner
William Inman, midshipman

Nathan Miller, carpenter
William Nichols, midshipman
William Peabody, midshipman
Henry R. Haskins, midshipman
William Vaughan, sailing master

Petty Officers
Caesar Bellamy, cook
Joseph Carey, carpenter's mate
John Carter, quarter gunner
Jesse Clark, quarter master
James Dunn, master's mate
William Eadus, pilot
John Elliott, quarter master
Gershom Fairchild, quarter gunner
John Gear, master at arms
Arthur Gladd, steward
Warren Green, clerk
Charles Hamilton, carpenter's mate
James Handy, steward
Henry Hastings, boatswain's mate
John Johnson, master's mate
William Ludlow, master's mate
Matthew McMurray, cooper
David Peirce, quarter gunner
Robert Quickly, quarter gunner
Nehemiah Root, master at arms
George Walker, quarter master
David Webber, quarter gunner
James White, quarter gunner
James Wilson, boatswain's mate

Seamen
Daniel Albro
John Alford
Abraham Babcock
Philip Brazier
Patrick Brick
John Bush
William Cable
John Clark
Thomas Cook
James Dutton
John Elliott
John Esling
Charles Foulks
Paul Gates
Willard Gates
William Grasey
John Grear
William Harrington
William Heaverin
James Higgins
Frederick Lepi
John Mahony
David Miller
Absalom Miner
Edward Moody
John Price
Guy Rickerson

Thomas Robinson
Daniel Rose
Asa Shadwick
George Thompson
George Walker
David Webber
John White
James Wilson

Ordinary Seamen
Andrew Brazier
John Bull
Thomas Burns
Israel Cain
John Calkins
John Carr
David Champlin
Joseph Crane
William Curview
Francis De Noyer
Joseph Dickenson
Alexander Ferguson
William Graham
Charles Gree
John Green
John Higgins
Michael Hughes
Charles Knowles
Elkane Magoon
Owen McGrath
Alexander Meville
Aubrey Meville
John Merris
David Miller
Edward Mitchell
James Murray
Abner Peirce
Samuel Reyolds
Samuel Rice
Jonathan Shaw
John Stollman
John Stone
John Thompson
Michael Turner
Edward Welsh
David Wilson
Isaac Wood

Landsman
William Bell

Boys
William Baker
Henry Briggs
John Calkins
Robert Davis
Richard Franks
John Hagens
John Harbison
John Le Courer

Alexander McCally
William McPhaggin
William Rickerson
John White Jr.
David White

U.S. Marines
William Hale, sergeant
James Cooper, corporal
John Graham, corporal

Privates
Peter Berriane
James Bird
John Dunn
John Heyer
Micah Jesson
Amasa Lounsberry
Michael McLeary
Lindsey Montgomery
Samuel Parr
Andrew Rogers
James Wark

U.S. Army
18 soldiers

Ontario [15]
Crew strength: 28 officers and men

Commanding Officer
Sailing Master Joseph Stevens

Petty Officers
William Pole, master's mate
Enoch Steelman, quarter gunner
Lewis White, steward
John Ratler, quarter masterWIA
Ephraim Hubble, pilot
Jeremiah Long, boatswain's mate

Seamen
Andrew Algerine
Silas Crary
John Edwards
Benjamin Hackner   WIA
Neil Heildersbrandt
Robert Milner
Philip Maxwell
William Robinson
Thomas Rogers
Arthur Saers
Thomas Sharp
James Young
Peter Young
William Tate

Ordinary Seamen
John Anderson
Paul Johnson
Isaac Johnson
Robert Kennedy
Thomas Milton

Landsman
William Elsworth
Michael Sands

Pert [16]
Crew strength: 27 officers and men

Commanding Officer
Lieutenant Samuel W. Adams

Warrant Officers
Eleazar H. Massey, midshipman

Petty Officers
John Clarkson, boatswain's mate
Matthew Kenny, steward
Andrew Rassmussen, pilot
John Thompson, quarter gunner
William Tracy, master's mate

Seamen
Thomas Bryan
John Cunningham
Fortune Howard
Samuel Howard
William Irvin
John Kindall
Gershom Moore
Allen Ramsay
Robert Relay
Allan Richardson
John White
Jonathan Wood

Ordinary Seaman
John Hubbard
Peter Dubois

Landsmen
Michael Brannon
John Dusenburry
Henry Griffith
Soloman Reynolds

Boys
Sidney Brown
Domingo Derin

Raven [17]
Crew strength: 28 officers and men

Commanding Officer
Sailing Master Thomas Almy

Petty Officers
Joseph Cotter, boatswain's mate
William Peckham, master's mate
Caleb Walker, master's mate

Seaman
Christopher Bayley
Joseph Brewer
Israel Clark   KIA
John Eckson

William Edwards
Adolph Fisher
Richard Lowes
Abraham Patch
Edward Polite
Peter Tomlinson
William Walker
James Williams

Ordinary Seaman
William Dickson
James Robinson

Boy
John Murray

Scourge [18]
Crew strength: 32 officers and men

Commanding Officer
Sailing Master Joseph Osgood

Warrant Officer
Philip Livingstone, midshipman

Petty Officers
Peter Bogardus, master's mate
John Christmas, quarter gunner
John Cochrane, steward
William Deer, boatswain's mate

Seaman
John Adams
Jacob Aldis
Louis Dousett
Henry Erekson
John Gregory
James Lawson
Edward Myers
George Pruence
William Southard
George Thornblood
William Vankown
John Wyatt

Ordinary Seaman
Lemuel Bryant   WIA
Ebenezer Duffie
Thomas Goldsmith
Simeon Grant
Roswill Hodge
William Johnson
Leonard Lewis
Peter Senis
William Smith
Tryal Way

Landsmen
Charles Edwin
Henry Greggs

Boys
Samuel Lott
Joseph Phillips

Casualties and Prisoners of War

In his classic work, *On War*, Carl von Clausewitz wrote, "Casualty reports on either side are never accurate, seldom truthful, and in most cases deliberately falsified."[1] The publication of casualty data following the battle at York lends credence to his assertion.

BRITISH/CANADIAN CASUALTIES

It is estimated that 82 regulars, militia and natives who defended York were killed in action, 91 were wounded (some of whom later died of their wounds) and 7 more were missing in action. There were at least 348 men taken captive, of whom 53 were wounded. The total of casualties and prisoners was about 475. The names of the casualties (including those known to have died of their wounds) are identified in Appendix 4, British Order of Battle at York, 27 April 1813, Appendix 5, Upper Canada Militia at the Battle of York and Appendix 9, The Terms of Capitulation.

Major General Sheaffe wrote his first report to Sir George Prevost on 30 April, while on his retreat to Kingston. In it he admitted, "I cannot inform Your Excellency what our loss has been."[2] He did not report any tallies of casualties in his formal reports, penned on 5 May, but when he issued a general order on 13 May he claimed there had been 130 killed and wounded, 63 short of the best estimate shown here. When a return was prepared on 10 May, it listed only members of the regular force. Subsequently, no one wrote an all-inclusive list of the casualties suffered by the British, Canadian and native forces at York. Information reported by the various sources was incomplete and conflicting, further confusing the situation. Major General Dearborn estimated that the British suffered 90-100 killed, 200 wounded and 300 taken prisoner. The best estimate is given in the following table, with the data for the different elements of the force discussed below:

	KIA	MIA	WIA	WIA/POW	POW	Total
Militia and Volunteers	4	-	-	6	264	274
Native Warriors	5	-	7	-	-	12
Dockyard Workers	2	-	-		15	17
Provincial Marine	-	-	-		6	6
Regulars	71	·7	31	47	10	166
Totals	**82**	**7**	**38**	**53**	**295**	**475**

Militia and Volunteers

The most widely used militia record concerned those taken prisoner and put on parole. Appended to the Terms of Capitulation signed on 28 April (transcribed in Appendix 9), it showed a tally of 264, although it did not refer to WIA/POWs, the numbers of which have been inserted based on casualty information:

	Lt Col	Mj	Cp	QM	Lt	En	Sg	Cr	Rank and File	Total[3]
Militia POWS	1	1	13	1	8	11	19	4	201	259
WIA/POW	-	-	1	-	1	-	-	-	3	5
										264

No comprehensive return was made of militia and volunteer casualties, but a variety of sources named these individuals:[4]

KIA	WIA
John Detlor	John Bassell
Donald McLean	Andrew Borland
Daniel Murray	Patrick Hartney
Matthias Saunders	William Jarvie
	William Jarvis
	Joseph Shepherd

Native Warriors

No one prepared a return of native casualties. Sheaffe made the clearest reference available when he remarked, "A few of the Indians (Mississaugas and Chippawas) were killed and wounded, among the latter were two chiefs."[5] For want of more precise information and given the ferocity of the first phase of the engagement, an estimate of 5 dead and 7 wounded does not seem inappropriate.

Dockyard Workers

No return was made of casualties among the dockyard crew, but letters referred to at least two KIA and the Terms of Capitulation showed 15 artificers taken prisoner and paroled.[6]

Provincial Marine

No return was made of casualties in the Provincial Marine. The Terms of Capitulation named 6 individuals taken prisoner and paroled.

British Regulars

Several conflicting reports concerning casualties suffered by the regulars were prepared. They are summarized below.

Prisoners of War Left at York

The Terms of Capitulation noted only 6 regulars taken prisoner and paroled, but the following reports reveal its inaccuracy.

1. Assistant Adjutant General for the militia, Captain Stephen Jarvis, 3rd York, completed a return on 1 May 1813 at York providing information about the number of WIA/POW and unwounded POW.[7]

	Sg	Cr	Dr	P	Total	
RA	-	-	-	1	1*	WIA/POW
	1	-	-	4	5	POW
8th Foot	2	2	-	23	27	WIA/POW
	-	-	-	1	1	POW
RNFR	3	-	-	8	11	WIA/POW
	-	-	-	2	2	POW
49th Foot	-	-	-	3	3	WIA/POW
Totals	6	-	-	44	50	

* This man identified as Private Patrick Hogen, "since dead".

2. Captain John Glegg, 49th Foot, signed a second undated report closely resembling Jarvis's. It added Lieutenant John de Koven to the list of the WIA/POW.[8]

	Lt	Sg	Cr	Dr	P	Total
RA	-	1	-	-	4	5
8th Foot	-	2	2	-	24	28
RNFR	1	3	-	1	10	15
49th Foot	-	-	-	-	3	3
Totals	1	6	2	1	41	51

3. Hospital Mate William Lee completed a return at York on 4 June 1813, revealing this data about wounded or sick men. At least 28 of the names match those on Jarvis's list (legibility made identification difficult). The two Glengarries were not among those in Captain Daniel McPherson's company:[9]

	WIA	Sick	Total
RA	1	-	1
8th Foot	21	3	24
RNFR	9	-	9
49th Foot	1	-	1
Glengarry	2	-	2
41st Foot	-	2	2
Militia	1	2	3
Totals	35	7	42

Casualty Lists

Officers prepared several lists of the casualties. Regimental records also noted casualties.

1. Captain John Glegg, 49th Foot, signed an undated report giving casualties for the 8th Foot alone as:

	KIA	MIA	WIA	POW	Total[10]
8th Foot	59	9	36	-	104

2. Captain Richard Leonard, 104th Foot, prepared lists of individuals and summaries, dated 10 May 1813, revealing this data:

	KIA	MIA	WIA	WIA/POW	POW	Total[11]
RA	3	1	-	1	4	9
49th Foot	-	-	-	3	2	5
RNFR	12	2	7	13	2	36
Glengarry	2	3	4	-	-	9
8th Foot	45	1	23	26	2	97
Totals	62	7	34	43	10	156

3. Regimental records reveal this summary of casualties.[12] The strengths are based upon data shown in Appendix 4, British Order of Battle at York, 27 April 1813. Casualty rates shown here are for KIA and WIA only.

	KIA	MIA	WIA	WIAd	WIA/POW	POW	Total	Strength	K+WIA Rate
RA	3	3	-	-	1	2	9	16	25%
41st Foot	-	-	-	-	-	-	0	4	0%
49th Foot	-	-	-	-	3	2	5	24	12.5%
RNFR	14	-	5	1	13	2	35	104	31.7%
Glengarry	-	2	4	1	1	4	12	62	9.6%
8th Foot	54	-	19	1	29	2	105	203	50.7%
Totals	71	5	28	3	47	12	166	413	36%

AMERICAN CASUALTIES

It is estimated that 57 Americans were killed and 264 wounded in the action. According to the official report of military casualties, and other sources, 53 soldiers were among the dead and 255 were wounded, while the navy suffered at least 4 dead and 9 wounded.

U.S. Army and Federal Volunteers

In his first despatch to the Secretary of War Armstrong on 28 April 1813, Major General Dearborn reported about 50 men killed and wounded during the landing and a number of casualties from the explosion of the grand magazine which "must I fear exceed one hundred."[13] Others in the American force gave estimates that varied between 240 and 400 casualties. Sheaffe did not speculate on the American losses, while William Powell, was one of the few British who offered his view, suggested that the explosion of the magazine caused 200 casualties.

Brigade Major Charles Hunter prepared a tally of the casualties suffered, breaking it into two categories: killed or wounded by ball; killed or wounded by the grand magazine explosion. Only two regiments, the Fifteenth Infantry and the Rifles suffered gunshot wounds. The distribution of the casualties across the regiments indicates how involved they were in the action at the landing, as opposed to how close they were to the magazine when it blew up. Hunter used "Subaltern" to refer to lieutenants and ensigns. The report (depicted below) was enclosed with Dearborn's despatch to Armstrong on 3 May 1813, although Colonel Pearce stated that Hunter presented the return to him while he was still in command on 27 or 28 April.[14] Whether the return Dearborn submitted was the original form or an updated one, including men who had died of their wounds by 3 May, is unknown.

No other official reports appear to have been prepared at the time and extant regimental records provide very little data pertaining to casualties. "Eaton's Compilation", a later report is shown here for comparison. The names of the casualties (including those known to have died of their wounds) are identified in Appendix 6, American Order of Battle at York, 27 April 1813.

Hunter's Report

Total Casualties

	KIA	WIA	Total
By gunshot	14	31	45
By explosion	39	224	263
Totals	53	255	308

Casualties by gunshot

		Mj	Cp	Sub	Sg	Cr	Mu	Pr	Total KIA	Total WIA
Fifteenth	KIA	-	-	1	1	1	-	3	6	
	WIA	-	1	1	1	1	-	4		8
Rifles	KIA	-	-	-	1	-	2	5	8	
	WIA	-	1	-	2	3	-	17		23

Totals 14 KIA + 31 WIA = 45

Casualties by explosion

		Lt Col	Mj	Cp	Sub	Sg	Cr	Mu	Pr	Total KIA	Total WIA
General Staff	KIA									1 (Pike)	
	WIA	3									3
Sixth	KIA	-	-	-	-	1	2	-	10	13	
	WIA	-	-	4	2	5	5	-	88		104
Fourteenth	KIA	-	-	-	-	1	-	-	-	1	
	WIA	-	-	-	-	-	-	1	3		4
Fifteenth	KIA	-	-	-	-	1	2	-	6	9	
	WIA	-	-	-	-	1	-	-	24		25
Sixteenth	KIA	-	-	1	-	-	-	-	4	5	
	WIA	1*	-	-	1	2	2	-	27		33
Twenty-first	KIA	-	-	-	-	1	-	-	-	1	
	WIA	1*	-	-	-	1	1	-	11		14
Rifles	KIA	-	-	-	-	-	-	-	1	1	
	WIA	-	-	-	-	-	-	-	1		1
Light Artillery	KIA	-	-	-	-	-	-	-	3	3	
	WIA	-	-	1	1	-	-	-	16		18
Third Artillery	KIA	-	-	-	-	-	-	-	3	3	
	WIA	-	-	-	1	2	-	-	13		16
Volunteers	KIA	-	-	-	-	-	-	-	2	2	
	WIA	-	-	1	2†	-	1	-	2		6

Totals 39 KIA + 224 WIA = 263

* Lieutenant Colonels Pearce and Ripley reported being wounded but they did not appear on Hunter's report.[15]

† This number includes the "friendly fire" wound (by bayonet) received by Lieutenant Irvine of the Baltimore Volunteers as his company landed, which Hunter did not include in his report.

Eaton's Compilation

Lieutenant Colonel Joseph Horace Eaton assembled this data, part of a compilation of casualties in actions between 1790 and 1848, in 1850-51. It includes naval casualties.[16]

	KIA	WIA	Total
General Staff	0	4	4
Sixth	13	103	116
Fifteenth	12	28	40
Sixteenth	5	36	41
Twenty-first	2	9	11
Artillery	3	16	19
Riflemen	9	18	27
Volunteers	2	5	7
Navy personnel	6	9	15
Totals	**52**	**228**	**280**

U.S. Navy

An official report on the casualties suffered by the U.S. Navy at York has yet to come to light, but the best evidence suggests that it was at least 4 killed and 9 wounded. Commodore Chauncey reported to Secretary Jones on 28 April "the death[s] of Midshipmen Thompson and Hatfield – the exact number I do not know as the returns from the different vessels have not been received."[17] Various newspaper published tallies. Muster and pay lists for the vessels also yielded pertinent data. As shown above, "Eaton's Compilation" listed 6 dead, 9 wounded.

Newspaper Accounts[18]

	KIA	WIA	Total
American Daily Advertiser	6	9	15
Centinel of Freedom	5	8	13
The Weekly Register	3	11	14

Squadron Muster and Pay Lists[19]

The lists of the various vessels provide the information shown here. Individuals were identified as killed or wounded at York or on 27 April. A number of men marked as "discharged, dead" (DD) early in May probably included individuals wounded at York. Names of all of these individuals are shown in Appendix 7, United States Navy Squadron, April 1813.

KIA	WIAd	WIA	DD, 7-12 May
4	1	8	5

The Terms of Capitulation

The Terms of Agreement for the Capitulation of the British forces at York, as settled and signed on 28 April 1813, were widely published in newspapers following the battle and have been a chief source of information about the force that defended the town ever since. Copies of the originals are held in the various archival records as well.[1]

It seems, however, that the original set of terms, as quickly negotiated at George Crookshank's house during the afternoon of 27 April 1813, have received no notice at all. The original agreement and two copies were prepared and one of these is held in the Special Collections of the Baldwin Room at the Toronto Reference Library.[2] Transcripts of this original set of terms and the 28 April version are presented below.

Although their wording is very much the same, the revisions made to the first document offer insight into the tension that developed between the officers of the U.S. Army and Navy over which service was foremost in capturing York. The navy gave in to the military argument even though the pugnacious Lieutenant Jesse Elliott represented the service afloat. Also obvious is Henry Dearborn's determination to claim responsibility for the victory at the expense of Cromwell Pearce, who tried to seize the laurels dropped by Zebulon Pike. It seems most likely that debate over these matters is what held up the negotiation process, which was not resolved until the early afternoon of 28 April.

The capitulation document that was agreed upon presents several problems regarding the list of paroled prisoners of war. It included only a small number of the regulars who fell into American hands. British regimental and casualty records identified wounded and unwounded prisoners (as shown in Appendices 4 and 5) but their names also appear on a return prepared on 1 May, as the Americans were withdrawing their force from the town. A transcript of this document is given below as an indication of a glaring omission in the ratified terms.

Dearborn and Chauncey appear to have agreed to the terms on 28 April, but as Lieutenant Ely Playter, 3rd York, noted in his diary, he and his friend Ensign Andrew Mercer did not sign the parole list until Friday 30 April.[3] Presumably, others did the same. It seems most likely that the lists were developed after the terms were signed, but were never fully completed, as the return of British regular POWs below shows. This notion is confirmed by a note that appears on the cover sheet of one of the copies of the terms held by the Library and Archives of Canada. The note, part of the second transcription below, suggests that the number of militia POWs was based on figures in the monthly garrison muster book for 24 April rather than a "head-count." It supports the idea that men not stationed at the garrison answered the alarm call and that by the time that Sheaffe began his retreat, most of the militia had left the scene.

At the very least, these three documents reveal the confusion that prevailed after the battle at York and the pitfalls of basing any historical account on one document, no matter who signed it or how often it has been published.

First Capitulation Agreement, 27 April 1813[4]
The document held by the Toronto Reference Library reads as follows:

> Terms of Capitulation entered into on the 27th April One Thousand eight hundred and thirteen for the Surrender of the Town of York in Upper Canada to the ~~navy~~ army and ~~army~~ navy of the United States under the Command of [*insertion*] > Majr Genl Dearborn and < Commodore Chauncey of ~~the Navy and of Colonel Pierce~~ of the Army."
>
> 1st. That the Troops Regular and Militia at this Post, and that the Seamen of his Britanic Majesty at this post, be surrendered prisoners of War The Troops Regular and Militia to ground their arms immediately on Parade – and with the seamen ~~this evening~~ [*insertion*] > confined [?] immediately.<
>
> That all public stores ordnance and ordnance stores be surrendered immediately to the commanding officer ~~of the Navy and~~ of the Army [*insertion*] > and Navy < of the United States
>
> that all private property be considered sacred and Guarenteed by the commanding Officers of the Army and Navy of the United States to the citizens of the Town of York – That the papers belonging to any of the Civil public officers be considered in the same light as private property.
>
> That such Surgeons as maybe procured to attend the sick ~~prisoners~~ and wounded may not be considered prisoners of war –
>
> The above terms subject to the Ratification or refusal of the Commanding officers of the Army and Navy
>
> > [Signed by]
> > G. O. Mitchell, Lt. Col. 3d Artillery USA
> > Wm. King, Majr 15th Infy
> > W. Chewett, Lt. Col. Commg 3rd Regt York Militia
> > W. Allan, Majr, 3rd Regt York Militia

Second Capitulation Agreement, 28 April 1813[5]
The ratification document that was widely published reads as follows:

> Terms of Capitulation, entered into on the 27th April One Thousand eight hundred and thirteen for the Surrender of the Town of York in Upper Canada to the army and navy of the United States under the command of Major General Dearborn and Commodore Chauncey.
>
> That the Troops Regular and Militia at this Post and Naval Officers and Seamen shall be surrendered Prisoners of War; the Troops Regular and Militia to ground their arms immediately on parade, and the Naval officers and Seamn be immediately surrendered.

That all Public Stores Naval and Militia shall be immediately given up to the commanding officers of the Army and Navy of the United States.

That all Private Property shal be Guarranteed to the Citizens of the Town of York.

That the papers belonging to the Civil officers shall be retained by them; that such Surgeons as may be procured to attend the wounded of the British Regular and Canadian Militia shall not be considered prisoners of war.

That one Lieut. Col., one Major, Thirteen Captains, nine Lieutenants, Eleven Ensigns, one Quarter Master and one Deputy Adjutant General of the Militia, Namely,

1 Lt. Col. Chewett	Lieutenants	Ensigns
1 Major W. Allan		
1 Captain John Willson	1 John Shultz	1 Andrew Thomson
2 John Button	2 George Mustard	2 Ared Smalley
3 Peter Robinson	3 Barnet Vandenburgh	3 Donald McArthur
4 John Arnold	4 Robert Stanton	4 William Smith
5 Jas Fenwick	5 George Ridout	5 Andrew Mercer
6 Jas Mustard	6 William Jarvis	6 James Chewett
7 Duncan Cameron	7 Edward McMahon	7 George Kuck
8 David Thomson	8 John Willson	8 Edward Thompson
9 John Robinson	9 Ely Playter	9 Charles Denison
10 Samuel Ridout		10 George Denison
11 Thomas Hamilton		11 Darcy Boulton
12 John Burn		Quarter Master Charles
13 Wm. Jarvie		Baynes

Nineteen Serjeants four corporals, two hundred and four rank and file
of the field train Department   1 William Dunbar
of the Provincial Navy   1 Lieut Francis Gauvreau
                                2 Lieutenant — Green
                                1 Midshipman John Ridout
                                2 — Louis Beaupré
                                Clerk Jas Longsden
one Boatswain, fifteen naval artificers.
of His Majesty's Regular Troops 1 Lt De Koven one Serjeant Major, and of the Royal Artillery one Bombardier and three Gunners
Shall be surrendered Prisoners of War and accounted for in the Exchange of Prisoners Between the United States and Great Britain.

[Signed}
G. E. Mitchell Lt. Col. 3r Artillery U.S.A.
Sam S. Conner Maj ADC to Majr Genl Dearborn
Willm King, Major 14 US Infy
Jesse D Elliott, Lt. US Navy

[Signed}
Wm Chewett Lt Col, 3d Regt York Militia
Wm Allan Major 3d Regt York Militia
F. Gauvreau Lt M Dept

York, 28 April 1813.
The foregoing agreement or Terms of Capitulation is approved by us

H Dearborn Maj General
Isaac Chauncey Commodore

Explanatory Remark on the List of Prisoners [written on covering page of at least one copy]

A great number of the Officers in the list were not on duty in the Garrison of York. Many of them arrived from their places of abode at various distances but [?] in time to be included in the Capitulation. The number of Non Commissioned Officers and Privates to be considered as prisoners was by agreement between the contracting parties decided by the muster roll of the previous 24th – the Number in which far exceeded that of the militia actually in arms when the regular forces retreated.

Regulars as Prisoners of War on Parole at York, 1 May 1813[6]

The following document shows the number of regulars who were prisoners of war at York after the battle. A second list of casualties at York on 4 June mentioned many of the same men.[7] This list shows fifty individuals, many more than the six referred to in the terms of capitulation. The document presents numerous problems for the researcher: the original tally chart conflicted with the actual numbers on the list; spelling varied from regimental and other records; two men listed here – Charles Pearson and Patrick Logan – do not appear on other regimental or casualty lists; at least five men listed elsewhere as WIA/POW are not included; and Richard Totten was shown as a corporal elsewhere. Alterations have been made in this transcript to make spellings and names consistent with those in other appendices and to correct tally errors.

Return of the Prisoners belonging to His Majesty's regular Forces on Parole to the United States Army at York 1st May 1813, signed by S. Jarvis, Assistant Adjutant General Militia

Regiments	Prisoners Wounded			Prisoners Not Wounded			Total		
	Sg*	Dr	RF	Sg	Dr	RF	Sg	Dr	RF
Royal Artillery	–	–	1	1B		4G	1		5
8th Regiment	2	–	25	–	–	1	2	–	26
49th Regiment	–	–	3	–	–	–	–	–	3
Royal Nfld. Regt.	3	–	8	–	–	2	3	–	10
Totals	5	–	36	1	–	7	6	–	44

*Sg, Dr, RF, B, G – sergeant, drummer, rank and file (corporals and privates), bombardier, gunner

Sergeant George Herne 8th Regt		5th Company	
	wounded	Felix Donnelly	not WIA
" Richard Totten	WIA	7th Company	
Corpl David Barry	WIA	John Wale	Sick
Privates Grenadiers			
Stephen Adams	WIA	Priv Thomas Boyce, 49th Regt	WIA
Squire Ackroyde	WIAd	John McCann	WIA
Henry Brainwhite	WIA	Thomas Reid	WIA
Thomas Day	WIA		
George Dixon	WIA	Sergeant John Chesney RNFL	WIA
Thomas Downes	WIA	" William Campion	WIA
Joseph Ellis	WIA	Drum major Sg Thomas Kelly	WIA
Samuel Henshaw	WIA	Private William Gardner (2)	
Robert Ireland	WIA		blind, not WIA
James Martin	WIA	Richard Beck	WIA
William Martin	WIA	Thomas Casey	WIA
Reuben Miller	WIA	Thomas Clarke 1st	WIA
Michael Murphy	WIA	Cornelius Fieley	WIA
Charles Pearson	WIA	Christopher Hughes	not WIA
Thomas Pope	WIA	Joseph Lannigan	WIA
Daniel Scary	WIA	Allan McDonald	WIA
Thomas Walker	WIA	William Maher	WIA
Joseph Wheelton	WIA	John Sparrow	WIA
6th Company		Royal Artillery	
Joseph Dayg	WIA	Bomd William Needham	not WIA
Thomas Singleton	WIA	Gunner John Bynon	not WIA
Henry Orford	WIA	John Henny	not WIA
Thomas Taylor	WIA	Patrick Hogan	WIA since dead
3rd Company		Thomas Hobroyd	not WIA
Corp. Charles Ogden	not WIA	James Lang	not WIA

Glossary

18-pounder: a piece of **artillery**, capable of firing a projectile rated as weighing 18 pounds; 6-pdrs., 9-pdrs., 12-pdrs, etc. fired shot and shell as per their calibre rating

adjutant: an administrative assistant to a commanding officer, distributing orders, writing reports., etc.

artillery: the **guns** of the military forces; also, that branch of the armed forces

baronet: a hereditary, British honour, above that of knight and below that of baron

bastion: a **gun** position, open to the inside of a **fortification**, extending from the perimeter and formed of four faces with **embrasures** allowing fire towards the field and enfilading the ditch along the perimeter

battalion: a complete second or third (or more) roster of a regiment, such as the 1st and 2nd battalions of the 8th Regiment of Foot; also used interchangeably with **regiment**, or a **unit**

battery: a position where a **gun** is mounted, such as a **redoubt**; also a **company** of **artillery**

bayonet: a three-edged piercing weapon, attached at the muzzle of a **musket** for hand-to-hand combat

bear up: steer a vessel toward the wind

beat to quarters: drummers aboard naval vessels "beat to quarters" to order the men to take their places in preparation for an engagement

blockhouse: a fortified structure, often two storeys tall, built to hold stores, act as a barracks and, during combat, serve as a defensive position

bomb: a **shell**

bombardier: a non commissioned officer in the **artillery**, roughly equivalent to a corporal in the **infantry**

boom: a large spar to which the bottom edge of one of the **fore and aft** sails might be attached

bower: an anchor

breastwork: a defensive barricade

breech: the aft end of a **gun**

breeching: the strong rope used to secure a **gun**

brig: a two-masted, **square-rigged** vessel

brigade: several **regiments**, or parts thereof, combined under one commanding officer

brigadier general: a general commanding a **brigade**

broadside: all the **guns** mounted on one side of a warship; also, the firing of them in unison or individually

buckshot: small lead pellets about one-tenth the size of a musket ball

bulwarks: the heavily planked sides of a naval vessel that rose above the level of the upper deck

canister: a projectile consisting of a tin can filled with small lead balls; also know as **case shot**

cannon: a term loosely referring to **long guns**

capstan: an upright, cylindrical, rotating device, to which capstan bars are attached so that seamen may turn the capstan to pull lines used for moving cables or **hawser** or other heavy objects

captain: the commanding officer of a military **company** or of a naval vessel

carriage: **guns** are mounted on carriages of different types such as **garrison carriages** and **field carriages**

carronade: a piece of **artillery**, its calibre being determined by the weight of shot it fired, lighter in construction than **long guns**, requiring smaller gun crews and smaller charges, though limited to a preferred range of only 500 yards

cartridge: the container of powder used in a **gun** or in one of the **small arms**

cascabel: the knob or "button" at the extreme end of the **breech** of a gun

case shot: see **canister**

cavalry: the mounted wing of the army

chain: a type of **shot**, consisting of two iron hemispheres (or the like) connected by a length of heavy chain

circle: essentially the same as a **traverse**

colonel: the commanding officer of a **regiment**

colours: the national standard and regimental flag issued to a **regiment**

column: the travelling formation for an armed force, consisting of the long **files** of foot soldiers, horsemen, **artillery** and baggage

commander: a **commissioned** Royal Navy rank for an officer one step below **captain**

commissariat: a department for the supply of provisions

commission: a certificate assigning an individual to serve in a specific position

commodore: the commanding officer of a naval **squadron**

company: a sub-unit of a **regiment**, generally comprising about 100 men

corporal: a member of the **rank and file**, one step above **private** and below **sergeant**

curtain: a wall in a fortification, sometimes joining one bastion to another

dirk: a short sword commonly worn by midshipmen

division: a military force, comprising two or more **brigades** or parts thereof

draft: the depth of water a vessel needs; also, in the **militia**, the drawing of names for required service

dragoon: a member of the mounted wing of an army

embrasure: the opening through which a gun in a battery fires

en barbette: **guns** mounted *en barbette* are mounted on platforms that allow them to fire over the **rampart** without the need of an **embrasure**

enfilade: to fire into an unprotected flank of an enemy position

engineer: a military officer in charge of building **fortifications** and other structures, as well as helping to lay sieges

ensign: the most junior of the **commissioned** military officers

exchanged: prisoners of war were sometimes repatriated in exchange for enemy prisoners of equal rank, or as part of a group of prisoners in return for an enemy prisoner of higher rank, after which the individuals involved could once more take up arms

expedition: an **operation** during a **campaign**, usually involving transport by water, quickness and surprise

fascine: a woven basket-like object, filled with earth, branches or litter, used in the hurried construction of batteries, etc. or carried into battle and used to fill ditches so they may be crossed more easily

fencibles: regular troops raised locally for local service only

field carriage: lighter in construction than a **garrison carriage**, this is equipped with large wheels so that it may be easily transported into the field

field gun: a light weight **gun** used on the battlefield

file: a line of men standing one behind the other

firelock: the same as a **flintlock**; also, a term often used synonymously with **musket**

flintlock: the hammer-like vice that held the flint of a **small arm**

fore-and-aft rigged: carrying sails set along the mid-line of the vessel

fortification: any of numerous structures erected for defense of a position or town

frizzen: the lid covering the **pan** of a **small arm**, which was forced open by the activation of the **flintlock** and against which the flint struck, creating sparks that fell into the pan, igniting the priming

frock: a knee length coat, square at the hem without tails, with flaps covering the shoulders, commonly worn by riflemen and fringed along all its edges

furnace: an oven used to heat **shot**

gaff: a large spar to which the top edge of one of the **fore and aft** sails might be attached

garrison: the force housed in a **fortification** for the purpose of defending it and the environs

garrison carriage: a strongly built **carriage** for mounting large guns, usually mounted on **trucks**

garrison gun: any gun mounted on a **garrison carriage** for use in a **fortification**

grape shot: a projectile comprising nine small iron **shot**, positioned around a centre spindle (mounted on a wooden base) and enclosed in quilted canvas that burst apart upon firing

grenadier: a member of the number one **company** of an **infantry regiment**, positioned on the right of the formation and usually manned by the strongest and most skillful individuals

gun: any of the different types of smooth bore **artillery**, including **long guns**, **field guns**, **carronades**, **howitzers** and **mortars**

gunboat: a small armed vessel, either decked or not, of various rigs, built to carry one or more guns or converted for service from a merchantman

gunner: a member of an artillery company, equal in rank to a private; also, a naval warrant officer in charge of the guns and their equipment and their supply of ammunition

halliard: a rope or tackle used to raise or lower a sail, a spar or a flag

hawser: a large rope, smaller than a cable, measuring about five inches in circumference

heave the lead: to cast a lead-line to determine the depth of water

howitzer: a short-barreled **gun**, usually mounted for field use, that could throw **shots** with a loftier trajectory than a **long gun** or **carronade**

infantry: the foot soldiers of the army

keel: the "backbone" of a vessel, formed from several heavy, shaped timbers, to which the frames are fastened

keelson: formed from several heavy, shaped timbers, the keelson lies atop the lower ends of the frames and is fastened through them to the **keel**

lieutenant: a **commissioned** rank, one step below **captain**

lieutenant colonel: a commissioned rank, one step below **colonel**

lieutenant general: a senior officer, commanding military **divisions**

larboard: the left side

larboard tack: on a course with the wind coming from the direction of the **larboard** side of the vessel

lead: a seven to fourteen pound lead weight, fastened to a "lead-line", cast ahead of a moving vessel to determine the depth of water as per "the mark" on the lead-line

lead-line: see **lead**

leeward: down wind

light infantry: that part of the military force involved in independent movements to feel out an enemy's strength and to cover the main body and its flanks during an attack or retreat

long gun: a piece of **artillery** with a long, smooth-bore barrel, its calibre determined by the weight of shot it fired, which was extremely heavy and required a large gun crew, though effective at longer ranges than **carronades**

loop-hole: a narrow opening cut into a **palisade** or **blockhouse** wall to allow a soldier to fire his **musket** at an enemy

magazine: a structure erected for the storage of ammunition

magistrate: a justice of the peace and primary level civil authority

major: a **commissioned** rank, one step below **lieutenant colonel**

major general: a **commissioned** rank for an officer commanding a **division**

master and commander: a **commissioned** naval commander in the Provincial Marine; also an old Royal Navy rank, replaced by **commander**

master commandant: a **commissioned** rank in the USN equivalent to a **commander** in the RN and a **master and**

commander in the PM

midshipman: a **non-commissioned** entry level rank for officers in the RN and PM; also, the same in the USN, except the young men received warrants

militia: the "citizen soldiers," male residents of a state or province expected to bear arms in time of insurrection and war

mortar: a short-barreled gun, mounted on a block at an angle allowing it to loft **shells** at the enemy

musket: a smooth-bore **small arm**, the most widely used weapon of the period

muzzle: the open end of a **gun** or **small arm**

non-commissioned officer: an officer without a **commission**, such as a **sergeant** in the military and a **midshipman** in the RN

operation: one of the various parts of a **campaign**, including **expeditions**, landings, attacks, advances, retreats, etc.

ordnance: generally referring to all **artillery** equipment as well as that of the **engineers**

palisade: a wooden wall on the perimeter of a **fortification**, consisting of stout, upright stakes, firmly anchored in the ground

pan: a fixture on a **small arm**, located next to the **vent** and covered by the **frizzen**, into which powder is poured as priming

parapet: a mound of earth in a **fortification**, raised for protection against enemy fire

parole: a promise made by a prisoner of war, usually a **commissioned** officer, not to exceed the limits of free movement put on him during captivity, or, if returned to his homeland, not to take up arms again until formally **exchanged**

picket: a **sentinel** on horseback

pike: a edged piercing weapon, comprising a long wooden pole and an iron blade measuring up to thirteen inches in length

platoon: a portion of a **company**

port: same as **larboard**

private: the lowest ranked soldier in an army, and most numerous member of the **rank and file**

prize: a captured vessel

puisne justice: the judge second in seniority to the chief justice

quarter master: an administrative officer in the military, with such duties as organizing a line of march and its encampments, accommodations, etc.

rampart: a mound of earth raised to cover the interior of a defensive position

ramrod: the pole used to push the **cartridge** and **shot** to the base of the barrel of a **gun** or **small arm**

rank: a line of men standing shoulder to shoulder

rank and file: the **privates** and **corporals** of a **regiment**

red ensign: a plain red flag with a Union Jack in the upper corner at the staff

regiment: a separate military body, ideally comprising ten **companies** and commanded by a **colonel**; also known as a **unit** or **battalion**

regulars: members of a national army

rifle: a **small arm** closely resembling a **musket**, but with a series of fine, spiraling grooves scored into the interior of its barrel to improve its accuracy

running rigging: the rigging used to adjust sails in a vessel

schooner: a two-masted, **fore-and-aft-rigged** vessel; some had **square** sails on their upper masts

sedentary militia: the part of the **militia** that waits to be called to service

sentinel: a guard

sergeant: a **non-commissioned** military officer with command over a portion of a **company**

shell: a hollow, iron projectile containing powder, and sometimes iron bits or balls, and fitted with a fuse that ignited upon firing from a gun and was trimmed to explode above or among the enemy; also referred to as a **bomb**

ship: a three-masted, **square-rigged** vessel

shipwrights: labourers skilled in the construction of vessels

shot: a projectile fired from a **gun**

skirmisher: a soldier specializing in **light**

infantry tactics

sloop: a one masted, **fore-and-aft-rigged** vessel

small arms: muskets, pistols, etc.

spherical case: a hollow spherical projectile, containing powder and small shot and fitted with a fuse so that it explodes like a **shell**, used only by the British

spring: a **hawser** fastened to an anchor cable, hauled to the other end of a vessel and pulled to turn the vessel

squadron: a force comprising a number of warships, smaller than a fleet and commanded by a senior **captain** or **commodore**; also, in the army a **company** of **dragoons**

square-rigged: carrying "square" sails, set across the mid-line of the vessel; all square-rigged vessels carried **fore-and-aft** sails, which were essential for manoeuvring

standing rigging: the rigging that secures the masts and spars of a vessel, such as the shrouds, braces and stays

starboard: the right side

starboard tack: on a course with the wind coming from the direction of the **starboard** side of the vessel

stem: the main timber forming the bow of the vessel

stern: the aft end of a vessel

stockade: a wooden wall, similar to a **palisade**

strakes: the runs of planking in a vessel's hull

strategy: the overall objectives for a **campaign** or an entire war

tack: changing a vessel's course so that the bow passes through the eye of the wind, allowing it to fill the sails on the other side

tactics: the methods by which an **operation** or engagement is conducted

traverse: in **artillery** terms, to move a gun laterally; also a **gun carriage** that allows the weapon to be swivelled laterally, widening its field of fire

truck: a small, but heavy iron wheel used on a **garrison carriage**; also, in a sailing vessel the circular cap on the top of a mast

trunnions: the iron lugs on each side of a **gun** by which it is fastened to its carriage and which permit it to be elevated (i.e., pointed higher or lower)

wear: changing a vessel's course so that the **stern** passes through the eye of the wind, allowing it fill the sails on the other side

wind gauge: a position at sea which is windward of an opponent, making it possible to sail "down" to meet him while he must flee before the wind or sail "up" into the wind to make contact

windward: upwind

vanguard: the foremost part of a military **column** or naval squadron

vent: the small hole drill into the base of **guns** and **small arms** by which the ignition of the fuse or of the powder in the **pan** is transmitted to the **cartridge** inside the base of the barrel

---

Weights and Measures

1 inch = 2.54 cm

1 foot = 0.305 m

1 yard = 0.915 m

1 mile = 1.6 km

1 pound = 0.45 kg

Metric equivalents for shot-weights:

6-pdr. = 2.7 kg

9-pdr. = 4.05 kg

12-pdr. = 5.4 kg

18-pdr. = 8.1 kg

24-pdr. = 10.8 kg

32-pdr. = 14.4 kg

Endnotes

Abbreviations

ADM Admiralty
ANB *American National Biography*
ASP:MA American State Papers: Military Affairs
ASP:NA American State Papers: Naval Affairs
CLB Chauncey Letter Books
CO Colonial Office
DCB *Dictionary of Canadian Biography*
DHC *The Documentary History of the Campaign upon the Niagara Frontier 1812-1814.* E.A. Cruikshank
DNB *Dictionary of National Biography*
EW *Encyclopedia of the War of 1812.* David S. and Jeanne T. Heidler
HDW *Historical Dictionary of the War of 1812.* Robert Malcolmson
HMG *His Majesty's Gentlemen: A Directory of Regular British Army Officers of the War of 1812.* Stuart Sutherland.
HRD *Historical Register and Dictionary of the United States Army from its Organization, September 29, 1789 to March 2, 1903.* Francis Heitman
LAC Library and Archives of Canada
LOC Library of Congress, Washington, D.C.
MG Manuscript Group
MS Microfilm Series
MU Manuscript
NAUK National Archives of the United Kingdom (Public Record Office, Kew)
NJHS New Jersey Historical Society
NWDH *The Naval War of 1812: A Documentary History.* William S. Dudley
NYSA New York State Archives
NYSL New York State Library
RG Record Group
SROLO *Service Records of U.S. Navy and Marine Corps Officers Stationed on Lake Ontario During the War of 1812.* Gary M. Gibson
TRL Toronto Reference Library
USNA United States National Archives and Record Administration
WCL William Clements Library, University of Michigan
WO War Office

Chapter 1: "Reared as if by enchantment." York, Upper Canada, 1812

1. Heriot, *Travels Through the Canadas*, 139.
2. Popular notions developed in the 1800s that "Toronto" was a Huron word meaning "meeting place" (Canniff, "An Historical Sketch of the County of York ...," v; Scadding, *Toronto: Past and Present*, 4-5) or "abundance" (*ibid.*), etc., and are still repeated in modern times (Kilbourn, *Toronto Remembered*, 70). These have been debunked by the native language expert John Steckley who proved the correct origin of the word in "Toronto: What Does It Mean?" See also Rayburn, "The real story of how Toronto got its name." A point of interest for War of 1812 students is that Benson Lossing used the "trees on the water" definition for Toronto in his 1868 classic *The Pictorial Field-book of the War of 1812*, 586; Scadding rejected Lossing's claim, *Toronto: Past and Present*, 6. Scadding referred to "The 'trees in the water' theory" as "a late afterthought, an ingenious guess," *History of the Old French Fort at Toronto*, 35. 60 miles = 97 km.

3. For a discussion of the origins of the Mississauga/Ojibwa and their land deals with the British, see: Smith, "The Dispossession of the Mississauga Indians"; Johnson, "The Mississauga-Lake Ontario Land Surrender of 1805"; Hathaway, "The River Credit and the Mississaugas." Also see: Benn, "The History of Toronto," <www.toronto.ca/culture/history>.

4. Simcoe to Clarke, 31 May 1793, Cruikshank, *The Correspondence of Lieut. Governor John Graves Simcoe*, 1: 338. Simcoe mentioned the temporary use of York as the capital to Clarke, 24 July 1793, *ibid.*: 396. For a discussion of the military importance of York, see Benn, "The Military Context of the Founding of Toronto." For a critique of Simcoe's ideas on defence, see, MacLeod, "Fortress Ontario or Forlorn Hope?" Cartwright expressed doubt about the feasibility and expenses in Simcoe's schemes to Todd, 14 October 1793, Cruikshank, *The Correspondence of Lieut. Governor John Graves Simcoe*, 2: 87. Secretary of State for War and the Colonies Henry Dundas agreed that "York is the most important ... as the Chief place of Strength and Security" to Simcoe, 16 March 1794, *ibid.*: 184.

5. Simcoe announced that York would be officially named the next day at noon in General order by Littlehales, 26 August 1793, *ibid.* 2: 46.

6. The layout of the town is based on the early town plans (1797 a, b and c, and 1818), reproduced and described, in Gentilcore and Head, *Ontario's Historical Maps*, 1984, 250-2. Population is based on "A List of Inhabitants in the Town of York March 1812," Mosser, *York, Upper Canada Minutes of Town Meetings*, 84. This record does not appear to be complete, as it omits, for instance, the family of James Chesney, headed by his widow, although the family appears in the 1808 (*ibid.*, 73) and 1813 (*ibid.*, 96). There does not appear to be a precise record of the number of houses in York in 1812, but this number is based on data showing a growth from 105 in 1807 to 110 in 1810 and 148 in 1820, Robertson, *Landmarks of Toronto*, 2: 995-7. The Don River bridges were described in a claim of a number of citizens for their destruction by the British during the war, LAC, RG 19 E 5 (a), vol. 3743, file 2.

7. Heriot, *Travels Through the Canadas*, 139. The "dirty little hole" quote comes from *The Canadian Freeman*, 1 January 1827, cited in Aitchison, "The Development of Local Government in Upper Canada," 580. Distances are based on the scale and details of two charts: Plan of York Harbour and Humber Bay – attributed to T. Chill-

ingsworth, E. W. C. R. Owen, E. E. Vidal and Joseph Bouchette, LAC, NMC 19400; and Plan of York, by Phillpotts, 24 May 1818, *ibid.*, NMC 17026.

8. Critical land distribution and ownership issues are discussed in Johnson, "Land Policy, Population Growth and Social Structure in the Home District, 1793-1851." The districts are described in Spragge, "The Districts of Upper Canada, 1788-1849." Population of the township in 1812 is recorded in Mosser, *York, Upper Canada Minutes of Town Meetings*, 89. The total population of the Home District is based upon the approximately 5,000 people living in the other townships in 1809, as shown in a census taken that year in Ridout, *Ten Years of Upper Canada*, 25.

9. Asa Danforth was contracted in 1799 to build the road east to the Bay of Quinte as noted in Russell to Portland, 19 June 1799, Firth, *The Town of York, 1793-1815*, 146. The spans of Dundas and Yonge streets are mentioned in the General Statement of Public Property ... by Russell, 2 July 1800, *ibid.*, 50. "Yorkville" being the southern terminus of Yonge Street is mentioned in Hathaway, *Jesse Ketchum and His Times*, 49.

10. Descriptions of the wildlife and vegetation are found in Firth, *Town of York*; Russell described the woods east of the Humber to Gray, 16 September 1793, 17; Elizabeth Simcoe refers to the various trees, flocks of fowl, redwing blackbirds, pigeons and clouds of mosquitoes in the excerpts from her diary in 213-23; Lord Selkirk's notes on York included comments about walnut, cherry and maple, 20 September 1803, 252; J. Willcocks described a wolf attack and the response, as well as the plentiful deer and fowl to Richard Willcocks, 3 November 1800, 236; vegetable and grains seeds and fruit trees were advertised in the 7 March 1801 and 20 February 1808 issues of the *Upper Canada Gazette*, 115 and 133. Isaac Wilson mentioned the fellow who caught 300 fish, among other relevant details, to Jonathan Wilson, 24 May 1812, AO, MS 199(5), Isaac Wilson Diaries.

11. The following note, "An ox attempting to wade through King Street, opposite the Church, sunk as if by magic, and must have perished in the mire unless for the exertions of six men, who rescued him from his perilous situation," appeared in the 2 May 1823 issue of the *Niagara Gleaner*, taken from the *York Observer*. Data regarding the number and types of houses from 1803-1809 (and extrapolated for use here) is in Robertson, *Landmarks of Toronto*, 1: 994-5. This description of the homes and other buildings based on: *ibid.*, 1: 1-5, 10-15, 88-93, 304-6; 3: 92-97; 5: 46-7, 290-3; Hounsom, *Toronto in 1810*, 52-68, 113; Martyn, *The Face of Early Toronto*. The report of more than 40,000 bricks fabricated for public and private use is mentioned in the General Statement of Public Property ... by Russell, 2 July 1800, Firth, *Town of York*, 50. Fence height is mentioned in the record of the 1810 town meeting, in Mosser, *York, Upper Canada, Minutes of Town Meetings*, 81. In 1807, 08 and 09 there were 60, 58 and 58 stills on record in the town, cited in Robertson, *Landmarks of Toronto*, 2: 995. The number of tavern licenses is noted on 28 December 1811 in "Minutes of the Court of General Quarter Sessions of the Peace for the Home District, 1800-1811," *Twenty-First Report of the Department of Public Records and Archives of Ontario*, 204. The church was not usually referred to as St. James until 1827, Benn, "A Georgian Parish, 1797-1839." For a note on the private library, see Firth, *Town of York*, 322n and for John Cameron the King's Printer of the *York Gazette*, *ibid.*, 133n. For Allan's career, see *DCB*, 8: 4 and Magill, "William Allan and

the War of 1812." The date of the building of his wharf is given as 1801 in Robertson, *Landmarks of Toronto*, 1: 251-2 and 3: 96, and 1803 in Hounsom, *Toronto in 1810*, 11. Cooper's is mentioned in Robertson, *Landmarks of Toronto*, 1: 245. Hounsom suggests that "Cooper's wharf" the second commercial dock was built in 1815. The location and size of the wharves is taken from the Plan of York, by Phillpotts, 24 May 1818, NMC 17026.

12. The suggested location for the naval dockyard is shown in the Plan of Toronto Harbour ... by Bouchette, probably 1792, LAC, NMC 145919. The "Merchant's Ship Yard" is shown on the Sketch of the ground in advance of and including York ...," by Williams, 7 November 1813, LAC, NMC 22820. The need for the vessel that became the *Toronto* was mentioned in Minutes of Executive Council, 17 January 1797, Firth, *Town of York*, 144. There are mentions of launches of three schooners (14 April 1803, 28 October 1804, June 1812), two of which were difficult, in Ely Playter's diary, AO, F 556. Plans to build the new schooner *Prince Regent* at York in June 1812 and use the reclaimed parts of the *Toronto* were mentioned in Gray to Prevost, 29 January 1812, LAC, RG 8, I, 728: 77. Since no other site was identified as a dockyard, it is assumed that the two vessels were built at the "Merchant's Ship Yard." The ill-fated *Speedy* and most public and private vessels were built at Kingston, O'Brien, *Speedy Justice: The Tragic Loss of His Majesty's Vessel* Speedy, 74-81. See also Malcomson, *Warships of the Great Lakes*, 40-54, 63 and 70.

13. Bruyeres to Prevost, undated, LAC, MG 11, CO 42, 146: 56. This report is grouped with Prevost's correspondence of March 1812 and, referring to Brock and his plans for subsequent defensive measures, was most likely written early in 1812. The lighthouse is described in the 5 August 1809 issue of the *York Gazette*. The first lighthouse at York had been built on top of the blockhouse in the garrison as mentioned by Russell to Simcoe, 9 December 1797, Cruikshank and Hunter, *The Correspondence of the Honourable Peter Russell*, 2: 38. All the blockhouses and other government structures are described in the General Statement of Public Property ... by Russell, 2 July 1800, LAC, RG 8, I, 1332: 99. See also Murphy, "Gibraltar Point Light." For a detailed description of the proposed Gibraltar Point blockhouse and battery, and the storage there of supplies sent from England see: Pilkington to Simcoe, 6 September 1793, Cruikshank, *The Correspondence of Lieut. Governor John Graves Simcoe*, 2: 47; Simcoe to Dundas, 20 September 1793, *ibid.*: 56; Simcoe to Richmond, 23 September 1793. Simcoe described his plans to Clarke, 31 May 1793, *ibid.*, 1: 338.

14. The garrison is described in Report of the State of the Public Works ... by Bruyeres, sent to Mann, 12 September 1802, LAC, RG 8, 383: 6. The appearance of the garrison is well-documented by the drawing "York Barracks, Lake Ontario, Upper Canada," 13 May 1804, by Stretton, LAC, C-014905. See also the General Statement of Public Property ... by Russell, 2 July 1800, Firth, LAC, RG 8, I, 1332: 99. For an explanation of the guns at York, see Appendix 3, British Artillery at York. The unhealthiness of the Town Blockhouse location is noted in Brock to Green, 29 July 1803, LAC, RG 8, I., 922: 91.

15. Prevost reported to Liverpool on 18 May 1812 that York's garrison "consists of three companies of the 41st Regiment," LAC, MG 11, CO 42, 146: 197. This is highly unlikely since the 41st was the only full regiment (its ten companies comprising about 1050 officers and men, General Monthly Returns, September 1812, LAC, MG

13, WO 17, 1515: 283-4) in the province, manning the frontier posts, the most important of which were on the Niagara and Detroit Rivers, not to forget Kingston and the St. Lawrence River posts, with others detached in Lower Canada. The best available returns of the force at York garrison in 1812 are from 12 November (LAC, RG 8, 1707: 60); 25 November (*ibid.*: 73); and 21 December (*ibid.*: 124). The first lists 2 Royal Artillerymen, 33 officers and men of the 41st Foot and 22 of the 49th Foot, 3 of the Royal Newfoundland Fencibles and 2 of the Canadian Fencibles, for a total of 62 officers and men. The second has a similar breakdown for a total of 71 and the third shows 68. The Report on the State of the Magazines, ..., by Glasgow, 18 September 1811, notes: "At York there are two light 6-pounders; neither magazine nor storehouse, one sergeant and one gunner," *ibid.*, 1706: 171.

16. The buildings were located at the modern Front Street end of the block between Beverley and Parliament streets. The most authoritative description of them, resulting from archeological studies, is Dieterman and Williamson, *Government on Fire*. The construction of the legislative buildings and funding limitations were mentioned in Russell to Simcoe, 9 December 1797, Cruikshank and Hunter, *The Correspondence of the Honourable Peter Russell*, 2: 37. The buildings are described in Heriot, *Travels Through the Canadas*, 139 and Dale, *"The Palaces of Government,"* 8-13. The inaccurate portrayal of the buildings as parallel to each other with their ends facing the town and the covered walkway at the rear/east end appeared in Robertson, *Landmarks of Toronto*, 1: 351-3 and is frequently repeated as in Martyn, *The Face of Early Toronto*, 25 and on the book jacket of Hounsom, *Toronto in 1810*. Re: government use of Elmsley House: Sheaffe to Bathurst, 15 May 1813, LAC, MG 11, CO 42, 354: 109. The home was located at the corner of modern King and Simcoe streets. It is described in Robertson, *Landmarks of Toronto*, 1: 304-6. For a note on the private library, see Firth, *Town of York*, 322n.

17. The design of the governor's house is seen in Plan and Elevation of the Lieut. Governor's House at York, Upper Canada, by Pilkington, 1800, LAC, NMC 5428. The lieutenant-governor's residence is seen on the left side of "Toronto or York, The Generals, The Barracks," 31 May 1803 by Stretton, LAC, C014822.

18. The six lieutenant-governors/head administrators were: Simcoe, 1791-96; Peter Russell, 1796-99; Peter Hunter, 1799-1805; Alexander Grant, 1805-06; Francis Gore, 1806-1811; Isaac Brock, 1811-12. Full details of offices and men holding them during this period are found in Armstrong, *Handbook of Upper Canadian Chronology and Territorial Legislation, passim*.

19. For Scott's career, see Riddell, "Thomas Scott: The Second Attorney-General of Upper Canada" and *DCB*, 6: 698. For Powell, see McKenna, *A Life of Propriety* and *DCB*, 6: 605. For the careers of McGill, Selby and Shaw see *DCB*, 5: 749 and 5: 752.

20. For Powell's career, see: McKenna, *A Life of Propriety*; TRL, L 16, Powell Papers; *DCB*, 6: 605. For Anne Murray Powell's biography, see *DCB*, 7: 638. Their home is described in Hounsom, *Toronto in 1810*, 65.

21. This description of the role of the magistrates/justices of the peace is based upon the following: Aitchison, "The Development of Local Government in Upper Canada, 1783-1850"; Wilson, "The Court of General Quarter Sessions of the Peace: Local Administration in Pre-Municipal Upper Canada"; Thompson, "Local Authority and District Autonomy: The Niagara Magistracy and Constabulary, 1828-1841"; Keele, *The Provincial Justice or Magistrate's Manual*; Schedule or Table of Fees and Costs, Payable to the Different Officers of the Quarter Sessions of the Peace; "Minutes of the Court of General Quarter Sessions ... 1800-1811"; *Twenty-First Report of the Department of Public Records*; Murray, *Colonial Justice*, 25-51.

22. For a complete study of influence among the leading citizens of York, see Burns, "The First Elite of Toronto: An Examination of this Genesis, Consolidation and Duration of Power in an Emerging Colonial Society."

23. An informal survey of "Minutes of the Court of General Quarter Sessions ... 1800-1811," *Twenty-First Report of the Department of Public Records*, reveals Allan, Cameron, McLean and Ridout attended numerous public meetings in 1811, while John Small (of York), Richard Beasley, (Flamborough), William Graham (Whitchurch), Richard Hatt (Flamborough), Samuel Smith (Etobicoke) and Archibald Thomson (Scarborough), William Applegarth, James Fulton, Alexander McDonell (their residences not certain) attended much less frequently. Other magistrates appointed since 1800 who did not attend in 1811 were William Baldwin, William Chewett, Alex Chisholm, Elisha Beman, John Erb, Samuel Hatt, William Jarvis, James McCauley, John McGill and Alexander Wood. Biographies in *DCB* pertinent to this study include Baldwin (7: 35), Chewett (7: 174), Ridout (5: 647), Small (6: 21), Wood (7: 919); and see Firth, "Alexander Wood, Merchant of York." Some other biographical data for these men and for Cameron and McLean may be found in the footnotes of Firth, *Town of York, passim* and in the appendix of Johnson, *Becoming Prominent, passim*. For Allan's career, see *DCB*, 8: 14 and Magill, "William Allan and the War of 1812."

24. The matter of attaining prominence is fully developed in Johnson, *Becoming Prominent: Regional Leadership in Upper Canada, 1791-1841*.

25. The boy was Robert Baldwin, son of William Baldwin and destined to help reform the government of Upper Canada, who was doted on by his father's father, as noted in the Diary of Elizabeth Russell, 10 January 1808, Firth, *Town of York*, 268. For Robert Baldwin's career, see *DCB*, 8: 45.

26. The law regarding slavery was "An act to prevent the further introduction of slaves, and to limit the terms for contracts of servitude within this province," 9 July 1793, *The Statutes of the Province of Ontario*, 1st Parliament, 2nd Session, Chapter 7, 41. The law allowed settlers to keep as slaves any person they had brought with them under such involuntary conditions up to that time, but thereafter no one else was to be allowed to enter the province as a slave, the purchase of slaves was illegal and the children of slaves were to be discharged from their mother's indenture at the age of twenty-five years. Examples of where people of colour are mentioned include: "Minutes of the Court of General Quarter Sessions ... 1800-1811," *Twenty-First Report of the Department of Public Records*, 124 and 199; Extracts from Joseph Willcocks' Diary, *Town of York*, 232 and 232n; Extracts of Elizabeth Russell's Diary, *ibid.*, 259-61.

27. For Givins's career, see *DCB*, 7: 347. Givins's property is described in Robertson, *Landmarks of Toronto*, 1: 1-3 and was located north of modern Queen Street at Givins Street, near the former Queen Street Mental Health Centre, now the Centre for Addiction and Mental Health. The road to the Humber began at Givins's property as noted in "Minutes of the Court of General

Quarter Sessions ... 1800-1811," *Twenty-First Report of the Department of Public Records*, 171.

28. This sketch of Ely Playter is based upon the following: Firth, *Town of York*, 93n, 99n; Firth, *The Town of York, 1815-1834*, 147n; Darke, *A Mill Should Be Build Thereon*, 32-4; The Playter-Beman marriage is noted in Robertson, *Landmarks of Toronto*, 3: 399; Mosser, *York, Upper Canada, Minutes of Town Meetings, passim.* Ely Playter's extensive diary forms a key resource in this study, AO, F 556. Ely owned "Lot No. 12, Concession 2 from the Bay, "located east of the Don River, just north of Danforth Avenue and astride Broadview Avenue. The author gratefully acknowledges Stephen Otto's assistance in identifying this location. George, Sr.'s land was located on the west side of the Don, near Castle Frank, Wise and Gould, *Toronto Street Names*, 166-7. For a discussion of the Late Loyalists, see Taylor, "The Late Loyalists."

29. This sketch of John Lyon is based on material given to the author by Bob Gregory of Kanata, Ontario, to whom the author extends his sincere gratitude. See also Firth, *Town of York*, 190n; Mosser, *York, Upper Canada, Minutes of Town Meetings, passim*; "Minutes of the Court of General Quarter Sessions ... 1800-1811," *Twenty-First Report of the Department of Public Records, passim.* His main residence was on Lot No. 32, Concession 1, Markham, east of modern day Yonge Street near Langstaff Sideroad while his mill sites were on Lot No. 36 on the same concession.

30. Little is known about Isaac Wilson other than what is found in AO, MS 199(5), which though labelled "Isaac Wilson Diaries, 1811-15," is actually a set of letters. The quotes used here are from, respectively: Wilson to his parents, 19 November 1811 and to his brother Jonathan, 24 May 1812 (their father had died shortly after returning). See also Firth, *Town of York*, 292n. For John Wilson: see *ibid.*, 67n; his Loyalty, militia service and advanced age are described in Chewett to Coffin, 21 June 1816, LAC, RG 9, 1B1, 5: unpaginated.

31. The play was advertised on 12 September 1810 in the *York Gazette*, Firth, *Town of York*, 275. In Ely Playter's diary, AO, F 556, there is mention of the meetings of Quakers and Methodists, (19 September 1802), hunting and fishing (28 April 1804).

32. The performance was advertised on 5 May 1810 in the *York Gazette*, Firth, *Town of York*, 274-5. Gore's annual celebration was reported in the 25 January 1809 issue of the *York Gazette*, *ibid.*, 273-4 and a fox hunt was reported on 14 February 1801, *ibid.*, 241. In "Extracts from Joseph Willcocks's Diary," *ibid.*, there is mention of duck hunting and fishing (232-3), a fox hunt and horse racing (233). In Ely Playter's diary, AO, F 556, there is mention of the orangutan (11 June 1804), playing billiards (29 October 1805) and the shivarees (12, 13, 14 October 1802, 21, 22, 25 August 1804 and 22 April 1805).

33. Strachan material most relevant to this study include: *DCB*, 9: 751; Spragge, *The John Strachan Letter Book: 1812-1834*; Henderson, *John Strachan: Documents and Opinions.* Also AO, F 983, Strachan Fonds, MS 35.

34. This quote, taken from Miles, *A School History of Canada*, (1870), 193-4, was used by Ryerson, *The Loyalists of America*, (1880), 2: 314n.

35. For Wood's career see: *DCB*, 7: 919; Firth, "Alexander Wood, Merchant of York"; Procter, "Silhouette of Alexander Wood"; and Proulx, "Tall, bronzed man moves to gay village." Wood's store was at the corner of King and Frederick Streets, Wise and Gould, *Toronto Street Names*, 16.

36. Powell quoted Robinson in a letter to William Jarvie to ask about his involvement in the controversy, 28 March 1832, TRL, L 16, Powell Papers, B 90: 71. The matter flared up in 1823 when Powell advised the lieutenant-governor against Wood's appointment to a commission on war claims. Wood eventually took him to court and Powell sought witnesses to the event. He also described the 1823 controversy, only alluding to the alleged sexual transgression, in a published pamphlet, Powell, *Letter from William Dummer Powell to His Excellency Sir Peregrine Maitland.*

37. Wood wrote this to Powell, 6 July 1810, TRL, L 16, Powell Papers, B 90: 1. Powell responded to Wood, 7 July 1810, *ibid.*: 2. Powell produced a declaration by James Ross, 5 March 1834, *ibid.*: 85. He had written to William Jarvie, who sent his recollection from Quebec, 4 April 1832, *ibid.*: 93. Powell mentioned the censure he suffered in the declaration of his 1823 trial, *ibid.*: 41. James Ross appears to have been living at York from 1807 with a wife and child as per Mosser, *York Upper Canada, Minutes of Town Meetings, passim.* Another of the oft-told scandals of York concerned the John White and John Small families, which involved infidelity, a deadly duel and years of repercussions, in which Anne Powell resolutely took a haughty and influential stance against immoral behaviour. It is detailed in McKenna, "The Role of Women in the Establishment of Social Status," and in Halliday, *Murder Among Gentlemen*, 41-7. See also the John Small and John White careers, *DCB*, 6: 721 and 4: 766.

38. Isaac Wilson to Jonathan Wilson, 5 December 1813, AO, MS 199(5), Isaac Wilson Diaries. Unrest among the general populace of the province is described in Sheppard, *Plunder, Profit and Paroles*, 13-39 and Cruikshank, "A Study of Disaffection in Upper Canada in 1812-15."

39. For Gore's career, see *DCB*, 8: 336. For Thorpe's career, see *DCB*, 7: 864. For Jackson's, see, *DCB*, 7: 438 and Jackson, *A View of the Political Situation of the Upper Canada in 1808.* Land ownership issues are discussed in Johnson, "Land Policy, Population Growth and Social Structure in the Home District, 1793-1851" and Fraser, *Sixteenth Report of the Department of Archives for the Province of Ontario*, 97-112. A comprehensive study of this period is found in Wright. "Law State and Dissent in Upper Canada," 226-85; also see the career of Joseph Willcocks, *DCB*, 5: 854. Another controversy concerned the incarceration of Robert Nichol, due to alleged misuse of public funds, *DCB*, 6: 539.

40. A deposition of the incident was made by Titus Geer Simons, 2 February 1807, Firth, *Town of York*, 176-7.

41. Brock to Prevost, 25 February 1812, LAC, RG 8, I, 676: 92.

42. Militia service was based on "An act to explain, amend and reduce to one act of Parliament the several acts now in being for the raising and training [of] the militia of this province," 16 March 1808, *The Statutes of the Province of Ontario*, 4th Parliament, Session 2, Chapter 1, 130. This law was revised during February and March 1812 as 5th Parliament, Session 2, Chapter 3, 169. Brock described the needs and changes in Brock to Baynes, 12 February 1812, Tupper, *The Life and Correspondence of Brock*, 147 and Brock to Nichol, 8 April 1812, *ibid.*, 163. According to the Annual Return of the Militia in Upper Canada on 4 June 1811, the 1st York comprised 1110 officers and men while the 2nd York had 467, LAC, RG 5, A 1, 13: 5437.

43. This excerpt from Ely Playter's diary is from 4 June 1802, AO, F 556. A similar scene was recorded on 4

June 1804, *ibid.*, 249. For Player's career, see *ibid.*, 99n
and Johnson, *Becoming Prominent*, 219-20. The alarm
post mentioned here might have been the garrison or
the Town Blockhouse or possibly Yorkville, since the
Playters had property on Yonge Street. The captains' returns were the musters and the "smoothe board guns"
were muskets. The 1804 entry shows that not all the
men were armed. Militia requirements are taken from
"An act to explain, amend and reduce to one act of
Parliament the several acts now in being for the raising
and training [of] the militia of this province," 16 March
1808, *The Statutes of the Province of Ontario*, 4th Parliament, Session 2, Chapter 1, 130.

44. G. Ridout to T.G. Ridout, 25 June 1812, AO, F 43, Thomas Ridout Family Fonds, MS 537. Brock explained the
organization and reasons for the flank companies to:
Baynes, 12 February 1812, Tupper, *The Life and Correspondence of Brock*, 147; Nichol, 8 April 1812, *ibid.*, 163;
and to Prevost, 22 April 1812, *ibid.*, 167. The 1808 law was
revised during February and March 1812, *The Statutes
of the Province of Ontario*, 5th Parliament, Session 2,
Chapter 3, 169.

45. This excerpt from Ely Player's diary is from 4 June 1812,
AO, F 556. The previous references are from 24 and 25
April and 4 May 1812, *ibid.* The reorganization of the
York regiments is mentioned in Firth, *Town of York*,
xlvi, and Regimental Orders, 2 May and 6 June 1812,
York Gazette, ibid., 82.

46. G. Ridout to T.G. Ridout, post script (27 June) on 25
June 1812, AO, F 43, Thomas Ridout Family Fonds, MS
537.

**Chapter 2: "Worthy of being at the head of affairs": The
Defence of Upper Canada**

1. Archibald McLean to unknown, 15 October 1812, *Quebec Mercury*, 27 October 1812.

2. For Prevost's career, see: Turner, *British Generals in the
War of 1812*, 24-57; Hitsman, "Sir George Prevost's Conduct;" [Brenton,] *Public Life of Sir George Prevost.* [Ri-
chardson], *The letters of Veritas*; *DCB*, 5: 693; *DNB*, 16:
320; *HMG*, 25-6, 304. Because of the size of Prevost's
command and the distance between Quebec and Halifax, the Atlantic centre, Lieutenant General Sir John
Coape Sherbrooke oversaw activity in the Atlantic
colonies, although he was subordinate to Prevost and
passed official correspondence with London through
Prevost's office.

3. Chief Justice Sampson Blowers of Nova Scotia made
this comment, cited in *DCB*, 5: 693.

4. Vicar General Edmund Burke of Nova Scotia made
this comment, cited in *DCB*, 5: 693. Major William
Cochrane's comment about Prevost's cheerfulness and
good nature is also found here.

5. Prevost announced his having arrived and taken command in a General Order issued by Edward Baynes,
the adjutant general for British North America, on 14
September 1811, LAC, RG 8, I, 1168: 4. For a comprehensive discussion of the causes of the War of 1812, see
Hitsman, *The Incredible War of 1812: A Military History*,
3-23, and Hickey, *The War of 1812: A Forgotten Conflict*,
5-28. An itinerary exists for a quick tour that Prevost
made from Quebec to Montreal at LAC, RG 8, I, 1708:
5. The itinerary is dated 1813, but probably represents
a trip made early in the governor-in-chief's term as it
appears to be arranged for him to observe the various
posts, as if he had never seen them before. It mentions
only "Thursday, the 26th" which may be Thursday, 26
September 1811; in *DCB*, 5: 693, it is stated that Prevost

did travel down to Montreal at this time.

6. Weak fortifications and no depots, Report of the State
of Fortified Military Posts, etc., by Bruyeres, 24 August
1811, *DHC*, 3: 19 and Report on the State of Magazines,
etc., by Glasgow, 18 September 1811, LAC, RG 8, I, 1706:
171. Brock discussed the other matters in letters to
Prevost, 2 December 1811, 25 February, 9 March and 22
April 1812, *DHC*, 3: 21, 43, 44 and 56. 20 miles = 32 km.

7. In the absence of a definitive return of the force in Upper Canada in December 1811, this number is based
upon the 1042 officers and men of the 41st Regiment
of Foot shown to be headquartered at Fort George at
the time, "Monthly Return of Officers …," 24 December 1811, LAC, MG 13, WO 17, 1515: 283-4, combined with
portions of the Royal Regiment of Artillery and 10th
Royal Veterans Battalion shown to be on detached duty
in the above return. A "General Return of the Troops
Stationed in Upper Canada …," dated 30 July 1812
(LAC, RG 8, I, 1707: 26) shows 80 officers and men of
the artillery and 196 of the veterans in the province at
that time and it is presumed they were present in 1811
as well. Brock described the situation in Upper Canada
and his ideas about striking American posts to Prevost
on 2 December 1811, LAC, MG 11, CO 42, 352: 55.

8. The history of the Provincial Marine has been described
in these sources: Douglas, "The Anatomy of Naval Incompetence: The Provincial Marine in Defence of Upper Canada Before 1813"; Malcolmson, "'Not Very Much
Celebrated: ' The Evolution and Nature of the Provincial Marine, 1755-1813;" Stanley, "The Army Origin of
the Royal Canadian Navy;" MacLeod, "The Tap of the
Garrison Drum: The Marine Service in British North
America, 1755-1813." The 1812 report was sent by Gray to
Prevost, 29 January 1812, LAC, RG 8, I, 728: 77.

9. Brock to Gordon, 6 September 1807, Tupper, *The Life
and Correspondence of Brock*, 64. For a defence of
Prevost's policy, see MacLeod, "Fortress Ontario or
Forlorn Hope?"

10. Prevost to Liverpool, 18 May 1812, LAC, MG 11, CO 42,
146: 197.

11. George Augustus Frederick, the Prince of Wales, King
George III's first son was acting as Prince Regent during this period when illness prevented the king from
performing his duties. Robert Banks Jenkinson, Lord
Liverpool, became prime minister shortly after the as-
sassination of Spencer Perceval on 11 May 1812. Prior
to that time he had been the secretary for war and the
colonies, a cabinet post which went to Henry Lord
Bathurst in the new government. Correspondence relevant to the issues discussed here include: Liverpool
to Prevost, 8 and 20 April and 15 May 1812, LAC, MG
11, CO 42, 146: 112, 152 and 170; Prevost to Liverpool, 3
March, 14, 20 and 21 April, 18 May and 15 July 1812, *ibid.*:
54, 134, 148, 154, 197 and 147: 19; Bathurst to Prevost, 4
July and 10 August 1812, *ibid.*, 146: 124 and 147: 94.

12. Liverpool to Prevost, 15 May 1812, LAC, MG 11, CO 42,
146: 170.

13. Liverpool to Prevost, 15 May 1812, LAC, MG 11, CO 42,
146: 170.

14. Liverpool to Prevost, 15 May 1812, LAC, MG 11, CO 42,
146: 170.

15. Prevost's efforts are detailed in the correspondence listed above. The distribution of the various regiments is
discussed in detail in Prevost to Liverpool, 15 July 1812,
LAC, MG 11, CO 42, 147: 19.

16. Prevost to Liverpool, 3 March and 14 April 1812, LAC,
MG 11, CO 42, 146: 54 and 134. The plan is described in
Bruyeres to Prevost, undated [probably late February

1812], *ibid.*: 56. Relocating the Provincial Marine and building up York's defences were proposed by Gray to Prevost, 29 January 1812, LAC, RG 8, I, 728: 77 and in Report upon the expediency of Removing the Marine Establishment from Kingston to York ..., 9 March 1812, *ibid.*: 94. Brock made similar suggestions in Memorandum to be Submitted to [Prevost] ..., undated [chronologically set in January 1812], *ibid.*: 68. Simcoe's ideas about York were described to Clarke, 31 May 1793, Cruikshank, *The Correspondence of Lieut. Governor John Graves Simcoe*, 1: 338.

17. Bathurst to Prevost, 4 July 1812, LAC, MG 11, CO 42, 146: 124.

18. For a full description of the battle, see Malcolmson, *A Very Brilliant Affair: The Battle of Queenston Heights, 1812.*

19. Susannah Sheaffe's letter to her brother Thomas Child in December 1767 is cited in Sabine, *Biographical Sketches*, 2: 280. For Sheaffe's career, see: Turner, *British Generals in the War of 1812*, 84-100; Whitfield, "The Battle of Queenston Heights: Sir Roger Hale Sheaffe"; *DCB*, 8: 792; *DNB*, 17: 1393; *HMG*, 330; obituary, *The Gentleman's Magazine*, 36 (1851), 318, Sheaffe Service Record to circa 1810, NAUK, WO 25, 748, unpaginated; Stephen Sheaffe, *The Sheaffe Family History*. The author gratefully acknowledges the assistance provided by Stephen Sheaffe, of Queensland, Australia, regarding family records.

20. For a biography of Percy/Lord Northumberland, see: *DNB*, 15: 865.

21. Simcoe to Hammond, 20 October 1794, Cruikshank, *Correspondence of Simcoe*, 3: 132. The Duke of Northumberland was a correspondent with Simcoe and once remarked in a post script "I cannot seal up this letter without thanking you for your goodness to my friend Capt. Sheaffe," Northumberland to Simcoe, 6 November 1795, *ibid.*, 4: 128. McGill, Selby and Shaw all worked with Simcoe as did other key Loyalists and would have been in Sheaffe's company on numerous occasions. After the Battle of York, 27 April 1813, Mrs. Anne Powell wrote to her husband with concerns about the Sheaffe's fate, showing consistent concern for "an unfortunate and injured friend," 20 May 1813, TRL, L 16, Powell Papers, Mrs. Powell's letters, A 93: 321. See also her letters of 10, 12, 16 and 31 May 1813, *ibid.*: 311, 315, 316 and 329.

22. The Lord Bishop of Quebec performed the nuptials for Sheaffe and Coffin on Wednesday, 31 January 1810 at Quebec as reported in the 5 February 1810 issue of the *Quebec Mercury*. Isabella Child Coffin and Susannah Child Sheaffe were sisters, as noted in Surveyer, "Nathaniel Coffin," 61.

23. Sheaffe's lifelong relationship with the Northumberland family is shown in Sheaffe to Mrs. Anne Powell, 8 August 1818, TRL, L 16, Powell Papers and in a quote from 1829, cited in Sabine, *Biographical Sketches*, 2: 291: "My friends in general seem to have expected that the Duke of Northumberland's recent appointment would have been productive to me; but it unfortunately happens that he has nothing in his gift suitable to a military man of my rank: he has asked for a Regiment or Government for me, and it is probably, with my admitted claims, that I shall get one." Winfield Scott reported hearing the same thing from Sheaffe himself, after he was captured at the Battle of Queenston Heights, 13 October 1813, "[Sheaffe was] adopted, when a boy, by Lord Percy (afterward Duke of Northumberland), then colonel of the 42d Foot, he was sent to England for his education, and that the duke continued his patron

through his whole military career," *Memoirs of General Scott, Written by Himself*, 1: 66-7. Hugh Percy, the 2nd Duke of Northumberland (1742-1817) was succeed by his son, the 3rd Duke (1785-1847).

24. Genealogical details about Sheaffe's children and those of his brother William are part of Stephen Sheaffe's *The Sheaffe Family History* which Stephen so generously shared with the author. Whitfield, "The Battle of Queenston Heights: Sir Roger Hale Sheaffe," 32 states that Sheaffe went to England in 1810 and probably did not return until the summer of 1812, but the shipping notices in *The Quebec Mercury*, which usually announced the arrival of British officers and distinguished citizens, made no mention of the departure of his wife and him nor their return between 1810 and summer 1812. Furthermore, Torrens stated that it was assumed that Sheaffe was in Canada in the autumn of 1811 and available for immediate appointment to Prevost, 18 October 1811, LAC, RG 8, I, 30: 105.

25. Sheaffe reported that the promotion to major general cost him the colonelcy of the 49th Foot and, therefore, half his income, to Susan Child, September 1811, Sabine, *Biographical Sketches of Loyalists*, 291. Sheaffe's changes in rank are seen in the Monthly Returns, Canada, 1808-1812, LAC, MG 13, WO 17, vols. 1514-1516. Sheaffe retained his rank and pay as lieutenant colonel of the regiment. The idea that he was in financial straits was repeated in Sabine, *Sketches*, 289 and in *DCB*, 8: 792. Sheaffe's belongings, and presumably those of other officers, were sold at an auction at Fort Niagara on 11 May. Surgeon William Beaumont estimated that Sheaffe's exquisite coat was worth $300 although it sold for $50. "His other things sold very high, being good and much wanted by our officers," noted Beaumont, *Wm. Beaumont's Formative Years*, 50. Other proofs of his wealth are that he spent over £600 during the auction of Brock's estate (List of Items in Brock's Estate and who purchased them, AO, MU 2143, F 775, Miscellaneous Collection, Folder 10) and a short time later he donated £200 to the Loyal and Patriotic Society as noted in *The Report of the Loyal and Patriotic Society*, 332.

26. The snuff box fell into American hands at the Battle of York, 27 April 1813 and ended up in Major General Henry Dearborn's possession as reported, along with details about its appearance and cost, by John Scott to Thompson, 17 May 1813, New Jersey Historical Society, MG 1044, Captain John Scott Letters. The story about the musical snuff box was repeated in the 12 June 1813 issue of *The Oleo* of New York. Later historians picked up the story: Ingersoll, *Historical Sketch of the Second War ...*, (1845), 273; and in Auchinleck, "History of the War," Chapter X," *Anglo-American Magazine*, (1863), 347; Lossing, *Pictorial Field-book of the War of 1812*, (1868), 333; and Beirne, *The War of 1812*, (1965), 160 ("Including among other trifles a musical snuffbox that delighted the Americans who already had established the national tradition for collecting souvenirs"). Scott mentioned that the box played several tunes while *The Oleo* reported that it played six. Music box experts claim it could not have played more than two; special thanks to Robert Ducat-Brown of the Musical Box Society of Great Britain, Michael Caulfield, Larry Karp, Robin Biggins and Frank Metzger of the Music Box Society International for their personal communications.

27. These descriptions are cited in Sabine, *Biographical Sketches*, 2: 292. Evidence of Sheaffe's close relationship with the Powells, in particular, is found in Anne Powell's letters to her husband on 10, 12, 16, 20 and 31

May 1813, *ibid.*: 311, 315, 316, 321 and 329, TRL, L 16, Powell Papers, Mrs. Powell's letters.

28. Tupper, *The Life and Correspondence of Brock*, 18.

29. Brock to Green, 8 February 1808, LAC, RG 8, I, 923: 12.

30. Cited in Sabine, *Biographical Sketches*, 2: 291. That Sheaffe was considered for the posting that Brock received (in lieu of Brock having received permission to return home to England) is shown in Torrens to Prevost, 18 October 1811, LAC, RG 8, I, 30: 105. This letter arrived months after Prevost had selected Brock. Prevost's arrival and Brock's appointment were announced in the same general order by Baynes, 14 September 1811, *ibid.*, 1168: 4. For biographies of Brock and Drummond, see *DCB*, 5: 109 and 8: 236.

31. Brock to his brothers, 3 September 1812, Tupper, *The Life and Correspondence of Brock*, 284. The next line in Brock's letter is: "Sir George Prevost has kindly hearkened to my remonstrations, and in some measure supplied the deficiency." Brock mentioned several officers he wished were assigned to his staff to Baynes, 12 February 1812, *ibid.*, 147. The author thanks Guy St. Denis for helping him reconsider the meaning of Brock's "necessary assistance" comment which, it was suggested in *A Very Brilliant Affair*, 96, referred to Sheaffe needing assistance in material goods or military competence. Brock complained about a lack of officers in his letter to Prevost, 29 July 1812, LAC, RG 8, I, 676: 239.

32. Executive Council of Upper Canada to Sheaffe, no date, NAC, RG 8, I, 688A: 6. Robinson, "Account of the Battle of Queenston Heights," 14 October 1812, AO, F44, John Beverley Robinson Papers.

33. *Kingston Gazette*, 24 October 1812. Report of a native council meeting, 6 November 1812, *DHC*, 4: 198.

34. Archibald McLean to unknown, 15 October 1812, *Quebec Mercury*, 27 October 1812.

35. Bathurst to Prevost, 8 December 1812, LAC, RG 8, I, 677: 237. Prevost to Bathurst, 21 October 1812, *DHC*, 4: 148. Sheaffe announced his activities to Bathurst on 20 October 1812, *DHC*, 4: 142. Prevost announced his appointment as government head in a General Order by Baynes, 21 October 1812, *DHC*, 4: 149. Prevost announced Sheaffe's baronetcy in a General Order by Rowan, 10 March 1813, *DHC*, 5: 104. The stipend amount is what Brock said it would be to his brother Irving, 30 October 1811, Tupper, *The Life and Correspondence of Brock*, 112.

36. Derenzy's suggestion is mentioned in Smith to Procter, 18 October 1812, USNA, RG 59, M588, unpaginated. The militia's willingness to join him is found in Crooks, "Recollections of the War of 1812," 39. The sidearms and indignation is mentioned in *The Niagara Bee*, 18 October 1812.

37. Crooks, "Recollections of the War of 1812", 40. Ensign John Smith, 41st Foot, reported in detail about the confusion to Procter, 18 October 1812, USNA, RG 59, M588, unpaginated. It was noticed by Winfield Scott, *Memoirs of General Scott, Written by Himself*, 1: 60. The term for getting a column into such a backwards situation is "clubbing". Sheaffe's predicament is described in full in Malcomson, "Clubbed Victory at Queenston Heights."

38. Prevost to Sheaffe, 27 October 1812, LAC, RG 8, I, 1220: 10.

39. Sheaffe to Prevost, 8 November 1812, LAC, RG 8, I, 677: 173. This was actually the second time that Prevost complained about Sheaffe's decision making. When he heard of an arrangement Sheaffe had made with Major General Stephen Van Rensselaer under the guidelines of the Prevost-Dearborn armistice of August 1812,

Prevost complained to Brock about Sheaffe's conduct, 30 August 1812, *ibid.*, 1218: 377. Brock was critical of the August armistice, too, as he informed his brothers, 3 September 1813, Tupper, *Life of Brock*, 284. Turner makes the point that "Sheaffe was treated in a more high-handed and critical manner than any other general in Prevost's command," *British Generals in the War of 1812*, 91.

40. Sheaffe to Bathurst, 20 October 1812, *DHC*, 4: 142. In this letter Sheaffe also added that he used the armistice "break" to go to York to formally assume his new post as government leader. Arrangements for transporting the American POWs can be seen in: the Garrison Orders, 16 and 20 October 1812, *DHC*, 4: 132 and 144; District General Order, 17 October 1812, *ibid.*: 134.

41. Sheaffe to Prevost, 8 November 1812, LAC, RG 8, I, 677: 173.

42. Brock complained about a lack of officers in his letter to Prevost, 29 July 1812, LAC, RG 8, I, 676: 239. For Myers's career, see *HMG*, 276. Glegg became Sheaffe's aide as per the District General Order of 16 October 1812, *DHC*, 4: 131. For Glegg's career, see *HMG*, 163. For Bisshopp's career, see: *DCB*, 5: 82; *HMG*, 65; Allan, "Bisshopp Papers." For Loring's career, see *DCB*, 7: 517 and *HMG*, 231.

43. For Nichol's career, see *DCB*, 6: 539. For Givins's career, see *DCB*, 7: 347. For Shaw's career, see *DCB*, 5: 752 and *HMG*, 328.

44. For Coffin's career, see Surveyer, "Nathaniel Coffin," and *DCB*, 7: 199. Sheaffe actually failed to mention Coffin in his report about the Battle of Queenston Heights, but corrected his omission in a note to Freer, 18 October 1812, LAC, RG 8, I, 677: 140.

45. Merritt, *A Desire of Serving*, 3. There were problems with conduct by men and officers alike during this period: widespread drunkenness, District General Order by Evans, 20 October 1812, *DHC*, 4: 141; problem of drunkenness continued, District General Order by Evans, 9 November 1812, *ibid.*: 188; a reminder of frequent drills was mentioned in the District General Order by Evans, 19 and 28 October 1812, *DHC*, 4: 138 and 169; the need for proper reporting was the subject of the District General Orders by Evans, 20 and 22 October, 1, 5, 11, 12 and 13 November 1812, *ibid.*: 141, 154, 174, 182, 202, 206 and 207.

46. Orders concerning the discharge, call up and organization of the militia were given on 16, 18, 20, 21, 23, 24, 25 and 29 October 1812, *DHC*, 4: 132, 137, 144, 153, 159, 161-2, 163-5 and 169. An example of urgent arrangements being made beyond the Niagara Peninsula is seen in Glegg to Talbot, 19 October 1812, Coyne, *The Talbot Papers*, 161.

47. Sheaffe to Prevost, 3 November 1812, LAC, RG 8, I, 677: 166.

48. Macdonell to Talbot, 12 October 1812, Coyne, *The Talbot Papers*, 160. John Strachan claimed that the militia "captured the greater part of the very arms by which [the province] was defended," Spragge, *Strachan*, 27. Following the battle at Queenston so many "French" muskets (of the calibre used by the American forces) were distributed among the militia that an order was issued for company commanders to exchange weapons with each other until their men had the same calibre of weapon which would make distribution of ammunition easier, District General Order by Evans, 21 October 1812, *DHC*, 4: 153. Sheaffe mentioned the problems with the delivery of clothing to Prevost, 16 December 1812, LAC, RG 8, I, 677: 260.

49. Mention of the arrival of supplies is in Sheaffe to Talbot, 7 November 1812 Coyne, *The Talbot Papers*, 163 and in Sheaffe to Prevost, 8 November 1812, *DHC*, 4: 186. Their distribution is noticed in Bisshopp to Claus, 10 November 1812, *DHC*, 4: 201 and the Militia General Order by Shaw and Sheaffe, 14 November 1812, *ibid.*: 211.

50. The clothing was delivered to Niagara in the second week of December as described in Strachan to Cameron, 7 December 1812, Spragge, *Strachan*, 28. See details in *The Report of the Loyal and Patriotic Society*, 3-5, 11-20. Elizabeth (Selby) Derenzy's part is mentioned in Shaw's biography, *DCB*, 5: 749.

51. The want of firewood and forage is mentioned in Militia and District General Orders by Bisshopp and Evans, 11 and 12 November 1812, *DHC*, 4: 202 and 207. Tailors were sought among the detachments, Militia General Order by Evans, 13 November 1812, *ibid.*: 210. In January Glegg declared "There is at this moment no fuel in the wood yard; the posts and guard making daily complaints for want of firewood, and the horses of the car brigade are actually perishing, owing to a want of forage," Glegg to unknown [probably Powell], 10 January 1813, *DHC*, 5: 31. The Canadian commissariat is described in Steppler, "A Duty Troublesome Beyond Measure." See pages 25-43 for its operation, alterations in 1811 and condition during 1812.

52. Glegg to unknown [probably Powell], 10 January 1813, *DHC*, 5: 31.

53. Nichol to Talbot, 12 December 1812, Coyne, *The Talbot Papers*, 167.

54. Evans to Powell, 6 January 1813, *DHC*, 5: 29. Nichol had to get Sheaffe to approve the pay of the officers as requested by Colonel Thomas Talbot in his letter to Sheaffe, 12 December 1812, Coyne, *The Talbot Papers*, 165. Nichol got Sheaffe's approval for Talbot's "estimates", Nichol to Talbot, 12 December 1812, *ibid.*, 167. On 18 December he wrote to Talbot, "Couche will not pay me for the provisions and other things furnished by your orders," *ibid.*, 170. Nichol, himself, had to petition headquarters for pay, claiming that he had not received any wages by mid-1813, Nichol to Brenton, 6 August 1813, Cruikshank, *Additional Correspondence*, 70.

55. Evans to Powell, 6 January 1813, *DHC*, 5: 29.

56. Samuel Jarvis to his parents, 8 November 1812, *DHC*, 4: 200. Sheaffe mentioned a similar rumour ("A frigate of thirty-two guns – keep it to yourself – was nearly ready to be launched") to Talbot in a letter on 25 November 1812, Coyne, *The Talbot Papers*, 163.

57. Sheaffe to Prevost, 8 November 1812, LAC, RG 8, I, 677: 173.

Chapter 3: "We have now the command of the lake": Chauncey's 1812 Campaign

1. Chauncey to Hamilton, 13 November 1812, USNA, RG 45, M 125, 25: 176.

2. In his annual message to Congress on 5 November 1811 President James Madison advised the legislators to take steps for "putting the United States in an armor and an attitude demanded by the [international] crisis," *Journal of the House of Representatives*, First Session, Twelfth Congress, 8: 7. The multi-pronged invasion strategy was championed by John Armstrong as shown in his letter to Eustis, 2 January 1812, Cruikshank, *DHC*, 3: 29 and by Henry Dearborn, as described in Brant, *James Madison, Commander in Chief*, 45 and Stagg, *Mr. Madison's War*, 193. Madison explained that one reason

for attacks on several fronts was to protect areas of the frontier, such as Detroit, from attack by the British and their native allies, Madison to Jefferson, 17 August 1812, Hunt, *Writings of James Madison*, 8: 210. A brief coverage of the plan is found in Malcomson, *A Very Brilliant Affair*, 28-30.

3. Jefferson to Duane, 4 August 1812, Ford, *Works of Thomas Jefferson*, 264. Among the negative representations of the nation's readiness to go to war are the following: Peter Porter, a key "war hawk," asked Secretary Eustis in April 1812 to delay the war until New York State was ready to fight it, as noted in Hatzenbuehler, "The War Hawks," 14-15; Winfield Scott's quote about most officers being "*utterly unfit for any military purpose whatever*" is well-known, Scott, *Memoirs*, 1: 35-6 and is somewhat supported by Skelton, "High Army Leadership"; among logistic problems was a lack of suitable clothing for the military, Chartrand, *Uniforms and Equipment of the United States Forces*, 31-4. Three descriptions of the U.S. Army during this period are found in: Crackell, *Mr. Jefferson's Army*; Skelton, *An American Profession of Arms* 3-105; and Coffman, *The Old Army*, 27-40. Also see Hickey, *The War of 1812: A Forgotten Conflict*, 29-51, for a description of war preparations and their results.

4. For a description of Hull's campaign and Brock's efforts: see Cruikshank, "General Hall's Invasion of Canada in 1812"; and Cruikshank, *Documents relating to the Invasion of Canada and the Surrender of Detroit, 1812*.

5. Armstrong to Eustis, 2 January 1812, *DHC* 3: 29. Hull wrote to then-Secretary of War Dearborn, 16 August 1807, in Fuller, "Documents Relating to Detroit and Vicinity, 1805-1813," 182. Hull repeated similar ideas to Eustis, 6 March 1812, in Fuller, "Documents Relating to Detroit and Vicinity, 1805-1813," 362. Woolsey appealed to Hamilton for additional support, 4 July 1812, USNA, RG 45, M 148, 10: 19: 82. Woolsey had sent frequent letters to Hamilton about British activities and the threat they posed: 23 and 30 July, 30 September 1811, *ibid.*: 17: 144, 88 and 140; 31 January 1812, *ibid.*: 19: 45. For Woolsey's career, see: *ANB*, 23: 860; *SROLO*, 166-8.

6. In August 1812 just before the fall of Detroit Madison wrote to Gallatin (Adams, *The Writings of Albert Gallatin*, 1: 526), "The command of the Lakes is obviously of the greatest importance, and has always appeared so. I am glad to find it not too late to have that on Ontario. There must have been some mistake as to the effort to obtain it." Madison later explained to John Nicholas, 2 April 1813 (Hunt, *The Writings of James Madison*, 8: 242), "The failure of our calculations, with respect to the expedition under Hull needs no comment. The worst of it was that we were misled by a reliance authorized by himself, on its securing to us the command of the Lakes. The decisive importance of this advantage has always been well-understood; but until the first prospect ceased, other means of attaining it were repressed by certain difficulties in carrying them into effect."

7. For Chauncey's career, see: *ANB*, 4: 750; Baillie, *American Biographical Index*, items 336-62; Gibson, *SROLO*, 45-7; *Preble's Boys*, 170-198.

8. Paul Hamilton sent Chauncey his orders on 31 August 1812, Dudley, *NWDH*, 1: 297. For a description of Chauncey's subsequent activities in September and October 1812, see Malcomson, *Lords of the Lake*, 43-8. An investigation into the use of the honorific "commodore" is presented in Malcomson, "'Stars and Garters of an Admiral', American Commodores in the War

of 1812." The other officers who were consistently addressed as "commodore" by the navy department during this period were William Bainbridge, Stephen Decatur and John Rodgers.

9. Captain Arthur Sinclair complimented Chauncey in a letter to Cocke, 25 August 1813, Malcomson, *Sailors of 1812*, 48. Chauncey announced his 6 October arrival at Sackets to Hamilton, 8 October 1812, USNA, RG 45, M 125, 25: 106

10. Chauncey described the events to Secretary of the Navy Paul Hamilton on 4 November 1812. Original copies of this letter are contained in USNA, RG 45, M 125, 25: 161. For a description of the *Oneida*, see Canney, *Sailing Warships of the US Navy*, 189-90; Chapelle, *History of the American Sailing Navy*, 229-30; Malcomson, *Lords of the Lake*, 17-22, *passim*; Malcomson, *Warships of the Great Lakes*, 55-8, *passim*; Palmer, "James Fenimore Cooper and the Navy Brig *Oneida*,"; The U.S. Frigate *Constitution* defeated HMS *Guerrière* on 19 August 500 miles southeast of Newfoundland.

11. According to a website of the National Aeronautics and Space Administration <http://sunearth.gsfc.nasa.gov>, the new phase of the moon began on 4 November 1812, meaning there was very little of the last quarter of the moon left when Chauncey set sail on 2 November. 35 miles = 56 km.

12. The *Oneida* carried approximately 126 officers and men and marines during November 1812, as shown in the Muster Roll for the U.S. Brig *Oneida*, June 1811–August 1813, USNA, RG 45, T 829A, roll 17. For career information on Ford and Vaughan, see *SROLO*, 71 and 158.

13. There is no indication in Chauncey's correspondence that he possessed dependable charts of any points on the Canadian shore. For want of a better map, he drew his own rough sketch of the approaches to Kingston and sent it to the navy department with a plan of attack he developed on 21 January 1813, USNA, RG 45, M 125, 26: 29. The lack of well-surveyed maps was not unusual during this age: a complete and accurate map of the south coast of England, for instance, was not available until 1837, Glover, *Peninsula Preparations*, 80. "In both India and the Peninsula, Wellington campaigned in a mapless country, almost as mapless as Alexander's Asia Minor…. In Portugal and Spain he was better provided for, though not much. Maps were few, incomplete and often very inaccurate," Keegan, *The Mask of Battle*, 134-5.

14. After seeing Earl's vessels at a distance on 3 November, Chauncey reported them to be "the *Royal George*, 26 guns; *Prince Regent*, 18 guns; *Duke of Gloucester*, 16 guns," in Chauncey to Hamilton, 4 November, USNA, RG 45, M 125, 25: 161. The *Duke of Gloucester* was not present, having already been laid up at York by this time and had been fitted out as a prison hulk, as noted in the York garrison orders 16 and 19 October and 3 November 1812, Ridout's York Garrison Orderly Book, LAC, RG 8, I, 1203. Very little biographical information about Hugh Earl has come to light. See: a petition for a financial settlement in Earl to Prevost, 15 October 1813, LAC, RG 8, I, 731: 42; a petition for pay, 24 March 1817, *ibid*. 739: 32; a report of a board of officers assembled to consider claims by Provincial Marine officers, 16 September 1813, LAC, MG 11, CO 42, 157: 81; and Preston, *Kingston Before the War of 1812*, 251*n*.

15. Chauncey reported on the strength of the British "as nearly as I can determine" in his letter to Hamilton, 6 November 1812, USNA, RG 45, M 125, 25: 167. He listed the other Provincial Marine vessels as: "Ship *Earl of*

Moira 18 guns 200 men; … *Taranto* 14 guns 80 men, *Governor Simcoe* 12 guns 70 men; *Seneca* 4 guns 40 men: making [combined with the other three] a Grand Total of 108 guns and 890 men." After seeing Earl's vessels at a distance on 3 November, Chauncey reported them to be "the *Royal George* 26 guns; *Prince Regent* 18 guns; *Duke of Gloucester* 16 guns," in Chauncey to Hamilton, 4 November, *ibid.*: 161. This report inflated the already incorrect information Woolsey had submitted to Hamilton on 23 July 1811, USNA, RG 45, M 148, roll 9, 17: 144, stating the *Royal George* to have 22 guns, the *Earl of Moira* 14, the *Duke of Gloucester*, 12, the *Simcoe* 14, the *Toronto* 8.

16. The history of the Provincial Marine has been described in these sources: Douglas, "The Anatomy of Naval Incompetence: The Provincial Marine in Defence of Upper Canada Before 1813"; Malcomson, "'Not Very Much Celebrated: ' The Evolution and Nature of the Provincial Marine, 1755-1813"; Stanley, "The Army Origin of the Royal Canadian Navy"; MacLeod, "The Tap of the Garrison Drum: The Marine Service in British North America, 1755-1813."

17. Fifty Provincial Marine officers and men were serving in the *Royal George* on 2 October 1812, supplemented by 64 officers and men of the Royal Newfoundland Regiment of Fencibles, as reported in a petition for prize money made on 15 October 1813 by Earl to Prevost, LAC, RG 8, I, 731: 42. The entire Provincial Marine squadron in 1811 was manned by a total of 42 officers and seamen, Return of the Effective Strength … by Pye, 21 June 1811 *ibid.*, 373: 26. The 1811 fire strength of the vessels was shown as: *Royal George*, 20 32-pdr. carronades, *Moira*, 10 18-pdr. carronades, *Duke of Gloucester*, 10 12-pdr. carronades, Return of HM Provincial Marine … by Pye, 16 September 1811, *ibid.*: 28. The *Gloucester* was to be replaced in 1812 but was armed with six 6-pdr. long guns (presumably) instead, as per a note by Pye, 9 December 1811, *ibid.*: 29 and Report upon the Provincial Marine … by Gray, 24 February 1812, *ibid.*, 728: 86. It had already been laid up at York by this time and had been fitted out as a prison ship, as noted in the York garrison orders 16 and 19 October and 3 November 1812, Ridout's York Garrison Orderly Book, LAC, RG 8, I, 1203. Prisoners from the Battle of Queenston Heights were held there temporarily before being put into the *Royal George* and *Prince Regent* for transport to Kingston, as noted in the garrison book. The "proposed" crew strengths for 1812 were to be: *Royal George*, 29, *Moira*, 19, *Gloucester*, 13, Proposed Establishment … by Pye, 30 August 1811, *ibid.*, 728: 60. Attempts to increase the crews were not successful as Prevost reported to Bathurst, 17 October 1812, LAC, MG 11, CO 42, 118: 273: "I have now to state the difficulties which attend providing [the Provincial Marine vessels] with proper officers and suitable crews." In January 1813 the *Royal George* was reported to have 80 officers and seamen and 22 soldiers, while the *Moira* had 35 sailors and 16 soldiers, as Gray reported to Vincent, 16 January 1813, LAC, RG 8, I, 729: 28. In an estimate of the preferred strength of the vessels prepared on 12 March 1813 for Prevost by Gray (*ibid.*: 118) the seamen needed were given as: *Royal George*, 80; *Moira*, 45; *Prince Regent*, 35; *Gloucester*, 20. At their strongest outfitting (August 1813) the principle vessels had these strengths: *Royal George*, 2 18-pdr. long, 16 32-pdr. carronades 2 68-pdr. carrronades guns, 155 seamen, 49 marines; *Moira*, 2 9-pdr. long guns, 14 24-pdr. carronades, 92 seamen, 35 marines; *Prince Regent* (renamed *Beresford*], 2 9-pdr. long guns, 10 18-pdr. car-

ronades, 70 seamen, 28 marines. The latter was reported by Yeo in his Comparative Statement of the Force ..., 24 July 1813, LAC, MG 11, CO 42, 151: 100.

18. Among the reports of the squadron carrying men and materiel are: Brock to Prevost, 3 July 1812, LAC, RG 8, I, 676: 115; Myers to Prevost, 17 August 1812, *ibid.*, 677: 47; Lovett to Alexander, 22 September 1812, Cruikshank, *DHC*, 3: 22; General District Order by Glegg, 20 October 1812, *ibid.*, 4: 144; Sheaffe to Prevost, 19 November 1812, *ibid.*: 222. Prevost's non-aggressive policy is seen in: Prevost to Brock, 24 December 1811 and 30 April 1812, Tupper, *Life of Brock*, 133 and 171. The attack on Sackets and raid at Charlotte are described in Woolsey to Hamilton, 21 July 1813, USNA, RG 45, M 148, 10: 19: 100; Preston, "The First Battle of Sackets Harbor"; Phelps to Tompkins, 4 October 1812, *DHC*, 4: 32 and Malcomson, *Lords of the Lake*, 31-6.

19. Chauncey to Hamilton, 6 November 1812, USNA, RG 45, M 125, 25: 167.

20. For data re: Chauncey's squadron see Appendix 7, United States Navy Squadron, April 1813. Jesse Elliott described this force to Peter B. Porter on 3 November 1812, *DHC*, 4: 177. For Elliott's career, see: *ANB*, 7: 431; *SROLO*, 64. For statistical data re: these schooners see: Silverstone, *The Sailing Navy*, 68-9; Malcomson, *Lords of the Lake*, Appendices A, B, D and E; and Malcomson, *Warships of the Great Lakes*, 65-71. Chauncey noted that he sailed with 430 seamen and marines in Chauncey to Hamilton, 6 November 1812, USNA, RG 45, M 125, 25: 168. Following a muster roll for the *Oneida* is a list of men, the vessels in which, and when, they were placed, which includes a notation that 165 seamen and marines arrived on 8 November and 42 more arrived on 19 November, USNA, RG 45, T 829A, roll 17.

21. Woolsey to Hamilton, 2 April 1809, USNA, RG 45, M 148, 6: 11: 3.

22. Myers, *Ned Myers*, 56-57.

23. *Myers*, 56.

24. Details about Chauncey's expedition may be found in: Chauncey to Hamilton, 6, 13, 17 and 21 November 1812, USNA, RG 45, M 125, 25: 167, 176, 183 and 185; Chauncey to Tompkins, 7 November 1812, WCL, CLB; Chauncey to Vincent, 16 November 1812, *ibid.*; Elliott to Porter, 3 November 1812, Cruikshank, *DHC*, 4: 177-8; Letter from an anonymous American officer, 15 November 1812, in the *New York Statesman*, 23 November 1812, *ibid.*, 4: 213-4; *Quebec Mercury*, 8 December 1812; Vincent to Sheaffe, 11 November 1812, NAC, RG 8, I, 728: 80; Distribution of the Forces in Canada, 12 November 1812, *ibid.*, 1707: 61; Gray to Prevost, 3 Dec. 1812, *ibid.*, 728: 135; Stacey, "Commodore Chauncey's Attack."

25. British reports on time of day during the War of 1812 tend to be one hour earlier than American reports. Colonel John Vincent, commanding at Kingston, noted that the exchange of fire began "at 2 o'clock", Vincent to Sheaffe, 11 November 1812, NAC, RG 8, I, 728: 80. An anonymous American officer wrote that Elliott opened fire at "Twelve minutes after 3" in a letter dated 15 November 1812, in the *New York Statesman*, 23 November 1812, *DHC*, 4: 213-4. He added that the squadron sailed out after 4:30 "as night was closing in". Vincent wrote that the firing continued "until it was dark." According to the U.S. Naval Observatory (website: <www.marinrowing.org>) sunset comes at 5:02 P.M. on 10 November. Since the American account compares better with modern records than the British version does, the American times given for this event are used here. Lieutenant Jesse Elliott joined Master Commandant

Oliver Perry at Erie, Pennsylvania, in the summer of 1813 and became embroiled in a vicious controversy following the Battle of Put-in-Bay. For Elliott's career, see: *ANB*, 7: 431; *SROLO*, 64.

26. Chauncey mentioned that the *Mary Hatt* was downbound from Niagara in his report to Hamilton, 13 November 1812, USNA, RG 45, M 125, 25: 268. Later, he noted that on board the *Hatt* was Captain James Brock, 49th Regiment of Foot, who had in his possession baggage belonging to the late Major General Isaac Brock, Chauncey to Hamilton, *ibid.*: 183. Captain Brock was allowed to return, on parole, to Kingston with the baggage.

27. The *Governor Simcoe* was one of the British private schooners said to have been heavily armed and manned, as Chauncey reported to Hamilton, 6 November 1812, USNA, RG 45, M 125, 25: 167. The account in the *Quebec Mercury*, 8 December 1812, states that the Americans "fired upwards of fifty shots at [the *Simcoe*]. But she escaped by the intrepidity and dexterity of the master and crew." Evidence that the *Simcoe* had stopped at York is found in merchant Alexander Wood complaining at York that he had lost cargo when the schooner sank, Wood to Stevens, 3 February 1813, Firth, *Town of York*, 289.

28. The account in the 8 December 1812 issue of the *Quebec Mercury*, states that "the sloop *Elizabeth* ... which sailed from York on Wednesday night, under convoy of the *Earl of Moira*, was taken ..."

29. Chauncey to Hamilton, 17 September 1812, USNA, RG 45, M 125, 25: 183.

30. Chauncey learned that the *Royal George*, the *Earl of Moira* and a schooner were loaded with military stores and clothing for Fort George, and that the British made four attempts to sail after 19 November, but the presence of Chauncey's schooners kept them in port, Chauncey to Hamilton, 9 December 1812, USNA, RG 45, M 125, 25: 210.

31. Chauncey to Hamilton, 13 November 1812, USNA, RG 45, M 125, 25: 176.

32. Chauncey announced the launch of the *Madison* in his report to Hamilton, 26 November 1812, USNA, RG 45, M 125, 25: 192. Chauncey had discussed a combined attack by 17 November (Chauncey to Hamilton, *ibid.*: 183) but by the time that Colonel Alexander Macomb, Third U.S. Regiment of Artillery, reached Sackets on 21 November, weather conditions and reports of enemy strength on land, put an end to such plans as mentioned in Chauncey to Hamilton, 22 November, *ibid.*: 187. Chauncey appears to have withdrawn the last of his patrols around 1 December, (Chauncey to Hamilton, 1 December, *ibid.*: 200) and the vessels were soon laid up for the winter (Chauncey to Hamilton, 12 December, *ibid.*: 211). For Macomb's career, see *ANB*, 14: 282.

33. Chauncey to Hamilton, 6 November 1812, USNA, RG 45, M 125, 25: 167. See details about the British vessels in note #17 above.

34. Chauncey to Hamilton, 13 November 1812, USNA, RG 45, M 125, 25: 176.

35. Chauncey first reported "from the best authority" 3,000 men at Kingston, of whom 1,000 were regulars, to Hamilton, 22 November 1812, USNA, RG 45, M 125, 25: 187. William Vaughan sailed to Kingston under flag of truce to return prisoners and talked to a Provincial Marine officer he had known for years and passed on the information to Chauncey about the 600 regulars of the 49th Foot and 500 of the Glengarry Regiment of Fencibles on the march and the 2,000 militiamen,

Chauncey to Hamilton, 9 December 1812, *ibid.*: 210.

36. Chauncey described the squadron's arrangement to Hamilton, 12 December 1812, USNA, RG 45, M 125, 25: 211. The new schooner was described in Chauncey to Bullus, 10 December 1812, WCL, CLB; work on the *Madison* in Chauncey to Woolsey and to Leonard, 10 December, *ibid.*

37. This description of Sackets Harbor based upon Wilder, *The Battle of Sackett's Harbour*, 31, 45 and Chauncey to Jones, 20 January and 5 February 1813, USNA, RG 45, M 125, 26: 25 and 50.

38. This comment made in a report by Surgeon William Ross to Jacob Brown at Sackets, 18 September 1813, in Wilkinson, *Memoirs of My Own Times,* 3: appendix. Surgeon James Mann noted bad conditions in the hospital and typical symptoms in *Sketches of the Campaigns in 1812, 1813 and 1814,* 57 and 12-19. A description of "lake fever" is found in Watkins, "On the Disease called the Lake-Fever," 359-61. The estimate of 500 dead was reported by Dwight, "'Plow-Joggers for Generals,'" 18. Chauncey mentioned to Jones that only 39 of the 100 or so marines were mustered early in March and that 16 of the men died in March alone, 5 and 22 March 1813, USNA, RG 45, M 125, 27: 13 and 74. An informal survey of available data in musters show these death numbers from the beginning of December 1812 to the end of March 1813 in the *Oneida* (7), the *Conquest* (2) and the *Governor Tompkins* (8), USNA, RG 45, T 829A, Rolls 15 and 17.

39. *Myers,* 58.

40. Among Chauncey's instructions were: Chauncey to Woolsey and to Leonard, 10 December 1812, WCL, CLB; Chauncey to Leonard, 1 February 1813, *ibid.*; General Order, 1 February 1813, *ibid.* His visit to Erie is described in Chauncey to Hamilton, 1 and 8 January, USNA, RG 45, M 125, 26: 1 and 13.

41. The situation at Sackets and his plans are noted in Chauncey to Jones, 20 January and 5 February 1813, USNA, RG 45, M 125, 26: 25 and 50. Chauncey proposed the new ship to the secretary on 20 January 1813, *ibid.*: 25. He outlined his plans for an attack on the shipping at Kingston to Jones on 21 January 1813, *ibid.*: 28. His brother Lieutenant Wolcott Chauncey who would soon join the squadron had proposed a fifty-man raid on Kingston to Jones, which Chauncey rejected in a letter to Jones, 21 February 1813, *ibid.*: 99. The preparations for the new vessel are in Chauncey to Jones, 15 February 1813, WCL, CLB. Only the *Elizabeth* ($3,500) and the *Mary Hatt* ($2,500) were brought into the service, Chauncey to Leonard and Anderson, 4 February, *ibid.*

Chapter 4: "Totally incompetent for the purpose":
Winter Plans for Upper Canada

1. Bruyeres to Prevost, 28 January 1813, LAC, RG 8, I, 729: 69.
2. Strachan to McGill, [late] November 1812, Spragge, *John Strahan Letter Book*, 25.
3. Wood to Stevens, 3 February 1813, Firth, *Town of York*, 289.
4. Scott to Sheaffe, 17 November 1812, LAC, RG 8, I, 688E: 3.
5. Sheaffe to Talbot, 25 November 1812, Coyne, *The Talbot Papers*,163. The vessel was the U.S. Ship *Madison* which carried a 12-pdr. long guns and 20 32-pdr. carronades. A Canadian who had just returned from New York State gave information to the British, including that the new vessel at Sackets carried 22 32-pdr. carronades, Statement of Alexander Galloway, taken by Evans, 14 No-

vember 1812, *DHC,* 4: 211.

6. Sheaffe to Prevost, 23 November 1812, LAC, RG 8, I, 728: 115. Sheaffe mentioned the inquiry in his letter to Prevost on 8 November 1812, *DHC,* 4: 186.
7. Prevost to Bathurst, 21 November 1812, LAC, MG 11, CO 42, 148: 50. Prevost's earlier appeals to Bathurst were 17 and 26 October and 5 November 1812, *ibid.,* 147: 215, 148: 3 and 7. Prevost's letter to Warren on 18 December 1812 finally reached the admiral at Bermuda in February and was forwarded with a letter from Warren to the Admiralty, 21 February 1813, LAC, MG 12, ADM 1, 503: 357.
8. Smyth to his Troops, 17 November 1812, *DHC,* 4: 215. Myers described the artillery duel in his report to Sheaffe, 22 November 1812, *DHC,* 4: 227. Sheaffe reported his motivations and movements to Prevost, 23 November 1812, LAC, RG 8, I, 677: 202. "Winter seems to have set in, a strong northwest wind has been blowing for nearly a fortnight," Sheaffe to Prevost, 19 November 1812, *ibid.*: 194.
9. For descriptions of Smyth's failed invasion, see: *HDW,* 534-5; Sheaffe to Prevost, 30 November 1812, LAC, MG 11, CO 42, 354: 9; Bisshopp to Sheaffe, 1 December 1812, *ibid.*: 11; Winder to Smyth, 7 December 1812, *DHC,* 4: 260. The British strength is based upon Monthly General Distribution …, 25 November 1812, LAC, RG 8, I, 1707: 73.
10. Statement attributed to W. D. Powell, no date, *DHC,* 5: 45.
11. District General Order by Evans, 20 November 1812, *DHC,* 4: 224.
12. Instructions Sent to Officers commanding Forts by Brock, probably late September 1812, "District General Orders of Maj.-Gen. Sir Isaac Brock," 34-41, 46.
13. Sheaffe to Bisshopp, 30 November 1812, *DHC,* 5: 36.
14. Officers to Sheaffe, 30 November 1812, *DHC,* 5: 36.
15. Sheaffe to Powell, 20 January 1813, *DHC,* 5: 45.
16. Scott, *Memoirs of General Scott, Written by Himself,* 1: 66-7. An example of Scott's inaccuracies is that he said the 31 July 1813 revisit to York happened in September and involved a fight against British troops, 1: 98. Typical of the way Scott's recollection about Sheaffe has been amplified by other authors is this: "Sheaffe had not wanted to fight the Americans and petitioned for assignment elsewhere. In this instance the British ministry sternly held to the right of expatriation, which it would not apply to the Irish soldiers in the American Army. Sheaffe's request was not granted and he was compelled to employ his best talents against his native people," Tucker, *Poltroons and Patriots: A Popular Account of the War of 1812,* 1: 244. Other creditable sources that have given varying degrees of credence to the story include: Wood, *Select British Documents of the Canadian War of 1812,* 1: 45; Cruikshank, *DHC,* 5: 35; Whitfield, "The Battle of Queenston Heights: Sir Roger Hale Sheaffe," 34; Turner, *British Generals in the War of 1812,* 99.
17. Evans to Powell, 4 December 1812, *DHC,* 5: 17.
18. Nichol to Talbot, 18 December 1812, Coyne, *The Talbot Papers,* 170. The militia discharge was announced in the Militia General Orders by Shaw, 16 December 1812, *DHC,* 4: 324 and Sheaffe to Bathurst, 31 December 1812, *ibid.*: 338. Sheaffe mentioned the problems with the delivery of clothing to Prevost, 16 December 1812, LAC, RG 8, I, 677: 260.
19. Gray was so described by Lieutenant John Le Couteur as cited in Graves, *Merry Hearts,* 112. For Gray's career, see *HMG,* 170 and Anonymous, "Sketch of the character of the late Capt. Gray …," *The Antijacobin Review*

and True Churchman's Magazine, 45 (July 1813): 390. Among Gray's reports to Prevost about the Provincial Marine were letters written on 29 January, 24 February and 9 March 1812, LAC, RG 8, I, 728: 76, 86 and 94.

20. Gray to Prevost, 11 December 1812, LAC, RG 8, I, 728: 119. Gray had also covered the situation from Kingston for Prevost on 3 December 1812, *ibid*.: 135. His later report to Prevost from Kingston was on 29 December 1812, *ibid*.: 142. Sheaffe to Prevost, 16 December 1812, *ibid*., 677: 260.

21. Gray to Prevost, 3 December 1812, LAC, RG 8, I, 728: 135.

22. Strachan to McGill, November 1812, Spragge, *Strachan: 1812-1834*, 25.

23. Donald McLean to Stewart, 11 January 1813, AO, MU 2036, F 895, Miscellaneous Military Records. Prevost rejected the idea to Gray, 19 December 1812, LAC, RG 8, I, 728: 125. The failure to attack Sackets was lamented by Johnson to Claus, 16 March 1813, *DHC*, 6: 116. The Executive Council had pointed out to Sheaffe the danger posed by the sudden growth of the U.S. Navy at Sackets Harbor on 17 November 1812, *ibid*., 688e: 3.

24. Difficulties in the launch of the *Prince Regent* were recorded in Ely Playter's diary: "6 June 1812, The Vessel was to be launched the P. M. and many attended, I went down 4 o'clock. She stoped 3 or 4 times on her ways and they did not get her into the water." "7 June they ware at work at the Vessel but did not get her off …" Ely Playter Diary, AO, F 556. A similar difficulty was experience with the launch of the smaller schooner *Governor Hunter* in October 1804: "28 October 1804, a vessel was to be launch'd and they started her about 1 o'clock but did not get her off that eveng;" "30 October 1804, they got the vessel into the water this eveng and christened her the Governor Hunter," *ibid*. The date of the building of Allan's wharf is given as 1801 in Robertson, *Landmarks of Toronto*, 1: 251-2 and 3: 96, and 1803 in Hounsom, *Toronto in 1810*, 11. The location and size of the wharf is taken from the Plan of York, by Phillpotts, 24 May 1818, LAC, NMC 17026. The shallow depths of the harbour are recorded on numerous charts, including: "Plan of the Town and Harbour of York, by Nicolls, 24 December 1833, in Firth, *The Town of York, 1815-1834*; A Plan of York Harbour in Upper Canada, Survey'd by Jos. Bouchette, 1794, LAC, NMC 145919. Both charts noted a depth along the shore of six feet or less and the growth of rushes (even in 1833) along the shore, and Nicolls's plan adds that at the end of Allan's wharf the water shelved at a rate of about one foot for every 100 feet. For Alexander Clerk's career, see *HMG*, 100.

25. HMS *Princess Charlotte* was a frigate launched at Kingston in April 1814. It measured 121 feet long by 37 feet, 8 inches in breadth and was not much bigger than the *Brock* would have been. It drew 16 feet, 4 inches of water when loaded, Malcomson, *Warships of the Great Lakes*, 110. Among the locals who doubted the project from the beginning were these: "I hope we shall regain the command of the Lakes so shamefully lost, but to me it appears doubtful, for I do not like the Idea of having our Navy at different Ports…. I much fear that our fleet will meet with difficulty in forming a junction in the Spring," Donald McLean to Stewart, 11 January 1813, AO, MU 2036, F 895, Miscellaneous Military Records. "As York was not a place of defence, I was rather astonished that a vessel was building there which could not be protected." Askin to Cameron, 3 June 1813, *DHC*, 5: 296. "There was not a man in the country… that did not predict that [the *Brock*] would be burnt at the opening of navigation, and … had it not been burnt

it was next to certain there was not enough water to launch it or soil to support the ways," McGillivray to McTavish, 7 June 1813, *DHC*, 6: 17.

26. Bruyeres described the building stage and the way it had been conceived to Prevost, 28 January 1813, LAC, RG 8, I, 729: 69.

27. Gray to Prevost, 11 December 1812, LAC, RG 8, I, 728: 119. Gray had also covered the situation from Kingston for Prevost on 3 December 1812, *ibid*.: 135. His later report to Prevost from Kingston was on 31 December 1812, *ibid*.: 142.

28. Plucknett described his experience in a memorial to the Duke of Richmond, 14 October 1818, LAC, RG 8, I, 189: 42. Prevost mentioned his dockyard experience in England to Gray, 19 December 1812, *ibid*. 728: 125. Gray reported to Prevost from Kingston on 31 December 1812, (*ibid*.: 142) that 128 carpenters had arrived. Freer had reported to Sheaffe on 8 December (*ibid*., 1220: 48) that 112 shipwrights, 8 sawyers and 8 smiths were on their way from Montreal with Plucknett.

29. Plucknett's instructions about the two 18-gun brigs were issued to him at Montreal by Baynes on 3 December 1812, LAC, RG 8 I, 189: 34. Plucknett later referred to having been made "Superintendent and Store Keeper of the Naval Department on the Lakes of Upper Canada," whereas his original orders specified York as his only post, Plucknett to the Duke of Richmond, 14 October 1818, LAC,. RG 8, I, 189: 42.

30. The term "combination" was used by Sheaffe in his letter to Powell, 20 December 1812, *DHC*, 5: 20. Prevost described the situation as "a disposition that has manifested itself in that province to cabal against the person administering the government of it," Prevost to Bathurst, 27 February 1813, LAC, MG 11, CO 42, 150: 76. The controversy is detailed with notes in *DHC*, 5: 35.

31. Glegg to Powell, 10 January 1813, *DHC*, 5: 31.

32. Glegg to Powell, 10 January 1813, *DHC*, 5: 31. This letter referred to Vincent's concerns.

33. Sheaffe to Powell, 20 December 1812, *DHC*, 5: 20. As concerns the weather, Glegg wrote to Powell on 10 January 1813 (*ibid*.: 31) "The very inclement state of the weather during the last seven days having nearly suspended all communications between our respective posts …." Other similar remarks on the weather are found in: Wood to Stevens, 3 February 1813, Firth, *Town of York*, 289; MacLean to Stewart, 11 January 1813, OA: MU 2036, F 895 Miscellaneous Military Records, folder 8; T.G. Ridout toWard 5 January 1813, OA Thomas Ridout Family Fonds, F 43.

34. Sheaffe to Powell, 20 January 1812, *DHC*, 5: 45.

35. Glegg to Powell, 10 January 1813, *DHC*, 5: 31.

36. Sheaffe to Procter, 29 January 1813, USNA, RG 59, M588, unpaginated.

37. Evans to Procter, 25 January 1813, USNA, RG 59, M588, unpaginated.

38. Sheaffe to Baynes, 9 February 1813, LAC, RG 8, I, 678: 86.

39. Sheaffe to Powell, 12 February 1813, *DHC*, 5: 69. Glegg reported Sheaffe's gradual improvement in a letter to Powell, 11 February 1813, *DHC*, 5: 67. No full description of Sheaffe's illness has come to light. There is no mention of one of the prevalent fevers or severe cold symptoms and whether he suffered an emotional collapse or not is unclear. "I have cut a finger and can scarcely write," he mentioned to Powell on 20 December 1812 (*DHC*, 5: 20), but whether this led to an infection that finally laid him low is not documented.

40. Plucknett to Myers, 27 January 1813, LAC, RG 8, I, 729:

62. The original site for the slipway was located near the foot of modern-day John Street where the CN Tower stands. Plucknett's site was at the foot of Bay Street near the east end of Union Station.

41. The events were described by Plucknett to Myers, 27 January 1813, LAC, RG 8, 729: 62 and Myers to Freer, 28 January 1813, *ibid.*: 58. Plucknett's subordination to Gray was plainly stated in Baynes to Plucknett, 3 December 1812, LAC, RG 8 I, 189: 34. For Bruyere's career, see *DCB*, 5: 118.

42. Myers to Plucknett, 27 January 1813, LAC, RG 8, I, 729: 56.

43. Bruyeres to Prevost, 28 January 1813, LAC, RG 8, I, 729: 69. Bruyeres had written more emphatically to Prevost about the advantages of concentrating the naval forces at Kingston, 19 January 1813, *ibid.*, 387: 10. Locals who doubted the project are cited in note 25 of this chapter.

44. Bruyeres to Prevost, 13 February 1813, LAC, RG 8, I, 387: 15.

45. Myers to Freer, 9 February 1813, LAC, RG 8, I, 729: 86

46. Merritt to Prendergast, February 1813, *DHC*, 5: 96. For descriptions of the actions at Lacolle (20 November 1812), Frenchtown and Ogdensburg, see *HDW*, 276, 196 and 392.

47. Prevost mentioned his intention to leave Quebec on 12 or 13 February 1813 to Bathurst on 6 February 1813, *DHC*, 5: 56 and repeated it in Prevost to Bathurst, 8 February 1813, LAC, MG 11, CO 42, 150: 37. An itinerary was not found for Prevost's journey but an itinerary exists for a quick tour that Prevost made from Quebec to Montreal, LAC, RG 8, I, 1708: 5. The itinerary is dated 1813, but probably represents a trip made early in the governor-in-chief's term as it appears to be geared for him to observe the various posts, as if he had never seen them. It mentions only "Thursday, the 26th" which may be Thursday, 26 September 1811; in *DCB*, 5: 693, it is stated that Prevost did travel down to Montreal at this time. The departure and arrival times, distances, use of post horses, accommodations, etc., are all fully detailed as his 1813 winter trip must have been. It makes reference to Prevost travelling twenty leagues (60 miles) on one day that had no visitation which does not conflict with the rate of travel he achieved during the winter trip when he went about 550 miles in eight days. Proof of excellent winter roads is: "Our Winter has set in unusually severe with plenty of snow, which will make good Roads to forward such supplies …," McLean to Stewart, 11 January 1813, OA: MU 2036, F 895 Miscellaneous Military Records, folder 8; "Our Canadian winter has set in to be very severe; all the great rivers and lakes are frozen over and the snow is four feet deep in our tractless forests, which makes sleighing excellent for about 12 miles thro' the country," T.G. Ridout toWard 5 January 1813, OA Thomas Ridout Family Fonds, F 43. 240 miles = 386 km. 550 miles = 886 km. 70 miles = 113 km.

48. Prevost to Bathurst, 6 February 1813, *DHC*, 5: 56. Writer and historian James Elliott suggests that the King's Head Inn would have been a likely place for the meeting. The inn is described in Robertson, *Diary of Mrs. Simcoe*, 320, 323, 324. Also known as "the Government House," it had been leased by the government for use as a post house since the mid-1790s, Minutes of the Executive Council, 9 March 1799, Cruikshank and Hunter, *The Russell Papers*, 3: 134.

49. Prevost to Bathurst, 27 February 1813, LAC, MG 11, CO 42, 150: 76. Prevost mentions having gone as far as Lake Erie and returned to Niagara by 27 February (to Bathurst, 27 February 1813, *ibid.*: 90). The round trip was 70 miles long and, given that he stopped to inspect the batteries and forts along the way, as well as observe the American preparations, Prevost must have spent one night away from Niagara which means he likely reached that town on 25 February, set out for Lake Erie the next day and returned on 27 February. He and his weary drivers and escorts then had several days to rest at Niagara before returning to York. Prevost had his adjutant general Edward Baynes express his dissatisfaction with Gray who replied to Baynes on 26 January 1813 (LAC, RG 8, I, 729: 26) that he was innocent of the allegations.

50. Prevost to Bathurst, 19 March 1813, LAC, MG 11, CO 42, 354: 104.

51. Sheaffe mentioned changes to the militia in Sheaffe to Baynes, 9 February 1813, LAC, RG 8, I, 678: 86 and Sheaffe to unstated, 7 January 1813, *ibid.*, 5: 30. General orders issued by Prevost were: Artillery Drivers, 3 March 1813, *ibid.*: 85; Provincial Artificers, 3 March 1813, *ibid.*: 85; Light Cavalry, 3 March 1813, *ibid.*: 86; personnel changes, 1 March 1813, *ibid.*: 84

52. Militia General Order by Shaw, 5 March 1813, *DHC*, 5: 88. Sheaffe "accompanied by a numerous staff," opened the session on 25 February as contained in a report about the session and the various speakers' remarks dated 8 March 1813, which begin at LAC, MG 11, CO 42, 354: 32. The session ended on 13 March as reported on 20 March 1813, in *ibid.*: 48. The details of the legislation are found in *ibid.*: 50.

53. Clerk to Gray, 24 March 1813, LAC, RG 8, I, 729: 175. The ship's name was mentioned in Minutes of the decision of the Commander of the Forces upon certain points relating to the Marine Department, by Freer, 3 February 1813, LAC, RG 8, I, 688E: 13.

54. Message to Prevost and his answer, 3 March 1813, *DHC*, 5: 99.

55. Prevost to Bathurst, 19 March 1813, LAC, MG 11, CO 42, 354: 104

Chapter 5: "A secondary, but still important object": American Campaign Goals for 1813

1. Note presented to the cabinet, on the 8th of February, 1813 by the Secretary of War, *ASP: MA*, 1: 439

2. For Eustis's career, see *ANB*, 7: 590. For Hamilton's career, see *ANB*, 9: 928 See: Eustis to Madison, 3 December 1812, Stagg *et al*, *The Papers of James Madison*, 5: 477; Madison to Eustis, 4 December 1812, *ibid.*: 479; Hamilton to Madison, 30 December 1812, *ibid.*: 534; Madison to Hamilton, 31 December 1812, *ibid.*: 535.

3. Madison informed Gallatin on 8 August 1812, "I am much worn down, and feel the approach of my bilious visitor," Adams, *The Writings of Albert Gallatin*, 1: 523. For a description of Madison's physical appearance, personality and persistent ill health (as well as on his hypochondriac concerns about epilepsy), see Matthews, *If Men Were Angels*, 4-7. Other material used here in reference to Madison includes: *ANB*, 14: 306; Hunt, *The Writings of James Madison*, vol. 8; Stagg, *Mr. Madison's War*, 270-347; Brant, *James Madison: Commander in Chief, 1812-1836*, 114-211; Stagg *et al*, *The Papers of James Madison*, vols. 4 and 5; Stagg, "James Madison and the Coercion of Great Britain"; Brant, "Timid President? Futile War?"

4. Calhoun to Macbride, 18 April 1812, Meriwether, *The Papers of John C. Calhoun*, 1: 99. President's message, 4 November 1812, *Journal of the House of Representatives*, 12th Congress, Second Session, 539.

5. Romaine to Romayne, 15 November 1812, Stagg *et al*, *The Papers of James Madison*, 5: 439, note 2a.

6. Monroe's report on military needs and strategy to the military committees in the Senate and House of Representatives and to several individuals accompanied his letter to Campbell, 23 December 1812, Hamilton, *The Writings of James Monroe*, 5: 227. Monroe's expectations about appointments to the war department or the army are the subjects of: Monroe to Crawford, 3 December 1812, *ibid.*: 227; Monroe to Madison, 25 February 1813, *ibid.*: 244; Monroe to Jefferson, 7 June 1813, *ibid.*: 259. For Monroe's career, see *ANB*, 15: 681. The financial situation was discussed in numerous documents, including: Gallatin to Madison, [mid-] autumn, 12 December 1812 and 5 March, Adams, *The Writings of Albert Gallatin*, 1: 527, 530 and 532; Monroe to Gallatin, 5 January 1813, *ibid.*: 531. The impact of financial considerations is fully described in Stagg, *Mr. Madison's War*, 278-86.

7. Armstrong to Spencer, 25 January 1813, cited in Skeen, *John Armstrong, Jr.*, 124. For Armstrong's career: see *ANB*, 1: 616; Skeen, "Mr. Madison's Secretary of War"; Skeen, "Monroe and Armstrong: A Study in Political Rivalry." Armstrong wrote to Eustis, 2 January 1813, *DHC*, 3: 29. Armstrong, *Hints to Young Generals by an Old Soldier*. Armstrong's nomination is noticed on 8, 12 and 13 January 1813 in the *Journal of the Executive Proceedings of the Senate*, 2: 315-6. Gallatin described the pros and cons of selecting Armstrong to Madison, 7 January 1813, Stagg *et al*, *The Papers of James Madison*, 5: 557. Armstrong formerly accepted his post in a note to Madison, 17 January 1813, *ibid.*: 593.

8. For Jones's career, see: *ANB*, 12: 256; Paullin, "Naval Administration Under Secretaries …"; Eckert, "William Jones: Mr. Madison's Secretary of the Navy." Jones declined the commissary general post in April 1812 as noted in Coxe to Madison, 13 August 1812, Stagg *et al*, *The Papers of James Madison*, 5: 150. When he thought he might be taking over the western army after Hull's defeat, Monroe proposed taking Jones with him to build gunboats to Madison, 6 September 1812, *ibid.*: 281. Madison sent Jones's commission to him on 12 January 1813, *ibid.*: 570, to which Jones replied, 14 January 1813, *ibid.*: 582.

9. Among the laws passed during this period were: 12 December 1812, "An act increasing the pay of non commissioned officers, …" 12th Congress, Session 2, Chapter 4, *Public Statutes at Large of the United States of America*, 2: 788; 2 January 1813, "An act to increase the navy of the United States," 12: 2: 6, *ibid.*: 789; 20 January 1813, "An act supplementary to … 'An act authorizing the more perfect organization of the army,'" 12: 2: 12, *ibid.*: 791; 29 January 1813, "An act in addition to … 'An act to raise and additional military force,'" 12: 2: 16, *ibid.*: 794; 24 February 1813, "An act making provision for an additional number of general officers," 12: 2: 24, *ibid.*: 801; 3 March 1813, "An act the better to provide for the supplies of the Army …," 12: 2: 48, *ibid.*: 816; 3 March 1813, "An act for the better organization of the general staff …," 12: 2: 52, *ibid.*: 819; 3 March 1813, "An act supplementary to the act for increasing the navy," 12: 2: 54, *ibid.*: 821; 3 March 1813, "An act making appropriations for the support of the navy …," 12: 2: 55, *ibid.*: 821; 3 March 1813, "An act making appropriations for the support of the army …," 12: 2: 57, *ibid.*: 822.

10. Colonel Charles Boerstler reported from Buffalo to Jones (and to Chauncey by separate letter) that deserters reported the two warships at York, with varying views of their armament, 24 January 1813, USNA, RG 45, M 125, 26: between items 33 and 34, without covering letter. Chauncey repeated the two-ship claim about York and mentioned the ship at Kingston to Jones, 20 January 1813, *ibid.*: 25. Thomas Plucknett's instructions about building two 18-gun brigs at York were issued to him at Montreal by Baynes on 3 December 1812, LAC, RG 8, I, 189: 34 and he travelled through Kingston later that month, when loose lips probably helped substantiate the reports Chauncey received.

11. Madison to Dearborn, 6 February 1813, Stagg *et al*, *The Papers of James Madison*, 5: 645. Monroe showed some uncertainty about controlling Lake Ontario in spring of 1813 in his report on military needs and strategy to the military committees in the Senate and House of Representatives and to several individuals as accompanied with his letter to Campbell, 23 December 1812, Hamilton, *The Writings of James Monroe*, 5: 227. Jones approved the new ship in his first letter to Chauncey, 27 January, USNA, RG 45, M 149, 10: 231.

12. Jones to Chauncey, 27 January, USNA, RG 45, M 149, 10: 231. Jones stressed the upper lakes to Chauncey in letters on 11 and 27 February 1813, *ibid.*: 251 and 285.

13. Jones to Chauncey, 27 January, USNA, RG 45, M 149, 10: 231. The commercial ties to the importance of regaining Mackinac are explored in Malcomson, "Carry Michilimackinac at all hazards."

14. Monroe expressed this idea in a lengthy report on military needs and strategy to the military committees in the Senate and House of Representatives and to several individuals as noted in his letter to Campbell, 23 December 1812, Hamilton, *The Writings of James Monroe*, 5: 227. Monroe's expectations about appointments to the war department or the army are the subjects of: Monroe to Crawford, 3 December 1812, *ibid.*: 227; Monroe to Madison, 25 February 1813, *ibid.*: 244; Monroe to Jefferson, 7 June 1813, *ibid.*: 259. Jefferson had made his oft-quoted remark to Duane, 4 August 1812, Ford, *The Works of Thomas Jefferson*, 11: 265.

15. Note presented to the cabinet, on the 8th of February, 1813 by the Secretary of War, *ASP: MA*, 1: 439.

16. Note presented to the cabinet, on the 8th of February, 1813 by the Secretary of War, *ASP: MA*, 1: 439. The St. Lawrence was generally open to navigation before 1 May, although this depended on the severity of the winter and ice build up. Kingston was completely clear of ice by 13 April 1814 as noted in Drummond to Prevost, 13 April 1814, LAC, RG 8, I, 732: 132. As will be seen, the ice clogged Kingston well past that date in 1813 as noted in Gray to Freer, 18 April 1813, LAC, RG 8, I, 729: 162.

17. "In choosing to take the offensive in this manner rather than waiting for better weather and more extensive preparations, Armstrong was probably governed by two motives: a desire to vindicate American honor speedily and the need to influence the outcome of the spring elections in New York," Stagg, *Mr. Madison's War*, 285. This speculation is not supported by any references. Stagg states on 335 that the victory at York on 27 April 1813, "undeniably assisted the Republican party in re-electing Governor Daniel Tompkins." Benn, *Historic Fort York*, 63, picks up on this idea and states that "victory proclamations circulated prior to the attack," was one contributing factor to the victory, referencing only Stagg. As will be shown in Chapter 15, news of the victory did not spread until the polling for the New York election was complete.

18. Dearborn expressed his thoughts on the strategy in a

long letter to Madison, 6 April 1812, Stagg *et al*, *The Papers of James Madison*, 4: 298. He went into detail about the attack on Quebec and briefly recommended a concurrent three-pronged attack on Upper Canada.

19. Scott to Thompson 17 November 1812, Scott, "The letters of Captain John Scott," 71. McDonogh described him as "a fine old gentlemen and makes a very soldierly appearance," to his parents, 13 September 1812, O'Reilly, "A Hero of Fort Erie," 71. For Dearborn's career, see: *ANB*, 6: 299; Smith, "General Henry Dearborn: A Biographical Essay"; Erney, *The Public Life of Henry Dearborn*. For a physical description of Dearborn, see *ibid.*, 331-3.

20. "Major Gen. Henry Dearborn, Commander in Chief of the Northern Army," was published in the *Boston Chronicle* and republished on 12 January 1813 in the *Quebec Mercury*.

21. Dearborn to Jefferson, 10 March 1812, cited in Erney, *The Public Life of Henry Dearborn*, 270. Monroe mentioned Dearborn's abilities in a letter to Jefferson, 7 June 1813 (Hamilton, *The Writings of James Monroe*, 5: 259): "he was advanc'd in years, infirm, and had given en no proof of activity or military talent during the year."

22. Eustis wrote to Dearborn, 4 and 26 June, 9 and 15 July and 1 August 1812, USNA, RG 107, Letters Sent by the Secretary of War, 5: 424 and 458, 6: 15, 26 and 199. Madison to Dearborn, 9 August 1812, Hunt, *The Writings of James Madison*, 8: 205. Dearborn expressed his misunderstanding of the span of his command to Eustis, 15 August 1812, USNA, RG 107, Letters Received by the Secretary of War, September 1811–December 1812 (C, D): unpaginated. Dearborn expressed his thoughts on the 1812 strategy in a long letter to Madison, 6 April 1812, Stagg *et al*, *The Papers of James Madison*, 4: 298. He went into detail about the attack on Quebec and briefly recommended a concurrent three-pronged attack on Upper Canada, adding that he thought the latter campaign would be handled by someone other than the general in charge of the former. He did not indicate which one he thought he would command, but may have been operating with that understanding, despite being stationed at Albany as senior general in the north. Tompkins expressed his frustration with Dearborn in a letter to him, 28 June 1812, *DHC*, 3: 83 and to Eustis, 27 June 1812, *ibid.*: 80.

23. "Granny Dearborn …" appears in "War and Proclamations", (from the *Connecticut Mirror*), republished on 2 March 1813 in the *Quebec Mercury*. The political cartoon (from a Montreal source) was described in the 23 February 1813 issue of the same paper. Other issues featured such satire as: "Dearborn's Campaign. A Song,"(Canadian source), 8 December 1812; "Third Invasion of Canada," (from Ballstown, New York), 26 January 1813; "The Carrier's Wish," (from the *Columbian Centinel*) 2 February 1813;

24. Thomas Leiper (an influential Philadelphia Republican) to Madison, 27 December 1812, Stagg *et al*, *The Papers of James Madison*, 5: 527.

25. Dearborn to Madison, 13 December 1812, LOC, James Madison Papers, Series 1: General Correspondence. Dearborn had already mentioned his willingness to stand aside in a letter to Lincoln, 27 September 1812, cited in Erney, *The Public Life of Henry Dearborn*, 304.

26. Monroe to Jefferson, 7 June 1813, Hamilton, *The Writings of James Monroe*, 5: 259. Monroe discussed these and other issues in a letter to Madison, 25 February 1813, *ibid.*: 244. He mentioned his near-appointment

to the campaign in the Northwest to Dearborn, 17 September 1812, *ibid.*: 223. Dearborn had already mentioned his willingness to stand aside in a letter to Lincoln, 27 September 1812, cited in Erney, *The Public Life of Henry Dearborn*, 304.

27. Dearborn expressed his ideas on improvements in the army, and mentioned the movement of British troops to Madison, 13 December 1812, and 14 February 1813, LOC, James Madison Papers, Series 1: General Correspondence. He described his attempts to improve recruitment (which were nullified, to his disapproval, by recent legislation creating military districts) and camp discipline and the movement of British troops to Armstrong, 14 February 1813, USNA, RG 107, M 221, roll 52: unpaginated.

28. Chauncey detailed his plan for an attack on Kingston to Jones on 21 January 1813, USNA, RG 45, M 125, 26: 28. 3 miles = 4.8 km.

29. Dearborn to Madison, 14 February 1813, LOC, James Madison Papers, Series 1: General Correspondence. Dearborn explained his plan to Armstrong, 14 February 1813, USNA, RG 107, M 221, roll 52: unpaginated.

30. The confusing and contradictory exchanges between Armstrong and Dearborn were, as follows. Armstrong explained the campaign goals to Dearborn on on 10 February 1813, USNA, RG 107, M 6, roll 6: 462. When he received Dearborn's suggestion about a March attack over the ice, written on 14 February, *ibid.*, M 221, roll 52: unpaginated, Armstrong wrote back to Dearborn to approve this scheme and offer some advice about it on 24 February, *ibid.*, M 6, roll 6: 467. In the meantime Dearborn wrote to Armstrong on 18 and 20 February, agreeing to undertake the larger plan approved by the cabinet, but expressing his concern about leaving the posts on Lake Champlain without proper defence and suggesting how militia regiments might be moved in to provide it, *ibid.*, M 221, roll 52: unpaginated. In his letter to Armstrong on 25 February, Dearborn wrote (with a complaining tone) that he had waited too long for Chauncey to return from New York and that it was too late to make an attack across the ice and that he was going ahead with Armstrong's plan, *ibid.*, M 221, roll 52: unpaginated. Armstrong finished the series with a letter to Dearborn on 4 March, leaving it up to him to choose which plan to follow, *ibid.*, M 6, roll 6: 302.

31. "Your movements …," wrote Armstrong to Dearborn, "… may be masked by reports that Sackett's Harbour is in danger," 10 February 1813, USNA, RG 107, M 6, roll 6: 462. Dearborn announced the British attack on Ogdensburg to Armstrong, 25 February 1813, USNA, RG 107, M 221, roll 52: unpaginated. He wrote to Armstrong about the situation at Sackets on 3 and 9 March 1813, *ibid.* For a description of the Ogdensburg raid, see Forsyth to Macomb, 22 February 1813, *ibid.* and Macdonell to Harvey, 25 February 1813, LAC, RG 8, I, 678: 100.

32. This description of Sackets Harbor based upon Wilder, *The Battle of Sackett's Harbour*, 31, 45. Wilder suggests that an abatis had been formed around the Harbor and its camps by the felling of timber to create a impenetrable tangle. As Gary Gibson pointed out in a private consultation, this was based on Macomb's stated intention to do the work as shown "in Macomb's orderly book [NYSL, 9962, Macomb Orderly Book, 1812-13] entry for 28 February 1813 which reads in part: 'My intention is to Abatis the rear of the whole place and the Militia are to be posted so as to extend all along it.'" A detailed map of the fortifications in the area, made

in late 1813, shows no evidence of any such obstacle, USNA, RG 77, Civil Works, Map File, D 15-1.

33. Dearborn to Armstrong, 14 March 1813, USNA, RG 107, M 221, roll 52: unpaginated. Chauncey requested Perry's services to Jones, 21 January 1813, USNA, RG 45, M 125, 26: 28. For Perry's career, see *ANB*, 17: 369.

34. Chauncey to Jones, 12 March 1813, USNA, RG 45, M 125, 27: 33. He mentioned his doubt of an attack to Jones on 8 March, *ibid.*: 20.

35. Chauncey to Jones, 18 March 1813, USNA, RG 45, M 125, 27: 58. Dearborn mentioned the date of the council to Armstrong, 16 March, USNA, RG 107, M 221, roll 52: unpaginated.

36. Chauncey to Jones, 12 March 1813, USNA, RG 45, M 125, 27: 33. He mentioned his doubt of an attack to Jones on 8 March, *ibid.*: 20. Writing at Kingston, Bruyeres had predicted this plan to Prevost in his 19 January 1813 letter, LAC, RG 8, I, 387: 10, noting: "the first effort of Commodore Chauncey will be to endeavour to destroy York previous to the ice being dispersed in the narrow part of the lake towards this place."

37. Chauncey to Jones, 18 March 1813, USNA, RG 45, M 125, 27: 58.

38. Chauncey to Jones, 18 March 1813, USNA, RG 45, M 125, 27: 58. Letters in which Jones stressed the importance of controlling the upper lakes included those to Chauncey, 27 January, 11 and 27 February 1813, USNA, RG 45, M 149, 10: 231, 251 and 285.

39. Chauncey to Perry, 15 March 1813, WCL, CLB.

40. Jones to Chauncey, 8 April 1813, *NWDH*, 2: 433. Evidence that Chauncey's plan was discussed with Armstrong is seen in Jones's mention of the use of batteaux and a larger force, points which Armstrong made to Dearborn on 10 and 29 March 1813, USNA, RG 107, M 6, roll 6: 314 and 338. Dearborn mentioned the change of plan to Armstrong, 16 March, USNA, RG 107, M 221, roll 52: unpaginated and the bare details of the plan in an undated note shown in *ASP: MA*, 1: 442. Dearborn suggested that he might not be able to accompany the expedition and mentioned his orders to the army officers to Chauncey, 31 March, enclosed with Chauncey to Jones, USNA, RG 45, M 125, 27: 157.

41. Armstrong to Dearborn, 29 March 1813, USNA, RG 107, M 6, roll 6: 338.

42. Armstrong to Dearborn, 29 March 1813, USNA, RG 107, M 6, roll 6: 338. Evidence for the policy of allowing field commanders to make the essential decisions includes Armstrong telling Dearborn on 4 March, to choose the form of attack he wanted to make against Kingston, *ibid.*,: 302 and Jones's comment to Chauncey, 8 April 1813, *NWDH*, 2: 433: " ... as nautical skill and experience can alone determine the time, circumstances and manner of employing that force, in cooperation with the military, of these you will be the exclusive judge." In discussing the 1813 campaign, Monroe wrote tpoHamilton on 23 December 1812, *The Writing of James Monroe*, 7: 235: "The plan of campaign must be formed by the general who commands the expedition. He alone can best decide at what points to make attacks and where to make feints, if any ought to be made."

43. Chauncey informed Jones of the various matters: the need for more marines, 5 March 1813, USNA, RG 45, M 125, 27: 13; arrival of seamen, 8 and 12 March 1813, *ibid.*: 20 and 34; expectation of more seamen, 18 March 1813, *ibid.*: 59; launch of the *Lady of the Lake*, and named the schooners, 6 April 1813, *ibid.*: 135; beginning the new ship (*General Pike*), 8 April 1813, *ibid.*: 152; the *Pike's* progress in Chauncey to Jones, 23 April 1813, *ibid.*, 28: 39.

Chapter 6: "Never more secure": Fortifying York

1. Comment by Strachan, March 1813, Spragge, *Strachan*, 10,

2. Ely Playter's diary entry of 18 October 1812, AO, F 556. He belonged to Thomas Hamilton's company and mentions the muster and draft and being on duty in the rest of his October entries. The diary stops at 25 October and resumes on 24 April 1813 by which time Hamilton's company had been put under command of Captain John B. Robinson. On 25 April 1813 Playter wrote, "the Men nearly all being employed daily at the Batteries and by the Engineer." Musters for the "Whitby Company" for August 1812, in Playter's diary, indicate names that have been drawn and in which order. Absenteeism is shown in the Returns of Subsistence paid to captain Ridout's Company ... from December 1812 to February 1813, AO, F 43, Thomas Ridout Family Fonds. For a full description of the militia at York, see Appendix 5, Upper Canada Militia at the Battle of York.

3. Isaac Wilson to Jonathan Wilson, 5 December 1813, AO, MS 199(5), Isaac Wilson Diaries. Wilson mentioned the use of a draft. He is shown as present in the Returns of Subsistence paid to Captain Ridout's Company ... from December 1812 to February 1813, AO, F 43, Thomas Ridout Family Fonds. He is shown as a corporal in the last of the Muster Roll and Pay Lists of Captain Sam Ridout's Company ..., 25 February to 24 April 1813, LAC, RG 9, IB7, 17: 187-8, 18: 430-1. Lyon's name appears on these payrolls: Muster Roll and Pay Lists of Captain Thomas Hamilton's and Captain John Beverley Robinson's Company ... 25 February to 24 April 1813, LAC, RG 9, IB7, 17: 222-3, 225-6, 18: 437-8 and Muster Roll and Pay Lists of Lieutenant William Jarvis's Company of Incorporated Militia, 25 March to 24 April 1813, *ibid.*, 18: 415. His pay was 14s for 28 days with Robinson and then 19s/3d for 25 days with Jarvis. 1 shillings equals 12 pence.

4. The best available returns of the force at York garrison in 1812 are from 12 November (LAC, RG 8, I, 1707: 60); 25 November (*ibid.*: 73) and 21 December (*ibid.*: 124). The first lists 2 Royal Artillerymen, 33 officers and men of the 41st Foot and 22 of the 49th Foot, 3 of the Royal Newfoundland Fencibles and 2 of the Canadian Fencibles, for a total of 62 officers and men. The second has a similar breakdown for a total of 71 and the third shows 68. Shortt was listed as the commander on the November return and mentioned in connection with the regulars at York in Sheaffe to Vincent, 29 March 1813, Sheaffe, "Letter Book," 370. Shortt also received allowances at York during this period as shown in the Fort York Account Book, City of Toronto Culture, Museum and Heritage Services. For his career, see *HMG*, 332.

5. For Clerk and Ingouville's careers see, *HMG*, 100 and 364. Ingouville was very likely at York in the autumn as one Royal Newfoundland lieutenant and one private were mustered there in November (Monthly General Distribution ..., 25 November 1812, LAC, RG 8, I, 1707: 73) and two lieutenants and one private were there late in December as noted in The Distribution of the Troops in Canada by Baynes on 21 December 1812, *ibid.*: 124-5. Sheaffe mentions his appointment of Ingouville to Prevost, 5A May 1813, LAC, MG 11, CO 42, 354: 132. Royal Engineer Lieutenant Colonel Philip Hughes complimented Ingouville's work as an assistant engineer at York to Sheaffe, undated (context strongly indicates early May 1813), LAC RG 5, A1, 17: 7305.

6. A sample of the correspondence during late winter and early spring of 1813 found in the Sheaffe "Letter Book" includes: Incorporated Militia – Sheaffe to Prevost, 13 March (p. 346) Loring to Baynes, 15 March (348), Sheaffe to Vincent, 17 March (349), Sheaffe to Prevost, 18 March (350); other posts – Loring to Freer, 13 March (346), Loring to Pearson, 18 March (350), Sheaffe to Freer 20 March (351), Sheaffe to Pearson, 21 March (352), Sheaffe to Baynes, 27 March (356), Sheaffe to Prevost, 5 April (361); native matters – Loring to Roberts, 25 March (354), Loring to Couche, 26 March (355), Sheaffe to Baynes, 29 March (356) Sheaffe to Procter, 6 April, (365); reinforcements – Sheaffe to Baynes, 25 March (353), Sheaffe to Myers, 29 March (357), Loring to Vincent, 30 March (359), Loring to Vincent, 31 March, (360).

7. Vigoureux's plan and Brock's influence were discussed in Bruyeres to Prevost, undated, LAC, MG 11, CO 42, 146: 56. This report is grouped with Prevost's correspondence of March 1812 and, referring to Brock and his plans for subsequent defensive measures, was most likely written early in 1812.

8. One of the most detailed descriptions of the fortifications at York in April 1813 was written by William Powell. It was in one of two accounts he wrote about the battle and which appear in *DHC*. It is referred to herein as [Powell A], "An Account of the Capture of York," *DHC*, 5: 175. He gives the distances to the Half Moon Battery and the Western Battery as 400 yards and 800 yards respectively. For this study of the battle the scales of these three maps were used to determine their locations: Sketch of the ground … York, by Williams, 7 November 1813, LAC, NMC 22820; Plan of the Town and Harbour of York …, by Bonnycastle, 1833, LAC, NMC 16818; an 1833 plan of the harbour (NAC, NMC 16817) in Benn, *Historic Fort York* 109. The Half Moon Battery only appears on Williams' map and appears to be about 390 yards west of western rampart of the fort, while the Western Battery is shown at 670 yards (613 m). The latter appears on the other two maps and is about 745 yards (682 m) west of the rampart. These measurements place the Half Moon Battery near the current intersection of Garrison Road and Fleet Street and the Western Battery just inside the Princes' Gates on Princes' Blvd. on the CNE grounds. The American column had advanced to the Half Moon battery at the time of the explosion on 27 April. Comments by witnesses as to the distances and fall of debris generally agree with the measurements above; see note 34 in Chapter 11 for the remarks. Beikie used the term "Government House Battery," John Beikie to John Macdonell, 5 May 1813, AO, F 548, John Macdonell Fonds. Finan briefly described the batteries, *Journal of a Voyage*, 283-91. See also: Major Abraham Eustis to his uncle the former Secretary of the Army, William Eustis, 11 May 1813, *Proceedings of the Massachusetts Historical Society*, 11 (1869-70): 492-5; and Trowbridge's description of York and account of the battle (hereafter "Trowbridge's account"), LOC, Trowbridge Papers. The continuing need to clear the woods west of the Western Battery which sat 50 yards from the edge of the woods was mentioned by Kitson to Vincent, 22 November 1813, LAC, RG 8, I, 388: 136.

9. "Near this [the magazine] was a Redoubt with five pieces of artillery, called the Governor's Battery," Trowbridge's account, LOC, Trowbridge Papers. Construction of a typical battery is described in Smith, *An Universal Military Dictionary*, 22. This 1779 record formed the basis of the description given in James's *New and*

Enlarged Military Dictionary, (1802), unpaginated.

10. Gray discussed the issue of fort designs in his Report upon the expediency of removing the Marine Establishment from Kingston to York, …, 9 March 1812, LAC, RG 8, I, 728: 94. He favoured "a *strong regular fort*, … "a small Pentagon or Square, with one of the sides of the Polygon upon the Lake (or Harbour), … [but] The neck of Land at the Gov't House is too much contracted, and irregular in its shape, for such a Work." Vigoureux's plan and Brock's influence were discussed in Bruyeres to Prevost, undated, LAC, MG 11, CO 42, 146: 56. In Brock to Prevost, 22 April 1812, LAC, RG 8, I, 676: 103, the general stated his intention to making a temporary magazine and "the excavation of the ditch for the proposed fortification on the spot where the government house stands." The best available contemporary graphic reference is Sketch of the ground in advance of and including York Upper Canada, by Williams, 7 November 1813 (drawn before major improvements were undertaken), LAC, NMC 22819 and 22820, H2, 440, Toronto, 1813. 50 yd. = 46 m. 7 feet = 2.1 m.

11. Gray to Prevost, 11 December 1812, LAC, RG 8, I, 728: 119. Sheaffe to Prevost, 16 December 1812, *ibid.*, 677: 260. Prevost reported to Gray, 19 December 1812, *ibid.*: 125, that one 18-pdr. and two 12s would be sent from Quebec and two more 12s from Montreal "as soon as it can be done consistent with the other services going on." Two more long 18-pdrs. and two 68-pdr. carronades were shipped in January, as noted in Freer to Gray, 9 January 1813, *ibid.*, 1220: 100. Regarding the arsenal at Quebec, see: Return of Brass and Iron Ordnance Mounted on Trailing and Garrison Carriages at the different Stations in Lower Canada and Upper Canada, by Glasgow, 19 December 1812, LAC, RG 8, I, 1707: 82. Of the British-made iron guns, there were 6 32s, 31 24s, 5 18s and 41 12s. The count of carronades was: 10 68s, 12 18s, 15 12s and 2 9s. There were also iron mortars, brass guns, howitzers and mortars mounted. There were a few other guns mounted on Martello towers at Quebec. There were very few guns mounted at Montreal, Chambly and Isle aux Noix. The delivery of guns to Kingston was minimal and even in June 1813 there were only 5 18-pdrs., 7 9-pdrs, 1 6-pdr. and 1 4-pdr. mounted, as noted in Return of Guns and Ammunition in the Batteries and Block Houses at the Post of Kingston, by Allan, 4 June 1813, LAC, RG 8, I, 688e: 96.

12. The guns at York in autumn 1812 were shown in the Return of Brass and Iron Ordnance Mounted on Trailing and Garrison Carriages at the different Stations in Lower Canada and Upper Canada, by Glasgow, 19 December 1812, LAC, RG 8, I, 1707: 82. The 6- and 12-pdr. long guns and 18-pdr. carronades at York in spring 1813 were listed in the Return of Ordnance Mounted on the Several Batteries with the Number of Rounds for Garrison Service at the undermentioned Posts, by James Gordon, 31 March 1813, *ibid.*, 387: 47 and mentioned in Bruyeres to Prevost, 13 February 1813, *ibid.*: 15 and in Myers to Freer, 2 April 1813, *ibid.*, 729: 153. Sheaffe noted on 7 April "2 12prs mounted – 6 18prs and hope to have more ready in a few days." Sheaffe to Baynes, 7 April 1813, Sheaffe, "Letter Book," 370. The field guns, limbers and ammunition are detailed in Return of the Field Ordnance and Traveling Carriages, with the Number of Rounds of Ammunition for Full Service at the undermentioned posts, by Gordon, 31 March 1813, LAC, RG 8, I, 387: 48. For a description of the artillery see: Appendix 3, British Artillery.

13. The condemned 18-pdrs. and their ammunition were

listed in the Return of Ordnance Mounted … by Gordon, 31 March 1813, LAC, RG 8, I, 387: 47. The condemned 12-pdr. was not on the list, but Sheaffe referred to its use during the battle to Prevost, 5B May 1813, LAC, MG 11, CO 42, 354: 119. This description of the 18-pdr. is based on an exhibit at Historic Fort York, Toronto, where it and an obsolete 9-pdr. are on display. This latter gun is without trunnions and cascabel and dates to about 1737 and does not appear to have been mounted in April 1813.

14. Brock to Prevost, 11 December 1811, Tupper, *Life and Letters of Brock*, 130. The description of typical magazines is based on archeological investigations and reconstruction of the magazine at Fort George as described in Desloges, *Structural History of Fort George*, 15-6, 55-6, 66-7, 148-69 and Benn, "Bombproof Powder Magazines."

15. 314 barrels of artillery powder were shown to be at York on the Return of Ordnance Mounted … by Gordon, 31 March 1813, LAC, RG 8, I, 387: 47. A vast number of solid projectiles and all the explosive shells are shown in the latter return and in the Return of the Field Ordnance … by Gordon, 31 March 1813, *ibid.*: 48. Nearly 40,000 English and French musket rounds and 11 barrels of fine powder were shown on the Return of Small Arms … by Gordon, 31 March 1813, *ibid.*: 49. Of special note is the fact that there was no spherical case in the arsenal at this time.

16. Trowbridge's account, LOC, Trowbridge Papers. This is a handwritten manuscript which formed part of the material Trowbridge submitted to Benson Lossing after they met at Watertown, New York as shown in Trowbridge to Lossing, 1 November 1855 and 10 April and 29 June 1856, *ibid.* Trowbridge's sketch of the attack on York is used elsewhere here. His record agrees with many details given by other eyewitnesses to the Battle of York and its aftermath. Trowbridge's Papers includes an autobiographical sketch, and his service as a surgeon to the New York Militia is confirmed by a General Order by Livingston, 10 October 1812 and Tompkins to Trowbridge, 10 October 1812, in Tompkins, *Public Papers of Daniel D. Tompkins*, 1: 412 and 3: 166. He joined the Twenty-first Regiment of U.S. Infantry as a surgeon on 1 August 1813, *HRD*, 1: 971. Lossing published *The Pictorial Field-book of the War of 1812* in 1868. Lossing visited Toronto and made sketches there, the one of the magazine almost certainly based on Trowbridge's description. Lossing did not refer to Amasa Trowbridge in relation to York; Dr. Josiah Trowbridge is mentioned in Lossing's Chapter XVIII. 30 feet = 9.2 m.

17. The detonation of the magazine on 27 April is detailed in Chapter 11 and in Appendix 2, The Explosion of the Grand Magazine.

18. For Baldwin's life, see: *DCB*, 7: 35; Thompson, *Spadina*, 45-77; Chadwick, *Ontarian Families*, 2: 34; Canniff, *The Medical Profession in Upper Canada 1783-1850*, 227-37. See also: Mosser, *York, Upper Canada Minutes of Town Meetings*, 95. The family lived in a house built for them by William Willcocks on the corner of Frederick and Palace Streets from 1803 until 1807 and then moved to the new home on the northeast corner of Bay and Front, Booth, *A View of Original Toronto*, 30. The Baldwin-Macdonell duel is described in Halliday, *Murder Among Gentlemen*, 50-3. See also Baldwin to Wyatt, 6 April 1813, Baldwin, "A Recovered Letter."

19. Baldwin to Wyatt, 6 April 1813, Baldwin, "A Recovered Letter."

20. Clerk to Gray, 25 March 1813, LAC, RG 8, I, 729: 175.

21. Gray described the beginning of the project at York to Prevost on 3, 11 and 29 December 1812, LAC, RG 8, I, 728: 135, 119 and 142. The pay lists in the Fort York Account Book, vol. 1, City of Toronto Culture, Museum and Heritage Services, unpaginated, showed the presence of skilled tradesmen and foremen and numerous shipwrights (without identifying the exact number) through the winter up until 24 April 1813. All but 50 of the 128 artificers who arrived at Kingston went to York with Plucknett as Gray reported to Prevost, 31 December 1812, LAC, RG 8, I, 728: 142. "A few days ago about Eighty Ship Carpenters arrived at this place from your Province; the Keel of a Thirty Gun Ship will soon be laid on the Stocks," Donald McLean to Charles Gray Stewart, 11 January 1813, OA: MU 2036, F895, Miscellaneous Military Records. For a description of the dockyard force see Appendix 4, British Order of Battle at York, 27 April 1813. The controversy over the building site was described by Plucknett to Myers, 27 January 1813, LAC, RG 8, I, 729: 62 and Myers to Freer, 28 January 1813, *ibid.*: 58.

22. This description of the state of progress on the *Brock* is based upon Return of the Work done to or for the Ship from the 7th to the 17th of April, by Leliévre, 19 April 1813, LAC, RG 8, I, 729: 166. Since details about the construction of the *Brock* are missing, the description of the ship and its components are based upon material in: Takakjian, *The 32-Gun Frigate* Essex; Goodwin, *The Construction and Fitting of the English Man of War*; Lees, *The Masting and Rigging of English Ships of War*; Gardiner, *Frigates of the Napoleonic Wars*. The 32-gun frigate *Essex* had over 30 strakes of planking to the top deck on each side (p. 54). Since the *Brock* was smaller and built for shallower water, it is presumed to have had fewer strakes. Lower masts of the *Essex* measured foremast – 79'; main mast – 85'; mizzen – 75' (p. 15). The building of batteaux was mentioned in Sheaffe to Baynes, 7 April 1813, Sheaffe, "Letter Book," 370. 90 feet = 27.5 m.

23. In October the *Duke of Gloucester* was laid up "in a proper situation between the Garrison and Mr. Crookshank's house (between modern Blue Jay Way and Bathurst Street)," and had been fitted out as a prison hulk, as noted in the York garrison orders 16 and 19 October and 3 November 1812, Ridout's York Garrison Orderly Book, LAC, RG 8, I, 1203. U.S. Surgeon Amasa Trowbridge mentions that it was at the area around the merchant dockyard at the time of the battle, Trowbridge's account, LOC, Trowbridge Papers. The six 6-pdrs. from the *Duke of Gloucester* were removed for use in the batteries as stated by Myers to Freer, 2 April 1813, LAC, RG 8, I, 729: 153. The purchase of the sloop *Mary Ann* and that it was not ready is in Sheaffe to Baynes, 14 April 1813, "Letter Book," 373 and in Loring to Freer, 19 April 1813, LAC, RG 8, I, 257: 78. The extreme disorder on board the *Prince Regent* when it arrived at Kingston was reported by Gray to Freer, 18 April 1813, *ibid.*, 729: 162. The lake being open for navigation between York and Niagara from 31 March was mentioned in Loring to Vincent, 31 March 1813, Sheaffe, "Letter Book," 360. There was still some ice in the bay at York 14 April, but Sheaffe was eager for the *Prince Regent* to sail, *ibid.*, 373.

24. Clerk described Plucknett's self-serving activities to Gray, 25 March 1813, LAC, RG 8, I, 729: 175. Myers described the state of things to Freer, 2 April 1813, LAC, RG 8, I, 729: 153.

25. Gray to Freer, 29 April 1813, LAC, RG 8, I, 729: 173.

26. Clerk mentioned the stoppage in pay to Gray, 25 March 1813, LAC, RG 8, I, 729: 175. Predictions about the completion of the vessel were: May (Pearson to Freer, 18 March 1813, *ibid.*: 124); June (Clerk to Gray, 25 March 1813, *ibid.*: 75); and "it is very doubtful when she will be ready" (Gray to Freer, 29 April 1813, *ibid.*: 173).

27. Freer to Gray, 29 January 1813, LAC, RG 8, I, 1220: 133. Requisitions for the guns for the two Lake Ontario ships and the one at Amherstburg were enclosed with Gray to Freer, 14 January 1813, *ibid.*, 729: 11. Ten 24-pdr. carronades, the only "set" of requisitioned guns specifically earmarked for the ship at Amherstburg (HMS *Detroit*), were not delivered to Burlington until late August or early September, as noted in Harvey to Procter, 17 September 1813, *ibid.*, 680: 75. This correspondence, and data regarding ordnance at York in the spring of 1813 as shown in previous notes, refutes the oft-made claim that a contributing factor for the British loss at the Battle of Put-in-Bay, 10 September 1813 was the capture or destruction of guns intended for the *Detroit* during the American attack on York, 27 April 1813. This was impossible since the guns were not there. For examples of the claim, see: Stacey, "Another Look at the Battle of Lake Erie," 131 and Drake, "Artillery and Its Influence on Naval Tactics: Reflections on the Battle of Lake Erie," 20. This misconception is discussed in full in Chapter 15 and Appendix 3, British Artillery.

28. Bruyeres to Prevost, 28 January 1813, LAC, RG 8, I, 729: 69.

29. The *Brock's* intended armament was described in 18 March 1813, Pearson to Freer, LAC, RG 8, I, 729: 124, as was the armament of the new ship and new schooner at Kingston. The revised plan for arming the *Brock* and the other vessels at York was described in Bruyeres to Prevost, 13 February 1813, *ibid.*, 387: 15 and by Myers to Freer, 2 April 1813, *ibid.*, 729: 153.

30. The frequent transactions with local merchants during this period are shown in the Fort York Account Book, vol. 1, City of Toronto Culture, Museum and Heritage Services. Profits enjoyed by local merchants are discussed in Magill, "William Allan and the War of 1812," and Sheppard, *Plunder, Profit and Paroles*, 145-7. Issac Wilson mentioned the many ways to profit at York, including one fellow's success in turning an outlay of $1500 into a net of $5000 within three months, Isaac Wilson to Jonathan Wilson, 5 December 1813, AO, MS 199(5), Isaac Wilson Diaries.

31. The employment of Playter, Stanton, Heward and Ridout is noted during this period in the Fort York Account Book, vol. 1, City of Toronto Culture, Museum and Heritage Services. Jarvis's appointment was mentioned in the militia general order of 14 March 1813, *DHC*, 6: 115 and in Jarvis, "Narrative of Colonel Stephen Jarvis," 253. Jarvis (1756-1840) came to York in 1809 and worked as a clerk in the office of Provincial Secretary William Jarvis and took over the store of an ex-American who returned to the United States after war was declared in 1812. For a brief biography, see "Narrative …," 149n. For George Jarvis's career, see *DCB*, 10: 379 and *HMG*, 205. Among the other gentlemen volunteers were Allan Napier MacNab, Donald MacDonell and John Mathewson (Mathieson), all of whom are all given credit for service at York in *HMG*, 205, 251, 239 and 258. For a discussion of this avenue into the service, see Hennell, *A Gentleman Volunteer*, 1-3.

32. Anne Powell believed that Grant and Elizabeth had too great a "wish to obtain what they call indispensables [and] I [call] superfluities" and were the agents of their own difficulties as she explained to William Powell, 29 May 1813, TRL, L 16, Powell Papers, Mrs. Powell's letters, A 93: 325. Anne mentioned to her brother that Sheaffe was going to recommend Grant for the post, 4 April 1812, *ibid.*: 305. For Grant's biography, see *DCB*, 7: 704. Brock recommended him to Prevost, 29 July 1812, LAC, RG 8, I, 676: 236. Grant's memorial about his service was written on 3 August 1813, *ibid.*, 84: 248. A Provincial Marine surgeon's annual salary was £182.10, as per the Proposed Establishment of the Provincial Marine … 1813, by Davis, *ibid.*, 230: 132.

33. Legg to Watson, 1 June 1816, Firth, *Town of York*, 142. Isaac Wilson described high inflation and going rates to Jonathan Wilson, 5 December 1813, AO, MS 199(5), Isaac Wilson Diaries. Strachan wrote to Bishop Mountain at Quebec on 15 September 1816 (Spragge, *Strachan*, 89), "During the War all articles of consumption were at this place four times their normal price." For a description of the financial boom and issues, see Sheppard, *Plunder, Profit and Paroles*, 134-50.

34. The four cases are mentioned in *The Report of the Loyal and Patriotic Society of Upper Canada*: Kennedy (31, 32), Major (31), Devins (38) and Smith (22, 25, 169, 173, 228-9). Correspondence regarding their provincial pensions are found in LAC, RG 9, IB4, 1: Kennedy (1: 10), Major (1: 33). For a description of Smith's death, see Malcomson, "Friendly Fire, War of 1812 Style."

35. Miss Baldwin is credited with designing the flag and organizing its fabrication in [no author indicated] "Toronto's Old Colours." *Heritage Columns* (Heritage Toronto), 1 (Spring, 2002): 3. Her life data is in Chadwick, *Ontarian Families*, 2: 35. The original regimental colour was held by the Archives and Museum of St. James Cathedral, Toronto until transferred to Fort York in June 2007, as per "1813 Colours Offered to Fort York." In a state of advanced deterioration, it measures 5' 2" by 9'. The account of the 23 March ceremony in the 20 April 1813 issue of the *Kingston Gazette* clearly refers to the conventional pair of flags in the "colours" presented to a regiment: the regimental colours, a homemade banner in this case; and the national standard, a Union Jack.

36. The quotes and description of events here are taken from the 20 April 1813 issue of the *Kingston Gazette*. Parts of the texts of the speeches are in *Strachan*, 10, but without clear indication of the speakers.

37. The history of the RNRF is described in Cruikshank, "The Royal Newfoundland Regiment" and *Selected Papers from the Transactions of the Canadian Military Institute*, 5 (1893-94): 5-15; Nicholson, *The Fighting Newfoundlander: A History of the Royal Newfoundland Regiment*, 1-88; Webber, *Skinner's Fencibles: The Royal Newfoundland Regiment, 1795-1802*; Fardy, *Before Beaumont Hamel: The Royal Newfoundland Regiment, 1775-1815*. For uniform details, see Summer and Chartrand, *Military Uniforms in Canada*, 60-1.

38. Prevost to Liverpool, 14 April 1812, LAC, MG 11, CO 42, 146: 134. An analysis of the detachment of 68 officers and men of the RNRF in the British squadron at the Battle of Put-in-Bay, 10 September 1813, showed that 41 of the men were born in the U.K., 22 in Canada, 1 in the U.S.A. and 4 born in other countries, Malcomson, "The Crews of the British Squadron …, Part I." The RNRF strength is based on the Monthly Returns recorded on 25 April 1813, LAC, MG 13, WO 17, 1517: 50-1. Prevost originally ordered five companies of the RNRF to Upper Canada as noted in Prevost to Liverpool, 14 April 1812, LAC, MG 11, CO 42, 146: 134. The Distribution of the Troops in Canada by Baynes on 21 December 1812

(LAC, RG 8, I, 1707: 124-5) showed 49 officers and men at Quebec, 82 at Prescott, 73 at Kingston, 3 at York, 115 at Fort George, 71 at Amherstburg and 150 "serving on the lakes." This changed little by the following spring when documents showed more than 90 of the regiment at Fort George on 24 March 1813 as per a Glegg memo, *DHC*, 5: 132 and more than 63 posted at Amherstburg in April, as noted in the Embarkation Return …, 23 April 1813, LAC, RG 8, I, 695a: 274. Turner makes the point that the garrison strength at York was 405 in March 1813 and 573 in June and July, *British Generals in the War of 1812*, 95, but this misconception is based upon the returns noted above and refers to the total strength of the unit which, as shown, was widely dispersed.

39. General Order by Baynes, 1 March 1813, LAC, RG 8, I, 1170: 126. The regimental pay list for March–June 1813 (Pay-List of the Royal Newfoundland Regiment of Fencible Infantry from 25 March to 24 June 1813, both days inclusive, NAUK, WO 12, 11027) showed five companies (about 220 men) at Kingston, with some of the men delegated to warships at Kingston before 27 April 1813 (the day of the York battle). The rest (about 160) were without apparent assignment, became casualties at York or were delegated to the Kingston vessels after the York survivors returned to Kingston in the first week of May. Most of this latter group is presumed to have marched to York with Heathcote. When the *Prince Regent* and *Duke of Gloucester* tied up at York in the autumn, any of the Royal Newfoundland Regiment then serving in them (if there were any) must have been sent to Kingston or Fort George as only two lieutenants and one private were mustered at York late in December, as shown in The Distribution of the Troops in Canada by Baynes on 21 December 1812, LAC, RG 8, I, 1707: 124-5.

40. Rules regarding women and children are found in the General Order of 17 March 1812, LAC, RG 8, I, 1168: 105. See also Nesbitt, "'Nothing More or Less than Devils'; Women of the Naval and Military Establishments in Upper Canada."

41. Finan, *Journal of a Voyage*, 270. For Bryan Finan's career, see *HMG*, 143.

42. Finan, *Journal of a Voyage*, 272-3.

43. According to *HMG*, 186, Heathcote was promoted to major in 1809 and did not achieve the rank of lieutenant colonel until June 1814. Documents from the spring of 1813, however, officially refer to him as lieutenant colonel and this rank will be used here for consistency purposes. For examples of such references, see Sheaffe to Prevost, 5A May 1813, LAC, MG 11, CO 42, 354: 132 and Proceedings of a Board of Officers [to examine claims following the battle], 18 May 1813, LAC, RG 8, I, 84: 167. For the careers of Blaskowitz, De Koven and LeLièvre, see *HMG*, 68, 122 and 225. For LeLièvre see also his service record NAUK, WO 25,765: 132. LeLièvre was forty years old when he received his first commission in 1795 as shown on his service record, although in a memorial to the Duke of York, through Prevost's office, he gave his age as sixty (in 1813), mentioning that he had started his career "with Lord Hood" in 1793 and that he had a wife and seven children, LeLièvre to the Duke of York, 25 September 1813, TRL, S 108, Sir George Prevost Papers, Memorial Book, 117; officially he was a "temporary" captain with the RNFR. The average age of the 68 RNRF officers and men in the British squadron at the Battle of Put-in-Bay, 10 September 1813, was 30 years, as presented in Malcomson, "The Crews of the British Squadron …, Part I."

44. Sheaffe to Bathurst, 16 March 1813, LAC, MG 11, CO 42,

354: 70. The dignity was announced in a General Order by Rowan, 10 March 1813, *DHC*, 5: 104.

45. The story about Mrs. Sheaffe comes from a letter from her mother to a niece, cited in Sabine, *Biographical Sketches of Loyalists of the American Revolution*, 2: 290.

46. Sheaffe to Bathurst, 5 April 1813, LAC, MG 11, CO 42, 354: 95. Sheaffe suggested Colonel Myers be given command of the Home and Durham Districts to Vincent and separately to Baynes, 29 March 1813, Sheaffe, "Letter Book," 357 and 359. On the premise that it would make performance of his quarter master general's department duties impossible, Myers asked Freer on 2 April 1813, to have Prevost veto the idea, LAC, RG 8, I, 729: 153. Sheaffe later recommended Colonel John Young of the 8th Regiment of Foot, but he was kept at Kingston until his entire regiment had passed through on its way west, Sheaffe to Prevost, 19 April 1813, *ibid.*, 678: 170.

47. Baldwin to Wyatt, 6 April 1813, Baldwin, "A Recovered Letter."

48. Freer to Sheaffe, 23 March 1813, LAC, RG 8, I, 688c: 28. Further evidence of the change in policy came soon after Commander Robert Barclay, Royal Navy, set out from Quebec to take command at Kingston, when Prevost wrote to him (26 April 1813, *ibid.*, 688e: 55), "I hope you found the King's Vessels on Lake Ontario Concentrated at Kingston Harbour on your arrival at Kingston and the New Ship Ready to Launch." It seems likely that the *Duke of Gloucester* was meant to sail for Kingston as well. Among Bruyeres's comments was the point that keeping the centre of the naval department at Kingston "would have saved much time and expense in Transport – united all the Workmen under one Head – And insured the armament of your ships," Bruyeres to Prevost, 19 January 1813, LAC, RG 8, I, 387: 10. In this long letter, written at Kingston, Bruyeres also correctly anticipated the American strategy when he told Prevost "that the first effort of Commodore Chauncey will be to endeavour to destroy York previous to the ice being dispersed in the narrow part of the lake towards this place." The decision to establish the headquarters for the Royal Newfoundland Regiment to York was announced in the General Order by Baynes, 1 March 1813, LAC, RG 8, I, 1170: 126, three weeks before Freer wrote to Sheaffe with the new intentions.

Chapter 7: "Be always ready": The Army Gathers at Sackets Harbor

1. This quote comes from Anonymous, "Biographical Memoir of the Late Brigadier General Zebulon Montgomery Pike," *Analectic Magazine*, 4 (1814), 382.

2. Pike to Wilkinson, 24 July 1812, cited in Hollon, "Zebulon Montgomery Pike and the York Campaign, 1813," 261. Pike was quoting from Shakespeare's "All the world's a stage" soliloquy in *As You Like It*, Act 2, Scene 7: "Then a soldier, / Full of strange oaths, and bearded like the pard, / Jealous in honour, sudden and quick in quarrel, / Seeking the bubble reputation / Even in the cannon's mouth."

3. For Pike's career, see: *HRD*, 1: 792; *ANB*, 17: 514; "Biographical Memoir of the Late Brigadier General Zebulon Montgomery Pike," *The Analectic Magazine*, 4 (1814): 380-91; Whiting, "Life of Zebulon Montgomery Pike"; Terrell, *Zebulon Pike: The Life and Times of an Adventurer*; Hollon, *The Lost Pathfinder: Zebulon Montgomery Pike*; Hollon, "Zebulon Montgomery Pike and the York Campaign, 1813;" Olsen, "Zebulon Pike and American Popular Culture." For Pike's father's career,

see *HRD*, 1: 792.

4. This quote comes from "Biographical Memoir of the Late Brigadier General Zebulon Montgomery Pike," *Analectic Magazine*, 4 (1814), 382.

5. Pike to Caesar A. Rodney, former attorney general in James Madison's cabinet, 24 January 1813, Zebulon Pike Papers, Chicago History Museum.

6. William Duane recollected this comment in a letter to Thomas Jefferson, 26 September 1813, Ford, "Letters of William Duane."

7. For the careers of Bloomfield, Fraser, Hayden, Hoppock, King, PerLee, Whitlock and Scott, see *HRD*, 1: 226, 434, 514, 542, 600, 784, 869 and 1030. Captain John Scott's letters are held by the NJHS, MG 1044, Scott Letters. Six of them covering the period from 24 August 1812 to 15 February 1813 were published as Scott, John "The Letters of Captain John Scott, 15th U.S. Infantry: A New Jersey Officer in the War of 1812." Edited by John C. Fredriksen. *New Jersey History* 107 (1989): 61-81. The regiment's strength is given in Scott to Thompson, 24 August, 24 and 25 September as between 750 and 850. Skelton makes the point about veteran officers being hesitant to go to new regiments in *An American Profession of Arms*, 49.

8. Scott to Thompson, 24 August 1812, NJHS, MG 1044, Scott Letters.

9. Scott to Thompson, 24 September 1812, NJHS, MG 1044, Scott Letters.

10. Scott to Thompson, 24 September 1812, NJHS, MG 1044, Scott Letters.

11. Scott described the expedition to Thompson, [no day] December 1812, NJHS, MG 1044, Scott Letters. For a brief description of the affair, see *HDW*, 276.

12. Beaumont, *Formative Years*, 11. William Beaumont, 1785-1853, won fame for his detailed examination in the 1820s of a severe gunshot wound to a man's stomach, eventually becoming known as the "Father of Gastric Physiology." For his career, see *HRD*, 1: 204 and <www.james.com/beaumont/dr_life.htm>.

13. Beaumont, *Formative Years*, 13.

14. "Gen. Z. M. Pike," obituary, 5 June 1813, *The Weekly Register*. The description of camp life on the Saranac comes from Pearce, "A Poor But Honest Sodger," 134-5. Pearce's narrative makes the point here and elsewhere that he never received due credit for his efforts on behalf of his regiment or his nation. John Scott described widespread illness and later recovery and named officers who were arrested and who left the service in his letters to Thompson, 16 January and 15 February 1813, NJHS, MG 1044, Scott Letters. Army Surgeon James Mann reported that 200 men at Burlington between November and February and the same number at Plattsburgh, *Sketches of the Campaigns*, 45. For Mann's career, see *HRD*, 1: 687.

15. This description of the march to Sackets Harbor is based on letters in WCL, Joseph Bloomfield and Zebulon M. Pike Letter Book: Pike to Bloomfield, 28 February 1813; to Dearborn, 28 February, 8, 13, 15, 18 and 26 March 1813; to Pearce, 1 and 7 March 1813; to Dearborn, 2 March; to Chandler, 2 and 13 March 1813; to King, 3 March 1813; to Fanning, 7 March; to Whitlock, 8 March 1813; to Woolsey, 13 March 1813. Pike informed Dearborn he would march with 400 men. The Joseph Bloomfield and Zebulon M. Pike Letter Book is held by WCL and is a single volume, of uncertain provenance, which was used by both Bloomfield and then Pike, or their secretaries, between September 1812 and April 1813. Chauncey noted that he was expecting Pike

to have 800 men to Jones, 8 March 1813, USNA, RG 45, M 125, 27: 20. John Scott noted 488 men equipped with snowshoes traveling in 130 sleighs to Thompson, 16 March 1813, New Jersey Historical Society, MG 1044, Scott Letters. 176 miles = 282 km.

16. Hoard to Rosseel, 6 April 1813, Parish-Rosseel Collection, Owen D. Young Library, St. Lawrence University. See also Hoard to Parish, 25 March and 16 June 1813, Daniel Hoard Letter Book, Young Library, St. Lawrence University. Similar claims were reported in: 11 February 1860, Court of Claims Reports 222, 223 and 224, 36th Congress, 1st Session, House of Representatives. Gary Gibson generously supplied these sources to the author.

17. For Muehlenberg, Brooks and Whitlock's careers, see *HRD*, 1: 734, 248, 1030.

18. This description of Sackets Harbor is based on: Spafford, *A Gazetteer of the State of New-York*, 6, 51, 80-1, 142 and 209; and Hough, *A History of Jefferson County*, 171-89. The village was actually within the township of Hounsfield, Jefferson County which had a population of 943 in 1810. See also Wilder, *The Battle of Sackett's Harbour*, 1-11.

19. The arrival of units, their total numbers and organization into brigades is mentioned to various extent in the following: Pearce, "A Poor but Honest Sodger," 134-5; Everest, *The War of 1812 in the Champlain Valley*, 92; Wilder, *The Battle of Sackett's Harbour*, 47; Walworth to "father" (this was actually his father-in-law Colonel Jonas Simonds, Sixth Infantry), 6 April 1813, LAC, MG 24, F 16, Jonas Simonds Papers, 1813, 1814; Chauncey to Jones, 8, 12a and 12b March 1813, USNA RG 45, M 125, 27: 13, 33 and 34. For Chandler's career, see *HRD*, 1: 295. Other data comes from Scott to Thompson, 28 October 1813 and (no date) December, NJHS, MG 1044, Scott Letters.

20. This description of the flow of business at Sacket's Harbor, Hooker's involvement and that of other individuals is based upon: Hooker's vouchers in Chauncey's accounts, USNA, RG 217, Entry 811; Turner to Chauncey, 3 March 1814, *ibid.*, Entry 810, 102; and Hough, *A History of Jefferson County*, 176-7. The Hooker House still stands at 100 Main Street, Sackets Harbor, <www.sacketsharborny.com/historical_society>. The author thanks Gary Gibson for his generous assistance in providing this data and other background material.

21. Pike to General Melancthon L. Woolsey (customs official at Plattsburgh), 13 March 1813, WCL, Bloomfield-Pike Letter Book.

22. Stacy, *Memoirs of the Life of Nathaniel Stacy*, 319-320.

23. Pike to General M. L. Woolsey, 13 March 1813, WCL, Bloomfield-Pike Letter Book. Pike to Chandler, 18 March 1813, *ibid*. "I have understood from Washington that I am held up as a Candidate to fill a Brigade appointment. Will you lend me a word (if you write) to some of your old friends at Washington to help me along?" Pike to C. A. Rodney, 24 January 1813, "Zebulon Pike Papers," Chicago History Museum. Chandler became a brigadier general on 8 July 1812, *HRD*, 1: 295. Pike's promotion was dated to 12 March 1813, *HRD*, 1: 792. Walworth mentioned that Pike heard of the promotion on 5 April to Simonds, 6 April 1813, LAC, MG 24, F 16, Jonas Simonds Papers, 1813, 1814.

24. Dearborn to Chauncey, 31 March 1813, enclosed with Chauncey to Jones, USNA, RG 45, M 125, 27: 157. Dearborn to Madison, 7 April 1813, LOC, James Madison Papers, Series 1: General Correspondence.

25. Dearborn to Madison, 13 March 1813, LOC, James

Madison Papers, Series 1: General Correspondence. Dearborn stated his willingness to be reassigned to Madison, 13 December 1812, LOC, James Madison Papers, Series 1: General Correspondence. He had already mentioned his willingness to stand aside in a letter to Lincoln, 27 September 1812, cited in Erney, *The Public Life of Henry Dearborn*, 304.

26. For the careers of Jones, Nicholson, Pinkney and Swan, see *HRD*, 1: 579; 747; 793; 938.

27. For a thorough discussion of the officer corps of the U.S. Army, see Skelton, *An American Profession of Arms*, 12-69.

28. Pike to C. A. Rodney, 24 January 1813, "Zebulon Pike Papers," Chicago History Museum. The issue of enlistment periods and their effects and the nature of the recruits is described in Stagg, "Enlisted Men in the United States Army, 1812-1815: A Preliminary Study" and Stagg, "Soldiers in Peace and War: Comparative Perspectives on the Recruitment of the United States Army, 1802-1815."

29. This description of the recruits is taken from Stagg, "Enlisted Men in the United States Army, 1812-1815: A Preliminary Study" and Stagg, "Soldiers in Peace and War: Comparative Perspectives on the Recruitment of the United States Army, 1802-1815." The data regarding appearance and size is based on the results of an informal study by the author of data regarding more than 500 American troops captured at the Battle of Beaver Dams, 24 June 1813, using the prisoner of war list found in the General Entry Book, LAC, RG 8, I, 694a. Age data in the latter also matches Stagg's findings in "Enlisted Men …," 633-4.

30. This description of the officers based on Skelton, "High Army Leadership in the Era of the War of 1812," and Skelton, *An American Profession of Arms*, 12-33. For the careers of Ripley and Pearce, see *HRD*, 1: 832, 778, and *HDW*, 411 and 474. For Ripley, also see *ANB*, 18: 530 and Anonymous, "Biographical Memoir of Major-General Ripley." For Pearce, also see, "A Poor but Honest Sodger," which was edited by John Fredriksen from the original "Biographical Memoir of Colonel Cromwell Pearce" at the Historical Society of Pennsylvania in Philadelphia. He was described as an "uncommonly stout man, six feet-two inches in height, erect and well-proportioned," "A Poor but Honest Sodger," 131. 6 ft. 2 in. = 1.9 m.

31. For the careers of Fanning, Hight, Hobart, McDowell and Thompson, see *HRD*, 1: 412; 529; 533; 664; 955.

32. Scott to Thompson, 16 January 1813, NJHS, MG 1044, Scott Letters.

33. Pearce, "A Poor but Honest Sodger," 134.

34. Scott to Thompson, 16 January 1813, Scott, NJHS, MG 1044, Scott Letters. For Dickerson and Whitehead's careers, see *HRD*, 1: 372 and 1029. Scott was wrong. Dickerson *did* return to duty and was honourably discharged as a first lieutenant in 1815. For controversies among officers in the various services, see: Skelton, *An American Profession of Arms*, 51-9; Altoff, "The Perry-Elliott Controversy"; Sugden, *Nelson, A Dream of Glory*, 272-7.

35. Dwight, "'Plow-Joggers for Generals,'" 17. For Dwight's career, see *HRD*, 1: 392.

36. Walworth to Simonds, 6 April 1813, LAC, MG 24, F 16, Jonas Simonds Papers, 1813, 1814. Walworth had praised Pike to Simonds, 29 March 1813, *ibid.* For Walworth's career, see *HRD*, 1: 1000.

37. Van de Venter to Armstrong, 31 March 1813, cited in Armstrong, *Notices of the War*, 1: 153-4.

38. For Forsyth's career, see *HRD*, 1: 430. He is mentioned throughout Fredriksen, *Green Coats and Glory*, which presents the history of the original Rifle Regiment, which became known as the First Rifles after the creation of the Second, Third and Fourth Regiments in 1814. Henry Whiting (1790-1851) wrote a rare and colourful description of Forsyth as part of his "Life of Zebulon Montgomery Pike," 300-4. Whiting was a first lieutenant of the Regiment of Light Dragoons and an aide-de-camp to Brigadier General John Boyd during this period and appears to have been an acquaintance of Forsyth's on the Niagara Frontier during the summer of 1813.

39. Whiting, "Life of Zebulon Montgomery Pike," 300-1.

40. Dearborn to Armstrong, 25 February 1813, USNA, RG 107, M 221, roll 52: unpaginated. "[Forsyth's] known zeal for a small partisan warfare has induced me to give him repeated caution against such measures on his part, as would probably produce some retaliating strokes as he would be unable to resist; but I fear my advice has not been as fully attended to as could have been wished." This letter enclosed the report of the defeat at Ogdensburg, Forsyth to Dearborn, 22 February 1813, *ibid.*

41. Thomson to his brother, 26 February 1813, NYSL, 17618, William Thomson Letter Book. "Forsyth is a perfect savage himself. He is as brave a brute as any in the woods…. He never obeys orders, yet he has turned the fate of the battle several times." Master Commandant Arthur Sinclair to Cocke, 4 July 1813, Malcomson, *Sailors of 1814*, 47. Sinclair made these comments after Forsyth's Rifles had played a leading role in the battles at York, 27 April 1813, and Fort George, 27 May 1813.

42. 6 February 1812, "An act authorizing the President of the United States to accept and organize certain Volunteer Militia Corps," 12th Congress, Session 1: Chapter 4, *Public Statutes at Large of the United States of America*, 2: 788. Supplementary legislation was passed on 6 July 1812, *ibid.*: Chapter 138. A brief discussion of the problems with the volunteer corps is in Stagg, *Mr. Madison's War*, 163. Problems with the program are discussed in: Madison to Gallatin, 8 August 1812, Stagg *et al*, *The Papers of James Madison*, 5: 128; Madison to Dearborn, 9 August 1812, *ibid.*: 133; Dearborn to Madison, 30 September 1812, *ibid.*: 364.

43. A description of New York State twelve-month volunteers who joined the army on the Niagara River in the summer and autumn of 1812 is found in Malcomson, *A Very Brilliant Affair*, 253. Information about McClure is drawn from: General Order by Livingston, 5 November 1812, Hastings, *The Public Papers of Daniel Tompkins*, 2: 274; Tompkins to Eustis, 21 April 1812, *ibid.*: 556; Tompkins to McClure, 20 June 1812, *ibid.*: 628. In this latter note Tompkins wrote, "If you let that unruly Irish blood of yours drive you into another fit, and to a resignation of the office of Lt. Col., I give you notice that I will get in a passion too and take you at your word." See also General Order by Macomb, 29 September 1812, *ibid.*, 1: 409. For the regiment's records see: NYSA, AGO, BO811, Box 9, Folder 2 and 6. See also Appendix 6, American Order of Battle at York, 27 April 1813.

44. The origins and nature of the Republican Albany Greens and their connection to McClure is found in: General Orders by Paulding, 27 May, 7 June, 19 September and 28 October 1811, Hastings, *The Public Papers of Daniel Tompkins*, 2: 222, 222, 229 and 309; Tompkins to Maher, 21 April and 8 May 1812, *ibid.*: 558 and 589; Tompkins to Eustis, 21 April 1812, *ibid.*: 559; General

Orders by Macomb, 29 September and 22 October 1812, *ibid.*, 1: 409 and 417. According to the website for the Historic St. Mary's Church in Albany, New York <www.hist-stmarys.org/Highlights.htm>, Maher was a catholic and prominent wholesale grocer Maher's Volunteers (or alternately the Albany Greens, Albany Rifles, the Greens) appear to have been separate from a twelve-month regiment, known as the Albany Volunteers, raised by Lieutenant Colonel John Mills during the winter of 1812-13 which was stationed at Sackets at the same time as Maher's men were, and which fought at the Battle of Sackets Harbor, 29 May 1813 as described in Mills's obituary, *National Intelligencer,* 22 June 1813. Dearborn informed Smyth on 21 October 1812 that he was ordering McClure's regiment forward, *DHC,* 4: 151. For the company's records see: NYSA, AGO, BO811, Box 7, Folder 10 and Box 9, Folder 6; and Appendix 6, American Order of Battle.

45. *The Weekly Register,* 28 September 1812. One reference notes the flag given to the Baltimore Volunteers was "placed on the highest pinnacle of the government house in the capital of Upper Canada," 12 June 1813, *ibid.* The company was also mentioned in *ibid.*, 12 September 1812. References to Moore are found in: William Kilty, *et. al.,* eds. *The Laws of Maryland …*, 3 February 1817, volume 192: 1942, <www.mdarchives.state.md.us>; Matchett's Baltimore Directory for 1833, 492: 16, *ibid.*; *Proceedings and Acts of the General Assembly,* 30 March 1968, 142: 1034, *ibid.* References to Irvine include: MSA SC 3520-18915, Archives of Maryland (Biographical Series), *ibid.*; Beirne, *The War of 1812,* 92; Brigham, *History and Bibliography of American Newspapers,* 2: 251-2.

46. Warner to his wife, 7 October 1812. Warner's letters are the private property of his fourth-generation grandson Gene Towner of Towson, Maryland, who published them on his website <www.haemo-sol.com/thomas/thomas.html> and donated them to the Flag House and Star-Spangled Banner Museum in Baltimore, Maryland. Mr. Towner provided genealogical information to the author.

47. Warner to his wife, 27 November 1812. Flag House, Baltimore. There were six companies in McClure's regiment, amounting to about 276 men, according to Smyth to G. McClure, Birdsall, *et. al.,* 3 December 1812, *DHC,* 4: 267. Smyth noted that they were prepared to join the invasion on 28 November and 1 December 1812 but saw no action.

48. Abel Grosvenor of Buffalo to his brother in Hudson, New York, 25 November 1812, *New-York Evening Post,* 10 December 1812, from the *Hudson Whig.* A second account of the riot was taken from the *Albany Gazette* and printed in the *New-York Evening Post,* 24 December 1812.

49. *The Weekly Register,* 20 February 1813. Thomas Warner made no mention of the riot in his letters. For the company's records see: NYSA, AGO, BO811, Box 9, Folders 2 and 3; and Appendix 6, American Order of Battle.

50. Warner to his wife, 19 April 1812, Flag House, Baltimore. McClure's movement to Utica is noticed in *The Weekly Register,* 20 February 1813. The illumination was reported in the *Albany Argus,* 2 March 1813. The regiment's move to Sackets was mentioned there as well and New York City's *Mercantile Advertiser,* 4 and 10 March 1813

51. Walworth to Simonds, 6 April 1813, LAC, MG 24, F 16, Jonas Simonds Papers, 1813, 1814.

52. Scott to Thompson, 16 January 1813, NJHS, MG 1044, Scott Letters.

Chapter 8: "Dashing evolutions": The Ways of War in 1813

1. Trowbridge's account, LOC, Trowbridge Papers.

2. Pike to Dearborn, 26 March 1813, WCL, Bloomfield-Pike Letter Book. Pike mentioned weak ice to Dearborn, 18 March 1813, *ibid.* "… the daily drills and parades by Pike on the ice, which lasted five to six hours," Trowbridge's account, LOC, Trowbridge Papers. The British practiced on the ice at Kingston in the spring of 1814 as noted in Le Couteur, *Merry Hearts Make Light Days,* 156.

3. Clausewitz, *On War,* 338. The concept of the strengths of the three arms is explained in 338-46.

4. For British recruitment practices and data, see Haythornthwaite, *The Armies of Wellington,* 43-51. British army recruiting standards for age and height were announced in General Order by Calvert and repeated by Baynes, 14 February 1812, LAC, RG 8, I, 1168: 140. The U.S. Army 5' 6" limit was stated on 16 March 1802 in "An act fixing the military peace establishment of the United States," 7th Congress, Session 1, Chapter 9, *Public Statutes at Large of the United States of America,* 2: 132. "An act to raise an additional Military Force," of 11 January 1812 did not state height, and gave the age range as 18 to 45, 12th Congress, 1: 14, *ibid.*: 671. Stagg discusses and explains subtle differences between the armies in age data in "Enlisted Men in the United States Army, 1812-1815: A Preliminary Study," 633-4, giving the average American recruit's age as 26.8 years. The average age of 28 and height of 5' 7" was found during the author's informal study of data regarding 481 infantry, cavalry and artillery privates of the U.S. Army captured at the Battle of Beaver Dams, 24 June 1813, as revealed in the prisoner-of-war list found in the General Entry Book, LAC, RG 8, I, 694a. Data for the RNRF was derived from prisoner-of-war information for the detachment of 68 RNRF officers and men in the British squadron at the Battle of Put-in-Bay, 10 September 1813, as presented in Malcomson, "The Crews of the British Squadron …, Part I," showing 41 of the men were born in the U.K., 22 in Canada, 1 in the U.S. A. and 4 born in other countries. A similar sample of 1000 fit recruits in Britain just after the war, showed 696 of them stood between 5' 6" and 5' 8", Haythornthwaite, *The Armies of Wellington,* 49.

5. Cooper, *Rough Notes of Seven Campaigns,* 14. For British recruits and recruiting, see: Haythornthwaite, *The Armies of Wellington,* 43-58; and Holmes, *Redcoat,* 135-56. Both authors refer to Wellington's famous 1831 "scum of the earth" comment and explain the context in which it was made.

6. Anonymous ["Saucy Tom"], *A Soldier of the Seventy-first,* xiii.

7. Baynes to Brock, 21 November 1811, Tupper, *The Life and Correspondence of Major-General Sir Isaac Brock,* 122. In an 1831 debate about discipline in the army, Wellington mentioned the low quality of the recruits and noted "it is really wonderful that we should have made them the fine fellows they are," quoted in Holmes, *Redcoat,* 149.

8. 11 June 1810, *Quebec Mercury.*

9. For British officers, see: Haythornthwaite, *The Armies of Wellington,* 22-42; and Holmes, *Redcoat,* 157-79. Being, officially, part of the Board of Ordnance rather than the army, artillery officers and engineers received thorough military schooling and advanced by seniority alone. For a discussion of this system and promotion in general, see Glover, *Peninsular Preparations,* 143-61.

10. Lawrence, *Autobiography,* 210-11. Sheaffe's reputation as

an officer is described in Chapter 2, referencing Brock's description of him to Green, 8 February 1808, LAC, RG 8, I, 923: 12.

11. Cooper, *Rough Notes of Seven Campaigns*, 10.

12. Anonymous ["Saucy Tom"], *A Soldier of the Seventy-first*, 33. Leisure pastimes of officers are described in numerous sources, including: daily life, museums, men and women of Madrid in Hennell to his brothers, 25 August and 1 and 19 September 1812, Hennell, *A Gentleman Volunteer*, 41-51; riding to the hounds and personal stables of horses, etc., Dyneley to his wife, 26 September 1811, 5 May 1812, Dyneley, *Letters*, 13, 23.

13. Anonymous ["Saucy Tom"], *A Soldier of the Seventy-first*, 60.

14. Sources for British uniforms include: Fletcher, *Napoleonic Wars. Wellington's Army*, 13-38, 50-1; Haythornthwaite, *The Armies of Wellington*, 83-4; Newfoundland and Glengarry Fencibles in Summer and Chartrand, *Military Uniforms in Canada*, 60-1, 72-3.

15. General Order by Baynes, 29 November 1812, LAC, RG 8, I, 1168: 58. Wellington's different approach is mentioned in Haythornthwaite, *The Armies of Wellington*, 83.

16. The regulation suit of clothing is described in 1 January 1812, "An Act to raise an additional Military Force," 12th Congress, Session 1, Chapter 14, *Public Statutes at Large of the United States of America*, 2: 671. Conditions of enlistment are found in this law and may be traced back to 16 March 1802, "An Act fixing the military peace establishment of the United States," 7th Congress, Session 1, Chapter 9, *Public Statutes at Large of the United States of America* 2: 132. Actual clothing issues are described in: Chartrand, *Uniforms and Equipment*, 24-42; and Coates, Kochan and Troiani, *Don Troiani's Soldiers in America*, 88-95. The matter of the different coloured uniforms issued to new recruits in the Sixth Infantry is mentioned in Simonds to Irvine, 16 February 1813, USNA, RG 98, Entry 176, Record of Units: Sixth Infantry, unpaginated.

17. Prevost explained about the shortage and change of colour to Sheaffe, 1 January 1813, LAC, RG 8, I, 1220: 83. Sheaffe noted to Baynes on 14 April 1813 (*ibid.*, 373), "The Militia Clothing is not arrived, but we have supplies of Shoes, Mogosins, Stockings and Flannel made and unmade." Sheaffe informed Prevost on 19 April 1813 (LAC, RG 8, I, 678: 170) that "5 boats go down the lake to bring up the Militia Clothing (which I have just learnt has been left about 70 miles from hence)." On 5A May 1813, (LAC, MG 11, CO 42, 354: 132) Sheaffe also informed Prevost that Captain William Jarvie had been sent with three boats to collect the uniforms and arrived at York on 27 April.

18. Anonymous ["Saucy Tom"], *A Soldier of the Seventy-first*, xiii.

19. Hanks, "Memoir," 29-31.

20. Le Couteur, *Merry Hearts Make Light Days*, 80. Punishments and everyday life of the soldier in the two services are described in: Haythornthwaite, *The Armies of Wellington*, 59-74, 313-19; and Holmes, *Redcoat*, 135-56. Hanks, "Memoir," Graves's introduction preceding it, 10-15.

21. Hanks, "Memoir," 24.

22. For a comprehensive description of muskets of the period see, Reilly, *United States Martial Flintlocks*, 17-97, with detail on French and British muskets on 20-25 and the U.S. Musket Model 1795 on 52–7. An India Pattern musket (0.753 calibre) fired a 0.683" diameter ball, manufactured at 14.5 balls per lb., had a 39" barrel (weighing 9 lb., 11 oz.), stood 55" in length, had a

15" bayonet (weighing 1 lb.), was 6' 1" long overall with bayonet affixed and weighed a total of 10 lb., 11 oz., as per "British Military Flintlock Arms from 1740," Blackmore, *British Military Firearms, 1650-1850*, 274 and 277. See also Darling, *Red Coat and Brown Bess*, 27-54. The U.S. 1795 model had a 0.69 calibre and fired a 0.63 ball manufactured at a rate of 19 balls per pound or a 0.64 ball manufactured at 18 balls per pounded, as noted in Lewis, *Small Arms and Ammunition*, 219. Buckshot was commonly manufactured at 180 per pound, *ibid.* The U.S. Model 1795 stood 59.5" in length, weighed about 9 pounds and was generally outfitted with a 15" bayonet, Chartrand, *Uniforms and Equipment*, 83-91, 94. Thanks, again, to Edward J. Anderson for his assistance in this regard. Brock complained to Prevost about "the 2329 French muskets which Your Excellency has directed to be sent here," on 11 December 1811, LAC, MG 11, CO 42, 352: 55. A Return of Small Arms, Accoutrements, …, by James Gordon, 31 March 1813, LAC, RG 8, I, 387: 49 showed nearly 2200 French muskets in the arsenals between York and Mackinac Island, only six of which were at York. Chartrand notes that the U.S. government bought about 11,000 India Pattern muskets for distribution in *Uniforms and Equipment*, 84-5. 0.75 inch = 1.9 cm. 0.69 inch = 1.75 cm. 0.68 inch = 1.73 cm. 0.63 inch = 1.6 cm.

23. This claim, made by a British officer, Colonel George Hanger in *To All Sportsmen* in 1814, is quoted in Haythornthwaite, *Weapons and Equipment*, 19. The European test figures quoted were from *Elements of the Science of War* by W. Muller in 1811 and quoted in *ibid.* The Canadian contest is described in *Quebec Mercury*, 17 November 1812 and discussed in Malcomson, "Silver Dollar Accuracy with a Musket?" Other factors affecting accuracy, and further challenging Hanger's view, are mentioned in Harding, *Small arms of the East India Company*, 291-2. 200 yd. = 183 m.

24. Among the many available descriptions of muskets, bayonets, ammunition, their use and training techniques are Haythornthwaite, *Weapons and Equipment*, 13-28; Haythornthwaite, *The Armies of Wellington*, 75-99; and Muir, *Tactics and the Experience of Battle in the Age of Napoleon*, 76-99. Contemporary examples of muskets being referred to as firelocks include: "The Grenadiers … [wading ashore at Sackets Harbor, 29 May 1813] raised their firelocks high," Le Couteur, *Merry Hearts Make Light Days*, 116; "We continued to advance, at double quick time, our firelocks at the trail, our bonnets in our hands," Anonymous ["Saucy Tom"], *A Soldier of the Seventy-first*, 60; and in claims by the British regiments for their losses at York, notably lists submitted by McPherson and Eustace, May 1813, LAC, RG 8, I, 84: 123 and 130.

25. Anonymous ["Saucy Tom"], *A Soldier of the Seventy-first*, 61.

26. Hanks, "Memoir," 43.

27. Anonymous ["Saucy Tom"], *A Soldier of the Seventy-first*, 100.

28. Sir David Dundas published *Principles of Military Movements* in 1788 which was approved for use with British infantry in 1792 and published in numerous editions among which was "Dundas's Regulations," *Rules and Regulations for the Formations, Field-Exercise, and Movements of His Majesty's Forces*, in 1801. For a discussion of training problems and solutions in the British army see, Glover, *Peninsular Preparation*, 111-22. An excellent description of the use of manuals in the U.S. Army is Graves, "Dry Book of Tactics." Alexander Smyth's *Regu-*

lations for the Field Exercise was approved in 1812 for the use of the army. It was an abridgement of the popular French guide. For samples of both books, see: Riling, *Baron Von Steuben and His Regulations*; Smyth, *Regulations for the Field Exercises, Manoeuvres and Conduct*; Duane, *A Hand Book For Riflemen*. For example of how such guides were adapted for use, see Malcomson, "'Encamped on the Field of Mars.'"

29. Pike's reference to the special outfitting of the third rank is mentioned in a letter to King, 3 March 1813, WCL, Bloomfield-Pike Letter Book. A brief discussion of the regiment's use of pikes and other American examples is in Chartrand, *Uniforms and Equipment*, 99-100. European-related descriptions are in: Fletcher, *Napoleonic Wars*, 105, 7; Haythornthwaite, *Weapons and Equipment*, 32; Haythornthwaite, *The Napoleonic Source Book*, 79. The lance had only recently been reintroduced to cavalry in Europe, with indifferent results, Muir, *Tactics and the Experience of Battle*, 110-11. 12 feet = 3.4 m.

30. This comment and details of the regiment's pikes are given by Scott to Thompson, 17 November 1812, NJHS, MG 1044, Scott Letters. Pike advised Whitlock to bring from Plattsburgh "the rifles and Snow Shoes," 8 March 1813, WCL, Bloomfield-Pike Letter Book. "[T]he small detachment of riflemen of the 15th and 16th Infantry" was mentioned in the Brigade Order by Jones, 25 April 1813, *DHC*, 5: 162.

31. The American rifles of the period are described in Reilly, *United States Martial Flintlocks*, 123- 33, with detailed notes on the 1803 Model on 125-6, and in Chartrand, *Uniforms and Equipment*, 91-2. The development of the rifle is detailed in George, *English Guns and Rifles*, in particular, 129-77. A .54 rifle fired a .525 ball manufactured at a rate of 32 balls per pound, according to Lewis, *Small Arms and Ammunition*, 220. For a demonstration of rifle use, see <www.lewis-clark.org/content/content-article.asp?ArticleID=1523>.

32. For a discussion of the development of the British rifle companies and regiments, Glover, *Peninsular Preparation*, 130-4. For the history of the U.S. Regiments of Rifles, see Fredriksen, *Green Coats and Glory*. The Muster Roll of Captain Robinson's Rifle Company was attached to the 1st Regiment of York Militia from the 25th October 1812 to the 24th November 1812, signed by Robinson, LAC, RG 9, IB7, 16: 57-58. "In a few minutes the sharp crack of the Indians' rifles waked me [5 July 1814, before the Battle of Chippawa]," McMullen, "The Narrative of Alexander McMullen," 69.

33. For a discussion of light infantry, see: Muir, *Tactics and the Experience of Battle*, 51-67; Glover, *Peninsular Preparation*, 122-34. John Le Couteur, a member of the light company of the 104th Foot, frequently referred to his men as the "light bobs," Le Couteur, *Merry Hearts Make Light Days*, passim.

34. T.G. Ridout to Betsey Ward, 5 January 1813, AO, F 43, Thomas Ridout Family Fonds. For a description of the Six Nations warriors at Queenston Heights, see Malcomson, *A Very Brilliant Affair*, 171-8. For a discussion of native tactics, see Benn, *The Iroquois in the War of 1812*, 67-85.

35. The Light Dragoons also suffered for a lack of horses as mentioned in Graves, "The Second Regiment of United States Light Dragoons, 1812-1814." See also McBarron and Finke, "United States Light Dragoons, 1808-1810." The Regiment of Light Dragoons was created in 1808 and was not referred to as the First Regiment of Light Dragoons until after the Second Dragoons were cre-

ated in 1812. Some purists prefer to omit the ordinal number of the original unit.

36. "Artillery intensifies firepower; it is the most destructive of the arms. Where it is absent, the total power of the army is significantly weakened. On the other hand, it is the least mobile and so make an army less flexible," Clausewitz, *On War*, 340-1. Among the many descriptions of how the guns were served are: Hughes, *Firepower*, 16-8, 66-71; Haythornthwaite, *Weapons and Equipment*, 61-64; and Holmes, *Redcoat*, 244-5. A favourite manual of the time was Adye, *The Bombardier and Pocket Gunner*.

37. This description of ammunition, ranges and use is based upon: Hughes, *Firepower*, 29-43, 59-65; Haythornthwaite, *Weapons and Equipment*, 55-61, 64-75. The photographs of massed troops standing 250, 500 and 600 yards down range from a field gun featured on pages 24 and 25 of Hughes's *Firepower* reveal how small a target a company of soldiers made. 1000 yd. = 915 m. 450 ft. = 137 m. 840 ft. = 256 m. 3.7 in. = 9.4 cm. 5.3 in. = 13.5 cm.

38. For a discussion of the Royal Artillery, see: Glover, *Peninsular Preparation*, 81-110; Haythornthwaite, *The Armies of Wellington*, 108-18; and Holmes, *Redcoat*, 128-30.

39. Standard ammunition for guns is described in Hughes, *Firepower*, 35-36, 59-65; Haythornthwaite, *Weapons and Equipment*, 64-71. The need for security during loading, including carrying cartridges in shirt sleeves is mentioned in Hughes, *Open Fire*, 15-17. Wellington's order at the Battle of Salamanca for cartridges to be stockpiled at the gun position is mentioned in *ibid.*, 26. "The enemy threw a shell directly into one of our limbers and blew it to atoms, killed the sergeant and wounded four men," Dyneley to Douglas, 25 August 1815, Dyneley, *Letters*, 65. 50 yd. = 46 m.

40. Dyneley reported the rounds fired at Salamanca to his brother, 25 July 1812, (Dyneley, *Letters*, 32) and that his battery had targetted a French battery and destroyed it. He later wrote his sister (23 November 1812) that his five guns fired from dawn to dusk, expending only 140 rounds and "we had received orders from his Lordship [Wellington] not to fire at artillery, or anything but formed columns," *ibid.*, 58. At the Battle of Waterloo, 18 June 1815, the average number of rounds per British gun was 129, with the highest count being 183, Hughes, *Firepower*, 64. Captain William Holcroft, RA, reported how he engaged American field guns across the Niagara River during the Battle of Queenston Heights, in the *Quebec Mercury*, 27 October 1812, cited in Malcomson, *A Very Brilliant Affair*, 170.

41. Hennell, *A Gentleman Volunteer*, 14.

42. Dyneley about the Battle of Salamanca to his brother, 25 July 1812, Dyneley, *Letters*, 32.

43. Hanks, "Memoir," 42.

44. Hennell, *A Gentleman Volunteer*, 91.

45. Hennell, *A Gentleman Volunteer*, 55. Cooper added up all the pieces of his equipment, clothing and necessaries to arrive at the weight of 55 pounds, *Rough Notes of Seven Campaigns*, 80-1. The weight of a single man's burden is also described in Anonymous ["Saucy Tom"], *A Soldier of the Seventy-first*, 50.

46. "It would be a serious mistake to underrate professional pride (*esprit de corps*) as something that may and must be present in an army to greater or lesser degree," Clausewitz, *On War*, 219.

47. Merritt, "Merritt's Journal," Wood, *Select British Documents*, 3: 545.

48. Pike to Wilkinson, 24 July 1812, cited in Hollon, "Zebulon Montgomery Pike and the York Campaign, 1813," 261. "A soldier, whether drummer boy or general, can possess no nobler quality [than boldness]; it is the very metal that gives edge and luster to the sword.... The higher up the chain of command, the greater is the need for boldness," Clausewitz, *On War*, 223.

49. Allan's quote comes from the 20 April 1813 issue of the *Kingston Gazette*. Parts of the texts of the speeches given that day are in *Strachan*, 10, but without clear indication of the speakers.

50. Anonymous ["Saucy Tom"], *A Soldier of the Seventy-first*, 2.

51. Trowbridge's account, LOC, Trowbridge Papers.

52. Walworth to Simonds, 19 April 1813, LAC, MG 24, F 16, Jonas Simonds Papers, 1813, 1814. In his 6 April letter to his father-in-law, Walworth stated that it was already known that Pike's brigade would go on the expedition.

53. Warner to his wife, 19 April 1812, Flag House, Baltimore.

Chapter 9: "Forebodings of an attack": The Day Approaches

1. Norton, *The Journal of Major John Norton, 1816*, 318-9.

2. For Norton's career, see *DCB*, 6: 550. For an additional explanation of Norton's role in the provincial and war affairs, see Benn, *The Iroquois in the War of 1812*, 7-8, 32-5, 104-6.

3. Sheaffe to Procter, 20 April 1813, "Letter Book," 377.

4. Norton, *The Journal of Major John Norton, 1816*, 318-9. Sheaffe and Norton maintained their friendship after the war as mentioned in an excerpt from J. B. Robinson's diary, 31 January 1816, in Robinson, C. W., *Life of Sir John Beverley Robinson*, 96.

5. The company's arrival is noted in Sheaffe to Baynes, 14 April 1813, "Letter Book," 373. The company's musters are preserved in NAUK, WO 10, 10800, Pay Lists of the Glengarry Regiment of Light Infantry Fencibles, from 25 December 1812 to 24 September 1813. See Appendix 4, British Order of Battle. The regiment's history is fully explained in Johnston, *The Glengarry Light Infantry*. For uniform data, see Summers and Chartrand, *Military Uniforms In Canada*, 72-3.

6. For McPherson's career, see: Service Record by McPherson, 1820, NAUK, WO 25, 766: 125-6; Johnston, *The Glengarry Light Infantry*, *passim* and 249; *HMG*, 252. The recruiting is mentioned in General Order by Baynes, 13 February 1812, LAC, RG 8, I, 1168: 93. Information about the Trades House of Glasgow and the Skinners and Glovers may be found at <www.tradeshouse.org.uk/>.

7. The Fort York Account Book, (City of Toronto Culture, Museum and Heritage Services) for this period shows the following information: Midshipman H. Gateshill was paid wages for fifteen seamen sent to Amherstburg in February and that another group went there around 17 April; Lieutenant F. Purvis was paid at York during the winter and had left for Amherstburg before 27 April; Lieutenant John Platt, Midshipmen Henry Putman and Richard Daverne were paid at York but were not present on 27 April, presumably having gone to Kingston with Lt. Fish (who was at York, too); Paid during the winter and present on 27 April were Lieutenant François Gauvreau and M. L Green, Midshipmen Louis Beaupré and John Ridout, Surgeon Grant Powell and Clerk and Stewart James Langdon. Also, see Appendix 4, British Order of Battle. There were also two gunners and two boatswains paid at York, only one

of which was confirmed as captured, the others having either gone to Amherstburg or Kingston.

8. Freer announced the policy change to Sheaffe, 23 March 1813, LAC, RG 8, I, 688c: 28. Sheaffe wrote to Baynes that there was still ice in the bay on 14 April and that he hoped to send the *Prince Regent* to Kingston at the first opportunity, "Letter Book," 373. The schooner reached Kingston on 17 April as Gray informed Freer, 18 April 1813, LAC, RG 8, I, 729: 162. According to the Proposed Establishment of the Provincial Marine Department ... for 1813 (*ibid.*, 230: 132), the *Prince Regent* was to have had a crew of 1 surgeon, 1 midshipman, 1 boatswain, 1 gunner, 1 carpenter, 40 seamen and 2 apprentices, but Gray reported to Prevost, 12 March 1813 (*ibid.*, 729: 117) that there were only about 150 seamen in total present for both the Lake Ontario and Lake Erie squadrons, making a reinforcement of RNRF necessary on the schooner. It is concluded that the *Prince Regent* was fully armed when it left York as Commodore Yeo reported in July that it still carried its original battery of 10 12-pdr. carronades and 2 6-pdr. long guns in Comparative Statement of the Forces ..., LAC, MG 11, CO 42, 151: 100. Notice that Sheaffe had purchased the *Mary Ann* and that it was not ready due to bad weather as Sheaffe wrote to Baynes, 14 April 1813, "Letter Book," 373. The vessel must have been readied and was sent off as it was not present during the battle.

9. The construction progress is based upon Return of the Work done to or for the Ship from the 7th to the 17th of April, by LeLièvre, 19 April 1813, LAC, RG 8, I, 729: 166. For the progress of work at Kingston, see Malcomson, *Lords of the Lake*, 94-100.

10. See Appendix 3, British Artillery, for a complete discussion of the artillery at York. Sheaffe mentioned the furnaces to Baynes, 7 April 1813, Sheaffe, "Letter Book," 370. "Shot oven" is not defined in either Smith, *An Universal Military Dictionary*, or James, *New and Enlarged Military Dictionary*. They have the same mention of "red hot shot" being heated in fire pits dug into the ground (19 and unpaginated, respectively) while Smith defines "furnace" as "a hollow or excavation" dug out when a mine is laid for blow up enemy works.

11. Bad weather was mentioned in Sheaffe to Baynes, "Letter Book," 373. Hughes's promotion is in a General Order, 13 March 1813, LAC, RG 8, I, 1203½G: 89. Sheaffe mentioned that Hughes, and his wife and children, arrived at York on 11 April to Vincent, 14 April 1813 and that he would remain there to deal with department matters, "Letter Book," 373. Sheaffe reported to Prevost on 8 May 1813 (LAC, RG 8, I, 678: 221) that he had repeated his censure of Hughes for taking a month to go from Montreal to York. Hughes was present at York during the battle on 27 April and reached Kingston after Sheaffe did. He was soon sent back to take command of the engineers at Montreal, General Order, 11 June 1813, *ibid.*, 1170: 241. Hughes complimented Ingouville and the Fencibles to Sheaffe in an undated letter at Kingston during May 1813, LAC, RG 5, A1, 17: 7305. The bridges were described in a post-war claim by a number of citizens for their destruction by the British during the war, LAC, RG 19 E 5 (a), vol. 3743, file 2. They mentioned Hughes's recommendation and wanted remuneration for their loss, but were unsuccessful.

12. Memorial by Ridout to Sheaffe, 19 March 1813, LAC, RG 8, I, 688c: 17. Ridout made a request for funds to cover the move to MacMahon, 11 April 1813, *ibid.*: 22. Alexander Wood's role as agent for the Elmsley estate is mentioned in Ridout to MacMahon, 14 June 1813, *ibid.*:

54. The location of Ridout's home (on Duke Street, facing Princess Street, and between Caroline and Ontario Streets) is taken from Robertson, *Landmarks of Toronto*, 1: 304-5, 317.

13. MacMahan to Small, 10 April 1813, LAC, RG 8, I, 688e: 35. MacMahon to Ridout, 10 April 1813, *ibid.*: 37. MacMahon to Jarvis, 10 April 1813, *ibid.*: 102. McGill expressed his confusion to Small, 13 April 1813, *ibid.*: 40. George Playter Jr. delivered the items to his father, George Playter, Sr., not to Ridout's home, as per his bill for services, 11 April 1813, LAC, RG 8, I, 688e: 39. Senior billed the government £7 for storing the materials at his house. Harley's bill was written on 27 April 1813, *ibid.*: 105. Jarvis's expenses were audited and approved by Thomas Scott, 29 October 1813, *ibid.*: 100. George Huck billed the government for £12 to store Jarvis's material at his home from 10 April to 30 June.

14. William Baldwin noted deserters described "the American forces at Niagara as very weak, that their great strength is at Sackets' from where we expect an expedition to this place – the papers of all the public offices are packed in chests ready for removal" to Wyatt on 6 April 1813, days before the official orders were made for their removal, Baldwin, "A Recovered Letter."

15. The *Madison* incident and Leonard's arrest is described in Chauncey to Jones, 16 April 1813, USNA, RG 45, M 125, 28: 2. Details of the matter are found in Leonard's court martial, 1 December 1813, USNA, RG 45, M 273, volume 4, case 151. See also Malcomson, *Lords of the Lake*, 93, 143-5, 244-5; Leonard was suspended from duty for one year, dating to his initial arrest and, though he remained in the service, never served afloat again. For Leonard's career, see, *SROLO*, 67-8.

16. Chauncey gave command of the *Madison* to Elliott, 17 April 1813, WCL, CLB. The dates of the lieutenants' commissions for Woolsey, Brown and Elliott were, respectively: 14 February, 1807, 27 March 1807, and 23 April 1810 as noted in *SROLO*, 166, 37 and 64. Seniority showed itself as an issue among the officers following the battle at York. When Chauncey left the squadron at York to sail to Fort Niagara and back, Woolsey raised a "commodore's" pendant and refused to follow any orders issued by Elliott. This raised Chauncey's ire who demanded an explanation, in which Woolsey apparently referred to the right of seniority which other officers also supported. Chauncey harshly rebuked him, Chauncey to Woolsey, 5 May 1813, WCL, CLB. Also see Chapter 13 for details. Problems with officers included the following. "Such is the tyranny practiced [by Chauncey] here," wrote Sailing Master John Hutton, after Chauncey had him arrested, in a letter to Jones, 25 April 1813, USNA, RG 45, M 148, 11: 21: 209, to which Hutton attached a petition to President Madison of the same date for the mitigation of his sentence. Chauncey described Hutton's repeated misconduct to Jones on 21 April 1813, USNA, RG 45, M 125, 28: 26. A bitter dispute among pursers was detailed in Chauncey to Jones, 18 April 1813, *ibid.*: 12. Lieutenant Sam Angus argued with Chauncey but eventually apologized as Chauncey explained to Jones, 20 April 1813, *ibid.*: 18. Midshipman Cadwallader Billings fought with a seaman and was arrested as noted in Chauncey to Billings, 10 December 1812, WCL, CLB. Midshipman Augustus Conkling struck a seaman and was arrested as per Chauncey to Conkling, 8 April 1813, *ibid.* For careers of Billings, Conkling, Darragh, Fry, Hutton, see *SROLO*, 20, 34, 38, 50 and 60.

17. Warner to his wife, 19 April 1812, Thomas Warner Letters, Flag House, Baltimore.

18. For details on the squadron and its crews, see Appendix 7, U.S. Navy. Chauncey had about 640 seamen and marines at Sackets by December 1812 according to the 430 mentioned in Chauncey to Hamilton, 6 November 1812, USNA, RG 45, M 125, 25: 168 and notes showing 165 seamen and marines arrived on 8 November and 42 more arrived on 19 November 1812, that follow the muster of the *Oneida*, USNA, RG 45, T 829A, roll 17. It is estimated here that about 600 seamen and marines were still on the rolls in April 1813 besides the 150 of Perry's detachment listed in a return by Hambleton, 24 February 1813, *ibid.*, M 148, 11: 21 and the 50 of W. Chauncey's detachment mentioned in Chauncey to Jones, 12 March 1813, *ibid.*, M 125, 27: 39. Chauncey describes his crew strength in his answer to Chandler's offer, 18 April 1813, WCL, CLB and Chauncey Letter Book and his plans to Pettigrew, 19 April 1813, *ibid.*

19. Chauncey mentioned the need of signal books to Jones, 23 April 1813, USNA, RG 45, M 125, 28: 40. His orders to the commanders were issued 23 April 1813, WCL, CLB.

20. Instructions are mentioned in Chauncey to Chandler and to Darragh, Fry and Anderson, 18 April 1813, WCL, CLB. There is no mention of horses being transported in any of the documents. Fraser mentioned that Mitchell "acted as a volunteer on the expedition," to "D … …" [William Duane?], May 1813, *The Weekly Register*, 5 June 1813. For Mitchell's career, see *HRD*, 1: 716. H. G. Armstrong gave a receipt to the York representatives for the provincial funds confiscated during the occupation as noted in E. Derenzy to Coffin, 25 June 1813, LAC, RG 9, 1B1, 1814, 2: 25. For his career, see *HRD*, 1: 170. The order of embarkation was given in the General Order by Hunter, 19 April 1813, First Brigade Order Book, Taliafera Papers, Minnesota Historical Society.

21. Armstrong informed Dearborn that there were forty batteaux suitable to carry thirty-five or forty men each at Oswego in a letter on 10 March 1813, USNA, RG 107, M 6, roll 6: 314. He strongly advised Dearborn to take the largest force possible on 29 March 1813, *ibid.*: 338 and backed it up with another one stating that President Madison agreed with him, 8 April 1813, *ibid.*: 354 and a further statement on 11 April (*ibid.*: 366) that there were enough batteaux at Sackets Harbor and Oswego to transport more than 5,000 men. Dearborn replied to Armstrong on 5 April that it was not safe to transport troops across the lake in batteaux and other flat-bottomed boats, *ASP: MA*, 1: 442.

22. Dwight described the three days of embarkation in "'Plow-Joggers for Generals,'" 18. Riggers were sent to Niagara in the *Lady of the Lake* by Chauncey's orders to "H. H" and Nichols on 22 April 1813, WCL, CLB. As noted in Walworth to "father" (this was actually his father-in-law Colonel Jonas Simonds, Sixth Infantry), 19 April 1813, LAC, MG 24, F 16, Jonas Simonds Papers, 1813, 1814 and Warner to his wife, 19 April 1813, Thomas Warner Letters, Flag House, Baltimore, the *Growler* had been out of the Harbor from 19 April. It returned in time to join the expedition and along with the *Gold Hunter* probably took on the additional 150 men. Use of the *Gold Hunter* is in Chauncey to Smith, 30 April 1813, WCL, CLB. Legal proceedings concerning the *Gold Hunter* are in United States vs. Schooner Gold Hunter, 12 August 1812 to 30 September 1813, M 919, Admiralty Case Files for the Southern District of New York, Roll 14, 1812. Dearborn reported to Armstrong on 23 April 1813, (USNA, RG 107, M 221, roll 52: unpaginated) that "1600 of the best men" had embarked. He expected to take on 150 more "if the sails for a new vessel arrive

... and a small sloop from Oswego [arrives]" The only new vessel was the *Lady of the Lake* and Chauncey had ordered a set of sails for it. It is speculated here that Dearborn mis-identified the *Gold Hunter* as the "small sloop" and was not aware of the *Lady of the Lakes*'s orders or the imminent return of the *Growler*.

23. Dearborn reported 1600 men plus 150 more to Armstrong on 23 April 1813, USNA, RG 107, M 221, roll 52: unpaginated. Dwight similarly note 1600 embarked by 21 April, followed by 150 more the next day, Dwight, "'Plow-Joggers for Generals,'" 18. Chauncey reported 1700 to Jones, on 28 April 1813, USNA, RG 45, M 125, 28: 63 and 1800 to Jones on 22 April 1813, *ibid.*: 30. Pearce reported 1700 in Pearce, "A Poor But Honest Sodger," 135. Eustis reported 2000, A. Eustis to his uncle, former Secretary of War W. Eustis, 11 May 1813, *Massachusetts Historical Society*, (1870), 492. See Appendix 6, American Order of Battle.

24. Dearborn's arrival and the salute on 20 April 1813 are mentioned in Dwight, "'Plow-Joggers for Generals,'" 18. Armstrong relayed the president's order for Dearborn to command the expedition on 8 April 1813, USNA, RG 107, M 6, 6: 354.

25. Mitchell's role was mentioned in Fraser to "D ... ..." [William Duane?], May 1813, *The Weekly Register*, 5 June 1813. Fraser noted that Mitchell "acted as a volunteer on the expedition." Lieutenants Benjamin K. Pierce and Charles M. Macomb and one private, all of the Third Artillery, accompanied Mitchell, as stated in Monthly report of strength of the Northern Army under the command of Genl. J. Chandler for the month of April, 1813, USNA, RG 94. H. G. Armstrong (*HRD*, 1: 170) was involved in collection of public funds after the battle as noted in Chapter 13; E. Derenzy named the men involved as did Armstrong in the letter and receipt sent by E. Derenzy to Coffin, 25 June 1813, LAC, RG 9, 1B1, 1814, 2: 25. Trowbridge described how he ended up on the expedition in Trowbridge's account, LOC Trowbridge Papers.

26. Chauncey to Jones, 24 April 1813, USNA, RG 45, M 125, 28: 51. Chauncey gave the dimensions of the Henry Eckford-designed *Madison* as "112 feet keel: 32½ feet Beam: 11½ feet Hold: 580 Tons," in his letter to Hamilton, 26 November 1812, *ibid.*, 25: 192. A similar ship designed by Eckford in 1819 with a beam of 32½ feet had a length of deck between perpendiculars of 124 feet (Chapelle, *History of the American Sailing Navy*, 340-1), which would be an appropriate length for the *Madison*. Length (124) x beam (32½) equals a rectangle of 4030 square feet. Upper deck space for the *Madison* mentioned here is an estimate based on this figure minus about 1/7 of the area to account for the ship's contours and wood work, about 3455 square feet.

27. Accounts of the two sailings appear in Dwight, "'Plow-Joggers for Generals,'" 18 and Pearce, "A Poor But Honest Sodger," 135.

28. Prevost to Bathurst, 21 April 1813, LAC, MG 11, CO 42, 150: 143.

29. Prevost to Bathurst, 21 April 1813, LAC, MG 11, CO 42, 150: 143. Prevost had been unhappy about Sheaffe's handling of naval requisitions during the winter, ordering Freer to inform Sheaffe, 3 February 1813, (LAC, RG 8, I, 688e: 18), "It would have been useful to the Commander of the Forces if you had transmitted by Captain Hall, your ideas on the Naval improvements which have been suggested by that Officer."

30. Prevost to Sheaffe, 27 October 1812, LAC, RG 8, I, 1220: 10.

31. Prevost to Barclay, 26 April 1813, LAC, RG 8, I, 688e: 55. Barclay to Freer, 9 May 1813, *ibid.*, 729: 183.

32. For the 8th's history, see Cannon, *Historical Record of the Eighth*, and <www.regiments.org>. The General Monthly Return of forces in Canada for April 1813 shows the 8th with 35 commissioned officers and 975 non coms, musicians and rank and file, LAC, MG 13, WO 17, 1517: 50-1. The company's arrival at York was noted by Finan, *Journal of a Voyage*, 282.

33. Data for the grenadiers of the 8th is based on Pay-List of the 1st Battalion of the 8th or King's Regiment of Infantry from 25 March to 24 June 1813, both days inclusive. NAUK, WO 12, 2575. For more details, see, Appendix 4, British Order of Battle. For McNeale's career, see *HMG*, 251.

34. Data for the company 3 of the 8th is based on Pay-List of the 1st Battalion of the 8th or King's Regiment of Infantry from 25 March to 24 June 1813, both days inclusive. NAUK, WO 12, 2575. The presence of men from other companies is evident from the casualty list, A Nominal List of the Number Killed, Wounded, Prisoners and Missing in the Action of 27th April 1813, signed by Richard Leonard, 10 May 1813, LAC, MG 11, CO 42 354: 123 and in the investigation of claims by the regiments for losses in May 1813, LAC, RG 8, I, 84: 127-30. Also see, Appendix 4, British Order of Battle. For Eustace's career, see *HMG*, 137. For the Ogdensburg despatch, see Macdonell to Harvey, 22 February 1813, LAC, RG 8, I, 678: 95.

35. Commins, "The War on the Canadian Frontier, 1812-14," 201. The editor of this article uses the sergeant's signature to establish the name as "Commins" rather than "Cummins" as noted on regimental paylists, Pay-List of the 1st Battalion of the 8th or King's Regiment of Infantry from 25 March to 24 June 1813, both days inclusive, NAUK, WO 12, 2575. Also, see Appendix 4, British Order of Battle.

36. Commins, James. "The War on the Canadian Frontier, 1812-14," 202.

37. Beaumont, *Formative Years*, 45. Dwight, "'Plow-Joggers for Generals,'" 18.

38. Brigade Order by Jones, 25 April 1813, *DHC*, 5: 162. Pearce mentioned that "All commanding officers of Corps summoned on board the ship *Madison*," "A Poor but Honest Sodger," 135.

39. General Order by Chauncey, 26 April 1813, WCL, CLB.

40. Cited in Hollon, *The Lost Pathfinder*, 217. Sunset and sunrise times are based on U.S. Naval Observatory data found at <http://aa.usno.navy.mil>. Monday, 26 April 1813: sunrise – 05: 18; midday – 12: 16; sunset – 19: 14. Tuesday, 27 April 1813: sunrise – 5: 15; midday – 12: 15; sunset – 19: 16.

41. Finan, *Journal of a Voyage*, 87, 282.

42. Two accounts of the battle at York are printed in *DHC* and said to have been taken from undated, original manuscripts in the handwriting of William D. Powell and are identified here in this manner: [Powell A], "An Account of the Capture of York", *DHC*, 5: 175 notes the use of the telegraph showing the Americans were "8 miles below the town" or to the east; [Powell B], "Narrative of the Capture of York," *DHC*, 5: 203 notes the squadron 10 miles east of York at 6: 00 and the signal guns being fired. Another long account of events at York written and signed by Chewett, Allan, Cameron, S. Smith, Strachan, Woods and Baldwin on 8 May 1813 and sent by Strachan to John Richardson, an influential merchant and politician in Montreal, on 10 May 1813, AO, F 983 Strachan Fonds, (also Spragge, *Strachan,*

37). The account, hereafter referred to as "Citizens' Account" (the original is at the TRL, York, Upper Canada, Papers Relating to the Capitulation, April 27–May 8 1813 and a version of it is printed in *DHC*, 5: 192) and mentions the express rider from Scarborough bringing news at 5: 00. The stationing of a corporal and three privates at the lighthouse is mentioned in the 20 September 1812 entry of Captain Samuel Ridout's Garrison Book, LAC, RG 8, I, 1203: 19. Five of the men in Willson's company of the 1st York Militia were stationed at the post as shown in the Muster Rolls and Pay Lists of Captain John Willson's Company of the 1st Regiment of York Militia, 25 January to 24 April 1813, LAC, RG 9, IB7, 18: 420-1, 20: 33-4, 37-8, 59-60. According to Hounsom, *Toronto in 1810*, 9, a Union Jack was raised to indicate vessels coming from the east and a red ensign for those coming from the west. 10 miles = 16 km.

43. Finan, *Journal of a Voyage*, 283.
44. Ely Playter's diary entry for 26 April 1813, AO, F 556. Sheaffe mentioned his order to the light company to Prevost, 5A May 1813, LAC, MG 11, CO 42, 354: 132.
45. Finan, *Journal of a Voyage*, 283.
46. [Powell B], *DHC*, 5: 203. Evidence that no definite plan was laid out may be seen in another comment made by Powell in this document: "[In the morning] some difference of opinion existed of opposing or admitting the landing." Powell did not identify whose views differed.
47. [Powell A], *DHC*, 5: 175. The uncertainty of where the Americans intended to land was expressed in several accounts as was the fact that troops were kept on both flanks of the town: Letter by British Anonymous B, at Kingston, 23 May 1813, published in the *Montreal Gazette*, 9 June 1813; "Truth," *Anglo-American Magazine*, December 1853, 565; Citizens' Account, 8 May 1813, TRL, York, U.C., Papers Relating to the Capitulation.
48. Ely Playter's diary entry for 26 April 1813, AO, F 556.
49. The Derenzy-Selby marriage is noted in Robertson, *Landmarks of Toronto*, 3: 407 as being on 31 January, but Nancy Mallett of the St. James Anglican Church Archives informed Carl Benn (with whom the author debated the marriage date) that the original registry shows 8 February 1813. Not wanting to be held responsible for the loss of the cash and also wanting reimbursement for her family's losses, E. Derenzy explained the situation in a memorial dated 5 July 1813 (LAC, RG 8, I, 688c: 57) and a latter to MacMahon, 23 July 1813, (*ibid.*: 70). The events are described in Robertson, *Landmarks of Toronto*, 1: 12-13 and in Selby's biography in *DCB*, 5: 749. The "Billy Roe" story is told in *Landmarks* but confuses the two sums and what happened to them. The notion that he did this on the day of the battle is also discounted here. McLean is shown to be residing in a dwelling owned by David Burns on Toronto Street, not marked on the contemporary maps, (LAC, RG 5, A1, 6: 2297), but whether he still lived there in 1813 is not clear.
50. Strachan to Brown, 26 April/14 June 1813, AO, F 983, Strachan Fonds. The first part of this letter is published in Spragge, *Strachan*, 36. An anecdote has it that Strachan told Allan McNab, Sr. about the alarm to which McNab replied, " Then all is up with the town, for Sheaffe is no commander!" Fitzgibbon, "A Historic Banner."

Chapter 10: "Disagreeable presages": The Americans Land

1. Strachan to Brown, 26 April/14 June 1813, AO, F 983, Strachan Fonds.
2. Sunset and sunrise times are based on U.S. Naval Ob-

servatory data found at <http://aa.usno.navy.mil>. Monday, 26 April 1813: sunrise – 05: 18; midday – 12: 16; sunset – 19: 14. Tuesday, 27 April 1813: sunrise – 5: 15; midday – 12: 15; sunset – 19: 16. This site, which also provides the phases of the moon through history, shows that the moon entered its last quarter on 23 April 1813 and the new moon phase on 30 April. Accounts of events during the war often reveal that British clocks were set one hour behind American clocks. The occasional mentions of time in the various accounts about the Battle of York do not show this as definitively. The times given here are counted from the time of sunrise given above and are based upon a comparison of times given in the accounts.

3. Reports on the number of vessels in the squadron varied among the British from 14 vessels (in five accounts) to 17 (in one account). Only Sheaffe mentioned the sixteen vessels in his reports about the battle to Prevost, 5A May 1813, LAC, MG 11, CO 42, 354: 132 and Sheaffe to Prevost, 5B May 1813, *ibid,*: 119. The 5B May letter was shorter than the first of that date and an excerpt of 5A May appears in *ibid.*: 126. Fourteen matches the data regarding the squadron as shown in Appendix 7, U.S. Navy. Surveys of the various accounts were made to determine the location of the anchorage in relation to the fort, with the range being 1-2 miles with 1.5 miles being most common and "opposite" Fort Rouillé consistently noted.

4. The following description of the Battle of York and subsequent events is based largely on primary sources. Nevertheless, previously published descriptions of the battle were studied in detail. Among the publications studied are: Benn, *The Battle of York*; Stacey, *The Battle of Little York*; Cumberland, *The Battle of York*; Hollon, "Zebulon Montgomery Pike and the York Campaign, 1813"; Humphries, "The Capture of York"; Quaife, *The Yankees Capture York*; Beirne, *The War of 1812*, 154-288. Hickey, *The War of 1812: A Forgotten Conflict*, 129-30; Kingsford, *The History of Canada*, 8: 246-63; Lucas, *The Canadian War of 1812*, 84-92; Mahon, *The War of 1812*, 140-5; Stanley, *The War of 1812: Land Operations*, 167-80; Tucker, *Poltroons and Patriots*, 1: 242-57;

5. Strachan to Brown, 26 April/14 June 1813, AO, F 983, Strachan Fonds.

6. The 1811 revision of uniform regulations for generals is described in Kosche, "Relics of Brock", 38. See also Katcher, *The American War of 1812-1814*, plate C.

7. Strachan wrote "Look through a glass find the vessels decks thickly covered with troops," to Brown, 26 April/14 June 1813, AO, F 983, Strachan Fonds. This description of anchoring is based upon Harland, *Seamanship in the Age of Sail*, 231-79.

8. British/Canadian confidence on the eve of battle was noted in a long account of events at York (hereafter referred to as "Citizens' Account"), written and signed by Chewett, Allan, Cameron, S. Smith, Strachan, Woods and Baldwin on 8 May 1813. The original is at TRL, York, U.C., Papers Relating to the Capitulation. Strachan sent a copy of it to John Richardson, an influential merchant and politician in Montreal, on 10 May 1813, Spragge, AO, F 983 Strachan Fonds, (also Spragge, *Strachan*, 37). British/Canadian confidence was also noted in Finan, *Journal of a Voyage*, 86. Sheaffe reported the "number of the enemy landed" to be between 1890 and 3000 in Sheaffe to Prevost, 5A and 5B May 1813, LAC, MG 11, CO 42, 354: 132 and 119. That up to 3000 men landed was reported in the letter by British Anonymous A, at Kingston 7 May 1813, published in the

Quebec Mercury, 25 May 1813 and in the letter by British Anonymous B, at Kingston, 23 May 1813, published in the *Montreal Gazette*, 9 June 1813.

9. Sheaffe to Prevost, 5B May 1813, LAC, MG 11, CO 42, 354: 119. In his 5A May report, Sheaffe mentioned only the individual regular units and "about three hundred militia and dockyard men," *ibid.*: 132.

10. [Powell A], *DHC*, 5: 175. In [Powell B], *DHC*, 5: 203 the total given is 600. Strachan stated 360 regulars and 350 militia to Richardson on 10 May 1813, Spragge, *Strachan*, 37 and between 650 and 700 to Brown, 26 April/14 June 1813, AO, F 983, Strachan Fonds. Thomas Ridout remembered 300 regulars and 208 militia, *Ten Years of Upper Canada*, 180. No other contemporary British/Canadian anecdotal records regarding Sheaffe's force were found.

11. The strength of Sheaffe's force, as reported here, nearly doubles what has been the traditional description of the matter. A full explanation of the figures used here and the documentary proof behind them is found in Appendix 4, British Order of Battle, Appendix 5, U.C. Militia, and Appendix 9, The Terms of Capitulation. Sheaffe noted his order about arming the dockyard and town men to Baynes, 7 April 1813, "Letter Book," 370.

12. In [Powell B], *DHC*, 5: 203.

13. Prevost to Sheaffe, 27 March 1813, LAC, RG 8, I, 1707: 154.

14. District General Order by Evans, 20 November 1812, *DHC*, 4: 224. Part of Brock's orders were "The officer in command will, of course, oppose him [the enemy who had landed] to the utmost in his endeavours to obtain a footing, but should he be at length compelled to retreat, he will, if practicable, fall back upon Chippawa, disputing manfully every step," Instructions Sent to Officers commanding Forts by Brock, probably late September 1812, "District General Orders of Maj.-Gen. Sir Isaac Brock," 34-41, 46. See Chapter 4 for the circumstances of Sheaffe's original order.

15. See data regarding the Royal Artillery in Appendix 4, British Order of Battle, and Appendix 8, Casualties and Prisoners of War. Captain McPherson reported that the arms and accoutrements of 22 of his men were lost "from the men being employed in a Battery when the magazine blew up by which they were destroyed," during the investigation of claims for losses in May 1813, LAC, RG 8, I, 84: 175, 176 after the retreat to Kingston.

16. Sheaffe to Prevost, 5A May 1813, LAC, MG 11, CO 42, 354: 132. In this letter he also wrote that Shaw "by some mistake drew away the Glengarry company from the direction assigned to it." Sheaffe mentioned the misdirection of the Glengarries in his shorter letter to Prevost, 5B May 1813, *ibid.*: 119, writing it had happened "by some mistake (not in the smallest degree imputable to its commander)." "From the garrison there ran parallel to the lake at a distance of about half to 3/4 of a mile from the water a road to the beach or Humber Bay," [Powell A], *DHC*, 5: 175. McPherson stated his men were ordered to leave great coats, etc. behind in their barracks in the morning, during the investigation of claims for losses in May 1813, LAC, RG 8, I, 84: 175, 176 after the retreat to Kingston.

17. "Our troops were ordered into the ravine in the rear of the Government garden," Sheaffe to Prevost, 5A May 1813, LAC, MG 11, CO 42, 354: 132. Eustace and Heathcote stated that their men and the handful from the 41st Foot, were ordered to leave great coats, etc. behind in their barracks in the morning, during the investigation of claims for losses in May 1813, LAC, RG 8, I, 84: 167

and 169, after the retreat to Kingston. In the same testimony Heathcote mentioned that the drummers were directed to arm themselves and leave their drums behind.

18. *Myers*, 59.

19. A typical British seaman's breakfast (in lieu of better American sources) is described in Robinson, *Jack Nastyface*, 32-3. Standard British naval rations are mentioned in Lavery, *Nelson's Navy*, 204-5.

20. Captain John Scott, Fifteenth Infantry, "they came to anchor at different distances from the shore from 1/4 to 1 mile Distant the Small Boats and Bateaus were immediately manned and filled with troops," to Thompson, 17 May 1813, NJHS, MG 1044, Scott Letters. Brigade Order by Jones, 25 April 1813, *DHC*, 5: 162. General Order by Chauncey, 26 April 1813, WCL, CLB. Batteau and boat data is taken, respectively, from Malcomson, "'Nothing More Uncomfortable Than Our Flat-Bottomed Boats,'" and May, *The Boats of Men-of-War*, 58-9. Major Abraham Eustis wrote, "There were boats sufficient to land something upwards of 300 men at once," to his uncle the former Secretary of the Army, W. Eustis, 11 May 1813, *Proceedings of the Massachusetts Historical Society*, 11 (1869-70): 492-5. The author gained some first-hand knowledge about handling small boats during a military landing while participating in a simplified re-enactment of the American landing at Fort George (27 May 1813) during the "School of the Sailor" event organized by Victor Suthren at Historic Fort George in Niagara-on-the-Lake, Ontario in July 2005. The General Order by Chauncey on 26 April 1813, (WCL, CLB) ordered troops to be landed from the *Conquest* and *Ontario* first, followed by the *Madison, Tompkins, Oneida, Raven, Gold Hunter, Hamilton, Scourge* and *Pert*, making no mention of the other vessels. This conflicts with the brigade order for embarkation by Hunter on 19 April 1813 (First Brigade Order Book, Taliafera Papers, Minnesota Historical Society), which put the riflemen in the *Hamilton* and *Julia*. It is assumed here that, since Chauncey's order was made on the day before the battle, the original embarkation plan must have been changed.

21. For data regarding the Regiment of Rifles, see Appendix 6, American Order of Battle. The mention of two large batteaux and Forsyth's pause was made by Fraser in a letter to "D … …" [William Duane?], May 1813, *The Weekly Register*, 5 June 1813. Fraser began this letter with an explanation that Pike, knowing he was mortally wounded, told him "write my friend D … … to tell him what you know of the battle." It is speculated that William Duane, editor of the newspaper *Aurora* of Philadelphia (where the letter was originally printed in May) and deeply involved with military affairs, was the recipient. Scott also mentioned Forsyth pausing his boats to Thompson, 17 May 1813, NJHS, MG 1044, Scott Letters. Forsyth's appearance, described in Chapter 7, is based on "he wore a broad-skirted coat of that color [green]. … He had on his head a broad-brimmed black hat," Whiting, "Life of Zebulon Montgomery Pike," 301. 200 yd. = 183 m.

22. This reference to McNeale taken from John Beikie to John Macdonell, 5 May 1813, AO, F 548, John Macdonell Fonds. Uniform details of the 8th Foot based on Koke, "The Britons who Fought on the Canadian Frontier," 169-70 and <www.warof1812.ca/8thregt.htm>. Daily diets in the British army are discussed in Henderson, "Marching on Its Stomach."

23. The "quick march" is defined in James, *A New and En-*

larged Military Dictionary, unpaginated. The destination for the 8th Foot was, at first the clearing around Fort Rouillé near the 1887 monument for the fort at the western end of the CNE grounds near Alberta Circle and Yukon Place. In January 2003 a lofty electricity-generating wind turbine went into operation near this spot and serves as a prominent landmark for judging distances visually. The distance from the 1887 monument to the fort is about 1.66 km.

24. Aspects of a lack of coordination in the deployment of the militia, and the presence of Plucknett's "artificers", are mentioned in several accounts, two clear examples being Citizens' Account, 8 May 1813, TRL, York, U.C., Papers Relating to the Capitulation and [Powell B], *DHC*, 5: 203. Sheaffe noted Jarvie's role to Prevost, 5A May 1813, LAC, MG 11, CO 42, 354: 132. Cruikshank's transcription of this latter document (*DHC*, 5: 188) incorrectly substitutes "Jarvis" for "Jarvie," an error in spelling and misidentification that may be found in others sources, too.

25. McLean is the best known of the volunteers and was frequently mentioned, an example being the John Beikie's letter, listed here, in which Alexander Wood is also mentioned. For Jarvis, see Jarvis, "Narrative of Colonel Stephen Jarvis,"252 and *DCB*, 10: 379. The Beikies are mentioned in J. Beikie to Macdonell, 5 May 1813 and Mrs. Penelope Beikie to John Macdonell, no date, AO, F 548, John Macdonell Fonds. For the MacNabs, see Beer, *Sir Allan Napier MacNab*, 6-7 and Coffin, *1812: The War and Its Moral: Canadian Chronicle*, 100. St. George, Wood, Beikie and McLean were mentioned in District General Order by Leonard, 13 May 1813, *DHC*, 5: 227. John Bassell, Keeper and Crier of the Court of General Sessions, was injured while on duty in the garrison as reported, in *The Report of the Loyal and Patriotic Society of Upper Canada*, 54-5. Jarvis, MacNab, MacDonell and Mathewson (Mathieson) were all young volunteers with the regulars and are all given credit for service at York in *HMG*, 205, 251, 239 and 258. See Hennell, *A Gentleman Volunteer*, 1-3 for an explanation of the role of a typical gentleman volunteer.

26. Sheaffe mentioned the use of the gun to Prevost, 5A May 1813, LAC, MG 11, CO 42, 354: 132. 1200 yd. = 1098 m.

27. Scott to Thompson, 17 May 1813, NJHS, MG 1044, Scott Letters. The American landing place was in the area of the lines of the current Dowling, Jameson and Dunn avenues.

28. This description of the warriors' clothing based on Johnson and Hook, *American Woodland Indians*, Plates F and G.

29. For a description of native tactics, see Eid, "'Their Rules of War,'"and Eid, "'A Kind of Running Fight.'" See also Benn, *The Iroquois in the War of 1812*, 53-4. Givins's uniform based on Chartrand and Embleton, *British Forces in North America 1793-1815*, Plate H. Norton's men at Queenston are described in Malcomson, *A Very Brilliant Affair*, 171-4.

30. For a description of the uniforms of the Regiment of Rifles, see Fredriksen, *Green Coats and Glory*, 12, 73-4. "The riflemen were hid behind the trees and logs and never appeared but when they fired, squatting down to load their pieces, and the cloaths being green they could not be distinguished from the bushes and trees," Citizens' Account, TRL, Papers Relating to the Capitulation.

31. John York, "The Battle of Toronto Bay – War of 1812."

32. Citizens' Account, TRL, Papers Relating to the Capitu-

lation. The death during the Battle of Yellowhead, and his grave in a native burial ground near Clover Hill, are mentioned in Scadding, *The 8th King's Regiment: A Curiosity in its Annals*, 8. Clover Hill was located near where St. Basil's Church stands on St. Joseph Street just west of Bay Street and east of Queen's Park. Scadding also repeated the gist of the story in *Toronto of Old*, 399.

33. John York, "The Battle of Toronto Bay – War of 1812."

34. Beikie to Miles Macdonell, 19 March 1814, in Firth, *Town of York*, 328.

35. "During the [first part of the] engagement two of the schooners hauled in near the shore, and threw grape-shot into the wood, which though it had no effect, served to alarm the militia and Indians who soon took to their heels," Eustis to W. Eustis, 11 May 1813, *Proceedings of the Massachusetts Historical Society*, 11 (1869-70): 492-5. "The schooners were required to beat up to their position," Chauncey to Jones, 28 April 1813, USNA, RG 45, M 125, 28: 63. A letter written to Elliott on 24 May 1821 by Joseph Macpherson, who commanded the *Hamilton*, stated his remembrance of Elliott resuming command of a schooner, Elliott, *Correspondence in Relation to the Capture of the British Brigs* Detroit *and* Caledonia … Philadelphia: United States Book and Job Printing, 1843, 10. Elliott was present in the *Conquest*, where he witnessed the death of John Hatfield as he revealed to Hatfield's father, 17 May 1813, *Otsego Herald*, 19 June 1813.

36. Scott to Thompson, 17 May 1813, NJHS, MG 1044, Scott Letters. 400 yd. = 366 m.

37. *Myers*, 59-60.

38. Scott to Thompson, 17 May 1813, NJHS, MG 1044, Scott Letters. Hoppock's wound is described in a letter by Lieutenant George Runk, Sixth Infantry, written at Sackets Harbor on 14 May 1813. Mr. Brian Murphy of Chester, New Jersey, owns the original copy and communicated its contents to the author, for which the latter is very grateful.

39. "Captain McNeil was the first who fell upon this melancholy occasion," Finan, *Journal of a Voyage*, 286. "Captain McNeal of the King's Regiment was early killed," Sheaffe to Prevost, 5A May 1813, LAC, MG 11, CO 42, 354: 132. "Repeated charges were made to get possession of the bank, in the first of these the gallant Capt. McNeil was shot thro' the head," "Truth," Letter to the *Anglo-American Magazine*, 3 (December 1853), 565-6. This latter writer claimed to have been at York during the battle and was writing to defend Sheaffe's reputation in rebuttal to an earlier article about the war in the magazine.

40. Fraser to "D … …" [William Duane?], May 1813, *The Weekly Register*, 5 June 1813.

41. Samuel E. Conner began his service as a major in the Twenty-first U.S. Regiment of Infantry on 12 March 1812. He was promoted to lieutenant colonel of the Fifteenth Infantry (upon Pike's promotion) on 12 March 1813, but remained as an aide to Dearborn instead of taking command of the regiment. For his career, see *HRD*, 1: 321. It appears that his promotion was yet to be confirmed and he felt himself still part of Lieutenant Colonel Eleazar Ripley's Twenty-first as implied in this statement regarding his role in the action at York: "The General [Dearborn] on this occasion, gave me liberty to join my Regiment on shore, and it afforded Lieut. Col. Ripley and myself particular pleasure to have rendered some little return for the confidence which it is understood the President reposed in us, but was withheld by the Senate," Conner to Armstrong, 4 May 1813,

USNA, RG 107, M 221 roll 51, item 153 [hereafter: roll: item, ie, 51: 153].

42. Dearborn to Armstrong, 28 April 1813, USNA, RG 107, M 221, 52: 125.

43. Fraser to "D … …" [William Duane?], May 1813, *The Weekly Register*, 5 June 1813.

44. "The Sergeant-Major of the 8th, a remarkably fine looking man, was the next, and the carnage soon became general," Finan, *Journal of a Voyage*, 286. "Mr. McLean … was killed at the landing, having joined the 8th grenadiers," [Powell B], *DHC*, 5: 203.

45. Among the several reports on Hartney's wound is the assessment of a medical board in 1816 which described the nature and severity of the wound, LAC, RG 9, I-B-4, 1: 51.

46. Scott to Thompson, 17 May 1813, NJHS, MG 1044, Scott Letters. Bloomfield's wound, as well as Hoppock's, is described in a letter by Lieutenant George Runk, Sixth Infantry, written at Sackets Harbor on 14 May 1813. Mr. Brian Murphy of Chester, New Jersey owns the original copy and communicated its contents to the author for which the latter is very grateful. See Appendix 8, Casualties and POWs for casualties suffered by the Fifteenth Infantry.

47. "Scott to Thompson, 17 May 1813, NJHS, MG 1044, Scott Letters. Pike's actions were described by Fraser to "D … …" [William Duane?], May 1813, *The Weekly Register*, 5 June 1813.

48. Whiting, "Life of Zebulon Montgomery Pike," 302.

49. "Their captain fell early and the company broke," British Anonymous B, at Kingston, 23 May 1813, published in the *Montreal Gazette*, 9 June 1813. "A large portion of the company dropped by the riflemen, …, it broke," [Powell A], *DHC*, 5: 175.

50. "The sound of Forsythe's *bugles* was heard, with peculiar delight," Fraser to "D … …" [William Duane?], May 1813, *The Weekly Register*, 5 June 1813. "The sound of Forsyth's bugle was heard indicating his success and the retreat of the enemy," Trowbridge's account, LOC, Trowbridge Papers. The tone and details of Trowbridge's memoir suggests he was familiar with the Fraser letter and relied upon it for part of his retelling.

51. Scadding describes the size of the clearing as 30 acres in *History of the Old French Fort*, 28. Casualty rates of the units (See Appendix 8, Casualties and POWs) were used here to determine their place in the fighting and was backed up by such statements as these: "The Glengarry company … [was] hardly in time to witness the retreat of the troops that had felt the enemy," Citizens' Account, TRL, Papers Relating to the Capitulation.

52. Sheaffe mentioned this episode to Prevost, 5A May 1813, LAC, MG 11, CO 42, 354: 132. "Two of the schooners … threw grape-shot into the wood, which, though it had no effect, served to alarm the militia and Indians," Eustis to to W. Eustis, 11 May 1813, *Proceedings of the Massachusetts Historical Society*, 11 (1869-70): 492-5.

53. The advance of the Fifteenth Regiment is described by Fraser to "D … …" [William Duane?], May 1813, *The Weekly Register*, 5 June 1813. Regimental colours and National Standards are discussed in Chartrand, *Uniforms and Equipment*, 112-15. "The troops fell back. I succeeded in rallying them several times," Sheaffe to Prevost, 5A May 1813, LAC, MG 11, CO 42, 354: 132. "The Newfoundland and militia destined to support the grenadiers were obliged to give way, … although they were rallied by Sir Roger in person," British Anonymous B, at Kingston, 23 May 1813, published in the *Montreal Gazette*, 9 June 1813. "The grenadiers and Newfoundland

division, with some militia who had joined, were so much galled by the fire of the enemy and had so many killed that they were obliged to retreat," Citizens' Account, TRL, Papers Relating to the Capitulation.

54. Among the several reports on Jarvie's wound is a series of four surgeons' assessments done in 1814 and 1815, explaining the nature and severity of the wound and Jarvie's subsequent loss of use of his right hand, LAC, RG 9, I-B-4, 1: 4. Murray's death was mentioned in several reports, including *ibid.*: 2. Borland received six wounds as noted in Ely Playter's diary entries for 28 and 30 April 1813 (respectively), AO, F 556. In an appeal to the Duke of Richmond for some additional compensation (14 October 1818, LAC, RG 8, I, 189: 42), Plucknett wrote, "I lost several men and all my effects while employed in this hazardous service." Daniel Daverne reported two of the men killed at York to Loring, 7 June 1813, LAC, RG 5, A1, 17: 7362. See also Appendix 8, Casualties and POWs.

55. "From the frequent halts made by our troops on their way to the scene of action and coming up in small divisions," Citizens' Account, TRL, Papers Relating to the Capitulation. [Powell A], *DHC*, 5: 175. Sheaffe ordered 20 of Chewett's militia to wait on the road in the woods near the Western Battery, [Powell A], *DHC*, 5: 175.

56. "Eventually left him with his aid-de-camp, Captain Loring, between the enemy and our retreating force," British Anonymous B, at Kingston, 23 May 1813, published in the *Montreal Gazette*, 9 June 1813. "[Sheaffe] twice rallied them and was fairly left with none but his A.D.C. Capt. Loring between the enemy and our retreating force," [Powell A], *DHC*, 5: 175.

57. Strachan to Brown, 26 April/14 June 1813, AO, F 983, Strachan Fonds.

Chapter 11: "The Stars are going up!": March to the Garrison

1. Fraser to "D … …" [William Duane?], May 1813, *The Weekly Register*, 5 June 1813.

2. "Gen. Dearborn at this time sent orders to Gen. Pike not to move from the plain, until the artillery was landed and the column perfectly formed," Conner to Armstrong, 4 May 1813, USNA, RG 107, M 221, roll 51, item 153 [hereafter: roll: item, ie, 51: 153]. For Conner rank and appointment see note 41 in the previous chapter. The mention of the fight "on the hill," was made in a letter by American Anonymous A, at Niagara, 9 May 1813, published in the *United States Gazette*, 24 May 1813, *DHC*, 5: 213.

3. "Brigade Major Hunter formed the troops for action as they landed and reached the plain," Fraser to "D … …" [William Duane?], May 1813, *The Weekly Register*, 5 June 1813.

4. Surgeon James Mann described a wound (Mann, *Sketches of the Campaigns*, 226) that must have been Irvine's: "An officer at Little York, was wounded by a bayonet, in the axilla [armpit], which divided by the artery; he bled until he fainted, when the hemorrhage ceased. This wound was cured without any unpleasant accident." The attribution of Irvine's wound to "friendly fire" is based upon the following. Captain Moore wrote to his brother from Niagara on 5 May that "Lieutenant Irvine received a bayonet through his right shoulder, at the moment of stepping out of the boat, but is doing well," Brannan, *Official Letters*, 151. Moore speaks in terms of "We" when describing the flow of the battle and closed with "My company distinguished themselves gloriously, and were noticed for their determined spirit." He does not mention their

specific involvement in the action on the beach. According to Pike's pre-battle order, the federal volunteers were put at the end of the column and, therefore, were among the last to be landed, Brigade Order by Jones, 25 April 1813, *DHC*, 5: 162. None of the accounts referenced in the previous chapter made any mention to the Baltimore Volunteers being involved in the first phase of the battle. Similarly, there is no mention of the British grenadiers ever descending to the beach. Most references to the volunteers involve their position on the flanks after the column had been formed, as seen in this example: "The column consisting of … Lieut. Col. McClures corps of Volunteers acted on the Flanks," Conner to Armstrong, 4 May 1813, USNA, RG 107, M 221, 51: 153. All other casualties among the volunteers were said to be due to the explosion of the magazine; see Appendix 8, Casualties and POWs.

5. Strachan to Brown, 26 April/14 June 1813, AO, F 983, Strachan Fonds.

6. The involvement of Baldwin, Aspinwall and Cawthra was mentioned in Citizens' Account, TRL, Papers Relating to the Capitulation. Cawthra is misidentified as "Cathray" in this account. For background on Aspinwall and Cawthra, see Firth, *The Town of York: 1793-1815*, lxxxiii and 130n respectively. Cawthra's home and apothecary was on the northwest corner of King Street and Caroline Street, which is modern-day Sherbourne Street, Robertson, *Landmarks of Toronto*, 4: 96. Aspinwall left York after the battle, joining the U.S. Army as a surgeon's mate for which see *HRD*, 1: 174. For the military surgeons, see Appendix 6, American Order of Battle, and Appendix 7, U.S. Navy.

7. John Beikie to John Macdonell, 5 May 1813, AO, F 548, John Macdonell Fonds.

8. Isaac Wilson to Jonathan Wilson, 5 December 1813, AO, MS 199(5), Isaac Wilson Diaries. Powell reported that "Capt. Cameron commanded the militia at the town blockhouse, and received orders which did not arrive in time for him to join the contest until it was over," [Powell B], *DHC*, 5: 203.

9. Ely Playter's diary entry for 27 April 1813, AO, F 556.

10. Wilmot and Fenwick's presence is shown in the Muster Roll and Pay List of a Detachment … retreating with the Army … 27 April to 13 May 1813, by Fenwick, LAC, RG 9, IB7, 16: 98. Playter wrote in his 27 April entry that after helping LeLiévre, he "came threw the town see a number of Country Ma. [presumably "Militia"] just come in," AO, F 556. See also Elizabeth Saunders's appeal for a pension mentions her husband's station and why he was mortally injured, 8 February 1814, LAC, RG 5, A1, 19: 7835: "he heard the signal for the alarm and ran to the action and was stationed at the twelve pounder and in trying to carry off the portable magazine was delayed and his leg shattered by the explosion of the magazine." The lists, made in 1814, of men who were taken prisoner after the battle include numerous individuals who were not shown on the pay rolls of the companies present at the garrison on 24 April 1813. While some of the men who were mustered on 24 April left the post the next day, it is assumed here that most of them stayed and were present on 27 April. Their numbers were strengthened by men who answered the call to arms and arrived through the day. For a full discussion of this data, Appendix 5, U.C. Militia, and Appendix 9, Capitulation.

11. Sheaffe referred to his guns as "this defective means," Sheaffe to Prevost, 5A May 1813, LAC, MG 11, CO 42, 354: 132. "[The naval commanders] perceived our guns were light and kept off, where we could not reach them," Ely Playter's diary entry for 27 April 1813, AO, F 556. "[Sheaffe] had no large guns. The fort was rendered untenable by the bombardment from the ships," Ridout, *Ten Years of Upper Canada*, 182. Sheaffe mentioned the furnaces to Baynes, 7 April 1813, Sheaffe, "Letter Book," 370. "Shot oven" is not defined in either Smith, *An Universal Military Dictionary*, nor James, *New and Enlarged Military Dictionary*. They have the same mention of "red hot shot" being heated in fire pits dug into the ground (19 and unpaginated, respectively) while Smith defines "furnace" as "a hollow or excavation" dug out when a mine is laid for blow up enemy works. Ned Myers described hot shot striking the *Scourge* and burning a man, *Ned Myers*, 60.

12. "Forty of their men were seen flying in the air," Trowbridge to John Trowbridge, May 1814, "Two Letters About the War of 1812." Trowbridge was on the *Oneida*, observing the action. The most thorough description of the incident was by Finan, *Journal of a Voyage*, 286-8, the gunner's careless, or accidental, use of the port fire and overcrowding of the battery also appearing in Citizens' Account, TRL, Papers Relating to the Capitulation and Commins, "The War on the Canadian Frontier, 1812-14," 202. Casualty counts ranged from 20 in British Anonymous A, at Kingston, 7 May 1813, published in the *Quebec Mercury*, 25 May 1813, to 30 in both John Beikie to John Macdonell, 5 May 1813, AO, F 548, John Macdonell Fonds and Isaac Wilson to Jonathan Wilson, 5 December 1813, AO, MS 199(5), Isaac Wilson Diaries, to "12-18 killed and many more wounded" in Citizens' Account, TRL, Papers Relating to the Capitulation. 50 yd. = 46 m.

13. John Beikie to John Macdonell, 5 May 1813, AO, F 548, John Macdonell Fonds. Jarvis's wound was confirmed in a note by William Allan, 16 June 1817, LAC, RG 9, IB4, 3: unpaginated. Other descriptions are from Finan, *Journal of a Voyage*, 287-8. For casualties, see Appendix 8, Casualties and POWs.

14. Isaac Wilson to Jonathan Wilson, 5 December 1813, AO, MS 199(5), Isaac Wilson Diaries. Wilson also wrote, "There was now much confusion, every man going where he would." "The militia began now to visibly melt away," Citizens' Account, TRL, Papers Relating to the Capitulation. "[There was a] considerable dispersion of the militia … the retreat was disorderly, but the regular force was kept together," [Powell A], *DHC*, 5: 175.

15. Grenadier Pond in Toronto's High Park is located two miles west of the battleground between Bloor Street and the lake, and between Parkside Road and Ellis Avenue. The Grenadier Restaurant is in the centre of the park while Grenadier Heights and Grenadier Road lie on either side of it. The grenadiers retreated eastward toward the fort, not to the west and it was no longer cold enough on 27 April 1813 for ponds to be frozen. The pond was actually informally named in the 1850s for the soldiers from Fort York who fished and relaxed there. Carl Benn succinctly debunked the legend with "The story is utter nonsense," *Historic Fort York*, 53. "By the vigour of Col. Hughes and Mr. Ingouville the battery was quickly cleared and the guns began again to play upon the enemy," Citizens' Account, TRL, Papers Relating to the Capitulation. Cruikshank transcription in *DHC* 5: 192 incorrectly suggested that Hughes was actually Heathcote.

16. Finan, *Journal of a Voyage*, 292.

17. The flight of the Baldwin family was described by

Mary-Warren (Baldwin) Breakenridge in Canniff, *The Medical Profession in Upper Canada*, 229-30. The same account appears in Robertson, *Landmarks of Toronto*, 1: 169-71. Von Horn is mentioned in Firth, *Town of York*, 67.

18. Anne Jane (Powell) Seymour gave this account as recorded in Robertson, *Landmarks of Toronto*, 3: 288-9. The Powells' home is described in *ibid.*, 1: 193 and was located at the southwest corner of Duke Street (modern day Adelaide Street) and George Street. The McGill "cottage" was located on the property of the Metropolitan United Church on the northwest corner of Queen and Church streets, *ibid.* 1: 193. See also Strachan to Brown, 26 April/14 June 1813, AO, F 983, Strachan Fonds.

19. Penelope Beikie to John Macdonell, 5 May 1813, AO, F 548, John Macdonell Fonds. The Givins anecdote is in Robertson, *Landmarks of Toronto*, 1: 1-3 while the Derenzy anecdote is in *ibid.*: The Givins home was on one of the park lots located north of modern Queen Street at Givins Street, near the site of the former Queen Street Mental Health Centre, now the Centre for Addiction and Mental Health.

20. *Myers*, 60-1. Myers mentioned that Chauncey travelled in a gig. When anchored, the schooner would have had its bow to the wind with its larboard facing the shore. Lieutenant Jesse Elliott relayed the story of Hatfield's death to his parents, 17 May 1813, which was published in the 19 June 1813 issue of the *Ostego Herald*.

21. Quotes in these paragraphs from *Myers*, 60-1. Myers mentioned that Chauncey travelled in a gig.

22. *Myers*, 60-61.

23. "The artillery, which was drawn by soldiers ...," Pearce, "A Poor But Honest Sodger," 136. The speculation about the length of the column is based upon the column advancing in sections, of four files each and each rank covering one yard of ground on the narrow road by the lake. Having suffered casualties, the American numbers were down to about 1700, 140 of these were the surviving Riflemen, 150 were the Volunteers who were on the flank, not in the column, bringing the number to about 1400. If there was one wagon for each gun and two for all the infantry and ten men hauling each gun and wagon, then a further 110 men, and another 60 spares, perchance, were not marching. 1200 men in formation, marching in four files with each rank covering one yard, takes up 300 yards without any "open column" spaces. If ten yards were needed for each gun or wagon, their length, without spaces would be [(6 + 6 + 2) × 10] = 140 yards (128 m.). If ten yards were allowed between each gun, wagon or section of infantry, another 200 yards might be added, making a total of (300 + 140 + 200) 640 yards (585 m.).

24. "The route was so much intersected by streams and rivulets, the bridges over which had been destroyed by the enemy as they retreated ... we collected logs and by severe efforts, at length contrived to pass over one field piece and a howitzer where were placed at the head of our column," Fraser to "D ... ..." [William Duane?], May 1813, *The Weekly Register*, 5 June 1813. "[The troops advanced] having a swamp and thick wood on their right and left," Pearce, "A Poor But Honest Sodger," 136.

25. The best description of the guns in the Western Battery is in Pearce, "A Poor But Honest Sodger," 136: "It mounted two long 18-pounders; one commanded the road in which the column was advancing; the other, the harbor. By the explosion of this battery in the morning,

the gun that commanded the road was dismounted.... The other gun of this battery was raised on a platform and could not be brought to bear on the column in the road. The only injury it did was cutting off some of the muskets of the advancing column."

26. Ely Playter's diary entry for 27 April 1813, AO, F 556.

27. [Powell A], *DHC*, 5: 175.

28. Citizens' Account, TRL, Papers Relating to the Capitulation. This document noted that Sheaffe "walked backwards and forwards on the road between the garrison and Mr. Haines's, more than half a mile from the troops."

29. The continuing need to clear the woods west of the Western Battery, which sat 50 yards from the edge of the woods, was mentioned by Kitson to Vincent, 22 November 1813, LAC, RG 8, I, 388: 136. The use of defensive barricades were successful at the Battle of Chateauguay, 26 October 1813, and the various battles at New Orleans, *HDW*, 85-6 and 365-72. Lieutenant General Gordon Drummond chose a rise of ground to defend at the Battle of Lundy's Lane, 25 July 1814, *ibid.*, 298-300. Among the battles where Wellington successfully chose a rise of ground as a defensive point were Vimiero, Portugal, in August 1808, Talavera, Spain in July 1809 and Busaco, Portugal in September 1810, Fremont-Barnes, *The Napoleonic Wars*, 33-4, 41-3 and 46-8. Wellington's defensive tactics are also described briefly in Muir, *Tactics and the Experience of Battle*, 16, 94 and 102 and in Haythornthwaite, *The Armies of Wellington*, 89-94.

30. A reference to Shaw's comments appears as a postscript on Citizens' Account, TRL, Papers Relating to the Capitulation.

31. Ely Playter's diary entry for 27 April 1813, AO, F 556.

32. The lack of grape or canister shot at the Western Battery was criticized in Citizens' Account, TRL, Papers Relating to the Capitulation, but the Return of Ordnance Mounted ... by James Gordon, 31 March 1813, LAC, RG 8, I, 387: 47 showed only 10 rounds of 18-pdr. grape shot at York and no canister at all for those guns. There were, however, over 1600 rounds or round shot. "Excepting some pikes broken and some bayonets bent, these guns gave us no annoyance," Fraser to "D ... ..." [William Duane?], May 1813, *The Weekly Register*, 5 June 1813. "The only injury it did was cutting off some of the muskets of the advancing column," Pearce, "A Poor But Honest Sodger," 136.

33. Walworth to his father-in-law, Colonel Jonas Simonds, Sixth Infantry, 13 May 1813, LAC, MG 24, F 16, Jonas Simonds Papers, 1813, 1814. See also Fraser to "D ... ..." [William Duane?], May 1813, *The Weekly Register*, 5 June 1813 and Pearce, "A Poor But Honest Sodger," 136.

34. Fraser to "D ... ..." [William Duane?], May 1813, *The Weekly Register*, 5 June 1813. There were nearly 3000 rounds of round shot, 200 of grape and 400 of canister for the 12-pdr. guns in the arsenal, as per the Return of Ordnance ... by James Gordon, 31 March 1813, LAC, RG 8, I, 387: 47. A full discussion of the location of Pike's column and its distance from the grand magazine is found in Appendix 2, Explosion.

35. There were at least two flags captured, a Royal Standard and another one. The Royal Standard, the mace and a carved lion were trophies of war that Chauncey sent to Jones and which he acknowledged on 14 June 1813 (USNA, RG 45, M 149, 10: 466), adding that they "will decorate the National Archives." The three items ended up in the museum of the U.S. Naval Institute in Annapolis, Maryland. The mace was returned to Toronto in a special ceremony held on 4 July 1934, as detailed

in the next day's issue of *The Globe*. The details of the second flag were not revealed, but it was the one that was brought to Pike as he died and which Chauncey later sent to his widow: "Permit me to send to you one of the British flags which were struck at York. It was the first that was brought on board of the Ship. I presented it to Genl. Pike before his death as a Trophy which he had so gallantly won," Chauncey to Mrs. Pike, 15A May 1813, WCL, CLB. This latter flag was almost certainly the Union Flag or Union Jack, as per: "It was the view of the King in Council 5th November 1800 that the Flag of Union could be flown on land only from His Majesty's forts and castles, and from His Majesty's ships at sea. It is the national official flag." NAUK, Sir A.Scott Gatty, Garter King of Arms in 1907, NAUK, HO 45, 10287: 109071, as cited in United Kingdom, Use and Status of the Flag, <www.flagspot.net/flags/gb-royal. html#exp>.

36. "I here proposed to General Pike to allow me to bring the two twelve-pounders to the front, reverse the battery, and fire under cover of it into the fort and blockhouse which we supposed still occupied by the enemy," Eustis to W. Eustis, 11 May 1813, *Proceedings of the Massachusetts Historical Society*, 11 (1869-70): 492-5. "Pike had come up to the second battery, and halted there, while he sent forward a corps to discover what was going on in the garrison as every appearance indicated its evacuation," T. Ridout, *Ten Years of Upper Canada*, 180.

37. Fraser to "D … …" [William Duane?], May 1813, *The Weekly Register*, 5 June 1813.

38. "Colonel Pearce was sitting on a stump facing General Pike, who was about 15 paces distant," Pearce, "A Poor But Honest Sodger," 137.

39. LeLièvre was forty-two years old when he received his first commission in 1795 as shown on his service record (NAUK, WO 25, 765: 132) where he also stated: "When the Americans attacked York in April [1813] … blew up the powder Magazine at the approach of the enemy, which occasioned him a loss of more than 200 men, our troops being then at nearly a mile and half in their retreat." A "Sergeant Marshall," was said to have claimed responsibility for blowing up the magazine in such works as: Auchinleck, "History of the War, Chapter X," *Anglo-American Magazine*, 344; and Cumberland, *The Battle of York*, 27. No contemporary documents were found to confirm this claim. The only "Marshall" on the rolls of the units at York was Corporal Seth Marshall of the Glengarry Light Infantry; see Appendix 4, British Order of Battle,.

40. The saucisson is described in the definition of "Mine" in James *New and Enlarged Military Dictionary*, (1802), unpaginated.

41. The moments before the explosion were described by Eustis to W. Eustis, 11 May 1813, *Proceedings of the Massachusetts Historical Society*, 11 (1869-70): 492-5; Fraser to "D … …" [William Duane?], May 1813, *The Weekly Register*, 5 June 1813; and Pearce, "A Poor But Honest Sodger," 137. They mentioned riflemen but did not identify them. Moore and the others are named here because he mentioned that his leg wound was caused by the explosion and "two of my company were killed at the same time, and four or five more of my brave fellows were severely wounded, now out of danger," Moore to his brother, 5 May 1813, Brannan, *Official Letters*, 151. See Appendix 8, Casualties and POWs, for confirmation of this data.

42. There are very few records of the time of the grand

magazine's detonation. The most reliable seems to be a diary entry by Lieutenant Colonel George McFeely, stationed at Fort Niagara, that the cannonade at York was distinctly heard to begin at 7:00 A.M. and continue until ending abruptly at 1:30 P.M. when the concussion of the explosion was clearly heard "which shook the buildings in Fort Niagara and made the glass in the windows rattle like what rolling thunder will do some times," "Chronicle of Valor," 257. Colonel Pearce, writing years after the war, remembered that the fighting began at 7: 00 and the Western Battery exploded "about 10:00 O'clock" and that "two hours after that explosion" the grand magazine blew up, "A Poor But Honest Sodger," 136 and 139. On 9 May 1813, American Anonymous A, wrote at Niagara that the fighting began at 7:00 and the explosion happened at 11:00, which was published in the *United States Gazette*, 24 May 1813, *DHC*, 5: 213;

43. A full discussion of the detonation of the grand magazine is found in Appendix 2, Explosion.

44. Fraser mentioned his first thought to "D … …" [William Duane?], May 1813, *The Weekly Register*, 5 June 1813. The four quotes that follow are from, in order: American Anonymous B, "The First Campaign of An A.D.C.," 1 (1833): 259; Beaumont, *Formative Years*, 16; Eustis to W. Eustis, 11 May 1813, *Proceedings of the Massachusetts Historical Society*, 11 (1869-70): 492-5; Conner to Armstrong, 4 May 1813, USNA, RG 107, M 221, 51: 153.

45. Finan, *Journal of a Voyage*, 289. Lieutenant Colonel George McFeely reported that about "half-past one … a tremendous explosion took place, which shook the buildings in Fort Niagara and made the glass in the window rattle like what rolling thunder will do some times," McFeely, "Chronicle of Valor," 257-8. The nature of the explosion at York was compared to the explosion of a munitions ship at Leiden, Holland in 1807, as described in: Reistma, H and A. Ponsen, "The Leiden disaster of 1807" and Reistma, H. J. "The explosion of a ship with black powder, in Leiden in 1807," *International Journal of Impact Engineering*, 25 (2001): 507-14. For a complete discussion, see Appendix 2, Explosion.

46. Descriptions of the wounds in this group are based on: Fraser to "D … …" [William Duane?], May 1813, *The Weekly Register*, 5 June 1813; American Anonymous E from York, 7 May 1813, *The Statesman*, 29 May 1813; Moore to his brother from Niagara on 5 May 1813, Brannan, *Official Letters*, 151.

47. American Anonymous B, "The First Campaign of An A.D.C.," 1 (1833): 259.

48. American Anonymous B, "The First Campaign of An A.D.C.," 1 (1833): 259.

49. Eustis to W. Eustis, 11 May 1813, *Proceedings of the Massachusetts Historical Society*, 11 (1869-70): 492-5.

50. The quotes here taken from, in order: American Anonymous A, at Niagara, 9 May 1813, published in the *United States Gazette*, 24 May 1813, *DHC*, 5: 213; American Anonymous B, "The First Campaign of An A.D.C.," 1 (1833): 259; Beaumont, *Formative Years*, 16.

51. For casualty figures, see Appendix 8, Casualties and POWs.

52. "The enemy sprung a mine upon us," Moore to his brother, 5 May 1813, Brannan, *Official Letters*, 151. "A tremendous explosion occurred from a large magazine prepared for the purpose," Dearborn to Armstrong, 28 April 1813, USNA, RG 107, M 221, 52: 125. "We at once understood that he had fired a train to the magazine," Eustis to W. Eustis, 11 May 1813, *Proceedings of the Massachusetts Historical Society*, 11 (1869-70): 492-5. "The

magazine was placed deep in the earth and surmount-
ed by an immense body of stone *probably for the purpose* of injuring an enemy *in case* it should be necessary
to explode it," Trowbridge to John Trowbridge, "Two
Letters."

53. "It was directly determined to conceal for the present
the fall of the General," Eustis to W. Eustis, 11 May 1813,
Proceedings of the Massachusetts Historical Society,
11 (1869-70): 492-5. Hunter and Mitchell's roles were
mentioned in Fraser to "D ... ..." [William Duane?],
May 1813, *The Weekly Register*, 5 June 1813. Fraser noted
that Mitchell "acted as a volunteer on the expedition."

54. American Anonymous A, at Niagara, 9 May 1813, published in the *United States Gazette*, 24 May 1813, *DHC*,
5: 213. "We were ready to give or receive a charge in
five minutes after the explosion," Fraser to "D ... ..."
[William Duane?], May 1813, *The Weekly Register*, 5
June 1813. "Not withstanding this calamity, the Troops
cheered, instantly formed and marched towards the
town," Conner to Armstrong, 4 May 1813, USNA, RG
107, M 221, 51: 153.

55. Ely Playter's diary entry for 27 April 1813, AO, F 556.
Sheaffe mentioned to Prevost (5A May 1813, LAC, MG
11, CO 42, 354: 132 and 8 May 1813, LAC, RG 8, I, 678:
227) that Loring and Davis were both injured by the
explosion and that Loring received a severe contusion
that was still affecting him ten days later. Also: "Captain Loring's horse was killed by the fall of a stone and
himself stunned," British Anonymous B, at Kingston,
23 May 1813, published in the *Montreal Gazette*, 9 June
1813. Myers saw an officer ride to the house before the
explosion and then speed away, *Ned Myers*, 64-5.

56. Isaac Wilson to Jonathan Wilson, 5 December 1813, AO,
MS 199(5), Isaac Wilson Diaries. For details about the
wounds Shepherd and Saunders suffered, see assessment of a medical board in 1816 which described the
nature and severity of the wounds, LAC, RG 9, IB4, 1:
32 and 2: 7 respectively. For Saunders, also see *The Report of the Loyal and Patriotic Society of Upper Canada*,
109, 232-3 and Elizabeth Saunders's appeal for a pension mentions her husband's station and why he was
mortally injured, 8 February 1814, LAC, RG 5, A1, 19:
7835: "he heard the signal for the alarm and ran to the
action and was stationed at the twelve pounder and in
trying to carry off the portable magazine was delayed
and his leg shattered by the explosion of the magazine."
Bassell's injury was noted in *The Report of the Loyal and
Patriotic Society of Upper Canada*, 54-5.

57. "The enemy did not escape the destruction of their
own works; hundreds were killed and wounded,"
Trowbridge to John Trowbridge, "Two Letters...." Ely
Playter's diary entry for 27 April 1813, AO, F 556.

58. Fraser to "D ... ..." [William Duane?], May 1813, *The
Weekly Register*, 5 June 1813.

59. American Anonymous D to friend in Northampton,
Massachusetts, May 1813, in *Otsego Herald* (New York),
19 June 1813.

60. Fraser to "D ... ..." [William Duane?], May 1813, *The
Weekly Register*, 5 June 1813.

61. Finan, *Journal of a Voyage*, 291. The flag was probably
one of the National Standards of one of the regiments,
featuring the eagle in flight amid a constellation of
seventeen stars as opposed to the "Stars and Stripes,"
although one reference notes the flag given to the Baltimore Volunteers by a group of patriotic ladies was
"placed on the highest pinnacle of the government
house in the capital of Upper Canada," 12 June 1813,
The Weekly Register. Finan's book was published in

1828, years after the term "Star-Spangled Banner" had
been popularized.

62. Sheaffe mentioned the meeting and his reasons for
retreat to Prevost, 5A May 1813, LAC, MG 11, CO 42,
354: 132. "The troops halted behind a ravine by Elmsley House.... it was now generally supposed that
General Sheaffe had abandoned all idea of further
resistance,"Citizens' Account, TRL, Papers Relating to
the Capitulation. Sheaffe's meeting, Heathcote and the
general's quick order were noted by [Powell A], *DHC*, 5:
175. Graves Street is currently known as Simcoe Street.

63. John Beikie to John Macdonell, 5 May 1813, AO, F 548,
John Macdonell Fonds.

Chapter 12: "Almost as bad as none": The Capitulation

1. John Beikie to John Macdonell, 5 May 1813, AO, F 548,
John Macdonell Fonds.

2. Chewett and Allan are mentioned in Citizens' Account,
TRL, Papers Relating to the Capitulation. Allan and
Robinson are mentioned in Ely Playter's diary entry for
27 April 1813, AO, F 556. Allan mentioned Chewett and
Strachan being involved to Sheaffe, 2 May 1813, LAC,
MG 11, CO 42, 350: 162.

3. American Anonymous Officer A mentioned "Young"
in his letter at Niagara, 9 May 1813, published in the
United States Gazette, 24 May 1813, *DHC*, 5: 213. White
Youngs was a captain in the Fifteenth U.S. Regiment
of Infantry; for his career, see *HRD*, 1: 1068. Pearce, "A
Poor But Honest Sodger," 137. Eustis to W. Eustis, 11
May 1813, *Proceedings of the Massachusetts Historical
Society*, 11 (1869-70): 492-5.

4. Crookshank's home was located west of the intersection of modern Front Street and Peter Street at its
southern end which is now known as Blue Jays Way.
In 1813 Peter Street was the western-most north-south
street of York, Robertson, *Landmarks of Toronto*, 4: 93.
The home is described in *ibid.*, 3: 65-9.

5. The anecdote was mentioned in a paper presented
in 1896 by Mary Agnes Fitzgibbon, "A Historic Banner." The anecdote says that Archibald McLean joined
Sheaffe's retreat. The next week, however, he wrote a
report giving day by day details of events at York, 4 May
1813, LAC, RG 8, I, 678: 190. The flag is said to have been
buried at the corner of modern Church and Shuter
streets, [no author indicated] "Toronto's Old Colours."
Heritage Columns (Heritage Toronto), 1 (Spring, 2002):
3. On 19 May 1813 a search party went to find the flag
which Samuel Ridout succeeded in doing, according
to Anne Powell to William Powell, 20 May 1813, TRL,
L 16, Powell Papers, Mrs. Powell's letters, A 93: 321. The
account of the 23 March ceremony in the 20 April 1813
issue of the *Kingston Gazette* clearly refers to the conventional pair of flags in the "colours" presented to a
regiment which were the regimental colours, a homemade banner in this case; and the national standard, a
Union Jack.

6. Ely Playter's diary entry for 27 April 1813, AO, F 556. The
transcript of this entry which appears in Firth, *Town
of York*, 280 shows "met Captn. Leatcover returning"
but an examination of the original entry in Playter's
diary in the AO F 556 makes "Lealeaver" a reasonable interpretation (the 't' is not crossed, something
Playter seems to have done consistently and the second
'e' matches the first and third). This is supported by
LeLièvre's own assertion in his service record that after
igniting the magazine, he "burned the Naval Stores and
a 20 gun ship then on the stocks," NAUK, WO 25, 765:
132.

7. LeLièvre's service record, NAUK, WO 25, 765: 132. "I and some others went with him and performed the service," Ely Playter's diary entry for 27 April 1813, AO, F 556. Plucknett appealed for compensation for his losses to Halton, 29 August 1816 (LAC, RG 19, E5, 3739, file 4, unpaginated) claiming that Sheaffe ordered Loring and him to burn the ship and dockyard, that he jumped on Loring's horse and went back and directed the burning. A conflict with this recollection is that Loring had been badly injured in the explosion before this and his horse was killed, as Sheaffe reported to Prevost, 8 May 1813, LAC, RG 8, I, 678: 227. In an appeal to the Duke of Richmond for some additional compensation (14 October 1818, LAC, RG 8, I, 189: 42), Plucknett repeated his claim about "destroying the ship and stores after the Troops with Major Genl, Sheaffe had evacuated the Place" without mentioning Loring. As shown elsewhere, notably in Chapter 6, Plucknett was self-serving and evasive to the extreme and inconsistently committed to his responsibilities.

8. Finan, *Journal of a Voyage*, 294. Sheaffe's order to the surgeons was harshly criticized in Citizens' Account, TRL, Papers Relating to the Capitulation. It was later revealed that Grant Powell retreated by his own volition as noted in Anne Powell to William Powell, 20 and 16 May 1813, TRL, L 16, Powell Papers, Mrs. Powell's letters, A 93: 321 and 316. These letters and others of 10, 12, 20 and 28 May identified the older local men who went with Sheaffe. Wilmot's detachment was shown in the Muster Roll and Pay List of a Detachment … retreating with the Army … 27 April to 13 May 1813, by Fenwick, LAC, RG 9, IB7, 16: 98. Evidence that the Don River bridge was intact was shown in Playter's diary where he noted that people were using the bridge by his father's place to cross the Don: "29 April – D. Brooks passed on his way to Kingston and many others also as the Enemy kept a Guard at the Don Bridge they came up here to cross," AO, F 556. 200 miles = 322 km.

9. This unattributed quote comes from a brief article in the 2 June 1813 issue of *The Statesman* of New York City, as taken from an unidentified issue of the *Boston Patriot*. Fraser to "D … …" [William Duane?], May 1813, *The Weekly Register*, 5 June 1813. Fraser began this letter with an explanation that Pike, knowing he was mortally wounded, told him "write my friend D … … to tell him what you know of the battle." It is speculated that William Duane, editor of the newspaper *Aurora* of Philadelphia (where the letter was originally printed in May) and deeply involved with military affairs, was the recipient. For details of Buchanan's service and treatment of Pike, see a memorial by Buchanan to Southard, 11 June 1824, USNA, RG 45, M 148, roll 35, 1824, 4: 106. "Permit me to send to you one of the British flags which were struck at York. It was the first that was brought on board of the Ship. I presented it to Genl. Pike before his death as a Trophy which he had so gallantly won," Chauncey to Mrs. Pike, 15A May 1813, WCL, CLB. This was not the Royal Standard which Chauncey sent to Secretary Jones, but possibly a Union flag. The Royal Standard, the mace and a carved lion were trophies of war that Chauncey sent to Jones and which he acknowledged on 14 June 1813 (USNA, RG 45, M 149, 10: 466), adding that they "will decorate the National Archives." The three items ended up in the museum of the U.S. Naval Institute in Annapolis, Maryland. The mace was returned to Toronto in a special ceremony held on 4 July 1934, as detailed in the next day's issue of *The Globe*. The flag brought to Pike was almost certainly the Union Flag or Union Jack, as per: "It was the view of the King in Council 5th November 1800 that the Flag of Union could be flown on land only from His Majesty's forts and castles, and from His Majesty's ships at sea. It is the national official flag." NAUK, Sir A. Scott Gatty, Garter King of Arms in 1907, NAUK, HO 45, 10287: 109071, as cited in United Kingdom, Use and Status of the Flag, <www.flagspot.net/flags/gb-royal.html#exp>. Such a flag can be seen flying in contemporary art of the military buildings at York.

10. American Anonymous D to friend in Northampton, Massachusetts, May 1813, in *Ostego Herald* (New York), 19 June 1813. This officer was on shore at the time of Pike's death, since he mentioned marching past him toward the garrison as the wounded Pike was being conveyed to the boat. For details of Buchanan's service and treatment of Pike, see a memorial by Buchanan to Southard, 11 June 1824, USNA, RG 45, M 148, roll 35, 1824, 4: 106.

11. Citizens' Account, TRL, Papers Relating to the Capitulation. This description of the 27 April meeting regarding terms is based on this document and Strachan to Brown, 26 April/14 June 1813, AO, F 983, Strachan Fonds. William Allan also described the negotiation process to Sheaffe, 2 May 1813, LAC, MG 11, CO 42, 150: 162. See Appendix 9 for a transcription of the 27 April terms.

12. Eustis to W. Eustis, 11 May 1813, *Proceedings of the Massachusetts Historical Society*, 11 (1869-70): 492-5.

13. Pearce, "A Poor But Honest Sodger," 141. Pearce's explanation was in response to a published account by Colonel Eleazar Ripley that he "pressed" him to proceed immediately into town, but that the delay prevented the capture of Sheaffe, *ibid.*, 140. The Ripley information comes from, Anonymous, "Biographical Memoir of Major-General Ripley," 115.

14. Playter wrote in his 27 April entry that after helping Leliévre, he "came threw the town see a number of Country Ma. [presumably "Militia"] just come in," AO, F 556. Detlor's nine children and their ages were listed in Ferusha Detlor's application for a pension, LAC, RG 9, I-B-4, 2: 8-9.

15. "As soon as I learned of Genl Pike being wounded I went on shore," Dearborn wrote to Armstrong, 28 April 1813, USNA, RG 107, M 221, 52: 125. Very similar statements were made in Conner to Armstrong, 4 May 1813, USNA, RG 107, M 221, 51: 153 and Chauncey to Jones, 28 April 1813, USNA, RG 45, M 125, 28: 63.

16. Pearce, "A Poor But Honest Sodger," 137. "General Dearborn assumed command the day after Pike's death, and remained on shore some days," Eustis to W. Eustis, 11 May 1813, *Proceedings of the Massachusetts Historical Society*, 11 (1869-70): 492-5. "The first appearance [Dearborn] made on shore was towards Sundown when we were Returning to the Garrison with the Prisoners we had taken," Scott to Thompson, 17 May 1813, NJHS, MG 1044, Scott Letters. Evidence that the Don River bridge was intact was shown in Playter's diary when he noted that people were using the bridge by his father's place to cross the Don because the American were guarding the other one: 29 April – "D. Brooks passed on his way to Kingston and many others also as the Enemy kept a Guard at the Don Bridge they came up here to cross," AO, F 556.

17. Transcriptions of the terms signed on 27 April and 28 April are found in Appendix 9 with a full discussion of their qualities and differences. Pearce alleged that the reason why Dearborn had the capitulation terms

revised "was to conceal the name of the officer upon whom the command and responsibility devolved on the fall of General Pike," Pearce, "A Poor But Honest Sodger," 139.

18. Pearce's arrangements for guards was mentioned in Pearce, "A Poor But Honest Sodger," 137 and Beaumont, *Formative Years*, 46. "The riflemen were appointed to protect it – a corps which bears the worst character in the American army…. The officers were liberated on their parole till next morning, and the privates were confined," Citizens' Account, TRL, Papers Relating to the Capitulation.

19. American Anonymous A, at Niagara, 9 May 1813, published in the *United States Gazette*, 24 May 1813, *DHC*, 5: 213.

20. Beaumont, *Formative Years*, 46. For the careers of Beaumont, Gilliland, Lawson, Mann and Trowbridge, see *HRD*, 1: 204, 457, 619, 687 and 971. Beaumont and Lawson were mentioned by American Anonymous A, at Niagara, 9 May 1813, published in the *United States Gazette*, 24 May 1813, *DHC*, 5: 213: "the surgeon and mate of the 6th Regiment took charge of the wounded." Mann declared he was an eyewitness to the battle in a letter to Dearborn, 6 July 1815, Lilly Library Manuscript Collection, University of Indiana. Mann also mentioned his involvement at York in Mann, *Sketches of the Campaigns*. James Bradford was a surgeon's mate with the Sixth Infantry and was present at York as stated in a petition for a pension to the American government, 15 October 1826, as noted in U.S. Serial Set, 25th Congress, 2nd Session, House of Representatives, Report 227, 28 December 1837. Trowbridge's career is detailed in the notes of Chapter 6, Trowbridge's account, LOC, Trowbridge Papers. Buchanan and Caton's careers, see *SROLO*, 38 and 44. In his memorial to Secretary of the Navy Southard on 11 June 1824 (USNA, RG 45, M 148, roll 35, 1824, 4: 106) Buchanan wrote that at York he "attended to the professional duties of not only the U.S. Madison but of every other vessel in the Squadron – the U.S. Brig Oneida excepted."

21. Canniff, *The Medical Profession in Upper Canada 1783-1850*, 230. A hospital building existed in the ravine on the east side of Garrison Creek about 300 yards from the lake as shown in "Plan of the Fort at York …" by Nicolls, June 1816 (LAC, NMC 23139) which may have existed in April 1813. Otherwise there must have been a building in the garrison or adjacent to it for this purpose.

22. "[Sheaffe] abandoned the sick and wounded, taking the two surgeons with him and leaving them without any medicine or medical assistance," Citizens' Account, TRL, Papers Relating to the Capitulation. The involvement of Baldwin, Aspinwall and Cawthra was mentioned in *ibid*. For background on Aspinwall and Cawthra, see Firth, *The Town of York: 1793-1815*, lxxxiii and 130n respectively. Cawthra's home and apothecary was on the northwest corner of King Street and Caroline Street, which is modern-day Sherbourne Street, Robertson, *Landmarks of Toronto*, 4: 96. Aspinwall left York after the battle, joining the U.S. Army as a surgeon's mate for which see *HRD*, 1: 174. For the military surgeons, see Appendix 6, American Order of Battle,.

23. Treatment of the various wounds is based upon: Beaumont, *Formative Years*, 10-51; Trippler and Blackman, *Handbook for the Military Surgeon*, *passim*; and Cushman, "Naval Surgery in War of 1812".

24. Beaumont, *Formative Years*, 46.

25. Mrs. Penelope Beikie to John Macdonell, no date, AO,

F 548, John Macdonell Fonds. Beikie's home was located where modern Windsor Street intersects with Front Street just east of the intersection with modern Blue Jays Way which is the southern extension of Peter Street. In 1813 Peter Street was the western-most north-south street of York, Robertson, *Landmarks of Toronto*, 4: 93. The home is described in *ibid.*, 3: 69-71. J. Beikie to Miles Macdonell, 19 March 1814, in Firth, *Town of York*, 328. The Powells' home is described in Robertson, *Landmarks of Toronto*, 1: 193 and was located at the southwest corner of Duke Street (modern-day Adelaide Street) and George Street. Petition of John Hunter, 11 March 1814, *The Journals of the Legislative Assembly*, 3: 105-6. The majority of claims for war losses are found in AO (and LAC) RG 19 E 5 (a), Board of claims for War of 1812 losses. They appear in various files in various forms, making one of the most convoluted record keeping systems imaginable. To simplify such references only the most complete descriptions available will be noted. In Allan's case it is *ibid*, vol. 3743, file 2. This was also published in Firth, *Town of York*, 301. The Givins home was on one of the park lots north of modern Queen Street at Givins Street, near the former Queen Street Mental Health Centre, now the Centre for Addiction and Mental Health, Robertson, *Landmarks of Toronto*, 1: 1-3.

26. American Anonymous C stated that "regulars and sailors were plundering and injuring private property. I believe Forsyth's corps did the principal mischief of this kind, professedly in retaliation of British outrages at Ogdensburg," in a 7 May 1813 letter to the *Baltimore Whig*, published in the 20 May 1813 issue of the *New York Statesman*, *DHC*, 5: 171. "The Enemy returned to the Garrison except the rifle corp, which is left under the pretense of protecting the town," Strachan to Brown, 26 April/14 June 1813, AO, F 983, Strachan Fonds. "The riflemen were appointed to protect it – a corps which bears the worst character in the American army…. If it had not been for the misconduct of the troops in pillaging at Ogdensburg many of them told us that there would have been little or no depredations committed here," Citizens' Account, TRL, Papers Relating to the Capitulation. One American officer openly showed his plunder, claiming "it was in compensation for his loss at Ogdensburg," [Powell B], *DHC*, 5: 203. Forsyth's lax attitude about discipline and looting is described in Whiting's rare and colourful description of Forsyth as part of his "Life of Zebulon Montgomery Pike," 300-4.

27. *Myers*, 62.

28. *Myers*, 63.

29. *Myers*, 63.

30. *Myers*, 64.

31. Strachan to Brown, 26 April/14 June 1813, AO, F 983, Strachan Fonds.

32. Ely Playter Diary, 30 April 1813, AO, F 556.

33. Citizens' Account, TRL, Papers Relating to the Capitulation. This account repeats the main gist of Strachan's private version of events (Strachan to Brown, 26 April/14 June 1813, AO, F 983, Strachan Fonds), in part because Strachan appears to have written most of the Citizens' Account, referring to himself throughout as a "Commissioner" of peace negotiations.

34. Transcriptions of the terms signed on 27 April and 28 April are found in Appendix 9 with a full discussion of their qualities and differences. Allan mentioned to Sheaffe that the terms were not signed until the afternoon, 2 May 1813, LAC, MG 11, CO 42, 150: 162.

35. Strachan to Brown, 26 April/14 June 1813, AO, F 983, Strachan Fonds.
36. Strachan to Brown, 26 April/14 June 1813, AO, F 983, Strachan Fonds.
37. Pearce, "A Poor But Honest Sodger," 137.
38. Pearce, "A Poor But Honest Sodger," 137.
39. Copies of it in the British/Canadian and American archives are identical: LAC, MG 11, CO 42, 150: 163; USNA, RG 45, M 125, 28: 64. The list of paroled men was made after the terms were signed as shown by "the officers were immediately set at liberty, and before sunset all the prisoners had left the garrison on their parole," Citizens' Account, TRL, Papers Relating to the Capitulation. More names were added over the next few days. Ely Playter, for instance, noted that he and Ensign Andrew Mercer did not register with the Americans until 30 April, Ely Playter's diary entry for 30 April 1813, AO, F 556. Others most certainly did the same. As pointed out later later in this chapter and in Appendices 8 and 9, the list was incomplete.
40. Elliott to Hatfield, 17 May 1813, *Otsego Herald*, 19 June 1813. Pearce mentioned that Hayden made his report to him on 28 April, Pearce, "A Poor But Honest Sodger," 138. The burials of Bloomfield, Hoppock and Lyon are mentioned in a letter by Lieutenant George Runk, Sixth Infantry, written at Sackets Harbor on 14 May 1813. Mr. Brian Murphy of Chester, New Jersey, owns the original copy and generously communicated its contents to the author. See Appendix 1, The Fort, the Graves, the Monuments, for details about the location of graves.
41. Fraser's full quote was "I have lost my best friend, except yourself." This was written in a letter to his father on 14 May at Sackets Harbor and printed in the *American Daily Advertiser* (Philadelphia), 10 May 1813. Fraser is not identified, but details of the letter point strongly at him.

Chapter 13: "This disgraced city": The Occupation of York

1. John Beikie to John Macdonell, 5 May 1813, AO, F 548, John Macdonell Fonds.
2. Strachan to Brown, 26 April/14 June 1813, AO, F 983, Strachan Fonds.
3. Ann Jane (Powell) Seymour's anecdote was recorded in Robertson, *Landmarks of Toronto*, 3: 289. Grant Powell's claim, noting destroyed furniture and stolen kitchen utensils and clothing, in LAC, RG 19 E 5 (a), Board of claims for War of 1812 losses, vol. 3745, file 1 and 3733, file 5, was fully approved.
4. William Powell's letter of 28 April is referred to in Ripley to Powell, 29 April 1813, *DHC*, 5: 173. Claims by Small, Shaw and Allan, respectively, are in LAC, RG 19 E 5 (a), Board of claims for War of 1812 losses: vols. 3733, file 5; 3744, file 2; 3753, file 1; and 3754, file 3. The latter is partially published in Firth, *Town of York*, 302. Reference to the looting of Crookshank's house is in [Powell B], *DHC*, 5: 203.
5. Ely Playter's diary entry for 28 April 1813, AO, F 556. Detlor's nine children and their ages were listed in Ferusha Detlor's application for a pension, LAC, RG 9, IB4, 2: 8-9. George turned nineteen on 24 July 1813.
6. Ely Playter's diary entry for 28 April 1813, AO, F 556.
7. Beaumont, *Formative Years*, 47. Saunders's and Jarvie's wounds are covered in, respectively, LAC, RG 9, I-B-4, 2: 7; and 1: 4. De Koven's wound was described by the Proceedings of a Medical Board, …, Montreal, 23 November 1818, LAC, RG 8, I, 721: 123.
8. Jordan was called to account for himself before the

Special Session of the Peace on 10 June 1813 and subsequently fined £2 which he agreed to pay, Firth, *Town of York*, 312. The bad weather and difficulties experienced in finding homes and medicines, etc., for the wounded was mentioned in Citizens' Account, TRL, Papers Relating to the Capitulation.
9. The quotes are from, respectively, Trowbridge to John Trowbridge, May 1814, "Two Letters" and Moore to his brother, 5 May 1813, Brannan, *Official Letters*, 151.
10. The quote is from Eustis, 11 May 1813, *Proceedings of the Massachusetts Historical Society*, 11 (1869-70): 492-5. One of several officers who wrote that more was captured than could be transported was Chauncey to Jones, 28 April 1813, USNA, RG 45, M 125, 28: 63. The *Hunter* is mentioned in Firth, *Town of York*, 308n. A large portion of the things taken at York was lost when the storehouses at Sackets Harbor were burned, mistakenly by the Americans, during the British attack there on 29 May 1813. This fact and the salvaged material, summarized here, was listed in a letter from Chauncey to the agent James Heard, 15 June 1813, WCL, CLB. Sheaffe noted to Baynes on 14 April 1813 (*ibid.*, 373), "The Militia Clothing is not arrived, but we have supplies of Shoes, Mogosins, Stockings and Flannel made and unmade." The loss of uniforms, arms and personal effects of the regulars was mentioned during the investigation of claims for losses in May 1813, LAC, RG 8, I, 84: 167-76. On 5A May 1813, (LAC, MG 11, CO 42, 354: 132) Sheaffe also informed Prevost that Captain William Jarvie had been sent with three boats to collect the uniforms and arrived at York on 27 April. The Simcoe-era materials were mentioned by Mrs. Penelope Beikie to John Macdonell, no date, AO, F 548, John Macdonell Fonds, and Isaac Wilson to Jonathan Wilson, 5 December 1813, AO, MS 199(5), Isaac Wilson Diaries.
11. At an auction near Fort Niagara on 11 May, Sheaffe's belongings, and presumably those of other officers, Sheaffe's coat, which Beaumont estimated was worth $300, was bought for $50. "His other things sold very high, being good and much wanted by our officers," he added Beaumont, *Formative Years*, 50.
12. Dearborn to Armstrong, 3 May 1813, USNA, RG 107, M 221, 52: 144. The matter of the snuff box was described by John Scott to Thompson, 21 May 1813, New Jersey Historical Society, MG 1044, Captain John Scott Letters. An undated story about the music box from the *Ontario Repository* was repeated in 12 June 1813 issue of *The Olio* of New York City.
13. Most of the squadron was at anchor in the bay by noon on 29 April and St. George's storehouse was being emptied as reported by Archibald McLean, 4 May 1813, LAC, RG 8, I, 678: 190. Locals using their wagons to remove stores at Elmsley House and Boulton's and assist the Americans were mentioned in a report by T.G. Ridout, 5 May 1813, *ibid.*: 188.
14. "The Enemy were joined by a number of vagabonds who gave them every information," reported by Archibald McLean, 4 May 1813, LAC, RG 8, I, 678: 190. Dearborn confirmed the safety of Ridout's papers in a note of 29 April 1813, AO, F43, Thomas Ridout Family Fonds. Not wanting to be held responsible for the loss of the $600 and also wanting reimbursement for her family's losses, E. Derenzy explained the situation in a memorial dated 5 July 1813 (LAC, RG 8, I, 688c: 57) and a letter to MacMahon, 23 July 1813, (*ibid.*: 70). The events are described in Robertson, *Landmarks of Toronto*, 1: 12-13 and in Selby's biography in *DCB*, 5: 749. Sheaffe reported the American threat to Bathurst, 13

May 1813, LAC, MG 11, CO 42, 354: 107. Elliott's parts in the threat was reported by Archibald McLean, 4 May 1813, LAC, RG 8, I, 678: 190, in which it was stated that Duncan Cameron handed over the money. E. Derenzy named the men listed here as did H. Armstrong in the letter and receipt sent by E. Derenzy to Coffin, 25 June 1813, LAC, RG 9, 1B1, 1814, 2: 25. Firth notes that £2144.11.4 was handed over in *Town of York*, 312n, but the receipt from Armstrong, enclosed with E. Derenzy to Coffin, gives the amount in dollars.

15. Sheaffe noted "the Legislative Council Room to be converted into a Barrack, and the Government House do [ditto] for the officers" to Baynes, 25 March 1813, Sheaffe, "Letter Book," 353. The buildings are described in: Heriot, *Travels Through the Canadas*, 139; Robertson, *Landmarks of Toronto*, 1: 351-3; Dale, "The Palaces of Government," 8-13; Martyn, *The Face of Early Toronto*, 25. An estimate to rebuild the wooden interiors was enclosed with a letter from Thomas Scott to McMahon, 1 October 1813, LAC, RG 5, A1, 18: 7594. Reconstruction of the Parliament Buildings is described in Dieterman and Williamson, *Government on Fire*, 20.

16. Gourlay, *Statistical Account of Upper Canada*, 1: 90-1.

17. Chauncey to Jones, 4 June 1813, USNA, RG 45, M 125, 29: 15. Scadding suggested the scalp was actually that of one of the native warriors, who was scalped by the Americans, *Toronto of Old*, 399. The story of the scalp was covered in Stacey, *The Battle of Little York*. Beirne repeated a British allegation that Chauncey had scalped the dead warrior, *The War of 1812*, 160, which Achinleck made in "History of the War," 347. The idea that the scalp was actually the speaker's wig was made in such places as Kingsford, *The History of Canada*, 1895. These were repeated by Tucker, *Poltroons and Patriots*, 1: 253.

18. Dearborn to Armstrong, 3 May 1813, USNA, RG 107, M 221, 52: 144. "... a scalp, which Major Forsyth found suspended over the speaker's chair," Auchinleck, "History of the War, Chapter X," *Anglo-American Magazine*, 347.

19. Re: W. Smith, see Special Session of the Peace, 15 May 1813, AO, RG, 22, 94, 0, 2, York County Court of General Sessions minute books, 1810-1822, 2: 142. Smith's claim for losses during the American visit at the end of July 1813 as noted in, LAC, RG 19 E 5 (a), Board of claims for War of 1812 losses, vol. 3733, file 5, was "Rejected, Major Allan stating that several articles plundered from the Government Stores whilst the Enemy was in York were found on claimants premises." Re: Thrall, see deposition by Cameron, 10 August 1813, LAC, RG 5, A 1, 16: 6554. Re: Lyon, deposition by Cutter, 15 August 1813, *ibid*.: 6538. Ketchum's property was bordered by modern Yonge and Bay streets and Queen and Adelaide (Newgate in 1813) streets as per Wise and Gould, *Toronto Street Names*, 210.

20. Deposition by Knott, 1 August 1813, Firth, *Town of York*, 309.

21. These men and others were listed with the charges against them in an enclosure sent by Ridout and other magistrates to de Rottenburg, 16 August 1813, LAC, RG 5, A 1, 16: 6667. Powell referred to Peters in [Powell B], *DHC*, 5: 203. An advertisement in the 12 September 1812 issue of the *York Gazette* stated that Peters had recently moved to York from Niagara to set up an office on Palace Street (modern Front Street) in the old town and was living with John Mills Jackson at Springfield Park, his farm three miles north on Yonge Street. For Peters's career, see *DCB*, 6: 578. For Bentley's career, see *DCB*, 5: 64.

22. Lyon's possession of the articles and how he got them was recorded in a deposition about Lyon by the constable George Cutter, 15 August 1813, LAC, RG 5, A 1, 16: 6538.

23. Jarvis, "Narrative of Colonel Stephen Jarvis,"254. The Jacksons and Ludden were mentioned in a report by T.G. Ridout, 5 May 1813, LAC, RG 8, I, 678: 188. For Jackson's career, see *DCB*, 7: 438. An Ely Luddon was noted as one of the York constables on 23 April 1811, in "Minutes of the Court of General Quarter Sessions ... 1800-1811," *Twenty-First Report of the Department of Public Records*, 183.

24. Chewett to Coffin, 6 July 1814, LAC, RG 9, 1B1, 1814, 3: unpaginated. American estimates of the numbers who got their paroles: 500 – Dearborn to Armstrong, 3 May 1813, USNA, RG 107, M 221, 52: 144; 1000 – John Scott to Thompson, 17 May 1813, New Jersey Historical Society, MG 1044, Captain John Scott Letters; 1200 – Beaumont, *Formative Years*, 47. 10 miles = 16 km.

25. Citizens' Account, TRL, Papers Relating to the Capitulation. The undated written statement to Dearborn, in Powell's handwriting, is printed in *DHC*, 5: 172 and Dearborn's general order, dated 30 April 1813, is in *ibid*.: 173. Original versions are [Powell to Dearborn], 30 April 1813 and Pinkney to [Powell], 30 April 1813, TRL, York, Upper Canada, Papers Relating to the Capitulation, April 27–May 8 1813. These events were described in [Powell B], *DHC*, 5: 203 and T.G. Ridout, 5 May 1813, LAC, RG 8, I, 678: 188.

26. Dearborn's views and the deployment of the Twenty-first Infantry were expressed by Ripley to Powell, 30 April 1813, *DHC*, 5: 173. William Allan mentioned "the Protection of Private Property was construed not to extend to your Baggage, having been abandoned by you, it is accordingly taken from the place of its deposit," to Sheaffe, 2 May 1813, LAC, MG 11, CO 42, 150: 162. Most of the officers lost their personal belongings as revealed in the inquiry regarding claims for losses held at Kingston in May 1813, LAC, RG 8, I, 84: 118.

27. Penelope Beikie singled out Swan for praise, to John Macdonell, no date, AO, F 548, John Macdonell Fonds. Beikie mentioned the two officers and a list of others in an undated memo, Names of Several Officers ..., LAC, RG 8, I, 1701: 74. Strachan wrote to Pelham after he was wounded at Crysler's Farm in November 1813 to offer his help, and that of his friends, in appreciation for the Pelham's conduct at York, 29 December 1813, AO, F 983, Strachan Fonds. John McGill's letter to Strachan on 13 May 1813, (*ibid.*) also referred to Pelham's efforts on his family's behalf. "All their officers disowned the plunder of private property, which they could not prevent," [Powell B], *DHC*, 5: 203.

28. Ely Playter's diary entry for 29 and 30 April 1813, AO, F 556. The family lost clothing, jewelry as per Playter's, LAC, RG 19 E 5 (a), Board of claims for War of 1812 losses, vol. 3733, file 5, which was approved as "strongly recommended Mr. Playter having been actively employed as a militia officer at the time."

29. Strachan to Brown, 26 April/14 June 1813, AO, F 983, Strachan Fonds. Mrs. Brown's claim appears in LAC, RG 9, 1B1, 1814, 2: Miscellaneous File, unpaginated. Strachan's reference to describing problems besides Mrs. Givins's is in Citizens' Account, TRL, Papers Relating to the Capitulation, but no specific incidents were given. Brown's is used here as an example of what one of the claims might have been. The loss of the flour was noted in Citizens' Account, TRL, Papers Relating to the Capitulation. Givin's claim for losses, noting de-

stroyed furniture, stolen dinnerware and clothing, etc. in LAC, RG 19 E 5 (a), Board of claims for War of 1812 losses, vol. 3733, file 5, was fully approved.

30. Citizens' Account, TRL, Papers Relating to the Capitulation. "From the judicious arrangements made by General Dearborn … the Troops will be ready to reembark tomorrow," Chauncey to Jones, 28 April 1813, USNA, RG 45, M 125, 28: 63.

31. The transfers of the wounded were mentioned in Beaumont, *Formative Years*, 16 and 47. The use of, and sailing orders for, the *Asp* and *Gold Hunter* and shipment of Pike's body were in Chauncey's order to J. Smith, 30 April 1813, WCL, CLB. For Aspinwall's career, see *HRD*, 1: 174; he was not assigned to a particular regiment as Beaumont was. Aspinwall was the only person listed in his residence in "A List of Inhabitants in the Town of York March 1812," Mosser, *York, Upper Canada Minutes of Town Meetings*, 88. His exertions were praised in the Citizens' Account, TRL, Papers Relating to the Capitulation. Hackett's return is noted in Canniff, *The Medical Profession in Upper Canada*, 230. Arrival of the other surgeons is in Strachan to unidentified, undated, and a petition for help with losses by Strachan, May 1816, AO, F 983, Strachan Fonds.

32. American Anonymous F, 14 May 1813, to the editors of the *American Mercury* (Connecticut), published 26 May 1813. Chauncey sent Green to Kingston on his parole on 14 May 1813 and mentioned his wish to have Lieutenant James Dudley who had been captured on the Niagara River on 13 April sent back in exchange, which was done – Chauncey to the commanding officer at Kingston, 14 May 1813, *CLB*. Green joined the PM on 25 March 1813 and was discharged in June as per the Nominal Return of the officers who served in the Provincial Marine …, 22 June 1821, by Lightfoot, LAC, RG 8, I, 741: 5. For Dudley's career, see *SROLO*, 63.

33. Mrs. Beikie to John Macdonell, no date, AO, F 548, John Macdonell Fonds.

34. *Myers*, 65.

35. John Beikie mentioned that the *Gloucester* was going to be a transport, to John Macdonell, 5 May 1813, AO, F 548, John Macdonell Fonds. Chauncey exaggerated the value of the *Gloucester* by reporting it "was undergoing a thorough repair and intended to mount 16 Guns," to Jones, 7 May 1813, USNA, RG 45, M 125, 28: 101. Myers called the *Gloucester*, a "man-o-war brig," *Myers*, 65. Chauncey mentioned Dearborn's deal with Kendrick to Jones, 7 May 1813, *op. cit*. This sum was equal to £300 according to Firth, *Town of York*, 308n.

36. American Anonymous F, 14 May 1813, to the editors of the *American Mercury* (Connecticut), published 26 May 1813. Destruction of the printing press was described in Cameron to Coffin, 16 May 1813, LAC, RG 8, 688c: 33 and de Rottenburg to Bathurst, 25 October 1813, LAC, MG 11, CO 42, 354: 150. Among the sources describing the destruction of public property was Beikie's letter to Miles Macdonell, 19 March 1814, in Firth, *Town of York*, 328.

37. *Myers*, 65. "Embarked on board of the fleet the 1st May in the afternoon after Destroying their Brest Works, taking some of the Guns on Board and Sinking the Remainder in the Lake," John Scott to Thompson, 17 May 1813, New Jersey Historical Society, MG 1044, Captain John Scott Letters.

38. *Myers*, 75. Archeologist Jonathan Moore, *et al.*, notes the replacement of the guns in "Fore-n'-Afters at Fifty Fathoms," 37-8. The number of "28 guns" taken at York was mentioned by Chauncey to Jones, 7 May 1813,

USNA, RG 45, M 125, 28: 101 (although Chauncey admitted no return had been made at that point) and by Trowbridge to John Trowbridge, "Two Letters…." When Chauncey submitted his list for the purpose of prize money, he listed only 16 guns, which was equal to the serviceable iron guns at York, Chauncey to Heard, 15 June 1813, WCL, CLB. The "sixteen cannon of different calibres" are mentioned in several court documents, 7 July, 10 August, 2 November 1813 and 30 May 1814, USNA, RG 21, M 886, roll 4, 1: 266, 405, 448 and 2: 79. Gary Gibson supplied this rarely accessed source, for which the author is grateful. The issue of the guns taken at York and the impact of later campaigning will be discussed in Chapter 15 and in Appendix 3, British Artillery.

39. The embarkation, retrieval of lingerers and position of the squadron were mentioned in a report by T.G. Ridout, 5 May 1813, LAC, RG 8, I, 678: 188. Chauncey described *Asp's* difficulties to Jones, 7 May 1813, USNA, RG 45, M 125, 28: 101.

40. Chauncey to Nichols, 22 April 1813, WCL, CLB. Chauncey to Jones, 7 May 1813, USNA, RG 45, M 125, 28: 101. Dearborn to Armstrong, 3 May 1813, USNA, RG 107, M 221, 52: 144.

41. American Anonymous B, "The First Campaign of An A.D.C.," 1 (1833): 259. Lieutenant Colonel George McFeely reported the shock of the explosion at Fort Niagara in his diary on 27 April and the next day wrote: "In the afternoon a sail was seen standing in … [and] She proved to be the *Growler* commanded by Lieutenant Meigs with dispatches for General Lewis and news of the capture of York." McFeely, "Chronicle of Valor," 257-8. Mix had command of the *Growler*, see Appendix 7, U.S. Navy. Peter Porter wrote "I have just returned from Fort Niagara, where I saw a Captain of the United States' navy" at the start of his letter from Manchester (Niagara Falls, NY) to J. Spencer, 28 April 1813 which was published in the 5 May issue of the *Geneva Gazette* and then picked up by numerous newspapers.

42. Chauncey to Jones, 7 May 1813, USNA, RG 45, M 125, 28: 101. Dearborn to Armstrong, 3 May 1813, USNA, RG 107, M 221, 52: 144.

43. John Scott to Thompson, 17 May 1813, New Jersey Historical Society, MG 1044, Captain John Scott Letters. Beaumont echoed Scott's uncertainty and described conditions on board the *Julia* in *Formative Years*, 48.

44. Chauncey to Woolsey, 4 May 1813, WCL, CLB. For a discussion of Department of the Navy use of the term 'commodore,' see Malcomson, "'Stars and Garters of an Admiral', American Commodores in the War of 1812."

45. Chauncey to Woolsey, 5 May 1813, WCL, CLB.

46. Chauncey to Jones, 7 May 1813, USNA, RG 45, M 125, 28: 101. Chauncey to Smith and Nichols, 4 May 1813, WCL, CLB. Beaumont, *Formative Years*, 48. For local comments about the weather, see: "9 May: This last week has been a most extraordinary week of wet weather as has been seen for many years," Diary of Thomas McCrae, who lived near Chatham, *DHC*, 5: 220; "The season is uncommonly wet. Old inhabitants say they have not seen so rainy a summer for twenty-five years," extract of letter (probably by Baptist Irvine) published in the 22 June 1813 issue of the *Baltimore Whig*, which appeared in the 9 July 1813 issue of the *New-York Evening Post*; "The last summer was reckoned to be the wettest ever known since this country was settled, May and June were wet, afterwards the weather was fine," Isaac Wilson to Jonathan Wilson, 5 December 1813, AO, MS 199(5), Isaac Wilson Diaries.

47. Ely Playter's diary entry for 2 May 1813, AO, F 556. Strachan and others reburied some of the dead on 11 May as per Anne Powell to W. Powell, 12 May 1813, TRL, L 16, Powell Letters, Mrs. Powell's letters, A 93: 315.

48. Mrs. Beikie to John Macdonell, no date, AO, F 548, John Macdonell Fonds.

49. Isaac Wilson to Jonathan Wilson, 5 December 1813, AO, MS 199(5), Isaac Wilson Diaries.

50. Citizens' Account, TRL, Papers Relating to the Capitulation. William Allan wrote to Sheaffe on 2 May 1813 (LAC, MG 11, CO 42, 150: 162), "the inhabitants were exposed to every sort of Insult and Depredation. But ... it is presumed that these depredations happened more from insubordination of the men than the wish of the officers."

51. Citizens' Account, TRL, Papers Relating to the Capitulation.

52. Strachan to Richardson, 10 May 1813, AO, F 983, Strachan Fonds. The declaration about civil control, an untitled statement issued on 3 May 1813, unsigned except for "high sheriff" (John Beikie), TRL, York, U.C., Papers Relating to the Capitulation. The investigation into men who had cheated on parole and the looters will be dealt with in Chapter 6teen. For sample evidence of this see, A Return of Paroled Men surrendered ... at York, [undated, probably spring 1814], LAC, RG 9, IB7, 16: 32. See also the case involving Hastings's theft of a musket on 12 June, York County Court of General Sessions of the Peace, AO, RG 22, 94,0,2, Minute Book, 2: 143-5.

53. [Powell B], *DHC*, 5: 203.

54. [Powell B], *DHC*, 5: 203. The other account was [Powell A], *DHC*, 5: 175.

55. All quotes in this section are taken from Citizens' Account, TRL, Papers Relating to the Capitulation. This latter document appears to be the original copy with few cross outs and insertions. Allan complained to Sheaffe about the lack of medical supplies, 2 May 1813, LAC, MG 11, CO 42, 150: 162.

56. Strachan sent the narrative and communicated the committee's wishes to Richardson, 10 May 1813, AO, F 983 Strachan Fonds. In mentioning the citizens' account, Anne Powell wrote that "our Neighbour has I hear give great offence by declining to add his signature to the list," to her husband, 12 May 1813, TRL, L 16, Powell Papers, Mrs. Powell's letters, A 93: 315. The erasure is apparent on the copy examined by the author but not clear enough to identify; Stacey wrote that it belonged to Ridout, *The Battle of Little York*, 21.

Chapter 14: "Great men in little things and little men in great things": Campaign Consequences

1. John Scott to Thompson, 17 May 1813, NJHS, MG 1044, Scott Letters.

2. Clausewitz, *On War*, 273. Sheaffe mentioned his order to the light company and meeting it to Prevost, 5A May 1813, LAC, MG 11, CO 42, 354: 132. A second shorter letter to Prevost on this date is 5B May 1813, *ibid.*: 119. An excerpt of 5A May appears in *ibid.*: 126.

3. Finan, *Journal of a Voyage*, 295-6. This description of the march is based upon *ibid.*, 95-100. Sergeant James Commins, 8th Foot, also mentioned encountering "many of the inhabitants who were disaffected," Commins, "The War on the Canadian Frontier, 1812-14," 201. 3 miles = 4.8 km.

4. Sheaffe noted that the column arrived at Kingston in stages to Prevost, 8 May 1813, LAC, RG 8, I, 678: 221. Wilmot's party is detailed in the Muster Roll and Payl-

ist of a Detachment ... from the 27th April to the 13th May 1813, LAC, RG 9, I-B-7, 16: 98. The order for them to return, Sheaffe to Wilmot, 7 May 1813, LAC, RG 9, 1B1, vol. 2, unpaginated.

5. The letter written on 12 May 1813 appeared in the 25 May 1813 issue of the *Quebec Mercury*. The full muster and pay lists of the six regiments involved at York were checked for "Derby" or similar names (sources for these are in Appendix 4, British Order of Battle,) with the closest candidate for the deed being Sergeant Daniel Darby of the 49th Foot, who was, however, declared an invalid in March 1813 and sent home, Pay List of the Forty-Ninth Regiment of Foot from 25th of March to 24th of June 1813, both dates inclusive, NAUK, WO 12, 6044.

6. See Muster Roll and Pay Lists of Captain John Button's Company of Cavalry of the 1st Regiment of York Militia, 25 March to 24 June 1813, LAC, RG9, IB7, 20: 324. The Lynde home was originally located on the south half of lot 31, concession 2, Whitby Township, 960 Dundas Street West. The home was preserved and moved to Cullen Gardens and Miniature Village on Taunton Road in Whitby, which closed in 2006. See <www.hpd.mcl.gov.on.ca>. Lynde filed a claim for damages, 5 May 1813, LAC, RG 5, A1, 17: 7299. Powell responded to an inquiry about it, pleading ignorance of the incident, to Loring, 28 May 1813, LAC, RG 8, I, 688c: 37. Sergeant James Commins, 8th Foot, mentioned encountering "many of the inhabitants who were disaffected," Commins, "The War on the Canadian Frontier, 1812-14," 201 as did Finan, *Journal of a Voyage*, 295-6.

7. Sheaffe to Prevost, 30 April 1813, LAC, RG 8, I, 678: 198.

8. Sheaffe's arrival was mentioned in the 4 May 1813 issue of the *Kingston Gazette* where the launch of the *Royal George* on Wednesday, 28 April was also noted.

9. Sheaffe to Prevost, 5A May 1813, LAC, MG 11, CO 42, 354: 132.

10. Sheaffe to Prevost, 5B May 1813, LAC, MG 11, CO 42, 354: 119.

11. "Casualty reports on either side are never accurate, seldom truthful, and in most cases deliberately falsified," Clausewitz, *On War*, 277. Plucknett referred to losing men in Plucknett to Richmond, 14 October 1818, LAC, RG 8, I, 189: 42.

12. See Appendix 8, Casualties and POWs, for data and sources regarding casualties and related data in Appendix 9, Capitulation. The 36% casualty rate suffered by British regulars alone at York is higher than normal when compared to rates suffered at the following well-known bloody affairs: 25% at Sackets Harbor, 29 May 1813, Malcomson, *Lords of the Lake*, 139; 17% at Crysler's Farm, 11 November 1813, Graves, *Field of Glory*, 269; 25% at Chippawa, 5 July 1814, Graves, *Red Coats and Grey Jackets*, 133, 167; 25% at Lundy's Lane, 25 July 1814, Graves, *Where Right and Glory Lead*, 195. Some of these figures include the militia involved, but even with their numbers and casualties taken out, there is little alteration to the basic rates. Furthermore, the 71 regulars killed at York compares well with the 45 KIA at Sackets Harbor, the 22 at Crysler's Farm, 148 at Chippawa, and 84 at Lundy's Lane, and attests to the murderous fire of Forsyth's Riflemen, as well. According to Sheaffe, he had 600 men in total (Sheaffe to Prevost, 5A May 1813, LAC, MG 11, CO 42, 354: 119), of whom 300 were militia and dockyard workers (Sheaffe to Prevost, 5A May 1813, *ibid.*: 132) which leaves 300 regulars and if this incorrect number is used, the regular losses exceeded 50%.

As argued elsewhere here, Sheaffe did not represent his strength accurately.

13. The Terms of Capitulation and list of POWs submitted by Sheaffe with his 5 May 1813 report is from LAC, MG 11, CO 42, 354: 121. William Allan mentioned "We have nearly forty wounded Men to take care of, some very badly," to Sheaffe, 2 May 1813, LAC, MG 11, CO 42, 150: 162. Regular POWs are found in Return of the Prisoners belonging to His Majesty's regular Forces on Parole to the United States Army at York, 1 May 1813, LAC, RG 5, A1, 17: 7292 and Return of sick in the hospital at York, 4 June 1813, *ibid.*: 7347. The latter list was made before the casualties from the battles at Fort George, 27 May and Stoney Creek, 6 June were transported to York. See Appendix 8, Casualties and POWs, and Appendix 9, Terms of Capitulation for the note at the end of this version of the Terms of Capitulation … 28 April 1813, LAC, RG 8, I, 695: 57, which mentions confusion and the use of the musters.

14. Sheaffe to Prevost, 8 May 1813, LAC, RG 8, I, 678: 221.

15. Powell and Scott's trip to Kingston is mentioned in McGill to Strachan, 13 May 1813, AO, Strachan Papers, F983. Re: lost provincial money, Sheaffe to Bathurst, 13 May 1813, LAC, MG 11, CO 42, 354: 107. Re: Elmsley House, Sheaffe to Bathurst, 15 May 1813, *ibid.*: 109. Re: increased provincial expenses, Sheaffe to Bathurst, 16 May 1813, *ibid.*: 111.

16. Talbot to Vincent, 18 May 1813, Coyne, *The Talbot Papers*, 189. The next two comments are from, respectively, Nichol to Talbot, 29 April 1813, *ibid.*: 189 and Burwell to Talbot, 21 May 1813, *ibid.*: 191.

17. Talbot to Vincent, 18 May 1813, *DHC*, 5: 234. The Sheaffe rumour was in the 18 May 1813 issue of the *Buffalo Gazette*, *ibid.*: 233.

18. District General Order by Leonard, 13 May 1813, *DHC*, 5: 227.

19. Yeo announced his arrival and the news of York to Croker, 5 May 1813, LAC, MG 12, ADM 1, 2736: 66.

20. Prevost wrote to Procter (LAC, RG 8, I, 678: 261) and Vincent from Montreal, (*ibid.*: 301) on 7 May via messengers sent forward by Sheaffe.

21. Prevost to Bathurst, 18A May 1813, LAC, MG 11, CO 42, 150: 156.

22. Prevost to Bathurst, 18B May 1813, LAC, MG 11, CO 42, 150: 169. Prevost to Bathurst, 18C May 1813, *ibid.*: 167. . Chauncey sent Green and two seamen to Kingston on parole on 14 May 1813 and mentioned his wish to have Lieutenant James Dudley who had been captured on the Niagara River on 13 April sent back in exchange, which was done – Chauncey to the commanding officer at Kingston, 14 May 1813, WCL, CLB. Dudley was exchanged as per *SROLO*, 63.

23. Chauncey to Jones, 11 May 1813, USNA, RG 45, M 125, 28: 136.

24. John Scott to Thompson, 17 May 1813, NJHS, MG 1044, Scott Letters. "[We] disembarked and lay all night on the beach in a cold rain storm without tents, blankets or fire," Dwight, "'Plow-Joggers for Generals,'" 19.

25. McFeely, "Chronicle of Valor," 259. The leaky roof of the mess house and deplorable conditions within were mentioned by American Anonymous B, "The First Campaign of An A.D.C.," 1 (1833): 261. Beaumont noted that tents were received at Four Mile Creek on 9 May 1813, Beaumont, *Formative Years*, 48. Dwight, noted the march to Fort Niagara and the camp at Two Mile Creek, Dwight, "'Plow-Joggers for Generals,'" 19.

26. Dearborn to Armstrong, 7 July 1813, USNA, RG 107, M 221, roll 52: 154. Armstrong's complaint was sent to

Dearborn, 21 June 1813, *ibid.*, M 6, 6: 470.

27. John Scott to Thompson, 17 May 1813, NJHS, MG 1044, Scott Letters. Among the places where the story about the musical snuff box was repeated were: Auchinleck, "History of the War, Chapter X," *Anglo-American Magazine*, 347; Tucker, *Poltroons and Patriots*, 1: 250;

28. Walworth to his father-in-law, Colonel Jonas Simonds, Sixth Infantry, 6 and 19 April 1813, LAC, MG 24, F 16, Jonas Simonds Papers, 1813, 1814.

29. This letter, "an extract to the Editor" of the *Whig*, was published in 29 May 1813 issue of *The Stateman* (New York City). "The object of General Dearborn was to conceal the name of the officer upon whom the command and responsibility devolved," Pearce alleged in regard to Dearborn's official report, "A Poor But Honest Sodger," 139. "Had [Pike] lived … we should have secured Sheaffe and every one who was under arms with him," Eustis to W. Eustis, 11 May 1813, *Proceedings of the Massachusetts Historical Society*, 11 (1869-70): 492-5. "[Pearce's] delay … enabled [Sheaffe] to make a precipitate retreat," Anonymous, "Biographical Memoir of Major-General Ripley," 115.

30. Moore to his brother, 5 May 1813, Brannan, *Official Letters*, 151. Moore's amputation is mentioned as happening on 3 May in McFeely, "Chronicle of Valor," 259.

31. Trowbridge to John Trowbridge, "Two Letters…."

32. Conner to Armstrong, 4 May 1813, USNA, RG 107, M 221, 51: 153.

33. American Anonymous B, "The First Campaign of An A.D.C.," 1 (1833): 264.

34. Dearborn to Armstrong, 28 April 1813, USNA, RG 107, M 221, 52: 125. Dearborn to Armstrong, 8:00 P.M., 27 April 1813, *ibid.* Dearborn also wrote to Governor Tompkins, 28 April 1813, which was published in such newspapers as the 8 May issue of *The Statesman*.

35. Dearborn to Armstrong, 3 May 1813, USNA, RG 107, M 221, 52: 144.

36. Conner to Armstrong, 4 May 1813, USNA, RG 107, M 221, 51: 153.

37. Chauncey to Jones, 28 April 1813, USNA, RG 45, M 125, 28: 63. He sent a brief notice of the victory to Jones, 27 April 1813, *ibid.*: 56. 200 yd. = 183 m.

38. Chauncey to Jones, 5 May 1813, USNA, RG 45, M 125, 28: 89.

39. Hunter's report was enclosed with Dearborn to Armstrong, 3 May 1813, USNA, RG 107, M 221, 52: 144. Pearce claimed that Hunter made his report to him first and also noted his wound in "A Poor But Honest Sodger," 138. Ripley's wound was mentioned in Anonymous, "Biographical Memoir of Major-General Ripley," 115. Among the numerous lists published in newspapers was a partial casualty list that included names of individuals in the units enclosed with a letter by an anonymous officer on 24 July 1813 at Fort George published in the 13 August 1813 issue of the *New-York Evening Post*. Other similar lists sent by unnamed individuals were published in such newspapers as *The Weekly Register* (12 June 1813), the *New England Palladium* (25 May 1813) and *The Centinel of Freedom* (1 June 1813). See Appendix 8, Casualties and POWs.

40. Pearce, "A Poor But Honest Sodger," 135.

41. Chauncey to Jones, 28 April 1813, USNA, RG 45, M 125, 28: 63. Chauncey reported the sick list size and dead sailing masters to Jones, 16 May 1813, *ibid.*: 144. Casualties in the squadron were reported by an anonymous officer (probably Lieutenant Donald Fraser), 14 May 1813 at Sackets Harbor, published in the 1 June 1813 issue of *The Centinel of Freedom*; similar reports appeared in

the 12 June 1813 issue of *The Weekly Register* (possibly by Baptist Irvine) and the 26 May 1813 issue of the *American Daily Advertiser*. See also Appendix 8, Casualties and POWs.

42. "I did not find the preparation at this place as complete as could have been expected," Dearborn to Armstrong, 3 May 1813, USNA, RG 107, M 221, 52: 144. Chauncey was more truthful when he explained to Jones on 11 May 1813 (USNA, RG 45, M 125, 28: 136), "Under these circumstances [the widespread sickness and high casualties] I thought with General Dearborn, that it would be unwise to make any attempt upon Fort George until we could receive reinforcements."

43. Chauncey sailed with the *Madison, Fair American, Hamilton, Julia, Growler, Asp, Raven* and *Duke of Gloucester* (and presumably the *Gold Hunter*) leaving the *Lady of the Lake, Governor Tompkins* and *Conquest* at Niagara, while he sent the *Oneida, Ontario, Scourge* and *Pert* to Oswego to pick up stores, Chauncey to Jones, 11 May 1813, USNA, RG 45, M 125, 28: 136. He mentioned the naval reinforcement to Jones on 16 May 1813, *ibid.*: 143. Most of the material taken at York were burned during the Battle of Sackets Harbor, 29 May 1813, and even when some of the material was salvaged the list did not identify quantities of most of the items, and Chauncey admitted, "I cannot get an inventory of the articles at this time" (and apparently never did), to James Heard, 15 June 1813, WCL, CLB.

44. *Myers,* 65.

45. Chauncey to Mrs. Pike, 15A May 1813, WCL, CLB. Extracts from letters written by two officers at Sackets Harbor (Lieutenant Colonel George Mitchell and an anonymous officer) on 14 and 13 May 1813, respectively, (published in the 28 May 1813 issue of the *National Intelligencer*) show the burial date as 13 May. Details about the iron casket, the window and alcohol are found in Hollon, *The Lost Pathfinder,* 214.

46. Chauncey to Mrs. Pike, 15B May 1813, WCL, CLB.

47. Regrets of Pike's death and homages to his memory appeared in such newspaper issues as: 10 May 1813, *The Statesman;* 12 May 1813, *Baltimore Patriot;* 28 May 1813, *Salem Gazette.* Mention of the Baltimore theatre is in the 5 June 1813 issue of *The Weekly Register.* Chauncey announced the launch of the new ship and its name hours after its launch on 12 June 1813 to Jones, USNA, RG 45, M 125, 29: 57. Madison's order was in Jones to Chauncey, 31 May 1813, USNA, RG 45, T 829, roll 453: 26.

48. "On the evening of 30th *Ultimo* [the previous month, May] I received an express from Lieutenant Chauncey, stating that the enemy was off Sackett's Harbor with his whole fleet. I immediately proceeded to leave Niagara with the squadron," Chauncey to Jones, 2 June 1813, USNA, RG 45, M 125, 29: 8. For a description of the attack and outcome of the action at Fort George, see Malcomson, *Lords of the Lake,* 124-9 and Cruikshank, *The Battle of Fort George.*

49. Citizens' Account, TRL, Papers Relating to the Capitulation. Prevost mentioned Green's information to Bathurst, 18 May 1813, LAC, MG 11, CO 42, 150: 156.

50. Commins, "The War on the Canadian Frontier, 1812-14," 201. McPherson was severely wounded in the battle. For a description of the attack and outcome of the action at Sackets Harbor, see Malcomson, *Lords of the Lake,* 129-40 and Wilder, *The Battle of Sackett's Harbour, 1813.* Among those who had long called for the attack on Sackets were: Strachan to McGill, November 1812, Spragge, *Strachan: 1812-1834,* 25; Donald McLean

to Stewart, 11 January 1813, AO, MU 2036, F 895, Miscellaneous Military Records; Johnson to Claus, 16 March 1813, *DHC,* 6: 116. Prevost rejected the idea to Gray, 19 December 1812, LAC, RG 8, I, 728: 125.

51. Prevost to Bathurst, 1 June 1813, LAC, MG 11, CO 42, 150: 175. Chauncey reported about the battle and shipyard loss to Jones, 2 June 1813, USNA, RG 45, M 125, 29: 8 and of his hesitation to leave Sackets on 11 June 1813, *ibid.*: 47. For a description of this phase of the struggle for control of Lake Ontario (including the controversy surrounding Wolcott Chauncey), see Malcomson, *Lords of the Lake,* 141-59.

52. Askin to Cameron, 3 June 1813, *DHC,* 5: 296.

53. McGillivray to McTavish, 7 June 1813, *DHC,* 6: 17. This letter was apparently forwarded to Lord Bathurst in August 1813.

54. Burwell to Talbot, 21 May 1813, *DHC,* 5: 239.

55. The article with a byline of Montreal, May 8th, 1813, appeared in the 11 May 1813 issue of *The Quebec Mercury.*

56. McGillivray to McTavish, 7 June 1813, *DHC,* 6: 17.

57. Anne Powell to W. D. Powell, 20 May 1813, TRL, L 16, Powell Papers. Mrs. Powell's other letters of this period mention Sheaffe's unpopularity, but she continued to be loyal to him as a valued family friend.

58. Anne Powell mentioned this to William Powell, 16 May 1813, TRL, L 16, Powell Papers, Mrs. Powell's letters, A 93: 316.

59. Sheaffe to "Dear General" [presumably Shaw], 9 June 1813, LAC, RG 9, IB1, 2: unpaginated.

60. Sheaffe to Mountain, undated [context suggests the fourth week of May 1813]. Edited by T. R. Millman. "Roger Hale Sheaffe and the Defence of York, April 27, 1813." *Canadian Church Historical Review Journal,* 5 (1963): 6-8.

61. Prevost to Bathurst, 26 May 1813, LAC, RG 8, I, 150: 171.

62. Prevost to Sheaffe, 22 July 1813, LAC, RG 8, I, 1221: 106.

63. Prevost to Bathurst, 24 June 1813, LAC MG 11, CO 42, 151: 37.

64. Prevost to York, 23 July 1813, LAC, RG 8, I, 1220: 408.

65. General order by Baynes, 6 June 1813, LAC, RG 8, I, 1170: 229. For de Rottenburg's career, see *HMG,* 320 and *DCB,* 6: 660. For Glasgow's career, see *HMG,* 163 and *DCB,* 5: 346.

66. Proclamation, 4 June 1813, LAC, RG 8, I, 688c: 42. District General Order by Sheaffe, 9 June 1813, *DHC,* 6: 61.

67. Executive Council to Sheaffe , 16 June 1813, LAC, MG 11 CO 42, 354: 137.

68. Sheaffe to Executive Council, 16 June 1813, LAC, MG 11 CO 42, 354: 138.

69. General order by Baynes, 6 June 1813, LAC, RG 8, I, 1170: 266.

Chapter 15: "A true account of our proceedings": Legacies of the Battle of York

1. Commins, James. "The War on the Canadian Frontier, 1812-14," 211.

2. News about the battle was published widely in American newspapers, a sample of which is provided here. The expedition's departure was reported in such 1813 issues and newspapers as 30 April, *National Intelligencer* and 3 May 1813, *Democratic Republican.* The capture of the warships and attack on Niagara appeared on 7 May in the *Baltimore Patriot.* Other quotes in this paragraph come from these sources, in order of their use: 10 May and 15 May, *The Statesman;* 10 May, the *American*

Daily Advertizer, 14 May, *The Statesman* and 13 May, *Boston Gazette;* 5 May, *Geneva Gazette* and 19 May, *Baltimore Patriot.* Lists of American casualties were in 10 May, the *American Daily Advertizer,* 1 June, *The Centinnel of Freedom,* 13 August, *New-York Evening Post.* Dearborn and Chauncey's reports were in 15 May 1813, *The Weekly Register* and 21 May 1813, *The Statesman.*

3. The toasts were mentioned in the 3 June 1813 issue of the *National Advocate.* The New York State elections were covered in these issues of the *New-York Evening Post,* a newspaper of Federalist persuasions: 24, 26, 27, 28 April, 1, 3, 5, 7, 12 May. As mentioned in the notes of Chapter 5, Stagg, *Mr. Madison's War,* 285, wrote, "In choosing to take the offensive in this manner rather than waiting for better weather and more extensive preparations, Armstrong was probably governed by two motives: a desire to vindicate American honor speedily and the need to influence the outcome of the spring elections in New York," without evidence of supportive references. He states on 335 that the victory at York on 27 April 1813, "undeniably assisted the Republican party in re-electing Governor Daniel Tompkins." No evidence was found in this project to show that rumours of the victory at York were widely circulated before the elections. 35 miles = 56 km.

4. The evening's entertainment was announced in the 2 June 1813 issue of *The Tickler.*

5. More's performance was described in the 2 June 1813 issue of *The Tickler.*

6. 13 May 1813, *New-York Evening Post.*

7. 25 May 1813, *Northern Whig.*

8. Armstrong to Dearborn, 29 March 1813, USNA, RG 107, M 6, roll 6: 338. For a discussion of American strategy development for this campaign see Chapter 5.

9. Chauncey to Jones, 18 March 1813, USNA, RG 45, M 125, 27: 58.

10. Armstrong to Dearborn, 15 May 1813, *Notices of the War of 1812,* 1: 226

11. Armstrong made this point in the 1840 *Notices of the War,* 1: 156.

12. Armstrong wrote this to Dearborn after reading his report on Stoney Creek, 19 June 1813, *APS: MA,* 1: 449.

13. A letter written on 8 June 1813 at Fort George (possibly by Baptist Irvine) and later published in the *Baltimore Whig* described the false alarm provoked by the known presence of Yeo's fleet and the approach under darkness of boats along the shore, which turned out to be American, but which drew fire nonetheless, *DHC,* 6: 30. For a description of the attack and outcome of the action at Fort George, see Malcomson, *Lords of the Lake,* 124-9 and Cruikshank, *The Battle of Fort George.* For a description, see Malcomson, *The Battle of Stoney Creek and the Blockade of Fort George, 1813.*

14. "The victory there [at York] achieved ... decides the command of the Lakes," Conner to Armstrong, 4 May 1813, USNA, RG 107, M 221, 51: 153. "Our gallant tars have either destroyed or obtained possession of a sufficient number of the enemy's ships to enable us very soon to chase the residue from the lake," editorial comments added to a letter from Porter to Spencer, 28 April 1813, at Niagara, and widely published, including the 5 May 1813 issue of the *Geneva Gazette.* The *Duke of Gloucester* was valued at $2,500 in several court documents and the sixteen guns were eventually valued at $28,804.46, 7 July, 8 October, 2 November 1813, 29 April and 30 May 1814, USNA, RG 21, M 886, roll 4, 1: 266, 405, 448 and 2: 10, 79. Apart from captured guns (discussed

below) only 3 bales of clothing (valued at $1,228.95) and 2 kegs of cartridges ($2,244.92) were included in these depositions. Gary Gibson supplied this rarely accessed source, for which the author is grateful.

15. Chauncey to Jones, 7 May 1813, USNA, RG 45, M 125, 28: 101.

16. Prevost to Bathurst, 20 July 1813, LAC, MG 11, CO 42, 151: 78.

17. Freer to Gray, 29 January 1813, LAC, RG 8, I, 1220: 133. Requisitions for the guns for the two Lake Ontario ships and the one at Amherstburg were enclosed with Gray to Freer, 14 January 1813, *ibid.,* 729: 11. Delivery of the ten 24-pdr. carronades is mentioned in Harvey to Procter, 17 September 1813, *ibid.,* 680: 75. When Chauncey submitted his list for the purpose of prize money, he listed only 16 guns (without details), which was equal to the serviceable iron guns at York, Chauncey to Heard, 15 June 1813, WCL, CLB. The "sixteen cannon of different calibres" were mentioned in several court documents and eventually valued at $28,804.46, 7 July, 10 August, 2 November 1813, 29 April and 30 May 1814, USNA, RG 21, M 886, roll 4, 1: 266, 405, 448 and 2: 10, 79. Gary Gibson supplied this rarely accessed source, for which the author is grateful. There were already 8 18-pdr. carronades, 7 12-pdr. and 9 6-pdr. long guns in Chauncey's squadron in the spring and no additions were made through the summer, Malcomson, *Lords of the Lake,* 333-4. The law then governing prize amounts allowed the commanding officer of a squadron 3/20s (7.5%) of the total prize value ($2,160.33 for the guns), 23 April 1800, "An act for the better government of the Navy of the United States," 6th Congress, Session, 1, Chapter 33, *Public Statutes at Large of the United States of America,* 2: 45. See Appendix 3, British Artillery.

18. James, *A Full and Correct Account of the Military Occurrences of the Late War between Great Britain and The United States of America,* 1: 142.

19. Roosevelt, *The Naval War of 1812,* 219. Hannay, *The History of the War of 1812,* 138.

20. Drake, "Artillery and Its Influence on Naval Tactics," 20. Similar claims are made in such works as: Mahan, *Sea Power in its Relations to the War of 1812,* 2: 40; Cruikshank, "The Contest for the Command of Lake Erie in 1812 and 1813, " 360; Stacey, C. P. "Another Look at the Battle of Lake Erie," 46; Stacey, *The Battle of Little York,* 21; Hitsman, *The Incredible War of 1812,* 171. For more detail on the Battle of Put-in-Bay, see Malcomson and Malcomson, *HMS Detroit: The Battle for Lake Erie,* 1990 and Skaggs and Altoff, *A Signal Victory.* Hickey discusses the York-Put-in-Bay link in *Don't Give Up the Ship,* 63-4. The Fort York Account Book (City of Toronto Culture, Museum and Heritage Services) for this period shows that on 9 March 1813 Angus McLauchlin was paid £46 for transporting stores to Amherstburg and that Midshipman H. Gateshill was paid wages for fifteen seamen sent to Amherstburg in February (possibly with another shipment of goods), that another group went there around 17 April and Lieutenant F. Purvis was paid at York during the winter and had left for Amherstburg before 27 April 1813.

21. Babcock, *The War of 1812 on the Niagara Frontier,* 82.

22. In September 1814 the Senate committee on foreign relations ordered an inquiry into "the authorized mode of warfare adopted by the enemy" and whether this was justified by similar American activities. The conclusion was that the British conduct had been unjustified. Notice of this, a long letter of explanation by Secretary of State James Monroe (23 February 1815) and other

letters, including one from Dearborn to Varnum, 17 October 1814, were published in the 18 March 1815 issue of *The Weekly Register*. A second longer letter by Dearborn to the committee, 11 November 1814, was attached to Quaife, *The Yankees Capture York*, 35-7. For details about Ross and Cockburn at Washington, see: Lord, *The Dawn's Early Light*, 145-87; Pack, *The Man Who Burned the White House*, 187-92; Pitch, *The Burning of Washington*, 99-129.

23. Burwell to Talbot, 21 May 1813, Coyne, *The Talbot Papers*, 161.

24. 15 May 1813, *The Weekly Register*.

25. Cochrane to Cockburn, 28 April 1814, Crawford, *NWDH*, 3: 51. Cochrane to Commanding Officers, 18 July 1814, *ibid.*: 140. The burnings at Havre de Grace, Niagara, Lewiston and Manchester, Black Rock and Buffalo and Port Dover are described in Malcomson, *HDW* 241, 374, 288, 38 and 431. The York-Washington connection is discussed in Hickey, *Don't Give Up the Ship*, 78-81.

26. 22 May 1813, *The Weekly Register*. Quaife, *The Yankees Capture York*. "No buildings, either public or private were destroyed either by my order or otherwise by the army or navy to my knowledge, excepting two military block houses and two or three sheds attached to the Navy Yard," Dearborn to the Senate committee, 11 November 1814, *ibid.*, 35. Stacey reviewed the correspondence and showed that Dearborn had admitted his embarrassment to York's headmen about the plundering and the burning of the Parliament Buildings (*The Battle of Little York*, 18) but there is no indication that he ordered or approved of such conduct. The general received support for his position from Surgeon James Mann who read about the issue and wrote to him, 6 July 1815, to state that he had not witnessed any burnings by the U.S. Army, Lilly Library, War of 1812 Manuscripts.

27. 19 June 1813, *The Weekly Register*.

28. Strachan wrote a long letter to Thomas Jefferson, 30 January 1815, after reading about American declarations of British barbarism. The letter unwittingly countered the points made by Secretary of State James Monroe to Bibb of the Senate committee investigating British conduct, 23 February 1815, published in the 18 March 1815 issue of *The Weekly Register*. Strachan's letter was published in: an 1815 issue of *The Antijacobin Review*, under Strachan's name and the title "On the Conduct of the Americans"; *The Report of the Loyal and Patriotic Society of Upper Canada ...*, 1817; and in Kingsford, *The History of Canada*, 8: 585. The author is grateful to Chris Raible, who brought this material to his notice and explained that the editors of the ongoing project publishing Jefferson's papers have no knowledge of Strachan's letter, suggesting that it was never sent. The story of the scalp and the burning was covered in Stacey, *The Battle of Little York*.

29. 29 May 1813, *American Daily Advertiser*.

30. 28 May 1813, *Salem Gazette*.

31. The Royal Standard, the mace and a carved lion were trophies of war that Chauncey sent to Jones and which he acknowledged on 14 June 1813 (USNA, RG 45, M 149, 10: 466), adding that they "will decorate the National Archives." The three items ended up in the museum of the U.S. Naval Institute in Annapolis, Maryland. The mace was returned to Toronto in a special ceremony held on 4 July 1934, as detailed in the next day's issue of *The Globe and Mail*. The trophies are described in detail in Robertson, *Landmarks of Toronto*, 5: 165-9. Dear-

born mentioned that he had the scalp in his letter to the Senate committee, 11 November 1814, Quaife, *The Yankees Capture York*, 35-7. Prompt return of the scalp to Dearborn is noted in Armstrong, *Notices of the War of 1812*, 1: 132.

32. Conner to Armstrong, 12 June 1813, *ASP: MA*, 1: 448.

33. Lewis to Armstrong, 14 June 1813, *APS: MA*, 1: 446. Other letters mentioning the illness and command changes include: Dearborn to Armstrong, 6, 8 and 20 June 1813, *ibid.*: 445 and 449 and Scott to Armstrong, 10 June 1813, *ibid.*: 447.

34. Gardner to Scott, 30 July 1813, New York State Library, 12914, Charles Kitchel Gardner Papers.

35. Scott to Gardner, 16 July 1813, New York State Library, 12914, Charles Kitchel Gardner Papers. Newspapers article that were very likely written by Irvine, and which were critical of Dearborn and others, include a letter dated 7 May 1813, at York Harbor, taken from the *Baltimore Whig* and published in the 29 May 1813 issue of *The Statesman* and a letter written on 8 June 1813 at Fort George, published in the *Baltimore Whig*, and included in *DHC*, 6: 30.

36. Armstrong to Dearborn, 6 July 1813, *APS: MA*, 1: 449. Armstrong later offered his criticisms of Dearborn in his *Notices of the War of 1812*, 1: 151-62 and explained how the impetus for his removal came from Congress, *ibid.*: 151n. Another criticism of Dearborn appeared in Monroe's letter to Jefferson, 7 June 1813 (Hamilton, *The Writings of James Monroe*, 5: 259): "he was advanc'd in years, infirm, and had given no proof of activity or military talent during the year."

37. The letter, dated 15 July 1813 at Fort George, Dearborn's reply and a description of the scene is from *DHC*, 6: 236-9.

38. Dearborn's reply, *DHC*, 6: 238.

39. American Anonymous B, "The First Campaign of An A.D.C.," 2 (May, 1834): 182.

40. American Anonymous B, "The First Campaign of An A.D.C.," 2 (May, 1834): 182.

41. Scott to Gardner, 16 July 1813, New York State Library, 12914, Charles Kitchel Gardner Papers.

42. Madison to Dearborn, 8 August 1813, Hunt, *The Writings of James Madison*, 8: 256. Dearborn's request of 24 July is mentioned in *ibid.*: 256n.

43. Monroe to Dearborn, 18 June 1814, Hamilton, *The Writings of James Monroe*, 5: 282.

44. Apart from biographical references noted earlier, see *HDW*, for biographies of Chauncey, 87; Dearborn, 136; Pearce, 411; Ripley, 474; Forsyth, 188; and Elliott, 164; and Myers, 359. Scott to Thompson, 2 June 1813, NJHS, MG 1044, Scott Letters. Biographical data from Scott, John. "The Letters of Captain John Scott." Dwight resigned over promotion issues as per his letter to the adjutant general's office, 12 August 1813, USNA, RG 94, M 566, 1813, roll 22: 2861. For his promotions and resignation, see *HRD*, 1: 392. Walworth, *HRD*, 1: 1000. For Warner, see <www.haemo-sol.com/thomas/thomas.html>. Strachan wrote to Pelham after he was wounded at Crysler's Farm in November 1813 to offer his help, and that of his friends, in appreciation for Pelham's conduct at York, 29 December 1813, AO, F 983, Strachan Fonds. For Pelham's parole, see Freer to Beckwith, 30 December 1813, Syracuse University Library, Manuscript Collections, MSS 64, Osborne Family Papers, Correspondence, Peter Pelham (1785-1826), Box 1. For Beaumont, see <www.james.com/beaumont/dr_life.htm>. For Elliott's see: ANB, 7: 431. Myers, *Ned Myers*.

45. These cases were: Casey, 26th Congress, Session 1, *Jour-*

nal of the House of Representatives of the United States, Report No. 450, 25 April 1814; Marshall, 27th Congress, Session 2, *Journal … Report* No. 439, 8 March 1842; Myers, 26th Congress, Session 1, *Journal …* Report No. 169, 5 March 1840.

46. Pike, *The Journal of Zebulon Montgomery Pike,* 2: 394-6. Hollon, *The Lost Pathfinder,* 216-7. Olsen, "Zebulon Pike and American Popular Culture." Appointment of a committee to discuss a national award for Pike, 13th Congress, 1st Session, *Annals of Congress,* 27 July 1813, 481. Details about the Pike family and children are from <www.historicmorrison.org/history/Pioneers/Gen-Pike.php>.

47. The newspaper quotes in this paragraph come from, in order, the following 1813 issues of the *Quebec Mercury*: 4 May; 11 May; 1 June 1813. Other information comes from the issues of 18 and 25 May. After the destruction of the printing press at York, the only newspaper operating in Upper Canada in the spring of 1813 was the *Kingston Gazette,* Benn, "The Upper Canadian Press, 1793-1815."

48. 11 May 1813, *The Quebec Mercury.* "We were in hopes to have seen, by this time, something official respecting the attack on York, but nothing of that nature having transpired, our readers must be satisfied with what private information has come to our hands on the subject," 25 May 1813, *The Quebec Mercury.* The anecdote about Derby appeared in this issue. Sheaffe's general order was in the issue of 22 June and the Executive Council's letter and Sheaffe's reply appeared in the issue of 29 June. The *Kingston Gazette's* first account of the battle was in its 25 May issue and comprised Peter Porter's letter at Niagara to J. Spencer, 28 April 1813, which was published in the 5 May issue of the *Geneva Gazette* and then picked up by numerous newspapers. Dearborn's 28 April report appeared in the 15 June issue of the *Kingston Gazette* and so did Sheaffe's general order about the battle. The Terms of Capitulation finally appeared a week later, long after they had appeared in American newspapers.

49. Re: limited resources and Warren, Prevost to Bathurst, 18A May 1813, LAC, MG 11, CO 42, 150: 156. Re: Sheaffe's inadequate defence, Prevost to Bathurst, 24 June 1813, LAC MG 11, CO 42, 151: 37. Re: concentrating the naval force at Kingston: Freer to Sheaffe, 23 March 1813, LAC, RG 8, I, 688c: 28; Prevost to Barclay, 26 April 1813, *ibid.,* 688e: 55.

50. Bathurst to Prevost, 1 July 1813, LAC, RG 8, I, 679: 164. Bathurst noted having only received Prevost's despatch of 21 April 1813 at this point, although he discussed the details of the loss at York in his letter, having obtained them from other sources, probably American newspapers.

51. "A distinguished commander without boldness is unthinkable. No man who is not born bold can play such a role, and therefore we consider this quality the first prerequisite of the great military leader," Clausewitz, *On War,* 226.

52. Anonymous, *The Letters of Veritas,* 31. Another contemporary criticism of Prevost's actions in relation to York was James, *A Full and Correct Account of the Military Occurrences of the Late War,* (1818), 1: 148-9. For assessments of Prevost's leadership, see: Turner, *British Generals,* 24-57, 141-55; and Hitsman, "Sir George Prevost's Conduct."

53. Bathurst to Sheaffe, 10 July 1813, *DHC,* 6: 214. Bathurst noted having only received Sheaffe's despatches written up to 5 April 1813 at this point. Bathurst had written to

Prevost, 1 July 1813, LAC, RG 8, I, 679: 164 to discuss the details of the loss at York in his letter, having obtained them from other sources, probably American newspapers.

54. Bathurst to Prevost, 11 August 1813, LAC, MG 11, CO 42, 151: 42. Bathurst noted receipt of all of Prevost's despatches from #58 (23 April) to # 72 (24 June).

55. York to Prevost, 10 August 1813, LAC, RG 8, I, 679: 382. De Rottenburg was recalled in the same despatch. He and Sheaffe were to be replaced by Lieutenant General Gordon Drummond and Major General Phineas Riall. Bathurst announced Sheaffe's removal to Prevost, 14 August 1813, *ibid.,* 230: 28. In anticipation that Sheaffe's frail health, as reported by Prevost during the winter, would require his removal, an order has been sent from Torrens at Horse Guard to Prevost on 9 May 1813, announcing that Major General Duncan Darroch and a Major General Steven were on their way to Canada and could replace him, LAC, RG 8, I, 229: 80.

56. Prevost to Sheaffe, 22 July 1813, LAC, RG 8, I, 1221: 106. Prevost wrote about a lack of discipline in the 2nd Battalion of Lower Canada Embodied Militia to Sheaffe on 15 July, asking him to look into the matter, *ibid.:* 104.

57. Sheaffe to Prevost, 25 July 1813, LAC, RG 8, I, 229: 136.

58. Sheaffe reassignment to the reserve force was announced in General Order by Baynes, 27 September 1813, LAC, RG 8, I, 1171: 33. Memorial by Sheaffe to Prevost, undated, sent with Prevost to Bathurst, 1 November 1813, *ibid.,* 1219: 133.

59. Sheaffe to Prevost, 13 November 1813, LAC RG 8, 230: 88. The British won the Battle of Crysler's Farm on 11 November 1813, putting an end to Wilkinson's invasion attempt.

60. Anonymous, *The Letters of Veritas,* 50.

61. Coffin, *1812: The War and Its Moral,* (1864), 106.

62. Turner, *British Generals,* 100. For Turner's chapter on Sheaffe and his comparison to the other generals, see 84-100, 141-55. Typical of the defences of Sheaffe is the letter by "Truth." Letter to the *Anglo-American Magazine,* 3 (December 1853), 565-6. Among the critics of Sheaffe's conduct were: Auchinleck, "History of the War, Chapter X," *Anglo-American Magazine,* 3 (October 1853), 338-48; and Hannay, *The History of the War of 1812,* (1905), 138.

63. "A general … is exposed to countless impressions, most of them disturbing, few of them encouraging…. If a man were to yield to these pressures, he would never complete an operation…. It is steadfastness that will earn the admiration of the world and of posterity," Clausewitz, *On War,* 227.

64. Excerpt from J.B. Robinson's diary, 31 January 1816, in Robinson, C.W., *Life of Sir John Beverley Robinson,* 96.

65. This account of Sheaffe's later years is based on the following: Sheaffe to Mrs. Anne Powell, 8 August 1818, TRL, L 16, Powell Papers; Stephen Sheaffe, *The Sheaffe Family History;* obituary, *The Gentleman's Magazine and Historical Review,* 36 (July–December, 1851), 318; Sabine, *Biographical Sketches,* 2: 290-2. As noted earlier, the author gratefully acknowledges the assistance provided by Stephen Sheaffe, of Queensland, Australia, regarding family records. Of particular interest is Sheaffe's continued relationship with the Northumberland family, as shown in a quote from 1829, cited in Sabine, *Biographical Sketches,* 2: 291: "My friends in general seem to have expected that the Duke of Northumberland's recent appointment would have been productive to me; but it unfortunately happens that he has nothing in his gift suitable to a military man of my

rank: he has asked for a Regiment or Government for me, and it is probably, with my admitted claims, that I shall get one." Hugh Percy, the 2nd Duke of Northumberland (1742-1817) was succeed by his son, the 3rd Duke (1785-1847).

66. Information on the careers of these men comes from these sources: LeLièvre, *HMG*, 225; MacPherson and his company – Johnston, *The Glengarry Light Infantry*, 249-50, 196-7 and *HMG*, 252; Hill, *HMG*, 191.

67. Merritt, *A Desire of Serving*, 54. For Robbins's career, see *HMG*, 317, and for Loring, *HMG*, 231, and *DCB*, 7: 517.

68. Quotes taken from Commins, "The War on the Canadian Frontier, 1812-14," 200 and 211.

Chapter 16: "A place equal to this": York After the Occupation

1. Isaac Wilson to his Jonathan Wilson, 5 December 1813, AO, MS 199(5).

2. Anne Powell to William Powell, 10 May 1813, TRL, L 16, Powell Papers, Mrs. Powell's letters, A 93: 311.

3. Anne Powell to William Powell, 10 May 1813, TRL, L 16, Powell Papers, Mrs. Powell's letters, A 93: 311.

4. Anne Powell to William Powell, 20 and 16 May 1813, TRL, L 16, Powell Papers, Mrs. Powell's letters, A 93: 321 and 316.

5. Anne Powell to William Powell, 10 and 12 May 1813, TRL, L 16, Powell Papers, Mrs. Powell's letters, A 93: 311 and 315. Other facts and comments are taken from Anne's letters of 16 and 20 May.

6. This section based on Ely Playter's diary entries 3–28 May 1813, AO, F 556. The family lost clothing, jewelry as per Playter's claim, LAC, RG 19 E 5 (a), Board of claims for War of 1812 losses, vol. 3733, file 5, which was approved as "strongly recommended Mr. Playter having been actively employed as a militia officer at the time." Anne Powell mentioned that the banner had been found to her husband, 20 May 1813, TRL, L 16, Powell Papers, Mrs. Powell's letters, A 93: 321.

7. Ely Playter's diary entries, the two quotes from 25 and 28 May, respectively, AO, F 556.

8. Anne Powell to William Powell, 31 May 1813, TRL, L 16, Powell Papers, Mrs. Powell's letters, A 93: 329. See also her letters of 6, 8, 10 and 12 June 1813, *ibid.*: 333, 337, 341, 343.

9. "The light company of the Newfoundland Regiment left York long ago as an escort to the prisoners taken at Stoney Creek," de Rottenburg to Baynes, 14 July 1813, LAC, RG 8, I, 679: 249. Coffin's frequent visits are mentioned in the Powell letters, noted above. Evidence of the militia continuing to operate at York, and be paid for it, is found in: Pay roll for commissioned officers of the 3rd York and Incorporated Militia, 25 April–24 May 1813, LAC, RG 9, 1B7, 18: 462; Jarvis's artillery payroll, same dates, *ibid.*: 465; Cavalry payroll, same dates, *ibid.*: 463; Jarvie's payroll, same dates, *ibid.*: 466. For payrolls for these companies through June, July and August, see *ibid.*: 484-488, 510, 537.

10. Chewitt to Denison and other commanding officers, 15 May 1813, AO, Thomas Ridout Family Fonds, F 43. Lists of the casualties, POWs and others was ordered by Chewitt to Denison and others, 10 May 1813, *ibid.* Sergeant George Cutter, 1st York, stated that he made out a list of illegal parolees and gave it to Lieutenant Colonel William Graham but the latter died soon after and nothing was done at the time with the list, Chewett to Coffin, 8 January 1817, LAC, RG 9, 1B1, vol. 5, unpaginated.

11. Proclamation by Sheaffe and the council, 4 June 1813,

LAC, RG 8, I, 688c: 42. Proclamation by Prevost, 14 June 1813, *DHC*, 6: 82. A deposition about Lyon by Cutter was made on 15 August 1813, LAC, RG 5, A 1, 16: 6538. Shaw ordered Colonel Graham to have Captain Thomas Selby take up a position on Yonge Street with a 35-man detachment of the 1st York "so that good order and tranquility may be preserved in this part of the province," 17 May 1813, LAC, RG 9, 1B1, 1814, vol. 2, unpaginated. A 17-man detachment under Major Samuel Wilmot, 1st York was on duty "at an Alarm" between 21 and 25 July 1813, LAC, RG 9, IB7, 16: 100. On 20 August Ely Playter noted that he and his brother George had been helping the magistrates examine the conduct of the "disaffected," Playter diary, AO, F 556.

12. Powell to Prevost, 28 June 1813, LAC, RG 8, I, 679: 148. Prevost asked for a report from Powell, 21 June 1813, *DHC*, 6: 102. Battersby's detachment included some of his own Glengarry Light Infantry, the light companies of the 1st and 89th Foot, five artillerymen, and the troop of the 19th Dragoons went with him, intended for service on the Niagara Peninsula, as did any other fit men from other regiments left to recuperate at Kingston, Garrison Order, by Baynes, 7 July 1813, *DHC*, 6: 202. De Rottenburg sent instructions and some light field artillery to Battersby at York on 14 July 1813, LAC, RG 8, I, 679: 249. For Battersby's career, see *HMG*, 59.

13. Smith's case was noted on 15 May 1813, Jordan's on 10 June and Hastings on 12 June, York County Court of General Sessions of the Peace, AO, RG 22 94,0,2, Minute Book, 2: 143-5. Smith's claim for losses, LAC, RG 19 E 5 (a), Board of claims for War of 1812 losses, vol. 3733, file 5, was "Rejected, Major Allan stating that several articles plundered from the Government Stores whilst the Enemy was in York were found on claimants premises." De Rottenburg's order for the arrests of Ketchum and Peters and John Young, Thaddeus Gilbert and Amasa Stebbins, was made by McMahon to Robinson, 9 July 1813, Firth, *Town of York*, 315. Ketchum and Peters were not tried as shown in their respective biographies in *DCB*, 9: 422 and 6: 578.

14. Battersby to Baynes, 31 July 1813, LAC, RG, 8, I, 679: 517. Colonel John Harvey had also ordered other elements to defend Burlington, based on the anticipated attack: Harvey to Claus, 28 July 1813, *DHC*, 6: 287; Harvey to Simons, 29 July 1813, *DHC*, 6: 291. The content of Battersby's note refutes the claim made by Sheppard, *Plunder, Proft and Paroles*, 87, that "Battersby fled at the first sight of the enemy fleet." This description of the July/August 1813 visit of the American squadron at York is based on the following: W. Powell to Prevost, 1 August, 1813, LAC, RG 8, I, 679: 309; Strachan and G. Powell to Baynes, 2 August 1813, *ibid.*,: 324; Allan to Baynes, 3 August 1813, *ibid.*, 688c: 84; Ely Playter's diary entry for 31 July and 5 August 1813, AO, F 556; Scott told Boyd they took one 24-pdr., 3 August 1813, *ASP: MA*, 1: 450; Chauncey told Jones they took five cannon without naming their calibres, 4 August 1813, USNA, RG 45, M 125, 30: 69.

15. Executive Council to de Rottenburg, 14 August 1813, LAC, RG 8, I, 688c: 87. The council's letter also included the evidence about the misconduct of John Young, Thaddeus Gilbert, Amasa Stebbins and William Peters. They were four of the five men ordered by de Rottenburg to be jailed in McMahon to Robinson, 9 July 1813, Firth, *Town of York*, 315 and were mentioned again after the second American visit to York in Allan to Baynes, 3 August 1813, LAC, RG 8, I, 688c: 84. Allan's letter prompted de Rottenburg to request the opinion of the

Executive Council in MacMahon to Small, 11 August 1813, *ibid.*: 81.

16. Lyon's undated note is placed among the documents passed between de Rottenburg's office and the Executive Council during this period of August 1813, LAC, RG 8, I, 688c: 80.

17. Lyon's possession of the articles, how he got them and what he said were recorded in a deposition about Lyon by the constable George Cutter, 15 August 1813, LAC, RG 5, A 1, 16: 6538.

18. Robinson to de Rottenburg, 20 August 1813, LAC, RG 5, A1, 16: 6532.

19. Ridout *et al* to de Rottenburg, 29 September 1813, LAC, RG 5, A1, 16: 6664. The first list prepared by the committee (signed also by Robinson), and in which they expressed their doubts about successful detention and conviction, was submitted on 16 August 1813, *ibid.*: 6667. The lists were attached to these letters.

20. Hastings case, 25 and 26 October 1813, Court of Queen's Bench Assize, Minute Books, AO, RG 22, 134, 0, 4, Criminal Assize, 1810-1814. Bentley's case, 26 October 1813, 31 March and 1 April 1814, *ibid.* Orton's indictment was noted on 30 March 1814, *ibid.*, but no further record appears. Jackson's conduct during the 27 April incident was mentioned in a report by T.G. Ridout, 5 May 1813, LAC, RG 8, I, 678: 188. No action was taken against Jackson as shown in his biography, *DCB*, 7: 438. The names of thirty-two men and their alleged misconduct were included with Ridout *et al* to de Rottenburg, 29 September 1813, LAC, RG 5, A1, 16: 6664.

21. John Lyon's wills and other (well referenced) documents and information about the man were supplied to the author by Bob Gregory of Kanata in June 2005, to whom the author extends his sincere appreciation.

22. Drummond's speech on 15 February 1814 to the Assembly and Legislative Council in which he recommended measures for dealing with the "malignant influence"was recorded in *Journal of the House of Assembly of Upper Canada*, 5th Session, 6th Parliament, 103-5. The acts passed by the provincial legislature are summarized on 14 March 1814 in *ibid.*, 163-4. Riddell, "The Ancaster 'Bloody Assize' of 1814."

23. Prevost proclamation was undated, but is said to have appeared in the *Kingston Gazette*, on 7 September, as per *DHC*, 8: 32. Playter mentioned the call, the parade, returns and service of the militia in his diary entries of 25 September–3 October 1813, AO, F 556.

24. The exchange was finalized on 18 April 1814 and announced in a militia general order by Foster, 24 April 1814, *DHC*, 9: 307. Correspondence concerning the inquiry and follow up events include: Proceedings of a Court of Inquiry, 4 July 1814, LAC, RG 9, 1B1, vol. 3, unpaginated; Chewett to Coffin, 6 July 1814, *ibid.*; Chewett to Foster, 23 February 1815, *ibid.*, vol. 4. Information about exchanges is one of the most difficult of War of 1812 records to track down comprehensively. The procedure to exchange men taken at York for Americans taken at Detroit in August 1812 began by September 1813 but was hindered by the lack of a list of the names of the 19 sergeants, 4 corporals and 204 privates on the list that accompanied the terms of capitulation as Thomas Barclay, the British agent for exchanges, explained to an unknown British recipient (possibly Prevost), 25 September 1813, LAC, RG 8, I, 690: 164; the list Barclay sent with his letter was identical to the authorized version prepared after the battle, dated 28 April 1813, LAC, MG 11, CO 42, 150: 163; USNA, RG 45, M 125, 28: 64. See Appendix 9 for a transcription of this docu-

ment. To date, the one American list of paroled militia POWs taken on 27 April that has come to hand shows only 99 names. It is filed after a list of POWs taken at Fort George on 27 May and is entitled List of Prisoners of War Paroled (exclusively of Regulars) at the taking of Little York, undated, USNA, RG 98, Districts, Divisions and Posts, Ninth Military District, Miscellaneous Records, vol. 1, unpaginated. Chewett mentioned that the militia had been paroled on 15 May 1814, which initiated an inquiry, "fearing there might be some misrepresentation," to Foster, 23 February 1815, LAC, RG 9, 1B1, vol. 4: unpaginated.

25. Re: Cutter's claims, including that he had made out a list of illegal parolees: Chewett to Coffin, 8 January 1817, LAC, RG 9, 1B1, vol. 5, unpaginated; Cutter died in the winter or early spring of 1817, as noted in Chewett to Coffin, 10 May 1817, *ibid.*; Cutter was one of the men who gave depositions to Robinson's committee at York in August and September 1813 as seen in 16 August 1813, LAC, RG 5, A1, 16: 6538. Re: Stooks's claims: Chewett to Coffin, 20 December 1816, LAC, RG 9, 1B1, vol. 5, unpaginated. Re: the inquiry, 10 May 1817, *ibid.* Chewett kept trying unsuccessfully to get access to Graham's papers through Wilmot who was about to resign his commission, as noted in Chewett to Coffin, 29 November 1817, *ibid.* The other two accusers, mentioned in these files, were Captain Jeremiah Travis and Private Michael Harmand. The next sets of files contain no further mention of the matter, except the confirmation of Hawlcy's guilt in the militia general order, 16 June 1818, LAC, RG 9, 1B3, vol. 2: 167.

26. Ryerson, *The Loyalists of America*, 2: 471. Similar comments are found in Edgar, *Ten Years of Upper Canada*, 6-7, and in Macdonell, "Address at the Brock Centenary,"327. For critics of the militia myth as well as the parallel Loyalist myth, see: Cruikshank, "A Study of Disaffection in Upper Canada in 1812-15"; Stanley, "Contribution of the Canadian Militia during the War"; Stacey, "The War of 1812 in Canadian History"; Errington, "Friends and Foes: The Kingston Elite and the War of 1812; Sheppard, "Deeds Speak: Militiamen, Medals and the Invented Traditions of 1812"; Sheppard, *Plunder, Profit and Paroles.*

27. Brock to Prevost, 25 February 1812, LAC, RG 8, I, 676: 92. Among the many examples of poor performance by American militia are their conduct at: Queenston Heights, 13 October 1812 (Malcomson, *A Very Brilliant Affair*, 177-8); Sackets Harbor, 29 May 1813, (Wilder, *The Battle of Sackett's Harbour*, 88-9); Bladensburg, 24 August 1814 (Whitehorne, *The Battle for Baltimore*, 132-3). See also a long description of American militia resistance to service and poor conduct in camp and the field in Bellesiles, "Experiencing the War of 1812."

28. For examples of Jackson's strong and decisive leadership, see: Remini, *The Battle of New Orleans*, 58-9, 97-8, 132-3; Reilly, *The British at the Gates*, 202-06. Bellesiles points out Jackson's effective management of the militia in, "Experiencing the War of 1812," 227-8. American estimates of the numbers who got their paroles: 500 – Dearborn to Armstrong, 3 May 1813, USNA, RG 107, M 221, 52: unpaginated; 1000 – John Scott to Thompson, 17 May 1813, New Jersey Historical Society, MG 1044, Captain John Scott Letters; 1200 – Beaumont, *Formative Years*, 47. Sheppard quotes a misprint in Firth, *Town of York*, 307 when he claims that Beaumont's estimate was 1700, *Plunder, Profit and Paroles*, 81. Even the estimate printed in *Beaumont's Formative Years* exceeded the actual strength of the 1st and 3rd York Regi-

ments. The strength of 559 officers and men for the 1st York is taken from a quarterly return dated 24 September 1813, LAC, RG 9, IB7, 16: 1 and that of 495 for the 3rd York is from a return dated 24 March 1813, *ibid.*: 12.

29. Jarvis, "Narrative of Colonel Stephen Jarvis," 254. For a full discussion of parole violators and disaffected individuals, see Appendix 5, U.C. Militia.

30. Chapin reported the request for protection to Dearborn, 2 June 1813, New York State Library, 12914, Charles Kitchel Gardner Papers. For a review of disaffection in Upper Canada, see Cruikshank, "A Study of Disaffection in Upper Canada in 1812-15." The populations of York and York Township are from "A List of Inhabitants in the Town of York, and York Township, July 1813," Mosser, *York, Upper Canada Minutes of Town Meetings*, 97 and 161. The strength of the 1st York is taken from a quarterly return dated 24 September 1813, LAC, RG 9, IB7, 16: 1 and that of the 3rd York is from a return dated 24 March 1813, *ibid.*: 12. American smuggling is detailed in: Alcock, "The best defence is … smuggling? Vermonters during the War of 1812"; Muller, "A 'Traitorous and Diabolical Traffic: ' The Commerce of the Champlain-Richelieu Corridor during the War of 1812"; Strum, "Smuggling in the War of 1812." The extensive looting at Washington is noted in: Lord, *The Dawn's Early Light*, 194-5; Pitch, *The Burning of Washington*, 150-1. There were problems of disaffection in Louisiana in 1814 prior to the British attack on New Orleans, as noted by General Thomas Flournoy to Armstrong, 31 January 1814, (cited in Owsley, *Struggle for the Gulf Borderlands*, 128): "I do believe there is not one person in twenty throughout this State, that is friendly to the United States, or who would take up arms in its defence."

31. Sheppard, *Plunder, Profit and Paroles*, 5.

32. Cash awards mentioned here are "best guesses" since the records of the distribution of funds mix the use of "dollars" and "pounds" and are contradictory about the actual amounts awarded. Reports of the following individuals were noted in *The Report of the Loyal and Patriotic Society of Upper Canada*: Borland, 54-5; Detlor, 67, 231; Murray, 67, 228-9; Saunders, 109, 233; McLean, 197, 228-9; Bassell, 228-9; Miller, 256-7. Mrs. Freel and Mrs. Tanning were mentioned in *The Report of the Loyal and Patriotic Society of Upper Canada*, 288-9. The closest names on the regimental musters and casualty lists to match these names are Private Cornelius Fieley, noted as WIA/POW, and Corporal John Fannen, KIA, both of the Royal Newfoundland Regiment, see Appendix 4, British Order of Battle, and Appendix 8, Casualties and POWs. Biographical information about Bassell is in Firth, *Town of York*, 186N.; he was mentioned in *The Report of the Loyal and Patriotic Society of Upper Canada*, 54-5; and in Mosser, *York, Upper Canada Minutes of Town Meetings*, passim.

33. Excerpt from J. B. Robinson's diary, April 1817, in C. W. Robinson, *Life of Sir John Beverley Robinson*, 124. Jarvie was back in Quebec in 1832 where he answered Powell's questions during the flare up of the Alexander Wood controversy (see Chapter 1), 4 April 1832, TRL, L 16, Powell Papers, B 90: 93. Jarvie wrote that he suffered from a "swimming in the brain with which I have been occasionally afflicted ever since the severe handling which I experienced from our unwelcome visitors at York in 1813." The details of the pension requests and medical board reports for the following individuals are found in LAC, RG 9, IB4, Jarvie, 1: 1, 4, 2: 1; Detlor, 1: 2, 70, 2: 8-9; Murray, 1: 2, 69, 2: 4; Saunders, 1: 2, 78, 2: 7-9;

Shepard, 1: 32, 2: 13 ; Hartney, 1: 51; Jarvis, 3: unpaginated.

34. Wood to Maitland and others, 21 February 1814, TRL, S 114, Wood, Alexander, Business Letter Books, vol. 3: unpaginated. De Koven ("Captain Decovin") is on the "List of Inhabitants in the Town of York, and York Township, 1816," Mosser, *York, Upper Canada Minutes of Town Meetings*, 116 and shown to have one male and one female under sixteen and two females older than that under his roof (see, also the following note). The proposal to put de Koven in the veterans unit was in Torrens to Prevost, 4 November 1813, LAC, RG 8, I, 230: 80, but most of his later correspondence indicated that he considered himself a lieutenant of the late Newfoundland Regiment. De Koven appears to have had a land grant of 500 acres which he tried to sell off in parcels, petition by de Koven, 14 March 1814, LAC, RG 5, A1, 19: 8058.

35. Proceedings of a Medical Board, …, Montreal, 23 November 1818, LAC, RG 8, I, 721: 123. Other documents about de Koven's condition include: de Koven to Addison, 21 October 1816, *ibid.*: 149; de Koven to Anthony, 23 October 1816, *ibid.*: 150; Return of Provisions, 24 October 1813 (showing one servant, two children, one woman and the officer), *ibid.*: 152; Memorials by de Koven, 11 January 1817, 8 October and 12 November 1818, *ibid.*: 155, 193 and 194. The author gratefully thanks Dr. J. Jakibchuk for his advice on de Koven's case.

36. Lieutenant John Kitson of the Royal Engineers reported on the work in progress on 22 November 1813, LAC, RG 8, I, 388: 136. William Powell reported on the timber resources and the town's accommodation resources to Prevost, 28 June 1813, *ibid.*, 679: 148; Ely Playter mentioned the draft of 100 "to carry on the public works" on 2 October 1813, Playter Diary, AO, F 556. Beikie described the batteries, etc., to Miles Macdonell, 19 March 1814, in Firth, *Town of York*, 328. Colonel Archibald Stewart, 1st Foot, held command of York from the autumn of 1813 through 1814 as shown in: Taylor to Ridout, 9 March 1814, Firth, *Town of York*, 328; and Harvey to Yeo, 9 April 1814, *DHC*, 9: 285. An estimate to rebuild the wooden interiors was enclosed with a letter from Thomas Scott to McMahon, 1 October 1813, LAC, RG 5, A1, 18: 7594. Reconstruction of the Parliament Buildings is described in Dieterman and Williamson, *Government on Fire*, 20.

37. Ely Playter mentioned the shortage of accommodations on 30 October 1813, Playter Diary, AO, F 556. Strachan described use of the church as a hospital and the number of patients to Owen, 1 January 1814, Spragge, *Strachan: 1812-1834*, 55.

38. Baldwin to St. George, 20 July 1814, Firth, *Town of York*, 332. In March 1814, steps were taken to remove all public papers out of town by 20 April in case the Americans attacked again, Executive Council to Drummond, 16 March 1814, LAC, RG 8, I, 688d: 20 and McGill to Scott, 13 April 1814, *DHC*, 9: 294. Chauncey to Scott and Powell, 14 November 1813, WCL, *CLB*.

39. These prices show a comparison between the information in Wilson to his parents, 19 November 1811 (AO, MS 199(5), Isaac Wilson Diaries) and that in Beikie to Miles Macdonell, 19 March 1814, in Firth, *Town of York*, 328. Wilson related his anecdote to his brother, 5 December 1813, AO, MS 199(5). The magistrates published their list of fixed prices on 25 April 1814, Firth, *Town of York*, 330; per pound, the price of beef was 7.5p and butter was 1s/3p. It became illegal to use grain for distillation purposes by the proclamation by Drummond, 14

March 1814, *DHC*, 9: 235. The imposition of martial law pertaining to the acquisition "of provisions and forage for the said troops," was announced by Drummond, 12 April 1814, *DHC*, 9: 292.

40. Wood's efforts to collect Plucknett's debt are shown in: Wood to Forsyth, 7 May, 1, 3, 5, 21 and 28 June 1813; Wood to McNaught and company, 22 June 1813, TRL, S 114, Wood, Alexander, Business Letter Books, vol. 3: unpaginated.

41. Plucknett to Richmond, 14 October 1818, LAC, RG 8, I, 189: 42. Note attached to this, 20 October 1818, *ibid.*: 45. Warrant of Plucknett's compensation and note re: same, 24 October 1818, *ibid.*: 40. Additional undated note by Thompson that suggests that Wood was successful in detaining some of Plucknett's funds or possessions, undated, *ibid.*: 38. Halton to Plucknett, 23 July 1816, LAC, RG 8, I, 189: 37. Plucknett's claim for personal baggage lost at York, 18 May 1813, *ibid.*, 84: 175. It appears that Plucknett also put in another claim for the same items which was rejected as in LAC, RG 19 E 5 (a), Board of claims for War of 1812 losses, vol. 3734, file 5.

42. Strachan was particularly offended by the way Prevost and Yeo failed to support the Lake Erie squadron under Commander Robert Barclay (one of Strachan's former students in Scotland) and criticized them both for this and other misdeeds. "Of the two Sir George and Sir Jas. I think the latter the worse – the former has not genius and was surrounded by wretched advisers the latter acted wrong from pure perverseness I hope the conduct of both will be strictly inquired into," Strachan to Harvey, 31 March 1815, Spragge, *Strachan*, 85. For Strachan's career, see earlier references and *DCB*, 9: 751.

43. For the Powells' biographies, see earlier references and *DCB*: William, 6: 605; Anne, 7: 638; Grant, 7: 704.

44. For the biographies, see earlier references and *DCB*: St. George, 6: 622; Wood, 7: 919; Allan, 8: 4.

45. For Baldwin's career, see earlier references and *DCB*, 7: 35.

46. Playter's diary, AO, F 556 provides the source for this information as well as a brief biographical note in Firth, *The Town of York, 1815-1834*, 147n.

47. Isaac Wilson to his Jonathan Wilson, 5 December 1813, AO, MS 199(5). The final quote in this chapter comes from Heriot, *Travels Through the Canadas*, 139.

Appendix 1: The Fort, the Graves, the Monuments

1. Benn, *Historic Fort York*, 134. The description of the fort through the 19th and 20th centuries here is largely based on Carl's fine work.

2. This information taken from these articles by Killan, "The First Old Fort York Preservation Movement," and "The York Pioneers and the First Old Fort York Preservation Movement," and Killan's *Preserving Ontario's Heritage*.

3. Geeson's letter was printed in the 4 October 1905 issue of *The Globe* and supported by an editorial that day. See also: Geeson, *A Brief History of the 'Old Fort' at Toronto*.

4. The controversy was summarized in Scott, "Fort York" and (no author), "Fort York Wins a Modern Battle." The controversy was covered almost daily in the local newspapers. A map showing the interchange between Highway 400 and the Gardiner Expressway was on the front page of the 2 January 1959 issue of the *Toronto Daily Star*.

5. 2 September 1958, *Toronto Daily Star*.

6. 23 September 1958, *Toronto Daily Star*. Letters supporting the editorial point of view appeared in the issues of

15 October, 27 November and 4 December 1958.

7. 12 June 1958, *The Globe and Mail*.

8. 7 June 1958, *Toronto Daily Star*.

9. Letter to the editor by Helen Dure of the Women's Canadian Historical Society of Toronto, 24 February 1958, *Toronto Daily Star*.

10. 6 January 1959, *Toronto Daily Star*.

11. 7 June 1958, *Toronto Daily Star*.

12. Stuart, "The Old Military Burial Ground, Toronto." Rudman, "The History of These Graves."

13. Elliott to Hatfield, 17 May 1813, *Otsego Herald*, 19 June 1813. The burials of Bloomfield, Hoppock and Lyon are mentioned in a letter by Lieutenant George Runk, Sixth Infantry, written at Sackets Harbor on 14 May 1813. Mr. Brian Murphy of Chester, New Jersey owns the original copy and generously communicated its contents to the author.

14. Yellowhead's death and burial, are mentioned in Scadding, *The 8th King's Regiment: A Curiosity in its Annals*, 8 and in *Toronto of Old*, 399.

15. The survey of Pike's burial plot is described in Burnham, "Finding Pike: Fort Drum Archeologist Searches for General's Remains," 9 October 2003, *Fort Drum Blizzard Online*, <www.drum.army.mil/sites/postnews/blizzard/blizzard_archives/news>. Lossing described the Madison Barracks burial ground in *The Pictorial Field-book of the War of 1812*, 615-18. Efforts to move Pike's remains to Colorado are found in the 27 April 1948 issue of *The New York Times* and Phillips, "New York Town Digs Our Hero Too," 12 May 2006, *The Gazette*, <www2.gazette.com/pikespeak/display.php?id>.

16. Scadding produced a pamphlet about McNeale's remains, *The 8th King's Regiment: A Curiosity in its Annals*. 14 May 1829, *The Colonial Advocate*.

17. Benn mentioned most of the discoveries in *Historic Fort York*. The topic of the burials is also covered in Otto, "Where the Bodies Lie Buried." The 1860 remains were also described in these newspapers: 13 August 1860, *The Globe*; 14 August 1860, *New York Times*.

18. The six-line story was in the 28 August 1888 issue of *The Globe*.

19. Scadding's *The 8th King's Regiment: A Curiosity in its Annals* was written to correct the misidentification of these remains as reported in 27 August 1894, *The Toronto Mail*; 27 August, 26 September and 5 October 1894, *The Globe*.

20. 27 October 1903, *The Globe*.

21. Sheaffe's grave is described and pictured at "Historical Narratives of Early Canada," <www.uppercanadahistory.ca/1812/18123.html>.

22. For a history of Brock's monuments, see: Malcomson, *Burying General Brock*. The 1853 meeting was described in the 20 October 1853 issue of *The Niagara Mail*.

23. Some of the Toronto monuments and plaques are described in Collins, *Guidebook to the Historic Sites of the War of 1812*, 146-9. Scadding, *History of the Old French Fort at Toronto and its Monument*. Unveiling ceremonies were described in: 23 and 25 September 1878, *The Daily Globe*; and 7 September 1887, *The Globe*.

24. The dedication of the monument and its completion are in 2 July 1902 and 7 January 1907, *The Globe*.

25. Details about the 1934 event and the return of the mace were covered in the following issues: 5 May, 1, 4, 5 and 15 July 1934, *The New York Times*; 5 July 1934, *The Globe* and *The Toronto Daily Star*. The quote is taken from the plaque mounted on the wall beside the sugar maple.

26. A valuable resource in the location of these plaques is Alan Brown's fine website, <torontohistory.org> at

<www.torontohistory.org/index.html>.

27. The quote is from the plaque. The event was noted in the 21 May 1968 issue of *The Globe and Mail.*

Appendix 2: The Explosion of the Grand Magazine

1. Finan, *Journal of a Voyage,* 289.

2. Lieutenant Colonel George McFeely reported that about "half-past one ... a tremendous explosion took place, which shook the buildings in Fort Niagara and made the glass in the window rattle like what rolling thunder will do some times," McFeely, "Chronicle of Valor," 257-8. 28 miles = 45 km. The casualties on the *Ontario* are described in Smith, *Legend of the Lake,* 121

3. Pearce, "A Poor But Honest Sodger," 139.

4. Eustis to W. Eustis, 11 May 1813, *Proceedings of the Massachusetts Historical Society,* 11 (1869-70): 492-5.

5. Conner to Armstrong, 4 May 1813, USNA, RG 107, M 221, 51: 153.

6. Dearborn to Governor Tompkins, 28 April 1813, in 8 May issue of *The Statesman.* "[T]he magazine ... was undoubtedly prepared by the enemy for that purpose," American Anonymous F, 14 May 1813, to the editors of the *American Mercury* (Connecticut), published 26 May 1813.

7. Conner to Armstrong, 4 May 1813, USNA, RG 107, M 221, 51: 153; Dwight, "'Plow-Joggers for Generals,'" 18; Pearce, "A Poor But Honest Sodger," 139; Trowbridge to John Trowbridge, May 1814, "Two Letters"; Beaumont, *Formative Years,* 46; Citizens' Account, TRL, Papers Relating to the Capitulation.

8. Dunbar's three reports, dated 31 March 1813, are found at LAC, RG 8, 1, 387: 47-9. Chauncey referred to only "tons" of shell and shot and some powder in his list of prize goods submitted to Heard, 15 June 1813, WCL, CLB.

9. The Fort George ordnance is described in Dunbar's three reports, dated 31 March 1813, are found at LAC, RG 8, 1, 387: 47-9. A barrel of powder weighed between 90 and 100 pounds (40.8 to 45.4 kg), Benn, "Bomb-proof Powder Magazines," 7-8, and judging that there were 300 barrels, at least, in the magazine, they contained about 30,000 pounds of powder. The weight of shot and shell is only an estimate as shot tended to weigh less than their calibre and shell weights varied according to whether or not they were filled. Weights for mortar shells are taken from Burney, *Falconer's New Universal Dictionary,* 50, and Tucker, *Arming the Fleet,* 125.

10. Burney, *Falconer's New Universal Dictionary,* 179-81. NOVA on line, Fireworks, <http://www.pbs.org/wgbh/nova/fireworks/anat_nf.html>.

11. <www.research.leidenuniv.nl> Reistma, H and A. Ponsen, "The Leiden disaster of 1807." <www.sciencedirect.com> Reistma, H. J. "The explosion of a ship with black powder, in Leiden in 1807," *International Journal of Impact Engineering,* 25 (2001): 507-14. 500 yd. = 455 m.

12. <www.museum.gov.ns.ca> Maritime Museum of the Atlantic, "The Halifax Explosion."

13. See Appendix 9, Casualties and POWs. Baltimore Volunteer Captain Stephen Moore claimed the explosion "destroyed about eight of his [the enemy's] own men," Moore to his brother, 5 May 1813, Brannan, *Official Letters,* 151. "About 100 of our men were killed and wounded by the explosion," Ridout, *Ten Years of Upper Canada,* 182.

14. Dearborn to Governor Tompkins, 28 April 1813, in 8 May issue of *The Statesman.*

15. *Myers,* 61.

16. Eustis to W. Eustis, 11 May 1813, *Proceedings of the Massachusetts Historical Society,* 11 (1869-70): 492-5. Beaumont, *Formative Years,* 46.

17. American Anonymous A, 9 May 1813, published in the *United States Gazette,* 24 May 1813, *DHC,* 5: 213.

18. Ely Playter's diary entry, 30 April 1813, AO, F 556.

19. Ely Playter's diary entries, 25 and 27 May 1813, AO, F 556.

20. T. Ridout to T.G. Ridout, 9 August 1814, Firth, *Town of York,* 332. Malcomson, *Lords of the Lake,* 290-2.

Appendix 3: British Artillery at York

1. The *Brock's* intended armament: was described in 18 March 1813, Pearson to Freer, 18 March 1813, LAC, RG 8, I, 729: 124. Revised plan: Bruyeres to Prevost, 13 February 1813, *ibid.,* 387: 15 and by Myers to Freer, 2 April 1813, *ibid.,* 729: 153.

2. Conner to Armstrong, 4 May 1813, USNA, RG 107, M 221, 51: 153. Twenty-eight guns: Chauncey to Jones, 7 May 1813, USNA, RG 45, M 125, 28: 101; Trowbridge to John Trowbridge, "Two Letters...." Disposal of guns: *Myers,* 65; John Scott to Thompson, 17 May 1813, New Jersey Historical Society, MG 1044, Captain John Scott Letters; American Anonymous F, 14 May 1813, to the editors of the *American Mercury* (Connecticut), published 26 May 1813. Sixteen guns: Chauncey to Heard, 15 June 1813, WCL, CLB.

3. Prevost to Bathurst, 20 July 1813, LAC, MG 11, CO 42, 151: 78.

4. James, *A Full and Correct Account of the Military Occurrences of the Late War between Great Britain and The United States of America,* 1: 142.

5. Drake, "Artillery and Its Influence on Naval Tactics," 20. Similar ideas are found in: Roosevelt, *The Naval War of 1812,* 219; Hannay, *The History of the War of 1812,* 138; Cruikshank, "The Contest for the Command of Lake Erie in 1812 and 1813, " 360; Stacey, "Another Look at the Battle of Lake Erie," 46; Stacey, *The Battle of Little York,* 21; Hitsman, *The Incredible War of 1812,* 171.

6. Simcoe described the guns to the Duke of Richmond, 23 September 1793, Firth, *Town of York,* 59. The 9-pdr. and one of the 18-pdrs. is on display at Historic Fort York, where their full history is described.

7. Report on the State of the Magazines, ..., by Glasgow, 18 September 1811, LAC, RG 8, I, 1706: 171. Return of Brass and Iron Ordnance ..., by Glasgow, 15 and 19 December 1812, *ibid.,* 1707: 82 and 121. Return of the Field Ordnance ..., by Gordon, 31 March 1813, LAC, RG 8, I, 387: 48.

8. Bruyeres to Prevost, 13 February 1813, *ibid.:* 15 and in Myers to Freer, 2 April 1813, *ibid.,* 729: 153. Return of Ordnance ..., by Gordon, 31 March 1813, LAC, RG 8, I, 387: 47. The delivery of guns to Kingston was minimal and even in June 1813 there were only 5 18-pdrs., 7 9-pdrs, 1 6-pdr. and 1 4-pdr. mounted, as noted in Return of Guns and Ammunition in the Batteries and Block Houses at the Post of Kingston, by Allan, 4 June 1813, LAC, RG 8, I, 688e: 96.

9. Sheaffe to Baynes, 7 April 1813, Sheaffe, "Letter Book," 370.

10. Sheaffe to Mountain, undated [context suggests the fourth week of May 1813]. Edited by T. R. Millman. "Roger Hale Sheaffe and the Defence of York, April 27, 1813." *Canadian Church Historical Review Journal,* 5 (1963): 6-8. Sheaffe to Prevost, 5A and 5 B May 1813, LAC, MG 11, CO 42, 354: 132 and 119.

11. [Powell A], *DHC,* 5: 175. Thomas Ridout, *Ten Years*

of Upper Canada, 180. Jarvis, "Narrative of Colonel Stephen Jarvis," 252. W. Eustis, 11 May 1813, *Proceedings of the Massachusetts Historical Society*, 11 (1869-70): 493. Pearce, "A Poor But Honest Sodger," 136; Trowbridge, "The Battle of York," LOC, Trowbridge Papers.

12. Powell noted that the Half Moon Battery was "thrown up without a gun," [Powell A], *DHC*, 5: 175, and most accounts of the battle do not state that this battery was armed: Stacey, *The Battle of Little York*, 5; Benn, *The Battle of York*, 10. Statements supporting the idea that the Half Moon Battery *was* armed include: "[after retreating from the Western Battery] our men retreated to the second battery, at about 300 yards distant from the garrison. Here they spiked the guns," Ridout, *Ten Years of Upper Canada*, 182; Finan seemed to be referring to the Half Moon Battery when he wrote, "there were only two or three guns at this battery and it but a short distance from the garrison, the troops did not remain in it but retreated to the latter. When the Americans … reached this small battery, instead of pressing forward they halted, and the general [Pike] sat down on one of the guns," *Journal of a Voyage*, 289; "This was a two-gun battery, on a small rising ground," A. Eustis to W. Eustis, 11 May 1813, *Proceedings of the Massachusetts Historical Society*, 11 (1869-70): 494; "The column … arrived at a second battery, which was deserted [as opposed to empty of guns]," Pearce, "A Poor But Honest Sodger," 136.

13. Chauncey to Jones, 7 May 1813, USNA, RG 45, M 125, 28: 101. Scott to Boyd, 3 August 1813, *ASP: MA*, 1: 450. Chauncey to Jones, 4 August 1813, USNA, RG 45, M 125, 30: 69.

14. Chauncey to Heard, 15 June 1813, WCL, CLB. *Myers*, 75. Archeologist Jonathan Moore, *et al.*, notes the replacement of the guns in "Fore-n'-Afters at Fifty Fathoms," 37-8.

Appendix 4: British Order of Battle at York, 27 April 1813

1. Sources of these anecdotal reports are, in order: Sheaffe to Prevost, 5B May 1813, LAC, MG 11, CO 42, 354: 119; [Powell A], *DHC*, 5: 175 and [Powell B], *ibid*: 203; Thomas Ridout, *Ten Years of Upper Canada*, 180; Strachan to Brown, 26 April/14 June 1813, AO, F 983, Strachan Fonds and Strachan to Richardson, 10 May 1813, Sprague, *Strachan*, 37.

2. McLean is the best known of the volunteers and was frequently mentioned, an example being the John Beikie's letter, listed here, in which Alexander Wood is also mentioned. For Jarvis, see Jarvis, "Narrative of Colonel Stephen Jarvis,"252 and *DCB*, 10: 379. The Beikies are mentioned in J. Beikie to Macdonell, 5 May 1813 and Mrs. Penelope Beikie to John Macdonell, no date, AO, F 548, John Macdonell Fonds. For the MacNabs, see Beer, *Sir Allan Napier MacNab*, 6-7 and Coffin, *1812: The War and Its Moral: Canadian Chronicle*, 100. St. George, Wood, Beikie and McLean were mentioned in District General Order by Leonard, 13 May 1813, *DHC*, 5: 227. Jarvis, MacNab, MacDonell and Mathewson (Mathieson) were all young volunteers with the regulars and are all given credit for service at York in *HMG*, 205, 251, 239 and 258. See Hennell, *A Gentleman Volunteer*, 1-3. Bassell's role as a volunteer was noted in *The Report of the Loyal and Patriotic Society of Upper Canada*, 54-5.

3. Although Sheaffe mentioned that there were 150 warriors encamped near York (to Baynes, 7 April 1813, "Letter Book," 370), he reported only 40 involved on 27 April (to Prevost, 5A May 1813, LAC, MG 11, CO 42, 354: 132), while Powell estimated 45 ([Powell A], *DHC*, 5: 175)

and Beikie estimated 100 (to Macdonell, 5 May 1813, OA, John Macdonell Fonds, F 548). The only native remembrance of the battle that was found during this project did not indicate their numbers and named no individuals (John York, "The Battle of Toronto Bay").

4. LeLièvre's presence is well established in the text. Among the several references to Daverne is the record of his pay, as a private citizen (he had property at Kingston), in the Fort York Account Book, City of Toronto Culture, Museum and Heritage Services, vol. 1, unpaginated.

5. The Provincial Marine contingent was named (there was no mention of other seamen) in the Terms of Capitulation Entered into on the 27th April 1813, …, by Mitchell, Conner, *et al.*, LAC, MG 11, CO 42, 354: 121, except for Langley and Cloutier who were listed with Green on a list of men who accepted parole at York as signed by Sailing Master Thomas Nichols, 2 May 1813, which was enclosed with a letter from Chauncey to Jones, 18 June 1813, M125, 29: 82. Some of the individuals were also named in the Nominal Return of the officers who served in the Provincial Marine …, 22 June 1821, by Lightfoot, LAC, RG 8, I, 741: 5.

6. Plucknett and Dennis's presence is well established in the text. McKay, Bennet, Lonnegan, and Patrick (the latter two were probably skilled workers, too) were paid through the winter until 24 April, according to pay lists of the Fort York Account Book, City of Toronto Culture, Museum and Heritage Services, vol. 1, unpaginated. The number of 70 artificers is an estimate based on the following. All but 50 of the 128 artificers who arrived at Kingston went to York with Plucknett as Gray reported to Prevost, 31 December 1812, LAC, RG 8, I, 728: 142. "A few days ago about Eighty Ship Carpenters arrived at this place from your Province; the Keel of a Thirty Gun Ship will soon be laid on the Stocks," Donald McLean to Charles Gray Stewart, 11 January 1813, OA: MU 2036, F895, Miscellaneous Military Records. The Fort York Account Book makes reference to the rations distributed to "sundry artificers" without defining how many men there were. Even dividing the number of rations by the number of days in each period does not produce an even figure: 25 December to 24 February, 3880 rations/62 days = 62.58; 25 February to 24 April, 3238 rations/59 days = 54.88. It is speculated that the number of artificers varied and gradually dropped. However, strong evidence for about 70 remaining in April results from a rough tally of them after the battle. Sheaffe ordered the artificers armed (Sheaffe to Baynes, 25 March 1813, "Letter Book," 353). He put Plucknett in command of them on 27 April with QMGD clerk Daniel Daverne in charge of one portion of them as stated in the claims for losses in May 1813, LAC, RG 8, I, 84: 175. He stated to Prevost that Plucknett arrived at Kingston on 8 May with 40 or 50, with another party following, 8 May 1813, *ibid.*, 678: 221. A return made by Daniel Daverne showed that 41 muskets, bayonets and cartridge boxes were collected from the artificers who reached Kingston, and "there were fifty men that came down from York – the number known to be killed there were – Two – and Missing about Eighteen, several of which were inhabitants of the Town of York," return enclosed with Daverne to Loring, 7 June 1813, LAC, RG 5, A1, 17: 7362. The Terms of Capitulation, cited above, listed 15 artificers paroled; see the transcription in Appendix 9.

7. The names of these men appeared on list of men who accepted parole at York as signed by Sailing Master

Thomas Nichols, 2 May 1813, which was enclosed with a letter from Chauncey to Jones, 18 June 1813, M125, 29: 82. As noted above, Daverne mentioned that some of the artificers were residents and two of these men have been so identified.

8. Sources of these anecdotal reports are, in order: Sheaffe to Prevost, 5A and 5B May 1813, LAC, MG 11, CO 42, 354: 132 and 119; [Powell B], *DHC*, 5: 203; Ridout, *Ten Years of Upper Canada*, 180; Strachan to Brown, 26 April/14 June 1813, AO, F 983, Strachan Fonds and Strachan to Richardson, 10 May 1813, Spragge, *Strachan*, 37; British Anonymous B, at Kingston, 23 May 1813, published in the *Montreal Gazette*, 9 June 1813.

9. Royal Artillery – This data based on casualty lists referenced above and Muster and Pay Rolls for 4th Battalion of the Royal Regiment of Artillery January–June 1813, companies of Major William Holcroft and Captains John Sinclair and Peter Wallace, NAUK, WO10, 976. See also Terms of Capitulation Entered into on the 27th April 1813, …, by Mitchell, Conner, *et al.*, LAC, MG 11, CO 42, 354: 121; see the transcription in Appendix 9.

10. 41st Foot – This data derives from the report of the board of inquiry convened at Kingston to investigate claims for losses resulting from the battle, May 1813, LAC, RG 8, I, 84: 171.

11. 49th Foot – This data based on casualty lists referenced above and Pay List of the Forty-Ninth Regiment of Foot from 25th of December 1812 to 24th of March 1813, both dates inclusive and from 25th of March to 24th of June 1813, both dates inclusive, NAUK, WO 12, 6044.

12. RNRF – The composition of the RNFR at York is based upon the following: Pay-List of the Royal Newfoundland Regiment of Fencible Infantry from 25 March to 24 June 1813, both days inclusive, NAUK, WO12, 11027; Return of non-commissioned officers, drummers, fifers and privates who have died, deserted, transferred to another regiment or been invalided home, 25 December 1812–24 June 1813, NAUK, WO25, 2206; A Nominal List of the Number Killed, Wounded, Prisoners and Missing in the Action of 27th April 1813, LAC, RG 8, I, 695: 192 and a revised form of the list, dated 10 May 1813 and signed by Richard Leonard, LAC, MG11, CO42 354: 123. Information about officers and the size of the detachment were revealed in the report of the board of inquiry convened at Kingston to investigate claims for losses resulting from the battle, May 1813, LAC, RG 8, I, 84: 118.

Members of this regiment who appeared on the casualty list were from Companies 1, 2, 3, 4, 6, 9 and 10. A portion of each of these companies (with the exception of Company 9) was shown to have joined specific warships at Kingston prior to 8 May so could not have been at York; furthermore, none of them were on the casualty list. The men shown here joined the warships at Kingston on or after 8 May or did not join the warships at all. It is speculated that most of these men were stationed at York on 27 April and retreated with Sheaffe to Kingston, arriving before 8 May, but all of them are listed here. The Drummer David Keeley is the only member of Company 9 on the York casualty list. More than half of Company 9 was on the casualty list for the Battle of Fort George, 27 May 1813, and it is speculated that most of the rest of the men were stationed there. For that reason only Keeley is listed here, although there may have been others from his company with him at York.

Captain John Evans is credited in *HMG*, 137, with having been at York, but he does not appear in any relevant documents. The same applies to Lieutenant Edward Enright (*ibid.*, 136) and Ensign Edward Gauvreau (*ibid.*, 159).

13. Glengarries – This data is based on casualty lists referenced above and Pay Lists of the Glengarry Light Infantry Regiment of Fencibles, from 25 December 1812 to 24 September 1813, NUAK, WO 12, 10800; Johnston, *The Glengarry Light Infantry, 1812-1816*. Details of the company's losses are in the report of the board of inquiry convened at Kingston to investigate claims for losses resulting from the battle, May 1813, LAC, RG 8, I, 84: 118. Sergeant Patrick Strange made a claim after the war for his kit and a large amount of other possessions worth £216.7 which was rejected, LAC, RG 19 E 5 (a), Board of claims for War of 1812 losses, vol. 3733, file 5.

14. 8th Foot – This data based on casualty lists referenced above and Pay-List of the 1st Battalion of the 8th or King's Regiment of Infantry from 25 March to 24 June 1813, both days inclusive, NAUK, WO12, 2575; Return of non-commissioned officers, drummers, fifers and privates who have died, deserted, transferred to another regiment or been invalided home, 25 December 1812–24 June 1813, NAUK, WO 25, 1549. Details about the regiment's losses and the names of the subalterns present at the battle are in the report of the board of inquiry convened at Kingston to investigate claims for losses resulting from the battle, May 1813, LAC, RG 8, I, 84: 171.

Appendix 5: Upper Canada Militia at the Battle of York

1. Regiment strength – Quarterly Return of the 1st Regiment of York Militia on 24 September 1813, by Wilmot, LAC, RG 9, IB7, 16: 1; Return of the 3rd Regiment of York Militia, 24 March 1813, by Chewett, *ibid.*: 12.

2. Thomas Ridout remembered 300 regulars and 208 militia, *Ten Years of Upper Canada*, 180; [Powell A], *DHC*, 5: 175; Sheaffe to Prevost, 5A May 1813, LAC, MG 11, CO 42, 354: 132; Strachan stated 360 regulars and militia to Richardson on 10 May 1813, Spragge, *Strachan*, 37. Cumberland mentioned 350 of the 3rd York only, *The Battle of York*, 11; Humphries stated 300 in "The Capture of York," 4; Benn stated 350 York and Durham militia in *Historic Fort York*, 50.

3. M – These totals are taken from muster and pay list referenced in full below.

4. P – Paroled men – The York Regiments made lists of men who had been paroled, properly and improperly, after the battle. Among the list of the 1st York are: an undated and unsigned list for the 1st York appears to have been done in the spring of 1814: A Return of Paroled Militia Officer, non-Commissioned Officers and Soldiers of the 1st Regiment York Militia surrendered Prisoners of War to the Americans at York, 27th April 1813, LAC, RG 9, IB7, 16: 32. Information for the 3rd York comes from the Return of Non Commissioned Officers and Privates of the 3rd Regiment of York Militia who were captured at York on the 27th April 1814 (sic), signed Chewett, 15 May 1814, LAC, RG 9, IB7, 16: 46; Return of Officers of the 3rd … who were surrendered by the capitulation at York on 27 April 1813, by Chewett, 15 May 1814, *ibid.*: 54.

5. VP – Voluntarily paroled – These men were suspected of having volunteered to be taken prisoner by the Americans on 28 April and after, as per: The 1814 list of prisoners in the 1st York identified six men as "sought his parole, a bad subject," A Return of Paroled Militia

Officers, ..., LAC, RG 9, IB7, 16: 32; Return of the Officers of the 3rd Regiment of York Militia who were obliged to surrender, or were taken prisoner at York, being surrounded by the Enemy on the 28th, 29th, 30th April 1813, signed by Chewett, York, 15 May 1814, *ibid.*: 42; Return of Privates of the 3rd Regiment York Militia, who were taken prisoner after the 28th April 1813, by Chewett, 15 May 1814, *ibid.*: 44; Men who "surrendered themselves or put themselves in the way of being made prisoners, all supposed to be disaffected persons," were listed on a return of the 3rd York, by Chewett, 15 May 1814, *ibid.*: 38: A court of inquiry, held on 4 July 1814 by officers of the 3rd York identified these men of having "put themselves in the way of being made prisoners," LAC, RG 9, IB1, 3: unpaginated.

6. POW – The single list of prisoners (other than regulars) taken at Little York found in an American source contained nearly 100 names. Spelling made identification difficult and only those that reasonably match names from the British and Canadian sources (about half the list) were identified here, "List of Prisoners of War Paroled/exclusive of Regulars at the taking of Little York," undated, unsigned, grouped with "List of British Prisoners after taking Fort George, May 1813," USNA, RG 98, Entry 57, Ninth Military District and Northern Army, 1812-1816, Miscellaneous Records, 1812-1816. See Appendix 9, Capitulation.

7. C – Most of the prisoners named were officers in the Terms of Capitulation Entered into on the 27th April 1813, ..., by Mitchell, Conner, *et al.*, LAC, MG 11, CO 42, 354: 121.

8. Terms of Capitulation, LAC, MG 11, CO 42, 150: 163. American estimates of the numbers who got their paroles: 500 – Dearborn to Armstrong, 3 May 1813, USNA, RG 107, M 221, 52: unpaginated; 1000 – John Scott to Thompson, 17 May 1813, New Jersey Historical Society, MG 1044, Captain John Scott Letters; 1200 – Beaumont, *Formative Years*, 47.

9. D – Disaffected – Most of these men were listed as suspected of having looted and acted in a disaffected manner during the 1813 investigation, T. Ridout *et al* to de Rottenburg, 29 September 1813, LAC, RG 5, A 1, 16: 6563. Several of them were identified by William Allan to Baynes, 3 August 1813, LAC, RG 8, I, 688c: 84. Others were named in a deposition given by former Sergeant Cutter, 1st York, as having "secreted and carried off the Stores belonging to the crown," attached to Chewett to Coffin, 8 January 1817, LAC, RG 9, IB7, 5: unpaginated.

10. W – Wilmot's retreat – Major Samuel Wilmot joined Sheaffe's retreat with Captain John Fenwick, five sergeants and ten privates, some from other companies in the 1st York, as shown in the Muster Roll and Pay List of a Detachment of the 1st Regiment of York Miltia under the Command of Major Wilmot retreating with the Army to Hamilton (Cobourg, Ontario) Court House from the 27th April to the 13th May 1813 inclusive, by Fenwick, undated, [part of 1814 documents] LAC, RG 9, IB7, 16: 98.

11. Richardson – Muster Roll and Pay List of Captain Reuben Richardson's Company of the 1st Regiment of York Militia, 25 March to 24 April 1813, LAC, RG 9, IB7, 18: 424-25. Also see: Muster Roll and Pay List of Captain Reuben Richardson's Company of the 1st Regiment of York Militia, 25 April to 27 April 1813, *ibid.*, 16: 111, 20: 68, which lists only commissioned and non commissioned officers and the note: "37 Privates ... The whole taken prisoners at the Battle of York never Mustered nor paid,

being stationed on actual service at York," by R. Richardson and Muster Roll and Pay List for 25 January to 24 February 1813, *ibid.*, 20: 71.

12. P. Robinson – Muster Roll and Pay List of Captain Peter Robinson's Company of the 1st Regiment of York Militia, 10 to 24 April 1813, LAC, RG 9, IB7, 18: 439-40. Some names taken from Muster Roll of Captain Robinson's Rifle Company attached to the 1st Regiment of York Militia from the 25th October 1812 to the 24th November 1812, signed by Robinson, *ibid.*, 16: 57-58. See also data for: 25 November to 24 December 1812, *ibid.*, 18: 212; 25 December 1812 to 24 January 1813, *ibid.*: 310; 25 to 31 January, *ibid.*, 16: 67. Although Andrew Borland was shown as discharged on 31 January 1813, he was present and wounded during the battle.

13. Willson – Muster Rolls and Pay Lists of Captain John Willson's Company of the 1st Regiment of York Militia: 9 to 15 September 1812, LAC, RG 9, IB7, 20: 41; 25 November to 24 December, *ibid.*, 18: 232 and 20: 27; 25 December 1812 to 24 January 1813, *ibid.*, 18: 314 and 20: 30; 25; 25 January to 24 February, *ibid.*, 20: 33; 25 February to 24 March, *ibid.*: 37 and 59; 25 March to 24 April 1813, *ibid.*, 18: 420 and 420-1, 20: 33-4, 37-8, 59-60, plus other lists in volume 20. Although Matthias Saunders did not appear on any of the musters reviewed, Willson certified that he had been a private in the company at the time he received his wound, LAC, RG 5, A 1, 19: 7839.

14. Fenwick – Muster Roll and Pay List for a company of the 1st Regiment of York Militia embodied at York at a General Call from the 27th to the 29th April 1813, inclusive, [Pringle commanding], LAC, RG 9, IB7, 20: 139. See also lists for Fenwick, 16 to 20 October 1812, *ibid.*: 134; 10 to 17 November, *ibid.*: 137. Wilmot – Muster Roll and Pay List of a Detachment of the 1st Regiment of York Miltia under the Command of Major Wilmot retreating with the Army to Hamilton (Cobourg, Ontario) Court House from the 27th April to the 13th May 1813 inclusive, LAC, RG 9, IB7, 16: 98. Oyster was not with the retreat, although he was listed in Fenwick's company in *ibid.*, 20: 137, A Detachment looking for deserters, 10-17 November 1812, and the 1814 POW list.

15. Selby – Muster Rolls and Pay Lists of Captain Thomas Selby's Company of the 1st Regiment of York Militia: 1 July–24 October 1812, LAC, RG 9, IB7, 20: 90; 25 November–24 December, *ibid.*, 18: 216 and 20: 94; 23 May–27 June 1813, 20: 98.

16. Button – Muster Roll and Pay Lists of Captain John Button's Company of Cavalry of the 1st Regiment of York Militia, 25 November to 24 December 1812, LAC, RG 9, IB7, 20: 324; 25 March to 24 April 1813, *ibid.*, 18: 413; 25 April to 24 May, *ibid.*: 463; 25 May to 24 June, *ibid.*: 486.

17. The only relevant muster and pay lists for Captain James Arnold is for 25 to 31 October 1812, LAC, RG 7, IB7, 18: 109 and 120.

18. No company records were found for Captain James Mustard during 1812 and 1813.

19. Hawley was court martialed on charges of giving himself up against the advice of his superiors and found guilty, Militia General Order, 16 June 1818, LAC, RG 9, IB7, 2: 167.

20. Cameron – Muster Rolls and Pay Lists of Captain Duncan Cameron's Company of the 3rd Regiment of York Militia: 25 November to 24 December 1812, LAC, RG 9, IB7, 18: 220; 25 January to 24 February 1813, *ibid.*, 17: 72; 25 February to 24 March, *ibid.*: 135, 138 and 141; 25 March to 24 April, 1813, LAC, RG 9, IB7, 17: 135-6 and

18: 427. Additional POW names are from Return ... by
Chewett, 15 May 1814, York, LAC, RG 9, IB7, 16: 46-53.
The transferred men all appeared as paroled in the 1814
lists. They have been listed here with the 1814 captains,
although they might have been Cameron's company at
the time of the battle.

21. Ridout – Muster Roll and Pay Lists of Captain Sam
Ridout's Company of the 3rd Regiment of York Militia,
25 November to 24 December 1812, LAC, RG 9, IB7, 18:
234 and 17: 152; 25 December to 24 January 1813, *ibid.*, 18:
316 and 17: 162; 25 February to 24 March, *ibid.*, 17: 187;
25 March to 24 April, *ibid.*, 18: 430. George Denison was
named as an ensign on the Capitulation list, which he
might have been promoted to by 27 April.

22. J. B. Robinson – Muster Roll and Pay Lists of Captain
Thomas Hamilton's and Captain John Beverley Robinson's Company of the 3rd Regiment of York Militia,
25 November to 24 December 1812, LAC, RG 9, IB7, 18:
236 and 17: 204; 25 December to 24 January 1813, *ibid.*,
18: 318 and 17: 204; 25 February to 24 March, *ibid.*, 17:
222 and 225; 25 March to 24 April, 18: 437-8; Return, 4
April, *ibid.*, 17: 24a. Daniel Murray's name did not appear on any of this company's lists, but Thomas Hamilton certified that he was killed while in his company,
2 December 1813, LAC, RG 9, IB4, 2: 4.

23. Denison – A Return of Non Commissioned Officers
and Privates of the 3rd Regiment York Militia who were
captured at York on the 27th April 1814 (sic), York, 15
May, Chewett, LAC, RG 9, IB7, 16: 46-53. For VP, see
Return of the Officers ... and Return of Privates ...,
by Chewett, 15 May 1814, *ibid.*: 42, 44 and Inquiry, 4
July 1814, LAC, RG 9, 1B1, 3: unpaginated and Return of
"disaffected", 3rd York, by Chewett, 15 May 1814, LAC,
RG 9, IB7, 16: 38. A number of privates from this latter
group had been mustered with other companies as of
24 April but, by the time the 1814 lists were made, they
had been moved to Denison's. For simplicity sake, their
parole record is shown only here. No records for Denison's company in 1812 and 1813 were found.

24. Heward – Besides the sources for P, VP, etc., noted
above, see records of Heward's company: 25 November to 24 December 1812, LAC, RG 9 IB7, 18: 225 and
17: 81; 25 December to 24 January 1813, *ibid.*, 17: 87; 25
January to 24 February, *ibid.*, 17: 93.

25. Thompson – Besides the sources for P, VP, etc., noted
above, no records for Thompson's company for 1812
and 1813 were found.

26. John Playter's officers from Return of the 3rd Regiment
of York Militia, 24 March 1813, LAC, RG 9, 1B7, 16: 12.

27. Although Detlor's name does not appear on any of the
reviewed militia records from this period, Chewett and
Allan certified that he was an ensign with the 3rd York
when he was killed, 17 November 1813, LAC, RG 9, IB4,
2: 8.

28. Yonge Street Company officers from Return of the 3rd
Regiment of York Militia, 24 March 1813, LAC, RG 9,
1B7, 16: 12.

29. Town Company officers from Return of the 3rd Regiment of York Militia, 24 March 1813, LAC, RG 9, 1B7, 16:
12.

30. Whitby Company officers from Return of the 3rd Regiment of York Militia, 24 March 1813, LAC, RG 9, 1B7, 16:
12.

31. Durham – Muster Roll and Pay List of Captain John
Burn's Company of the 1st Regiment of Durham Militia, 25 November to 24 December 1812, LAC, RG 9, IB7,
18: 230; 25 December to 24 January 1813, *ibid.*: 312; 25
March to 24 April, *ibid.*: 434.

32. Jarvie – Muster Roll and Pay Lists of Captain William
Jarvie's Company of Incorporated Militia, 25 March to
24 August 1813, LAC, RG 9, IB7, 18: 416, 466, 488 and
537.

33. Jarvis – Muster Roll and Pay Lists of Lieutenant William Jarvis's Company of Incorporated Militia, 25
March to 24 April and 25 May to 24 July 1813, LAC, RG
9, IB7, 18: 415, 465, 487, 510.

34. T. Ridout *et al* to de Rottenburg, 29 September 1813,
LAC, RG 5, A 1, 16: 6563. Several of them were identified
by William Allan to Baynes, 3 August 1813, LAC, RG 8, I,
688c: 84.

35. Deposition given by former Sergeant Cutter, 1st York,
as having "secreted and carried off the Stores belonging
to the crown", attached to Chewett to Coffin, 8 January
1817, LAC, RG 9 1-B-1, 5: unpaginated.

**Appendix 6: American Order of Battle at York, 27 April
1813**

1. Chauncey to Jones, 1700 on 28 April 1813, USNA, RG
45, M 125, 28: 63 and 1800 to Jones on 22 April, *ibid.*:
30. Pearce, "A Poor But Honest Sodger," 135. Dearborn
to Armstrong on 23 April 1813, USNA, RG 107, M 221,
roll 52: unpaginated. Dwight, "'Plow-Joggers for Generals,'" 18. Beaumont, *Formative Years*, 16. Eustis to to
W. Eustis, 11 May 1813, *Proceedings of the Massachusetts
Historical Society*, 11 (1869-70): 492. Trowbridge to John
Trowbridge, May 1814, "Two Letters."

2. The exact strength of the American artillery is unclear.
The best anecdotal information includes the following: Fraser mentioned the Third's field gun and howitzer and an artillery battery under Eustis to "D ...
..." [William Duane?], May 1813, *The Weekly Register*,
5 June 1813; Anonymous American Officer A reported
Fanning's howitzer and a 6-pdr. Pike referred to two
pieces of Fanning's and Eustis's train supported by his
own infantry in the Brigade Order by Jones, 25 April
1813, *DHC*, 5: 162. Eustis only mentioned that six pieces
of artillery were embarked, adding that two 12-pdrs.
and one 6-pdr. [apparently Fanning's] was brought
into action to W. Eustis, 11 May 1813, *Proceedings of the
Massachusetts Historical Society*, 11 (1869-70): 492-5;
two 6-pdrs. and 4 12-pdrs. were mentioned in the British Citizens' Account, TRL, Papers Relating to the Capitulation.

3. Staff and Volunteers – Staff participation is confirmed
by various reports, including: Dearborn to Armstrong,
3 May 1813, USNA, RG 107, M 221, 52: unpaginated.
Conner to Armstrong, 4 May 1813, USNA, RG 107,
M 221, 51: 153. Fraser to "D ... ..." [William Duane?],
May 1813, *The Weekly Register*, 5 June 1813. Chauncey to
Jones, 28 April 1813, USNA, RG 45, M 125, 28: 63. Officer-Volunteers were noted in: Lieutenants Benjamin
K. Pierce and Charels M. Macomb and one private, all
of the Third Artillery, accompanied Mitchell, as stated
in Monthly report of strength of the Northern Army
under the command of Genl. J. Chandler for the month
of April, 1813, USNA, RG 94. Armstrong was involved in
collection of public funds after the battle, E. Derenzy to
Coffin, 25 June 1813, LAC, RG 9, 1B1, 1814, 2: 25.

4. Sixth Infantry – This data taken from Sixth Infantry
musters and pay lists, USNA, RG 94: Box 262C, Captain
Humphreys, 31 December 1812 to 31 July 1813; Box 262A,
Captain Muhlenberg, 31 December 1812 to 31 July 1813;
Box 263, Captain Sadleir, 28 February to 31 July 1813;
and Box 263E, Captain Walworth, 31 December 1812 to
31 July 1813.

5. Walworth to Simonds, 6 May 1813, LAC, MG 24, F 16,

Jonas Simonds Papers, 1813, 1814. Beaumont, *Formative Years*, 44.

6. Fourteenth Infantry – This data taken from Fourteenth Infantry musters and pay lists, USNA, RG 94: Box 341A, Captain Grindage, 12 October 1812 to 30 December 1813 and 31 December 1812 to 1 March 1813. The field and staff officers are taken from *ASP: MA*, 1: 398.

7. Dwight, "'Plow-Joggers for Generals,'" 17-19. Return of force at Sackets Harbor, 1 March 1813, NYSL, 9962, Macomb Orderly Book, 220.

8. Fifteenth Infantry – This data taken from Fifteenth Infantry musters and pay lists, USNA, RG 94: Box 343, Pay Roll of the Field and Staff of the Sixteenth Regiment of Infantry from 28 February to 30 June 1813; Box 343E, Captain Hunter, 31 December 1812 to 30 June 1813; Box 344, Captain Rossell, 31 December 1812 to 30 June 1813; Box 344, Captain Scott, 31 December 1812 to 30 June 1813; Box 344A, Captain Van Dalsem, 1 January to 28 February 1813, July to December 1813; Box 344B, Captain Youngs, 30 June to 31 July 1812, 31 December 1812 to 28 February 1813, 31 August to 30 November 1813.

9. New Jersey Historical Society, MG 1044, Captain John Scott Letters. Dwight, "'Plow-Joggers for Generals,'" 17-19.

10. Sixteenth Infantry – This data taken from Sixteenth Infantry musters and pay lists, USNA, RG 94: Box 345G, Pay Roll of the Field and Staff of the Sixteenth Regiment of Infantry commanded by Colonel Cromwell Pearce for March and April 1813; Box 346A, Captain Steele, 28 February–30 June 1813; Box 346B, Lieutenant Machesney, 28 February–30 June 1813. (Note: Machesney was promoted to captain on 13 March 1813 (*HRD*, 1: 668), and apparently assumed command after Steele was captured at the Battle of Stoney Creek, 6 June 1813, as noted in the rolls); Box 346A, Captain Lyon, 1 October 1812 to 28 February 1813; Boxes 345 and 345D, Captain McEwen, 1 January to 28 February 1813 and 28 February to 30 June 1813 (this latter list included most of the men from Lyon's company, suggesting that McEwen took command of them after Lyon's death).

11. Twenty-first Infantry – This data taken from Twenty-first Infantry musters and pay lists, USNA, RG 94: Box 357, Pay Roll of the Field and Staff of the Sixteenth Regiment of Infantry commanded by Lieutenant Colonel E. W. Ripley for March through June 1813; Box 357C, Captain Grafton, January and February 1813, March to June 1813, July and August 1813. The General Order by Hunter, 19 April 1813, First Brigade Order Book, Taliafera Papers, Minnesota Historical Society, shows that 250 of the Twenty-first were expected to embark. A thorough search of regimental documents at the USNA revealed that only the men listed here were probably present at York. As pointed out in note 20 of Chapter 10, the details of Hunter's order conflicted with an order by Chauncey on the day before the battle.

12. Rifles – This data taken from Rifle Regiment musters and pay lists, USNA, RG 94: Box 131A, Captain Forsyth, 31 August to 30 December 1812, Captain Smyth, 31 December to 30 November 1813. The General Order by Hunter, 19 April 1813, First Brigade Order Book, Taliafera Papers, Minnesota Historical Society, shows that 250 of the Rifles were expected to embark. The same research and conflict mentioned in note 11 above applies to this data also.

13. Dwight, noted 150 riflemen in "'Plow-Joggers for Generals,'" 18. Scott said there were 200 to Thompson, 17 May 1813, New Jersey Historical Society, MG 1044, Captain John Scott Letters. Trowbridge reported 300

to John Trowbridge, May 1814, "Two Letters."

14. Third Artillery – This data taken from Third Artillery musters and pay lists, USNA, RG 94: Boxes 47A and 48, Captains Brooks and Fanning, April to June 1812, 30 June to 31 August 1812, 1 January to 30 June 1813, September to November 1813; Box 47A, Pay Roll of the Field and Staff of the Third Regiment of Artillery commanded by Colonel Alexander Macomb, 1 January to 31 August 1813. Only those men listed at Niagara are shown here, some of whom might not have been with the expedition to York.

15. Light Artillery – This data taken from Light Artillery musters and pay lists, USNA, RG 94: Boxes 102 B, Captain Andrew McDowell, 1 March to 30 June 1813 and June 1813; Box 100A, A. Eustis, 31 October to 31 December 1810 and 28 February to 30 April 1811 and Marie Boisaubin, March and April 1812. Boisaubin was Eustis's lieutenant on the previous drafts and some of their men appeared in McDowell's company. Lieutenant Gates (probably John Jr., possibly William) was assigned to Eustis's detachment just before embarkation as per the brigade order of 22 April 1813 in Orderly Books of the Adjutant at Sackets Harbor, USNA, RG 98, Entry 42.

16. W. Eustis, 11 May 1813, *Proceedings of the Massachusetts Historical Society*, 11 (1869-70): 492-5. Dwight, "'Plow-Joggers for Generals,'" 18. Pearce, "A Poor But Honest Sodger," 135. Conner to Armstrong, 4 May 1813, USNA, RG 107, M 221, 51: 153. Beaumont, *Formative Years*, 16. American Anonymous A, at Niagara, 9 May 1813, published in the *United States Gazette*, 24 May 1813, *DHC*, 5: 213. Scott to Thompson, 17 May 1813, New Jersey Historical Society, MG 1044, Captain John Scott Letters. Brigade Order by Jones, 25 April 1813, *DHC*, 5: 162.

17. Warner to his wife, 19 April 1812, Thomas Warner Letters, Flag House, Baltimore.

18. McClure's Volunteers – This data taken from McClure's Volunteers musters and pay lists, NYSA, AGO, B0811: Box 9, Folders 2 and 6, Payrolls for Field and Staff of Francis McClure's Volunteer Regiment, September 1812 to 30 September 1813. Also see Box 9, Folders 4, 5 and 6 for the other companies in McClure's regiment of volunteers.

19. Albany Greens – This data taken from musters and pay lists, NYSA, AGO, B0811: Box 7, Folder 10 and Box 9, Folder 6, James Maher's company of Francis McClure's Volunteer Regiment, Oct. 1812 to 30 April 1813.

20. Baltimore Volunteers – This data taken from musters and pay lists, NYSA, AGO, B0811: Box 9, Folders 2 and 3, Stephen H. Moore's company of Francis McClure's Volunteer Regiment, Oct. 1812 to 30 Sept. 1813.

Appendix 7: United States Navy Squadron, April 1813

1. Trowbridge to John Trowbridge, "Two Letters...." Beaumont, *Formative Years*, 16. Sheaffe to Prevost, 5A and 5B May 1813, LAC, MG 11, CO 42, 354: 132 and 119. John Beikie to John Macdonell, 5 May 1813, AO, F 548, John Macdonell Fonds. Citizens' Account, TRL, Papers Relating to the Capitulation Strachan to Brown, 26 April/14 June 1813, and Strachan to Richardson, 10 May 1813, AO, F 983, Strachan Fonds.

2. Chauncey's orders to his commanders, 23 April 1813, WCL, CLB and to Nichols, 22 April 1813, *ibid*. Use of the *Gold Hunter* is in Chauncey to Smith, 30 April 1813, *ibid*. He reported his strength as 430 to Hamilton, 6 November 1812, USNA, RG 45, M 125, 25: 168. Notes showing 165 seamen and marines arrived on 8 November and 42 more arrived on 19 November 1812, are with

the muster of the *Oneida*, USNA, RG 45, T 829A, roll 17. The force was weakened by illness but there were still about 550 seamen and marines fit for duty in April 1813 besides the 150 of Perry's detachment listed in a return by Hambleton, 24 February 1813, USNA, RG 45, M 148, 11: 21 and the 50 of W. Chauncey's detachment mentioned in Chauncey to Jones, 12 March 1813, *ibid.*, M 125, 27: 39. Chauncey describes his crew strength in his answer to Chandler's offer, 18 April 1813, WCL, CLB and his plans to Pettigrew, 19 April 1813, *ibid.* The July report was A Return of Vessels of War, by Chauncey, 18 July 1813, *ibid.* The small number of marines shown on the musters is due to illness as Chauncey mentioned to Jones that only 39 of the 100 or so marines were mustered early in March and that 16 of the men died in March alone, 5 and 22 March 1813, USNA, RG 45, M 125, 27: 13 and 74.

3. A Return of Vessels of War, by Chauncey, 18 July 1813, WCL, CLB. The additional guns for the *Scourge* are mentioned in *Myers*, 75.

4. The casualty list was A Return of Killed and Wounded … in the attack on York …, by Chauncey, 29 May 1813, in the 10 June 1813 issue of the *National Intelligencer*. In addition to the individual documents found in the USNA, RG 45, T 829A, the following crew lists were based on material in *SROLO*, Gibson, *Service Records of U.S. Navy and Marine Corps Officers Stationed on Lake Ontario During the War of 1812.* 27 March 1812, "An act to provide a Naval Armament,"3rd Congress, Session 1, Chapter 12, *Public Statutes at Large of the United States of America*, 1 : 350; 21 April 1806, "An act in addition to an [supplementary naval] act, ….". 9: 1: 35, 2: 390; 30 March 1812, "An act concerning the Naval Establishment." 12: 1: 47, 2: 699.

5. *Asp* – This data taken from Muster and Pay Lists for the U.S. Schooner *Asp*, February–December 1813, USNA, RG 45, T829A, Rolls 13, 18, 193 and 194.

6. *Conquest* – This data taken from Muster and Pay Lists for the U.S. Schooner *Conquest*, August 1812–December 1813, USNA, RG 45, T829A, Rolls 15, 193 and 194 and Lake Ontario Squadron Muster, November 1812, *ibid.*, Roll 17.

7. *Fair American* – This data taken from Muster and Pay Lists for the U.S. Schooner *Fair American*, August 1812– December 1813, USNA, RG 45, T829A, Rolls 14, 16, 18, 193 and 194 and Lake Ontario Squadron Muster, November 1812, *ibid.*, Roll 17.

8. *Governor Tompkins* – This data taken from Muster and Pay Lists for the U.S. Schooner *Governor Tompkins*, November 1812–December 1813, USNA, RG 45, T829A, Roll 15 and Lake Ontario Squadron Muster, November 1812, *ibid.*, Roll 17.

9. *Growler* – This data taken from Muster and Pay Lists for the U.S. Schooner *Growler*, August 1812–August 1813, USNA, RG 45, T829A, Roll 15 and Lake Ontario Squadron Muster, November 1812, *ibid.*, Roll 17.

10. *Hamilton* – This data taken from Muster and Pay Lists for the U.S. Schooner *Hamilton*, August 1812–August 1813, USNA, RG 45, T829A, Rolls 15, 193 and 194 and Lake Ontario Squadron Muster, November 1812, *ibid.*, Roll 17.

11. *Julia* – This data taken from Muster and Pay Lists for the U.S. Schooner *Julia*, August 1812–December 1813, USNA, RG 45, T829A, Roll 16 and Lake Ontario Squadron Muster, November 1812, *ibid.*, Roll 17.

12. *Lady of the Lake* – This data taken from Muster and Pay Lists for the U.S. Schooner *Lady of the Lake*, April–December 1813, USNA, RG 45, T829A, Rolls 16, 193 and 194.

13. *Madison* – This data taken from Muster and Pay Lists for the U.S. Ship *Madison*, and the rest of the squadron, August 1812–August 1813, USNA, RG 45, T829A, Rolls 13-18, 193 and 194. The list presented here is more speculative than the other squadron compliments as the data regarding the *Madison*'s complement at the end of April 1813 proved to be the most difficult to gather, sort out and synthesize with certainty.

14. *Oneida* – This data taken from Muster and Pay Lists for the U.S. Brig *Oneida*, June 1811–December 1813, USNA, RG 45, T829A, Roll 17.

15. *Ontario* – This data taken from Muster and Pay Lists for the U.S. Schooner *Ontario*, August 1812–December 1813, USNA, RG 45, T829A, Rolls 14, 18, 193 and 194 and Lake Ontario Squadron Muster, November 1812, *ibid.*, Roll 17.

16. *Pert* – This data taken from Muster and Pay Lists for the U.S. Schooner *Pert*, February–August 1813, USNA, RG 45, T829A, Rolls 16, 193 and 194 and Lake Ontario Squadron Muster, November 1812, *ibid.*, Roll 17.

17. *Raven* – This data taken from Muster and Pay Lists for the U.S. Schooner *Raven*, February–August 1813, USNA, RG 45, T829A, Roll 18, 193 and 194.

18. *Scourge* – This data taken from Muster and Pay Lists for the U.S. Schooner *Scourge*, February–August 1813, USNA, RG 45, T829A, Rolls 18, 193 and 194 and Lake Ontario Squadron Muster, November 1812, *ibid.*, Roll 17.

Appendix 8: Casualties and Prisoners of War

1. Clausewitz, *On War*, 277.

2. Sheaffe to Prevost, 30 April 1813, LAC, RG 8, I, 678: 198. Sheaffe to Prevost, 5A and 5B May 1813, LAC, MG 11, CO 42, 354: 132 and 119. District General Order by Leonard, 13 May 1813, *DHC*, 5: 227. Dearborn to Armstrong, 3 May 1813, USNA, RG 107, M 221, 52: 144. Conner estimated 300 killed and wounded and 400 POWs to Armstrong, 4 May 1813, *ibid.*, 51: 153.

3. The first terms of capitulation signed at Crookshank's house on 27 April (an original copy is held by the TRL, York, U.C., Papers Relating to the Capitulation) did not list any POWs. The second set of terms, complete at the garrison on 28 April, eventually listed names and numbers and virtually identical copies of it were widely published and are held by the Canadian and American archives: LAC, MG 11, CO 42, 150: 163; USNA, RG 45, M 125, 28: 64. See Appendix 9 for transcriptions of these documents.

4. Return of Militia Killed in the Action of the 27th April 1813 at York, Signed by S. Jarvis, Assistant Adjutant General, Militia, no date, LAC, RG 9, IB7, 16: 56A. See files in *ibid.*, 1B4, 1 and 2, and notes in *The Report of the Loyal and Patriotic Society of Upper Canada* and Gray, *Soldiers of the King*. To simplify the data, the volunteers McLean and Bassell were included with the militia, although Bassell's status as a prisoner is unknown.

5. Sheaffe to Prevost, 5A May 1813, LAC, MG 11, CO 42, 354: 132.

6. A return stated "the number known to be killed there were – Two – and Missing about Eighteen, several of which were inhabitants of the Town of York," return enclosed with Daverne to Loring, 7 June 1813, LAC, RG 5, A1, 17: 7362. "I … succeeded in destroying the Ship and stores … [and] lost several men," Plucknett to Richmond, 14 October 1818, LAC, RG 8, I, 189: 42.

7. Return of the [Regular] Prisoners belonging to His Majesty's regular Forces on Parole to the United States Army at York, by Jarvis, 1 May 1813, LAC, RG 5, A1, 17:

7292. See Appendix 9 for a transcription of this document.

8. Return of prisoners belong to His Majesty's regular forces now on parole at York, all of whom are wounded except five: no date, signed by Glegg, *DHC*, 5: 229.

9. Return of sick in the hospital at York, 4 June 1813, by Lee, LAC, RG 5, A1, 17: 7347.

10. Casualties in a detach't of the 8th or King's Regt. stationed at York in Upper Canada when that place was captured by the Americans, 27th April, signed by J.B. Glegg, Brigade Major, *DHC*, 5: 215.

11. A Nominal List of the Killed, Wounded, Prisoners and Missing of the Troops Engaged at York under the command of Sir Roger Hale Sheaffe on the 27th Ulto, and summaries of the same, by Leonard, 10 May 1813, LAC, MG 11, CO 42, 354: 123-25. Leonard signed a second nominal list, dated 10 May, which had several slight variations, LAC, RG 8, I, 695: 192.

12. The development of this data involved cross checking casualty information the report by Leonard, 10 May 1813, LAC, MG 11, CO 42, 354: 123-25, mentioned above, with the following regimental records: Muster and Pay Rolls for 4th Battalion of the Royal Regiment of Artillery January–June 1813, companies of Major William Holcroft and Captains John Sinclair and Peter Wallace, NAUK, WO10, 976; Pay List of the Forty-Ninth Regiment of Foot from 25th of December 1812 to 24th of March 1813, both dates inclusive and from 25th of March to 24th of June 1813, both dates inclusive, NAUK, WO 12, 6044; Pay-List of the Royal Newfoundland Regiment of Fencible Infantry from 25 March to 24 June 1813, both days inclusive, NAUK, WO12, 11027; Return of non-commissioned officers, drummers, fifers and privates who have died, deserted, transferred to another regiment or been invalided home, 25 December 1812–24 June 1813, NAUK, WO25, 2206; Pay Lists of the Glengarry Light Infantry Regiment of Fencibles, from 25 December 1812 to 24 September 1813, NUAK, WO 12, 10800; Johnston, *The Glengarry Light Infantry, 1812-1816*; Pay-List of the 1st Battalion of the 8th or King's Regiment of Infantry from 23 March to 24 June 1813, both days inclusive, NAUK, WO12, 2575; Return of non-commissioned officers, drummers, fifers and privates who have died, deserted, transferred to another regiment or been invalided home, 25 December 1812–24 June 1813, NAUK, WO 25, 1549.

13. Dearborn to Armstrong, 28 April 1813, USNA, RG 107, M 221, 52: 125. Trowbridge suggested 40 KIA and 200 WIA in Trowbridge, "Two Letters," while Beaumont gave 60 KIA and 300 WIA in *Formative Years*, 46 and Dwight reckoned 300-400 in Dwight, "'Plow-Joggers for Generals,'" 18. [Powell A], *DHC*, 5: 175. Reports of casualties appeared in numerous newspapers such as the issues of 25 May 1813, the *American Daily Advertiser* and 13 August 1813, *The New York Evening Post*.

14. Dearborn to Armstrong, 3 May 1813, USNA, RG 107, M 221, 52: 144. Pearce claimed that Hunter made his report to him first in "A Poor But Honest Sodger," 138.

15. Pearce noted his wound in "A Poor But Honest Sodger," 138. Ripley's wound was mentioned in Anonymous, "Biographical Memoir of Major-General Ripley," 115.

16. USNA, RG 94, M 1832, Returns of Killed and Wounded in Battle or Engagements with Indians and British and Mexican Troops, 1790-1848, Compiled by Lieutenant Colonel Joseph Horace Eaton (Eaton's Compilation).

17. Chauncey to Jones, 28 April 1813, USNA, RG 45, M 125, 28: 63.

18. Newspaper accounts: 6 May 1813, *American Daily Advertiser*; 1 June 1813, *Centinel of Freedom*; 12 June 1813, *The Weekly Register.*

19. For the squadron musters and pay lists see Appendix 7. This data incorporates the names on A Return of Killed and Wounded … in the attack on York …, by Chauncey, 29 May 1813, in the 10 June 1813 issue of the *National Intelligencer.*

Appendix 9: The Terms of Capitulation

1. Newspapers in which the terms were published include: 15 May 1813 issue of *The Weekly Register*; 21 May 1813 issue of *The Statesman*; 22 June issue of the *Kingston Gazette*. The terms have been key sources used in: Hannay, *The History of the War of 1812*, 141-2; Kingsford, *The History of Canada*, 258; Cruikshank, *DHC*, 5: 164, which contains several misspellings, notably Jarvis for Jarvie; Sheppard, *Plunder, Profit and Paroles*, 79-80.

2. "At length the following articles were agreed upon, after much altercation … When two copies had been signed this gentleman [Major William King] took them away and promised to return in a few minutes with the ratification," Citizens' Account, TRL, Papers Relating to the Capitulation.

3. Ely Playter's diary entry for 29 and 30 April 1813, AO, F 556.

4. Terms of Capitulation … 27 April 1813, TRL, York, U.C., Papers Relating to the Capitulation.

5. Terms of Capitulation … 28 April 1813, LAC, RG 8, I, 695: 57. Copies are found in other archival records, such as: TRL, York, U.C., Papers Relating to the Capitulation; LAC, MG 11, CO 42, 150: 163; USNA, RG 45, M 125, 28: 64.

6. Return of the Prisoners …1 May 1813, LAC, RG 5 A1, 17: 7292.

7. Return of Sick in Hospital at York, 4 June 1813, LAC, RG 5 A1, 17: 7347.

Captions to Pictures

1. Richard Cartwright to Isaac Todd, 14 October 1793, Cruikshank, *The Correspondence of Lieut. Governor John Graves Simcoe*, 2: 87.

2. Strachan to Prevost, October 1812, Spragge, *Strachan: 1812-1834*, 12.

3. Anne Powell to George Murray, 31 March 1807, TRL, L 16, Powell Papers, Mrs. Powell's letters, A 93.

4. Prevost to Liverpool, 14 April 1812, LAC, MG 11, CO 42, 146: 134.

5. The excerpt from the 1809 letter is quoted in Sabine, *Biographical Sketches*, 2: 289.

6. Sheaffe to Powell, 20 December 1812, *DHC*, 5: 20.

7. Madison to Dearborn, 7 October 1812, Stagg, *The Papers of James Madison*, 5: 371.

8. Chauncey to Hamilton, 8 October 1812, USNA, RG 45, M125, 25: 106.

9. Armstrong to Eustis, 2 January 1812, Armstrong, *Notices of the War*, 1: 234.

10. Jones to Chauncey, 27 January, USNA, RG 45, M 149, 10: 231.

11. Mitchell's assignment is noted in a general order by Shaw, 30 March 1813, LAC, RG 9, IB3, 2: 75.

12. Anonymous, "Biographical Memoir … Pike," 382.

13. Anonymous, "Biographical Memoir … Ripley," 114.

14. McLean to Stewart, 11 January 1813, AO, MU 2036, F 895, Folder 8.

15. Adam and Mulvany, *History of Toronto*, 2: 27.

Bibliography

PRIMARY SOURCES: UNPUBLISHED

Archives of Ontario, Toronto
F 43, Thomas Ridout Family Fonds
F 44, John Beverley Robinson Papers
F 548, John Macdonell Fonds
     Beikie Letters
F 556, Ely Playter Fonds, 1801-1853
F 775, Miscellaneous Collection
     MU 2143, Folder 10, Brock Estate papers
F 895, Miscellaneous Military Records
     MU 2036, Folder 8, Donald McLean letter
F 983, John Strachan Fonds
MU 4198, John Fisher Papers, *The Niagara Bee*
MS 199(5), Isaac Wilson Diaries, 1811-1845
RG 22-94,0,2, Minute Book, York County Court of General Sessions of the Peace

Chicago History Museum
Zebulon Pike Papers

City of Toronto Archives

City of Toronto Culture, Museum and Heritage Services
X.3019.1, Fort York Account Book, vol. 1, December 1812–June 1815

The Flag House and Star-Spangled Banner Museum, Baltimore
2004.2, Thomas Warner Letters

Historical Society of Pennsylvania, Philadelphia
Biographical memoir of Colonel Cromwell Pearce

Jefferson County Historical Society, Watertown, N.Y.

Library and Archives of Canada, Ottawa
MG 11, CO 42, Original Correspondence, Secretary of State, Lower and Upper Canada
MG 12 ADM 1, Secretary's Department, In Letters from Captains
MG 13, WO 17, Monthly Returns, Canada, 1808-1814
MG 24, F 16, [Walworth Letters] Jonas Simonds Papers
RG 5, A1, Civil Secretary's Correspondence, Upper Canada
RG 8, I, British Military and Naval Records, United States, War of 1812, 1806-1834
RG 9, 1B1, Department of Militia, Adjutant General's Office, Upper Canada Militia, Correspondence
RG 9, IB4, Department of Militia, Adjutant General's Office, Upper Canada Militia, Pension and Land Records
RG 9, IB7, Department of Militia, Adjutant General's Office, Upper Canada Militia, Proceedings of Medical Boards

RG 19 E5, Department of Finance. Upper Canada: War of 1812 Losses Claims

Library of Congress, Washington, D.C.
James Madison Papers, Series 1: General Correspondence
Amasa Trowbridge Papers

Lilly Library Manuscript Collection, University of Indiana, Bloomington
James Mann letter to Henry Dearborn, 6 July 1815

Minnesota Historical Society
Taliafera Papers, (Pike's) First Brigade Order Book

National Archives of the United Kingdom (Public Record Office), Kew
Home Office 45, 24746, Sir A. Scott Gatty, Garter Principle King of Arms, re: Colours
WO 10, 976, Muster and Pay Rolls, 4th Battalion of the Royal Regiment of Artillery
WO 12, Regimental Pay Lists: 2575, 1st Battalion, 8th Foot; 6044, 49th Foot; 10800, Glengarry Light Infantry; 11027, Royal Newfoundland Fencibles
WO 25, Casualty Returns: 1549, 1st Battalion, 8th Foot; 2206, Royal Newfoundland
WO 25, 748, Returns of Officers' Services

New Jersey Historical Society, Newark
MG 1044, Captain John Scott Letters

New York City Public Libraries: Humanities and Social Sciences Library

New York State Archives, Albany
B0811, Transcriptions of War of 1812 Payrolls for New York State Militia units, 1812-1815, New York (State) Adjutant General's Office

New York State Library, Albany
905, Daniel Parker letter, 18 May 1813
9962, Macomb Orderly Book, United States Army, Third Artillery Regiment, Orderly Book, 1812-1813
12914, Charles Kitchel Gardner Papers
14403, General Orders, 1802-1875, New York (State) Adjutant General's Office
17618, William Thomson Letter Book

Owen D. Young Library, St. Lawrence University, Canton, N.Y.
Daniel Hoard Letter Book
Parish-Rosseel Collection

Starsmore Center for Local History, Colorado Springs Pioneers Museum, Col.

Syracuse University Library, Syracuse, N.Y.
Manuscript Collections, MSS 64, Osborne Family Papers, Correspondence, Peter Pelham (1785-1826), Box 1

Toronto Reference Library
L 16, Powell Papers
S 108, Sir George Prevost Papers, Memorial Book
S 114, Wood, Alexander, Business Letter Books, vol. 3, 1810-22
York, Upper Canada, Papers Relating to the Capitulation, April 27–May 8 1813
    [Powell to Dearborn], 30 April 1813
    Pinkney to [Powell], 30 April 1813
    Declaration regarding civil control, 3 May 1813
    Citizens' Account, by Strachan, *et al*, 8 May 1813

United States National Archives and Records Administration, Washington, D.C.
RG 21, Records of Federal District Courts of the United States
    M 886, Minutes and Rolls of Attorneys … New York
    M 919, Admiralty Case Files for the Southern District
    M 928, Prize and related records for the War of 1812, Southern District of New York, 1812-1816, First Series
RG 45, Naval Records Collection
    M 125, Letters Received by the Secretary of the Navy from Captains
    M 147, Letters Received by the Secretary of the Navy from Masters Commandant
    M 148, Letters Received by the Secretary of the Navy from Officers Below Command and from Warrant Officers
    M 149, Letters Sent by the Secretary of the Navy to Officers
    M 273, Records of Courts Martial and Courts of Inquiry of the Navy Department
    T 829, 829A, Miscellaneous Records of the Navy Department; Secretary of the Navy's Private Letter Book; Musters and Paylists, Lake Ontario Vessels
RG 59, General Records of the Department of State, War of 1812 Papers, Miscellaneous, M 588, Intercepted Correspondence
RG 77, Civil Works, Map File
RG 94, Records of the Adjutant General's Office, 1780's-1917
    Muster Rolls of Regular Army Organizations
    Monthly report of strength of the Northern Army under the command of Genl. J. Chandler for the month of April, 1813
    M 566, Letters Received by the Adjutant General
    M 1832 Returns of Killed and Wounded in Battle or Engagements with Indians and British and Mexican Troops, 1790-1848, Compiled by Lieutenant Colonel Joseph Horace Eaton (Eaton's Compilation).
RG 98, Records of the United States Army Commands
    Entry 42, Ninth Military District and Northern Army, 1812-1814. Second Division, 1812-13. Orderly Book of the Adjutant at Sackett's Harbor, September 1812-September 1813
    Entry 57, Ninth Military District and Northern Army, 1812-1814. Miscellaneous Records, 1812-16. Lists of British prisoners after taking Fort George, May 1813
    Entry 176, Records of Units. 6th Regiment, 1811-1815. Letters sent and received, June 1811-October 1813

RG 107, Records of the Office of the Secretary of War
    M 6, Letters Sent by the Secretary
    M 221, Letters Received by the Secretary of War, Registered Series
RG 217, Records of the Accounting Officers of the Department of the Treasury
    Entry 810, Miscellaneous Letters
    Entry 811, Settled Accounts of Navy Paymaster and Pay Agents, 1798-1915 (4th Auditor's Settled Accounts, Alphabetic Series, Chauncey, Isaac)

William Clements Library, University of Michigan, Ann Arbor
Chauncey Letter Books, September 1812–August 1813
Joseph Bloomfield and Zebulon M. Pike Letterbook, February–April 1813

PRIMARY SOURCES: PUBLISHED

American State Papers: Military Affairs. Washington, D.C.: Gales and Seaton, 1832, vol. 1.
American State Papers: Naval Affairs. Washington D.C.: Gales and Seaton, 1834, vol. 1.
Annals of Congress. Debates and Proceedings of the Congress of the United States. Washington, D.C.: Gales and Seaton, 1854.
Anonymous [American]. "The First Campaign of An A.D.C.." *Military and Naval Magazine of the United States,* 1 (1833): 153-62, 257-67; 2 (1833-34): 10-20, 73-82, 200-10, 278-88; 3 (1834): 258-66, 329-38, 437, 446; 4 (1834): 26-34; 5 (1835): 85-93, 253-61.
Anonymous ["Saucy Tom"]. *A Soldier of the Seventy-first: The Journal of a Soldier of the Highland Light Infantry, 1806-1815.* Edited by Christopher Hibbert. Warren, Mich.: Squadron/Signal Publications, 1976.
Armstrong, John. *Notices of the War of 1812.* New York: General Dearborn & Wiley and Putnam, 1840, 2 vols.
Baldwin, William W. "A Recovered Letter: W. W. Baldwin to C. B. Wyatt, 6th April, 1813." Edited by J. McE. Murray. *Ontario History,* 35 (1943): 49-55.
Beaumont, William. *Wm. Beaumont's Formative Years: Two Early Notebooks, 1811-1821.* Edited by Genevieve Miller. New York: Henry Schuman, 1964. In *The Career of William Beaumont and The Reception of His Discovery,* edited by I. Bernard Cohen, i-xv, 1-87. New York: Arno Press, 1980.
Bisshopp, Cecil. "The Bisshopp Papers during the War of 1812." Edited by Robert S. Allen. *Journal of the Society for Army Historical Research,* 61 (1983): 22-9.
Brock, Isaac. "District General Orders of Maj.-Gen. Sir Isaac Brock from June 27th, 1812–Oct. 16th 1812." *Transactions of the Women's Canadian Historical Society,* No. 19 (1920), 5-48.
Commins, James. "The War on the Canadian Frontier, 1812-14. Letters Written by Sergt. James Commins, 8th Foot." Edited by Norman Lord. *Society for Army Historical Research,* 17 (1939): 199-211.
Cooper, John Spencer. *Rough Notes of Seven Campaigns in Portugal, Spain, France and American During the Years 1809-1815.* Staplehurst, UK: Spellmount, 1996.
Coyne, James H., ed. *The Talbot Papers ….* Transactions of the Royal Society of Canada, 1909.
Crawford, William J. ed. *The Naval War of 1812: A Docu-*

mentary History. Washington, D.C.: Naval Historical Center, 2002, Vol. 3.

Crooks, James. "Recollections of the War of 1812." *Niagara Historical Society*, No. 28 (Niagara-on-the-Lake, Ont., 1916), 28.

Cruikshank, E. A., ed. *The Documentary History of the Campaign upon the Niagara Frontier 1812-1814*. Welland, Ont.: Lundy's Lane Historical Society, 1896-1908, 9 vols.

— . *Documents relating to the Invasion of Canada and the Surrender of Detroit, 1812*. Ottawa: Government Printing Bureau, 1912.

— . *The Correspondence of Lieut. Governor John Graves Simcoe* …. Toronto: Ontario Historical Society, 1923, 5 vols.

— and A. F. Hunter, eds. *The Correspondence of the Honourable Peter Russell* …. Toronto: Ontario Historical Society, 1932, 3 vols.

Duane, William. "Letters of William Duane, communicated by Worthington C. Ford." *Proceedings of the Massachusetts Historical Society*. Second Series, 20, 1906-07, 257-394.

Dudley, William S. ed. *The Naval War of 1812: A Documentary History*. Washington, D.C.: Naval Historical Center, 1985, 1992, Vols. 1 and 2.

Dwight, Joseph Hawley. "'Plow-joggers For Generals': The Experiences of a New York Ensign in the War of 1812." Edited by John C. Fredriksen. *Indiana Military History Journal*, 11 (1986): 16-27.

Dyneley, Thomas. *Letters Written by Lieut.-General Thomas Dyneley, C.B., R.A., While on Active Service between the Years 1806 and 1815*. Arranged by F. A. Whinyates. London: Ken Trotman, 1984.

Elliott, Jesse Duncan. *Correspondence in Relation to the Capture of the British Brigs* Detroit *and* Caledonia *on the night of October 8, 1812*. Philadelphia: United States Book and Job Printing, 1843.

Eustis, Abraham. A. Eustis to his uncle, former Secretary of War William Eustis, 11 May 1813. *Proceedings of the Massachusetts Historical Society*, 11 (1869-70): 492-5.

Finan, P. *Journal of a Voyage to Quebec in the year 1825: with recollections of Canada during the late American war in the year 1812-13*. Newry, Ireland: Peacock, 1828.

Firth, Edith G., ed. *The Town of York, 1793-1815*. Toronto: Champlain Society, 1962.

—. *The Town of York, 1815-1834*. Toronto: Champlain Society, 1966.

Ford, Paul L. *The Works of Thomas Jefferson*. New York: G.P. Putnam's Sons, 1905, 12 vols.

Fraser, Donald. Fraser to D … … [William Duane?], May 1813. *Niles Weekly Register*, 5 June 1813.

Fuller, George N., ed. "Documents Relating to Detroit and Vicinity, 1805-1813." *Michigan Historical Collections*, 40, Lansing: Michigan Historical Commission, 1929.

Hanks, Jarvis. "The Memoir of Drummer Jarvis Frary Hanks." In *Soldiers of 1814: American Enlisted Men's Memoirs of the Niagara Campaign*, edited by Donald E. Graves, 18-49. Youngstown, N.Y.: Old Fort Niagara Association, 1995.

Hennell, George. *A Gentleman Volunteer: The Letters of George Hennell form the Peninsular War, 1812-13*. Edited by Michael Glover. London: Heinemann, 1979.

Hunt, Gaylord, ed. *The Writings of James Madison*. New York: Knickerbocker Press, 1908, 9 vols.

Jarvis, Stephen. "Narrative of Colonel Stephen Jarvis." In *Loyalist Narratives from Upper Canada*, edited by James Talman, 149-266. Toronto: Champlain Society, 1946.

Journal of the Executive Proceedings of the Senate of the United States of America. Washington, D.C., 1828, vol. 2.

Journal of the House of Assembly of Upper Canada. Ninth Report of the Bureau of Archives for the Province of Ontario. 1912. Toronto: Cameron, 1913.

Journal of the House of Representatives of the United States. Washington, D.C., 1826, vols. 8 and 9.

Journal of the Senate of the United States of America. Washington, D.C., 1821, vols. 5 and 6.

Journals of the Legislative Assembly of Upper Canada for the Years 1792-94, 1798-1804. Toronto: Ontario Archives, 1909, vol. 1.

Knowlton, Minor. "An American Spy's Report on Fort George, 1840." Edited by Carl Benn. *The York Pioneer*, 98 (2003): 18-22.

Lawrence, William. *The Autobiography of Sergeant William Lawrence, a Hero of the Peninsular and Waterloo Campaigns*. Edited by George Nugent Bankes. London: Sampson Low, Marston, Searle and Rivington, 1886.

Le Couteur, John. *Merry Hearts Make Light Days. The War of 1812 Journal of Lieutenant John Le Couteur, 104th Foot*. Edited by Donald E. Graves. Ottawa: Carleton University Press, 1993.

List of the Officers of the [British] *Army and* [Royal] *Marines* …. London: C. Roworth, 1790-1815.

Malcomson, Robert, ed. *Sailors of 1812: Memoirs and Letters of Naval Officers on Lake Ontario*. Youngstown, N.Y.: Old Fort Niagara Association, 1997.

Mattern, David B., ed. *James Madison's "Advice to My Country."* Charlottesville: University Press of Virginia, 1997.

McDonogh, Patrick, "A Hero of Fort Erie: Letters relating to the Military Service, Chiefly on the Niagara Frontier, of Lieutenant Patrick McDonogh." Edited by Miss O'Reilly. *Publications of the Buffalo Historical Society*, 5 (1901).

McFeely, George. "Chronicle of Valor: The Journal of a Pennsylvania Officer in the War of 1812." Edited by John C. Fredriksen. *Western Pennsylvania Historical Magazine*, 67 (1984): 243-84.

McMullen, Alexander. "The Narrative of Alexander McMullen, a Private Soldier in Colonel Fenton's Regiment of Pennsylvania Volunteers." In *Soldiers of 1814: American Enlisted Men's Memoirs of the Niagara Campaign*, edited by Donald E. Graves, 60-79. Youngstown, N.Y.: Old Fort Niagara Association, 1995.

Meriwether, Robert L., ed. *The Papers of John C. Calhoun*. Columbia: University of South Carolina Press, 1959, 10 vols.

Merritt, William Hamilton. "Merritt's Journal, 1812-1815." In *Select British Documents of the Canadian War of 1812*. Edited by William Wood. Toronto: Champlain Society, 1920, 1923, 1926, 1928, 3 vols.

Merritt, William Hamilton. *A Desire of Serving and Defending my Country": The War of 1812 Journals of Wil-*

liam Hamilton Merritt. Edited by Stuart Sutherland. Toronto: Iser Publications, 2001.

"Minutes of the Court of General Quarter Sessions of the Peace for the Home District, 1800-1811." Twenty-First Report of the Department of Public Records and Archives of Ontario. Edited by Alexander Fraser. Toronto: Herbert H. Ball, 1933.

Moore, Stephen. Letter to his brother, 5 May 1813. In Official Letters of the Military and Naval Officers of the United States during the War with Great Britain in the Years 1812, 13, 14 and 15 with some additional letters and documents elucidating the history of that period. Collected by John Brannan. Washington: Way and Gideon, 1823.

Myers, Mordecai. Reminiscences 1780 to 1814 Including Incidents in the War of 1812-14. Washington, D.C.: Crane, 1900.

Myers, Ned. Ned Myers; or A Life Before the Mast. Edited by James Fenimore Cooper. Philadelphia: Lea and Blanchard, 1843. Reprint, Annapolis: Naval Institute Press, 1989.

Norton, John. The Journal of Major John Norton, 1816. Edited by Carl F. Klinck and James J. Talman. Toronto: The Champlain Society, 1970.

Pearce, Cromwell. "'A Poor but Honest Sodger': Colonel Cromwell Pearce, the 16th U.S. Infantry and the War of 1812." Edited by John C. Fredriksen. Pennsylvania History 52 (1985): 131-61.

Pike, Zebulon. The Journals of Zebulon Montgomery Pike with Letters and Related Documents. Edited by Donald Jackson. Norman: University of Oklahoma, 1966, 2 vols.

Preston, Richard A., ed. Kingston Before the War of 1812: A Collection of Documents. Toronto: Champlain Society, 1959.

Public Statutes at Large of the United States of America …. Boston: Little and Brown, 1845, vol. 2.

Ridout, Thomas. Ten Years of Upper Canada in Peace and War, 1805-1815; being the Ridout Letters. Edited by Matilda Ridout Edgar. Toronto: William Briggs, 1890.

Roach, Isaac. "Journal of Major Isaac Roach, 1812-1824." Pennsylvania Magazine, 17 (1893): 129-315.

Robertson, J. Ross, ed. The Diary of Mrs. John Graves Simcoe …. Toronto: William Briggs, 1911. Reprint, Toronto: Prospero, 2001.

Rudman, Michael J. "The History of These Graves." The York Pioneer, 94 (1999): 17-28.

Schedule or Table of Fees and Costs, Payable to the Different Officers of the Quarter Sessions of the Peace … for The London District. London: 1839.

Scott, John. "The Letters of Captain John Scott, 15th U.S. Infantry: A New Jersey Officer in the War of 1812." Edited by John C. Fredriksen. New Jersey History. 107 (1989): 61-81.

Scott, Winfield. Memoirs of General Scott, Written by Himself. New York: Sheldon, 1864, 2 vols.

Sheaffe, Roger Hale. "Letter Book of Gen. Sir Roger Hale Sheaffe" Publications of the Buffalo Historical Society, 17 (1913), 271-381.

Sheaffe, Roget Hale to Bishop Jacob Mountain, May 1813. Edited by T. R. Millman. "Roger Hale Sheaffe and the Defence of York, April 27, 1813." Canadian Church Historical Review Journal, 5 (1963): 6-8.

Spragge, George W., ed. The John Strachan Letter Book: 1812-1814. Toronto: Ontario Historical Society, 1946.

Stagg, J. C. A. et al, ed. The Papers of James Madison, Presidential Series. Charlottesville: University of Virginia Press, 1984-2004, 5 vols.

The statutes of the province of Upper Canada : together with such British statutes, ordinances of Quebec, and proclamations, as relate to the said province. Kingston, Ont.: Thomson and MacFarlane, 1831.

Tompkins, Daniel. Public Papers of Daniel D. Tompkins, Governor of New York 1807-1817. Edited by Hugh Hastings, Albany, N.Y.: J.B. Lyon, 1902, 3 vols.

Trowbridge, Amasa. "Two Letters About the War of 1812." Edited by Francis Bacon Trowbridge, 537-8. The Trowbridge Genealogy. History of the Trowbridge Family in America. New Haven, Conn.: Tuttle, Morehouse and Taylor, 1908.

"Truth." Letter to the Anglo-American Magazine, 3 (December 1853), 565-6.

Tupper F. B., ed. The Life and Correspondence of Major-General Sir Isaac Brock, K.B. London: Simpkin, Marshall, 1845.

Wilkinson, James. Memoirs of My Own Times. Philadelphia: Abraham Hall, 1816, 3 vols.

Wood, William C. H., ed. Select British Documents of the Canadian War of 1812. Toronto: The Champlain Society, 1920-28, 3 vols.

York, John. "The Battle of Toronto Bay – War of 1812." In "Ojibwa Myths and Tales," edited by G.E. Laidlaw, 87-8. In Twenty-eighth Annual Archaeological Report, 1916, being part of the Appendix to the Report of the Minister of Education, Ontario by R.B. Orr. Toronto: A. T. Wilgress, 1916.

SECONDARY SOURCES

Reference Books

American National Biography. New York: Oxford, 1999, 25 vols.

Baillie, Laureen.ed., American Biographical Index. London: K.G. Saur, 1993.

Burney, William, ed.. Falconer's New Universal Dictionary of the Marine. 1815 edition. Reprint: London: Chatham Publishing, 2006.

Dictionary of Canadian Biography. Toronto: University of Toronto, 1976-88, vols. 5–9.

Dictionary of National Biography. London: Smith, Elder, 1885, 65 vols.

Gibson, Gary M. Service Records of U.S. Navy and Marine Corps Officers Stationed on Lake Ontario During the War of 1812. Sackets Harbor, N.Y.: Sackets Harbor Battlefield Alliance, 2005.

Heidler, David S. and Jeanne T. Heidler, eds. Encyclopedia of the War of 1812. Santa Barbara, Cal.: ABC-CLIO, 1997.

Heitman, Francis B., ed. Historical Register and Dictionary of the United States Army from its Organization, September 29, 1789 to March 2, 1903. Washington: 1903. Reprint, Baltimore: Genealogical Publishing, 1994.

James, Charles. A New and Enlarged Military Dictionary …. London: T. Egerton, 1802.

Malcomson, Robert. Historical Dictionary of the War of

1812. Lanham, Md.: Scarecrow Press, 2006.

Sabine, Lorenzo. *Biographical Sketches of Loyalists of the American Revolution ….* Kennikat Press: Port Washington, N.Y., 1864, 2 vols.

Smith, George. *An Universal Military Dictionary: A Copious Explanation of the Technical Terms, etc., Used in the Equipment, Machinery, Movements and Military Operations of an Army.* London: J. Millan, 1779. Reprint, Ottawa, Ont.: Museum Restoration Service, 1969.

Sutherland, Stuart. *His Majesty's Gentlemen: A Directory of Regular British Army Officers of the War of 1812.* Toronto: Iser Publications, 2000.

General Titles

Adam, G.M. and C.P. Mulvany. *History of Toronto and County of York, Ontario: containing an outline of the history of the Dominion of Canada; a history of the City of Toronto and the County of York, with the townships, towns, villages, churches, schools; general and local statistics; biographical sketches, et., etc… .* Toronto: C.B. Robinson, 1885, 2 vols.

Adye, Ralph Willett. *The Bombardier and Pocket Gunner.* London: T. Egerton, fourth edition, 1804.

Anonymous. *The Letters of Veritas Republished from the Montreal Herald; containing a Succinct Narrative of the Military Administration of Sir George Prevost, During his Command in The Canadas.* Montreal: W. Gray, 1815.

Anonymous. *Some Account of the Public Life of the late Lieutenant-General Sir George Prevost, Bart., …* [from] *An Article in the Quarterly Review for October, 1822.* London: T. Cadell and T. Egerton, 1823.

Armstrong, Frederick H. *Handbook of Upper Canadian Chronology and Territorial Legislation.* London, Ontario: University of Western Ontario, 1967.

Armstrong, John. *Hints to Young Generals by an Old Soldier.* Kingston: J. Buel, 1812.

Babcock, Elkanah. *A War History of the Sixth U.S. Infantry from 1798 to 1903, …* Kansas City: Hudson-Kimberley, 1903.

Babcock, Louis L. *The War of 1812 on the Niagara Frontier.* Buffalo: Buffalo Historical Society, 1927.

Beer, Donald R. *Sir Allan Napier MacNab.* Hamilton: Dictionary of Hamilton Biography, Inc., 1984.

Beirne, Francis F. *The War of 1812.* Hamdon, Conn.: Archon Books, 1965.

Benn, Carl. *The Battle of York.* Belleville, Ont: Mika, 1984.

—. *Historic Fort York: 1793-1993.* Toronto: Natural Heritage/Natural History, 1993.

—. *The Iroquois in the War of 1812.* Toronto: University of Toronto Press, 1998.

—. *The War of 1812.* Oxford: Osprey Publishing, 2002.

Birkhimer, William E. *Historical Sketch of the Organization, Administration, Matériel and Tactics of the Artillery, United States Army.* Washington: James J. Chapman, 1884. Reprint, New York: Greenwood Press, 1968.

Boorman, Sylvia. *John Toronto.* Toronto: Clarke, Irwin and Company, 1969.

Boulton, D'Arcy. *Sketch of His Majesty's Province of Upper Canada.* London: n. p., 1805. Reprint: Toronto: Baxter Publishing, 1961.

Brackenridge, H. M. *History of the Late War Between the United States and Great Britain, containing a Minute Account of the Military and Naval Operations.* Baltimore: Cushing and Jewett, 1818.

Brant, Irving. *James Madison: Commander-in-Chief, 1812-1836.* New York: Bobbs-Merrill, 1961.

Brereton, J. M. *A Guide to the Regiments and Corps of the British Army on the Regular Establishment.* London: Bodley Head, 1985.

Brigham, Clarence S. *History and Bibliography of American Newspapers.* Westport, Conn.: Greenwood Press, 1972, 2 vols.

Canney, Donald L. *Sailing Warships of the US Navy.* London: Chatham Publishing, 2001.

Canniff, William. *The Medical Profession in Upper Canada 1783-1850.* Toronto: William Briggs, 1894.

Cannon, Richard. *Historical Record of the Eighth or, The King's Regiment of Foot … to 1844.* London: Parker, Furnivall and Parker, 1844.

Carter-Edwards, Dennis. *At Work and Play: The British Junior Officer in Upper Canada, 1796-1812.* Ottawa: Parks Canada, 1985.

Chadwick, Edward Marion. *Ontario Families: Genealogies of United-Empire-Loyalist and other Pioneer Families of Upper Canada.* Toronto: Rolph, Smith and Co., 1895, 2 vols.

Chapelle, Howard. *The History of the American Sailing Navy: The Ships and Their Developments.* New York: Bonanza, 1949.

Chartrand, René. *Uniforms and Equipment of the United States Forces in the War of 1812.* Youngstown, N.Y.: Old Fort Niagara Association, 1992.

Chartrand, René and Gerry Embleton. *British Forces in North America: 1793-1815.* London: Osprey Publishing, 1998.

Chichester, Henry Manners and George Burges-Short. *The Records and Badges of Every Regiment and Corps in the British Army.* London: Gale and Porden, 1900.

Clausewitz, Carl Von. *On War.* Edited and translated by Michael Howard and Peter Paret. New York: Alfred A. Knopf, 1993.

Coates, Earl J. And James L. Kochan, art by Don Troiani. *Don Troiani's Soldiers in America, 1754-1865.* Mechanicsburg, Penn.: Stackpole Books, 1998.

Coffin, William F. *1812: The War and Its Moral: Canadian Chronicle.* Montreal: Lovell, 1864.

Coffman, Edward M. *The Old Army: A Portrait of the American Army in Peacetime, 1784-1989.* New York: Oxford University Press, 1986.

Collins, Gilbert. *Guidebooks to the Historic Sites of the War of 1812.* Toronto: Dundurn Press, 1998.

Crackell, Theodore J. *Mr. Jefferson's Army: Political and Social Reform of the Military Establishment, 1801-1809.* New York: New York University Press, 1987.

Cruikshank, E. A. *The Battle of Fort George.* Welland, Ont.: Tribune Print, 1904. Reprint, Niagara-on-the-Lake, Ont.: Niagara Historical Society, 1990.

—. *The Battle of Stoney Creek and the Blockade of Fort George, 1813.* Niagara Historical Society, No. 3, Niagara-on-the-Lake, Ont.: Times Book, 1917.

Cumberland, Frederick Barlow. *The Battle of York: An Account of the Eight Hours' Battle from the Humber Bay to the Old Fort and Defence of York on April 27, 1813.* Toronto: William Briggs, 1913.

Dale, Clare A. *"The Palaces of Government": A History of the Legislative Buildings of the Provinces of Upper Canada, Canada and Ontario, 1792-1992.* Toronto: Ontario Legislative Library, 1993.

Darke, Eleanor. *A Mill Should Be Build Thereon: An Early History of the Todmorden Mills.* Toronto: Natural Heritage, 1995.

Darling, Anthony D. *Red Coat and Brown Bess.* Alexandria Bay, N.Y.: Museum Restoration Services, 1991.

Deiterman, Frank A and Ronald F. Williamson. *Government on Fire: The History and Archaeology of Upper Canada's First Parliament Buildings.* Toronto: eastendbooks, 2001.

Desloges, Yvon. *Structural History of Fort George. History and Archaeology 3.* Ottawa: National Historic Parks and Sites Branch, Parks Canada, Environment Canada, 1980.

Duane, William. *A Hand Book For Riflemen containing the First Principles of Military Discipline ....* Philadelphia: the author, 1813.

Duncan, Major Francis. *History of the Royal Regiment of Artillery.* London: John Murray, 1879, 2 vols.

"Dundas's Regulations." *Rules and Regulations for the Formations, Field-Exercise, and Movements of His Majesty's Forces.* London: Adjutant Generals' Office, War Office; J. Walter, 1801.

Edgar, Matilda Ridout, ed. *Ten Years of Upper Canada in Peace and War, 1805-1815; being the Ridout Letters.* Toronto: William Briggs, 1890.

Egerton, Ryerson. *The Loyalists of America and their times: from 1620 to 1816.* Toronto: William Briggs, 1880, 2 vols.

Erney, Richard Alton. *The Public Life of Henry Dearborn.* New York: Arno Press, 1979.

Everest, Allan S. *The War of 1812 in the Champlain Valley.* Syracuse, N.Y.: Syracuse University Press, 1981.

Fardy, Bernard D. *Before Beaumont Hamel: The Royal Newfoundland Regiment, 1775-1815.* St. John's, Newfoundland: Creative Publishers, 1995.

Flint, David. *John Strachan: Pastor and Politician.* Toronto: Oxford University Press, 1971.

Fraser, Alexander. *Sixteenth Report of the Department of Archives for the Province of Ontario.* Toronto: Clarkson W. James, 1921.

Fraser, Robert L., ed. *Provincial Justice: Upper Canadian Legal Portraits.* Toronto: University of Toronto, 1992.

Fredriksen, John C. *Officers of the War of 1812 with Portraits and Anecdotes: The United States Army Left Division Gallery of Honor.* Lewiston, N.Y.: Edwin Mellen Press, 1989.

—. *Green Coats and Glory: The United States Regiment of Rifles, 1808-1821.* Youngstown, N.Y.: Old Fort Niagara Association, 2000.

Fremont-Barnes, Gregory. *The Napoleonic Wars: The Peninsular War 1807-1814.* London: Osprey Publishing, 2002.

Gardiner, Robert. *Frigates of the Napoleonic War.* London: Chatham Publishing, 2000.

Geeson, Jean Earle. *The Old Fort at Toronto: 1793-1906.* Toronto: William Briggs, 1906.

George, John N. *English Guns and Rifles; being an account of the development ... and users of these arms.* Plantersville, South Carolina: Small-Arms Technical Publishing, 1847.

Gilleland, J. C. *History of the Late War between the United States and Great Britain; containing an Accurate Account of the Most Important Engagements by Sea and Land.* Baltimore: Schaeffer and Maund, 1817.

Glazebrook, G. P. *The Story of Toronto.* Toronto: University of Toronto Press, 1971.

Glover, Richard. *Peninsular Preparation: The Reform of the British Army, 1795-1809.* Cambridge: Ken Trotman, 1988.

Godfrey, Sheldon and Judy. *Stones, Bricks and History: The Corner of "Duke and George", 1798-1984.* Toronto: Lester and Orpen Dennys, 1984.

Gooding, S. James. *An Introduction to British Artillery in North America.* Alexandria Bay, N.Y.: Museum Restoration Service, 1986.

Goodwin, Peter. *The Construction and Fitting of the English Man of War, 1650-1850.* London: Conway Maritime Press, 1987.

Gourlay, Robert. *Statistical Account of Upper Canada.* London: Simpkins and Marshall, 1822. Reprint: New York: Johnson Reprint Corporation, 1966, 2 vols.

Gray, Hugh. *Letters From Canada Written During a Residence There in the Years 1806, 1807 and 1808 ..* London: Longman, Hurst, Rees and Orme, 1809.

Gray, William. *Soldiers of the King: The Upper Canadian Militia, 1812-1815.* Erin, Ont.: Boston Mills, 1995.

Halliday, Hugh A. *Murder Among Gentlemen: A History of Duelling in Canada.* Toronto: Robin Brass Studio, 1999.

Hannay, James. *The History of the War of 1812 between Great Britain and the United States of America.* Toronto: Morang and Co., 1905.

Harding, D. F. *Smallarms of the East India Company, 1600-1856, Vol. 3: Ammunition and Performance.* London: Foresight Books, 1999.

Harland, John. *Seamanship in the Age of Sail.* Annapolis: Naval Institute Press, 1984.

Hathaway, E. J. *Jesse Ketchum and His Times.* Toronto: McClelland and Stewart, 1929.

Haythornthwaite, Philip J. *The Napoleonic Source Book.* New York: Facts on File, 1990.

—. *Weapons and Equipment of the Napoleonic Wars.* London: Arms and Armour, 1979.

—. *The Armies of Wellington.* London: Brockhampton Press, 1998.

Head, George. *Forest Scenes and Incidents in the Wilds of North America ....* London: John Murray, 1829.

Heriot, George. *Travels Through the Canadas ....* London, Richard Philips, 1807.

Hickey, Donald R. *The War of 1812: A Forgotten Conflict.* Urbana: University of Illinois Press, 1990.

—. *Don't Give Up the Ship! Myths of the War of 1812.* Toronto: Robin Brass Studio. 2006.

Hitsman, J. Mackay. *The Incredible War of 1812: A Military History.* Toronto: University of Toronto Press, 1965. Revised edition, Toronto: Robin Brass Studio, 1999.

Hollon, W. Eugene. *The Lost Pathfinder: Zebulon Montgomery Pike.* Norman: University of Oklahoma Press, 1949.

Holmes, Richard. *Redcoat: The British Soldier in the Age of*

Horse and Musket. London: Harper Collins, 2002.

Hough, Franklin B. *A History of Jefferson County in the State of New York from the Earliest Period to the Present Time.* Albany: Joel Munsell, 1854.

Houlding, J. A. *Fit For Service: The Training of the British Army, 1715-1795.* Oxford: Clarendon Press, 1981.

Hounsom, Eric Wilfrid. *Toronto of 1810.* Toronto: Ryerson Press, 1970.

Howison, John. *Sketches of Upper Canada, Domestic, Local and Characteristic, … and some Recollections of the United States of America.* London: Whittaker, 1821. Reprint: Toronto: Coles, 1980.

Hughes, B. P. *Firepower: Weapons Effectiveness on the Battlefield, 1630-1850.* New York: Charles Scribner's Sons, 1974.

—. *Open Fire: Artillery Tactics from Marlborough to Wellington.* Strettington, England: Antony Bird Publications, 1983.

Irving, L. Homfray. *Officers of the British Forces in Canada During the War of 1812-15.* Toronto: Canadian Military Institute, 1908.

Ivison, Stuart and Fred Rosser. *The Baptists in Upper and Lower Canada before 1820.* Toronto: University of Toronto Press, 1956.

Jackson, John Mills. *A View of the Political Situation of the Upper Canada in 1808.* The Author: Southampton, 1809.

James, William. *A Full and Correct Account of the Military Occurrences of the Late War between Great Britain and The United States of America.* London: the author, 1818, 2 vols.

Johnson, J. K., ed. *Historical Essays on Upper Canada.* Ottawa: McClelland and Stewart, 1975.

—. *Becoming Prominent: Regional Leadership in Upper Canada, 1791-1841.* Montreal and Kingston: McGill-Queen's University Press, 1989.

Johnson, Leo A. *A Pioneer Era In Vaughan Township.* No location: no publisher, *ca.* 1966.

Johnson, Michael G. and Richard Hook. *American Woodland Indians.* London: Osprey, 1990.

Johnston, Winston. *The Glengarry Light Infantry, 1812-1816: Who Were They and What Did They Do in the War?* Charlottetown, Prince Edward Island: Benson Publishing, 1998.

Katcher, Philip and Bryan Fosten. *The American War 1812-1814.* London: Osprey Publishing, 1990.

Keegan, John. *The Mask of Command.* London: Jonathan Cape, 1987.

Keele, W. C. *The Provincial Justice or Magistrate's Manual ….* Toronto: H. and W. Rowsell, 1843.

Kilbourn, William. *Toronto Remembered. A Celebration of the City.* Toronto: Stoddart, 1984.

Killan, Gerald. *Preserving Ontario's Heritage.* Ottawa: Love Printing, 1976.

Kingsford, William. *The History of Canada.* London: Kegan Paul, Trench Trübner and Co., 1895, vol. 8 of 10.

Laws, M. E. S. *Battery Records of the Royal Artillery, 1716-1859.* Woolwich: Royal Artillery Institute, 1952.

Lees, James. *The Masting and Rigging of English Ships of War, 1625-1860.* London: Conway Maritime Press, 1984.

Lewis, Berkeley R. *Small Arms and Ammunition in the United States Service.* Washington: Smithsonian Institute, 1956.

Lord, Walter. *The Dawn's Early Light.* New York: W.W. Norton, 1972.

Lossing, Benson. *The Pictorial Field-book of the War of 1812.* New York: Harper and Brothers, 1868.

Lucas, C.P. *The Canadian War of 1812.* Oxford: Clarendon Press, 1906.

Mahan, Alfred T. *Sea Power in its Relations to the War of 1812.* London: Sampson, Low, Marston and Co., 1905, 2 vols.

Mahon, John K. *The War of 1812.* Gainesville: University of Florida, 1972.

Malcomson, Robert. *Lords of the Lake: The Naval War on Lake Ontario, 1812-1814.* Toronto: Robin Brass Studio, 1998.

—. *Burying General Brock: A History of Brock's Monuments.* Niagara-on-the-Lake: The Friends of Fort George, 1996.

—. *Warships of the Great Lakes: 1754-1834.* London: Chatham Publishing, 2001.

—. *A Very Brilliant Affair: The Battle of Queenston Heights, 1812.* Toronto: Robin Brass Studio, 2003.

— and Thomas Malcomson. *HMS Detroit: The Battle for Lake Erie.* St. Catharines, Ont.: Vanwell Publishing, 1990.

Mann, James. *Sketches of the Campaigns of 1812, 1813, and 1814 to which are Added Surgical Cases; Observations on Military Hospitals; and Flying Hospitals Attached to a Moving Army.* Dedham, Massachusetts: H. Mann and Co., 1816.

Martyn, Lucy Booth. *The Face of Early Toronto: An Archival Record, 1797-1936.* Sutton West, Ontario: Paget Press, *ca* 1982.

Matthews, Richard K. *If Men Were Angels: James Madison and the Heartless Empire of Reason.* Lawrence: University of Kansas Press, 1995.

May, W. E. *The Boats of Men-of-War.* Annapolis: Naval Institute Press, 1999.

McAlexander, U. G. *History of the Thirteenth Regiment United States Infantry.* Regimental Press, Frank D. Gunn, 1905.

McConnell, David. *British Smooth-Bore Artillery: A Technological Study.* Ottawa: Parks Canada, 1988.

McKenna, Katherine M. J. *A Life of Propriety: Anne Murray Powell and her Family, 1755-1849.* Montreal and Kingston: McGill-Queen's University Press, 1994.

Miles, Henry H. *A School History of Canada prepared for Use in the Elementary and Model Schools.* Montreal: Dawson Brothers, 1870.

Mosser, Christine, ed. *York, Upper Canada Minutes of Town Meetings and Lists of Inhabitants, 1797-1823.* Toronto: Metropolitan Toronto Library Board, 1984.

Muir, Rory. *Tactics and the Experience of Battle in the Age of Napoleon.* New Haven, Conn.: Yale University Press, 1998.

Murray, David. *Colonial Justice: Justice, Morality, and Crime in the Niagara District, 1791-1849.* Toronto: University of Toronto Press, 2002.

Nicholson, G. W. L. *The Fighting Newfoundlander: A History of the Royal Newfoundland Regiment.* Ottawa: Government of Newfoundland, *ca* 1964.

O'Brien, Brendan. *Speedy Justice: The Tragic Last Voyage of His Majesty's Vessel* Speedy. Toronto: University of Toronto Press, 1992.

Owsley, Frank Lawrence, Jr. *Struggle for the Gulf Borderlands: The Creek War and the Battle of New Orleans, 1812-1815*. Gainesville: University of Florida Press, 1981.

Pack, James. *The Man Who Burned the White House: Admiral Sir George Cockburn, 1772-1853*. Annapolis: Naval Institute Press, 1987.

Petre, F. Loraine. *The Royal Berkshire Regiment (Princess Charlotte of Wales's), 49th Foot and 66th Foot*. Reading, England: The Regiment, 1925, 2 vols.

Pitch, Anthony S. *The Burning of Washington: The British Invasion of 1814*. Annapolis: Naval Institute Press, 1998.

Powell, William Dummer. *Letter from William Dummer Powell to His Excellency Sir Peregrine Maitland regarding the Appointment of Alexander Wood as a Commissioner for the investigation of claims ...*. York: the author, 1831.

Pratt, Fletcher. *Preble's Boys: Commodore Preble and the Birth of American Sea Power*. New York: William Sloane Associates, 1950.

Quaife, Milo M. *The Yankees Capture York*. Detroit: Wayne University Press, 1955.

Reid, William D. *Marriage Notices of Ontario*. Lambertville, New Jersey: Hunterdown House, 1980.

Reilly, Robert M. *United States Martial Firelocks: A Comprehensive Illustrated History of the Flintlock in American from the Revolution to the Demise of the System*. Lincoln, R.I.: Andrew Mowbray, 1986.

Reilly, Robin. *The British at the Gates: The New Orleans Campaign in the War of 1812*. New York: G.P. Putnam's Sons, 1974. Revised edition, Toronto: Robin Brass Studio, 2002.

Remini, Robert V. *The Battle of New Orleans*. London: Penguin Books, 1999.

The Report of the Loyal and Patriotic Society of Upper Canada with an Appendix and a List of Subscribers and Benefactors. Montreal: William Gray, 1817.

Riling, Joseph R., ed. *Baron Von Steuben and his Regulations*. Philadelphia: Ray Riling Arms Books, 1966.

Robertson, Robert Ross, ed. *Landmarks of Toronto: A Collection of Historical Sketches ...*. Toronto: Robertson, 1894-1914. Reprint: Belleville, Ont.: Mika, 1976, 6 vols.

Romney, Paul. *Mr Attorney: The Attorney General for Ontario in Court, Cabinet and Legislature, 1791-1899*. Toronto: University of Toronto Press, 1986.

Roosevelt, Theodore. *The Naval War of 1812*. New York: G.P. Putnam's Sons, 1882. Reprint, Annapolis: Naval Institute Press, 1987.

Scadding, Henry. *Toronto of Old*. Toronto: Adam, Stevenson and Co., 1873. Abridged and edited by F. H. Armstrong. Toronto: Oxford University Press, 1966.

—. *Toronto: Past and Present, Historical and Descriptive: A Memorial Volume for the Semi-Centennial of 1884*. Toronto: Hunter, Rose, 1884.

—. *Memoirs of Four Decades of York, Upper Canada*. Toronto: Hunter, Rose and Co., 1884.

—. *History of the Old French Fort at Toronto and its Monument*. Toronto: Copp Clark, 1887.

—. *The 8th King's Regiment: A Curiosity in its Annals*. Toronto: Copp, Clark and Co., 1894.

Sheaffe, Stephen. *The Sheaffe Family History*. Brisbane, Australia: the author, 1988.

Sheppard, George. *Plunder, Profit and Paroles: A Social History of the War of 1812 in Upper Canada*. Montreal and Kingston: McGill-Queen's University Press, 1994.

Shepperd, Alan. *The King's Regiment*. Reading, England: Osprey, 1973.

Silverstone, Paul H. *The Sailing Navy: 1775-1854*. Annapolis: Naval Institute Press, 2001.

Skaggs, David Curtis and Gerard T Altoff. *A Signal Victory: The Lake Erie Campaign, 1812-1813*. Annapolis: Naval Institute Press, 1997.

Skeen, C. Edward. *John Armstrong, Jr., 1758-1843: A Biography*. Syracuse, N.Y.: Syracuse University Press, 1981.

Skelton, William B. *An American Profession of Arms: The Army Officer Corps, 1784-1861*. Lawrence: University Press of Kansas, 1992.

Smith, Arthur Britton. *Legend of the Lake: The 22-Gun Brig-Sloop Ontario, 1780*. Kingston: Quarry Press, 1997.

Smyth, Alexander. *Regulations for the Field Exercise, Manoeuvres and Conduct of the Infantry of the United States: Drawn Up and Adapted to the Organization of the Militia and Regular Troops*. Philadelphia: Anthony Finley, 1812.

Spafford, Horatio G. *A Gazetteer of the State of New-York; ...*. Albany: H. C. Southwick, 1813.

Stacey, C. P. *The Battle of Little York*. Toronto: Toronto Historical Board, 1971.

Stacy, Nathaniel. *Memoirs of the Life of Nathaniel Stacy Preacher of the Gospel of Universal Grace*. Columbus, Pennsylvania: Abner Vedder, 1850.

Stagg, J. C. A. *Mr. Madison's War: Politics, Diplomacy, and Warfare in the Early American Republic, 1783-1830*. Princeton: Princeton University Press, 1983.

Stanley, George F. G. *The War of 1812: Land Operations*. Ottawa: Canadian War Museum, 1983.

Stevenson, D. Alan. *The World's Lighthouses Before 1820*. London: Oxford University Press, 1959.

Stewart, Charles H. *The Service of British Regiments in Canada and North America*. Ottawa: Department of National Defence Library, 1994.

Sugden, John. *Nelson, A Dream of Glory*. London: Jonathan Cape, 2004; Pimlico, 2005.

Summers, Jack L. and René Chartrand. *Military Uniforms in Canada: 1665-1970*. Ottawa: Canadian War Museum, 1981.

Swinson, Arthur, ed. *A Register of the Regiments and Corps of the British Army*. London: Archive Press, 1972.

Takakjian, Portia. *The 32-Gun Frigate Essex*. London: Conway Maritime Press, 1990.

Terrell, John Upton. *Zebulon Pike: The Life and Times of an Adventurer*. New York: Weybright and Talley, 1968.

Thompson, Austin Seton. *Spadina: A Story of Old Toronto*. Toronto: Pagurian Press, 1975.

—. *Jarvis Street: A Story of Triumph and Tragedy*. Toronto: Personal Library Publishers, 1980.

Threlfall, T. R. *The Story of the King's (Liverpool Regiment) Formerly the Eighth Foot*. London: George Newnes, 1916.

Trippler, Charles S. and George C. Blackman. *Handbook for the Military Surgeon.* Cincinnati: Robert Clarke and Co., 1861.

Tucker, Glenn. *Poltroons and Patriots: A Popular Account of the War of 1812.* New York: Bobbs-Merrill, 1954, 2 vols.

Tucker, Spencer. *Arming the Fleet: U.S. Navy Ordnance in the Muzzle-Loading Era.* Annapolis: Naval Institute Press, 1989.

Turner, Wesley. *British Generals in the War of 1812: High Command in the Canadas.* Montreal: McGill-Queen's University Press, 1999.

Webber, David A. *Skinner's Fencibles: The Royal Newfoundland Regiment, 1795-1802.* St. John's, Nfld.: Newfoundland Naval and Military Museum, 1964.

Whitehorne, Joseph A. *The Battle for Baltimore, 1814.* Baltimore: Nautical and Aviation Publishing, 1997.

Wilder, Patrick. *The Battle of Sackett's Harbour, 1813.* Baltimore: Nautical and Aviation Publishing, 1994.

Wise, Leonard and Allan Gould. *Toronto Street Names: An Illustrated Guide to their Origins.* Willowdale, Ont.: Firefly Books, 2000.

Wright, N. Hill. *Monody on the Death of Brigadier General Zebulon Montgomery Pike: and Other Poems.* Middlebury, Vt.: Slade and Ferguson, 1814.

Articles

"1813 Colours Offered to Fort York." *The Fife and Drum: Newsletter of the Friends of Fort York and Garrison Commons.* 11 (July, 2007): 1.

"Fort York Wins a Modern Battle." *Ontario History*, 51 (1959): 22-4.

Alcock, Donald G. "The best defence is … smuggling? Vermonters during the War of 1812," *Canadian Review of American Studies*, 25 (1995): 73-91.

Altoff, Gerard T. "The Perry-Elliott Controversy." *Northwest Ohio Quarterly*, 60 (1988): 135-52.

Anonymous. "Biographical Memoir of Major-General Ripley." *The Port Folio*, 6 (1815): 108-36.

Anonymous. "Biographical Memoir of the Late Brigadier General Zebulon Montgomery Pike." *The Analectic Magazine*, 4 (1814): 380-91.

Auchinleck, G. "History of the War …, Chapter X." *Anglo-American Magazine*, 3 (October 1853), 338-48.

Bellesiles, Michael A. "Experiencing the War of 1812." In *Britain and America Go to War: The Impact of War and Warfare in Anglo-America, 1754-1815.* Edited by Julie Flavell and Stephen Conway. Gainesville, Florida: University Press of Florida, 2004: 205-40.

Benn, Carl. "The Upper Canadian Press, 1793-1815." *Ontario History*, 70 (1978): 91-114.

—. "The Military Context of the Founding of Toronto." *Ontario History*, 81 (1989): 303-22.

—. "Bombproof Powder Magazines of the War of 1812 Period in Upper Canada." *Arms Collecting*, 29 (1991): 3-13.

—. "The Blockhouses of Toronto: A Material History Study." *Material History Review*, 42 (Fall 1995): 22-38.

—. "British Army Officer Housing in Upper Canada, 1784-1841." *Material History Review*, 44 (Fall 1996): 79-96.

—. "A Georgian Parish, 1797-1839." In *The Parish and Cathedral of St. James', Toronto, 1797-1997.* Edited by William Cooke. Toronto: University of Toronto Press, 1998: 3-37.

—. "Aboriginal population movements in southern Ontario, 1600-1800: a historian's perspective." In *Celebrating one thousand years of Ontario's history.* Toronto: Ontario Historical Society, 2001: 53-60.

—. "John Graves Simcoe, the birth of Ontario, and the frontier crisis of the 1790s." In *Celebrating one thousand years of Ontario's history.* Toronto: Ontario Historical Society, 2001: 257-64.

—. "The York Militia Colours." *The Fife and Drum: Newsletter of the Friends of Fort York and Garrison Commons.* 11 (July, 2007): 5-6.

Brant, Irving. "Timid President? Futile War?" *American Heritage: The Magazine of History*, 10 (1959): 46-7, 85-9.

Buano, Jose M. and René Chartrand. "Upper Canada Militia and Provincials, 1812-1815." *Military Collector and Historian*, 28 (1976): 14-16.

Canniff, William. "An Historical Sketch of th County of York …." *Illustrated Historical Atlas of the County of York …*. Toronto: Miles and Co., 1878, v-xiii.

Chartrand, René. "Uniforms of the Canadian Voltigeurs and the Glengarry Light Infantry, 1812-1816." *Military Collector and Historian*, 26 (1974): 14-18.

Chartrand, René. "Notes on the Uniforms of the British Indian Department." *Military Collector and Historian*, 29 (1979): 114-7, 141.

—. "British and Canadian Royal Artillery Drivers, 1812-1815." *Military Collector and Historian*, 56 (2004): 239-45.

Cruikshank, E.A. "The Royal Newfoundland Regiment." *Selected Papers from the Transactions of the Canadian Military Institute*, 5 (1893-94): 5-15.

—. "The Contest for the Command of Lake Erie in 1812 and 1813." *Transactions of the Royal Society of Canada*, 6 (1899): 359-86.

—. "General Hull's Invasion of Canada in 1812." *Proceedings and Transactions of the Royal Society of Canada*, Series 3, 1 (1907): 211-90.

—. "A Study of Disaffection in Upper Canada in 1812-15." *Transactions of the Royal Society of Canada.* Third Series, vol. 6, section 2 (1912): 11-43.

—. "Additional Correspondence of Robert Nichol." *Ontario History*, 26 (1930): 37-96.

—. "The 'Chesapeake' Crisis as it Affected Upper Canada." *Ontario History*, 24 (1927): 281-322.

—. "The Garrisons of Toronto and York, 1750-1815." *Selected Papers from the Transactions of the Canadian Military Institute*, 31 (1934-35): 17-65.

Cushman, Paul. "Naval Surgery in War of 1812." *New York State Journal of Medicine*, 72 (1972): 1881-7.

Douglas, W. A. B. "The Anatomy of Naval Incompetence: The Provincial Marine in Defence of Upper Canada Before 1813." *Ontario History*, 71 (1979): 3-25.

Douglas, W. A. B. "The Anatomy of Naval Incompetence: The Provincial Marine in Defence of Upper Canada Before 1813." *Ontario History*, 71 (1979): 3-25.

Drake, Frederick C. "Artillery and Its Influence on Naval Tactics: Reflections on the Battle of Lake Erie." In *War on the Great Lakes: Essays Commemorating the 175th Anniversary of the Battle of Lake Erie*, edited by William J. Welsh and David C. Skaggs, 17-29. Kent, Ohio: Kent State University Press, 1991.

Dudley, William S. "Commodore Isaac Chauncey and the U.S. Joint Operations on Lake Ontario, 1813-14." In *New Interpretations of Naval History: Selected Papers from the Eighth Naval History Symposium*, edited by William B. Cogar. Annapolis: Naval Institute Press, 1989: 139-155.

Eckert, Edward K. "William Jones: Mr. Madison's Secretary of the Navy." *The Pennsylvania Magazine of History and Biography*, 96 (1972): 167-82.

Eid, Leroy V. "'Their Rules of War': the Validity of James Smith's Summary of Indian Woodland War." *Register of the Kentucky Historical Society*, 86 (1988): 4-23.

—. "'A Kind of Running Fight': Indian Battlefield Tactics in the Late Eighteenth Century." *Western Pennsylvania Historical Magazine*, 71 (1988): 147-71.

Erickson, Arvel B. "Abolition of Purchase in the British Army." *Military Affairs*, 23 (1959): 65-76.

Errington, Jane. "Friends and Foes: The Kingston Elite and the War of 1812 – A Case Study in Ambivalence." *Journal of Canadian Studies*, 20 (1985): 58-79.

Ferguson, Allan J. "Trumpets, Bugles and Horns in North America." *Military Collector and Historian*, 36 (1984): 2-7.

Firth, Edith G. "Alexander Wood, merchant of York." *The York Pioneer*, 54 (1959): 5-29.

Fitzgibbon, Mary Agnes. "A Historic Banner." Transactions of the Women's Canadian Historical Society of Toronto, 1 (1896): 6-22.

Fredriksen, John C. "Green Coats and Glory: The United States Regiment of Rifles, 1808-1821: Parts 1 and 2." *Military Collector and Historian*, 50 (1998): 2-11, 58-64.

Fuller, J. F. C. "Sir John Moore's Light Infantry Instructions of 1798-1799." *Journal of the Society for Army Historical Research*, 30 (1852): 68-75.

Gero, Anthony F. and Philip G. Maples. "Notes on the Dress of the 13th Regiment, United States Infantry, 1812-1813." *Military Collector and Historian*, 38 (1986): 167-8.

Graves, Donald E. "The Second Regiment of United States Light Dragoons, 1812-1814." *Military Collector and Historian*, 34 (1982): 101-08.

—. "'Dry Books of Tactics': US Infantry Manuals of the War of 1812 and After, Parts I and II." *Military Collector and Historian*, 38 (1986): 50-61, 173-7.

—. "Field Artillery of the War of 1812: Equipment, Organization, Tactics and Effectiveness." *Arms Collecting*, 30 (1992): 39-48.

—. "American Ordnance of the War of 1812: A Preliminary Investigation." *Arms Collecting*, 31 (1993): 111-20.

Hathaway, Ernest J. "The River Credit and the Mississaugas." *Ontario History*, 26 (1930): 432-44.

Hatzenbuehler, Ronald L. "The War Hawks and the Question of Congressional Leadership in 1812." *Pacific Historical Review*, 45 (1976): 1-22.

Henderson, Robert. "Marching on Its Stomach: Diet and Messing Arrangements of the British Army in Upper Canada at the Opening of the War of 1812." *Military Collector and Historian*, 49 (1997): 175-81.

Hitsman, J. Mackay. "Sir George Prevost's Conduct of the Canadian War of 1812." *The Canadian Historical Association*, (1962): 34-43.

Hollon, E. W. "Zebulon Montgomery Pike and the York Campaign, 1813." *New York History*, 30 (1949): 259-75.

Humphries, C. W. "The Capture of York." *Ontario History*, 51 (1959): 1-21.

Innis, Mary Quayle. "The Industrial Development of Ontario, 1783-1820." In *Historical Essays on Upper Canada*, edited by J. K. Johnson, 140-52. Ottawa: McClelland and Stewart, 1975.

Johnson, Eric. "The Baltimore Volunteers: Maryland's elite militia company." *The Journal of the War of 1812*, 10 (2006): 5-9.

Johnson, Leo A. "Land Policy, Population Growth and Social Structure in the Home District, 1793-1851." In *Historical Essays on Upper Canada*, edited by J. K. Johnson, 32-57. Ottawa: McClelland and Stewart, 1975.

—. "The Mississauga-Lake Ontario Land Surrender of 1805." *Ontario History*, 83, (1990): 233-55.

Kerr, W. B. "The Occupation of York (Toronto), 1813." *Canadian Historical Review*, 5 (1924): 9-21.

Killan, Gerald. "First Old Fort York Preservation Movement, 1905-1909: An Episode in the History of the Ontario Historical Society." *Ontario History*, 64 (1972): 162-80.

—. "The York Pioneers and the First Old Fort York Preservation Movement." *The York Pioneer*, 68 (1973): 2-15.

Koke, Richard J. "The Britons who Fought on the Canadian Frontier: Uniforms of the War of 1812." *The New-York Historical Society Quarterly*, 45 (1961): 141-94.

Kosche, Ludwig. "Relics of Brock: An Investigation." *Archivaria*, 9 (1979), 33-103.

MacDonell, Angus Claude. "Address at the Brock Centenary, 1912." In *The Defended Border: Upper Canada and the War of 1812*, edited by Morris Zaslow. Toronto: Macmillan, 1964, 324-8.

MacLeod, Malcolm. "Fortress Ontario or Forlorn Hope? Simcoe and the Defence of Upper Canada." *Canadian Historical Review*, 53 (1972): 149-78.

Magill, M. L. "William Allan and the War of 1812." *Ontario History*, 64 (1972): 134-41.

Malcomson, Robert. "'The Crews of the British Squadron at Put-in-Bay: A Composite Muster Roll and Its Insights." *Inland Seas*, 51 (Spring, 1995): 16-29; (Summer, 1995): 43-56.

—. "'Not Very Much Celebrated:' The Evolution and Nature of the Provincial Marine, 1755-1813." *The Northern Mariner/Le Marin du nord*, 11 (2001): 25-37.

—. "'Nothing More Uncomfortable Than Our Flat-Bottomed Boats:' Batteaux in the British Service During the War of 1812." *The Northern Mariner/Le Marin du nord*, 13 (2003): 17-28.

—. "'Stars and Garters of an Admiral', American Commodores in the War of 1812." *The Northern Mariner/Le Marin du nord*, 16 (January 2006): 53-63.

—. "Silver Dollar Accuracy with a Musket?" *Strategy and Tactics*, #235 (2006): 25-6.

—. "Friendly Fire, War of 1812 Style." *Strategy and Tactics*, #236 (2006): 32-3.

—. "'Encamped on the Field of Mars': Van Rensselaer's Army on the Niagara, 1812." *Journal of Early American Wars and Armed Conflicts*, 1 (2006): 56-68.

—. "'Carry Michilimackinac at all hazards' How the capture of Michilimackinac affected American campaign plans in the War of 1812." *Inland Seas*, 62 (2006): 197: 206.

—. "Clubbed Victory at Queenston Heights." *MHQ, The Quarterly Journal of Military History*, 19 (Spring, 2007): 64-7.

McBarron, Hugh Charles. "American Military Dress in the War of 1812." *Journal of the American Military Institute*, 4 (1940): 55-64, 185-96.

—. "American Military Dress in the War of 1812." *Military Affairs*, 5 (1941): 138-144.

— and Delmar H. Finke. "United States Light Dragoons, 1808-1810." *Military Collector and Historian*, 32 (1980): 125.

McKenna, Katherine. "The Role of Women in the Establishment of Social Status." *Ontario History*, 83 (1990): 180-205.

Muller, H. N. III. "A 'Traitorous and Diabolical Traffic:' The Commerce of the Champlain-Richelieu Corridor during the War of 1812." *Vermont History*, 44 (1976): 78-96.

Murphy, Rowley. "Gibraltar Point Light." *Inland Seas*, 3 (1947): 150-4.

Nesbitt, Kelly. "'Nothing More of Less than Devils': Women of the Naval and Military Establishments of Upper Canada." In *Celebrating one thousand years of Ontario's history* (Toronto: Ontario Historical Society, 2001): 165-71.

Olsen, Michael L. "Zebulon Pike and American Popular Culture, or, Has Pike Peaked?" *Kansas History: A Journal of the Central Plains*, 29 (Spring 2006): 48-59.

Otto, Stephen. "Where the Bodies Lie Buried." *The Fife and Drum: Newsletter of the Friends of Fort York and Garrison Common*, 10 (2006): 1-2.

Palmer, Richard F. "James Fenimore Cooper and the Navy Brig *Oneida*." *Inland Seas*, 40 (1984): 90-9.

Patterson, Richard. "Lieutenant Colonel Benjamin Forsyth." *North Country Notes*, no. 106 (1974): 2-3.

Paullin, Charles O. "Naval Administration Under Secretaries of the Navy Smith, Hamilton, and Jones 1801-1814." *Proceedings of the United States Naval Institute*, 32 (1906): 1289-1328.

Procter, Lorna. "Silhouette of Alexander Wood." *The York Pioneer*, 54 (1959): 25-8.

Proulx, Shaun. "Tall bronze man moves to gay village." *The Globe and Mail*, 21 May 2005, M1, 6.

Riddell, William Renwick. "The Ancaster 'Bloody Assize' of 1814." *Ontario History*, 20 (1923): 107-25.

—. "Thomas Scott: The Second Attorney-General of Upper Canada." *Ontario History*, 20 (1923): 126-44.

Scott, John. "Fort York." *The York Pioneer*, 54 (1959): 2-6.

Sheppard, George. "Deeds Speak: Militiamen, Medals and the Invented Traditions of 1812." *Ontario History*, 83 (1990): 207-32.

Skeen, C. Edward. "Monroe and Armstrong: A Study in Political Rivalry." *New-York Historical Society Quarterly*, 57 (1973):121-47.

—. "Mr. Madison's Secretary of War." *Pennsylvania Magazine of History and Biography*, 100 (1976): 336-55.

Skelton, William B. "High Army Leadership in the Era of the War of 1812: The Making and Remaking of the Officer Corps." *William and Mary Quarterly*, 51 (1994): 253-74.

Smith, Donald B. "The Dispossession of the Mississauga Indians: A Missing Chapter in the Early History of

Upper Canada." *Ontario History*, 73 (1981): 67-87.

Smith, Hermon Dunlap. "General Henry Dearborn: A Biographical Essay." In *Revolutionary War Journals of Henry Dearborn, 1775-1783*, edited by Lloyd A. Brown and Howard H. Peckham, 3-33. Chicago: Caxton Club, 1939.

Spragge, George W. "The Districts of Upper Canada, 1788-1849." *Ontario History*, 39 (1947): 91-100.

Stacey, C. P. "Commodore Chauncey's Attack on the Kingston Harbour, November 10, 1812." *Canadian Historical Review*, 32 (1951): 126-38.

—. "Another Look at the Battle of Lake Erie." *Canadian Historical Review*, 39 (1958): 41-51.

—. "The War of 1812 in Canadian History." *Ontario History*, 50 (1958): 153-8.

Stagg, J. C. A. "James Madison and the Coercion of Great Britain, Canada, the West Indies and the War of 1812." *William and Mary Quarterly*, 3rd Series, 38 (1981): 3-34.

—. "Enlisted Men in the United States Army, 1812-1815: A Preliminary Study." *William and Mary Quarterly*, 43 (1986): 615-45.

—. "Soldiers in Peace and War: Comparative Perspectives on the Recruitment of the United States Army, 1802-1815." *William and Mary Quarterly*, 57 (2000): 79-120.

Stanley, George F. G. "The Army Origin of the Royal Canadian Navy." *Journal of the Society of Army Historical Research*, 32 (1954): 64-73.

—. "Contribution of the Canadian Militia during the War." In *After Tippecanoe: Some Aspects of the War of 1812*, edited by Philip Mason, 28-48. Toronto: Ryerson Press, 1963.

Steckley, John. "Toronto: What Does It Mean?" *Arch Notes*, 92-3 (May/June 1992): 23-32.

Strachan, John. "On the Conduct of the Americans." *The Antijacobin Review, and True Churchman's Magazine, or, Monthly, Political and Literary Censor*, 49 (January-June 1815): 652-62.

Strum, Harvey. "Smuggling in the War of 1812." *History Today*, 29 (1979): 532-7.

Stuart, Jacqueline. "The Old Military Burial Ground, Toronto." *The York Pioneer*, 78 (1983): 1-7.

Surveyer, E. Fabre. "Nathaniel Coffin" (1766-1846)." *Transactions of the Royal Society of Canada*, Series 3, 42, section 2 (1948): 59-71.

Taylor, Alan. "The Late Loyalists: Northern Reflections of the Early American Republic." *Journal of the Early American Republic*, 27 (2007): 1-34.

Thatcher, Joseph M. "A War of 1812 Gunner's Haversack." *Military Collector and Historian*, 49 (1997): 190.

—. "American Artillery Caissons of the War of 1812." *Military Collector and Historian*, 50 (1998): 29-40.

"Toronto's Old Colours." *Heritage Columns* (Heritage Toronto), 1 (Spring 2002): 3.

Watkins, John W. "On the Disease called the Lake Fever …" *Medical Repository*, 3 (1800): 359-61.

Webb, Catherine. "1989 Fort York Archaeology Project." *Archæological Report*, 1 (1990): 137-38.

—. "1992 Fort York Archaeology Project: Investigation of the 1813-1814 Blockhouses and the 1826 Kitchen Wing of the 1814/1815 Officers' Quarters." *Archæological Report*, 4 (1993): 115-20.

Whitfield, Carol. "The Battle of Queenston Heights: Sir

Roger Hale Sheaffe." *Occasional Papers in Archeology and History*, No. 11, Parks Canada, 1974, 9-59.

Whiting, Henry. "Life of Zebulon Montgomery Pike." In *The Library of American Biography*, second series, vol. 5, edited by Jared Sparks, 219-314. Boston: Little and Brown, 1845.

Wilson, Pearl. "Consumer Buying in Upper Canada." In *Historical Essays on Upper Canada*, edited by J. K. Johnson, 216-25. Ottawa: McClelland and Stewart, 1975.

Young, Richard. "Blockhouses in Canada: 1749-1841: A Comparative Report and Catalogue." *Occasional Papers in Archeology and History*, No. 23, Parks Canada, 1980, 5-116.

Zlatich, Marko. "Uniform of the 15th United States Infantry Regiment, 1812." *Military Collector and Historian*, 54 (2002): 130-1.

Dissertations and Private Papers

Aitchison, James H. "The Development of Local Government in Upper Canada, 1783-1850." Ph.D. Thesis. Department of Political Economy, University of Toronto, 1953.

Burns, Robert Joseph. "The First Elite of Toronto: An Examination of this Genesis, Consolidation and Duration of Power in an Emerging Colonial Society." Ph.D. Thesis. Department of History, University of Western Ontario, 1974.

Letter by Lieutenant George Runk, Sixth U.S. Regiment of Infantry, 14 May 1813, owned by Mr. Brian Murphy of Chester, New Jersey.

MacLeod, Carol. "The Tap of the Garrison Drum: The Marine Service in British North America, 1755-1813." Parks Canada, Historical Research and Records Unit, 1983.

Moore, Jonathan, Ian Morgan and John Ames. "Fore-n'-Afters at Fifty Fathoms: The Wrecks of the *Hamilton* and *Scourge*." 2002.

Steppler, Glenn A. "'A Duty Troublesome Beyond Measure' Logistical Considerations in the Canadian War of 1812." M.A. Thesis. Department of History, McGill University, Montreal. 1974.

Thompson, Frances Ann. "Local Authority and District Autonomy: The Niagara Magistracy and Constabulary, 1828-1841." Ph.D. Thesis. History Department, University of Ottawa, 1996.

Wilson, James K. "The Court of General Quarter Sessions of the Peace: Local Administration in Pre-Municipal Upper Canada." M.A. Thesis. History Department, McMaster University, Hamilton, Ontario, 1991.

Wright, James B. "Law State and Dissent in Upper Canada." J.D. Thesis. York University, Toronto, 1989.

Newspapers

Albany Argus
American Daily Advertizer, Philadelphia
American Mercury, Hartford, Conn.
Baltimore Patriot
Boston Gazette
The Centinel of Freedom, Newark, N.J.
The Chronicle of Harrisburgh, Penn.
The Colonial Advocate, Toronto
Democratic Republican, Walpole, N.Y..
Geneva Gazette, Geneva, N.Y.

The Globe, Toronto
The Globe and Mail, Toronto
Kingston Gazette, Upper Canada
Mercantile Advertiser, New York City
National Advocate, New York City
National Intelligencer, Washington, D.C.
New England Palladium, Boston
New-York Evening Post
The Niagara Mail
Northern Whig, Hudson, N.Y.
Otsego Herald, Ostego, N.Y.
The Quebec Mercury
Salem Gazette, Salem, Mass.
The Statesman, New York City
The Tickler, Philadelphia
Toronto Daily Star
The Toronto Mail
The Weekly Register, Baltimore
York Gazette

Selected Websites

Archives of Maryland. <www.mdarchives.state.md.us>

Beaumont, William. <www.james.com/beaumont/dr_life.htm>

British Army Regiments. <www.regiments.org>

British Flags. <www.flagspot.net/flags/gb-royal.html#exp>

Burnham, Travis. "Finding Pike: Fort Drum Archeologist Searches for General's Remains," 9 October 2003, Fort Drum Blizzard Online. <www.drum.army.mil/sites/blizzard>

8th Regiment of Foot. <www.warof1812.ca/8thregt.htm>

Historic Plaques in Toronto. <www.torontohistory.org/index.html.

Historical Narratives of Early Canada. www.uppercanada-history.ca/1812/18123.html

The History of Toronto. An 11,000 Year Journey. By Carl Benn. <www.toronto.ca/culture/history>

Jabez Lynde home. <www.hpd.mcl.gov.on.ca>

National Aeronautics and Space Administration. <www.sunearth.gsfc.nasa.gov>

Phillips, "New York Town Digs Our Hero Too," 12 May 2006, The Gazette. Pikes Peak Bicentennial, 8 August 2007. <www.gazette.com/pikespeak/display>

Pike genealogy. <www.historicmorrison.org/history/Pioneers/Gen-Pike.php>

Sackets Harbor <www.sacketsharborny.com/historical_society.html>

Thomas Warner letters, Gene Towner, Towson, Maryland. <www.haemo-sol.com/thomas/thomas.html>

Toronto: The Real Story of How Toronto Got Its Name, by Alan Rayburn. <www.geonames.nrcan.gc.ca/education/toronto_e.php>

U.S. Naval Observatory. <www.marinrowing.org>

U.S. Rifle, Model 1803. <www.lewis-clark.org/content/content-article.asp?ArticleID=1523>

<www.research.leidenuniv.nl> Reistma, H and A. Ponsen, "The Leiden disaster of 1807."

<www.sciencedirect.com> Reistma, H. J. "The explosion of a ship with black powder, in Leiden in 1807," International Journal of Impact Engineering, 25 (2001): 507-14.

Index

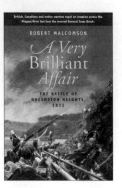
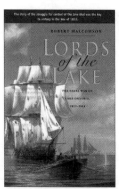